ALSO BY JOANNE B. FREEMAN

Affairs of Honor: National Politics in the New Republic
Alexander Hamilton: Writings
The Essential Hamilton: Letters & Other Writings

THE FIELD OF
BLOOD

B. Thurston, Steam Printer.

THE FIELD OF
BLOOD

VIOLENCE IN CONGRESS AND
THE ROAD TO CIVIL WAR

JOANNE B. FREEMAN

FARRAR, STRAUS AND GIROUX   NEW YORK

Farrar, Straus and Giroux
175 Varick Street, New York 10014

Copyright © 2018 by Joanne B. Freeman
All rights reserved
Printed in the United States of America
First edition, 2018

Library of Congress Cataloging-in-Publication Data
Names: Freeman, Joanne B., 1962– author.
Title: The field of blood : congressional violence and the road to civil war /
    Joanne B. Freeman.
Description: First edition. | New York : Farrar, Straus and Giroux, 2018. |
    Includes bibliographical references and index.
Identifiers: LCCN 2018010176 | ISBN 9780374154776 (hardcover)
Subjects: LCSH: United States—Politics and government—1815–1861. |
    United States—Politics and government—1861–1865. | United States.
    Congress—History—19th century. | Legislators—United States—
    History—19th century. | Legislators—Violence against—United States. |
    Political violence—United States—History—19th century. | Political
    culture—United States—History—19th century. | United States—
    History—Civil War, 1861–1865.
Classification: LCC E338 .F735 2018 | DDC 973.7—dc23
LC record available at https://lccn.loc.gov/2018010176

Designed by Jonathan D. Lippincott

Our books may be purchased in bulk for promotional, educational, or business use.
Please contact your local bookseller or the Macmillan Corporate and Premium
Sales Department at 1-800-221-7945, extension 5442, or by e-mail at
MacmillanSpecialMarkets@macmillan.com.

www.fsgbooks.com
www.twitter.com/fsgbooks • www.facebook.com/fsgbooks

3   5   7   9   10   8   6   4

Frontispiece: The caning of Sumner; detail of a print from
the presidential election of 1856 (Courtesy of the Library of Congress)

To my students past and present:
They have given me more than they know

That blood would flow,—*somebody's* blood, . . . before the expiration of your present session on that field of blood, the floor of Congress, I have fully expected.
    —John T. Sargent to Charles Sumner, May 25, 1856

CONTENTS

LIST OF ILLUSTRATIONS

AUTHOR'S NOTE

Writing this book was an emotional process. Immersing myself in extreme congressional discord and national divisiveness at a time of extreme congressional discord and national divisiveness was no easy thing. At various points, I had to walk away and get some distance. At other points, unfolding events sent me scurrying to my keyboard to hash things out. Of course, there are worlds of difference between the pre–Civil War Congress and the Congress of today. But the similarities have much to tell us about the many ways in which the People's Branch can help or hurt the nation.

Many years ago, when I began researching this book, it was far less timely and far more puzzling. There seemed to be *so* much violence in the House and Senate chambers in the 1830s, 1840s, and 1850s. Shoving. Punching. Pistols. Bowie knives. Congressmen brawling in bunches while colleagues stood on chairs to get a good look. At least once, a gun was fired on the House floor. Why hadn't this story been told?

That question is answered in the pages that follow, which reveal for the first time the full scope and scale of physical violence in Congress between 1830 and the Civil War. Yet even knowing that answer, I didn't fully grasp how such congressional fireworks could remain undercover until last year. In a long and intimate *Politico* interview, former House Speaker John Boehner revealed that some time ago, during a contentious debate over earmarks (items tacked onto bills to benefit a member of Congress's home state), Alaska Republican Don Young pushed him up against a wall in the House chamber and threatened him with a knife.[1] According to Boehner, he stared Young down, tossed off a few cusswords, and the matter ended. According to Young, they later became friends; Boehner was best man at Young's wedding. And according to the press reports that addressed the incident, it wasn't the first time that Young pulled a knife in the halls of Congress. In 1988, he reportedly waved one at a supporter of a bill that would have restricted logging in Alaska. (He also angrily shook an oosik—the penis bone of a walrus—at an Interior Department official who wanted to restrict walrus hunting in 1994, but that's an entirely different matter.) Two of these confrontations made the papers when they happened, but only recently has the Boehner showdown come to light. Remarkably, even in an age of round-the-clock multimedia press coverage, what happens in Congress sometimes stays in Congress.

From a modern vantage point, it's tempting to laugh—or gasp—at such outbursts and move on, and sometimes that's merited. (The oosik incident is definitely worth a chuckle.) As alarming as Young's knifeplay seems, it says less about a dangerous trend than it does about a somewhat flamboyant congressman.

And yet congressional combat has meant much more than that—especially in the fraught final years before the Civil War. In those times, as this book will show, armed groups of Northern and Southern congressmen engaged in hand-to-hand combat on the House floor. Angry about rights violated and needs denied, and worried about the degradation of their section of the Union, they defended their interests with threats, fists, and weapons.

When that fighting became endemic and congressmen strapped on knives and guns before heading to the Capitol every morning—when they didn't trust the institution of Congress or even their colleagues to protect their persons—it meant something. It meant extreme polarization and the breakdown of debate. It meant the scorning of parliamentary rules and political norms to the point of abandonment. It meant that structures of government and the bonds of Union were eroding in real time.[2] In short, it meant the collapse of our national civic structure to the point of crisis. The nation didn't slip into disunion; it fought its way into it, even in Congress.

The fighting wasn't new in the late 1850s; it had been happening for decades. Like the Civil War, the roots of congressional combat ran deep.[3] So did its sectional tone and tempo; Southern congressmen had long been bullying their way to power with threats, insults, and violence in the House and Senate chambers, deploying the power of public humiliation to get their way, antislavery advocates suffering worst of all. This isn't to say that Congress was in a constant state of chaos; it was a working institution that got things done. But the fighting was common enough to seem routine, and it mattered. By affecting what Congress did, it shaped the nation.

It also shaped public opinion of Congress. Americans generally like their representatives far more than they like the institution of Congress.[4] They like them all the more if they are aggressive, defending the rights and interests of the folks back home with gusto; there's a reason why Don Young's constituents have reelected him twenty-three times. The same held true in antebellum America; Americans wanted their congressmen to fight for their rights, sometimes with more than words.

This was direct representation of a powerful kind, however damaging it proved to be. The escalation of such fighting in the late 1850s was a clear indication that the American people no longer trusted the institution of Congress to address their rights and needs.[5] The impact of this growing distrust was severe. Unable to turn to the government for resolution, Americans North and South turned on one another. The same held true for congressmen; despite the tempering influence of cross-sectional friendships, they, too, lost faith in their sectional other.[6] In time, the growing fear and distrust tore the nation apart.

Toward the start of my research, I discovered poignant testimony to the power of congressional threats and violence. It took the form of a confidential memorandum with three signatures on the bottom: Benjamin Franklin Wade (R-OH), Zachariah Chandler (R-MI), and Simon Cameron (R-PA).[7] And it told a striking story.

One night in 1858, Wade, Chandler, and Cameron—all antislavery—decided that they'd had enough of Southern insults and bullying. Outraged by the onslaught of abuse, they made a difficult decision. Swearing loyalty to one another, they vowed to challenge future offenders to duels and fight "to the coffin." There seemed to be no other way to stem the flow of Southern insults than to fight back, Southern-style. This was no easy choice. They fully expected to be ostracized back home; in the North, dueling was condemned as a barbaric Southern custom. But that punishment seemed no worse than the humiliation they faced every day in Congress. So they made their plans known, and—according to their statement—they had an impact. "[W]hen it became known that some northern senators were ready to fight, for sufficient cause," the tone of Southern insults softened, though the abuse went on.

The story is dramatic, but what affected me most when I first read it was the way the three men told it; even years later, they could barely contain themselves. "Gross personal abuse" had an impact on these men, and it was mighty. Not only did it threaten "their very manhood" on a daily basis, but by silencing Northern congressmen, it deprived their constituents of their representative rights, an "unendurable outrage" that made them "frantic with rage and shame." To Wade, Chandler, and Cameron, sustained Southern bullying wasn't a mere matter of egos and parliamentary power plays. It struck at the heart of who they were as men and threatened the very essence of representative government. They *had* to do something. And they did.

These men were doing their best to champion their cause and their constituents in trying times, and they said so in their statement. They had written it "for those who come after us to study, as an example of what it once cost to be in favor of liberty, and to express such sentiments in the highest places of official life in the United States." They were pleading with posterity—with *us*—to understand how threatened they had felt, how frightened they had been, how much it had taken for them to fight back, and thus how valuable was their cause. In a handful of paragraphs, they bore witness to the presence and power of congressional violence.[8]

When I first read their plea, it brought tears to my eyes. It was so immediate and yet so far away. It was also stunningly human, expressing anger and outrage and shame and fear and pride all in one. Not only did it bring the subject of this book to living, breathing life, but it showed how it felt to be part of it. By offering a glimpse of the emotional reality of their struggle, Wade, Chandler, and Cameron opened a window onto the lost world of congressional violence.

The lessons of their time ring true today: when trust in the People's Branch shatters, part of the national "we" falls away. Nothing better testifies to the importance of Congress in preserving and defining the American nation than witnessing the impact of its systemic breakdown.[9]

Joanne B. Freeman
January 11, 2018

THE FIELD OF
BLOOD

INTRODUCTIONS

TOBACCO-STAINED RUGS AND BENJAMIN BROWN FRENCH

Charles Dickens was intrigued by many things during his 1842 visit to America, but in Washington one thing stood out: tobacco chewing. The practice repulsed him wherever he found it, but it was "in its full bloom and glory" in the nation's capital, "the head-quarters of tobacco-tinctured saliva."[1] Looking on from a seat of honor on the House floor, he found it "remarkable . . . to say the least, to see so many honorable members with swelled faces," their chairs tilted back and their feet on their desks, shaping a "plug" with their penknives, "shooting" the old plugs from their mouths "as from a popgun" and "clapping the new one in its place." And heaven help anyone who dropped something on the spit-spattered floor. "I strongly recommend all strangers not to look at the floor," he advised, "and if they happen to drop anything . . . not to pick it up, with an ungloved hand on any account."[2]

It's a striking image that's all the more striking because it was true.[3] Congressmen habitually tilted back their chairs and put up their feet—at least in the House. When Representative John Farnsworth (R-IL) did so during a visit to the Senate in the 1850s, a page reprimanded him. "You're more dignified over here," Farnsworth joked. (He "was certainly right about that," the page later huffed.)[4] And the floors were revolting. Although there were well over a hundred spittoons scattered around the House and roughly half that number in the Senate, congressional chewers often missed their mark—in part, because they could.[5] Covering the carpets only made matters worse because congressmen didn't think twice about dirtying the mats.[6] Dickens was describing just what he saw.

The tobacco-juiced rugs of the House and Senate are an apt metaphor for Congress in the decades before the Civil War. Yes, there was soaring oratory on occasion. Yes, there were Union-shaking decisions being made. But underneath the speechifying, pontificating, and politicking was a spit-spattered rug. The antebellum Congress had its admirable moments, but it wasn't an assembly of demigods. It was a human institution with very human failings.

This is a far cry from its conventional image as a lofty pantheon of Great Men like Henry Clay and Daniel Webster. The names alone call forth images of staid men in black frock coats striking classical debating poses, one finger thrust in the air in emphasis. Even their contemporaries arrived in Washington expecting a string of bravura performances, particularly in the Senate. Writing home to his wife, the freshman representative David Outlaw (W-NC) declared himself disappointed; most speeches didn't even stand up to stump speeches back home.[7] The average member of Congress was just that: average. We forget that when we highlight the standouts.

Even if Congress *had* been filled with Clays and Websters, the times were demanding in ways that weren't always awe-inspiring. Nations don't tear themselves in two accompanied by poetic strains of eloquence alone. Congressional proceedings in the 1830s, 1840s, and 1850s weren't pretty. The high-stakes political struggles of those decades were accompanied by insults and brawls as often as they were quieted—temporarily—by strategic compromises. Even the worthiest of congressional worthies had their ugly moments; swearing, blustering, threats, and personal insults (known as "personalities") were coin of the congressional realm, and fisticuffs were common enough to seem routine. ("This session is like all other sessions that I have seen—except there has, as yet, been no fighting," noted one onlooker, the "as yet" showing that he fully expected it.)[8]

To some degree, violent outbursts in the antebellum Congress are no surprise. These were violent times. There was the expulsion of Native Americans from their native lands and sweeping massacres of their people. There was rampant mobbing for a whole host of reasons: anti-abolitionism, racism, nativism. Between July and October 1835 alone,

there were 109 riots nationwide.[9] There was the war with Mexico between 1846 and 1848, a battle that enflamed the nation's slavery problem and stoked sectional passions, laying the groundwork for violence
to come. In the 1850s there was the murderously brutal fight over slavery and statehood in "Bleeding Kansas"; western expansion forced a national reckoning with slavery's future that was bloody and fiercely
fought. And of course, there was the institution of slavery itself and the
violence and cruelty at its core.

Politics was also violent.[10] There was hand-to-hand combat and
rioting at polling places. On one memorable occasion in Washington
in 1857, three nativist gangs—the Plug Uglies, the Chunkers, and the
Rip-Raps—joined forces to terrorize immigrants casting votes, causing
a riot. When the panicked mayor called in the Marines, the three
gangs hauled a cannon into play, though they never fired it. By the time
the brawl subsided, several people had been killed.[11] State legislatures
also erupted into uproars from time to time. In 1857, there was an all-
out row in the Illinois legislature featuring "considerable wrestling,
knocking over chairs, desks, inkstands, men, and things generally."[12] In
1858, state assemblies in both New York and Massachusetts dissolved
into fisticuffs. "[T]here was a most heavenly time in the House for an
hour or two," gushed a *New York Times* reporter about the Boston outbreak. It "would have made a sensation even in Congress."[13] The Arkansas House deserves special mention. In 1837, when a representative
insulted the Speaker during debate, the Speaker stepped down from
his platform, bowie knife in hand, and killed him. Expelled and tried
for murder, he was acquitted for excusable homicide and reelected, only
to pull his knife on *another* legislator during debate, though this time the
sound of colleagues cocking pistols stopped him cold.[14]

Congressional violence was of a piece with this world. As I researched
this book, I discovered that between 1830 and 1860, there were more
than *seventy* violent incidents between congressmen in the House and
Senate chambers or on nearby streets and dueling grounds, most of them
long forgotten.[15] This isn't to say that all such fighting has vanished from
view. Many studies of the coming of the Civil War note a surge of fighting
in Congress in the 1850s. Most such books—and many more besides—
offer a vivid account of the most famous violent incident: the caning of
the abolitionist senator Charles Sumner (R-MA) in 1856.

My archival digging revealed much more. (See Appendix B for details on the digging.) I found canings, duel negotiations, and duels; shoving and fistfights; brandished pistols and bowie knives; wild melees in the House; and street fights with fists and the occasional brick.[16] Not included in that number is bullying that never went beyond words. Therein lies a problem, because the *threat* of violence had an enormous impact on congressional debate, but proving that someone has been bullied into silence is no easy matter. Some such episodes appear throughout the book, but only when substantiated by concrete evidence. There was far more bullying than appears on these pages. There was also more violence. The words that people used to describe these fights and showdowns—thrashing, bullying, pistoleering, stampeding—offer a revealing ground-level glimpse of the antebellum Congress. They expose the tobacco-stained rugs.

Detecting those rugs can be difficult; politics is often Janus-faced, presenting a composed public face to the world while masking a less savory private one. This was especially true in the first half of the nineteenth century. Washington newspapers had a tangled relationship with Congress; many of them survived on government printing contracts, and Congress did the granting, so local newsmen were well advised to make Congress look good by not recording the gritty details of congressional threats and violence. Describing congressional rumbles was also dangerous for reporters; record an insult the wrong way—or the *right* way—and you might become entangled in an honor dispute and get pounded by a congressman. As a result, when it came to fighting, the Washington press offered bare-bones details when it mentioned it at all, showing plenty of bravado but few fists and weapons. For a time, these partially censored newspaper accounts were the nation's main news source for congressional proceedings, and the basis of the *Congressional Globe*, the period's equivalent of the *Congressional Record*. Not until the rise of a commercially independent national press brought out-of-town reporters to Washington in large numbers was congressional violence reported in some detail, gaining its maximum impact through new technologies such as the telegraph in the 1850s—just as the nation's slavery crisis began to peak.

Given such subterfuge, uncovering Congress's rough realities isn't easy. It requires an on-site witness. Yet not just any witness will do. To be of value, he must be a congressional insider, but not too far inside because he needs some perspective. He needs to be observant, with an eye for detail, an ear to the ground, and a flair for saying the unsaid. He needs to focus his attention on Congress and congressmen, routinely and religiously. And he needs a sense of humor and some self-awareness, two necessary gifts in the art of gaining insight into human nature. Benjamin Brown French was all of these things.

A House clerk from New Hampshire, French arrived in Washington in 1833 at the age of thirty-three to take up his job, and though he initially expected to stay only for a year or two, he ultimately made the nation's capital his home. French wasn't new to politics or to clerking; a loyal Democrat, he had been a clerk in his state senate and a member of his state house. Nor was he unschooled in the ways of the world; remarkably good-natured ("the king of pure drawling good nature," according to one acquaintance), he made friends easily.[17] French had a sense of humor and some self-awareness, and his job required them; first as a House clerk and then as *the* House Clerk, he spent his time serving congressmen, not all of them hail fellows well met.

In his new post, French was a professional Congress-watcher. He spent most of his working hours recording the House's proceedings along with roughly ten other clerks. At first, his main job was copying documents.[18] Promoted to assistant clerk in 1840, then elected Clerk of the House in 1845, French did less copying and more organizing, monitoring, record-keeping, and vote-tabulating, becoming a renowned expert on parliamentary points of order. He also spent lots of time in the House chamber, often at the Speaker's table, reading reports or documents aloud, taking notes, and watching. Always watching.

In all of these ways, French is an ideal witness: a likeable insider with a sense of perspective, a deep and abiding interest in politics, and a job that forced him to focus on Congress. But there's more. French was a writer. In New Hampshire, he edited a newspaper; in Washington, he published poetry, songs, and newspaper articles, and—most significant of all for our purposes—he kept a diary for much of his adult life. And not the kind of diary containing personal reflections and little else. French recorded what he did and described what he saw: the goings-on in the Capitol, the mood on the House floor, the stories that he heard, the tics and quirks of congressmen, and the choreography of

The eleven volumes of French's diary (Courtesy of the Library of Congress)

their brawls, sometimes offering blow-by-blow narratives complete with sound effects (the pounding of the mallet, the Speaker's cries of "order—order," the countercries of "Damn him . . . Where are your Bowie knives? . . . Knock him down," and the Clerk of the House screaming, "Order gentlemen, for God's sake come to order").[19]

Although he missed stretches of time, French was a dedicated diarist. Between 1828 and 1870, he filled eleven volumes—more than 3,700 pages. At first, in New Hampshire, he kept a diary to remember things, but like most people who vow to keep a diary, he had his doubts. ("God only knows how long this *fit* will last. I may journalize this once & never more."[20]) Alone in Washington without his wife, he wanted his diary to enable them to "live over again *together* the time that was passed in separation."[21] After his wife joined him, he used his diary to organize his thoughts and—he hoped—his life.[22] Eventually, he realized that a "faithful journal" would be "a transcript of his life," and from that point on, he was committed to it.[23] (French's twelve-year-old son Francis tried to live up to his father's example with mixed results: "Thursday, February 7. I'll be gaul darned if I know what I did today.")[24]

For thirty-seven years, this self-described "journalizer" was surrounded by congressmen. During his first five years in Washington, he shared a boardinghouse with more than a dozen of them, first on his own and then with his wife. Later, as a house-renter and then a homeowner, he wined and dined them.[25] (In a strange twist of historical fate, French's house was torn down in 1895 to make way for the Library of Congress, which now houses his papers.) Always up for a friendly chat, he dropped in on congressional friends after hours. He even had a few short-term congressional boarders.[26] And of course, during his fourteen years clerking in the House, French's workday revolved around congressmen. Even after he lost the clerkship in 1847, he remained in Congress's orbit, clerking for committees, filling in as a House clerk when needed, and, for a short time, struggling to earn a living as a lobbyist.[27]

It's hard to imagine a better guide. French shows us a Congress of friendships and fighting; of drinking and dallying; of the passions of party and the prejudices of section and how they played out on the floor. He reveals the human dynamic of debate and the interaction of personality, partisanship, and policy. He shows how life in Washington affected politicking in Washington, and personally demonstrates how that politicking was advertised throughout the nation through the vehicle of the press.

He also shows how Congress and the nation changed over time, because he embodied those changes, most dramatically in his gradual conversion from a loyal Democrat eager to appease Southern allies to a devoted Republican with a deep-seated hatred of the Southern "slaveocracy." By 1860, this most genial of men was armed and ready to shoot Southerners, a change of mind and heart experienced throughout the North.

French's diary shows what fueled that transformation. It shows him kowtowing to Southerners to save the Union and serve himself; the gains of party dominance could be sweet. It shows him learning—gradually and with difficulty—how Southerners were all too willing to abandon Northern allies for the sake of slavery. It shows the grating impact of the threats and violence that Southerners deployed to get their way.

It was a hard lesson for Northerners, but a lesson well learned. Particularly concerning the charged issue of slavery, you needed to think twice before messing with a slaveholder. Not only did slaveholders have an advantage of numbers through the U.S. Constitution's Three-fifths

Compromise, but they had a cultural advantage that extended their influence. Northerners who ranted about a despotic Slave Power dominating the national government were not delusional. There *was* a domineering block of slaveholders at the heart of the national government who strategically deployed violence to get their way.[28] The tobacco-stained rugs are even more apt as a metaphor; the floors of the Capitol were fouled with the yield of a Southern cash crop cultivated by the enslaved. Slavery tainted everything.

As we will see, French doesn't merely describe these rough realities; he explains how they felt, and in so doing, bears witness to the human reality of the antebellum Congress and the *emotional logic of disunion*.[29] French's evolving fears and growing sense of betrayal show that the breaking of national bonds wasn't a detached argument about sovereignty and rights. Disunion wasn't born of cool appraisal. Nor was it a product of events in the 1850s alone. The rending of the Union was a long and painful process that spawned jarring instabilities and vast unknowns. It was a wrenching experience for those who lived through it, shaped by habits, resentments, and assumptions that built up over decades. Sectional fighting had a history, and that history mattered.[30]

At the core of French's experience was the emotional power of the Union and all that it represented; French's love of the Union was profound. He fretted about it in his diary, sang about it in campaign songs, and praised it in poetry. His heartfelt concern for the Union colored the fabric of his life. Born of a compromise and sustained by bonds of brotherhood, the Union wasn't an abstract political entity in antebellum America. It was a state of being, and all the more fragile because of it. Today, we take the Union for granted as a structure of government. In antebellum America, it was more of a pact, grounded on conceptions of rights, fairness, and equal membership. Pacts are inherently vulnerable and unstable, open to reinterpretation by different peoples at different times; western expansion and the spread of slavery exposed and intensified those tensions. Thus the shared sense of political crisis throughout this period as the nation's founding compact was questioned and renegotiated time and again.[31]

The Democratic Party had an equally powerful hold on French's emotions, embracing his entire worldview. Structured national parties first rose to power in this period, inspiring the intense devotion of a cause.[32] Party membership was more than a label; it was a kind of pledge, a statement of loyalty to a political worldview that bound men together in reputation and purpose. Manhood and honor were fundamental to this band-of-brothers form of politics, particularly in the public forum of Congress. And abuse of one party member potentially abused them all. Fighting was more complex than throwing a punch.

It was also inspired by more than outrage. For the most part, political principles fueled congressional combat. In the 1830s, most fighting centered on party differences. In the 1840s and 1850s it became slavery-centric, sparked by western expansion; Congress was the nation's proving ground on the issue of slavery, the only institution capable of outlawing the interstate slave trade and abolishing slaveholding in the District of Columbia and western territories. Trace patterns of congressional violence and you expose the nation's shifting fault lines. Congress was a representative institution in more ways than one.

But French wasn't thinking of fault lines when he lost faith in Southerners. He was thinking of rights. For Northerners, Southerners, and Westerners alike, having one's rights within the Union challenged was a form of degradation that required resistance; fighting for those rights was a test of manhood. This was as true for congressmen as it was for their constituents. As tempting as it is to blame disunion on blundering politicians—as some historians did a generation ago—congressmen were bound to the folks back home in purpose and feeling.[33] Nothing shows this link more dramatically than people who sent guns to their representatives in the late 1850s.[34] They wanted their representatives to fight for their rights. And fight their representatives did. Reporters who branded some of these fights "battles" were more accurate than they knew; in a sense, the first battles of the Civil War were waged in Congress itself.[35]

It was French's fate to rise to national politics during this crisis-ridden period. A time of unsettled, unbalanced, and unpredictable politics, the 1830s, 1840s, and 1850s were uneasy decades of national unknowing. To fully grasp the meaning of that moment, we need to understand the process of discovery of those who lived through it. We need to view events "in forward motion, as they were lived," with their contingency intact.[36] Looking through French's eyes reveals these eventful decades as they unfolded, removing them from the shadow of a war yet to come.

For all of these reasons, in the ensuing chapters, French will be our guide to the sometimes familiar, often alien world of the antebellum Congress; his emotional arc forms the core of this book and his lived experience structures it. There are risks to this book's approach. More important men might have broader perspectives. But precisely because French *wasn't* exceptional, his vantage point has value. However likeable he was and however useful he proved to be, French was an ordinary man who found his way into national politics like thousands of people before and after him, experiencing these turbulent decades from a front-row seat. His feelings and reactions are larger than the limits of his life.

THE RISE OF BENJAMIN BROWN FRENCH

If you met French, you may well have liked him. Most people did. Stocky in build, with an easy laugh, he enjoyed people, had a good sense of fun, and loved a zesty round of cribbage. His diary is filled with dinners and picnics, whiskey punch and good cigars. It's also filled with his family. Widowed once and married twice, he was miserable without his wife and sons, Frank and Benjamin. Home alone for a few weeks in 1838, he hid their things—his wife's pincushion, Frank's pillow with "the exact print of his little head in it"—because they made him weepy.[37] He chided himself for being sentimental, but so he was.[38]

Before coming to Washington, French had been living an exceedingly local life—like most Americans—eking out a living in small New Hampshire towns with friends and family close by.[39] His travels were bumpy jogs on rickety stagecoaches (in one case led by a blind horse, a broken-down nag, and two colts who had never before been harnessed to a carriage; after jumping out of the coach in a panic more than once, French ended up walking most of the way).[40] He had never been south of Boston. Antebellum America was a large-scale nation of small-scale horizons.[41] Other regions were faraway places filled with strange people with strange habits.

Chester, French's birthplace, was a small farming town of 2,000 people in 1800, the year that French was born.[42] His father, Daniel, was a big fish in that small pond: a wealthy lawyer (he bought the town's first "cooking stove"), the state's attorney general during the War of 1812,

Benjamin Brown French at the age of thirty-eight. Friends and family called him "the Major" due to a stint in the state militia. (Courtesy of the Library of Congress)

and "quite a farmer," as a town history described him.[43] French's mother, Mercy, was the daughter of the town's leading merchant, Benjamin Brown; she died eighteen months after her son was born, at the age of twenty-three.[44] Daniel married twice more in coming years, expanding his brood exponentially. All told, Benjamin had four half brothers and seven half sisters; he was close to most of them for most of his life.

Daniel French was a difficult man; a contemporary described him as fair and faithful to his legal clients, but "rather sharp in his practice."[45] Benjamin thought him harsh. But raising the younger French was a challenge. The good-natured sense of fun that earned him countless friends as an adult was more of a rebellious streak when he was young. (Offered gin for the first time at the age of fourteen, Benjamin didn't just take a sip; he guzzled mouthfuls, got "gloriously drunk," and pitched "head foremost into a snowbank, as I then thought 'just for fun.'")[46] Sent to Maine for much of his schooling (he had an uncle and a grandfather in North

Yarmouth), by his own account he studied "deviltry" more than anything else, until he clashed with a "drunken tyrant" of a teacher. As French later recalled it, he told the man "exactly what I thought of him" and then "marched out of the Academy, never again to enter it, or any other school." Back in Chester, his father pushed him to study law, but after two years, at the age of nineteen, French ran away to go to sea; unable to find a berth on a ship, he enlisted in the U.S. Army. It took his family months to track him down and bring him home.[47] However harsh his father was, French mused in later years, "I do not doubt I deserved it."[48]

Although he went back to studying law after his military adventures, French hadn't yet started to practice when—at the age of twenty-four—he married Elizabeth Richardson, five years his junior. Her father, William Richardson, chief justice of the New Hampshire Supreme Court, was a formidable no-nonsense man with a chilly disposition, literally as well as figuratively; during brutally cold New England winters, he was miserly with firewood and never wore gloves. One of his law clerks, noting how the ink froze in the inkwells in Richardson's law office, described him as "somewhat puritanic." The more charitable French said that he had "stern integrity," though once French got to know him, he thought him kind.[49]

Richardson disapproved of French's courtship, which wasn't surprising given that French had no job or income. So the ever-impulsive French eloped with the no-less-impulsive "Bess"—a thickset brown-haired groom and his wisp-thin brown-haired bride—and they kept the marriage secret for six months. (Family legend has it that the frightened newlyweds revealed the truth to Bess's father by placing their marriage certificate on a windowsill and waiting for him to find it.)[50] Once the secret was out, the couple set up house in the rustic little town of Sutton, forty miles northwest of Chester, with the idea that Benjamin would practice law—the first lawyer in town.[51]

But Benjamin had no liking for lawyering. Within two years, the Frenches had moved to Newport, New Hampshire, where he had been appointed Clerk of the Courts in newly created Sullivan County. Two years later, in 1829, he became one of three owners of the Jacksonian *New Hampshire Spectator* as well as its editor, a position that he held during his tenure as clerk until he left for Washington.[52]

The *Spectator* was a launching point for French. Not only did it capitalize on his scribbling impulse, but it plunged him into New Hampshire politics at a key moment of change. French joined the paper just as one of the state's foremost politicos, Isaac Hill, was becoming a power-house organizer for what would eventually become the Democratic Party. Editor of the Concord *New Hampshire Patriot*, Hill was at the center of the drive to promote the presidential candidate Andrew Jackson and his supporters in New Hampshire.

In many ways, Hill was a perfect spokesman for Jackson's common-man message.[53] Born in poverty, largely self-taught, lamed by a child-hood injury, and afflicted with what French called a "splutter" (Hill's thoughts seemed to outpace his mouth), Hill was a lifelong scrapper.[54] He was "emphatically a political man" whose "whole soul" was devoted to politics, French thought.[55]

Hill wasn't new to politics in the 1820s. But his organizing efforts gained steam and power with the rise of Jackson. In New Hampshire, Hill coordinated the efforts of the state's Democratic newspapers, helped establish new papers where needed, and allied himself with editors in other states. He created committees of correspondence to organize local efforts before elections.[56] He helped stage elaborate celebrations of Jackson's War of 1812 victory at the Battle of New Orleans on January 8, which grew to become a local holiday second only to the Fourth of July—and not by much. He stumped all over the state giving speeches (always reading them; he didn't splutter when he read aloud), preaching Jackson's common-man message in his all-too-appropriate black printer's coat.[57] In the process, Hill revolutionized New Hampshire politics, helping to set the stage for what would eventually become structured national political parties.[58]

Newspapers were central to that change.[59] As Thomas Jefferson had put it during his own campaign for president, they were the "engine" of a democratic politics.[60] Editors were the engineers. They were also pol-iticians, in fact if not in name. Smack in the middle of the political fray, tied in with politicos and the man on the street, their energies aimed at scoring points and winning elections, editors gained political office by the score during the so-called Age of Jackson.[61]

French's rise was typical of many. His pro-Jackson *Spectator* elec-tioneering made him a local politico in his own right. His clerking duties gained him further influence, as did his membership in the Masons, which placed him amid powerful public men—though he was drawn to the order not by its clout but by its spirit of brotherhood as witnessed at a Masonic funeral.[62] By 1831, two years after joining the *Spectator*, French had won a seat representing Newport in the New Hampshire House of Representatives.

There, in Concord, the state capital, French got his first taste of legislative politics. Some of it he relished, particularly the camaraderie— the Madeira-drinking, cigar-smoking, storytelling evenings spent with fellow legislators. Five or six of them, he felt sure, would be friends for life.[63] One such "good fellow" was Franklin Pierce. Elected to the New Hampshire House in 1829, Pierce became Speaker two years later at the age of twenty-six. The governor's son, Pierce had something of the "golden boy" about him. French saw it the first time he spotted Pierce in a crowd. Pierce was "full of fun and frolic," French thought, and he exuded charm.[64] Strikingly handsome—athletic and slender in an age of stocky, stodgy men—he had an appealing speaking voice that he used to full effect, and a warm, graceful manner; he was famed for swaying juries as well as partisans. A college friend perhaps best summed him up: Pierce had "no very remarkable talents" but a lot of personal appeal.[65]

The two men got to know each other when French joined the New Hampshire House, and they became fast friends. Renting rooms across the hall from each other at Gass's Eagle Hotel, they spent many an evening talking politics and occasionally arm wrestling; French lost every time.[66] Judging from French's diary, he and Pierce spent a lot of time together. Pierce appears all over its pages, singing at the piano at parties with French, sitting by his side at dinners, riding around the countryside for pleasure, even visiting Chester with French—meeting French's old friends and walking out to the town's "great rock." In decades to come, in ways that French could not even begin to fathom, Pierce would dramatically shape French's life.

French generally liked the business of politics; he was one of the most frequent speakers in the House. The *New Hampshire Sentinel* dubbed him the House's "leading man" based on the sheer number of times that he rose to his feet.[67] But his job didn't suit him and he knew it.[68] He was too impulsive, a realization that hit home when Speaker Pierce called him to order; "a desire to do everything that I happen to think should be done at the moment the thought occurs" had led him into many "embarrassing situations," he admitted in his diary that night.[69] And as ardent a Jacksonian as French was, as fervent an organizer, coordinator, and party drum-banger as he would become, he couldn't stomach partisan dirty business. He didn't have the temperament for it. He had a hard time holding grudges ("I do really believe I could not retain malice against the worst scoundrel that ever existed over half an hour," he thought), and he agonized when asked to fire Whigs as a party hatchet man.[70] The mere idea of such "indiscriminate political slaughter" kept him up nights, so what would "the performance of the odious duty cost me in wear & tear of heart & feelings?"[71] French simply wasn't in his element as a party combatant.

But he was a superb party operative, an organizer and coordinator par excellence. He was perfectly suited to it: responsible, thorough, diligent, detail-minded, and almost preternaturally good with people in a sincere, straightforward kind of way. His genial personality made him an ideal person for drumming up enthusiasm; joined with his other skills, it virtually guaranteed that he was made an officer (often the secretary) of almost every organization that he joined, and he joined dozens over the course of his life. This was the great age of associations and organizations; charities, reform movements, and social clubs as well as political parties were multiplying, expanding, and trying for national or even international reach. With skilled secretaries in constant demand, French's skill set was perfectly attuned to the times.[72]

French found politics exciting, even fun. But its intensity sometimes scared him. It seemed as though the nation was involved in an "all-engrossing" war that could tear it in two; his fears about the state of the Union run through his diary like a whisper of doom.[73] Past political excitement had seemed grounded on an "honest difference of opinion," French thought. Current politics seemed fueled by "aspiring office seekers & political demagogues."[74] Upset by men who seemed intent on winning power with orchestrated public appeals, French was unsettled by the rise of structured party politics.

But he was also swept up in it, entertained and even amused by it, and nowhere was it more amusing than in Washington. There was something undeniably funny in watching the leaders of the land throw punches. "Don't you think the members of Congress are carrying on quite a little business in the way of pounding & shooting & being pounded & shot?" French asked his half brother Henry in 1832. "I expect some of them will get a hole made in their *bread baskets* yet."[75]

French was referring to a series of violent clashes involving former (and future) congressman Sam Houston, who had assaulted a congressman for slandering his name, battering him with a cane on Pennsylvania Avenue; not long after, there was an assassination attempt on the steps of the Capitol against another congressman who had insulted Houston, followed by a near-duel involving yet another congressional Houston detractor.[76]

In future years, when the implications of congressional violence became clear, French wouldn't be laughing. But for the present, like thousands of other men with ambitions and a sense of adventure, French tied his life and livelihood to a leader whose violent outbursts were legend. Andrew Jackson swept French into the national political world.[77]

In June 1833, Jackson was on a New England victory lap at the start of his second presidential term. Hoping that he would stop in Concord, the New Hampshire House sent French and two colleagues to Boston to invite him in person. Recalling the events of that June a few weeks later, French thought that more had been "crowded into one little month than has often passed before me in a year."[78]

Arriving in Boston on a Friday morning, the three legislators did first things first: they conferred with the editor of the Jacksonian *Boston Statesman & Morning Post*. Then they took in some sights, two of the men visiting Bunker Hill while French went art-gazing at the Athenaeum.

Then came Jackson.

French was watching from his hotel window when a flag raised on the statehouse signaled Jackson's arrival and the city went wild. Cannon fired. Bells were ringing. Fire engines paraded. Harvard students in full regalia stood in formation. And the crowd! It was unlike anything that French had ever seen. It was immense, a "solid mass of heads" as far as he could see, with soldiers, coaches, horsemen, children and adults, white and black so densely packed that "a person could have walked upon the heads and shoulders of the multitude." When the president's open carriage entered the heart of the city and his shock of white hair came into view, the crowd burst into the heartiest cheering that French had ever heard.

Later that day, French and his cohort met the president, who accepted their invitation. Then the next day, more festivities: a formal address by the governor at the statehouse, followed by a never-ending crowd of people surging toward Jackson, who bowed to each and every one until the doors were closed so he could catch his breath. "Heaven only knows how long they would have kept him there bowing," French thought. A lavish feast in the Senate chamber followed, and then a formal review of Massachusetts infantry on Boston Common, attended— French guessed—by a hundred thousand people. "How small *one* man was among all that multitude," he marveled, and yet *"one* man had caused its assemblage and on one alone every eye rested." A few days later, Concord feted Jackson on a somewhat smaller scale, with yet another endless bout of bowing; Bess came to town to join in the fun. Moved by the power of it all, French became teary; thrilled with the implications of such power, Isaac Hill, now a U.S. senator and a member of Jackson's Kitchen Cabinet, took a pinch of snuff and laughed.[79]

Andrew Jackson. The man was a phenomenon. A war hero. A tough-guy fighter; a duelist who killed his man. A self-made symbol of the American frontier. For French, Jackson's coolness under fire during an 1835 assassination attempt would only add to his legend; as French wrote admiringly to his father after the would-be assassin fired off two pistols—which miraculously *both* misfired—the sixty-eight-year-old president had shoved people aside so he could "get at" the man himself.[80] Jackson's passions got the better of him time and again, and in this violent and passionate age, many Americans loved him the better for it.[81]

Friend and champion of the common man, Jackson could be trusted with power—or so the party line went, a one-two political punch that won him a lot of political muscle. The fact that Jackson championed the *white* common man often went unvoiced but was no less central to his broad appeal. French couldn't praise him enough. "Only second in our annals to the Father of His Country . . . the bravest of her brave," Jackson was "the venerated[,] the admired, the beloved Chieftain, whom any true democrat delights to honor."[82]

To French, Jackson's party was no less remarkable. Grounded on the seductive combination of Jackson's war-hero popularity, an ambiguous common-man message, and the assurance that a national party would combat sectionalism and strengthen the Union, the Jacksonian Democrats electrified popular politics; in the presidential election of 1828, there was a massive increase in voter turnout wherever the party took hold, and it took hold with a vengeance in New Hampshire, with "Dictator" Isaac Hill, leader of the so-called Concord Regency, at its head.[83] It was the first organized national political party of its kind.

French came of age when this political machine was first gunning its engines. A small-town boy with no sense of direction, he lurched from one vocation to another—a soldier, a lawyer, a ne'er-do-well knock-about, a clerk—until he stumbled, or rather plunged into the world of party politics, gaining a network of allies and influence in the process; for French and countless others, their life paths and the rise of the "Second Party System" were intertwined. A little over five months after feting Jackson, French was offered a House clerkship, and a week later he was headed for Washington.

1

THE UNION INCARNATE FOR BETTER AND WORSE

THE UNITED STATES CONGRESS

In the middle of December 1833, the thirty-three-year-old French set off for the nation's capital and a new life as a clerk for the U.S. House of Representatives. Duty drove him more than anything else; as he explained in his diary, he needed to earn money to pay his debts. He was too extravagant with his earnings, he knew, and now he was paying the price. His wife—"all I love on this earth"—was back in New Hampshire. And he was trundling in a stagecoach, then three steamboats, then another stagecoach to Washington.[1]

During his trip, French bumped up against concrete evidence of just how localized the nation and he himself were. State banks printed their own currency, so interstate travel required preparation, and French wasn't prepared. In Pennsylvania, he discovered that his New Hampshire bills weren't much good. When his wife followed him to Washington a few months later, he had sage advice: "Use New Hampshire or Massachusetts money until you get to New Haven, and then begin upon your Southern money. I had some trouble in Philadelphia to get rid of my New Hampshire money."[2]

Southern money in hand, French arrived in Washington on December 21, 1833—at 1:30 a.m. on a cold morning, to be precise—and he spent the day doing what any visitor would do; he toured the capital with fresh eyes.[3] What he saw was a raw young city with pretensions of becoming something more.

A view of Washington from Capitol Hill in 1834, one year after French arrived.
Pennsylvania Avenue is to the left. (By J. R. Smith and J. B. Neagle. Courtesy of the Library
of Congress)

Planned in the 1790s and first serving as the seat of government in
1800, Washington was a new capital for a new nation. Boosters called
it the City of Magnificent Distances; critics called it the City of Magnificent Intentions. Either way, it embodied big hopes and an uncertain
future.

You could see the city's rawness everywhere: in its sprawling dimensions and empty expanses; in its clusters of low wood houses and straggling rows of buildings pocked by vacant lots; in the odd isolated splendor
of its scattered handful of large government buildings (as if "the British
Museum . . . suddenly migrated to the centre of an exhausted brick-
field"); in its broad unpaved avenues and its seemingly permanent blan-
ket of dust from ongoing construction.[4] As late as 1850, houses weren't
numbered, street signs weren't mandatory, there were no streetlights,
"and the visitor who wanted to find a residence had to depend upon the
hack-drivers, whose method of memory seemed to be that each person
lived 'just a little way from' somewhere else."[5] Thanks to poor planning,
sewage pooled in low-lying areas; there was a "miasmatic swamp" near

the White House, and in 1857 a sewage-induced dysentery outbreak in the National Hotel killed three and sickened dozens, including the president-elect.[6] Cows, geese, and pigs roamed the streets. Over the years, French had countless livestock run-ins; on one evening in 1838, he was convinced that "nearly all the dogs in Washington" were behind his boardinghouse barking at cows. A few years later, a cow wearing a bell woke him night after night for months; even as he was complaining in his diary, the cow seemed to "gingle" her bell "as if she knew that I was writing about her. . . . D—n that cow."[7]

In a city networked by more roads and alleys than New York or Philadelphia, the streets themselves seemed to rise up in rebellion.[8] Crossing one of the broad avenues could be an adventure. When it rained, they were mired in mud. When it didn't, the wind stirred up dust clouds so dense that people were choked and blinded. The wise Washingtonian carried a handkerchief to cover nose and mouth when crossing the street.[9] ("You have no idea of the dust," noted a clerk searching for a place to board that wasn't enveloped in a thick cloud of it.)[10] In the summer of 1856, Congress spent nearly $2,000 watering down Pennsylvania Avenue, roughly equivalent to $56,000 in 2017; French, commissioner of public buildings at the time, supervised the watering.

Of course, Washington changed during its first five decades, transforming from a town of roughly 8,000 people in 1800 to a city of more than 50,000 in the 1850s.[11] But one thing didn't change: Washington revolved around the openings and closings of Congress. Just before the start of every session, a migrant group of politicians and their families trouped to the capital, joined by a throng of hangers-on: "distinguished foreigners, gentlemen who are traveling for amusement, political demagogues, claimants, patentees, letter writers, army and navy officers, office hunters, and a host of gamblers and blacklegs"—not to mention socialites eager for fun.[12] (One congressman included "lunatics" in this group, noting that Washington had more than its share because some government claimants literally went insane waiting for Congress to act.)[13] To French, it was a "cloud . . . equalled only by the locusts in Egypt."[14]

French was part of that cloud in 1833. He spent his first day seeing the sights with two New Hampshire congressmen, including Franklin

A view of the Capitol as seen from Pennsylvania Avenue in 1834. (By Milo Osborne. Courtesy of the Library of Congress)

Pierce.[15] The three men probably saw the White House and strolled down Pennsylvania Avenue, the city's main thoroughfare (known as "*the Avenue*"), with its array of houses, hotels, churches, saloons, small businesses, and newspaper offices. But of all that French saw on that first day, one thing stood out: the United States Capitol. "I viewed it with thoughts and emotions which I cannot express," he confessed in his diary that night.[16]

Perhaps he was struck by the grand sweeping architecture; the iconic statues and artwork in the rotunda; the look, sound, and feel of the House and Senate chambers. Perhaps he was anticipating this new phase of his life on an elevated stage. He was certainly excited to hear "the great men of the land debate." But more than anything else, French was struck by the symbolism of his surroundings. Thus his reaction to viewing the Capitol for the first time: "*will it always be the capitol of my happy country?* I fear the seeds are already sown whose fruit will be disunion, but God forbid it!"[17] French was responding to the Nullification Crisis of 1832–33, a standoff between the national government and South Carolina, which had nullified a federal tariff; for a time, the threat of federal military intervention had been all too real. French may have been looking at a brick-and-mortar structure, but he was seeing the Union incarnate.

The Capitol encouraged this kind of thinking by design. Not only was it an architectural anchor of the city—an enormous structure at one end of Pennsylvania Avenue, in a permanent showdown with the White House at the other end—but it was also a national monument of sorts, open to the public and filled with commemorative works of art.[18] The exterior was adorned with "colossal" allegorical statues: the *Genius of America, War, Peace, Hope,* and *Justice* (though somewhat forebodingly, in 1842 "Justice" was damaged, her arm and hand—clutching the Constitution—broken off and smashed on the Capitol's steps).[19] The interior was filled with statues and portraits of Great Americans and paintings of Great American Moments, most notably John Trumbull's iconic paintings in the rotunda: the *Surrender of General Burgoyne at Saratoga,* the *Declaration of Independence,* the *Surrender of Lord Cornwallis at Yorktown,* and *General George Washington Resigning His Commission.*[20] American values, American heroes, and American history, all on display.

The building's scope and scale were equally symbolic, designed to capture the spirit of American governance. The imposing rotunda with its impressive dome signaled the high ambitions—even the majesty— of popular representation, as did the House and Senate chambers, open to public view: the House, grand in scale, with a dramatic domed ceiling and crimson drapery; the Senate with its clubby intimacy and luxurious red Moroccan leather chairs. The concentric arc-shaped rows of simple desks in both houses captured the other half of the republican equation: a plainspoken, straightforward approach to business with little to no frippery to get in the way. (Newspaper ads seeking craftsmen to build them requested "strong, neat and plain" furniture "without any superfluous ornament.")[21] The desks were the only offices that congressmen had, aside from their paper-strewn boardinghouse or hotel rooms.[22] In his first months in office French saw it all, touring the building from bottom to top, glorying in its wonders, and laughing at how the "superb" view from the dome made people in the rotunda look like "little squab looking fellows."[23]

All in all, the Capitol's structural design was intended to have an impact, and French got the message. He could think of "no more imposing spectacle" than an evening session of the House: the light "equal to that of at least 1,000 candles," the galleries jammed with the Washington "gentility," the "vast pillars," the plush drapery that looked "richer, if possible, by artificial light than by the light of day." If conditions were right—"If the House happens to be in good humor, & some interesting subject is under debate"—it was a magnificent sight, suggesting all that Congress was supposed to be.[24]

And Congress was supposed to be quite a lot; in the first half of the nineteenth century it had a particularly large role to play. By the time of French's arrival in 1833, the government had been in operation for forty-four years. On the one hand, this was long enough to prove that one stupid policy or one sweeping crisis wouldn't dash it to ruins. America's survival through the War of 1812, the nation's second war against Great Britain, suggested that the American experiment might just have legs. On the other hand, forty-four years wasn't long enough to take things for granted; there were kinks to be worked out, fundamental understandings yet unreached, major decisions yet to be made, and large, looming power vacuums waiting to be filled. Here, too, the Capitol embodied the Union; it was still under construction, and would be into the Civil War and beyond.

There was also the destabilizing influence of national expansion. The young nation was still in its adolescence, spreading across the North American continent at a remarkable rate. Between 1840 and 1860, seven new states were added to the Union; in 1860, fifteen out of thirty-two states were less than forty-five years old. For many Americans, it was exciting and empowering, seemingly the groundwork of a future empire. It was also unsettling, because each new state raised fundamental questions about the nature of the nation. The question of slavery was front and center—would it, should it, spread and survive?—but it wasn't the only one. What of native peoples who owned western lands? How far could new states go in setting their own terms? What was the relationship between periphery and center? And what about the logistics? How would this far-flung nation be interconnected? By toll roads? Canals? Railroads? Who would fund and manage their development, and how? And speaking of funding, how active should the national government be in harmonizing the nation's unsteady and diverse economy as the Industrial Age began to unfold? What role should the government play in handling the period's many financial panics? There were endless uncertainties, logical enough in a new and growing nation, but unsettling nonetheless.

Congress would help to answer many of these questions, establishing vital precedents. It would play a role in crisscrossing the continent with roads and canals. It would foster industry with protective tariffs on imported goods—or not, depending on which party was in power. It would weigh in on the terms of statehood for every new state, but not without turmoil; although the Constitution and subsequent legislation outlined this process, it left room for interpretation, and the question of slavery expanded to fill much of it. In one way or another, during the first half of the nineteenth century, Congress was shaping the scale, scope, and influence of the national government and how far it could go in shaping the nation.

And the American people knew it. Congress was where the action was. Although the presidency got its share of press coverage—and more during election years—Congress got the lion's share of column inches.[25] Newspapers routinely printed lengthy summaries of congressional debates as well as congressional commentary. Popular culture kept pace. By the 1850s, there was a virtual school of Congress-bashing in squibs, plays, cartoons, even mock epic poetry. All of these efforts were filled with inside jokes grounded on the assumption that the reading public was remarkably knowledgeable about the day-to-day happenings in Congress.

They were certainly well versed in the words of Congress's star orators. This was the great age of speechifying, and the Senate was its national headquarters, though the House held its own. Oratory was a vastly popular form of entertainment through much of the nineteenth century. People would flock to hear stump speeches and lectures that went on for hours (testimony to the long-lost art of having a long attention span). This was the realm of Henry Clay and Daniel Webster, as well as a number of their peers who have since lost their luster. When these men were due to give speeches, crowds packed the galleries, Senate attendance improved remarkably, and Representatives migrated from the House to hear them. One 1848 speech by Clay—before the American Colonization Society, after hours in the House—attracted a crowd of thousands who not only filled every square inch of the chamber but packed the rotunda and the space outside the windows. (One disgruntled congressman quipped that Clay, a repeat presidential contender, "could get more men to run after him to hear him speak, and fewer to vote for him, than any man in America.")[26] Such grandstand performances didn't necessarily change congressional votes. But they might change public opinion, and that could change everything. A reliable source of praise and fame, impressive oratory was political muscle. As one reporter put it, "Eloquence, in this empire, is power."[27]

At their best, the best speakers voiced shared sentiments so elo-quently and forcefully that their words became a kind of patriotic gos-pel; generations of schoolchildren memorized and delivered Daniel Webster's speeches as American anthems. Even French, a firm Demo-crat when he arrived in Washington, almost genuflected at the men-tion of the mighty Whig's name. Webster was a New Hampshire native *and* the voice of America: it was impossible for French not to be proud. When French was accused of attacking Webster in his newspaper col-umn, he anxiously checked every column he'd ever written, breathing a sigh of relief when he came up empty-handed: he was "[t]oo proud of being a native of the same state with him to abuse him." As much as he disapproved of Webster's Whig politics, French considered him "one of the greatest men in this Union."[28]

It's no wonder that some people viewed Congress as the land of Great Men. French did at first. "The color of the rose was about everything I saw," he later recalled.[29] Even congressmen themselves could be im-pressed by some of their fellows. French's friend John Parker Hale (D-NH) acknowledged as much when he asked big-name colleagues to frank his letters home so his wife could save their autographs.[30]

This was the Congress enshrined in the Capitol's architecture and artwork, the Congress that took French's breath away. But there was another Congress, a place of negotiating and compromising, of parlia-mentary power plays on the floor and politicking in back rooms, of ego, bravado, and boozy backslapping with an occasional ultimatum deliv-ered behind closed doors. The man-to-man challenges and the sense of community; the heated debate and drawn-out pauses; the quiet asides, muttered insults, and fistfights: this was the ground-level workaday Congress, an often contentious, sometimes tumultuous, and occasionally even dangerous assembly charged with crafting policies and precedents that would shape the nation, a fitting reflection of a restless people pushing the bounds of empire.

THE "AUGUST PRESENCE" OF
THE AMERICAN CONGRESS

As impressive as the House sometimes seemed to French, evening sessions rarely ended that way. Sometime around midnight, with the audience long gone and members straggling off, the mood often changed. The niceties of debate would break down. Men would become tired and testy. There would be interruptions and constant (desperate) calls to adjourn. The Speaker's pounding gavel and screams for order would only add to the prevailing noise and confusion. Members would be sleeping in their seats or on the sofas bordering the room, some stretched out on the carpet behind the Speaker's chair. (It wasn't only the House that was sleeping; partway through a twelve-hour Senate session in 1843, the ever-energetic Thomas Hart Benton [D-MO] declared himself "quite fresh and vigorous," having "just waked up from the sofa.")[31] At about 2:00 a.m., someone would make a call of the House, summoning all members to the floor; by 5:00 a.m., the sergeant at arms would be dragging them into the chamber half-dressed, their hair uncombed, their faces unwashed and unshaven, looking "as little like 'the first gentlemen in America' as possible," French thought.[32]

It's hard to imagine a more human Congress: an assemblage of sleepy, grouchy, disheveled men. But this was what most evening sessions were like. French saw "this farce" time and again. And this wasn't the worst of it. Take, for example, the last night of the session in 1835. A military bill had been bouncing back and forth between the two houses all night, the Senate rejecting a House amendment granting President Andrew Jackson three million dollars to spend on the military, the House standing firm. Although a conference committee devised a compromise, it wasn't enough for House Democrats, who defeated it by stopping any and all action until the session expired. To hasten the end along, they played the rule-stickler card, refusing to vote after the session's formal closing hour of midnight; at various points, between seventy and one hundred Democrats left their seats in protest, and they didn't leave quietly.[33] Drunk and belligerent, they were, as French put it, "laughing and scolding, swearing and joking, hissing & cheering & all sorts of things." Reflecting that he was "in the August presence of the American Congress," French felt "a sort of sickness at the heart."[34] Here was rug-level politics at its best, or rather its worst: drunken chaos as a political ploy. And it worked. Nothing got done. And Congress adjourned at 3:00 a.m.[35]

This was hardly a typical day in the House.[36] Even so, it reveals much about the routine dynamics of Congress. It reminds us that the everyday business of legislating had rough edges—sometimes very rough. Alongside the debating, discussing, conferring, and voting was a healthy (or rather, unhealthy) dose of belligerence, violence, and drunken swaggering with its own logic and tempo. The *Congressional Globe* often glossed over such things; its account of March 3, 1835, looks remarkably sedate. But they were there, and they shaped what Congress did and how it evolved.[37] It's an obvious fact with broad implications: What a legislature does and how it does it are direct reflections of how its members get along. Of course, "getting along" is a hard thing to measure, and that's precisely the point. People are unpredictable, and for that very reason their interactions matter, affecting outcomes in unexpected ways.

Look closely at the Capitol's working spaces in action and you can see the rough edges. These weren't pristine stages for speechifying and voting. Take, for example, the House chamber. The *Congressional Globe* makes it seem calm and orderly, with a smattering of sniping and scattered interruptions, but in truth the chamber was a roiling sea of noise and motion. Members were continually coming and going, chatting and laughing and arguing, reading newspapers, writing letters, franking printed speeches, and tossing off quips at a speaker's expense or urging him on. Men who wanted the floor were shouting to the Speaker and waving their arms; those already speaking were gesturing dramatically, pounding their desks, sometimes yelling to be heard. During the debate over Oregon statehood, Senator William Allen (D-OH) pounded his desk hard enough to draw blood, leading one newspaper to declare it "the first and only blood shed in the Oregon war." (Allen must have

The crowded and chaotic House floor in 1857, not long before it moved to larger quarters (*The Meeting of Congress—Hall of Representatives, December 1857*, by Winslow Homer, *Harper's Weekly*, December 12, 1857. Courtesy of HarpWeek)

been quite a performer; another paper described him as "a cross between William Pitt and an angry cockatoo.")[38]

All in all, the House was in a constant state of organized chaos. Looking down from the gallery, one reporter thought that a deaf man "would be apt to think himself in a spacious gymnasium" filled with men practicing "odd exercises of the arms and legs and head."[39] Add the comings and goings of clerks shuffling papers, the pages darting between desks running errands, and the buzz from the galleries, punctuated by an occasional hiss or cheer, and you get a sense of working conditions on the House floor.[40]

In part, this was a product of numbers; there were too many people in too small a space. When the chamber was completed in 1807, there were 145 seats representing seventeen states; fifty years later, there were thirty-one states represented by roughly 240 men: nearly a hundred more men, desks, and chairs crammed onto the floor. (French prided himself on learning their names faster than anyone.)[41] The acoustics didn't help matters. Ironically, the room's symbolic grandeur wreaked

havoc on the *actual* voice of the people. The high-domed ceiling created strange echoes and the crimson drapery absorbed sound, bouncing voices all over the hall or swallowing them entirely.[42] The end result
was laughable. People would call to the Speaker from one side of the
room and he would turn to the other to recognize them, mistaking the
echo for the voice. Whispers inaudible only inches away were quite
audible in random pockets around the room; once, a young man's "whis-
perings" from the "love corner" of the ladies' gallery made it all the way
down to the Speaker's chair. New members had to learn the tricks of
the chamber, the "modulations of the voice" and "turns of the body" that
were likely to get them heard.[43] Thus the "odd exercises" of the arms,
legs, and head. People were battling the acoustics.

All this in a room that was hot, stuffy, and smelly. At the end of a
typical day, with the galleries full and hours of body heat trapped in
the chamber, French thought that reading aloud to members was like
reading "with his head stuck into an oven."[44] When the House moved
to larger windowless quarters in 1857, the acoustics improved but the
air didn't. This wasn't just a matter of cigar smoke, whiskey fumes, and
body odor. A series of climate studies revealed the scope of the problem: no air was circulating in the chamber, and the wisp of a draft that
rose through the floor grates had to pass through a layer of "lint, dirt,
tobacco quids, expectoration, and filth of every sort."[45] One member
claimed that the "confined and poisonous" air had caused "much sickness and even several deaths," and indeed, a handful of congressmen
died during an average session, though not necessarily because of the
air.[46] Ongoing whimpering from the floor produced another study,
this one demonstrating that it was thirty degrees warmer inside than
outside and that the chamber smelled of sewage from the basement.[47]
Visiting the new chamber not long after it opened, French wasn't impressed. The idea of "shutting up a thousand or two people in a kind of
cellar, where none of God's direct light or air can come in to them . . .
does not jump with my notions of *living*," he groused.[48] Thirty years later,
members *still* declared the House "the worst ventilated building on the
continent."[49]

Clearly there were limits to politicking on the House floor. Extended
debates on fine points of legislation were difficult at best. Declaratory
speeches were easier, assuming that you had mastered the acoustics and

weren't banking on the room's rapt attention; often such efforts were aimed at a home audience. Group efforts were more effective. Tag-team obstruction was part of the parliamentary game and backup usually was right at hand. Anyone making a proposal, refuting a ruling, or hungry for a few extra minutes of speaking time only had to call out for the help of "political friends," as did Francis Rives (D-VA) when denied a chance to refute an accusation; when he asked, "have I no friend in this House that will move a suspension of the rules, in order that I may be heard?" a "political friend" immediately did just that.[50]

Sometimes the hubbub was handy. If you played the acoustics right, you could confer quietly around the edges of the chamber without being overheard. And if you lowered your voice to just the right pitch, you could threaten someone on the sly. In 1840, Daniel Jenifer (W-MD) suddenly dropped his voice in the middle of a speech to deliver what must have been either a threat or an insult; witnesses didn't know what he said, but they saw its impact on the victim's face.[51]

This spat went no further, but that wasn't always the case. Given conditions on the floor, it's easy to see how angry words could spark a chain reaction. Colleagues on left and right were little more than an elbow away, some routinely wore weapons, many had short fuses (growing shorter all the time given the working conditions), and it was an easy slide from hard words to jostling, clenched fists, shoving, punching, and bowie knives.

The House floor didn't always feel safe, and in fact it sometimes wasn't; standing up for yourself meant running a risk. In 1837, when Committee on Ways and Means member Richard Fletcher (W-MA) asked John Quincy Adams (W-MA) if he should respond to a "coarse and abusive" verbal assault by Democratic committee-mates, Adams advised silence. The attack was a "party movement to bully down" Fletcher, he thought, and resistance would result in a fistfight or worse.[52] Not only did Fletcher remain silent, but he resigned from the committee. As far as the Democratic bullies were concerned, it was a job well done.

The Senate chamber was a very different place, though it had some of the same problems. It was noisy, though to a lesser degree. (French was put out by the "buzzings" of ladies admitted on the floor, as they were from time to time.)[53] And the heat and foul air did their dam-

age. Sweating profusely in his shirtsleeves one July afternoon, the normally good-humored John Parker Hale was the absolute "picture of
discomfort," noted a colleague. Hale considered the Senate "the most
unhealthful, uncomfortable, ill-contrived place I was ever in in my
life."[54]

Hot air of all kinds to the contrary, the Senate was generally calmer
than the House. Smaller in size, with its acoustics in working order and
its members a little older, more established, more experienced, and
sometimes higher on the social scale, it was a true forum for debate as
well as a proving ground for future presidential hopefuls. There was less
competition to be heard on the floor; every senator had the right to speak
for as long as his lungs could carry him. And there was more of a sense
of community: senators put down roots because they served for six years,
as opposed to the two-year terms in the House.

Debate in the Senate was thus more of a dialogue—long-winded,
agenda-driven, and something of a performance, but a dialogue just the

The Senate chamber in 1846. This composite of daguerreotype portraits—all
of them taken for this image—was four years in the making. (*United States Senate
Chamber* by Thomas Doney, after James Whitehorn. Courtesy of the National Portrait Gallery, Smithsonian Institution)

same. This doesn't mean that the Senate was a haven of safety. It wasn't. There were plenty of threats and insults on the floor. Henry Clay (W-KY) was a master. His attack in 1832 on the elderly Samuel Smith (J-MD), a Revolutionary War veteran and forty-year veteran of the Senate, was so severe that senators physically drew back, worried that things might get ugly.[55] Clay called Smith a tottering old man with flip-flopping politics; Smith denied it and countered that he could "take a view" of Clay's politics that would prove *him* inconsistent; and Clay jeered, "Take it, sir, take it—I dare you!" Smith defended himself, but when he later sought the advice of John Quincy Adams (clearly, Fight Consultant Extraordinaire), Smith was so deeply wounded that he was on the verge of tears.[56]

Some such exchanges escalated into duel challenges, which were far more common in the Senate than in the House. Not only were formal duels more likely among the Senate's somewhat more elite membership, but they preserved its sense of community by channeling violence off the floor. Even senatorial fistfights often took place elsewhere—on the streets or in boardinghouses or hotels.[57]

The different spirit in the two chambers was readily apparent in the wake of a fight. Clashes in the House triggered calls to the Speaker for protection; clashes in the Senate led senators to appeal to one another and their shared sense of respect.

"THE DAMP DUNGEONS OF THE CAPITOL".

Of course, there were other working spaces in the Capitol, some public, some private. The library and the lobbies were in the former category. The library was available for milling about of all kinds. Tourists wandered through while congressmen chatted about doings in the chambers or bided time to avoid a vote, and pages dashed in to fetch books for congressmen. The lobbies, as one might expect, were for lobbying as well as lingering, and typically were filled with tourists, reporters, people who wanted to hear the debates but were crowded out of the galleries, and assorted others ("lobbyists") demanding things of congressmen. In later years, when French had lost his clerking job due to the shifting tides of politics, he tried to bank on his congressional connections by earning a living as a lobbyist, without much success.[58]

But some things weren't fit for the open air; some topics needed closed-door privacy, frank unhurried conversations, and, in the case of the House, decent acoustics. Thus the importance of committees. Not only did they allow for the practice of politics by other means, but they shunted work off the floor, a growing necessity given the increasing complexity and quantity of congressional business; for many scholars, the rise of a committee system marks the modernization of Congress.[59] Much of the institution's real work took place in committees, particularly in standing committees overseeing ongoing concerns such as foreign relations or military affairs. As one congressman put it, committees were appointed "to facilitate and mature business" for the body as a whole; they shaped legislation, conducted investigations, and collected information, among other things. In essence, committees were legislatures by proxy, though their recommendations were more likely to be challenged on the floor than their equivalent today.[60]

Yet they were legislatures with a difference: committee-room doors were firmly closed. Private rooms where men could hash things out, they had the look and feel of gentleman's clubs, with plush Turkish rugs, deep leather chairs, bookshelves filled with spillover from the congressional library, and sideboards stocked with whiskey and cigars.[61] Their privacy served a purpose. As one congressman put it, he "had said many things in committee which he could not say" in the House.[62]

And yet closed doors weren't always an advantage. Off-limits to both the public and the press, documented only by formal reports that were often biased and selectively censored, committee meetings were dark voids where anything could happen. Short-term select or special committees were especially problematic; often focused on sensitive matters of immediate concern, their members bound to work together for only a short time, they could be dangerous terrain.[63] If he were ever unfortunate enough to be involved in a brawl, observed one congressman in 1840, "he would never consent to be tried in the damp dungeons of the Capitol by any committee."[64]

Finding out precisely what happened in these "dungeons" isn't easy. Their closed-door policy was so effectively maintained that even today it's hard to get past it; you have to find a leak. Daniel Jenifer (W-MD) spilled the truth in the House in 1840. Outraged at a biased report from the Committee on Elections concerning a contested election, he ranted for days, insisting that Democrats on the committee had bullied two Northern Whig members into accepting the report (and thus, new Democratic congressmen). The Democrats succeeded because the Northerners were easy targets who wouldn't "resent an injury done them"—meaning, they didn't abide by the code of honor and wouldn't fight back.[65] Jenifer's charges were so inflammatory that the *Globe* didn't record them, reporting only that he "spoke with great acrimony"; they appeared in print only when a Democrat refuted them.[66] When Henry Wise (W-VA) mentioned a committee member who had threatened to pummel whoever disagreed with him, he was promptly scolded for exposing "the secrets of the prison house . . . before the world."[67]

Wise caused his own share of problems in committee-rooms. That same year, he took part in an armed showdown. To slap at President Jackson, Wise and his friend Balie Peyton (W-TN) had pushed for a House investigation of the president's "pet banks" (state depositories for public funds that replaced what Democrats called the "Monster" Bank of the United States). In the days before testifying to the investigative committee, an agent for several of those banks, Reuben M. Whitney, had called Peyton a liar in the press. So when Whitney sneered at Peyton during his testimony, all hell broke loose. Peyton jumped to his feet and threatened to kill Whitney; Wise, who had been regaling committee members with amusing anecdotes on a couch across the room, caught the drift, rushed over, and joined in. At this point, Whitney jumped to his feet, Peyton reached for his gun, and Wise positioned himself within firing range of Whitney, his hand on his gun, his gaze fixed on Whitney's hand in his pocket.

If Whitney had moved his arm one inch as if to pull a pistol, Wise later admitted, he would have killed him on the spot. (Had Whitney "but fingered his 'gold boys,'" joked a reporter, he would have been a dead man.[68]) Although Wise eventually saved the day, calming Peyton long enough for Whitney to escape, he never lived it down. French told a Wise joke two years later: the Virginian had lost his luggage—containing his pistols—on the way to Washington, so a committee that he served on couldn't meet, because he couldn't shoot the witnesses.[69]

Guns, threats, insults, and bullying: a lot was happening behind closed doors. There was a reason why congressmen called committee-rooms the "black holes of the Capitol."[70] They also called them bar-rooms, again for good reason; not only were they stocked with liquor for committee meetings, but during evening sessions they were on call for the House and Senate chambers—"[c]onverted into a bar-room," as one senator put it.[71] (Not all of those howling Democrats on the last night of the session in 1835 got drunk over dinner.) Rumor had it that more than one page got his drinking legs from "contraband" liquor filched from committee-rooms.[72]

Nor was that all as far as booze was concerned. There were two bars in out-of-the-way corners of the Capitol, one near the House, and the aptly named "Hole in the Wall" behind the Senate post office.[73] There was also a "refectory" serving food and drink of *all* kinds, and beginning in 1858, a members' dining room that served hard liquor to those in the know; rumor had it that if you wanted gin or whiskey in the refectory, you should ask for "pale sherry" or "Madeira," neither one a "spirituous" liquor.[74] If you were friendly with Daniel Webster, he might invite you to his "Wine Room," a private wine cellar of sorts in a small room on the Capitol's third floor, just above the Senate chamber.[75] And then there were the whiskey jugs stashed in clerks' offices.[76] All told, rivers of liquor flowed through the Capitol, and had been flowing for quite some time. As early as 1809, the Senate was billing a hefty supply of "syrup" to its contingent fund, an expense laughingly pointed out by a Senate committee on contingent expenses in 1874.[77] Of course, this was an age of remarkably heavy drinking, every day, all day, all the time. There were well over one hundred ways to call someone drunk, including long-lost classics such as *has a pinch of snuff in his wig*; *clips the king's English*; *takes a lunar*; and *chases geese.*[78] In this sense, Congress was indeed representative.[79] The temperance movement had a point.

Attempts to stem the flow of liquor didn't do much. The Congressional Temperance Society was a fine idea with little influence.[80] Even after an 1837 joint rule banned the sale of "spirituous liquors" in the Capitol or on its grounds, the problem persisted; there were too many loopholes—in an assembly of lawyers.[81] Thus the remarkable precision of the 1867 amendment to the joint rule; it prohibited "spirituous or malt liquors or wines" from being "offered for sale, exhibited, or kept within the Capitol, or any room or building connected therewith, or on the public grounds adjacent thereto."[82] But even this didn't fully dry out the Capitol.[83] With the institutional equivalent of a wink and a nod, Congress essentially sanctioned drinking, yet another factor contributing to the unpredictability of the House and Senate floors.

There are no boozy congressmen in the *Globe*, though there's plenty of denial. Whenever some brave soul raised the issue, he was invariably called a liar. The chorus of outrage (Liquor? What liquor?) greeting Massachusetts Republican Henry Wilson's charges about booze in the Capitol in 1867 is laughable alongside his detailed account of precisely what liquor was kept where.[84] Along similar lines, when Henry Wise (W-VA) claimed that Democrats were drunk at the close of the 1835 session, an outraged Democrat immediately denied it and demanded that Wise name names. "The gentleman might feel unhappy" if he did, Wise wryly replied.[85]

"IF THE WHOLE PEOPLE . . . KNEW AS MUCH AS I DO ABOUT THESE SESSIONS . . ."

Of course, Congress was *not* a pit of abandon. It was a working institution doing its job: creating and debating legislation, considering and acting on petitions, attending to ongoing business and special circumstances in committees, and more. This is the Congress that we know and (occasionally) love.

And yet the potential for dramatic confrontations and violence could have a profound impact. It certainly filled the galleries; the likelihood of a showdown packed them full. Debate "great measures of policy" and the galleries were empty, complained Franklin Pierce (D-NH) in 1838. But hint at the chance of "personalities" the next day, and the galleries and lobbies were "crowded almost to suffocation," the halls and doorways "literally blockaded." As long as the public craved such things, it was useless to assume that their elected representatives would behave any differently.[86] Gallery rubberneckers reflected public opinion, and the public seemed to glory in congressional clashes, a hunger that would bear bitter fruit with passing decades.

It was another reality of being a congressman: the constant presence and overriding influence of the American public in the galleries and beyond. Sitting above the members' heads was a watchful audience, studying their actions, listening to their words, and forming their own opinions. Sitting alongside them were people who were trying their best to shape those opinions: the reporters of the American press. Congressmen ignored this audience at their peril. In the same way that the Capitol's art and architecture expressed Congress's symbolic meaning, and the rug-level realities of its working spaces shaped congressional proceedings, the galleries imposed the influence of Congress's ultimate judges and juries: the public and the press.

French's diary is littered with references to them: the mumbling, "buzzing," whispering gallery-sitters of the House and Senate.[87] Members on the floor could see who was up there. Sometimes they scanned the crowd for familiar faces.[88] People in the galleries did the same looking down at the assembly below. But they couldn't see everything—certainly not the worst of it, as French well knew. Irritated at a proposal to start the next session early to avoid undone business at its close, he felt sure that the House could finish "every whit" of business if members would stop wasting time on selfish whims and fancies, like figuring out how to buy themselves books with government funds. If the "whole people of this Union knew as much as I do about these sessions of Congress," he fumed, they might actually try to "reform their representation." But instead, they were "outrageously humbugged by their representatives."[89]

French had a point. Even looking down from the galleries, onlookers missed a lot. Mostly, they saw heads—not heads of state, but rather foreheads and hair. The noted British traveler Harriet Martineau was struck by the sight; entering the Senate galleries in the 1830s, she immediately concluded that she had never seen "a finer set of heads."[90] American writers were no less impressed. Daniel Webster's brow seemed uniformly awe-inspiring. "The forehead is remarkable," enthused one magazine writer. "You follow its bold curve with fear and trembling."[91] John C. Calhoun, on the other hand, had "a frizzly head, and an eye like a hawk" with a "mouth partly open," not quite as awe-inspiring a sight as "Black Dan".[92] Foreheads were humbler in the House. Henry Wise sadly lacked "the Shakespearian pile of forehead," and Vermonter Samuel S. Prentiss's (AJ-VT) head was "large and out of proportion to the rest of his frame," though somehow "not ugly."[93] Americans who encountered Charles Dickens after his Washington visit had the same strange obsession, repeatedly asking if the legislators' heads had impressed him. Given that some of them belonged to bullying slaveholders, he wasn't much moved.[94]

In part, this focus on congressional heads reflects the period's faddish interest in phrenology, the pseudoscience of determining a person's character by studying the shape of his skull.[95] French had his skull read in 1841 and found the reading eerily accurate: he was sensitive, "inclined to literature," a good neighbor and a good friend, "liked a good dinner & a glass of wine & enjoyed company," and was "rather disposed to be indolent," though he could work hard when he felt like it. His one qualm was the phrenologist's claim that he didn't remember people; he remembered the names and faces of congressmen better than anyone he knew. Of course, any phrenologist who met French and noted his stout build and good humor would have given the same reading; clearly, this was a man who relished dinners with friends. Even so, French thought there was "something in it."[96]

In this sense, heads were descriptive shorthand: describe a head and you described a person, character and all. But the head-centric accounts of the House and Senate also say something about a gallery-sitter's perspective; literally and figuratively, it was only an overview. They heard a sampling of oratory, saw a smidgen of legislation-in-the-making, learned a bit about policy and party politics, got a sense of the hum of business, and had a glance at the people behind the names. Depending on their timing, they might also witness a congressional clash, though again from a distance, perhaps seeing some shoving in the House or hearing a deliberate insult in the Senate. Sometimes they didn't hear anything at all. A self-described "Mechanic" told one congressman, "I *felt* . . . that I was listening to eloquence and was well content to wait for the words until I could see them in The Globe."[97]

Enter the press, a shaping influence on what happened on the floor. During testy proceedings, congressmen often looked up to the galleries and pleaded with reporters to be fair.[98] If they weren't "fair and impartial," it would be near impossible for congressmen to "keep themselves erect before their constituents," Francis Rives told reporters when he was accused of bullying people in a committee-room.[99] Thomas Hart Benton made a similar plea in 1834 after insisting that the sergeant at arms arrest people hissing and cheering in the Senate galleries. Colleagues protested that arresting gallery sitters seemed to pit the Senate against the American public. Not surprisingly, Benton did some hasty backpedaling, pleading with onlooking reporters to report his meaning accurately.[100]

Here we see the power of gallery-sitters and what they represented. Benton's impulsive swipe at some gallery rowdies became a strike at the American public in the blink of an eye—a rather large leap, but a largely accurate one. In a sense, gallery onlookers *did* stand in for the public. They were doing on-site what others did from a distance: evaluating their representatives and registering their opinions, though with hissing and cheering instead of votes and petitions, and perhaps unintentionally with clumps of dirt; a sign on the Senate gallery door stated: "Gentlemen will be pleased not to put their feet on the board in front of the gallery, as the dirt from them falls upon Senators' heads."[101]

Like the public writ large, all kinds of people looked on from the galleries. In addition to the press, the Washington gentility was there in force, as were tourists, visitors, and the general public, including French's young son Frank in the 1850s.[102] Women were there in such large numbers that they crowded men out.[103] After being squeezed out of the Senate gallery, the legal scholar Francis Lieber (of "Lieber Code" fame) joked that he wanted to found the "Polite anti-ladies-thronging-poor-men-out-of-every-chance-of-seeing-anything-Society."[104] By the 1850s, there were also women reporters in the galleries. In Washington, women had a very public presence.

Sometimes that presence was felt on the floor. Merely by sitting in the galleries, women occasionally discouraged bad behavior. Congressional combatants sometimes glanced at the galleries before throwing an insult or taking a swing, and managed to contain themselves if women were present (though in the 1820s, the erratic and eruptive Representative John Randolph [R-VA] doubled down on his insults when told that his victim's wife was in the audience).[105] Congressmen who sprinted to the galleries to shield women during brawls were drawing gendered lines in the sand, protecting allegedly fragile flowers from the rough-and-tumble of politics.[106] The creation of a ladies' gallery in both houses was more of the same, protecting women from lower-class men, though "gentlemen" who accompanied ladies were admitted.[107]

This isn't to say that women wanted protection. Men and women alike often came to the galleries explicitly for the fights, driven by the same urges that draw crowds to professional wrestling matches and hockey games: a love of sport and spectacle, and the thrill of a contained risk. (Wrestlers, hockey players, and congressmen rarely kill one another, though they make a good show of it.) People enjoyed cheering on their champions to fight the good fight. They loved the bold gesture, the cutting comment, the "personality" thrown down like a gauntlet; a rousing congressional brawl was the icing on the cake. As much as French recognized the dire implications of congressional chaos at key moments like session openings and closings, he perked up when he saw a good man-to-man brawl. It was one of the things that he liked about his job; when fists flew, he had a ringside seat. He reveled in what he called the *"great fight"* of 1841, which began when Edward Stanly (W-NC) and Henry Wise (W-VA) exchanged insults. When Wise slugged Stanly, "nearly all the members" rushed over and began pummeling one another in a wild melee. "[T]he Speaker & I had the best chance to see all the fun," French wrote to his half brother, "& while he stood at his desk pounding & yelling, I stood at mine 'calm as a summer's morning'— enjoying the sport, *and keeping the minutes of the proceedings!*"[108]

In this sense, one of the period's much-used metaphors is strikingly apt: politics was a kind of war. We make that same link today when we speak of political campaigns, but given the routine electoral violence in antebellum America, it had the ring of truth.[109] Some campaigns even featured mock soldiers on parade.[110] Looking back in the shadow of the Civil War, such military fervor seems unfortunate, even ghoulish. But it captured the raw bluster and bravado of the period's politics, and acknowledged—even celebrated—its violent undertow. As Franklin Pierce suggested, the American people had a passion for violent clashes of principle and purpose, including the kind playing out in the Capitol, one of many political battlefields.

So when French gazed at the Capitol on that cold December day in 1833 and worried about the fate of the nation, he had good reason. Congress *was* the Union incarnate, for better and worse, and its collapse could bring down the nation in its wake. On December 10, 1839—six years later, almost to the day—he thought that his worst fears were playing out. For ten days, the House had been unable to elect a Speaker and organize, and the hall was in a state of chaos. At one point that afternoon, more than twenty men were on their feet screaming for order, for the floor, for attention, with all their might. When someone challenged the vote of a man whose election was contested, he was up in an instant, howling about his rights and waving his written commission so violently that French was surprised that it didn't rip to shreds. At least once, he feared "personal violence."[111]

To French, this wasn't just a momentary outbreak of congressional chaos. It was the state of the nation. It made the national government seem surprisingly fragile, and in so doing, it put the Union's survival in doubt. Indeed, maybe this was the beginning of the end. Sitting at home at the end of the day, exhausted and losing hope, he confessed to his sister that he felt like "a mourner, following my Country to its grave." Years from now, he imagined, when the Constitution was "a thing that *was*, the pen of the historian" would date "the commencement of its overthrow" to this congressional breakdown and all that it revealed. This was "an era in the history of our Country," French thought, a period of enormous and eventful change.[112] He was right in ways that he couldn't even begin to fathom.

2

THE MIX OF MEN
IN CONGRESS

MEETING PLACE OF
NORTH AND SOUTH

rench's early years in Washington were full of firsts. Mingling
with people from around the country, working to expand the
national reach of his party, seeing the South and plantation
slavery: all of it was new, and its impact was mixed.[1] On the one hand,
he felt the bonds of Union as never before. On the other hand, he saw
firsthand how fragile those bonds could be. Such was the paradox of
political life at the national center: sectional differences were never as
apparent as when Northerners, Southerners, and Westerners lived,
worked, and played side by side.

Party loyalties sometimes bridged such divides, particularly the
divide over slavery. When it came to the South's "peculiar institution," many a Northern Democrat like French was more than willing
to appease Southern allies for the sake of the Union, their party,
and their careers; the South reigned supreme in Washington in more
ways than one. Such negotiations were part of the business of Congress. There—as nowhere else—French saw the working reality of
the complex shifting balance of section and party that kept the Union
as one.[2]

French's Congress was a sprawling mix of men. Spawned by the rise
of the Jacksonian "common man" and all that came with it, a wide range of
people found their way into Congress, many of them figures of local prom-
inence who served a term and then went home, sometimes vanishing

from public life and even from the public record, often without a single portrait or photograph left behind. They are literally faceless names long gone. Scene-stealers like Henry Clay make it easy to forget the mass majority that profoundly shaped the human reality of the antebellum Congress.[3]

Given the brisk turnover, both houses were filled with a shifting cast of freshmen, particularly the House with its two-year terms; roughly half of every House was new.[4] Regardless of their talents, these men mattered. They registered their opinions, defended the rights and interests of their constituents, supported their party, and countered their foes. Some of them threw an occasional punch. They were a center of gravity in Congress, an anchoring reality beneath the highfliers, a shaping influence on the texture and tone of congressional proceedings, and, through sheer force of numbers, the ultimate arbiters of what got done. It is impossible to fully understand the antebellum Congress without acknowledging their presence and influence.

Photographs are a good starting point; these men were part of the first generation to be captured on film. To French, history itself was like a photograph. A good historian should produce "a daguerreotype of the times he writes about," he thought, preserving on paper realities great and small—the "minutia of existence."[5] Photographs capture some of this minutia, revealing very real people in the clothing, postures, and attitudes of a very different time.

Yet photographs can be deceiving; they show how congressmen *wanted* to appear. Taken collectively, they form a parade of self-importance, jaws set, faces unsmiling, dressed in black almost to a man, with starched white collars and cravats tied at the neck. A few strike a Napoleonic pose, one hand thrust in their vest. Many try for grim dignity and achieve it. Some have their life experiences etched on their faces. Others show a flash of the charisma that won them office. A few are simply homely. (According to acquaintances, *Globe* editor Francis P. Blair's charms far outweighed his looks.)[6] They all convey a certain congressional gravitas, forward-looking, farseeing, serious of purpose: the "National Statesman" that each wanted to be.

So much for the image of the antebellum congressman. What of the reality? Demographics help to fill this gap. Collect and analyze broad sweeps of data and you find that between 1830 and 1860, the average

A composite photograph of the members of the Thirty-sixth Senate (1859–61) from the work of the famed photographer Mathew Brady (Courtesy of the Library of Congress)

member of both houses was a college-educated lawyer in his forties with experience in public office. In the House, roughly half the members fit this description; in the Senate, significantly more.[7]

There aren't many surprises here. But demographics can be deceptive; they tend to sacrifice gritty human realities in favor of assembled portraits, and when studying past peoples whose lives and habits are dramatically different from our own, minutiae matter. For example, take John B. Dawson (D-LA). Forty-three when he entered the House in 1841, he was a college-educated planter and newspaper publisher from a well-to-do family with an unsuccessful run for governor, fourteen years as a parish judge, and two years of state legislative experience; he served two terms in Congress. Demographically speaking, Dawson is the virtual embodiment of the typical representative. But look for him in Congress and you find a man who routinely wore both a bowie knife and a pistol, and wasn't shy about using them in the House chamber, threatening to slash one man's throat and cocking his pistol at another, among his many moments of congressional glory.[8] Dawson—the hands-down winner of the Frequent Weapon Wielder award—is a reminder that tidy demographics can mask messy realities.

Look beneath that mask and you can see it: the mix of men in the antebellum Congress. In addition to sons of privilege who attended Ivy League schools, you see men who were schooled at local academies and colleges, as well as men with catch-as-catch-can educations with little more than a few years at the local "common" school, like 98 percent of all white American men.[9] French's hodge-podge education was typical of many; he bounced from ill-equipped tutors (his father's law clerks), to the local common school, to a "commoner, if possible" local academy ("taught by a numbskull named Johnson"), to his preoccupied uncle Revevend Francis Brown, and ultimately to an academy in Maine, picking up some grammar here, some ancient history there, a splash of Latin someplace else.[10] Education was patchy and erratic in early America, ranging from the systematic order of New England to some virtually unschooled portions of the South and West.[11] Some virtually unschooled men found their way into Congress.

So did men who worked with their hands before entering politics, like the wagon maker Charles Bodle (J-NY), the gunsmith Ratliff Boon

(J-IN), and the iron furnace operator Martin Beaty (AJ-KY). Statistically speaking, there weren't many such congressmen, and they're often hard to spot in demographic studies, which tend to lump people into broad bucket categories: farmers, lawyers, merchants.[12] But they were there. So were growing ranks of newspapermen. Include the many men like French who served stints as editors in their youth, and the congressional contingent of newsmen is yet more striking.[13]

Even the teeming multitude of lawyers holds surprises. While there were accomplished scholars such as Senator Rufus Choate (W-MA)— *"he knew everything,"* French marveled—there were far more men who fell into the law as the path of least resistance. Legal education requirements collapsed amid the democratic upsurges of Jacksonian America; by 1851, four states had no educational requirements at all, simply declaring that any citizen of good moral character with a minimal amount of study could be admitted to practice.[14] For an ambitious young man searching for a livelihood with some prestige, lawyering was the answer, particularly if he had political ambitions; given the vast number of lawyer-politicians, a law career was a virtual bid for political power. The 1830s was the first decade in which at least 60 percent of new House members were lawyers; in the Twenty-third Congress alone—French's first—69 percent of the House were lawyers, as were 83 percent of the Senate.[15] Of the fifteen men in French's boardinghouse, only one wasn't a lawyer. He was a newspaper editor: Isaac Hill. "He is a bitter enemy to the gentlemen of the bar and often abuses them very unreasonably," French noted, adding wryly, "Every gentleman who boards at this house, except him, is a lawyer."[16] Clearly, Hill lived something of an uphill life.

For every Choate in Congress there was a ream of less-educated and sometimes less-polished members from a wide range of backgrounds—men like Senator Thomas Morris (J-OH), an Indian fighter, store clerk, and lawyer with only a few months of common schooling. Morris sprinkled his speeches with verses from the Bible, one of the few books in his childhood home. Like many of his congressional colleagues, he went from humble beginnings to the practice of law, to his state legislature, to Congress.[17]

Highborn and not-so-highborn, educated and not-so-educated, gruff and crude, sophisticated and worldly: increasingly in the 1830s and beyond, all of these men found their way into political office, broadening their horizons through the national power networks of their party and in some cases finding their way into Congress. The nation's political elite was more diverse than facts and figures let on.

A CITY OF EXTREMES

Of course the city of Washington was even more diverse. In fact, its sectional diversity was its hallmark, and people had high hopes that it would unify the nation. The "social collisions" of living in Washington would "erode sectional prejudices," enthused one writer, "and the East and West, the South and North, thus brought into closer intimacy, become cemented by more enduring ties."[18] Even regional accents seemed likely to fade. As the linguist George P. Marsh (W-VT) put it, "Many a Northern member of Congress goes to Washington a *dactyl* or a *trochee*, and comes home an *amphibrach* or an *iambus*."[19] Bringing together peoples and customs from throughout the nation, Washington was a city of cultural federalism.[20]

It was also a city of extremes. In part, this was a product of drunkenness. Much like the Capitol, Washington was awash in alcohol.[21] In 1830 alone, the city granted almost two hundred liquor licenses.[22] French saw liquor everywhere he looked. There were saloons on almost every corner, stinking of "tobacco smoke[,] bad cabbage & unmentionable mixtures of villainous smells."[23] Porter houses, hotel bars, dram shops, and groceries: they served liquor too, the latter two in handy gulp-sized portions. (The grocery near the Capitol did a particularly brisk business.)[24] Even the lobby of the National Theater seemed like little more than a drinking hole. "If Heaven should be located here," French thought, "there would certainly be a grog shop in one corner!" Everything in Washington seemed "contaminated by haunts of dissipation— even the Capitol itself has not escaped."[25]

French's father had feared as much when his son headed south. "You are now stationed in a land of trials & temptations beyond your [vaunted] experience," he warned not long after his son arrived in Washington. "Theatres, Balls, gambling tables, riots . . . & unlawful assemblies are all before you." Knowing full well his son's rebellious streak, the elder

French could only pray: "God grant that your choice shall obtain the smiles of an approving conscience."[26]

For the most part, French's conscience remained clear; a wavering but enthusiastic temperance supporter, he wasn't much of a drinker. But some people let loose in Washington in ways that they didn't dare back home. The whirl of diversity, the city's notorious "floating population" of residents who came and went with Congress, the many men who left their wives and families back home: the "bachelor-life" of Washington "was not conducive to moral restraint," noted an observer with marked understatement. Even staid Northerners sometimes went to extremes.[27] "Many of our best men are . . . giving a loose rein to their ambition & their appetites," worried Robert McClelland (D-MI) in a letter filled with misbehaving Northerners.[28] Amasa Dana's (D-NY) friends despaired when he befriended Felix Grundy McConnell (D-AL), a hard-drinking, "all-round, all-night man about town." McConnell liked to swagger into saloons and invite everyone "'to come up and licker.'" (French liked him fine when he was sober, but refused to commit McConnell's witty "vulgarisms" to paper.)[29] Once, at a party, thoroughly soused and with a woman on each arm, McConnell teetered up to President James K. Polk and toasted him, insisting that Polk drain his glass in a gulp, calling out, "No heel taps, Jimmy." With McConnell by his side, Dana transformed from "a sober, steady, modest & sedate man . . . into a perfect rake."[30] Franklin Pierce didn't fare much better. He hit an alcoholic low in 1836 when he and two drinking buddies, Edward Hannegan (D-IN) and Henry Wise (W-VA)—the three of them a case study in national diversity—got drunk and caused a ruckus at a theater when Hannegan got into a fistfight and pulled a gun; the rumble nearly sparked a duel.[31]

Drunken congressmen were the stuff of legend; newly arrived members looked for each session's hard drinkers. "Gov. [John] Gayle [W-AL] and a man by the name of [John] Jameson [D-MO] . . . are the only members I have seen drunk," David Outlaw (W-NC) reported in 1848 within his first months in office, the word *only* revealing his expectations.[32] Diaries and letters describe men too drunk to speak clearly, too drunk to leave their lodgings, even too drunk to stand; they matter-of-factly note that one or another congressman is out on a drinking bout, called a "breeze" or a "spree."[33] In 1841, French saw a remarkable before-and-after performance by Thomas Marshall (W-KY), nephew of the renowned Chief Justice John Marshall and a self-described member of the "spreeing gentry."[34] On August 23, Marshall—"for a rarity, sober," French noted—gave an eloquent speech that "enraptured" everyone, including the not easily impressed John Quincy Adams (W-MA), who praised its "beautiful flights of fancy." Two days later, Marshall gave a ranting, raving speech while "three sheets in the wind," forcing his way onto the floor, ignoring calls to order, and draping himself all over his desk, at one point leaning so far back that he was virtually lying on it. French considered it "a most disgusting exhibition."[35] (The *Globe* said only that Marshall "further continued" the debate.)[36]

Some men were surprisingly functional when boozy, even chairing the House, as did George Dromgoole (D-VA) in 1840. ("Drunk in the chair," Adams observed matter-of-factly.)[37] Others became master orators under the influence. Some of Senator Louis Wigfall's (D-TX) most stingingly bitter and effective speeches were supposedly a product of the Hole in the Wall.[38] Even the overindulgent Thomas Marshall had his moments when sloshed; Adams summed up his "peculiar style of eloquence" as "alcohol evaporating in elegant language."[39]

But other men were overcome. James McDougall (D-CA) became a staggering drunk in Washington, falling off his horse on Pennsylvania Avenue, even lying in the gutter. "The temptations of the Capital were too strong for him," a friend noted.[40] Pierce's drinking buddy Edward Hannegan suffered the same fate for much the same reason.[41] A few men paid the ultimate price for their sins. In 1834, James Blair (J-SC) committed suicide due to drink, shooting himself in a state of sodden despair. Blair was a man "of sterling good sense, and of brilliant parts," noted Adams, but "the single vice of intemperance . . . bloated his body to a mountain, prostrated his intellect, and vitiated his temper to madness." Blair once drunkenly fired a pistol at an actress on a Washington stage; he carried a loaded gun to the House every day. Adams thought the "chances . . . quite equal that he should have shot almost any other man than himself."[42] Most shocking of all was the death of Felix McConnell, who butchered himself with a pocketknife in 1846. According to Polk, a shaky and pale McConnell, probably "just recovered from a fit of intoxication," came to the White House, borrowed one hundred dollars, dallied at a bar, loaned some money to the barkeep, retired to his room, and killed himself.[43] If a congressman was "at all inclined to dissipation," observed one writer, "an easy and pleasant road is opened to him; and not a few yield to the temptation."[44]

Formal congressional privileges sometimes made matters worse. According to Article 1, Section 6 of the Constitution, congressmen were protected from arrest while attending Congress. The fine art of flaunting this privilege has a storied history and it started early.[45] According to French, in 1838, when police stopped the *"Honorable"* John Brodhead (D-NY) from picking flowers on the Capitol grounds, Brodhead replied, "I am a member of Congress, & I'll let you know I shall do just what I please," proving his point by grabbing clumps of flowers and "strewing them about."[46]

This isn't to say that all congressmen were boozed up rowdies or that all socializing was a back-slapping, booze-drinking bonanza. There were genteel receptions, parties, dinners, "hops," and fancy balls galore.[47] French and Bess attended and hosted many, though even tame events could have a risqué undertow; one congressman noted a string of colleagues cheating on their wives.[48] Nor were the city's freedoms restricted to partying. The New York writer Anne Lynch loved the "intellectual superiority" born of the city's "delightful freedom," particularly for women. Washington wasn't "hedged round by so many conventionalities," she thought.[49]

All in all, Washington's diversity was a mixed bag, forging cross-regional friendships even as it fostered the city's turbulent spirit. On both counts, it influenced not only the Washington community but also the community of Congress.[50] One reporter said so outright: "The disagreeable, shocking scenes which are so often witnessed in both Houses of Congress, would perhaps not occur, if there were an independent and sufficiently consequential society in Washington, capable of punishing offenders against the proprieties of life."[51] An unfettered Washington meant an unfettered Congress. Washington's gloriously freeing diversity set the stage for congressional violence.

LIVING IN SLAVE-LAND

French did some moderate dissipating. During his first spring in Washington, he went to the city's wildly popular horse races and loved it. The excitement, the fighting, the gambling, the drinking: French had never seen anything like it. "[V]ery many honorable members of Congress were—not exactly sober," he reported to his half sister Harriette, swearing that he "drank nothing, not even a glass of water."[52] Within a year or two, he had learned to play billiards (or as he put it in his diary, "have learned to play billiards!").[53] But the appeal of cockfighting was beyond him: "pah. It almost made me sick."[54]

Horse racing, gambling, and cockfighting: some of Washington's most popular pastimes had a distinctly Southern flavor. In fact, national city that it was, Washington was Southern at its core. As one Ohio congressman attested, the city's "fixed population" was "intensely southern."[55] In 1830, roughly 60 percent of its permanent white residents were from Southern states or had strong Southern ties, and about a third of the city's residents were black; the fact that more than half of these black residents were free made Washington a true border-state town.[56] Even the city's town houses, with their back-lot outbuildings for housework, mirrored the layout of plantations.[57] In more ways than one, the South reigned supreme in Washington.

Of course, the most obviously Southern aspect of Washington was the ubiquitous presence of slavery. The auction blocks and slave pens, one of them clearly visible from the Capitol's windows; the cuffed slave gangs; the brutality that infused a slave regime: although Washington wasn't a central hub of the slave trade, slavery's grim realities struck Northerners in the face when they first arrived.[58] ("Here I am in slaveland again," reported the Massachusetts Free-Soiler Horace Mann upon arriving in Washington in 1852.)[59] Not long after his arrival, Joshua Giddings (W-OH) was stunned to see a slave gang of sixty-five shackled men, women, and children being marched down the street.[60]

French was stunned to be *living* with slaves; New Hampshire was overwhelmingly white in 1830, with 602 free black citizens and 5 enslaved people out of a total population of 269,328.[61] I have "a servant to wait on me whenever I call," he wrote wonderingly to Bess during his first days in his boardinghouse. "There are about a dozen or fifteen servants about the house, all *negro slaves*."[62]

Not all of New England was as free of slavery as New Hampshire, where it had never really taken hold; for a time, the nation's "free states" weren't entirely free. Slavery was scattered throughout New England in small numbers, and it shaped the region dramatically, enabling it to shift

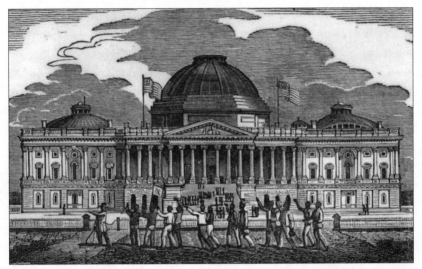

Detail from an American Anti-Slavery Society broadside showing chained slaves in front of the U.S. Capitol (*The Home of the Oppressed* by William S. Dorr, 1836. Courtesy of the Library of Congress)

from subsistence farming to a market economy.[63] It was also entrenched. Emancipation in most Northern states didn't come easily; it was a complex process that took decades and introduced new complications; for some Northern whites, disapproving of slavery was one thing and living among free blacks was quite another.[64] Slavery and race were very real problems in New England, and New Englanders like French arrived in Washington with their home-born prejudices intact.

But Southern plantation slavery was an entirely different thing. Many Northern congressmen had never seen a plantation or talked slavery with slaveholders. Curious Northerners sought out such encounters, sometimes at the encouragement of Southerners, who were all too eager to free their Northern allies of their "temporary . . . prejudices," as one Southerner put it.[65] The abolitionist Harriet Martineau experienced this Southern charm campaign firsthand; on her first day in Washington she was visited by several Southern senators and their wives, who pledged their services and invited her to their homes to see plantation slavery for herself.[66]

French's friend and fellow New Hampshirite John Parker Hale (D-NH) couldn't wait to talk slavery with slaveholders. "I have had an opportunity which I have long wanted, viz. a full unreserved & frank conversation with a Southerner, an intelligent & gentlemanly man, on the subject of Slavery," he told his wife during his first weeks in Congress in 1844. The man was "not only willing, but I thought quite as willing to answer as I was to ask questions." Two more conversations revealed something that would shock most Northerners, Hale thought: white Southerners were "hard-working people." One South Carolina congressman even made his own hoe handles.[67] Four years later, Hale advanced his slavery schooling by spending a weekend with four wealthy planters at a nearby plantation, discussing slavery.[68]

Many Northerners made similar visits.[69] French did. In 1851, he and his family visited the Maryland plantation of his fellow Mason Michael Carroll, and French was pleasantly surprised.[70] Carroll's slaves seemed well-off; the house slaves were "dressed better than N.[ew] H.[ampshire] Farmers' wives & daughters." And Carroll seemed to care about them, almost sobbing over a beloved slave's recent death. French's diary account virtually oozes relief, suggesting that as dedicated a Democrat as he was, he'd had his doubts about plantation slavery. His visit eased his conscience and made him roaring mad at abolitionists who were threatening the Union. God sanctioned slavery, he insisted in his diary a few days later: "the old Testament abounds with evidence." And abolitionists were fanatical Union-busting blasphemers with baseless claims; to prove his point, he attached a newspaper clipping about recent New Hampshire antislavery resolutions that seemed to violate "in spirit, the Holy Word of God."[71] When Carroll died a month later, French's obituary sang his praises as a "good, generous, and noble-hearted master" and condemned Northern "fanaticism."[72] His plantation visit had had an impact.

But so did other visits. Witness French's tangled trajectory: As a Northern Democrat, he had come to Washington as a self-described "ultra" on the issue of slavery, so firmly convinced that only slaveholding states had the right to act on it that he didn't think that people in free states had even the right to *petition* against it.[73] A conversation with the Ohio abolitionist Joshua Giddings in 1849—a mere two years before his plantation visit—changed his mind. After hearing Giddings argue in the House that slaves weren't property, French had been so intrigued that he went to Giddings's boardinghouse to chat about it. He came home vowing to help abolish slavery in the District of Columbia.[74] Two years later, French would be declaring slavery God-sanctioned after visiting Carroll's plantation. The following year he devoted himself to promoting Franklin Pierce's South- and slavery-friendly presidential bid. Yet not quite a month after Pierce's nomination, French wrote a poem honoring Giddings for a speech *condemning* Pierce's proslavery views.[75] French wavered on slavery, and he wasn't alone; for many Northerners, living in Washington put their politics to the test.

"A NEW HAMPSHIRE BOY"

For a time, the bonds of party overcame such sectional fluctuations— or at least, they outweighed them, particularly in Washington, where many people experienced their party as a national organization for the first time. Fragile though they were, political parties of the 1830s forged vital national ties. A far cry from today's top-down enterprises, they were essentially national leagues of local organizations. Cities and towns had party clubs and committees; county, district, and state organizations fostered and corralled those local efforts; and politicians in Washington helped as best they could, coaching and guiding more than anything else.[76] Well into the 1840s there was no central party management and no clear chain of command; party organization stemmed from local organizers like Isaac Hill. Even national party conventions, which had their start in the 1830s, were initially centered on *creating* party unity, gathering together a far-flung group of allies to hash things out.[77] National party politicking was much like the Union: decentralized, localized, and bound by ties of sentiment more than structure.

Thus the novelty of politicking in Washington. Local politicos like French suddenly found themselves banging the party drum with allies from near and far, particularly in Congress, the national center of partisan "slang-whanging."[78] French was a noteworthy cog in the congressional slang-whanging machine. He was a congressional correspondent for Democratic newspapers in New Hampshire, Washington, and Chicago. (Isaac Hill's brother Horatio co-owned the *Chicago Democrat*.)[79] As an active member of the city's Jackson Democratic Association and ultimately its president, French corresponded with sister clubs around the country, collecting information and spreading the party line. He helped stage massive celebrations and lavish banquets with guest lists of hundreds of prominent Democrats from around the country and national press coverage that preached the glories of their visibly national party to a widespread audience. In Washington, French forged national party ties.

For much of the 1830s, Whig and Democratic party ties alike centered on the iconic figure of Andrew Jackson. The early Whig Party was a conglomerate of interests bound together by their hatred of "King Andrew's" polarizing politics.[80] The "wiggies" were an "unholy league" of "ites" ("Bank-ites," "Tariff-ites") formed "of the odds & ends of disappointed factions," French thought. They were a blend of "Abolition, Antimasonry, old Federalism & humbug, mingled with drunkenness and dissipation," and little else.[81]

For the Democrats, of course, love of Jackson knew no bounds. French virtually genuflected at the mention of his name. Even in his diary, he gushed.[82] The magic at the heart of the Democracy was the rhetorical link between Jackson and the Union; in the Democratic cosmos, they were lastingly entwined. At the events that French organized, these polestars of the party almost always led the way. Promoting Jackson would promote the Union; worshiping Jackson was worshiping the Union; national party unity would breed national unity: Jacksonian Democrats north, south, and west joined in singing one song. And French was a choirmaster, a fount of Democratic songs and poems.[83]

An 1852 Battle of New Orleans dinner was typical of many. The Washington Jackson Democratic Association sent invitations to Jackson's "friends" throughout all thirty-one states, inviting them to a banquet that would bolster party bonds and Old Hickory's beloved Union, and promote Franklin Pierce's presidential bid in the process. The lavish gathering, attended by five hundred people, featured three hours of speechifying, a B. B. French song ("The Altar of Liberty"), and at least sixty toasts, with French—a man with a "pair of lungs admirably calculated to keep order," according to the *Baltimore Sun*—repeating the toasts so that everyone could hear. ("I almost split my lungs," he later groused.)[84]

So routine were such pro-Jackson fanfares that they became a standing joke. An 1828 newspaper parody caught the parade of excess perfectly. Predicting how that night's Battle of New Orleans celebration would go (because "it can be predicted with as much certainty as the weather in an almanac"), it described an elaborate banquet featuring half an alligator, and if necessary, eaten words; a series of ridiculous toasts; and a grand triumphal song, heralded with trumpets, bagpipes, gongs, and a "Grand Shout," followed by the song's opening lines, "Strike the Tunjo! Blow the Hugag!"—a B. B. French song on steroids. This "famous 'hugag and tunjo' article" so perfectly captured the pomp and nonsense of the period's politicking that satirists mined it for decades.[85] But silly or not, such grandstanding worked: it fueled passions powerful enough to bridge sectional divides.

Yet those divides persisted, even for a devoted national party operative like French. Given his party electioneering, his decades in Washington, and his congressional career, it's hard to imagine someone more national in perspective or Washingtonian in spirit. It becomes harder still when his endless stream of civic responsibilities is thrown into the mix. French was president of the City Council, an alderman, a cofounder of one local charity and active in several others, a trustee of the public schools and a supporter of a school for free black girls, assistant secretary for the Smithsonian Board of Regents, and a lecturer for clubs and societies all over town. As commissioner of public buildings under Presidents Franklin Pierce, Abraham Lincoln, and Andrew Johnson, he repaired bridges, watered down the dusty avenues, and oversaw the Capitol's extension and new dome, which featured French's name inscribed on the "Goddess of Freedom" sculpture at its top.[86] As Grand Master of the District of Columbia Masons, he even laid the cornerstones of three of the city's most iconic buildings: the Smithsonian Institution, the Washington Memorial, and the Capitol extension.[87]

But as dedicated a national organizer and Washingtonian as French was, he viewed the world through a New Hampshire lens. He was looking through that lens when he attended a Democratic rally in Maryland in 1840. Curious to see "how they manage political meetings in this part of the Union," he was impressed. The speeches—given by

congressmen—were just the thing to "tickle the ear & stir up the feelings of the multitude." But the flagpole! No one from the Granite State
would have settled for such a puny flagpole. New Hampshire poles stood
one hundred feet high; this one was so short that if the wind hadn't been
blowing, the flag "would have trailed upon the ground!"[88] (Competitive
pole-raising ran rampant during electoral campaigns, adding a whole
new dimension to the manly art of politics.)[89] Even amid a crowd of
people who were virtually—if not literally—singing his song, French
was a Granite State man to the core.

In fact, he was never more a Granite State man than when he was
in Washington. He praised New Hampshire in poems and toasted it at
dinners. ("New Hampshire!—Before my heart shall forget thee, it must
become harder than thy granite.")[90] He sang its glories in songs, as in
one that he wrote for the 1849 "Festival of the Sons of New Hampshire," a celebration of native sons living "abroad" (in foreign countries
like Boston and Washington):

> *Our granite race are* every where,
> *Where man can find employ;*
> *If ever man* was *in the moon,*
> *'T was a New Hampshire boy.*[91]

He was a virtuoso of the New Hampshire non sequitur. Unexpectedly
called to the podium during a St. Patrick's Day dinner in 1843 and casting about for kinship with the Irish, he came up with this: "it was said
that the Emerald Isle rested upon a bed of granite, and he himself
was born in the 'Granite State.'"[92] Even in death he salutes his home
state; he lies beneath a granite obelisk in Washington's Congressional
Cemetery. To say that French was proud of his birthplace (as he himself
couldn't say often enough) is a colossal understatement.[93]

French identified just as much with his home region. His writings
are filled with references to his "Yankee ears" and "Yankee blood." He
was quick to praise Yankee ingenuity and just as quick to see the Yankee in people he liked; he thought the "very amiable" Charles Dickens
looked far more like a Yankee than a Brit.[94] His closest friends in
Washington were from Maine and New Hampshire. And he wasn't a
lone Yankee fan; he was an active member of the New England Society

of the District of Columbia, a club devoted to celebrating "the land of the Pilgrims" and promoting Yankee charity.[95] His New England accent was just as steadfast; more than a decade after arriving in Washington, his Yankee twang remained so sharp that even New Englanders noted it.[96] An 1849 newspaper sketch put it best: French "retains a deep and ardent love for New England, of which time does not seem, in any degree, to abate the fervency."[97]

This reporter was more accurate than he knew. Because not only didn't French's time in Washington cool his love of New England; it intensified it. Watching New Englanders mingle with Southerners and Westerners, French gained a new understanding of what set them apart. His writings are filled with lessons learned: Yankees are industrious; Yankees are brave; Yankees can hold their own in a fight. French developed a new and stronger image of New England in Washington; in the process, he learned just how different the rest of the Union could be.[98] He was experiencing in person the ultimate lesson taught by life in the nation's capital: the Union truly was the "Glorious Whole of glorious Parts."[99]

The same held true for many congressmen: being in Washington revealed and reinforced regional views. This was as true for Southerners as it was for Northerners. The presence of Northern "he-women" taught Representative David Outlaw of North Carolina just how superior Southern women were. "There is a boldness, a brazenfacedness among the Northern city women, as well as a looseness of morals which I

Caricatures of the stereotypical unpolished Western congressman, starchy Northerner, and swaggering Southerner (*Harper's Weekly*, April 10, 1858. Courtesy of HarpWeek)

hope may never be introduced south," he complained to his wife, who was safely and permanently ensconced in North Carolina.[100]

Some Southerners found Northern men no more impressive. Back home after a term in Congress in 1841, Charles Fisher (D-NC) announced his findings in a speech. "Why is it that the condition of the people of the Southern States, is not as good as that of the people of the Northern States?" he asked. Some "among us . . . say it is owing to the superior sagacity, & greater industry of the people of these states over our people." This was untrue, Fisher stated, and he had proof: "We meet them in Congress—are they sup[erio]r there?"[101] The reluctance of Northern congressmen to brawl or duel was just as striking; Southern scorn of Northern cowardice was a constant.[102] Here was the flip side of cross-regional bonding: familiarity could breed contempt.

In this sense, being in Congress required an internal balancing act. Congressmen were in a national institution doing the nation's work with a national sampling of colleagues tied to national parties; but doing that work highlighted what set them apart. Although party loyalties often reigned supreme, for most congressmen, as for French, sectional preferences framed their vision of the world.

DOCILE DOUGHFACES

At no time was this balancing act more apparent than when casting votes, because every vote was a statement of priorities. Thus the creative ways in which congressmen dodged vote calls. Such personal compromises were the stuff that the Union was built on, makeshift as they might be.

Northern Democrats were notorious for this kind of dodging, largely because of the problem of slavery. When it came to that seemingly irreconcilable difference, preserving party unity and preserving the Union required dodging and weaving on all sides. Some evasive measures were more successful than others. Sweeping stratagems like gag rules that prohibited discussion of slavery petitions were stereotypically Southern; uncompromising, unapologetic, aggressive, and heavy-handed, they did more to stoke antislavery fires than to slake them.

Subtler strategies were better at smoothing the waters, and when it came to subtleties, Northern Democrats like French were virtuosos. As Northerners, some of them weren't entirely comfortable with slavery's morality or realities; by the 1830s, many of them viewed it as both Southern and foreign.[103] They also were keenly aware of the precarious balance of power between states slave and free, so the addition of new slave states couldn't help but give them pause. Many of them had racist fears that freed slaves would head north, as well as realistic fears that attacking slavery would destroy both the Union and their party.[104] Some worried that slavery would overrun Western territories and outpace yeoman farming. Yet their support of states' rights gave them a hands-off policy concerning slavery. For Northern Democrats, there was a brutal bargain at the heart of party membership: the rewards of party power were tied to preserving slavery. In exchange for the former, they accepted the latter. In the Democracy, as in Washington, Southerners held sway.

French's views were typical of many Northern Democrats, a messy, shifting blend of generalization, distraction, abstraction, and denial. As he put it when pressed on the matter in 1855, he was

> so much a Freesoiler as to be opposed to the addition of any more slave territory to this Union—but utterly opposed to the agitation of the question of slavery if it can be avoided, &, although abhorring slavery in the abstract, defending it to the utmost of my power so far as it is tolerated or justified by the Constitution.[105]

French abhorred slavery, wanted no new slave states, defended slavery, and didn't want it discussed. His one tangled sentence exposes an internal tug-of-war felt by many Northern Democrats.

There was a word for men like French: *doughface*. Coined by the acerbic and eccentric Representative John Randolph of Virginia, it referred to Northerners who catered to Southern interests. As defined by Bartlett's *Dictionary of Americanisms* (1848), *doughface* was a "contemptuous nickname, applied to the northern favorers and abettors of negro slavery."[106] The term first gained popularity after the Missouri Compromise of 1820, and it had a sting, particularly in Congress. By implication, doughfaces were servile, docile, and all-around unmanly. Working side by side with slaveholders, congressional doughfaces risked being these things *in person*. When they responded to proslavery blustering by backing down or making nice, they seemed to prostrate themselves before their slaveholding colleagues. In Congress, the challenges of balancing section and party could be painfully personal.

It makes perfect sense that Randolph coined this notorious slap at Northerners; he was a master of Southern swaggering. Famed for his brilliant, rambling, and sometimes drunken oratory, his razor-sharp wit, his fighting temper, and his shrill, piping voice, Randolph stalked around the House booted and spurred, riding crop in hand and hunting dogs at foot, beating men down with withering insults and tossing off duel challenges, a virtual caricature of a Southern slave lord. He has the dubious distinction of being the only person to have challenged both Henry Clay and Daniel Webster to duels, though only the Clay duel advanced to a dueling ground, with no blood shed. When Thomas Hart Benton solemnly delivered Randolph's challenge to Webster, who was relaxing on a sofa on the outskirts of the House, Webster was nonplussed, to say the least; he read it, carefully folded it, paused, unfolded it, reread it in seeming disbelief, and wiped his brow.[107] Randolph ultimately retracted the challenge.

Although the term *doughface* has puzzled people almost from the moment that Randolph uttered it—Doe face? Dough face?—in fact, he was referring to a children's game involving dough masks donned to frighten people. Using the term in 1809, Randolph said that passing a nonintercourse act against Great Britain was equivalent to dressing up in a dough face to frighten people "who may blow our brains out."[108] He used the term again in 1820 during the crisis over Missouri's admission to the Union. Speaking of Northerners who had voted with the South to admit Missouri as a slave state, Randolph mocked their "conscience, and morality, and religion," declaring:

> I knew *these would give way*. They were scared at their own dough faces—yes, they were scared at their own dough faces! We had *them* and if we had wanted *three* more, we could have had them; yes, and if *these* had failed we could have had three more.[109]

As appreciative as he was of Northern supporters, Randolph couldn't stomach their seeming servility. By his logic, these men had prostrated themselves before the South out of fear of fracturing their party and perhaps the Union. Thirty years later, Walt Whitman echoed the thought in a poem titled "Song for Certain Congressmen," later retitled "Dough-face Song":

> We are all docile dough-faces,
> They knead us with the fist,
> They, the dashing southern lords,
> We labor as they list.[110]

For both Randolph and Whitman, doughfaces were cowards who had betrayed their home region.

For Northern congressmen working alongside Southerners, such blows hit hard, particularly given Northern parliamentary acrobatics aimed at sidestepping slavery; in their flagrant attempts to flee the issue—sometimes literally—Northerners looked cowardly. Some of them routinely dodged problem votes; in 1850, during voting over the controversial Fugitive Slave Act mandating that runaway slaves anywhere in the country must be returned to their masters, a pack of Northerners had a sudden urgent need to visit the congressional library. William Seward's (W-NY) son saw them aimlessly milling about and knew enough to ask what was happening in the House.[111] Their absence was duly noted—and mocked; once the bill passed, Thaddeus Stevens (W-PA) wryly suggested sending a page to the library to tell the dodgers "that they may now come back into the Hall."[112]

Vote changing was another doughface dodge. For example, at the opening of Congresses between 1835 and 1843, some Northern Democrats routinely voted against a rule "gagging" discussion of slavery petitions, well aware that their constituents might object to it. Later in the session when the rule was no longer in the spotlight, these doughfaces would drift back to the "pro–Gag Rule fold"—and national party unity— for the rest of the session.[113]

Some Northerners were equally adept at dodging problem Southerners, fleeing the chamber rather than endangering party unity by confronting aggressively proslavery allies. After just one week in Congress, William Fessenden (W-ME) had already fled the House several times. The need to adopt rules for the session had raised talk of a gag rule, sparking a slew of Southern insults about Northern fanatics oppressing the South. Afraid of being "forced into a reply & defiance," Fessenden and a number of other Northern Whigs left the chamber to avoid "disappointing our friends, & ruining the party." A few times, "pushed beyond all power of human patience," he tried to get the floor, "thanking God afterwards that I did not succeed."[114] Fessenden was afraid of being defiant to brother Whigs—striking testimony to the tangled emotions behind Northern party loyalties. "Selfish" Southern Whigs didn't struggle that way, he grumbled; they lashed out at their Northern allies thinking only of themselves. Such selfishness was the flip side of being a doughface: being disloyal to one's party for the sake of one's section. "The truth is that we are cursed with a set of allies who are enough to ruin any party," he told his father.[115] Sustaining the balance of section and party was no easy thing.

Dodging, fleeing, and flip-flopping: many a new congressman was stunned by such spinelessness. Within his first two weeks in Congress, the abolitionist Joshua Giddings was shocked to find "our Northern friends so backward and delicate."[116] John Parker Hale (D-NH) said virtually the same thing during his first term.[117] Even Southerners who banked on doughface votes sneered at Northern servility, stirring up sectional discord in the process. To Henry Clay, the two words *dough* and *face* with which John Randolph had "rated and taunted our Northern friends . . . did more injury than any two words I have ever known."[118]

Antislavery advocates had more reason than most to denounce doughface treachery. Giddings declared even slaveholders more honorable. "I may be led to confide in the honor of a slave-holder," he said during debate in 1843, "but a 'servile doughface' is too destitute of that article to obtain credit with me."[119] Hale found the "servility of some of the Northern democrats to Southern dictation . . . humiliating and disgusting to the last degree."[120] Doughfaces were "white slaves," charged one congressmen; they suffered from "slavery of the mind," said another.[121] The only way to defeat slavery was for free-state congressmen to assume "a bolder tone, and rise above the unmanly fear of slaveholding 'chivalry.'"[122]

Clearly, *doughface* was more than a political label in Congress. It was a personal insult that put one's manhood on the line.[123] Franklin Pierce (D-NH) felt this firsthand during an 1836 debate over slavery in the District of Columbia. To prove that abolitionism was a looming threat, Senator John C. Calhoun (N-SC) claimed that Northern Democrats routinely underplayed the number of abolitionists in their home states in the hope of soothing Southern allies. As proof, he cited a newspaper article that accused Pierce of committing that sin and branded him a doughface. Isaac Hill immediately leaped to Pierce's defense, as did Thomas Hart Benton after a hasty consultation with Pierce, who had entered the Senate chamber as the article was being read, and blanched. Calhoun apologized to Pierce at least three times in the next few days, during debate and man-to-man. It was a good thing, too, noted John King (D-GA), for "what encouragement did such treatment afford to our friends at the North to step forth in our behalf?"[124]

But Calhoun's apologies weren't enough for Pierce. A few days later in the House, still visibly upset, he fought back. He first justified his claims about the paltry threat of New Hampshire abolitionism (by poohpoohing the importance of antislavery petitions signed by women, among other things).[125] Then he addressed the second charge. He had been called an epithet coined by "one of the ablest debaters of any age" that in the North "was understood to designate a 'craven-spirited man.'" It was a lie to say he was a doughface, he declared, and he would physically fight anyone who dared declare it true. He didn't want to "provoke an assault." He had nothing against Calhoun, who had apologized. But for all other comers, Pierce hereby declared, "once for all, that if any gentleman chose to take that statement as correct, he might put Mr. P's spirit to the test when, and where, and how he pleased."[126] By this point, Pierce was so wound up that he had to sit down. But he made his point. Accused of being a cowardly tool of slave-driving Southerners, Pierce had demonstrated his manliness by pronouncing himself willing to fight.

New Englanders got the message. John Fairfield (D-ME) proudly declared Pierce just the man to stand and fight.[127] Even Whig newspapers offered grudging respect. The *Connecticut Courant* noted Pierce's "gallantry, show of fight, and real spunk," concluding, "Pretty well for New Hampshire."[128] The Democratic *New Hampshire Patriot* went one step further: not only was Pierce brave, but the "nullifying bravadoes" had "quailed" in response. These "southern *nullies*" were "the greatest cowards in the world," the writer scoffed. Though they "bluster and talk big, yet they quail and cower when they are before a yankee that faces them in their own manner."[129] By the *Patriot's* logic, Pierce had saved his reputation and asserted his manhood by acting like a Southerner.

FIGHTING MEN AND NON-COMBATANTS

The *Patriot* was voicing a popular notion that seemed readily apparent in the mix of men in Congress: many a Southerner or Southern-born Westerner was what French called "a hard customer."[130] They talked big and blustered. ("[B]ombastical heroics," French called it.)[131] They strutted and swaggered. They met challengers with fist-clenched or pistol-gripping or knife-wielding defiance; armed and ready, they flaunted their willingness to fight.[132]

Take for example the frequent weapon wielder John Dawson (D-LA). It's hard to tell what Dawson was like in the Louisiana legislature. Maybe he had more self-control. Maybe not; this was a violent age of aggressive manhood, and Louisiana in the 1840s had some rough edges, as did Dawson, a self-described man of "malignant hatred" who had a penchant for fighting duels with the aptly named cut-and-thrust sword.[133] Given his relative obscurity on the national stage, it's also hard to tell how others judged him, though there are clues. John Quincy Adams summed him up as a "drunken bully," and thanks to his 1842 threat to cut a colleague's throat "from ear to ear," he became something of a byword for bullying on the floor. Threats were sometimes met with a mocking "Are you going to cut my throat from ear to ear?"[134] All in all, it's entirely possible that Dawson was a blade-wielding charmer wherever he happened to be; when he died in 1845, even his congressional eulogists couldn't avoid mentioning unnamed "grave faults."[135]

But what's most telling about the congressional Dawson are his literal and figurative trigger points. In one way or another, it was opposition to slavery that galled him enough to wave a weapon. His throat-cutting victim, a Whig Southerner, had been defending John Quincy Adams's right to speak during a ruckus over antislavery petitions. The outspoken Joshua Giddings was honored by Dawsonian ire

This portrait of the knife-bearing, pistol-wearing frequent fighter John Dawson of Louisiana hints at his inner demons. (*Gen. the Hon. John Bennett Dawson of Wyoming Plantation, West Feliciana Parish, ca. 1844–1845*, by C. R. Parker. Courtesy of Neal Auction Company)

A bowie knife of the sort worn by congressmen in the 1830s (Photograph by Hugh Talman and Jaclyn Nash. Courtesy of National Museum of American History, Smithsonian Institution)

more than once. In the midst of an antislavery speech by Giddings in 1843, Dawson shoved him and threatened him with a knife. ("I take it, Mr. Speaker, that it was not an attempt to cut his throat from ear to ear," Adams joked darkly.)[136] Two years later, during another Giddings antislavery speech, in what may rank as the all-time greatest display of firepower on the floor, Dawson, clearly agitated, vowed that he would kill Giddings and cocked his pistol, bringing four armed Southern Democrats to his side, which prompted four Whigs to position themselves around Giddings, several of them armed as well. After a few minutes, most of the pistoleers sat down.[137] Dawson may or may not have been a troublemaker in the Louisiana legislature, but he was one in Congress for one central reason: face-to-face attacks on slavery.

In the South, most Southerners didn't confront open opposition to slavery in their everyday lives. Even in *print* it was beyond the pale; a flood of abolitionist tracts mailed south in 1835 prompted panic, mass protest rallies, vigilante violence, and bonfire burnings of sacks of mail.[138] It's not surprising then that confrontational antislavery talk in Congress was a challenge that some Southerners handled better than others; many took it as a personal affront that they felt bound to avenge. As John C. Calhoun said in 1836, there were only two ways to respond to the insults proffered in antislavery petitions: submit to them or "as a man of honor, knock the calumniator down."[139] Many slaveholders chose the path of most resistance, even on the House and Senate floors.

In part, this was a matter of custom. Such man-to-man encounters were semi-sanctioned in the South; authorities rarely intervened.[140] Southerners were accustomed to mastery in more ways than one. Indeed, their lives depended on it. By definition, a slave regime was violent and imperiled; the chance of a slave revolt inspired a wary defensiveness on the part of slaveholders, making them prone to flaunt their power and quick to take violent action.[141] When it came to leadership, violent men—sometimes *very* violent men—had a popular advantage. Robert Potter (J-NC) was elected to his state legislature after his release from jail for castrating two men he suspected of committing adultery with his wife; when he committed the crime, he was a member of the U.S. House of Representatives. William Lowndes Yancey (D-AL) was elected to the Alabama House and then the U.S. House of Representatives after killing an unarmed man by shooting him in the chest, pistol-whipping his head, and stabbing him with a sword cane.[142]

Appearances mattered in such a world; authority and power were contained in a man's person as well as his property. Thus the public-minded nature of Southern violence and its notorious brutality. It was meant to impress.[143] Honor culture was of a piece with this world. A man was only as honorable as others thought him to be.[144] Duels were more about parading manhood and showing coolness under fire than they were about killing. Cower before a duel challenge and you were no man at all.[145]

Northern violence was different. This isn't to say that Northerners couldn't be savagely violent or that they were immune to the power of honor culture. The "Yankee code of honor," as French called it, had its own logic and power.[146] Less grounded in gunplay, it was no less centered on manhood.[147] Canings were common in the North, as were ritualistic "postings"—printed insult-filled public attacks on offenders who refused to defend or take back their offensive words. After a particularly heated congressional election, two of French's Maine friends in Congress posted each other.[148] Mainers were New England's frequent fighters, partly a product of the young state's frontier spirit; it had achieved statehood as recently as 1820.

Yet as belligerent as Northerners could be, many were slower to fight than Southerners and quicker to call in the law. In the North, when assaults went too far or rioting erupted, authorities often imposed order. Most casualties in Northern riots were killed by authorities trying to rein people in; in contrast, Southern rioters tended to kill one another.[149] Thus the Northern response to violent displays in Congress; more often than not, Northerners turned to the Speaker or chair to enforce the rules. John Quincy Adams dubbed their pleas "lamentation speeches."[150]

These sectional styles of fighting bumped up against each other in Congress.[151] In congressional lingo, most Northerners were "noncombatants" and many Southerners were "fighting men," which gave them a literal fighting advantage.[152] In essence, some men were willing—even eager—to back up their words with weapons, and some men weren't, which compelled them to back away from confrontations and risk looking cowardly in the process. The British visitor Harriet Martineau thought that Northern servility was palpable in Washington. With their "too deferential air" and habitually "deprecatory walk," New Englanders seemed to "bear in mind perpetually" that they "can not fight a duel, while other people can."[153] Southerners, in contrast, used violence as a "device of terrorism" to force compliance to their demands—and they did so with pride.[154] Southerners and Westerners "would do these things now and then, and man could enact no laws that would prevent them," declared William Wick (D-IN) in 1848 after two congressmen flipped a desk and started slugging each other. If the House formally reprimanded the combatants, "the country would laugh it to scorn—at least, all that country west of the mountains."[155] The matter ended in something of a compromise: a formal resolution that the House accept a public apology, and no further action. The final vote was 77 to 69; no New Englander supported the resolution, regardless of party. Even in the realm of *settling* disputes, Southern mores often prevailed.

Different men from different regions had different ideas about manhood, violence, lawfulness, and their larger implications—enough so that they sometimes required translators. Border-state congressmen often filled this gap.[156] Hailing from Maryland, Delaware, Kentucky, Missouri, and northern Virginia, many of them were slaveholders but their home states had mixed views about slavery, and their border location ensured ongoing interaction with the free-labor north.[157] Border states had prosperous cities—Baltimore, St. Louis, Louisville—that followed a Northern model, with diverse populations and many free blacks. And perhaps most important of all for the purposes of congressional conciliation, border-state political passions often centered more on nativism than on slavery; even abolitionists were sometimes tolerated.[158]

Culturally bilingual, less defensive about antislavery rhetoric than their deeper south peers, and likely to be law-and-order Whigs, border-state congressmen were perfectly positioned to negotiate fights.[159] It's no accident that the period's most renowned legislative compromisers were virtually all from border states, nor is it any more accidental that these same men were fight mediators of the first order.[160]

Fighting men, non-combatants, and compromisers: when congressmen studied pathways of power to chart a legislative course, they knew which men were in which categories and planned accordingly. The personal dynamics of the antebellum Congress were shaped by sectional patterns of violence. In ways that went beyond policies—even beyond the simmering issue of slavery—sectionalism mattered, shaping the balance of power on the floor.

French factored these patterns into his congressional calculations on an ongoing basis. When an argument moved from animated debate into head-to-head nastiness, he did what most of the congressional community did. He sized up the fighters and their grievances, decided what course of action would redeem reputations, watched closely to see what happened, and assessed the outcome. Men who behaved "manfully" earned kudos and clout; men who didn't were scorned as cowards and their power on the floor fell accordingly. It was the calculus of congressional reputations, and fighting was a major variable.

Such calculations could be complex. French usually flipped through a mental fight checklist. *Who was arguing?* Were they Southern, Northern, or Western? Were they "honorable & fearless?"[161] Had they dueled in the past? Was either man a proven coward, a noncombatant, a clergyman, or elderly? For Southerners, Southern-born Westerners, and fighting men generally, the fighting bar was set high and failing to meet it meant a lot. *How serious was the offense?* Was it words or a blow? Who witnessed it? Had either man used a hot-button insult? *Puppy, rascal, scoundrel, coward,* and *liar* were virtual invitations to duel. In certain circles, so was *abolitionist. Were there any special circumstances?* Was there a long-standing feud at play? Did the two men simply hate each other? Was one of them drunk? Were both of them drunk?

Almost every serious spat set French to calculating. In 1834, when Senator George Poindexter (AJ-MS) and Senator John Forsyth (J-GA) had a "gladiatorial *set too*" over Poindexter's slurs against the Jackson administration, and Forsyth threw the lie (accused Poindexter of lying), French predicted a duel but the Senate settled it in "some way in secret session."[162] In 1838, when Henry Wise (W-VA) and Samuel Gholson (D-MS) exchanged harsh words (Gholson called Wise a "cowardly scoundrel"—a double whammy), French expected a fistfight given the two men's track records, but Gholson's arm was in a sling so "he could not make much of a fight."[163] Identifying each season's best fighters, figuring the odds of a clash, sizing up likely winners and losers, watching for playoffs on the field of honor: in a sense, congressional fighting was a spectator sport.

And Congress was the major league. Although legislatures all over the Union had flash fights and bullying, clashes in Congress had added weight. Precedent-setting national policy was under debate. A national audience was judging the state of the nation by watching proceedings on the House and Senate floor. The Union-busting problem of slavery was never far from sight. And sectional habits gave some men a fighting advantage. It could have spelled disaster, and it ultimately did. But during the 1830s and 1840s, party bonds provided a vital counter-balance.[164] Each party had its share of fighting men and non-combatants, and for the most part, parties cared for their own; attack a non-combatant and you risked a comeuppance from his combatant allies. In a very real way, there was safety in numbers.

But sometimes the demands of pride, section, and party pushed even non-combatants into combat. French discovered this for himself in 1838. When a New England Democrat was challenged to a duel, French had a surge of Yankee pride for a countryman and ally who was holding his own. But when things went horribly wrong and the unthinkable happened, French crossed a line. He plotted an assault on a congressman.

3

THE PULL AND POWER OF VIOLENCE

THE CILLEY-GRAVES DUEL (1838)

Staring out at the House for fourteen years, French saw a lot of fighting. He saw screaming matches, finger-pointing, and desk-pounding. He saw Southerners rise en masse in a chorus of fist-clenched outrage, bellowing for all they were worth. He saw men so red-faced and angry that they could barely speak. (John Quincy Adams's bald head was a barometer of anger; the redder it got, the madder he was.)[1] He saw stamping and shoving, fistfights and flipped tables. He saw a few all-out melees—"*interesting and intellectual* exhibitions," he called them—with dozens of congressmen pounding one another or standing on chairs to get a good look. He saw bowie knives brandished and pistols drawn, and even saw one gun fired on the floor. Most of it didn't faze French, not even the stray bullet that wounded his hunting buddy, Capitol police officer John Wirt. He was "in very great pain," French reported to his brother, but because he was "a Democrat, with *of course* a clear conscience, he will no doubt soon get over it."[2]

Amid all this mayhem, for French one fight stood out: the 1838 duel between Representative Jonathan Cilley (D-ME) and Representative William J. Graves (W-KY), the only fatal congressional clash in Washington.[3] A fellow New England Democrat—a New Hampshire–born family man, no less—had engaged in deadly combat with a fellow congressman. It shook French to his core; he couldn't get over it. He discussed it in letters. He ranted about it in newspaper columns. He debated its ins and outs in his diary for days, even visiting the dueling ground and sketching the details for himself.[4] Twenty-six years later, when he published a memoir in magazine installments, he devoted two entries to the duel and its aftermath, the only event that received so much coverage.[5]

Routine "rough play" had led to a death.[6] This wasn't how congressional violence was supposed to work. Although threats, weapons, and fistfights were common, once the initial flashpoint of conflict had passed, friends and allies usually smoothed things over and avoided extremes, testimony to the congressional community's powers of self-preservation and the degree to which fighting—but not killing—was a congressional norm. Most congressional bullying wasn't about bloodlust, although some blood was shed. It was grounded on the gut-wrenching power of public humiliation before colleagues, constituents, and the nation-at-large. Fighting men used that power, joined with the threat of physical harm, to intimidate rivals and get their way.

The Cilley-Graves duel shows that power in action. It wasn't caused by anger or a thirst for revenge; the two men had no ill will between them. Rather, Cilley and Graves were *pulled* into fighting. Like most congressmen, both men assumed that their honor was bound up with the honor of all that they represented: their party, their constituents, even their section of the Union. When insulted, both men took dishonor seriously. And when the congressional community failed to negotiate a settlement, both men felt compelled to fight.

As suggested by French's prolonged gasp of a response, few things so effectively prompt earnest and ample testimony to the rules of the game than the game gone awry. In the wake of the duel, people inside and outside Washington weighed in on what had been wrong—and right—about it, highlighting the norms of congressional violence in the process. Indeed, virtually everyone even remotely involved in the duel registered his opinion during the formal congressional investigation that followed, resulting in a remarkable 175-page committee report full of sworn testimony to the pull and power of violence in Congress.[7]

Feelings were an important part of that power; fighting men put fear, shame, and anger to political use. And the Cilley-Graves duel certainly provoked strong feelings. French wasn't alone in his fascination. Sermons condemned it. Town meetings raged about it. Petitions denounced it. Newspaper headlines literally screamed bloody murder. Congressmen filled their letters and diaries with it. And the surviving participants justified their actions in letters, newspapers, and even on the House floor. Perhaps the best documented duel in American history, the Cilley-Graves duel presents a perfect opportunity to pierce the veil of congressional violence, revealing its internal logic and what it meant to congressmen, to Congress, and to a watchful public, horrified, fascinated, and admiring all in one.

"THE FIRST FATAL CONGRESSIONAL DUEL"

French immediately grasped the duel's historic significance: it was "the first fatal Congressional duel that has ever occurred."[8] Yet it was hardly his only brush with history. He had an uncanny knack for being in the right place at the right time. In 1835, when a deranged man tried to assassinate President Andrew Jackson, French was there.[9] He dined with Charles Dickens during the writer's 1842 tobacco-spit tour.[10] Not long after John Quincy Adams's fatal stroke in the House in 1848, French was by his side, his eyes filled with tears.[11] And he was at President Abraham Lincoln's deathbed in 1865, comforting his wife, Mary.[12] In a sense, French was a professional history-stalker. But the Cilley-Graves duel was different.

In part, this was because he was smack in the middle of it. French saw the debate that set things off, tracked the circulating gossip, and even saw Cilley write the letter that invited Graves's challenge. (When Cilley ducked into the Clerk's office to write it, French was there.)[13] On the day of the duel, French tried to intervene. Hours later, he saw a carriage with the victim's body ride by, and days later, he attended the victim's funeral.[14]

French also knew Cilley and Graves, and he liked them. They were pleasantly conventional. Graves—tall, dark, and strapping—was a "good-natured, pleasant" man, so much so that French deemed him "the last man . . . of all the members of the House" who seemed likely to duel (though this may say more about the good-natured French than about Graves; one New England congressman deemed Graves an "insolent . . . Kentucky rowdie."[15] The thin, bespectacled Cilley was "gentlemanly" and "seldom without a smile," though when excited, "there was a curl

Jonathan Cilley, ca. 1838
(Courtesy of the Library of
Congress)

William Graves, ca. 1840
(Courtesy of the Library of
Congress)

of the lip indicative of firmness and determination."[16] That curled lip was in evidence more than once during Cilley's time in Congress. According to French, he had "an excitable temperament," and it's obvious in his letters. He was given to blustery warnings like "They shall hear from me."[17]

In a sense, Graves and Cilley were average congressmen; they certainly fit the profile. Not quite forty (Graves was thirty-three; Cilley was thirty-five), both men were well educated; Cilley had a brief stint as a newspaper editor while studying law. Both men served in local office before coming to Congress. Both were loyal party men; like French, Cilley was a dedicated doughface Democrat. And both came from established families, particularly Cilley, who spoke often and proudly of the Cilley name: his grandfather, the Revolutionary War general Joseph Cilley, appears in one of John Trumbull's epic paintings in the Capitol rotunda; his uncle Bradbury was in the House during the Madison administration; and his brother Joseph would be an abolitionist senator under President James K. Polk.[18]

Yet in one way, Cilley *wasn't* average. He was unusually aggressive for a New England congressman. In part, this was a matter of circumstance; for years, he had been fighting for his political life in Maine against a league of friends turned enemies, usually emerging victorious. (Oddly enough, his foremost opponent would unintentionally play a role in the duel.) Elected to the Maine legislature in 1831 at the age of twenty-nine—a young man on the fast track to political power, much like his college friend Franklin Pierce in New Hampshire—Cilley held his own by taking strong stands. "I know that by many here, I am hated & feared," he wrote to his wife in 1833. "I am hated because I am feared."[19] He was rewarded for his efforts by being elected Speaker in 1835; in the fall of 1836 he was elected to the U.S. House, following Pierce's path to power. During a visit the summer before Cilley left for Washington, his college friend Nathaniel Hawthorne thought him a strange mix of sincerity and ambition, a shrewd "daring fellow"—"fierce as a tiger" if need be—who had fought his way into Congress by sheer force of will. Indeed, Hawthorne thought him a bit overconfident: "Hardly anybody, probably, thinks him better than he is, and many think him worse." He predicted that Cilley wouldn't be prominent in Congress.[20] Sadly, it was a prediction that proved wrong for all the wrong reasons.

Spurred by the financial panic of 1837, the Twenty-fifth Congress convened three months early for a short six-week session, and Cilley took his seat in September with a reputation as a man of mettle. French later recalled that Cilley "came to Washington with the endorsement that he would fight"; already, French's congressional calculations were under way.[21] As a fellow New England Democrat, French doubtless cheered the news. And Cilley delivered, though his wife counseled otherwise. "Why do you want me to keep still," he asked her on September 24. "It will not do for one who is sustained by the democracy to shrink from responsibility. . . . I never felt stronger or more confident in my life."[22] His confidence was apparent during the following session. Six weeks in, he was on his feet making speeches. "I made quite a sensation in the house, I assume," he told his wife in January 1838, the "I assume" suggesting that perhaps he didn't.[23] He was doing well socially, mingling with his messmates and attending parties. And then he got into an argument with Henry Wise (W-VA).

By 1838, the thirty-two-year-old Wise had served two terms in Congress, and in some ways he was much like Cilley and Graves. Similar in age, college-educated and trained in the law, Wise came from good Virginia stock; his father had been a Federalist presidential elector in the contest of 1800 that elected Thomas Jefferson.[24] But there all similarity ended, because Wise was the virtual epitome of a Virginia gentleman, almost to the point of caricature. He was a man of extremes: blustering, flamboyant, impulsive, high-strung, even violent, yet a remarkably genial jokester when he wanted to be; once, during an endless evening session, French saw him sneaking up on sleeping congressmen and tickling their noses with a slip of paper.[25] People who expected a firebrand when they met him were disappointed. As Wise himself put it, he was "warm in his affections" and "generous in his disposition," but could make a man "hate him with a bitter hate."[26] The phrenologist who examined his skull and said that he made a "bitter enemy" had it right.[27] Like many a Southerner, Wise was an inveterate tobacco chewer; he could spit to the impressive distance of fifteen feet. (Someone saw him do just that on a White House portico.)[28] Tall, thin, and "ghastly" pale, his clothes and long hair usually a bit askew, Wise had a long, striding gait and a short fuse.

On the floor, Wise was a frequent, fiery, and eccentric speaker who

sprinkled his invective with strange streaks of humor; once, when someone protested against a call to order by insisting that he could ask what
he liked, Wise jumped to his feet and asked the Speaker "how to spell
apple pie."[29] (He made his point.) Prone to dramatic displays of bravado,
Wise seemed to revel in waging war, but his passions got the better of
him time and again. By the time of the Twenty-fifth Congress, he already
had fought a duel, started a fistfight, and nearly gunned down Reuben
Whitney in a committee-room—and he was just getting started.[30] Cred-
iting Wise with "a dozen brawls," French considered him the king of
disorder, and many agreed. He was "an impudent & fancy fellow," Cilley
thought. "I do not like him at all."[31] So renowned were Wise's congressional exploits that during Charles Dickens's 1842 House visit, Wise
was one of two men whom he wanted pointed out. (The other was the
knife-wielding John B. Dawson; Dickens clearly had the inside scoop
on misbehaving congressmen.) Just a few days before Dickens's visit,
Wise had denounced a visiting British abolitionist during debate, dramatically turning to face him when delivering his most biting barbs, a
bit of stage business that Cilley would come to know all too well. Dickens described Wise as "wild looking . . . with a great ball of tobacco in
his left cheek." Wise undoubtedly contributed amply to the spit-spotted
rug that so disgusted Dickens.[32]

In all these ways, Wise was the epitome of a congressional "fighting
man," even staking his reputation on it. As he explained to his constituents during the furor over the outcome of the Cilley-Graves duel, to
properly fulfill his duties as their representative, all he needed was the
protection of his "own trusty weapon, and a trusty friend."[33] A gun and a
friend to fight by his side: these were the tools of Wise's trade. He was
even more explicit a year later when his role in the duel came up during
debate. "In the face of an approaching election, I say to my good constituents . . . 'If you are determined I shall not defend myself when assailed, like a true knight, do not send me to Congress, for I shall just as
surely fight.'"[34] His constituents *approved* of his fighting, he declared,
and indeed they did, electing him to Congress a remarkable six times.
He went on to become Virginia's governor in 1855, the man responsible
for signing the abolitionist John Brown's death warrant in 1859.

Wise first clashed with Cilley on January 23, 1838, while debating
the ongoing war against the Seminole Indians in Florida. When Wise

sympathized with the Indians to malign the Van Buren administration's handling of the war, Cilley erupted in defense of the Democratic president. "[W]hat was to become of the poor Indians?" he mocked. Far more important to worry about "poor Whites." To Cilley, sympathy for "the dark red man" seemed "to be akin to that expressed in some quarters for the man of a yet darker hue." Cilley was taunting Wise with abolitionism, and Wise felt the blow. He "cowered under the charge more than I have ever seen him before," observed John Quincy Adams.[35]

Three weeks later, Wise returned the favor. He was in full form on February 12 when he rose to his feet with a newspaper in hand. The matter was "of the deepest importance," he announced dramatically; two Whig newspapers had made charges of corruption against an unnamed Democratic congressman.[36]

Reading aloud the charges from the *New York Courier and Enquirer*, Wise demanded an investigation. Cilley objected. A free press could say what it pleased, he argued. Why credit one newspaper's dark hints? He didn't know the *Enquirer's* editor, James Watson Webb, personally, Cilley added, but if he was the same man who had attacked the Bank of the United States in his paper and then changed his tune after it granted him a loan, he didn't deserve much credit in Congress.

Whigs persisted. Democrats objected. The debate grew heated. The appropriately named tough guy Ratliff Boon (D-IN) growled that if anyone accused *him* of corruption he would settle it "by applying my *fist* to his spectacles," an open threat to the author of the *Enquirer* piece, Matthew "Old Specs" Davis, a man who seemed to court controversy; he was an Aaron Burr supporter in times past. James W. Bouldin (D-VA) deemed the charge yet another example of Wise's ongoing crush-the-Democrats blame game, played so artfully three years past when he had falsely accused Democrats of being drunk at the close of the session. Wise replied that they *had* been drunk and he could prove it. "So much for that."[37]

Now it was Cilley's turn to face Wise's fire. A true man of honor wouldn't quibble over details, Wise sneered, and as a Democrat, Cilley *certainly* shouldn't quibble, given that he himself might be the anonymous culprit mentioned in the *Enquirer*. When Cilley predictably bristled at hearing "the basest charges insinuated against himself," Wise stopped him mid-sentence and played the honor card. Dramatically turning to face Cilley, seated behind him, he asked if Cilley had meant to accuse him of making "base charges." This was moving into duel territory. Cilley said that Wise had been "ungenerous." Unsatisfied, Wise asked again and Cilley repeated himself. So Wise upped the stakes. Was Cilley *deliberately* insulting him? An answer of "yes" would have justified a duel. No, Cilley insisted, but he knew his rights and the rights of his constituents; he had every right to speak his mind. A little more taunting and sneering by Wise and the moment had passed. (The *Globe* summed up this spicy exchange as "some mutual explanations.")[38]

But the impact lingered. This was harsh stuff. It impressed French. Flipping through his mental checklist, he decided that it seemed to require something more. Yet recently Wise had let someone get away with a "gross insult," so perhaps he was too cowardly to push things further—a stellar example of the high price of letting insults pass.[39] And what about Cilley? As a non-combatant Northerner, what would he do? Being a combative non-combatant could be hard to manage, and Cilley's situation reveals why. His defense of his party had become self-defense within seconds. Soon, his life would be in the balance. In Congress, party politics could be a matter of life and death.

KNOCKING DOWN WHIGS

It's hard to believe that the Cilley-Graves duel stemmed from vague charges of corruption in the Democratic Party, but so it was. Underneath all of its twistings and turnings, it was a good old-fashioned party battle at heart. It started as a Whig attack on Democratic corruption; touched on the Bank of the United States, a third-rail source of party strife; involved one of the nation's most powerful Whig newspapers, James Watson Webb's *New York Courier and Enquirer*; and pitted a team of Whigs against a team of Democrats.

In 1838, this battle was intensifying because of the financial panic the year before. In the wake of massive economic instability, party differences clarified and a united Whig Party was born. No longer an amalgamated cluster of "ites," as French put it, the Whigs had cohered into a party that championed the use of government programs to develop the nation's infrastructure and promote economic growth; they favored protective tariffs and the return of the Bank of the United States. The states' rights Democrats, in contrast, blamed the nation's problems on corrupt banking men, sometimes summed up as a "Money Power." Thus the power of Wise's charge of corruption in the Democratic Party; he was turning the table on his foes. And thus the Democratic sensitivity to such charges.[40]

Agenda-driven as this battle was, however, it was also profoundly personal. "The Whiggery" and "the Democracy" were enduring entities with an emotional heft that went beyond mere institutional loyalty. French's love for his party ran deep. Its purpose, its principles, its founder, its revelry: he loved it all. The Democratic Party was more of a brotherhood than a political organization to French, and he wasn't alone.

Cilley's eight-year-old son, Greenleaf, had imbibed such lessons well. Not long before his father's duel, Greenleaf told him that he couldn't wait to knock down Whigs, bragging that "I guess I culd knock one of them down as fast as he could get up." Cilley laughingly told Greenleaf to bide his time. "You are not quite large enough yet to knock down Whigs," he chided. "Better wait till your beard & whiskers grow."[41] French's five-year-old son, Frank, was also an early adopter of party politics, though he had little sense of its meaning; in 1842, seeing a massive crowd gathered at the White House to pay a call on President John Tyler on New Year's Day, Frank asked with great seriousness if the people were going to "head Captain Tyler"—a phrase used by irritated Whigs who wanted to force Tyler to comply with their demands.[42]

Join the passions and ideals of party membership with its newly energized team-sports mentality, its political benefits, the confines of the congressional community, and the pressures of performing in the public forum of Congress, and you begin to see the many ways that party bonds inspired violence. They certainly did in the Twenty-fifth Congress. During the eight months of its first two sessions alone, in addition to the Wise-Cilley spat, there were at least nine nasty encounters—eight in the House and one in the Senate—most of them not degenerating into all-out fights but coming close.

Most of the clashes pitted Whigs against Democrats, though a brawl between the Tennessee Whigs William Campbell and Abram Maury was particularly dramatic. During an evening session, Campbell had gone home at 3:00 a.m. and was dragged back by the sergeant at arms; when Maury complained about slackers, Campbell took it personally and slugged him, nearly crashing him through a window. (Campbell later apologized.)[43] Not surprisingly, Democratic newspapers put the fight to good use, branding it a sign of "Whig Manners and Decency."[44]

Without a doubt, Henry Wise was the session's most frequent fighter. There was a reason for this beyond his persistent floor-rage problem. He was in the midst of an extended campaign against Speaker James K. Polk (D-TN) and, through him, the Democratic Party. With the presidential election of 1840 looming and candidates gunning their engines, Wise was campaigning for a Whig president in the way he knew best: by dishonoring leading Democrats with man-to-man showdowns, with Polk at the top of his list. And he wasn't alone. Joining him in his crusade were John Bell (W-TN) and his "trusty friend" Balie Peyton (W-TN).

The inner logic of this Whig onslaught was the inner logic of many a fight: insult one party member and you insult them all. The reverse was true too: disgrace a party and you disgrace its members. No man was an island when it came to party politics—a reality that brought Wise and Cilley to their feet. Wise was attacking a party; Cilley was defending it. And the consequences were profoundly personal as well as political. Two years later, when Edward Black (D-GA) attacked Whig policy and Waddy Thompson (W-SC) jumped to his feet as though personally insulted, Black confronted the problem outright: "Had it come to this, that a member could not get up here to question the course of a party, without being required to make personal explanations?"[45] The answer, at least sometimes, was yes. Here is one explanation for congressional violence. A simple equation: my party, myself.

The impact of such thinking could be severe, as the Cilley-Graves duel shows all too well.[46] That same thinking was in play a few months later during yet another battle in Wise's anti-Democracy campaign, though this time Wise's buddy John Bell did the dirty work, calling Polk supporter Hopkins Turney "the tool of tools" during debate. Seated directly in front of Bell, the "strongly excited" Turney wheeled around and declared Bell a liar (or as French recorded it: "Tis false—tis false"). Bell responded by slugging Turney, setting off a full-fledged rumble.[47]

Calculating outcomes in a letter to Wise two weeks later, Balie Peyton wondered if there would be a duel. If so, then Bell should

> load up those rifle barrel pistols of his which will kill a Buffaloe 50 yards and meet him, shooting the first at the distance of at least 30 yards—holding it like a rifle in both hands, and aiming low, with a heavy charge. Bell can out shoot any man in that way you ever saw. He has a steadiness of nerve which I never witnessed in any other man. He would be hell in a street fight—rather too slow in a duel—but very deliberate anywhere.

Bell was no duelist, so Peyton went further. Wise should take him out shooting and test different stances to see "how he will be most certain" to get his man.[48]

This is congressional violence in all its glory: calculated, deadly, and close at hand. Bell had insulted Turney; Turney had insulted Bell; and now Peyton was plotting Turney's death. Peyton's tone is so casual and his plans so bloodthirsty that he almost seems to be joking. Except that he wasn't.

Most fighting men didn't seek bloodshed so blatantly, and not all bullying prompted violence; often a display of bravado or a dose of humiliation was enough. Nor was all violence this deliberate. Fatigue, frustration, testy tempers, and the ready availability of booze all played a role. Even so, people who were defiant or confrontational on the floor took their chances and they knew it, which is precisely what congressional bullies counted on: intimidating their opponents into silence.

"AS I AM FROM NEW ENGLAND, I AM TO BE 'BLUFFED'"

Cilley knew what Wise had done when he spoke of "base charges." He had thrown down the code of honor as a gauntlet to prove Cilley a coward for not taking it up, a cat-and-mouse game that fighting men used to great advantage against non-combatants; indeed, most clashes were sparked by Southerners and Southern-born Westerners who abided by the code.[49] Wise's parting words to Cilley drove this lesson home; as he turned away, he dropped his voice and sneered, "But what's the use of bandying words with a man who won't hold himself personally account-able for his words?"[50] Wise was all but calling Cilley a coward for being a Northerner, and Cilley felt the sting, a sting felt by many Northern-ers. Cilley's subsequent struggle to chart the right course shows the complications of sectionalism in the national arena of Congress, and the ways that it sometimes put Northerners and non-combatants at a dis-advantage; with their manhood at stake and their political clout at risk, they were pulled into violence.[51]

Within one day of Cilley's clash with Wise over the *Enquirer* story, Whig newspapers already were mocking Cilley's manhood, playing the New England coward card for all it was worth, as in this article from the *Baltimore Sun* which someone placed in his hand. In Cilley's part of the country, it scoffed,

> duelling is considered an irresponsible and an irreligious pur-suit, and the man who flogs his neighbor with any thing larger or more violent than an ox-gourd is set down for a rap-rascal, and is voted out of church by the pious deacons and deacon-esses. As Mr. Cilley is a man of great practical and devotional piety, he may possibly eschew the pistol and seize the ox-gourd.

The message was clear. As Cilley's second later put it, the article "was calculated to make the impression that Mr. Cilley was not a gentleman, or brave man."[52]

Cilley had been scorned during debate and now the press was following suit. What should he do? How much damage had been done? And how could he fix it? The answers weren't clear. Ignoring such insults could have a high price. Cilley's manhood was at stake, as was the manhood of any congressman in the give-and-take (and push-and-shove) of congressional debate. Fighting men were quick to remind their victims of this fact, as Wise had done during Cilley's first weeks in the House, lambasting not one but *all* Democrats as cowards. They re-minded him of

> scenes of fright in the haunted house. A ghost is seen—who shall go and see what it is? Will you? will you? or you? No: no:

no. At last one poor trembling wretch, by volition or force, accident or half resolve, is pressed or ventures to totter forward, with broom-stick in hand—the rest pressing him on from behind—when, lo! a sound scatters them in backward flight, tumbling one over another in fright.[53]

Wise's attackers "would make very brave starts, and march fiercely up to a certain line, but then they stopped." Wise, according to Wise, was braver than them all. This was macho posturing to the point of absurdity. But it amply shows how manhood was coin of the realm in Congress.

Ignoring personal attacks also slashed at a man's political power and influence. Cilley's friend Franklin Pierce said as much not long after the duel. "You know well what is the consequence, if personalities are directed to you, and you allow them to pass in silence," he noted.[54] Disrespect and disempowerment in Congress and back home were sure to follow. Yet responding to insults was risky, particularly for a Yankee. By the 1830s, many New Englanders condemned dueling as irresponsible, irreligious, barbaric, and unequivocally Southern. As Pierce put it, on this "the tone of feeling in our section of the country" was quite clear.[55] So when it came to dueling, Northern congressmen had a double burden: their constituents disapproved of it and they themselves lacked the expertise and easy familiarity of their Southern-born colleagues; thus the appeal of honor-taunting by fighting men. Those Northerners who did venture into dueling territory virtually all chose duel-savvy Southern or Southern-born Western allies as their seconds or "friends."[56]

The "tone of feeling" was equally clear in the South. Dueling was respected and praised, with a dash of mournful regret thrown in. Although there were anti-dueling laws throughout the region, they were rarely enforced, and duelists were widely respected and routinely raised to high office, as Andrew Jackson's political career shows all too well.[57] The Southern dueling mantra was voiced by Senator William Campbell Preston (N-SC) after the Cilley-Graves duel. "Duelling had undoubtedly produced much folly and much misery," he admitted, "but at the same time it had mitigated the indulgence of revengeful passions . . . Was it not . . . manifestly less outrageous upon receiving offense to send a challenge than to draw a dirk?"[58] Dueling *restrained* violence, Preston argued; indeed, even the mere threat of a duel urged good behavior. Wise agreed. When it came to slander, he noted, "The law cannot restrain it—a pistol sometimes will."[59] All in all, many Southerners considered dueling an unfortunate but necessary civilizing force. It was also becoming a symbol of the South, perhaps even a matter of pride; in response to rising antislavery sentiment in the 1830s, defensive Southerners began aggressively touting all things Southern, including the code of honor.[60]

In the national center, charting a middle course between sectional customs and national demands could be challenging, particularly for men who didn't abide by the code of honor; in a sense, sectionalism was *always* in play in Congress, shaping how men interacted, if not always shaping their votes. This was cultural federalism with a vengeance.

As tangled as Cilley's situation was, the arrival of the *Enquirer* editor James Watson Webb in Washington brought new challenges. Intent on defending his name against Cilley's claims about the Bank and bribery, Webb came to the capital ready to fight. Though by no means a Southerner, the native New Yorker was a fighting man's fighting man. The editor of a powerful and notably aggressive Whig newspaper, he talked big and backed up his words with weapons. Often. Over the course of his eventful career, he threatened, caned, horsewhipped, and dueled with his antagonists and was himself threatened, beaten, and shot, partly a product of his job, partly a product of his temperament, and partly a holdover from his eight years in the army; military men were connoisseurs of the fine art of personal chastisement.

When it came to threatening violence against Washington politicos, Webb was a repeat offender; he had a habit of racing from New York to the capital to clear his name. In 1830, he had attacked the Washington *Telegraph* editor Duff Green for insulting Webb in his paper, lunging at Green on the Capitol steps. But Green had greater fire power—literally; when he cocked a pistol, Webb backed down.[61] He was foiled again in 1837 when he confronted yet another offender. As was his wont, Wise had insulted the Democrats during debate, and Samuel Gholson (D-MS) had defended them, denouncing Webb in the process. When Webb confronted Gholson and called him a liar—a virtual invitation to fight a duel—Gholson declared Webb too lowly to fight, and there things ended thanks to Webb's friends, who intervened out of fear that Webb's second would be forced to fight in his place as demanded by the code of honor.[62]

Now, five months later, Webb was trying the same move with Cilley. And like Gholson, Cilley wanted nothing to do with Webb. He didn't think much of him, didn't like his politics, was well aware of his fighting record, and didn't want to be drawn into a "personal difficulty" with every editor who disliked what he said on the floor. Plus, he had the sneaking suspicion that Webb had pegged him as an easy mark. "I see into the whole affair," Cilley told one of his duel advisors. "Webb has come on here to challenge me, because *he*, and perhaps others, think that, as I am from New England, I am to be '*bluffed*:' and Mr. Webb will then proclaim himself a *brave man*."[63] Here is the logic of bullying in plain view: fighting-man Webb would promote himself by humiliating a non-combatant.

Webb took a step in that direction when he confronted Cilley. But in compliance with the code of honor, rather than approaching Cilley himself, he sent his friend William Graves (W-KY) in his place. Graves and Webb had come to know each other when Graves had visited New York some time past; Webb had been more than welcoming, and Graves wanted to return the favor, but they weren't close friends.[64] Wise later would scold Graves for entangling himself in an honor dispute for anyone less than a bosom friend.[65]

On the morning of February 21, Graves spotted Webb hobnobbing in the House lobby and went over to shake his hand. Democrats so detested the Whig press warrior that his mere presence raised hackles; when Jesse Bynum (D-NC) spotted him, he immediately asked the Speaker why Webb had been allowed in the hall.[66] A few minutes later, Webb pulled Graves aside, and the two men stepped behind a screen at the edge of the chamber. When Webb asked a favor, Graves was more than willing, but then he handed Graves a letter to deliver to Cilley. "I paused," Graves later recalled. "It instantly struck me that the paper was a challenge." If it was, he wanted nothing to do with it, he told Webb. Plus, he was "totally ignorant of the etiquette of duelling," so he wasn't the man for the job. Webb assured him that it wasn't a challenge; it was a letter of inquiry. As the code dictated, before things went further, Webb was giving Cilley a chance to explain or retract his remark about Webb and Bank bribery. If Webb sent a challenge, he assured

Graves, someone else would be his second, the man responsible for fighting in Webb's place if necessary. "Totally unconscious . . . that any possible mischief could arise out of my carrying a simple paper of interrogation from one gentleman to another," Graves took the note.[67]

He immediately sent a page to fetch Cilley, and the two men stepped behind another screen. (The Cilley-Graves duel negotiations are a prime example of how much was happening around the edges of the bustling House chamber.) Graves held out the letter and Cilley reached for it, but when Graves said that it was from Webb, Cilley dropped his hand. Graves assured him that the note was "respectful," but Cilley wanted none of it. He didn't want to be "drawn into personal difficulties with the conductors of public journals" for what he said during debate, and he hadn't insulted Webb as a gentleman; he didn't even know Webb.

So now what to do? Neither man was sure. Acknowledging that he didn't know much about the code of honor, Graves said that Cilley's refusal to accept the letter seemed to put him in an "unpleasant" situation. Cilley apologized. He meant no disrespect. But he knew even less than Graves about the code; he needed time to think. A short time later, they met again behind the screen, but Cilley hadn't changed his mind. He still wouldn't take the letter. They were at a standoff. And so they parted, two men on dangerous ground without a map. They were fighting a party battle with a sectional weapon that could easily misfire in their hands.

A COMMUNITY AFFAIR

Well aware that they had wandered onto the thin ice of an honor dispute, both men immediately turned to knowledgeable friends to lead them to safety, as was the norm in congressional clashes. Cilley went straight to the Senate lobby and beckoned to Franklin Pierce, who had five years of congressional experience. Pierce didn't know what to do but he knew whom to ask. Darting off to consult with Southern friends, he returned moments later, reporting that Cilley had done right; he shouldn't accept Webb's note. But he'd better arm himself, Pierce advised, because with a duel off the table, Webb would probably assault Cilley on the street.[68] Such was the conventional alternative to a duel; if someone proffered an insult but refused to meet on the field of honor, a sound beating was the likely result.

So off Cilley went in search of a pistol. He first tried Alexander Duncan (D-OH), a large man—six feet tall and stout—known for his loud, confrontational style of debate. John Quincy Adams considered him "coarse, vulgar, and impudent . . . a thorough-going hack demagogue . . . with a vein of low humor exactly suited to the rabble of a populous city, and equally so to the taste of the majority of the present House of Representatives."[69] (Adams had a way with an insult.) An in-your-face Westerner, Duncan was a likely gun owner, but he only had a rifle, so he brought Cilley to gun provider number two, John F. H. Claiborne (D-MS), Gholson's second in *his* dispute with Webb, who was happy to lend his pistols. "Now, Cilley, for God's sake, don't be drawn into a duel with Mr. Graves," Claiborne jokingly advised as they parted. "No danger of that," replied Cilley. "Mr. Graves and myself are not enemies; I never had a difficulty with but one person in the House"—Henry Wise.[70]

It's easy to see how the process of collecting duel consultants could snowball; negotiating fights was a community affair. When a fight threatened to escalate, fighting experts often rushed into the breach to forge a compromise or devise a strategy. Indeed, given the high stakes, negotiating a fight often required a virtual board of advisors with varied levels of fighting expertise, institutional savvy, and congressional clout. This was especially true for Northern non-combatants, who relied on Southern party allies to decode the code of honor. In Congress, cross-sectional party bonds did more than win elections or shape legislation; they forged crucial cross-sectional personal bonds as well.[71]

Cilley had dire need of such bonds because, like most Northerners, he was unversed in the details of the *code duello*. Between February 21 and 23, he and his friends consulted at least ten Democrats, including Cilley's New England messmates, other Maine and New Hampshire representatives, Southerners and Westerners who understood the code of honor, and the *Globe* editors Francis P. Blair and John C. Rives, who each offered Cilley a rifle, giving an entirely new meaning to the idea of a supportive party press. Cilley and Pierce alone worked their way through much of the Missouri delegation—including the longtime senator and past duelist Thomas Hart Benton—desperate for border-state men who could translate the code and act as Cilley's second in case of a duel.[72]

Aware that Cilley's refusal to accept Webb's letter was an affront, Graves also went on a consultation spree, though a modest one given the many duel-savvy fellow Kentuckians offering advice. In that same three-day period, he talked to his three Kentucky messmates—including friend and fight expert Henry Clay (W-KY)—as well as two other Kentuckians and two notoriously confrontational Southerners, Waddy Thompson (W-SC) and Henry Wise, both experienced in the subtleties of duel challenges.[73] During negotiations, Clay did his duty as a border-state man, translating the meaning of some of Cilley's befuddling choices by explaining Yankee logic. For example, after Cilley's initial refusal of Webb's letter, Clay supposedly explained that the clueless Northerner probably assumed it was a challenge, and told Graves how to explain things to a Yankee.[74]

All told, in a three-day period, at least twenty-four congressmen and sundry congressional staffers, including French, learned of the looming threat of a duel—roughly 10 percent of the House. Not only did the business of Congress spark fights, but negotiating fights was sometimes the business of Congress. The Graves-Cilley tangle was negotiated almost entirely in the Capitol.[75] Endorsed by the congressional community, fighting was woven into the fabric of Congress.

And no endorsement could be more apparent than the routine spurning of "privilege of debate," a hallowed parliamentary rule that could have quashed any number of disputes. Embedded in Article 1, Section 6 of the U.S. Constitution, it gave congressmen the right to "not be questioned in any other place" for words spoken during debate.[76] But hiding behind an institutional shield seemed cowardly, so congressmen routinely cast it aside when embroiled in a fight. The 1837 exchange between Gholson and Webb was typical of many. When Webb called Gholson a coward for insulting him on the floor while shielded by his privileges, Gholson renounced them. "I claim no privilege from my situation as a member of the House of Representatives," he wrote in his formal reply to Webb's opening letter. Cilley followed Gholson's lead.[77] Even on the dueling ground, when Wise virtually begged him to plead privilege of debate, he refused.[78]

Even so, under different circumstances, Cilley might have found a way out. He had every right to refuse to duel with an inferior; the tradition of treating editors like lower-class artisans wasn't entirely a thing of the past in the 1830s, and duels were fought only between equals. Five months earlier, Gholson had refused to meet Webb on those grounds, scorning him as "unworthy of any notice."[79] This snub was precisely why Webb was so fired up to fight Cilley. As Webb put it, the "true secret of my repeated difficulties, is to be found in . . . the abominable doctrine, that in *becoming an editor I ceased to be a gentleman!*"[80]

Cilley might have traveled down that path if it hadn't been for the fact that his encounter with Graves involved the community of Congress. By spurning Webb, Cilley insulted Graves, Webb's friend and envoy. In past congressional spats, Webb had chosen congressional outsiders as seconds, making it easier for congressmen to snub him without serious repercussions. The involvement of a brother congressman complicated matters.[81] Dishonor him and you dishonored all that he represented, as Graves well knew, mentioning it more than once during negotiations. For the honor of himself, of his constituents, of Kentucky, and of the South, Graves felt that he couldn't let Cilley's implied insult slide, and his advisors agreed.

Cilley had no desire to inflict that sort of damage. Yet he couldn't treat with Webb without dishonoring himself and all that *he* represented, as his advisors noted more than once in the days before the duel. Even merely insulting Webb required careful calculations. When Duncan— not a man of subtleties—suggested that Cilley write Webb a letter denouncing him as "an unprincipled scoundrel, a degraded coward, and a bought-up vassal" who was unworthy of meeting, even through Graves, Pierce quickly said no. Such an answer might do for a "Southwestern man," he advised, but given New England's hatred of dueling, it was "of the first importance that Mr. Cilley should only act in the defensive, and be clearly in the right." If Cilley ended up fighting a duel, "it must clearly appear that he is forced to do so in defence of his honor and of his rights."[82]

In the end, struggling to defend his honor without offending his constituents, Cilley decided he'd have to fight if challenged. "My people will be better pleased if I stand the test, than disgrace myself by humiliating concessions," he reasoned.[83] That said, he insisted that no "Northern friend" risk his reputation back home by acting as his second. He wouldn't even let Pierce join him on the dueling ground; with elections coming in the fall, the risk to Pierce's career was too great. "I'll never be able to get any recognition in Maine after this," Cilley told his second, even as he headed to the dueling ground.[84] It's easy to understand Cilley's takeaway lesson about being in Congress, written to his wife in the midst of his wrangle: "[A] man, if he think free & boldly must take his life in his hand."[85]

And so on the morning on February 23, Graves sent Cilley a formal challenge, noting that he was "left no other alternative but to ask that satisfaction which is recognized among gentlemen."[86] That evening, Cilley accepted. And the duel that no one wanted advanced to the dueling ground.

"AN AGITATION IN THE HOUSE"

By the day of the duel—February 24—both men had assembled teams of advisors to guide them through the coming confrontation. As a Southerner, Graves didn't have to go far to find duel-savvy men whom he knew and trusted. He ultimately chose frequent fighter Henry Wise as his second, U.S. Navy surgeon Jonathan M. Foltz as his doctor, and Richard H. Menefee (W-KY) and John J. Crittenden (W-KY) as his secondary "friends," the latter a mild-mannered senior senator with a national reputation who might be able to wield his influence to settle the fight.[87] As Graves explained it, Crittenden's presence "would be the best evidence I could offer at home, that I did not intend to act rashly."[88]

As a congressional newcomer, Cilley had a harder time of it. With no close duel-savvy friends, he assembled a team of relative strangers with a history of fighting: his second was George W. Jones, a delegate from the Wisconsin territory, recommended by Missouri men as an experienced second (he had four duels under his belt); his doctor was the rifle-ready Alexander Duncan; and his secondary "friends" on the field were Jesse Bynum (D-NC), a veteran of two congressional duels, once as a second and once as a principal (plus a fistfight with Henry Wise two years past); and Jones's college friend Colonel James W. Schaumburg, a hot-tempered Louisianan renowned for fighting a duel with swords on horseback and accidentally killing his unfortunate horse. Schaumburg became involved only because Pierce spotted the famous duelist on Pennsylvania Avenue and sought his advice. Well aware of Schaumburg's hair-trigger temper, Jones blurted out, "For God's sake, don't take him," but he was too late.[89] Whigs had good reason to question the influence of Cilley's "violent political friends."[90] As for Cilley's closest nonviolent friend, Franklin Pierce, by the morning of the duel, he was beside himself with worry, walking into Cilley's room and immediately walking out, too disturbed to speak.[91]

A few hours later at a little past noon, Cilley, Jones, Bynum, and Schaumburg met Duncan at his boardinghouse and set out for the Anacostia bridge, where they were to meet Graves and his friends and leave the District together. After a brief wait at the bridge, two carriages drove up, one carrying Graves, Wise, and Menefee, the other Crittenden and Foltz. All three carriages then set out for Maryland. A short time later, Whig representatives John Calhoon and Richard Hawes of Kentucky followed in their tracks, equipped with blankets in case Graves was shot.[92] All told, ten congressmen were present that day.

From start to finish, the duel was a very human affair, as were all duels, but few were documented beyond bare-bones reports by the seconds. The Cilley-Graves committee report offers an intimate view of a duel's gritty realities: the misunderstandings and mistakes, the offhand jokes, the quirky side stories, the surprises and oversights. It shows a group of men gingerly feeling their way through a deadly encounter, clinging to rules and rituals in the name of fairness, for the sake of honor, but hoping to end things with bloodless gunplay, a parting handshake, and nothing more.

Some of the duel's details are almost funny: no one knew where the District's border was, so they had to ask a stranger; a random tourist with a lifelong desire to witness a duel shadowed the carriages and insisted on watching; Menefee loaded Graves's rifle incorrectly before the first shot, leading Wise to joke about so-called Kentucky riflemen; Cilley's carriage driver and the son of the farmer who owned the field chatted with Graves between shots, the boy peppering him with questions (Are you fighting a duel? Are you members of Congress? Where are you from? Are you fighting over a debate?) until Graves asked him to stop.

The report also reveals that neither Cilley nor Graves was good with a rifle, something that the two seconds deliberately suppressed in their joint post-duel account of their proceedings; it wouldn't have done much for their principals to expose them as bumblers who misfired. But so they were. As a rifleman, Cilley had a slight advantage, but very slight. He hadn't shot a gun in at least five years, and even then he'd been hunting squirrels—badly, because he was nearsighted. Graves was so bad with a rifle that his friends felt sure that he'd be killed; thus the presence of Calhoon and Hawes with blankets. (Menefee said that Graves fired "with an awkwardness very remarkable in one educated and residing in Kentucky.")[93] Graves's friends filed down his gun's trigger to keep him from firing prematurely, but during the second exchange of fire he did precisely that. Cilley misfired during the first exchange. Both men had practice sessions before the duel and they needed them.[94]

But for the most part, events went as planned. The three carriages arrived at the chosen spot, stopping just outside the fence surrounding the field. Wise and Jones, the two seconds, surveyed and measured the ground, linking arms and taking extra-large paces so that what was supposed to be a distance of eighty yards was closer to ninety-two. Then they signaled for everyone to "come on," with Cilley and Graves arriving last, their places marked, their rifles loaded.

The two men walked to their designated spots, Cilley standing on a slight rise, Graves standing in front of a fence near a small wood; such things mattered because they might affect one's aim. Graves faced the sun. There was a strong wind blowing against Cilley; it was a cold winter day.

The two men angled their left sides toward each other to narrow themselves as targets. They were handed their rifles. Jones, as deter-

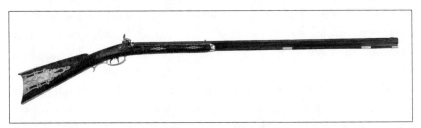

The rifle used by Jonathan Cilley in his duel (Photograph by Hugh Talman and Jaclyn Nash. Courtesy of National Museum of American History, Smithsonian Institution)

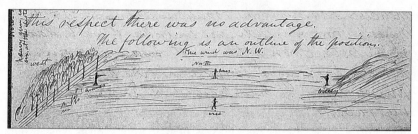

A few weeks after the Cilley-Graves duel, French visited the dueling ground to chart the duel's logistics. Later that day, he drew it in his diary. (Courtesy of the Library of Congress)

mined by a coin toss, said, "Gentlemen, are you ready?" and when neither man said no, continued: "Fire—one, two, three, four." (No one was to fire after the count of four). Cilley fired first before he'd fully raised his gun. Graves fired a second or two later and missed.

Now, as was customary, the seconds and friends assembled halfway between the principals and conferred; neither Graves nor Cilley could hear them. Jones asked Wise if Graves was satisfied. If so, they could shake hands and leave. "These gentlemen have come here without animosity towards each other," Wise replied. "Cannot Mr. Cilley . . . make some disclaimer which will relieve Mr. Graves from his position?" Jones spoke with Cilley and returned: Cilley said that he meant no disrespect to Graves, "because he entertained for him then, as he now does, the highest respect and the most kind feelings." He refused Webb's note because he didn't want to be drawn into a "controversy" with him, and didn't "choose to be drawn into an expression of opinion as to him." After a brief discussion, both men checked with their principals and returned, Wise stating that Cilley's answer left Graves "precisely in the position in which he stood when the challenge was sent," Cilley's friends insisting that the exchange of fire and Cilley's "peril of life" should satisfy Graves's honor. Roughly twenty minutes were spent in "earnest conversation," Graves and Cilley watching from afar.

But because nothing had changed, Wise and Menefee determined that the fight should continue. Cilley and Graves got back into position, and this time Graves fired before fully raising his gun and Cilley missed. Graves staggered back so violently at the misfire that his friends thought he'd been hit; embarrassed and frustrated, he demanded another shot.[95] Again, the seconds and friends conferred. Jones insisted that Cilley had proven himself "a brave man" and had given satisfaction to Graves by risking his life. "The matter should end here." But Wise, speaking for Graves, wanted Cilley to acknowledge that Webb was a gentleman, otherwise Graves had "borne the note of a man who is not a man of honor" and dishonored himself in the process.[96]

Meanwhile, off to the side, Cilley's carriage driver chatted with Graves. He thought that Graves had been hit during the second fire. "I didn't feel the ball or hear it," Graves replied. The driver asked the distance between Graves and Cilley. "Eighty yards," was the answer. "[I]t was a chance shot to hit a man at that distance, as the wind was blowing." At that moment, the two seconds began reloading the rifles. "I am very sorry to see them rifles loaded again," said the driver. Graves dropped his head and murmured, "So it is."

As the reloading continued, Wise pulled Jones aside for one last stab at settling matters. Couldn't Cilley claim privilege of debate? Cilley wouldn't, Jones knew. Cilley's team now objected "in the strongest language" to continuing, but Wise and Menefee wanted Cilley to either admit that Webb was a gentleman or plead privilege of debate. When Jones reported this to Cilley, he replied, "They must thirst for my blood mightily."[97] Here, Schaumburg's hair-trigger temper did its damage. Arguing with Wise and Menefee about whether honor had been satisfied, he snapped, "[G]o on, and load and fire until you are satisfied." And the two men stalked off and did just that.[98]

Again, Jones gave the count. Both men took aim and fired, nearly simultaneously. This time, Graves's shot rang true. Dropping his rifle and grabbing his abdomen, Cilley reached for his friends and cried, "I am shot," falling into Schaumburg's arms. The ball had passed through Cilley's body, severing his abdominal aorta. He died within minutes, his friends in tears.[99] The random tourist (clearly not shy) arrived at Cilley's side as his friends closed his eyes; walking back to his horse, he passed Wise, then Graves and the others, all of them asking after Cilley. "He is dead, sir," was the answer. Crittenden asked him to deliver a note to Clay reporting the outcome. Wise, in tears, sent word of the outcome to his drinking buddy Pierce, who shunned Wise for the next fourteen years.[100] Graves and his friends walked to their carriages, Graves's face masked in his cloak. Cilley's friends carried his body to their carriage. And they all headed back to town.

Back in Washington, the Capitol was abuzz. The duel was virtually common knowledge, though few had expected it to happen; given the involvement of a non-combatant Northerner and the mere "punctilio" at the heart of the conflict, until the morning of the duel most people had assumed that the combatants would find a way out. Thus French's ability early in the dispute to joke that Cilley had been invited to "stand up and be shot at."[101]

But there wasn't much joking on the morning of the duel. Congressmen were clustered on the Capitol grounds, looking up the road, waiting for news. Inside the House chamber no one could concentrate. "There was an agitation in the House, different from that which is occasioned by an irritated debate," reported John Quincy Adams. "[A] restless, uneasy, whispering disposition, clustering into little groups with inquisitive looks, listening ears, and varying reports as one member or another went out of, or came into the Hall."[102]

Hoping to prevent gunplay, the congressional community kicked into gear. People were scampering all over town trying to intervene. Maine Democrats John Fairfield and Timothy Carter ran to a carriage that they thought contained Cilley and his friends, but were mistaken.[103] French tried to pry the duel's location from Carter, but Carter "pretended not to know anything." (French's phrasing would prove significant in events to come.)[104] Hearing of the duel early that morning, two of Webb's friends had rushed to Clay's boardinghouse, waking him from a dead sleep. Stunned to hear that the duel was taking place (he thought that Whig delaying tactics had kept Graves from finding a rifle), but as Graves's friend unable to intervene, Clay sent them to the district attorney and to the frequent fight mediator Charles Fenton Mercer (W-VA), who he knew would do all that they could.[105] The district attorney promptly rushed to the Capitol to find out where the duel was taking place, then raced off to arrest the participants—at the wrong location.

And then there was the perennial loose cannon, James Watson Webb. Horrified to find that Graves was fighting in his place, he came up with a series of increasingly outrageous and *un*gentlemanly plans. First, he and two friends, all of them well armed, went to Cilley's boardinghouse intending to give him two options: duel Webb immediately or swear to do so before fighting Graves. If Cilley refused, Webb would shatter his right arm so he couldn't duel Graves. Finding that Cilley had already left, the desperados opted for Plan B: run onto the dueling ground and insist that Webb take Graves's place. If Cilley resisted, they'd shoot him. If Graves and Wise ordered them off the field . . . they'd shoot Cilley. The three men spent much of the morning racing to dueling grounds all over the District and beyond with the dignity and aplomb of the Keystone Kops, but after visiting three wrong locations they returned to the city to await the result. (Clearly, congressional duelists had a wide range of playing fields.)

French's various writings describe what came next; as always, he witnessed it all. He was lounging at a "billiard saloon" when someone burst in yelling that the parties were returning from the dueling ground, leading French and a pack of billiard loungers to make a mad dash for the windows. Moments later, French emerged from the building as the carriage bearing Cilley's corpse passed by, trailed by an immense crowd. Rushing around the corner, French watched as the body was carried into Cilley's boardinghouse. A few moments more and French was home at his window with Bess, watching the angry, milling crowd and the agitated comings and goings at the dead congressman's door.[106]

Cilley's body lay in state in the Capitol's rotunda before his funeral, not far from the Trumbull painting that included his grandfather's portrait, an eerie coincidence that came to light when a little girl, standing before the painting with an explanatory card in her hand, asked her father, "Which is Colonel Cilley?"[107] Then came Cilley's enormous funeral in the House chamber, attended by the president, vice president, cabinet, Congress—and French, followed by a funeral procession to the Congressional Cemetery that extended for half a mile.[108] It was a "political parade," thought Wise.[109] "The funeral of a saint," Adams groused. But with a difference; the Supreme Court refused to attend the funeral of a duelist, as did some Massachusetts congressmen.[110] On the opposite end of the dueling spectrum, some Southern congressmen were offended by the preacher's anti-dueling sermon.[111]

Not surprisingly given the uproar, Cilley's burial didn't calm things in Washington. French noticed handbills announcing that Wise and Webb were to be burned in effigy near City Hall, Webb for causing the tragedy and Wise for pushing it to its violent close.[112] For a short time,

An 1838 cartoon mocking James Watson Webb's post-duel strut up and down the Avenue, daring people to assault him. In reality, he was armed, but not with quite so many weapons. (Courtesy of the Library of Congress)

there was talk of a mob forming to hang Graves and Wise.[113] Webb was threatened with a beating, even a lynching. True to form, he responded by taking a long, deliberate stroll up and down the Avenue—twice—daring his attackers to strike, combative, unrepentant, and heavily armed to the end.[114]

Four years later, Webb finally succeeded in dueling a congressman but it didn't end well. He and Representative Thomas Marshall (W-KY)—of the "spreeing gentry"—had been sniping at each other for months over a bankruptcy law that Marshall wanted repealed, and that Webb dearly needed. When Marshall went to New York City on business, the sniping got more serious, leading Marshall to issue a duel challenge. In the subsequent duel, Webb was shot in the leg; not long after, New York's Democratic district attorney indicted him under the state's anti-dueling law. Arguing that he hadn't bothered to obey a law that was never enforced, Webb was tried, found guilty, and sentenced to two years in the notorious Sing Sing penitentiary, but was pardoned by the governor after 14,000 New Yorkers petitioned for his release.[115] Clearly, dueling had not yet had its day in the North.

Nor had it had its day in Washington. How long would "this tragical event" prevent congressional dueling? wondered British visitor Fredrick Marryat. "Well, I reckon three days, or thereabouts," a stranger sarcastically shot back.[116] In fact, it was three years until the next challenge, four years until the next duel, and three months until the next fistfight.[117]

"GO TO THE BALLOT BOXES"

Meanwhile, the North exploded in outrage. There were demonstrations and public meetings throughout New England and the Middle Atlantic states. Writing from Chester, New Hampshire, French's half brother Henry reported that Cilley's death had "created a great sensation." He felt sure that "New England would be glad to have Wise hanged—I should."[118] Maine was in an uproar. "You can form no conception of the excitement here," wrote one of John Fairfield's (D-ME) constituents.[119] Scores of petitions spilled into the House and Senate demanding an anti-dueling law and the expulsion of the duel's participants, particularly Graves and Wise.[120]

The Northern press seethed with outrage of all kinds. Anti-dueling advocates saw a golden opportunity to push their point; antislavery advocates saw a chance to condemn slaveholders and the South; and Whigs and Democrats saw a chance to condemn one another.

Democratic papers were particularly passionate in denouncing "the murder of Cilley" at the hands of a gang of Whig assassins. Isaac Hill's former paper, the *New-Hampshire Patriot*, wins the prize for headline creativity (and excessive capitalization): "BANK RUFFIANS, HIRED TO SHOOT DOWN [Democratic-] REPUBLICAN MEMBERS OF CONGRESS." The remedy, of course, was to "GO TO THE BALLOT BOXES."[121] *The United States Magazine and Democratic Review* published a lengthy article whose title said it all: "The Martyrdom of Cilley."[122] Given that the dead man was a Democrat, Whig papers were at a disadvantage, but they took their share of swings. Many chided the Democrats for using a "bloody tragedy . . . for electioneering

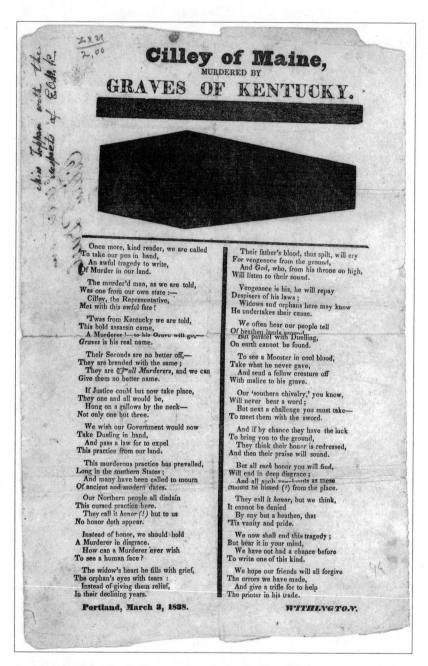

An example of the flood of commentary in the duel's wake, this 1838 anti-dueling broadside asserts the superiority of Northern culture and mocks Southern "honor." (By William Withington. Courtesy of the George J. Mitchell Department of Special Collections and Archives, Bowdoin College Library, Brunswick, Maine)

purposes," then turned around and did the same, claiming that Cilley's friends—a gang of assassin Democrats—had sacrificed Cilley to get at Webb.[123]

Not surprisingly, the response was more subdued in the South and West. Crittenden was appalled by the "faint, puny, stinted sort of defense" of Graves in Kentucky newspapers.[124] With anti-dueling laws on the books throughout much of the nation and reformers of all kinds condemning the practice, it was difficult to publicly defend dueling with gusto, even in dueling country.[125]

Given the uproar and the risk to reputations and careers, many participants tried to spin things their way in public statements. Wise and Graves addressed their constituents; Webb published a statement in the *Courier and Enquirer*; Benton wrote a letter to the *Washington Globe*; and Pierce wrote a letter to the investigative committee that was later published in the press. Not surprisingly, all five men sent the same message: don't blame me. Webb and Graves took the extreme Whig approach, accusing Cilley's "violent political friends" of pushing him into a fight.[126] Benton denied any real involvement, admitting only to being consulted on the day of the duel.[127] And Pierce refuted a stream of accusations flooding Whig newspapers in New England: no, he hadn't been Cilley's second; no, he hadn't urged Cilley to fight; no, after the duel, he hadn't raced down the street with a smile on his face, eager to hear that Cilley had slaughtered Graves.[128]

Wise's and Graves's statements had an added dimension because they directly addressed their constituents, Wise in a written statement, Graves in a speech in Louisville that later appeared in print. Both defended themselves at length for the same stated reason: they were being accused of dishonorable behavior, and their honor and their constituents' honor were intertwined. "Your Representative is accountable to you for his *personal* as well as his political conduct," Wise wrote, "for, by it he is worthy of you, or you are dishonored." Graves was even more explicit. He had fought for his honor and the honor of Kentucky, and if his constituents continued to support him, he would continue to "preserve your honor with my own," a declaration that drew "Great cheering."[129] Crittenden said the same in a private letter: Graves felt that "the honor of *his State* is in *his hands*."[130] Wise and Graves were advancing the same argument: a dishonored congressman dishonored all that he represented. In a very real way, congressmen *were* their constituents, states, and regions personified; they practiced a kind of *performative representation*, acting as physical surrogates for all that they represented.[131]

Cilley had made this argument in the days before the duel. His rights were his constituents' rights; his humiliation was their humiliation. They were one and the same. By this logic, as much as his constituents might disapprove of dueling, they would disapprove far more of being publicly disgraced. Several times, he even hinted that he was defending the honor of New England as a whole. Given the circumstances, he thought it better to fight.[132]

This wasn't clouded thinking in the heat of the moment. It was the truth; as a fellow New Englander, French felt the power of Cilley's logic, heart and soul. When Wise and Cilley had first clashed on the floor, French had gloried that a New Englander—even better, a Granite State native—was standing firm in rough waters. Wise had tried to "brag off" Cilley, but Cilley "would not budge an inch," French gloated. He was holding his own "with an unflinching eye." Then, even more remarkably, Cilley stood up to Webb in the face of a duel. "Yankees are not the fellows to *back out* of any thing when they are once in," French crowed, pleased that Webb had found "a customer."[133] To French, Cilley was upholding New England's honor as well as the honor of the Democracy.

This wasn't French's first praise of an embattled New Englander. One year earlier, when John Bell (W-TN) had called Leonard Jarvis (J-ME) a liar during debate, Jarvis had stood Bell down, insisting that the matter "must be settled *elsewhere* Sir, & in another manner than by words, yes sir—*in another manner sir*"—rather heavy-handedly hinting at a duel. When colleagues pushed for apologies, Jarvis held his ground, demanding an unconditional withdrawal of the insult, which Bell delivered after *hours* of negotiations that occupied the House for an entire afternoon, with Henry Wise acting as Bell's second. French was lost in admiration. "[N]o man could have taken higher & more honorable ground than Jarvis did. He was as firm as a rock."[134]

Like Jarvis, Cilley had "stood his ground manfully," and to French that meant something.[135] It showed that Northerners were men—that they wouldn't be cowed. It showed that Northern qualms about dueling needn't hamstring them in Washington. It showed that the North was fully and fairly represented—that the rights of Northerners were being defended on the floor. Although French disapproved of dueling and deplored Cilley's death, he admired Cilley's bravery and cheered him on. Even John Quincy Adams craved some Northern fire. On the same day that Wise and Cilley clashed over corruption charges, Adams was yearning for some "bold, dashing, fluent, and eloquent" Northerners who could "raise the reputation of New England" in Congress by overcoming its "tameness."[136]

This was just what Cilley had hoped: given the peculiar logic of cross-sectional politics in Washington, Northerners would support him regardless of hometown habits and ideals. And indeed, although the mode of his death was deplored far and wide, he himself was exalted as a courageous champion. To Southerners, he was the very model of a loyal Northern Democrat, making the ultimate sacrifice to uphold Southern interests. Southern Democrats spilled over with praise. Cilley "was the most gallant man I ever saw from the North," declared Francis Pickens (D-SC). He was "the first northern man who openly denounced the Abolitionists and spoke as a Southern man." He even looked Southern.[137] New Englanders of all political stripes praised Cilley for defending New England's honor, with even the staunchest anti-dueling Whigs doing little more than condemning his "violent friends."[138] The Maine Democrats who announced his death in the House and Senate likewise praised his "manly bearing towards opponents" and his desire to avoid "disgrace to himself, to his family, and to his constituents."[139]

The ever-clear-eyed John Quincy Adams characteristically stripped away the posturing and emotion. "The Career of Mr. Cilley is that of an ambitious Northern young man, struggling to rise on a Southern platform," he explained to his son. Cilley

> had already announced that he had no sympathies for Indians or for human beings of a darker hue; and this declaration had already brought him golden opinions from the carnation colour of the South. He seized the first possible opportunity to announce and prove himself an unerring marksman with the rifle, and to select it as his favourite weapon for settling his points of honour. . . . All this was to display to the South and West how high he soared above the region of Yankee prejudices.

Adams charged Cilley with adopting Southern standards to promote his reputation. Pierce had done the same to redeem his name when denounced as a doughface two years past. Cilley's fate showed the price of this logic. It was a "monumental warning to his successors," Adams thought—a warning that would go unheeded.[140]

Of course, not every Northerner followed Cilley's lead. Many wouldn't, even couldn't, go that far. Take, for example, Cilley's roommate Timothy Carter (D-ME). Already in ill health, the thirty-seven-year-old lawyer lapsed into a state of delirium on the day of Cilley's death, raving that he had been challenged to a duel. Given French's comment that Carter "pretended" not to know the duel's location, it's tempting to attribute at least some of his suffering to a guilty conscience. Regardless of the cause, he died two weeks later, depriving Maine of another representative.[141] The stunned French wrote and published a eulogy.[142] Carter's gravestone bears witness to his ultimate trial. It reads simply: "Died while a member of the 25th Congress at Washington, D.C."[143] For some, the complications of cross-regional conflict were simply too challenging.

Others tried to level the playing field by demanding formal institutional retribution. On February 28, John Fairfield (D-ME) proposed an investigation into the causes of Cilley's death, immediately provoking what the *Globe* might have called a "lively debate." Whigs roared that emotions were too heated for a fair investigation. Democrats demanded justice.[144] And then a handful of Southern Whigs essentially threatened violence, warning that because an investigation would touch on matters of honor, it was bound to cause *more* bloodshed. "It would require more than ordinary nerve to serve" on that committee, warned Cost Johnson (W-MD), advising its members to arm themselves. And what right did Congress have to investigate such matters anyway? This was an affair of honor, a private matter between gentlemen. In the end, the vote was 152 to 49 in favor of an investigation, but the results were strikingly sectional. With the exception of one lone Rhode Island Whig, *every* New Englander supported an investigation, regardless of party.[145] Clearly, the threat of a duel was a powerful weapon in the Southern and Western arsenal.[146]

The investigative committee was no less divided, though in more complex ways. Consisting of four Democrats and three Whigs, it ultimately produced three different reports.[147] The majority—three Northern Democrats and a Southern Whig—exonerated Cilley, recommending expulsion for Graves and the censure of Wise and Jones for breach of privilege.[148] In a separate report, two Northern Whigs protested that the committee had no right to take sides or suggest punishments.[149] And in the third report, a Southern Democrat recommended a mild punishment given that none of Congress's many duelists and near-duelists had been formally punished since the launching of the government.[150] All in all, the results were partly partisan and partly sectional, an accurate reflection of congressional culture overall. Northern Democrats favored punishment. Northern Whigs didn't. And Southerners were divided. Not surprisingly, the equally divided House tabled the report, effectively "smothering it," noted John Quincy Adams, though the suggested punishments remained "suspended over the heads" of Graves, Wise, and Jones.[151] Although one congressman had killed another for words spoken during debate—a flaming violation of a fundamental privilege—no one was punished. By the congressional community's standards, no rules had been broken.

But the hovering threat of a duel remained a problem for noncombatant Northerners. So they pursued an anti-dueling law in earnest, with Samuel Prentiss (AJ-VT) shepherding it through the Senate and Adams (W-MA) seeing it through the House. Given that it prohibited giving, delivering, or accepting a challenge in the District of Columbia only, it was essentially a congressional anti-dueling law, a specific solution to the specific problem of an imbalance of power. And it had teeth: ten years' imprisonment at hard labor if someone was killed or mortally wounded in a duel, five years for dueling without a casualty, and three years for assaulting someone who refused to accept a challenge, the latter provision the most blatant Northern protective measure of all. Ironically, due to its harsh penalties, the law was rarely enforced, as some people warned when debating it.[152] Although it ultimately discouraged duels, it didn't prevent them, and it had little impact on congressional threats and violence.

Discussing the bill wasn't easy, even in the abstract. Although Northern congressmen opposed dueling, supporting a law that seemed aimed at protecting themselves seemed cowardly. Thus, even as they supported the bill and condemned dueling with fist-clenched righteousness, they did some symbolic chest-beating, insisting that they weren't afraid to play rough. New England congressmen might need protection from "those gentlemanly assassins . . . who might seek to call them out for words spoken during debate," argued Perry Smith (D-CT). But he himself "was not afraid of any man."[153] Nor was Franklin Pierce. New Englanders didn't need any "*special* protection," he insisted; if they failed to fend off a conflict, they would face the consequences like men. Enactment of an anti-dueling law was a purely *moral* matter.[154] Given the formidable presence of fighting men and the implications of cowering before them, even the mere mention of avoiding a duel required compensatory swaggering. (Of course, it was no easier to *oppose* an anti-dueling law; when the bill passed in the House, roughly 40 percent of its members didn't vote.)[155]

Ultimately, few men were immune to the sway of congressional violence, not even the good-natured French. When the harried Henry Wise publicly insulted him for mumbling while reading the investigative committee report aloud, French, still reeling in the wake of Cilley's death, considered flogging him. If he himself wasn't a family man, French fumed in his diary, he "would have inflicted personal chastisement on Wise, *at any risk*," adding for good measure that he feared no man. French wasn't alone in his fight calculations. Two congressmen offered to help him "chastise Mr. Wise personally" and to stand by French "through any result," clearly anticipating a duel or an assault. Fight calculations were going full-force, but in the final analysis French held back. Nine years later, he read through his diary and stopped at this point. "Never should have been written," he wrote in the margin, sorry to have documented his surrender to the passions of the floor, but not apologetic for having felt them.[156]

To French and his colleagues, congressional violence was routine. Party loyalties pulled them into fighting; concern for manhood pushed them into fighting; the community of Congress sanctioned fighting; and holding one's own before a hometown audience sometimes seemed to require it. In the case of the Cilley-Graves duel, it was also rewarded and even praised by congressmen and constituents alike. Virtually every participant won reelection the following session: Bynum, Graves, Wise, Crittenden, Duncan, and Pierce. Only Wisconsin delegate Jones lost his seat, a casualty of wavering support in an eastern area settled largely by New Englanders. But even he suffered no permanent damage, winning a Senate seat in Iowa ten years later.[157] The same holds true for most of Congress's frequent fighters: many were reelected. Not only did Congress endorse fighting, but by reelecting combatants, the nation did the same, encouraging their representatives to literally fight for their rights. Here, perhaps, is the most fundamental reason for congressional violence. When it came to earning influence in Congress and back home, it worked all too well.

4

RULES OF ORDER AND THE RULE OF FORCE

DANGEROUS WORDS AND THE GAG RULE DEBATE (1836–44)

Yankees were brave: for French, that was the moral of Cilley's death. Years later, in a song written for the 1849 Festival of the Sons of New Hampshire, French set this theme to music, lauding Cilley as the "bravest of the brave."[1] As horrible as the duel had been—"never to be forgotten," said French—it had proven Cilley a "fearless and honorable" man who had done New England proud.[2]

French was less philosophical about clashes that stopped the wheels of government. Outbreaks of pandemonium that prevented sessions of Congress from formally opening or closing almost always sent him into a frightened tailspin of doom. Maybe this time there would be no compromise. Maybe this time the government would break down. Maybe this time the Union would dissolve.

These thoughts tormented French at peak moments of strife during the nine-year conflict over instituting a gag rule to silence antislavery petitions.[3] Beginning in the 1830s, antislavery sentiment reached the floor of Congress with a new and growing power due to the founding of the American Anti-Slavery Society in 1833 and its organized campaigns that flooded Congress with hundreds of thousands of petitions from petitioners black and white, male and female, many seeking the abolition of slavery in the District of Columbia, which was under congressional jurisdiction.[4] French probably handled many of them; the House Clerk's staff shouldered much of the workload. On one day in

February 1838 alone—the month that Cilley died—John Quincy Adams presented 350 antislavery petitions to the House featuring roughly 35,000 signatures.⁵ The spate of anti-dueling petitions following Cilley's death only added to the onslaught. If this "petition mania" lasted much longer, French griped a few weeks after the duel, the Capitol would need a new wing for storage, staffed by armies of clerks to sift through the paper.⁶

The flood of petitions was for good reason. Slavery was expanding. Beginning in the early nineteenth century, industrialization and urbanization led to massive demands for new kinds of raw materials, and the practice of slavery evolved to fill that need, shifting to new technologies and spreading to new territories. As tempting as it is to dismiss American slavery in the pre–Civil War decades as an antiquated holdover doomed to extinction, in the early decades of the nineteenth century it was flourishing.⁷

Spurred by the expansion of slavery, the rise of antislavery sentiment, and the onslaught of petitions, and encouraged by the abolition of slavery in the British Empire in 1833, a few congressmen broached the issue of slavery in earnest, most aggressively and consistently in the House, aided and abetted by a cluster of antislavery lobbyists eager to promote their cause on the national stage.⁸ Between 1836 and 1844, outraged slave-state representatives and concerned free-state colleagues responded by promoting a series of gag rules to keep antislavery petitions off the floor. French wholeheartedly supported this strategy. "If fanatics will persist in petitioning," he thought, "the less debate there is, the better."⁹

To French, the alternative was terrifying. An 1837 outburst sparked by the abolitionist William Slade (W-VT) showed how a worst-case scenario might play out. Sixteen days into the second session of the Twenty-fifth Congress, he presented some antislavery petitions and moved their consideration by a select committee to consider the abolition of slavery; his request for a committee entitled him to discuss the issue, and on December 20 he did just that, ranging far and wide over the history of slavery and its inhumanity, persisting even as Southerners roared out objections. "Nothing could stop him," John Fairfield (D-ME) marveled. The impact of Slade's stand was dramatic: three Southern-state delegations stormed out of the hall. That night, a larger group of Southerners devised a new gag rule that they presented and carried the next day. It was a good thing too, thought Fairfield, though he would have preferred a slightly different rule. "We were obliged to take that or let the whole subject remain open for a long violent, angry & dangerous discussion. I say dangerous because I believe the permanency of the Union would be endangered if not destroyed by it."[10] French wasn't alone in his fears.

It was a strikingly simple solution to a menacing problem: stop the words. Its underlying logic was straightforward, if flawed. If we can stifle antislavery talk in Congress, we can keep its Union-threatening dissonance to a low hum. We can preserve national party bonds. We can deny a national forum to troublemaking "fanatics," the favored word for abolitionists, who seemed maniacally hell-bent on destroying the Union. No less important, we can keep that national forum calm and functional (at least, by congressional standards).[11] Slaveholders had the added impetus of staunching slave resistance; in the South, dangerous words could set off mass rebellion. For people on both sides of the aisle, including some Northern Whigs and most Northern Democrats, when it came to antislavery petitions, gag rules made sense.[12]

John Quincy Adams was of another mind. Elected to Congress in 1830 after losing the presidency to Andrew Jackson two years earlier, Adams had entered the House with the Union on his mind, intending no dramatic action on the issue of slavery, but the gag rule debate changed his thinking. Opposed to slavery and enraged at this blatant violation of the constitutional right of petition, he launched a campaign of resistance. Fearless and equipped with a keen intellect, a penchant for sarcasm, a lifetime of political training, and a profound knowledge of rules of order, Adams circumvented gags time and again, sometimes with creative parliamentary maneuvering, sometimes by forcing his way onto the floor. French couldn't understand it. Why stir up trouble? Was it ego? Was Adams senile? By 1842, after years of watching Adams's efforts, French was ready to expel "the old gentleman, for really, I do not believe him sane on the subject of petitions." Adams seemed to be deliberately driving slaveholders—and the Union—to the breaking point.

And he was. Raising a ruckus served Adams's purpose. What mattered most to him was forcing the issues: forcing the issue of slavery onto the floor, forcing the right of petition into play, and forcing slave-holders to display their brutality for all the world to see. As Adams well knew, imposing a gag revealed a harsh reality in stark relief: to a certain degree, in Congress, slaveholders ruled, much as they did in the federal government as a whole. As he explained in a speech to his constituents in 1842, slaveholding congressmen "marching in solid phalanx" had a preponderance of power. Gag rules were born of this regime; by drawing a line in the sand about slavery, slaveholders set the terms of debate.

Henry Wise—an "ultra anti abolitionist" according to French—did his best to defend that regime. When it came to opposing Adams's gag rule campaign, Wise was bully-in-chief. But in this war, he couldn't use his full arsenal of weapons, because Adams was above assault.[13] Elderly (sixty-three years old when he entered the House), a former president of the United States, and the son of a president who was also one of the nation's foremost founders, Adams suffered more than his fair share of insults, threats, and parliamentary blows during his gag rule campaign. But he was never physically attacked by a congressman. In the gag rule debate, this gave him a special power that he used to full advantage.

To counter Adams, Wise and his allies would have to fight with rules of order alone, even as Adams gleefully taunted them, almost daring them to take a swing. Wise could barely restrain himself. After one slashing exchange with Adams, he admitted it. "If the Member from Massachusetts had not been an old man, protected by the imbecility of age," Wise warned, "he would not have enjoyed, as long as he has, the mercy of my mere words."[14] Adams got the message. That night in his diary, he wrote: "Wise then replied to me in his own way, closing with a threat of murdering me in my seat."[15]

The abolitionist Joshua Giddings (W-OH) was also threatened for his antislavery views, but he most decidedly was *not* above assault; during his lengthy congressional career, he was attacked at least seven times, and like Adams, he seized such moments to put Slave Power brutality on display. Giddings was ideally suited to this strategy of attack because of his imposing size, strength, and spirit; over six feet tall and brawny—grown strong from years of homesteading—he was daring enough to taunt slaveholders and confident that he could hold his own.

John Dawson's knife didn't scare him. "[H]ad I struck him," Giddings told his wife after Dawson attacked him, his "bowie knife would have been of little avail."[16] In essence, Giddings was an antislavery toreador, waving the red flag of abolitionism in front of roaring slaveholders, confident that they would reveal their bloodlust in response before a national audience. Other antislavery toreadors had different strategies, and they needed them; standing down the Slave Power was dangerous without a plan.

Performed properly, abolitionist stands on the floor of Congress sent a strong message, because attempts to gag such men—whether with gag rules, other rules of order, or the rule of force—did slaveholders damage, galvanizing not only abolitionists, but also Northerners whose right of petition was being compromised.[17] According to the First Amendment in the Bill of Rights, Congress could make no law abridging the "right of the people . . . to petition the Government for a redress of grievances." Curtailing that right was a serious step indeed (though French got past it by declaring that slavery wasn't a Northern grievance, so Northerners had no right to petition against it.)[18]

Northern rights of representation and free speech also became entangled in the gag rule debate, to the point that even Southerners occasionally had qualms, as did William Graves (W-KY), of duel fame, who defended Adams's right to express his opinion in 1837 and was roundly reprimanded by Southerners for doing so.[19] Endangered rights gripped Northern onlookers with a guttural power that abolitionists used to full advantage. As one congressman noted in later years, violating "great principles of constitutional right" drove people to take action as nothing else could.[20]

Thus the stalwart efforts of men such as Adams, Giddings, and their lobbyist allies to advertise that threat by stirring up slaveholders in the halls of Congress. They well knew that in the battle against slavery, gags were gifts and words were weapons.

THE RULE WARRIORS AND THEIR WAR

Antislavery petitions were bringing Congress to a literal shrieking halt. But how to stop them? Should they be tabled and removed from discussion? Should they be referred to a committee, and if so, what next? Should the House simply refuse to accept them? Was that even possible? Could petitions—the almighty voice of the public—be pushed aside? Would a simple resolution to reject them be enough, or was a permanent rule of order required? Could the latter be carried and sustained? One seething Southerner even suggested a petition bonfire.[21]

This wasn't a problem for the House alone, though things unfolded differently in the Senate for several reasons: with its staggered six-year terms, the Senate was a continuing body that didn't adopt rules at the start of every session; it received fewer petitions than the House; and, for a time at least, there were fewer firebrand senators pressing the issue, though the same qualms about stifling the right of petition were ever present.[22] In 1836, John C. Calhoun raised those qualms when he proposed that the Senate reject antislavery petitions outright. After extended wrangling, they devised a roundabout solution: when an antislavery petition was presented, a senator would question whether it should be received, and another senator would table the question of its reception. By tabling that *question* rather than the actual petition, the Senate effectively sidestepped First Amendment complications by neither accepting nor rejecting the petitions themselves.[23] This somewhat indirect mode of stifling antislavery petitions continued until 1850, when John Parker Hale (FS-NH) exposed its crass reality, noting that the Senate routinely accepted Southern petitions and rejected Northern ones.[24]

The House sometimes practiced the same sleight of hand, but because each Congress had to adopt rules of order, they followed a different path, passing one session-long gag resolution after another until they built up enough steam to pass a standing rule: House Rule 21. Their first resolution, passed in May 1836 after months of wrangling, provided that "all petitions, memorials, resolutions, propositions, or papers relating in any way or to any extent whatever to the subject of slavery shall, without being printed or referred, be laid upon the table and that no further action whatever be taken thereon."

Yet this hardly settled the matter. Such restrictions did nothing to stop Adams's petition campaign or the rage that it provoked. "The House of Representatives are doing more now towards dissolving this glorious Union than has been done . . . since the adoption of our Constitution," French fretted.[25] Rules of order were causing disorder.

A draft of the House's second gag rule of December 21, 1837, declaring "that all petitions, memorials, and papers touching the abolition of slavery or the buying, selling, or transferring of slaves in any state, district or Territory of the United States be laid upon the table without being debated, printed, read, or referred and that no further action whatever shall be had thereon." (Courtesy of the National Archives)

As a House clerk from 1833 to 1845 and *the* House Clerk from 1845 to 1847, French's life revolved around those rules. He recorded or engrossed House documents as prescribed by the standing rules. He made sure that every member had a copy of those rules. On duty at the Clerk's table in front of the Speaker, he focused on broken rules, transcribing objections and recording points of order for inclusion in the House Journal, which Adams used frequently during the gag rule debate as he wended his way through thickets of gags.[26] It's no wonder that French became a recognized expert on parliamentary procedures and precedents. In 1850, when the Committee on Rules wanted to write a manual, it turned to him.[27] Even as he conducted business at the Clerk's table, people tried to stump him with questions about tangled points of order, and they usually failed.[28]

Thus his utter frustration with Adams for routinely, deliberately, even gleefully breaking rules for almost a decade. In some ways, Adams seemed to be at war with Congress itself. And it was an extended war; of the fourteen years that French clerked for the House, nine were pocked with the outbursts born of Adams's "petition flourishes," as French called them.[29]

Adams was just the man to fight this battle. As Ralph Waldo Emerson put it in 1843, he was a "bruiser" who "loves the melee."[30] His talents were in full view in 1839 when Joshua Giddings (W-OH) gave his first declarative antislavery speech. With roaring slaveholders jumping to their feet in outrage, the stunned Giddings noticed Adams at his desk laughing heartily.[31] Another time, during a routine roll-call vote, Adams challenged the constitutionality of gag rules, again bringing howling slaveholders to their feet, Adams continuing to speak all the while. When the agitated Speaker pleaded for order, Adams "suddenly dropped into his chair and the uproar instantly ceased," leaving Adams convulsed with laughter.[32]

But challenging gag rules wasn't usually a laughing matter. Slaveholders viewed antislavery petitions as "assaults" and treated Adams accordingly.[33] Many a slavery supporter stalked over to him during his petition rants and glowered. During one staring match in 1838, Ratliff Boon (D-IN)—"the thickest skull in the House," according to Adams—

Seventy-six-year-old Representative John Quincy Adams in 1843. He was the first U.S. president to be photographed. (By Albert S. Southworth and Josiah J. Hawes. Gift of I. N. Phelps Stokes, Edward S. Hawes, Alice Mary Hawes, and Marion Augusta Hawes, 1937. Courtesy of the Metropolitan Museum of Art)

seemed ready to land a punch. A colleague's joking offer to fight along-side Adams to even out the odds wasn't far off the mark; later that day, one of Boon's messmates warned Adams that Boon had threatened to assault him, though in the end even Boon knew better than to cross that line.[34]

Public onlookers were no less hostile. Even as abolitionists flooded Adams with petitions, slaveholders sent death threats; by 1839 he was getting roughly a dozen per month.[35] One letter told him to prepare to be "unexpectedly . . . hurried into eternity." Another featured a drawing of him with the mark of a rifle ball on his head and the biblical phrase *Mene mene tekel upharsin* (Your days are numbered).[36] Adams dismissed them all as "the natural offspring of slave-breeders and slave-traders."[37]

Every controversy served Adams's purposes. Correcting a reporter's notes of one of his speeches in 1839, Adams was most concerned that they include the "desperate struggle" to take the floor from him. Press coverage of that attempt would be "much more valuable than that of my speech," he reflected in his diary that night.[38] Ironically, the campaign to gag Adams was spreading his message by offering the world an image of screaming, stomping, threatening slaveholders imposing their will. On the floor of Congress there *was* a Slave Power: a violent, domineering slavery defense team that did whatever it took to stay in power.[39]

Thomas Marshall (W-KY) and Henry Wise were part of that Slave Power, as they demonstrated in 1842 when they led an attempt to censure Adams. (Forty-one years earlier—almost to the day—Adams's father had made Marshall's uncle John the fourth chief justice of the United States.) Adams had invited the attack by presenting a petition from forty-six of his constituents calling for the dissolution of the Union because Northern resources were being drained to sustain the South. The entirely predictable stir that followed gave Adams a chance to attack slavery and defend the right of petition.[40] Indeed, when a motion to censure him was first mentioned, Adams's immediate response was: "Good!"[41]

On the morning of Tuesday, January 25, the galleries were packed with people eager to see this battle. As expected, Marshall and Wise held forth with lengthy anti-Adams, proslavery diatribes. (The "insolence of these Southern boys is intolerable," fumed William Fessenden [W-ME].)[42] And then—also as expected—Adams let loose, savaging both men and demolishing their arguments. French had never seen such biting fury, and given Isaac Hill's way with an insult, that was saying something.[43] Scoffing at Marshall's "puny mind," jeering at his supposed adherence to a temperance pledge, and noting that he most assuredly had not gotten his law from his uncle John, Adams suggested that Marshall go back to law school to learn what he missed the first time around, and then proceeded not just to refute but to *correct* Marshall's speech.[44] Marshall made a great show of rising to his feet and staring Adams down during the tirade. But to a friend on the floor he admitted, "I wish I were dead."[45] He was still shuddering years later when he recalled for a reporter how Adams had pressed his hands on the arms of his chair and slowly risen to his feet, unleashing "such a torrent of eloquence" that Marshall had wanted the floor to open so he could drop out of sight.[46]

Wise received even harsher treatment. Adams insisted on his right to a fair hearing by recalling a time four years past when Wise had demanded the same: after the Cilley-Graves duel. Wise had entered the House "with his hands and face dripping with the blood of murder, the blotches of which were yet hanging upon him," Adams charged, yet although Democrats had proposed trying him for murder, he had received no punishment because the House wasn't a fit tribunal for such a crime. Stunned by Adams's bloody accusation, Wise blasted back that it was "as base and black a *lie* as the *traitor* was black and base who uttered it." But despite the bravado, Adams's words ate at Wise, who refuted them almost literally until the day he died.[47] Robert Barnwell Rhett (D-SC) spoke for many when he stated—after a brief contretemps with Adams—that "everyone who has had any experience in this Hall . . . understood the adroitness, in matters of controversy of this kind, which the gentleman possessed."[48] French's friend "Long John" Wentworth (D-IL) had good reason to praise Adams's "sledge-hammer" eloquence.[49]

Adams used rules to force his way onto the floor. Wise used rules as muzzles. Throughout his eleven-year congressional career, he hounded opponents with calls to order and stymied their efforts with meandering speeches that tested the bounds of the relevant. (In 1836, he wearily sighed that "he should remember that word *relevant* to the day of his death.")[50] His tirades routinely drove men to distraction; once, he worked himself into such a lather that he fainted.[51] Speaker of the House James K. Polk (D-TN) was hard put to stop him; Wise alternately mocked, ignored, insulted, and challenged him in his ongoing campaign to advance his cause and destroy his foes, including Polk himself. Wise was a master of the legislative roadblock, a champion rule warrior.

For years, Wise and Adams engaged in an intricate game of point-counterpoint, sometimes fighting a war of rules, sometimes a war of words. Almost by signal, when Adams spoke, Wise jumped up in protest. Adams returned the favor, objecting so frequently during one debate that a *Globe* reporter described him as "jumping up and down like the key of a piano." ("Mr. A. to all appearance, did not listen . . . with much patience," he added with marked understatement.)[52] The two were a matched set: the brash young Virginian, twenty-seven years old when

Thirty-four-year-old Henry Wise in 1840 (By Charles Fenderich. Courtesy of the Library of Congress)

he took his seat in 1834, and the acerbic senior statesman, fearless in a fight. They were the "ruling spirits of disorganization and confusion in this House," complained a colleague, "such a complete match . . . that if they were put in a bag together, and well shaken, he did not know which would fall out first."[53]

RULES AS WEAPONS

The destructive power of rule warfare wasn't lost on French. Years later, when he devised rules of order for the Masons, he did his best to counter it.[54] Unlike congressmen, Brother Masons shouldn't be able to silence one another with charges of irrelevance, French insisted. Petitions were to be accepted or rejected with no debate, though debate was allowed once they were accepted. The presiding Master had "supreme command," so there could be no appeal from his rulings. And unlike House rules, Masonic rules would be permanent. In French's world of Masonic brotherhood, there would be no squabbles over rules or petitions, no gags imposed by calls to order, and an all-powerful presiding officer to keep things calm.[55] The gag rule debate taught French some hard lessons.

A "known system of rules" was supposed to impose order. So stated Thomas Jefferson's 1801 *Manual of Parliamentary Practice*, a guidebook based on his time presiding over the Senate as vice president.[56] Decorum was key, Jefferson insisted. Personal attacks and insults were strictly out of bounds. No one should address fellow members by name or speak to them directly; comments should be directed to the chair. There would be no hissing or coughing to drown someone out, no insulting or "nipping" words. Nor was anyone to speak "tediously"—surely wishful thinking on Jefferson's part. Attacking someone's motives was a "personality" and thus forbidden. "Disorderly words" would be documented by the Clerk and discussed. And in case of "warm words, or an assault," members had to "declare in their places not to prosecute any quarrel"—meaning, there would be no duel.[57]

A system of rules also was supposed to keep things fair. More than anything else, parliamentary rules are grounded on a sense of fair play. Particularly in America's democratic system of governance, for people to be invested in it, they need to believe that their representatives have a fair chance of advancing their goals. They need to believe that all representatives—all states, all regions, all parties—fight as equals on even ground; equal membership is the heart of American federalism and its human embodiment in Congress. As Wise put it, to represent his constituents properly, he required "an open field and a fair fight."[58] By setting limits, structuring debate, and equipping everyone with the same weapons, rules of order encouraged a fair fight.

Wise was speaking as a member of the House's Whig minority, so his words had added meaning. As Jefferson acknowledged in his *Manual*, faced with a powerful majority, a minority had one weapon of defense: "the forms and rules of proceeding."[59] To protect their rights and stick a foot in the door of legislation, minority members could enforce close adherence to shared rules. In this sense, a system of rules maintained a balance of power.[60] But as fair-minded as this sounds in theory, applied to real debates between warring teams, be they sectional factions or political parties, rules were more than minority ballast. They were malleable tools of legislative obstruction, and by the 1830s congressmen had perfected the fine art of using them to bring things to a standstill. Rules became weapons that were used to full effect during the gag rule debate.[61]

This form of warfare was more genteel in the smaller and more manageable Senate. According to Senate rules and customs, any senator who sought the floor had the right to be recognized, there were no regulations imposing relevance during debate, and it was difficult to force an immediate vote.[62] Senators bent on obstruction could talk on any topic as long as their lungs could carry them. In essence, senators enjoyed broad freedom of debate with few limits.[63]

They also thought twice about calling colleagues to order because in the intimacy of the Senate, it seemed insulting. As Vice President Millard Fillmore (W-NY) explained in 1850, "The reason why Senators so seldom interfere by calling each other to order is, doubtless, because they fear that their motives may be misunderstood."[64] Senator Lewis Linn (D-MO) would be "among the last to call either a personal enemy or a political opponent to order; he would not do it," he declared in 1842. "When any one transgressed the bounds of propriety in relation to Mr. L. he knew how to seek redress, and to obtain it in his own way."[65] Better to launch duel proceedings than to hide behind rules of order.

The House played a rougher game in the realm of rule warfare, as Adams and Wise knew all too well. Take, for example, the knife-wielding John Dawson's (D-LA) reaction when Thomas Arnold (W-TN) called a Democrat to order to allow Adams to speak. Stalking over to Arnold's seat, Dawson sneered, "I understand you are a great hand at keeping order, sir."[66] When Arnold didn't take the bait, Dawson called him "'a d—d coward' and 'a d—d blackguard,'" and threatened to cut his throat. A few days later, Arnold mentioned the incident when discussing disorder in the House. Joking that "if the Democracy employed persons to bully members here, he hoped that if any of them came to cut his throat he would make a mistake and cut his own which would be a great deal better," he got a laugh. But when called to order for irrelevance, he bridled: "[H]e was speaking of the disorders of this House, and if there could be a case more directly relevant to that subject on the face of God Almighty's globe, he should be glad to hear it."[67] Dawson had picked a poor target; Arnold wasn't easily cowed. Ten years earlier on the steps of the Capitol he had subdued an armed assassin intent on murdering him for insulting Sam Houston and President Jackson by association.[68]

Even apart from men like Dawson, in the unwieldy House, rule warfare could be savage because it was grounded on obstruction. Minori-

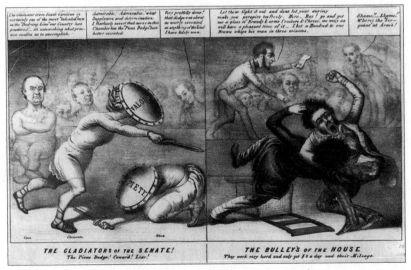

A caricature of the different modes of fighting in the somewhat genteel Senate and the "bear garden" House (By John L. Magee, ca. 1852. Courtesy of the Library of Congress)

ties delayed voting by interrupting one another with calls to order, calling for the previous question (demanding an immediate vote on the question under debate), refusing to vote (known as "disappearing quorums"), and making motions for adjournment.[69] Representatives had to compete for the floor and defend it once gained; House proceedings were based on competition for a scarce resource. The House was called a "bear garden" for good reason.[70] And not surprisingly, talk of slavery made matters worse. By 1842, Adams was using a one-word shorthand in his diary for petition flare-ups: "Explosion."[71] Recalling years later an insult-laden, fist-waving, foot-stamping debate about a "bomb shell . . . in the form of a petition," French dubbed it the customary "manner of debate in our House."[72]

In this setting, Henry Wise was a self-proclaimed champion. As he explained in 1843 during the gag rule debate, his habitual "mode of warfare" consisted of contesting motions, "calling upon the Speaker to decide points of order; . . . [and] asking that the rules of the House may be enforced."[73] All three techniques immediately halted debate. Contested motions and points of order took precedence over the topic at hand, and demands for enforcement shifted attention to the rules and the chair's ability and willingness to enforce them. It was a devastatingly effective way to stymie debate.

For example, on January 21, 1841, a day dedicated to petitions, Adams presented "a preamble and resolution of the anti-slavery society of Pennsylvania" to the House. Wise immediately called him to order and continued to do so—loudly—as Adams continued to read. The Speaker favored Wise. Wise next protested that Adams's "paper" was a series of resolutions and not a petition, so it had no place on the floor that day. Adams denied it. The Speaker favored Adams. Wise next moved that the question of receiving the petition be tabled—the conventional way of taking antislavery petitions off the floor. The House passed the motion. Adams then moved that the paper be printed. Wise objected that the House hadn't received it so it had no business printing it. Adams objected, but when others joined with Wise, Adams folded, only to immediately present another antislavery petition that Wise attacked in like manner. It's no wonder that Adams sometimes couldn't contain himself, as in this *Globe* account of him gaining the floor: "Mr. Adams [much excited and raising his voice] Yes, sir, provided there is no point of order raised—no fifty or one hundred questions of order raised to gag me."[74]

On this occasion as always, Adams gave as good as he got, insisting on his right to read aloud a letter from Wise to his constituents to prove a point, which Adams did "exultingly" according to the *Globe*, though Wise didn't protest. "He was so used to the gentleman pouring out the vials of his wrath on his head," Wise explained, "that he really now did not regard it."[75]

Adams's wording is worth noting. Points of order were being raised "to gag me," which indeed they were. There were countless ways to use parliamentary procedures as gags. Peppering people with objections was one way. Taunting them and denying them the chance to respond was another. It was "the usual practice of the Whigs," complained gag victim Jesse Bynum (D-NC), "after having two or three bullies to attack a gentleman and do him injustice, to refuse to let him reply to such attacks." Calling for the previous question—demanding an immediate vote—was yet another "gag system," as Charles Brown (D-PA) phrased it: "A member moved the previous question; another member of the same political sentiments asked him to withdraw it; he consented, provided that member would renew it; that member renewed the motion, and then withdrew it at the request of another of his political friends."[76] This was tag-team obstruction at its finest, but unfortunately for the minority, because demanding the previous question was a way to force an immediate vote, it tended to work best for the legislation-wielding majority.[77]

As Adams showed time and again, such gags could be resisted. But it took a certain kind of man with a certain kind of nerve to stand down angry men bellowing calls to order. Called to order for irrelevance in 1840, Wise declared himself one of these men: "Let me tell gentlemen, that if they ever attempt to apply the screws to me for this irrelevancy in debate, I will throw them into a scene of disorder which it will not be so easy to get out of. This would be easy for a man of nerve to do when he was determined to maintain his rights."[78] On June 14, 1841, he asserted that nerve during a six-hour diatribe defending a gag rule, probably leading many to want *him* gagged.[79]

In 1842, the abolitionist Theodore Dwight Weld saw what such men of nerve faced when they attacked slavery. When Adams told him that he planned to put slaveholders "in a blaze" the next day, Weld went to watch. "Such a scene I never witnessed," he told his wife, Angelina, and sister-in-law Sarah Grimke, themselves leading abolitionists. Scores of slaveholders shouted points of order, "every now and then screaming at the top of their voices: 'That is false.' 'I *demand* Mr. Speaker that you *put him down*.' 'What are we to sit here and endure such insults.'" Hoping to silence Adams, a pack of glowering Southerners gathered around his seat, but their threats and interruptions only earned them scorn from Adams, who shot back barbed comments, such as "I see where the shoe pinches, Mr. Speaker, it will pinch *more* yet."[80] The din was so deafening that reporters couldn't hear a word.[81] There was a "glorious row in the House," French reported to his brother, "& in the midst thereof the House adjourned, & to day I expect we shall have an elegant time."[82]

And where was the Speaker in the midst of such mayhem? Couldn't he keep order? Often, the answer was no. In part, this was a matter of logistics. Presiding over a testy band of roughly 240 men crowded into a room and competing for attention was no easy task, and things could turn ugly in a flash. An alert Speaker could make all the difference. Once, in the middle of a personal insult (halfway through the word *malignant*), Wise saw Speaker John Bell shaking his head, and stopped, adding, "Sir, I leave the blank to be filled by the House."[83]

The Speaker's ultimate tool of order was supposedly the House mace, a ceremonial staff that sits on a pedestal to the right of the Speaker when the House is in session.[84] Carried by the sergeant at arms into the midst of tumults at the Speaker's request, it was supposed to shame men to their senses. More common was the response to an 1841 eruption. When Wise and Edward Stanly (W-NC) launched a fistfight, most of the House rushed over, some to intervene, some to cheer on their favorite, others to join in. Sitting at the Clerk's desk, French saw it all: the pandemonium on the floor, the Speaker screaming for order; the crowd yelling "Damn him . . . Knock him down"; Thomas Arnold's (W-TN) lucky escape from having his head bashed in by George Houston's (D-AL) cane. Although the House Clerk rushed into the uproar with the mace, yelling, "Gentlemen, respect the symbol of authority, respect yourselves," it did nothing. According to French, order was restored by the enormous Dixon Lewis (D-AL), who positioned himself between Wise and Stanly "like an elephant among a parcel [of] dogs, keeping them all at bay."[85]

It was hard to preserve order in the House, but most Speakers were somewhat arbitrary in their efforts because they were blatantly partisan, sometimes according to party, sometimes according to region.[86] Biased Speakers shaped the House in their own image. They stacked committees with like-minded men, buried their opponents in hopeless minorities, and shut some men out; abolitionists sometimes served on no committees at all. They favored allies during debate: friends were recognized first, got the floor more easily, could rain down abuse on their enemies, and were upheld more often. As Alexander Duncan (D-OH) complained when called to order for insulting Whig president-elect William Henry Harrison, why weren't Whigs "called to order when they called Van Buren a jackass?"[87] There were limits to such favoritism; Congress's credibility and utility rest on credible debate and compromise. But all in all, Speakers skewed the balance of power. Thus the elections for Speaker that provoked fistfights and dragged on for weeks.[88] And thus the despair of the losing side. When the speakership went to a Southerner in 1849 (as it had in every Congress between 1827 and 1845), abolitionists despaired. "Now we shall have all proslavery committees," lamented Horace Mann (W-MA). Sure enough, within two weeks, Mann reported that abolitionists were "so buried" in committees full of Southern Democrats that "they cannot get their heads high enough up to breathe."[89]

By *not* imposing routine order, presiding officers had a tremendous impact, making gag campaigns with points of order that much more offensive. They were like "throwing firebrands into the House," thought Charles Brown. They were virtually guaranteed to "kindle the flame of discord" and have "injurious consequences."[90] Whereas Jefferson's *Manual* stated that calls to order and demands for the previous question could halt discussions "of a delicate nature," it didn't consider that it could cause them.[91]

Adams courted such chaos in his fight against the gag rule. He was a master at orchestrating the House's sounds and silences, driving the chamber into a frenzy and then dropping into his seat to cut it off, only to immediately rise to his feet and start again. Two years into the gag rule controversy, French couldn't see a way out. If rules of order couldn't silence Adams, what could? "[T]he end must come," he predicted, but "God only knows what that end will be."[92]

THE LAW OF FORCE AND ITS ENFORCERS: CONGRESSIONAL BULLIES

Wise knew full well what could silence most antislavery advocates when rules failed to do the job. Like many, when it came to fending off attacks on slavery, he believed in the almighty power of the "law of force."[93] Adams was exempted from this reign of violence, but most men weren't, and Wise was a prime practitioner. As much as he objected to the term, Wise was a "bully." (He preferred the phrase "troublesome fellow.")[94] Bullies were fighting men with a legislative agenda; as "political champions," they routinely and strategically used threats, insults, and physical force to intimidate opponents out of their objections and potentially their votes. Adams sometimes called them "destructives."[95] So regular was congressional bullying that it was frequently condemned as a "system" of intimidation, beginning as early as the 1820s and continuing through the 1850s. Rejecting a duel challenge in 1824, David Barton (NR-MO) hurled defiance at the congressional "system of bullying and pistoleering," a system that would frame the gag rule debate.[96]

No one liked being called a bully, particularly given its implications of cowardice: bullies targeted the weak.[97] Wise said as much in 1836 after a screaming match with Jesse Bynum of North Carolina, the alleged "champion" of the Democrats and a bully himself; within four years, he fought a duel with a colleague, almost provoked at least two more, and sparked two fistfights on the floor, one time wielding a knife.[98] Bynum had called Wise a bully; Wise had scoffed that he "would as soon think of bullying a fly"; and then all hell had broken loose as the two sprang at each other crying, "Scoundrel!," "rascal," and "contemptible puppy," duel-worthy insults all. (According to French, Wise pulled a gun.) After frantic negotiating on the floor to avoid a duel, Wise explained that "an epithet had been applied to him, which he despised, and which no one should make to him without receiving the proper response." Apparently, the proper response to a charge of bullying was . . . bullying.[99]

Every Congress had its bullies, and like Wise, many of them threatened to pound their accusers, with no apparent sense of irony.[100] Most such men were Southerners or Southern-born Westerners, though not all bullying was slavery-centric, and not all fighting men were bullies. (Adams described one debate as pitting "bullies" against "Yankees.")[101] Whigs and Democrats were almost equally represented; even law-and-order Whigs were pushed to extremes in the congressional combat zone.[102] Bullying was gentler in the Senate but it *was* there, tending toward threats of duel challenges or street fights that funneled violence off the floor.

Wise was a bully of the first order. His talents were in full view in 1841 when he tried to make the entire Georgia delegation support a tariff bill by bullying its most mild-mannered member, Eugenius Nisbet (W-GA)—"gentle, inoffensive, and no duellist," John Quincy Adams noted pointedly.[103] Speaker James K. Polk was a constant target; Wise bullied him for years as a way of smacking at President Jackson, Polk's close friend.[104] At first, Wise tried open contempt during debate, refuting Polk's rulings loudly, frequently, and with flair. A typical Speaker faced a sprinkling of challenges; Polk suffered seventy-eight such objections, largely from Wise.[105] When that didn't faze Polk, Wise insulted him to his face, ambushing him by the House door and spouting a string of insults, adding for good measure: "I mean it personal . . . damn you. Pocket it."[106] A deliberate personal insult virtually demanded a duel challenge, but Polk resisted the temptation and the Whig press shamed him accordingly.[107] Democrats, on the other hand, sang his praises in an electioneering song for his presidential run in 1844, praising his resistance to "a ruffian named Henry A. Wise . . . Who sought to repulse him with insults and lies."[108]

Clearly, bullying could backfire. Not only did it enhance Polk's image among his supporters, but it inspired him to bury Wise in committees packed with Jackson supporters. And Wise's bullying invited more in return; in 1837, President Andrew Jackson announced that the Virginian and his fellow Polk-provocateur Balie Peyton (W-TN) "should be . . . chastised in the public streets," a virtual invitation to a Jacksonian champion to pummel them. Jackson was so taken with the idea that he coined a word for it, saying that Wise and Peyton should be "Houstonized," a reference to Sam Houston's vicious caning of William

Stanbery (AJ-OH) five years past. Both men took Jackson's threat seriously enough to remain armed at all times, showing how quickly threats could spiral into violence.[109]

Attacks on Northerners—"Cilley scenes," as Adams phrased it—displayed the power of bullying in all its glory.[110] Given the gaping holes in the parliamentary safety net, many Northerners silenced themselves rather than face violent or humiliating repercussions. As ever, Adams stripped this logic bare. "Languid, compromising, non-resistants of the North" allowed gag rules to prevail because they feared "the attitude of defiance, flung in their faces by the bullying threat of readiness to meet them 'here or elsewhere'"—the customary invitation to fight a duel.[111] Fearful of the price of resistance, Northerners were victims of the gag of violence.

Joshua Giddings (W-OH) noticed this sectional imbalance during his first weeks in Congress in 1838, and it struck him to the core. Irritated when the Democratic delegate George W. Jones—unseated because of his involvement in the Cilley-Graves duel—claimed travel fees and a per diem that he didn't deserve, Giddings discovered that his Northern colleagues refused to protest "on account of Mr. Jones's duelling character." Stunned by such cowering, Giddings took action. "I have myself come to the honest conclusion that our Northern friends are in fact afraid of these Southern bullies," he wrote in his diary.

> I have bestowed much thought upon the subject. I have made inquiry, and think we have no Northern man who dares boldly and fearlessly declare his abhorrence of slavery and the slave-trade. This kind of fear I never experienced, nor shall I submit to it now. When I came here I had no thought of participating in debate at all, but particularly this winter. But since I have seen our Northern friends so backward and delicate, I have determined to express my own views and declare my own sentiments, and risk the effects. . . . I would rather lose my election at home than suffer the insolence of these Southerners.[112]

Risking life, limb, and potentially his reelection, Giddings took slaveholders on.

Swaggering bravura was part of Giddings's method; in a sense, he

"Antislavery toreador" Joshua
Giddings, ca. 1855–65 (Courtesy of
the Library of Congress)

fought Southerners with their own weapons. For example, in 1845, when
he criticized Georgia slaveholders for claiming government compensation for unborn children of fugitive slaves, Edward Black (D-GA) fired
off a volley of abuse and then approached Giddings's seat, threatening
to knock him down (after glancing up at the galleries to be sure that no
ladies were watching.)[113] Giddings responded:

> The gentleman talked about knocking him down. Did he [Black]
> think the people he [Giddings] represents would send a cow-
> ard here? One gentleman had once drawn a bowie knife on him,
> and others had used menacing and insulting language towards
> him. Did gentlemen think to brave the freemen of the North
> because we are modest and unassuming, and disapprove of fight-
> ing duels?

When Black persisted, Giddings replied that he had "never seen an
internal coward that did not talk loud"—strong words, for according to
the code of honor, "coward" was a grievous insult that virtually demanded

a duel challenge or a beating. Black opted for the latter. The *Globe* describes what happened next: "[Mr. Black was here observed rushing into the bar towards Mr. G., with a cane upraised, but was seized and withheld from entering the bar by Mr. Hammett (D-MS) and other southern gentlemen.]"[114]

Black's attack had little impact; Giddings continued to speak as the "dancing raving and prancing" Georgian was restrained by friends.[115] Nor did John Dawson's armed posse silence Giddings that same year.[116] Not even the likelihood of a street fight stopped him; one friend was so sure that Giddings would be assaulted that he offered him his knife, which the Ohioan declined.[117]

Giddings was standing down the Slave Power, which responded with gusto, attacking him in ways that they didn't dare with Adams. Since Adams was "too old a man to be the object of personality," explained one congressman to his wife, Southern abuse was "principally levelled at Mr. Giddings of Ohio."[118] Shunned, insulted, threatened, shoved, and attacked with guns, knives, and canes, Giddings persisted, partly to advance the antislavery cause, partly to expose Southern barbarism, partly to show that the North could—and would—stand up to Southern bullying, and partly because Giddings "enjoyed the sport . . . first-rate."[119] Giddings was indeed an antislavery toreador, performing death-defying feats in the congressional arena before cheering and booing crowds in the Capitol and beyond.

"SOUTHERN DOULOCRACY AND NORTHERN SERVILITY"

In later years, French would be part of that cheering crowd. But for the present, when it came to slavery, he preferred gag rules and a reign of silence. Although Giddings routinely shattered that silence, French vented most of his spleen at Adams, whose interruptions and tossed-off barbs were a constant irritant on the floor. They were also disappointing; French expected more from a "great man."[120] In truth, apart from the gag rule debate and a few wild and woolly Whig moments, French deeply respected and liked the elder statesman, taking careful note of what Adams thought about his colleagues (not much), about the

Capitol's artwork (not bad), and about Andrew Jackson (not good). On Jackson, French recorded a story that Adams told about a woman who called her husband a "crack-louse" so often that he dunked her head underwater, at which she raised her hands and gestured "crack-louse" with her fingers. That was Jackson on the Bank of the United States, said Adams: on a sickbed, on his way out of office, thrusting his hands above the waves to signal "crack-louse" one last time.[121] For French, the best way to redeem Adams and save Congress was for his constituents to keep him home in Braintree, where he could happily write poetry with his dignity intact.[122]

It's hard to imagine a more un-Adams-like image: a passive poet surveying the national scene from afar. Adams was a congressional warrior in every sense of the word and he had nothing but scorn for "Northern political sopranos" who silently stood by.[123] Yet even Adams was sometimes cowed by bullying. In 1842, listening to a Southerner rant about "liberty and the natural inalienable rights of man" while decrying debtor laws—"as if there was not a slave in his State or in this District," griped Adams—he feared that if he "said one word about slavery I should have had the whole pack of Southern doulocracy and Northern servility upon me, produced merely a brawl, and been branded as a firebrand in my own land of the Pilgrims." So in utter disgust, he stayed silent, "leaving six thousand slaves to drag their lengthened chains for life."[124] He did the same in 1844 after a pro-gag rule onslaught of "overbearing insolence and bullying" by the "slavers." Although he longed to lash out, he dreaded the consequences: "To leave it all without reply would be tame submission. To reply in the same tone might breed a brawl; for which I should be held responsible by the public. To say just what will be proper, and nothing more, requires counsel from above. May it not be withheld!"[125] As much as he relished baiting slaveholders, deliberately launching a full-fledged brawl was beyond the pale. In this case, although Adams was safe from physical attack, public opinion silenced him. Even he could be silenced by the gag of violence.

Thus his strong support of the 1839 anti-dueling law to loosen that gag. "There is not a point in the affairs of this nation more important than this very practice of dueling," Adams argued. Why? Because it allowed "members from that section of the Union whose principles are against duelling . . . to be insulted upon every topic of discussion, because it is supposed that the insult will not be resented, and that 'there will be no fight.'" Adams refused

> to sit any longer here and see other members from my own sec-
> tion of country, or those who may be my successors here, made
> subject to any such law as the law of the duellist. . . . It goes to
> the independence of this House; it goes to the independence
> of every individual member of this House; it goes to the right
> of speech and the freedom of debate in this House.[126]

Adams was testifying to the impact of bullying. Northerners were in-sulted and shouted down because they were too scared to fight back and face the repercussions back home. Adams's anti-dueling rant was an attack on the gag of violence.

Congressmen alone didn't impose that gag. The American public held it in place. Adams restrained himself for fear of disapproval back home, as did Northerners who dodged duel challenges. Those who *didn't* dodge challenges—like Cilley—worried about constituent disapproval even more.[127] Giddings thought that his tough-guy theatrics might lose him his seat.[128] All of these men assumed that a Northern audience would condemn their aggression.

Southern audiences were different, Southern congressmen insisted. In Georgia, Giddings would be lynched for his words and actions, ar-gued Edward Black (D-GA). Should Black "sit silently and take what his people would not take?" Moments later he was running at Giddings, brandishing his cane.[129] Adams echoed this idea in his 1842 speech to his constituents. Most Southern congressmen weren't bad people, he said. Their bullying was "dictated far more by the passions and prejudices of their constituents than by their own."[130] Adams's point was startling but true. Some bullying was performed for the folks back home, though it was no less real or damaging because of it.[131]

Wise's career was a case in point. His exploits earned him the praise and votes of his constituents, who hailed him as their "peculiar cham-pion" in the House and reelected him six times in an age of one-term wonders.[132] Indeed, for a Southerner, *avoiding* a fight could be a serious liability, as Edward Stanly discovered in 1842. When Stanly's horse jostled Wise at a racetrack, Wise struck Stanly with his cane. A physical blow was a serious offense, but Stanly negotiated an apology rather than issue a duel challenge, leaving himself open to charges of cowardice that opponents in North Carolina used to full advantage. One election broadside joked that his campaign motto of "On, Stanly, on!"—had been "Wise-ly changed to 'Run, Stanly, run!'" According to some, Stanly's duel dodge cost him the election.[133]

By discouraging Northern violence and encouraging Southern violence, the American people fostered the imbalance of power in Congress. The gag rule debate began to shift this balance. The imposition of gag rules galvanized the North by attacking their fundamental rights of petition, representation, and free speech, and highlighting the degree to which a tyrannical Slave Power held the reins of power in Washington. Northerners responded by demanding that their congressmen fight for their rights, though with words and votes rather than fists and weapons.

John Parker Hale felt the impact of that message. French's friend from New Hampshire Assembly days and Pierce's classmate at Bowdoin, "Jack" Hale (as French called him) was like French in many ways: a stocky, good-natured Granite State man whose life was transformed by the Democratic Party. When Hale first took his House seat in 1843, he was "as good a Democrat . . . as there was in the world," he later recalled. But the gag rule debate brought his scruples about slavery and the right of petition to the fore.[134] So on the opening day of the Twenty-eighth Congress—Hale's first day in the House—when Adams proposed adopting the rules of the previous Congress without House Rule 21, its standing gag rule, Hale was the only New Hampshire delegate who supported him.

Hale's vote earned him fan mail praising his manly resistance to "Southern dictation" and urging him on.[135] The antislavery advocate Amos Tuck praised Hale for "daring to be a man, a whole man." Another writer fumed that Northern rights and character had "been trampled upon *long enough* by *such* . . . Southern Bullies." Yet another worried about how those bullies would respond to Hale's vote. "Should any of the southerners be rash and mean enough, to challenge a New Hampshire Representative to fight," he counseled, "I trust New Hampshire men have sufficient courage to refuse a challenge."[136] As much as Hale's constituents wanted him to fight the gag rule, their disapproval of dueling remained a powerful counterforce.

Hale's constituents continued to urge him on at the session's end, much to the dismay of Franklin Pierce, retired from Congress but a leading New Hampshire Democrat who feared a split in the party. The two men went head-to-head at a Concord town meeting in March 1844. When attendees proposed resolutions upholding the right of petition, denouncing New Hampshire congressmen who up-held the gag rule, and urging them to join Hale in "manfully" sustain-ing their rights, Pierce pleaded the case of the slavery-bedeviled South with the kind of all-stops-pulled speechifying that usually earned him kudos. He concluded by chiding abolitionists for disrupt-ing the meeting and leading him into the uproar, at which someone fired back that he was "sorry that friend Pierce should consent to be led by anybody," a slap at Pierce's doughface willingness to be led by the South.[137] Others scolded Pierce for his pro-gag-rule voting rec-ord, which haunted him for years to come; when he stood to speak during a meeting of New Hampshire Democrats in 1846, people yelled "Gag! Gag!" to drown him out.[138] The mighty New Hampshire Democracy was dividing, with French's longtime friends Frank Pierce and Jack Hale leading the way. For French, it was a bellwether of things to come.[139]

Perhaps the most dramatic demonstration of the gag rule's galva-nizing power was the censure of Joshua Giddings in 1842. Two months earlier, an attempt to censure Adams had failed, partly because of his status, partly because of his parliamentary skill, and partly because he had invoked the right of petition. But Giddings had no shield, few de-fenders, and, due to some skillful parliamentary maneuvering, no chance to defend himself. So on March 21, 1842, when Giddings offered reso-lutions defending the rights of rebelling slaves on a slaving ship to go free, a fellow Ohioan—Democrat John B. Weller—moved to censure Giddings for promoting mutiny and murder, and then immediately moved the previous question, effectively gagging him.[140] The next day, the House voted to censure him without even giving him the chance to speak, arguing the question with what Adams described as two hours of "twistings, decisions by the Speaker reversed by the House," and "mo-tions that he should have permission to be heard in his defence, by reconsideration, by suspension of the rules, by general consent."[141] That same day, Giddings suffered his punishment; called up to the front of the House, he received a formal censure read aloud by the Speaker. Although the rule of force didn't gag him, the rules of order did.

From the beginning of Giddings's congressional career, Adams had advised him to insist upon his rights and "not to be intimidated by the course taken by the Southern men."[142] The two had been comrades in arms throughout the gag rule struggle, strategizing in league with a core group of antislavery lobbyists based in Washington; Giddings dubbed the group the "Select Committee on slavery."[143] During the gag rule debate, that committee devoted itself to causing congressional chaos.[144] The dangerous words that so upset French were of great service to the antislavery cause; when the Southern hysterics that resulted were transmitted to the nation through the vehicle of the press, they exposed the tyrannical force of the Slave Power for all to see. But those same words were nothing but trouble to the Whig and Democratic parties, whose survival depended on some degree of conciliation between North and South. Giddings's censure was the result.

The elder statesman hadn't foreseen this outcome. "I can find no language to express my feelings at the consummation of this act," the stunned Adams confessed.[145] But Giddings had the last word. Upon suffering the humiliation of being censured, he resigned his seat and went home to his constituents, who applauded his "manly" fight against "congressional tyranny." Town meetings throughout his district passed resolutions upholding his antislavery sentiments, denouncing the violation of their rights, and insisting that Giddings's censure had insulted "the whole North."[146] He was reelected by a whopping 7,469 to 393 votes over a proslavery Democrat and returned to Congress stronger than before with an antislavery mandate. Wise ruefully deemed it "the greatest triumph ever achieved by a member of the House."[147]

Eventually, even the rule's staunchest supporters saw its failings. Instead of stifling dangerous talk, gag rules inspired it, causing dissension on the floor, drastically increasing the number of antislavery petitions, and rousing the Northern public to demand their rights of representation, petition, and free speech, and to elect congressmen who shared their convictions.[148] French saw the irony, noting that gag rules caused more talk than "the confusion of tongues" at Babel, and as he well knew, more talk meant more violence to stifle it.[149] Indeed, two of the five most violent Congresses between 1827 and 1861 met during the gag rule debate. (The other three met during the five years before the Civil War.)[150]

For both Wise and Adams, such vitriol had costs. Somewhat chastened in later years, Wise confessed that his congressional sparring had almost destroyed him. "It shattered my health almost to atoms, nearly lost me my voice, and was so fraught with actual personal danger and bro[ugh]t me so shockingly & often into violent collisions with both party and personal malignity as to acquire for me a character in the country which I never coveted & now deeply regret. I was earnestly actuated by a zeal for the public good which made me really forget myself."[151] Adams likewise was caught up in the moment, heaping abuse on "the gentleman from Accomac" to the point of exhaustion. After one particularly scathing attack, he confessed in his diary, "my feelings are wound up to a pitch that my reason can scarcely endure. I trust in God to control me."[152]

Wise admitted failure on December 21, 1843, beckoning reporters to listen closely, then dramatically declaring "that now, henceforth, and forever, he ceased to contend in the war which was being carried on in that House by certain men against the South." Defending Southern rights was too grave a matter to defend with points of order, he explained, never stating, but surely knowing, the power of gag rules to rouse Northern fury over violated rights. Not all of his slaveholding colleagues agreed. Isaac Holmes (D-SC) immediately urged them to take up Wise's mantle. When the notoriously fight-prone Wise asked to respond, Holmes's hasty backpedaling produced roars of laughter.[153] Wise must have gotten some Southern flak, because soon he was back at his post as the gag rule's chief defender. But like the rule, he was on his way out. In February 1844 he resigned his seat; in poor health and seeking the refuge of a diplomatic post, he had been appointed minister to Brazil in January. Roughly ten months later, on December 3, the day after the Twenty-ninth Congress opened, Adams proposed and carried the repeal of House Rule 21, due largely to an influx of freshman Northern Democrats who opposed the rule.[154] "Blessed, forever blessed, be the name of God!" he wrote in his diary that night.[155]

Thus ended the nine-year gag rule struggle. The rule's opponents had won a battle—but not a war, as the Kentuckian Thomas Marshall made clear in an address to his constituents. The slave interest had accomplished something important, he charged. By tormenting Adams, they had advertised the price of opposing slavery.[156] The gag of violence was still in place. And words were still weapons, provoking words, dangerous words, Union-splitting words that needed to be stopped, if not by formal rules, then by the rule of force.

5

FIGHTING FOR THE UNION

THE COMPROMISE OF 1850 AND THE BENTON-FOOTE SCUFFLE (1850)

As luck would have it, French reached his peak moment of congressional power as the nation's next sectional crisis was taking form. At the time, his private life was going swimmingly. In 1837, he and Bess had had their first son, Frank. Five years later, he had built his family a large, comfortable house at 37 East Capitol Street, replete with an arbor-graced garden that boasted a three-tiered fountain with goldfish—the only goldfish in Washington aside from the fishpond on the Capitol grounds. His Washington insider status was apparent in his home decor; his lush red, gold-fringed parlor curtains were from the Supreme Court, bought by French when the Court was redecorated. His comfy, much-used study was on the top floor.[1]

French gained the House clerkship in December 1845 (and gained his second son, Ben, in February). That same year, the United States annexed Texas. Texans had declared independence from Mexico in 1836 with the aid of Southern militias and the Southern press, after which Southern settlers had flocked into the territory, exponentially increasing its slave population in the process. Their aim was Texas as a slave state.[2]

The vote over annexing Texas had been close. Just as Southerners hoped, adding it to the Union was an unequivocal boost to the spread of slavery and the Southern balance of power in the Union. Thus the flood of anti-annexation antislavery petitions to Congress throughout this period. And thus Adams's continued insistence that the acquisition of Texas was a nefarious Southern ploy to expand slavery's reach.[3]

Adams also insisted that the annexation of Texas was immoral. Mexico hadn't conceded Texan independence, so annexing it was as good as declaring war. Sure enough, less than six months after Texas joined the Union, Mexican-American relations unraveled. When the newly elected president James K. Polk, an ardent expansionist, ordered troops into Texas to protect American claims, President Mariano Paredes of Mexico countered with troops of his own. By May 1846, a series of skirmishes had launched the Mexican War.

The Wilmot Proviso of 1846 was a direct result of that conflict. Proposed by Representative David Wilmot (D-PA) at the start of hostilities and unsuccessfully proposed twice more, each time failing in the South-friendly Senate, it banned slavery in land gained from Mexico. Although voted down, the proviso became a litmus test of loyalties: if you supported it, you were no friend of the South.

Whigs used this logic to tar French in his race for reelection in 1847. Given the House's small Whig majority and the fact that some Northern Whigs had promised French their votes, the contest was close. Some Whig newspapers thought that French's skills and popularity might preserve him his job.[4] To prevent this outcome, Whigs put the proviso to use, telling their Southern wing that French supported the slavery-banning proposition and their Northern wing that he opposed it.[5]

It's hard to say if that scheme cost French the clerkship, but whatever the reason, the former House member Thomas Campbell (W-TN) won by four votes. All but one of the Whig votes promised to French went to Campbell. For the most part, French took it in stride, happy to surrender the immense workload and "wear and tear of lungs."[6] But he was surprised that his friends and talents hadn't kept him in office. He could only assume that he had lost his job for no sin other than being a Democrat.[7] Convinced that he had taken a hit for the Democracy, French concluded that it owed him and looked forward to regaining the clerkship in the next Congress.

The lone Whig who stayed true to his word was John Quincy Adams—ever the contrarian—who told French that although the press said that no Whig would vote for him, "I profess to be a whig, and I *shall* vote for Mr. French."[8] After the election, the grateful French thanked him in person, little knowing that these would be his last words to Adams, who suffered a stroke in his House seat two months later, on February 21, 1848. Carried into the Speaker's chamber, he lingered for two days; French made a tearful visit to the comatose Adams before he died.[9] Appropriately enough, Adams's last word on the floor was "No." Near the end, he murmured thanks to the officers of the House.[10] It was a fitting end for a man who had dedicated most of a decade and all of his energies to bedeviling Speakers and challenging clerks with his war against gag rules.

When the next Congress opened in 1849 with a Democratic majority, French felt sure that he'd regain the clerkship, but America's victory in the Mexican War in 1848 complicated matters. The United States gained new lands whose slavery status had to be reckoned with, as did the national government's right to restrict slavery in these territories, and a tangle of related issues: the boundaries of Texas, slavery in the District of Columbia, and the problem of fugitive slaves. By forcing the issue of slavery on Congress, national expansion raised fundamental questions about the sectional balance of power, the nature of the Union, and what kind of nation the United States would be.

Primed for the fateful decisions at hand, Northern and Southern congressmen arrived in Washington eager to seize every advantage, launching three weeks of savage, foot-stamping, name-calling arguments about selecting a Speaker. The stakes seemed too high for good faith or compromise. Accusations abounded as congressmen tried to determine the precise loyalties of each and every candidate. Did they favor the Wilmot Proviso? Did they advocate disunion over any and every compromise on slavery? Even nature seemed eager to tear the Capitol in two. Afraid that lightning would strike the building's ninety-two-foot-tall mast "and kill Congress at a lick," French joked darkly, Congress had taken down the mast.[11]

Ten days in, the House reached a breaking point.[12] While discussing the speakership, William Duer (W-NY) called Richard Kidder Meade (D-VA) a disunionist. When Meade denied it, Duer called him a liar, Meade lunged at him, and the chamber went wild. The sergeant at arms from the previous Congress ran to Duer's side to fend off raging slaveholders, but became so alarmed that he ran back for the mace—which did absolutely nothing to stem the tide of fury. Had "a bomb exploded in the hall, there could not have been greater excitement," he later reported. (According to a more poetically inclined *Globe* reporter, "The House was like a heaving billow.")[13] Alarmed congressmen hustled to the galleries to protect their families; with no officers elected and no way to impose order, people feared a full-fledged riot and almost got one. They also almost got a duel, though Meade and Duer ultimately settled their differences.

It took some time to return the House to order. But minutes later, there was talk of disunion yet again. Enraged at the idea of Northerners branding Southerners disunionists, Robert Toombs (W-GA) swore his loyalty to the Union, but declared that if the House planned "to fix a national degradation upon half the states of this Confederacy, *I am for disunion.*" Other Southerners vowed that if the South was treated unfairly, they would keep the House disordered forever.[14] Writing to his wife amid the "indescribable confusion," David Outlaw could only moan, "I most sincerely wish I was at home."[15]

Northerners responded to Southern threats as Northerners were wont to do: they demanded orderly debate. But some of them did so with defiance, dismissing threats as bluster and asserting their rights on the floor. Edward Baker (W-IL) met Toombs's ultimatum by refusing to be "intimidated by threats of violence. . . . We are here as freemen, to speak for freemen; and we will speak and act as becomes us, in the face of the world."[16] Chauncey Cleveland (D-CT) took the same stand. Did the South expect the North to "forget that we are freemen—the representatives of freemen?" Did they think that the North "should yield our opinions, our principles to their dictation?"[17] Both men were refusing to be gagged by threats of violence. It was an echo of six years past, but magnified by a mandate; Northerners wanted their congressmen to defend their rights. To make matters worse, by dismissing Southern bullying as bluster, Northerners threw the lie at Southerners and scoffed at their manhood, raising tempers even higher.

With Congress at a standstill, Meade pleaded for a compromise. Would no Northerner offer an olive branch? It would never happen, replied Joseph Root (FS-OH). After more than a week of Southern threats and grandstanding, no Northerner would dare appease a Southerner. His constituents would scorn his cowardice. (Or as Root more colorfully put it, any such Northerner should tell his children to "get their Sunday clothes on, for they would want to see their daddy for the last time.")[18] Several Northerners privately said the same thing to speakership candidate Howell Cobb (D-GA). Although they wanted to support him, "the threats and menaces of southern men . . . would destroy their position at home" by suggesting that they had voted "under the influence of these belligerent taunts."[19]

After a three-week wrangle, Cobb was elected Speaker and attention turned to the election of the Clerk. Assuming that the Democracy owed him their support given his lost election, French was stunned to find several Democrats running against him. "My notions of honor do not exactly square with the idea of placing myself *in the way* of any democrat who has been immolated on the political altar," he fumed in his diary. Even so, he thought that he could win. But Democrats chose the *Philadelphia Pennsylvanian* editor John Forney, "a peculiarly faithful ally of the south," as their nominee.[20] To French, it was a staggering display of party faithlessness. (In true French form, he dubbed this sin "Forneycation.")[21]

Disappointed as he was, French resolved to hold back; his party had made its choice and he would let things play out. But when he heard that some Southern Democrats absolutely *refused* to vote for him, his "Yankee blood was up at once" and he declared himself a candidate.[22] He later regretted it; his Yankee foot-stamping peeled away Democratic votes for Forney, as Forney later grumbled in the press.[23] But French didn't decide the election, although he tangled it; in a close contest with convoluted twists and turns that lasted for a week and twenty ballots, he received only a smattering of votes.[24] The tide was turned by eight Southern Democrats who reelected the Tennessee Whig Thomas Campbell, putting section above party to give the clerkship to a Southerner.[25] In 1847, French had lost the clerkship for being a Democrat. Now he had lost it for being a Northerner.

For French, a loyal doughface and longtime clerk with supportive friends on both sides of the Mason-Dixon Line and both sides of the aisle, it was a stunning betrayal. For two decades, he had worked to preserve party ties between North, South, and West, singing a song of Union and Jackson, playing down talk of slavery and playing up talk of states' rights. He had done this and more for the Democracy and the Union, pouring his heart, soul, and energies into an organization that he felt sure had the nation's—and his—best interests at heart. Yet in French's hour of need, his party had abandoned him. The Democracy had done what it did so often and so well: Southerners had served themselves and Northerners had knuckled under, and together they had cast him aside.[26]

This stark imbalance of power was nothing new. But in 1849, it had a sharp personal edge that forced French to reckon with some ugly truths; the corrupt bargain at the heart of the Democracy had been exposed. "One thing I have learned, and I intend to make a note of it," he told his brother not long after his loss: "if a northern man will not bow, & knuckle, & prostrate himself in the dust before their high mightiness of the South, he must hope for nothing."[27] Doughface congressmen, "moulded into any shape their Southern taskmasters choose," were little more than "whipped puppies," he fumed, never saying—but surely knowing—that he himself had long fit that mold. French himself was through with such cowering: "I will see the South all d—nd to everlasting perdition before I will ever crook my thumb & forefinger, or open my lips in their defence." Let Southerners turn to their "own servile race" for support.[28] Northerners should defend their rights and interests and stop enslaving themselves. Though still loyal to the Democracy, French no longer trusted Southern Democrats.

His feelings mirrored the mood in Congress. The weeks of ultimatums set the tone for the session. Sectional passions were reaching new heights. Northerners were more confrontational than ever before. And a watchful, wary public was a palpable presence. Slaveholders and free-state men were throwing down.

Remarkably, this strife-ridden Congress produced one of the most famous compromises in American history: the so-called Compromise of 1850.[29] A patchwork cluster of bills that occupied the entire ten-month session—the longest session since the founding of the government—it soothed but didn't solve the slavery crisis. Men who were literally at each other's throats ultimately came together for the sake of the Union; indeed, the raging sectional fury made the need for a national compromise that much more urgent. This volatile blend of intense sectionalism and intense nationalism would characterize congressional politics for years to come.

At the heart of this standoff were sectional rights: Southerners demanded equal rights in the territories, Northerners demanded equal rights on the floor. The alternative was unthinkable—*degradation*, a key word throughout the Compromise debate.[30] Sectional honor was at stake in 1850, but not as a tool of debate as in "Cilley scenes" of times past. During the crisis of 1850, with the balance of power in the Union in question, sectional honor *was* the debate. Thus the newfound Northern belligerence.

And thus a shift in Southern bullying as well. Southerners had long held sway with man-to-man threats. Now, with the expansion and survival of slavery at stake, they began to threaten the institution of Congress and the Union with a new power, depicting the nation's end times with alarming precision. The halls of Congress bloodied, disunion, civil war: Southerners paraded an array of horrors in this politics of ultimatums.[31] Southern bullying had expanded exponentially, embracing the entire Union in its reach.

But even now, apart from a few stellar outbursts, Congress didn't dissolve into a den of furies. Violence continued apace, but so did some degree of self-restraint. Even as they shoved, slugged, and threatened one another in the cross-fire of a crisis—indeed *because* of that crisis—congressmen abided by informal rules of combat that kept fighting fair, though like the terms of Union as a whole, these customs skewed Southern, compelling non-combatants to fight or risk dishonor.[32] In essence, congressional combat was grounded on a South-centric spirit of compromise. And like the bonds of Union, without some degree of cooperation and mutual trust, Congress's institutional bonds wouldn't survive.

To see the rising tensions between fighting and fairness, it's hard to think of a better case study than the dramatic 1850 clash between Senator Thomas Hart Benton (D-MO), the storied champion of the nation's "manifest destiny" to spread across the continent, and Senator Henry Foote (D-MS), Benton's far less storied colleague.

The two men had long disliked each other, and their mutual dislike had blossomed in the summer before the opening of the session. Early in 1849, Senator John C. Calhoun (D-SC) had orchestrated what came to be known as the Southern Address, a statement signed by a small group of Southern congressmen denouncing Northern aggression against Southern rights, denying Congress's right to forbid slavery in new territories, and threatening secession. Not long after, the Missouri State Assembly adopted similar resolutions.[33] Disturbed by Southern extremism and its implications for the Union, and eager to prevent agitation of the slavery question, Benton attacked the measures in electioneering speeches throughout Missouri for months, denouncing the extreme claims and downplaying the threat of secession.[34] "There has been a cry of wolf when there is no wolf," he later quipped.[35]

Alarmed by Benton's politics and outraged at his implied sneer at Southern threats, several Southerners took him on. Foote did so with verve. Egged on by his friend Henry Wise—now a bullying consultant from afar—he published a lengthy letter to Wise full of abuse of Benton, accusing the Missourian of being willing to "sacrifice southern honor and southern prosperity on the altar of his own political advancement." He continued in that vein for twenty pages.[36] His sniping continued once Congress was in session.

Foote played a leading role in this slavery showdown. His first attempt to get what he wanted reached far beyond Benton; he threatened a mass Southern assault on Congress and civil warfare if a South-friendly bundle of compromises wasn't hammered out in private—and soon. This was Southern bullying on a massive scale, so massive that few people believed it. But some did, and that meant something. They saw sectional combat in the Capitol as not only possible, but imminent.

When Foote failed to get his way with bullying writ large, he turned to bullying writ small, focusing his sights on Benton, a loud and aggressive opponent of his plan. Hoping to defeat Benton's influence by damaging his reputation, Foote insulted him for weeks, with Benton grasping at rules and customs to defend himself without losing control and thereby losing the fight.

Finally, on April 17, 1850, Benton snapped. Throwing back his chair, he lunged at Foote, who responded by pulling a pistol and aiming it at Benton. Predictably, this produced chaos. Congressmen stampeded through the Senate to break up the fight (or get a better look). Some of their fellows howled for order in a panic. Mass pandemonium erupted in the galleries. A few moments later, Foote's gun was taken from him and the chamber regained some semblance of order.

A crisis had been averted. But Benton refused to let the matter drop. The ensuing debate centered not on the simple fact of Foote's gunplay, but rather on his motives and intentions: had he been fighting fair? After what the *Globe* might call a "lively debate," with Northerners pushing for a formal investigation and Southerners dismissing the episode as too trivial to merit one, Vice President Millard Fillmore (W-NY) appointed an investigative committee. The next day, the Senate got back to business, eventually making its way to the subject of . . . the acceptance of antislavery petitions.[37]

The Senate committee then went to work. Over the course of several weeks, it examined forty-three witnesses, including senators, congressional staff, newspapermen, personal friends of both combatants, and even the shop clerk who sold Foote a pistol. The resulting 135-page report—filled with people's thoughts about a fight and its fighters—reveals the patchwork of intricate and sometimes contradictory compromises that kept fighting fair and bridged divides, much like the Compromise of 1850 itself.

French emerged from his lost clerkship battle with his own patchwork of contradictions and compromises. For income, he patched together several jobs, cashing in on his congressional know-how by opening a claims office; doing some lobbying; and serving as a director and stockholder of the Magnetic Telegraph Company, and from 1847 to 1850 as its president. But his hard work didn't garner much reward. His finances fluctuated throughout this period; neither lobbying nor lawyering promised a stable income. "We have plenty of business," he wrote of his claims office in December 1850, "but it is of that sort which only pays *if we are successful.*"[38] His loss of the clerkship—the office that his wife, Bess, said he preferred "to any other in the Union"—was a mighty loss indeed.[39]

By 1849, French's politics were something of a patchwork as well. The betrayal of Southern Democrats in his election for Clerk had opened his eyes; although he remained a party activist, he no longer saw the Democracy as a forge of Union. From this point on, the Constitution would be French's political touchstone. Fidelity to the Constitution—to French, "the wellspring of wisdom and concession"—would bind the nation, section to section, state to state, and man to man.[40] The fellow feelings of Americans would secure those bonds; French saw the unifying power of such feelings among the Masons, a national brotherhood that came to play an increasingly central role in his life.[41] With sectional tensions on the rise, French grasped at what he perceived as the nation's fundamental spirit of fellowship and compromise.

Yet even as French fretted for the Union, he turned his face north. Convinced that Southern domination meant national ruin, he saw Northern resistance as the only way to level the balance of power: Northerners needed to fight for their rights. French's near idol worship of Joshua Giddings in the 1850s was of a piece with his new state of mind; he deeply admired the Ohioan's willingness to risk life and limb battling the Slave Power. French had long admired Northerners who stood down Southern bullies. Now he wanted a league of such men, and he wanted them to fight. And he wasn't alone. During the debate over the Compromise of 1850, fighting for the Union began to take on troubling new dimensions—for French, for Congress, and for the nation.

THE FIGHTERS AND THEIR FIGHT

When the dust had settled after the tumultuous opening of the Thirty-first Congress, French did what came naturally: he wrote a poem—a *"rather patriotic piece,"* his twelve-year-old son, Frank, judged after reciting it.[42] Alarmed at the sectional uproar (or as French's poem put it: "That dark and dismal cloud that seems / Our Union to enfold"), French published "Good Wishes for the Union," a call to arms for compromisers everywhere. His message was captured in the poem's refrain: "Our Union cannot fall— / While each to all the rest is true, / Sure God WILL prosper all." With selfish Southerners and faithless Democrats fresh on his mind, French was preaching national brotherhood and loyalty. Yet even in this ode to nationalism, he planted seeds of sectionalism; his poem cites every Northern and Middle Atlantic state by name, even encompassing Western territories, but mentions no state south of Virginia. His wounds were fresh and deep.

French had good reason to be alarmed. Political bonds of all kinds were fraying. Not only were the Whig and Democratic parties collapsing under the strain of sectional tensions, but even sectional allies were at odds. All told, Congress was split four ways over the issue of a compromise on slavery. There was a mix of Free Soilers, Northern Whigs, and Northern Democrats who opposed compromise and thought that slavery should be excluded from the West. There were Whigs who favored compromise and felt that the federal government had power over slavery in the territories. There were Democrats (Northerners and some Southerners) who favored compromise and thought that new territories should decide the issue of slavery for themselves. And there were Southern Democrats who opposed compromise, denied the federal government's power over slavery, and demanded slavery's expansion west.[43] Even slaveholders were divided on the best way to handle the issue of slavery, as the Benton-Foote conflict shows all too well.

In a sense, the two men were bound to create conflict because their politics clashed and their practices didn't; both men were congressional bullies of the first order. Forty-six years old, the Virginia-born Foote was slight, short, bald, and none too strong; he had a slight limp from a wound received in a duel.[44] But he was a fighter; as a friend put it, Foote was "liable, somewhat, to be involved in disputes and personal difficulties."[45] That was an understatement. Foote fought legislative battles by insulting, belittling, and threatening his foes; at peak moments of oratorical wrath, he stamped his feet. (In the committee report, several observers noted that he barely had time to stamp each foot once before Benton exploded.)[46] He earned his nickname—"Hangman Foote"—in 1848 when he told the aggressively antislavery John Parker Hale that if he ever set foot in Mississippi he'd be hanged, with Foote standing by to help. Foote called the nickname the most "severe humiliation" of his life, which was saying something given his congressional shenanigans.[47]

Not surprisingly, Foote was a frequent fighter. He fought four duels during his political career and was shot in three of them, suggesting that he was far better at shooting off his mouth than his gun.[48] In addition, during his five years in the Senate he was involved in at least four brawls with senators, once exchanging blows with Jefferson Davis (D-MS) in their boardinghouse, an episode that prompted two near-duels; once exchanging blows with Simon Cameron (D-PA) on the Senate floor (as Sam Houston [D-TX] put it, the "eloquent and impassioned gentlemen got into each other's hair"[49]); once slugging John C. Fremont (D-CA)—Benton's son-in-law—just outside the Senate door, again raising talk of a duel (Fremont asked Cilley's second, George W. Jones, to be his second); and once getting into a scratch fight with Solon Borland (D-AR) over the politics of John C. Calhoun.[50] He also routinely bullied

Henry Foote, ca. 1845–60
(Courtesy of the Library of
Congress)

Northern non-combatants.[51] So notorious was Foote's fighting problem
that a journalist set it to music, writing a mock "moral song" for
children—and senators:

> *Grave Senators should never let*
> *Their angry passions rise,*
> *Their little hands were never made*
> *To scratch each other's eyes.*[52]

Despite the mayhem, Foote was an educated man with refined
tastes, as were many bullies; the fine art of congressional bullying went
beyond back-alley brawling. Having pursued classical studies before
training in the law, Foote sprinkled his lengthy and frequent oratorical forays with learned references, accompanied—as one reporter
described it—by the "eloquent gestures of a galvanized frog."[53] Watching Foote perform in the Senate, Representative David Outlaw
described him as a "talking machine" who quoted "Greek, Latin, the

Bible, Shakespeare, Vattel, and heaven knows what else." Foote was his "evil genius," Outlaw groused to his wife, "for it so happens I hardly ever go into that chamber, and remain for half an hour, without [him] either making a speech, or interrupting some person who is speaking." All in all, Outlaw concluded, "of all the men I ever heard, he is to me the most disagreable."[54]

Many found the sixty-eight-year-old Benton equally disagreeable. French thought him the vainest man he'd ever known, citing as proof a time when he had seen Benton point to his signature on a document and pronounce it (with a portentousness that "Doct. Johnson could not have surpassed") a name of world renown. But Benton had a right to be vain, French thought, ranking him as one of the nation's greatest statesmen.[55] Personally, French liked him. During the friendly house calls that filled most New Year's days, the French family often called on the Bentons.

Born in North Carolina, Benton practiced law in Tennessee before moving to St. Louis; a notorious street brawl with Andrew Jackson featuring pistols, knives, fists, a whip, and a sword cane probably influenced the move, since it complicated Benton's place in Tennessee politics, to say the least. (As Benton himself put it, "I am literally in hell.")[56] But in Missouri, Benton was no less combative; in 1817, he fought a duel with the opposing lawyer in a court case and killed him.[57]

In Congress, Benton's fighting reputation preceded him; even as a newcomer, French was already factoring it into his congressional calculations.[58] It was for good reason that Cilley's friends turned to Benton for fighting advice. During the Missourian's many years in the Senate, he came close to fighting a duel three times in addition to his 1850 fight with Foote, in one case throwing the lie at Henry Clay, who threw it right back. (Clay claimed that Benton had once said that if Andrew Jackson became president, congressmen would have to be armed at all times; they settled the matter off the floor.)[59] Most recently, after an argument sparked by a debate over the slavery status of the Oregon Territory in 1848, Senator Andrew Butler (D-SC) had commenced duel negotiations with Benton, with Foote acting as Butler's second. Foote's delivery of Butler's opening letter had so alarmed the entire Benton family, that—partly out of disdain for Foote—Benton had refused to act on it.[60] Rumor also had it that Benton, a devoted family man who was so publicly affectionate with his children that he almost charmed the formidable John Quincy Adams, had promised his wife that he would never duel

Thomas Hart Benton,
ca. 1845–55 (Courtesy of
the Missouri History
Museum, St. Louis)

again.[61] During the 1850 encounter, Foote's sneering reference to Benton's alleged cowardice in the Butler affair made matters worse.

Physically, Benton was Foote's polar opposite. A large, hulking man, muscular, powerful, roughly six feet tall, he was an imposing figure when fully fired up. His towering temper matched his size. He "was not only a man of tremendous passions," recalled Representative George Julian (FS-IN), but he was "unrivaled as a hater. . . . He was pre-eminently unforgiving."[62] Watching him in one of his rages, the ever-sardonic Adams described him as "the doughty knight of the stuffed cravat" abating "his manly wrath."[63] None too challenged in the ego department, Benton veered toward pomposity. Foote stamped; Benton strutted.[64]

One of Missouri's first senators, Benton served in the Senate for a remarkable thirty years, and he never forgot it; in 1850, he was the senior senator in point of service. Foote wasn't the only man to denounce him as a self-proclaimed Senate patriarch who routinely bullied men into compliance. Like Foote, "Old Bully Bottom Benton"—to quote Henry Wise—had a sarcastic turn.[65] "When he wanted to torture an opponent," a contemporary later recalled, "he had a way of elevating his voice into a rasping squeal of sarcasm which was intolerably exasperating and sometimes utterly maddening" and he used the word *sir* as "a formidable missile," as during the exchange that led Andrew Butler to challenge him to a duel.[66] When Butler accused Benton of leaking a document to the press, Benton declared, "I don't quarrel, sir. I have fought several times, sir, and have fought for a funeral; fought to the death, sir; but I never quarrel."[67] (True to form, the *Globe* summed up the fiery exchange by noting: "[The scene was more than usually exciting at one time.]")[68]

In personality alone, the two seemed destined to clash, but their clashing politics guaranteed it. Although both men were Southern Democrats hoping to save the Union, they differed in their views of sectionalism, slavery, and compromise—and in 1850, all three were bound in a bundle of controversy. Fearful that Southern ultimatums would destroy the Union, Benton opposed the expansion of slavery into the territories, a stance that Foote couldn't fathom. California statehood proved their breaking point. When the state requested admission to the Union as a free state, Benton supported it but Foote wanted a bundled compromise hammered out privately in committee with California as a bargaining chip—to him, the best way to protect Southern rights and interests.[69] Benton objected to this proposed "lump" of legislation, unwilling to allow the threats of a Southern minority to awe the majority into concessions.

To defeat Benton's influence, Foote turned to bullying, attacking the Missourian's reputation. By his logic, to prevent the South's degradation, he had to degrade Benton. But even as his anti-Benton campaign began to build momentum, Foote attempted something far more dramatic. He tried to force through his plan of compromise by threatening the institution of Congress and the Union as a whole.

SECTIONAL DEGRADATION AND THE POLITICS OF ULTIMATUMS

Foote wasn't alone in this politics of ultimatums. Disunion and civil war were topics of debate throughout the session. Southern congressmen had long used such threats to good effect. But in 1850, with a Union-shaping cluster of concerns on the table and sectional hostilities reaching new heights, those threats became more detailed, more violent, and more ambitious.[70] Sectional bullying was coming into its own.

In the same way that the threat of a duel challenge had tipped the balance of power toward Southerners for decades, the threat of disunion held that balance in place during the crisis of 1850. In both cases, Southerners didn't really want to follow through; few if any men wanted to fight a duel or dissolve the Union. During the speakership wrangle, Richard Kidder Meade had lunged at William Duer for suggesting as much. Threats don't need to be fulfilled to be effective; the power of a threat is in the *chance* of its fulfillment, and Southerners had been flaunting their collective itchy trigger finger for decades.

The power behind these threats was the power behind all bullying: fear of humiliation and dishonor. Indeed, the entire Compromise debate was infused with talk of degradation and submission, honor and bravery, manhood and power, defiance and pride.[71] Northerners, Southerners, and Westerners saw their rights under attack, and rights talk is honor talk; men who surrender their rights without resistance are cowards.[72] So a discussion of sectional rights was bound to be painfully personal for congressmen and constituents alike.

This amped-up style of bullying began not long after the speakership contest was settled. While discussing California's slavery status on January 22, 1850, Representative Thomas Clingman (W-NC) gave a speech so extreme that at least one newspaper editor thought that telegraph transmissions had mangled it. If the North intended "to degrade and utterly ruin the South, then we resist," Clingman declared. "We do not love you, people of the North, enough to become your slaves."[73] To prevent such degradation, he proposed a Southern one-two punch. First, Southerners would fight as "Northern gentlemen" did, using calls for adjournment and calls for yeas and nays to bring the government to a dead halt. If that failed, then they would fight like Southerners—with violence. If Northerners tried to expel Southern troublemakers, there would be bloodshed. "Let them try that experiment," he warned. Washington was slaveholding country, and "[w]e do not intend to leave it." The end result would be a "collision" as electric as the Battle of Lexington, followed by the collapse of Congress.[74] Clingman was describing the opening vista of a civil war. He was also offering fair warning.

A few weeks later, Foote took Clingman's threats one step further.

On February 18, free-state congressmen in the House had used the previous question to try to force through a resolution admitting California as a free state. In response, Southerners did what Clingman said they would do: they used parliamentary weapons to halt the debate until midnight, at which point the resolution would have to wait until March 4.[75] Three days later, Foote rose to his feet in the Senate and proposed his solution to the California standstill: a select committee to hammer out a bundled "scheme of compromise." To get his way, he issued an ultimatum: if a committee didn't devise a compromise by Saturday, March 2—the last workday before the postponed California resolution would return to the House—then "so help me Heaven . . . during the next week occurrences are likely to take place of a nature to which I dare not do more than allude." He knew what he was talking about, he insisted. "I have looked into the matter. I have conversed with members of both Houses of Congress; and I state, upon my honor, that unless we do something during the present week, I entertain not the least doubt that this subject will leave our jurisdiction, and leave it forever."[76]

What did Foote mean? Newspapers were quick to tell the tale.[77] According to unnamed congressional insiders, if no plan was forged by March 2, a pack of armed Southern congressmen would "break up the House." Rumor had it that they would pick a fight and spark a melee as their opening gambit. Once open warfare broke out in the House, there would be no turning back. The Compromise debate would move to broader fields of battle than the floor of Congress. Foote was bringing Clingman's threat to life.

Armed warfare in the House: the threat is so extreme that it's hard to take seriously, particularly given its author, who was all too fond of what one newspaper called "gassing."[78] Thus the *Globe*'s nonresponse to Foote's dire warning; it barely mentioned his ultimatum, even on the dreaded date of March 4. Within the context of the *Globe*, Foote's threat doesn't seem different from the rest of the session's flame-throwing rhetoric.

But dig deeper and the threat's full impact becomes clear: some people seriously considered its implications and some few believed it. Even dubious congressmen couldn't rule out such an onslaught. In private, there was talk. North Carolina Whigs Willie Mangum and David Outlaw calculated how many of their colleagues were armed. Mangum thought seventy or eighty men—a third of the House. Outlaw thought fewer, though he was struck that some Northerners were armed.[79] However unlikely bloodshed seemed at present, there were some "acts of aggression which will call for resistance, at any and every hazard," he thought. "Death itself is preferable to degradation and dishonor."[80] To even the most moderate of men, some insults required violent resistance. However much Foote was gassing, there could come a time when his words would bear true.

Much of the press reached similar conclusions. Although a few Northern newspapers bought Foote's threat wholesale, most considered gunplay possible but not probable. Armed Southerners probably wouldn't break up the House, they advised, but hadn't Southern congressmen proven time and again that they were capable of it?[81] Here was the power of bullying firsthand. Although most threats were bluster, some of them weren't, and it was hard to predict which ultimatums would be backed up with force. As Horace Mann (W-MA) put it when discussing three fights that broke out at the close of the previous session, "the spirit of fighting" was a hard thing to predict; it all "depends upon the men." (In that case, the spirit of fighting had been clear; all three fights had featured a Southerner assaulting a Northerner.)[82]

A full-fledged battle within the walls of the Capitol was unlikely: so judged congressional insiders and the press. But what of the public? They showed what they thought in the days leading up to March 4. In anticipation of the congressional day of reckoning, people began streaming into Washington, fully prepared to see armed warfare between North and South in the House. Only after the day passed without bloodshed did the "great crowds which assembled here to see the Union dissolved by a general battle in the House of Reps" drift home, Outlaw told his wife.[83]

To these people, congressional ultimatums weren't bluster; they seemed real enough to justify a visit to the Capitol—or to require some reassurance, as stray letters from congressmen comforting their friends and family make clear.[84] Dangerous words were having an impact. And congressmen couldn't help but notice. Some fretted about the damage that their extreme language could cause throughout the Union by fostering extremists. Others—particularly Southerners—thought that such language might do some good; as much as he regretted the repeated threats of disunion, Outlaw hoped that they would "cause the North to pause in their career before it is too late."[85]

This was bullying writ large—very large. It was bullying as state-craft, and it had an impact, though not as planned. Like Outlaw, many Southerners were counting on its power to quell Northern aggression and resistance. It had worked one year past. After the passage of a reso-lution to end the slave trade in the District of Columbia, Southerners had threatened to dissolve the Union and then met in private to dis-cuss "what they are pleased to denominate Southern Rights," John Parker Hale told his wife. Frightened Northerners had responded by voting to reconsider the resolution. The end result, Hale had felt sure, would be "some insipid unmeaning motion for an inquiry into the expediency of doing something instead of the bold and manly resolution" that had al-ready passed.[86] In these cases, as in others, Southerners didn't punch and shoot their way to victory. They used intimidation; they played on the fact that disunion seemed possible, if not probable. And in 1850, with South-erners mouthing *plans* of disunion instead of mere threats, it seemed more possible than ever before.[87]

But although a politics of ultimatums sometimes worked magic, during the high-stakes debate of 1850 it backfired, compelling North-ern congressmen to dig in their heels and meet strut with strut. They boasted of their bravery in facing Southern threats. They bellowed about their right of free speech. And most of all, they presented themselves as champions of Northern rights. By standing up to slave-state men, they were defending the interests and honor of the North, just as bullying Southerners championed the South. In confronting their sectional antagonists, congressmen were literally and figuratively fighting for sectional rights.

To a certain degree, this had always been true in Congress. Both Jonathan Cilley and William Graves felt that they were fighting for "their people" and their section, Cilley—the taunted New Englander—perhaps most of all. Both men likewise felt that their honor and the honor of all that they represented were intertwined. But in 1850, sectional honor *was* the debate. This was performative representation of a powerful kind; con-gressmen were performing sectional rights on the floor, and their actions would shape sectional rights in the Union, though only if sustained by their home audience.

French counted on that fact, telling his brother that once North-erners knew "the game that is playing" in Congress, they would elect men who would fight for their rights.[88] He himself reached new heights of respect for Northern fighting men during the 1850 debate, particu-larly for Joshua Giddings. Although French had long questioned Giddings's aggressive abolitionism, he had always liked the Ohioan's down-to-earth honesty; for French, "down-to-earth" was the highest praise that he could give. But during the Compromise crisis, he couldn't praise Giddings's manliness enough. Giddings was "one of the great men of this Nation," French effused, "a high-minded *fearless* man, who is ready, I know, to become a martyr in a righteous cause." French felt sure that Giddings, aided by "the God of battles," would defeat "the oppres-sors" and save the Union.[89]

Giddings had pitted himself against Southern "oppressors" in 1849 during debate over slavery in California at the close of the previous ses-sion. When Southerners had threatened to rip out the hearts of antislav-ery men, Giddings scoffed. Richard Kidder Meade (D-VA) responded by bragging that the best way to manage antislavery congressmen was to keep them afraid for their lives. Unwilling to be bullied, Giddings condemned Meade's words to his face, prompting Meade to grab Gid-dings's collar and raise his fist, at which Southerners pulled the Virgin-ian away. One reporter saw "a couple of gray heads bobbing about, and directly saw one of them hustled down the aisle . . . his arms seeming to be held in constraint by several friends."[90] At a time when French was raging against Southern dictation, this sort of display did his heart proud. Giddings was his beau ideal of a champion, a man who would stand up to bullying Southerners and right the balance of Union.

Senator John Parker Hale received similar praise from friends, con-stituents, and the press for his defense of Northern rights. When An-drew Butler (D-SC) called him a "mad man" during discussion of an antislavery petition, the normally genial Hale lost his temper, shooting back that Butler would have to "talk louder, and threaten more, and de-nounce more before he can shut my mouth here." Northerners weren't to be "frightened, sir, out of our rights . . . we are not to be frightened even by threats of danger personally to ourselves." New Hampshire men would proudly defend their rights in Congress or in battle, let the enemy "come when they will, and where they will, and how they will."[91] Given

Hale's typically jovial style, this combative defense of Northern rights received ample press coverage.

So did his skillful skewering of ranting Southerners, as on May 20, 1848, when he responded to one of Foote's taunts by asking for a dictionary so he could find the insult's meaning, playing up the comedy of the moment and bringing down the house.[92] In the Thirty-first Congress, the ongoing contest between Foote and Hale was much like the gag rule battle between Henry Wise and John Quincy Adams; the two men were partners in taunt and torment. Like Adams and Giddings, Hale was an antislavery toreador, but whereas Giddings fought with physical bravado and Adams fought with sarcasm and parliamentary savvy, Hale's chosen weapon was humor. He was a master at deflating Southern bravado by reducing the Senate to laughter.

Such energized Northern resistance was striking. More striking still were the energized fears of congressmen about their safety on the floor. With hundreds of people milling about the Capitol, Joseph Woodward (D-SC) thought that if the Duer-Meade scuffle at the start of the session had been more serious, "in less than three minutes three hundred strangers would have rushed into this Hall" and produced a bloody melee, a scenario that was strikingly close to Foote's doomsday threat.[93] David Outlaw agreed. "In times of great excitement, as upon the slavery question[,] armed men might be admitted into this Hall, and in case of a personal collision this place might become a scene of bloodshed and confusion."[94] The press came to the same conclusion; a "bloody row" fueled by "outsiders" could happen at any time, and "civil war would thus commence in the Capitol."[95] The South's "new game of frustration, or parliamentary hindrances," could end no other way.[96] Southern threats of civil war didn't seem so outrageous after all, but the American public—not congressmen—would bring them to fruition.[97]

The session's intense focus on bloodshed and sectional degradation is a reminder that sectional rights weren't ethereal abstractions. They were close at hand and deeply personal, which gave them a special kind of power. As Volney Howard (D-TX) put it in 1850, if the Union was ever dissolved, it would be done not by calculation but as "a matter of feeling."[98] Fellow feeling might hold the Union together, but feelings of degradation could tear it apart. The gag rule debate had shown the importance of such feelings all too well. Northerners with little to say about the rule's impact on slavery had plenty to say about its violation of their rights of free speech and representation, and the rule's opponents played on that fact to bring it down.

Fairness, honor, rights, and feelings: the Union was built on these dangerously subjective constructs, as were the workings of its legislative branch. The constitutional pact was just that—a pact—and violating that founding compromise was dishonest and dishonorable. On this all sides could agree. But the precise boundaries and implications of that pact were still up for debate in 1850, so violations were often in the eye of the beholder.[99] French's ode to the Union confronted that challenge by asking each state to be true to the others. To French, fellow feeling and good faith were the Union's only hope.

But fellow feeling was in short supply in 1850, even for French, who hoped that Northerners would remember "the spirit of '76" and do all that they could to ensure that "the North is no longer cheated of its rights."[100] Cross-sectional trust was failing and fears of the consequences of that collapse were mounting. "At the very moment when forbearance and conciliation are of the first importance," said David Outlaw, "these cardinal virtues, so essential to the peace of the country and the preservation of the Union, seem to have departed from our Legislative Halls."[101] Concern for the terms of Union was driving men apart.

THE IMPORTANCE OF FIGHTING FAIR

Ultimately, Foote's large-scale sectional bullying campaign failed. As was ever his way, he went too far, making a threat too extreme to be believed—except by the people who came to Washington to witness the congressional apocalypse. But in the end, stalwart Northerners held firm, the day of reckoning passed without incident, and the torturous Compromise debate continued, as did Foote's ongoing assault on Benton's power and influence.

Opposed to the extension of slavery, disapproving of Foote's backroom mode of compromise, and detesting Foote personally, Benton was a hulking roadblock of a problem. He was also a formidable opponent. Never a graceful speaker, his power was in the reach and recall of his knowledge. A master at amassing facts and figures, he wielded them like weapons during debates.

But Benton was a vulnerable target. His ambivalence toward slavery had long made him suspect among Southerners, who were more on guard than ever with its future at stake; Benton's fight with Foote was one of many tussles between Southerners during that session.[102] Much like French's, Benton's views on slavery were a web of contradictions; he disliked the institution, didn't want to agitate the issue, disapproved of its extension, yet was willing to protect enslaved people as property. Neither a full Free Soiler nor a loyal Democrat, Benton embodied the mixed views of his home state of Missouri, which was grappling with the problem of slavery on the border of North and South. Many Southerners considered him downright traitorous; he was one of only two Southern senators not invited to Calhoun's Southern caucus. His habit of dismissing Southern threats as empty bluster only made matters worse. Thus Benton's nickname during the Compromise struggle: "Tommy the Traitor."[103]

Foote seized on this logic in combatting Benton, trying repeatedly to prove that the Missourian was no Southerner and thus couldn't be trusted with Southern rights. If Foote managed things deftly, he might even hurt Benton's chance for reelection.[104] With such clear benefits in mind, he held nothing back. As the committee report phrased it, Foote "indulged in personalities towards Mr. Benton of the most offensive and insulting character, which were calculated to arouse the fiercest resentment of the human bosom."[105]

For Foote, such displays came naturally; he enjoyed Benton-baiting. Benton's "overbearing demeanor," his "boisterous denunciation," his "sneerful innuendo": Foote hated it all.[106] On March 26, two weeks before his most renowned confrontation with Benton, Foote upped the ante. Eager to cut Benton off, Foote unleashed a string of insults, stating that Benton's refusal to duel Butler had dishonored him, hinting at the possibility of a Foote-Benton duel, and accusing Benton of cowardice for tossing off insults while hiding behind privilege of debate and his refusal to obey "the obligatory force of the laws of honor."[107]

Foote's strategy was ingenious. By insulting Benton personally and to his face, he was daring Benton to challenge him to a duel. For Benton, this was a lose-lose situation. He didn't want to fight a duel. But refusing to do so could destroy his reputation. So thought David Outlaw (W-NC). Although he detested the practice of dueling, he believed that some situations demanded it, and Benton was "in my judgement in that predicament." To avoid "degradation," the Missourian needed to "fight the first man who gives him occasion."[108] But given Benton's foot-dragging in his near-duel with Andrew Butler two years past, Foote didn't expect a challenge. And therein lay the power of his punch. He was trying to prove that Benton wasn't a full-fledged Southern man and thus wasn't loyal to the South. He drove that point home after each barrage of insults, asking Benton repeatedly: Do you abide by the code of honor?[109] If the answer was yes, then a duel challenge was almost mandatory. If the answer was no, then Benton wasn't a true Southerner. Clearly, Southerners could be bullied as effectively as Northerners.

For a long time, Benton didn't rise to the challenge. Perhaps he held back for the sake of the Senate; patriarch that he was, maybe he was upholding its status. Perhaps at the age of sixty-eight, he wasn't eager to fight. A devoted family man, maybe his violent days were past. Perhaps he was preserving his congressional gravitas. Or perhaps he was simply doing his best to advance the Compromise debate.

Whatever the reason, Benton restrained himself, defending his reputation by resorting to time-honored congressional traditions that kept fighting fair. For example, on one occasion, when Foote's insults became too much for him, Benton magisterially gathered up his cloak and left the Senate chamber. Attacking a man in his absence was unfair and thus frowned upon; it was "not in accordance with what a gentleman should do," one victim argued.[110] By leaving the room, Benton was trying to cut Foote off.[111] But Foote continued his "personalities" long after Benton had gone.[112]

On other occasions, Benton defended himself with a "personal explanation." According to custom, an embattled congressman had the right to demand a few minutes to "defend himself as a man of honor" before colleagues, the press, and the nation.[113] Unless there was an objection—which almost never happened—people who requested personal explanations were immediately given the floor, overriding all formal rules of order, and they couldn't be interrupted.[114] These explanations weren't without their difficulties; as one Speaker complained, when the rules were suspended, it was near impossible to determine "what language is strictly in order," and indeed, Benton's explanations were sometimes filled with threats and personalities.[115] But given their national audience, congressmen wanted a fair chance to defend their name.

Most explanations were sparked by newspaper accounts of congressional debates. Newspapers assailed congressmen beyond their reach; personal explanations were safe havens for fighting back. And fight back Benton did. The day after Foote taunted him on March 26, he declared the *National Intelligencer*'s version of Foote's remarks "a lying account from the beginning to the end." According to the *Intelligencer*, Foote had accused Benton of talking big because he couldn't be attacked: he was "shielded by his age, his open disavowal of the obligatory force of the laws of honor, and his senatorial privileges." Foote was calling him a coward. Foote had said no such thing, Benton roared—plus, it was a lie. He wasn't too old to fight; insult him off the floor and you would know his age "without consulting the calendar." He decided honor disputes on a case-by-case basis. And he never hid behind his privileges. If the Senate allowed these kinds of insults to continue, he concluded, "I mean from this time forth to protect myself—cost what it may."

That statement would come back to haunt him. Hearing it, many onlookers—including Foote—thought that Benton was giving Foote fair warning of a pending street fight. It followed the conventional format exactly and was a favorite ploy of non-duelists who wanted to defend their name. In place of a duel, they typically declared that they would defend themselves "wherever assailed."[116] Once fair warning had been given, both parties would arm themselves with weapons and friends, and watch for a chance encounter on the street, which usually involved "pushing, scuffling, pointing of pistols, calling of names, and great disturbance of peaceable bystanders."[117]

These "irregular" or "informal meetings" were substitute duels. Understood to be "the usual last resort of the non-duellist," they became increasingly common in the 1850s with the rise of Northern resistance to Southern threats.[118] Onlookers expected one after the Meade (D-VA) versus Duer (W-NY) outburst that started the session, given the involvement of a feisty Northerner.[119] Street fights were a sectional compromise that enabled non-duelists to defend their name on equal terms. They made fighting fair.

Thus Foote's assumptions about Benton's declared willingness to defend himself, come what may. Foote "expected to be attacked on his way going to or returning from the Senate, and about the capitol buildings," he told one friend.[120] Benton was "a man of courage," warned another. "[H]e would do whatever he said he would, and . . . Mr. Foote ought to be prepared to defend himself."[121] A fellow senator later chided Foote and Benton for *not* fighting on the street. "There is plenty of room out of the Senate," he scolded. "[T]he streets are large, the grounds are spacious; and it is said there are good battlegrounds, if gentlemen choose to occupy them."[122]

So Foote donned a pistol, watched, and waited. Several times, he asked friends if he should challenge Benton to a duel. Did public opinion seem to demand it? Foote, for one, preferred it. Given that "this matter was destined to terminate in a difficulty," he preferred to settle it honorably in a duel than to grapple on the street, where Foote was bound to lose, though given Foote's track record, a duel wasn't likely to go better.[123] But Benton never attacked. Even when the two brushed past each other on Pennsylvania Avenue, nothing happened. Foote could only conclude that Benton was "a recreant coward."[124]

It was Foote's renewed and reinforced charge of cowardice that pushed things too far on April 17, the day Benton snapped. A few days after passing Benton in the street, Foote threw the charge at Benton, but had gotten only halfway through the insult when Benton sprang to his feet, kicking aside his chair so violently that he toppled a glass from his desk. (Reporters in the galleries described the "breaking of glass, a movement among the desks, a rising among the crowd in the galleries," and "a sort of crashing in the neighborhood of Benton's seat.")[125] On seeing Benton head his way "with an expression of countenance which indicated a resolve for no good purpose," Foote retreated backward down the aisle toward the vice president's chair, pistol in hand. In a moment "almost every Senator was on his feet, and calls to 'order'; demands for the Sergeant-at-Arms; requests that Senators would take their seats, from the Chair and from individual Senators, were repeatedly made."[126]

Henry Dodge (D-WI) tried to restrain Benton, who dramatically bared his breast and yelled, "'I have no pistols!' 'Let him fire!' 'I disdain to carry arms!' 'Stand out of the way, and let the assassin fire!'"[127] Witnesses saw him open his jacket and bare his breast as he bellowed. At this point, a senator grabbed Foote's pistol and locked it in his desk, and for the moment the fireworks were over.

But the controversy wasn't. Foote and Benton immediately began to argue about motives and intentions. Foote insisted that he had acted

An 1850 cartoon depicting the Benton-Foote scuffle. Benton is throwing open his coat and bellowing, "Let the assassin fire!" as people in the galleries flee in panic. (*Scene in Uncle Sam's Senate, 17th April 1850*, by Edward W. Clay, 1850. Courtesy of the Library of Congress)

in self-defense. Benton insisted that Foote was an assassin inventing excuses—a serious charge because it suggested that Foote had taken "unmanly" advantage; by pointing a pistol at an unarmed man, he wasn't fighting fair.[128] Benton had opened his jacket to prove that he had no gun for just this reason.[129] Foote's howling objections to the charge suggest its seriousness.

To prevent such unfair matches, when two men seemed likely to fight, brother congressmen usually did an instinctive weapon check, eyeing jackets and vest coat pockets for the bulge of a gun or a flash of metal. If one man was unarmed, people typically intervened. When no one was armed, the fighters often were left to their own devices; it seemed only fair. In 1858, this scenario played out in the House when Augustus Wright (D-GA) noticed a fist-clenched stranger standing in front of Francis Burton Craige (D-NC); convinced that Craige was the stronger man, Wright went back to work—which speaks volumes about the level of violence that seemed normal on the floor. But when Wright spotted a weapon under the stranger's coat, he leaped to his feet to prevent an "assassination." Even then, he held back as the two men wrestled, ready to intervene if the stranger reached for his weapon. (And he had two: a knife and a revolver.)[130]

The confrontation between Foote and Benton was similarly unbalanced, but it fell to an investigative committee to determine the details and pass judgment. In the meantime, the Senate got back to business. And much as people had flocked to Washington in March to see a whole-House rumble, they filled the galleries the day after the Foote-Benton fracas to see what came next. As the *Boston Courier* reported, the galleries were jammed full of people expecting something "in the shape of a grand finale." When business got under way and Foote rose to complete the speech that Benton had "so unceremoniously cut short," the room hushed and the audience leaned forward. Benton sat nearby, nervously twirling a piece of paper. Would there be "another rush, another melée, another scamper, and another pistol drawn?" The entire chamber was "in an agony of suspense." But Foote merely surrendered the floor and sat down, at which Benton took an audibly deep breath. Later that day, he sarcastically noted how "harmonious" the Senate seemed.[131] With disharmony relegated to an investigative committee, the Senate was moving on.

"PUBLIC EXPLANATION IS NECESSARY"

As dramatic as the events of April 17 had been, in the end not much happened. The investigative committee did little more than condemn "personalities" and the wearing of arms in the halls of Congress, advising the Senate to take no action, which is precisely what the Senate did.[132] Given this nonresponse, it's tempting to dismiss the episode as political theater. But in his testimony, Foote noted that he had planned a path of retreat from Benton that put fewer senators in the path of his gun if he fired it. And many people assumed that Benton would have mauled Foote had he gotten hold of him.[133] To the fighters and their audiences alike, the chance of bloodshed was very real.[134]

And the nation was watching. With the rise of the telegraph, the American public was witnessing congressional scuffles with ever-increasing speed and efficiency. "Washington is as near to us now as our up-town wards," gushed the *New York Express* in 1846. "We can almost hear through the Telegraph, members of Congress as they speak."[135] Beginning with a small-scale experiment in Washington in 1844, the telegraph was spreading throughout the country, drastically reducing the news lag around the nation, and congressmen had to grapple with the impact.[136] Not only did they have less time and power to tame their words, but it was difficult if not impossible to speak to different audiences with different voices. When the abolitionists Benjamin Wade (W-OH) and Charles Sumner (FS-MA) denounced the Slave Power while in their home states, Clement Clay (D-AL) took offense in Washington: How could these men "who profess to abhor and contemn us" up north "make the acquaintance of slaveholders, salute them as equals," and "cordially grasp their hands as friends" in Washington?[137] By networking the nation during a rising sectional crisis, the telegraph complicated national politics.

Ever and always at the crossroads of history, French played a role in this dramatic transformation; from 1847 to 1850 he was president of the Magnetic Telegraph Company, an enterprise that he discovered through his friend F.O.J. Smith (his son Frank's namesake), one of three men that Samuel Morse chose to promote telegraphy at the dawning of the enterprise.[138] The company had incorporated to create a telegraph line from Washington to New York, accomplishing the task in June 1846. The job not only sent French traveling about on telegraph business, occasionally putting him out in the field stringing wires, but it also made him something of an innovator in the use of telegraphy in politics. The presidential election of 1848 was the first election in which all states voted on the same day, and thus the first election in which the telegraph gathered returns. In preparation for it, French kept the telegraph offices in Washington, Baltimore, Philadelphia, and Jersey City open all night from November 7 through November 10, paying workers overtime and urging them to "avoid any partiality . . . during the excitement" so that biased reporting wouldn't sway the results—a new fear for a new age.[139] Six months earlier, he had paid for the telegraphic transmission of the Democratic Convention out of his own pocket.[140] (French also may have been a telegraph pioneer outside of politics; according to one source, the first poem to be telegraphed was written by B. B. French.)[141]

After reading his first telegraph transmission in 1843, French had immediately grasped its political impact: whatever happened in "the *heart* here in Washington, will be instantly known to all the extremities of this widespread Union!"[142] In the aftermath of the Foote-

Benton clash, this realization caused a shock of recognition. Minutes after people settled back into their seats, Henry Clay—ever the great compromiser—followed the lead of Jefferson's *Parliamentary Manual* and asked both men to "pledge themselves, in their places, to the Senate, that they will not proceed further in this matter," meaning they would promise not to duel. Both men refused, Benton declaring that he would rather "rot in jail" than pledge to anything that implied his guilt, and Foote insisting that he had done nothing wrong and would take "no further remedy," though as a "man of honor" he would do whatever he was "invited" to do, meaning that if Benton challenged him to a duel, he would accept. Sensing a stalemate and hoping for better luck out of the public eye, Willie Mangum (W-NC) suggested closing the Senate doors.

"I trust not," Foote blurted, as senators echoed, "oh, no." "I hope my friend will not insist upon it, when public explanation is necessary on my part." Hale agreed, noting that due to the telegraph's "lightning speed," by sundown in St. Louis, it would be rumored "that there has been a fight on the floor of the American Senate, and several Senators have been shot and are weltering in their gore." The image brought a laugh, but Hale had a point. A formal investigation was essential, not just for "vindicating the character of the Senate, but to set history right, and inform the public as to what *did* take place." If the Senate didn't take immediate action, public opinion would run wild. (The challenges of viral news coverage have long roots.)

Indeed, even with immediate action, news of the encounter spread with lightning speed. The next day, headlines were screaming in Boston and New York, and within forty-eight hours the *Milwaukee Sentinel and Gazette* announced: "By Telegraph. A ROW IN THE SENATE! COLLISION BETWEEN FOOTE AND BENTON! PISTOL DRAWN!" Just as Hale predicted, the facts got scrambled. Even before April 17, news had spread nationwide that Foote was going to challenge Benton to a duel; one newspaper even reported Benton's death at Foote's hand (though the report came from an April Fools' Day telegraph transmission). Here was the answer to the question asked by countless congressmen. Why bother with the tedium of an investigation if no action was ever taken? Because it would set the record straight and suggest to the public that Congress had taken matters in hand. It would preserve the image—and ideally, the reality—of Congress as the headquarters of national compromise.

The public *was* watching. Indeed, the dispute was partly caused by the public eye. It was the publicity of Foote's insults that most riled Benton. From the start of the session, Foote's ongoing onslaught had received ample press coverage, and Benton was up for reelection. During the investigation, he questioned committee witnesses on this very point: Had they heard Foote say anything about drumming him out of the Democratic Party? Did Foote have correspondents in Missouri? Was he involved in a recent attack on Benton in the *Missouri Statesman*? More than fifty pages of the report center on newspaper accounts of the two men's exchanges. Benton and Foote were fighting for public opinion.

The two men were equally obsessed with the written coverage of Foote's insults. Foote had tampered with the press coverage of their confrontations to make himself look good, Benton told the committee, and it was bad form to privately edit the record of a personal insult after the fact. Far fairer to correct newspaper accounts of fights and insults in person in the Senate before the people who had heard them spoken and could distinguish right from wrong. To Benton, this was "the only way that honor can ever do. . . . A public correction of public personalities is the only thing that can be endured in a land of civilization."[143]

Seconds later, Foote admitted that he had indeed tampered with the press coverage of his insults, but for good reason: he spoke quickly and was hard to hear. But he had made his edits "hurriedly" in his seat and hadn't changed his meaning. If anything, he had softened his insults, he claimed. On the floor, he had attacked Benton for his cowardice in his 1848 honor dispute with Andrew Butler, now amicably settled. But because a senator sitting nearby murmured to Foote that mentioning a settled honor dispute was an "indiscretion," Foote removed all mention of it from a reporter's notes—though he'd be happy to restore it, he sneered.[144]

The tables were turned when Foote read the *National Intelligencer's* account of the scuffle. In a statement published in the paper and reprinted around the country, he protested that he hadn't "retreated" from Benton, as the *Intelligencer* reported. He had "glided" into a "defensive attitude."[145] This wasn't mere silliness on Foote's part, as silly as it was. Two senators had told him that he shouldn't have run from Benton:

Andrew Butler had blurted it out as Foote dashed past, and Willard Hall (D-MO) thought that Foote's "enemies might say that he was actuated by fear."[146] Foote didn't want to look like a coward in the public eye.

Both men were grappling with the challenges of national press coverage in the age of the telegraph. Reporters saw things differently and reported different things for different reasons, news spread with its own speed and logic, facts got scrambled with no time for correction, the public drew its own conclusions, and congressmen didn't control this process, try as they might. Both Foote and Benton tried to shape their spin, but neither emerged from the episode unscathed.[147]

Many newspapers berated one or the other combatant with regional flair. Southern writers focused on the code of honor. Benton hadn't fought fair, one paper argued. "This swearing one's life against a man . . . so feeble in health as Gen. Foote" was not "entirely *comme il faut*."[148] As the "assailed party" (an arguable point), Foote had done right, claimed another. Under the code of honor, Foote had the choice of weapons, and a pistol was the most "Patrician" choice.[149] Northern newspapers focused on parliamentary rules, denouncing Southern violence and insisting that someone should have called Foote to order. Reporting for the *New-York Tribune*, the antislavery advocate Jane Swisshelm—the first woman admitted to the reporters gallery (on the very day of the scuffle)—approved of Benton's politics but regretted that he had "meditated any personal chastisement," the product, she assumed, of a Southern education.[150] The Foote-friendly *Richmond Enquirer* countered by playing the gender card, denouncing Swisshelm as "a disgrace to her sex" who was ill equipped to judge "a champion of the South."[151]

Some newspapers condemned both men as well as Congress. A Pennsylvania paper took the long view, declaring the incident "a disgrace to the Nineteenth Century."[152] A Vermont paper waxed histrionic: "O Senators and Pistols! O Gunpowder and dignity! O Law-makers and bullets! Shame, shame!"[153] The real villains were "Senatorial bullies," charged a New Jersey paper: "instead of minding the business of their constituents, they—these grave Senators—only think of it!—are daring one another, almost daily, like schoolboys, to knock chips off their hats."[154] The solution was simple, claimed the *Boston Herald*: "If one-half of our Congressmen would kill the other half, and then commit suicide themselves, we think the country would gain by the operation."[155]

Fighting was deplorable and something should be done: it was a lamentation speech writ large. But just as such hand-wringing accomplished little, its press equivalent rang hollow. Even as the press condemned congressional fisticuffs, it cheered and booed combatants with full force. National compromises were being forged by congressional gladiators egged on by a national audience, North, South, and West, and the nation's ongoing slavery debate gave them plenty to fight about. Fence straddlers on the issue of slavery would find it increasingly hard to find electoral traction. Benton suffered this fate. With his mixed views on slavery, he lost reelection to the Senate in 1851, a stunning defeat after thirty years of service. There were bad times ahead.

For the moment, however, there was peace. Four months after the Foote-Benton scuffle, the Senate passed a series of bills that the House passed one month later. California was admitted as a free state; popular sovereignty would decide the fate of slavery in New Mexico and the Utah Territory; slavery was preserved in the national capital, though the slave trade was banned; a stronger Fugitive Slave Act would require all U.S. citizens to assist in the capture and return of runaway slaves; and Texas gave up some of its western land and received compensation.

Compromise and community had prevailed in Washington—a fact worth celebrating—and on the evening of Saturday, September 7, with California newly granted statehood, celebrate Washington did. Fireworks boomed. There was a hundred-gun salute. The Marine Band marched down Pennsylvania Avenue playing "The Star-Spangled Banner" and "Yankee Doodle." Crowds went from boardinghouse to boardinghouse applauding congressmen, who were all too happy to speechify in response. According to one onlooker, it was "a night on which it was the duty of every patriot to get drunk," and congressmen did their duty. (The next day, a badly hungover Henry Foote blamed his stomach trouble on "bad fruit.") Dr. Jonathan Foltz, an attending physician to presidents and duelists (he was present at the Cilley-Graves duel), noted that he had "never before known so much excitement upon the passage of any law."[156] Congress was receiving an all-too-rare standing ovation, evidence of how dire the crisis had seemed.

But as much as the Compromise soothed a sectional crisis, it had a mixed impact on sectional sensibilities. The sustained Southern bullying campaign had schooled Northern onlookers in the gut realities of

Slave Power dictation. Proudly proclaimed a policy and expanded to include the institution of Congress and the Union, Southern ultimatums and threats drove home the power and humiliation of Southern bullying. Just as French hoped, Northerners were seeing Congress's skewed dynamics for themselves—not for the first time, but with a new power. They emerged from the crisis of 1850 with a keener sense of their rights and a sharper understanding of the power of Southern threats.

They also gained powerful models of resistance. The many men who vocally defended Northern rights on the floor taught home audiences what Northern resistance felt like. A letter to John Parker Hale in April 1850 shows the personal impact of this sectional combat on a home audience; the writer praised Hale for standing up to the Slave Power but worried about "the degradation of the North," which would inspire feelings of "self degradation." For constituents as well as congressmen, the link between sectional honor and personal honor was profound, and congressmen were an all-important link between the two in North and South alike.[157]

Thus the paradoxical outcome of the 1850 Compromise crisis. On the one hand, Americans gained a deeper appreciation of the Union and its fragility—an appreciation born of that fragility. On the other hand, they gained deeper convictions and stronger feelings about the very things that were threatening that fragile Union: slavery, sectional rights, and fear of sectional degradation.

It was both the nation's and Franklin Pierce's bad fortune for him to become president in 1853 at this time of tensions and paradoxes. A man with a foot in both sectional camps, a Northerner who catered to Southern interests for the sake of the Union and his party, Pierce was the ultimate compromise candidate, a logical choice at a time of crisis-born compromises. But his concessions would prove deadly. In 1854, when the slavery status of the Kansas and Nebraska territories came up for debate, Pierce's South-centric statecraft would rekindle the crisis of 1850 and magnify it tenfold, launching a national crisis that would catch French in the cross-fire.

As Pierce's longtime friend and supporter, French gave the Pierce campaign his all, though it wasn't easy. It was hard to wage a national campaign at a time of sectional strife, and as a disillusioned Democrat, French faced personal challenges in waving the party flag. But he so deeply believed in Pierce as the man of the hour, so firmly believed that Democratic policies could save the Union, and was so good at the letter-writing, backslapping, hand-shaking, and songwriting that went into successful campaigning, that he devoted himself to the cause. In a sense, French had been training for the Pierce campaign for decades.

Perhaps Pierce could bind North and South. Perhaps he could steer the ship of state through the slavery crisis. Perhaps he would reward French with a plum job; the spoils of victory could be sweet, and French was struggling to get by. (He was voted out of the presidency of the Magnetic Telegraph Company in 1850.)[158] French hoped for all of these things. But in the end, he was disappointed. He didn't get the reward that he was yearning for: the well-paid position of marshal of the District of Columbia. He rarely even managed to get Pierce's ear, though he dreamed about it—literally; in December 1852, worried that Pierce didn't "see how the wires are pulled" in Washington, French dreamed that he and Pierce went into a stable loft and "sat down on the hay & talked over things."[159]

Ultimately, Pierce's disastrous slavery policies proved disastrous for his friendship with French. By the end of 1855, French's thirty-year friendship with Pierce had fallen victim to the slavery crisis, and French was on his way out of the Democratic Party.

6

A TALE OF
TWO CONSPIRACIES

THE POWER OF THE PRESS AND
THE BATTLE OVER KANSAS (1854–55)

F ranklin Pierce's presidency was ravaged by ill omens, but none more tragic than the death of his only child in a train accident on January 6, 1853, as the president-elect and his family traveled home to Concord after the holidays. Not more than an hour into their trip, a broken axle sent their train car tumbling down an embankment; eleven-year-old Benjamin Pierce was the only immediate fatality.[1] Franklin and Jane Pierce entered the White House in a state of collapse. When Pierce was inaugurated on March 4, there were few festivities; what little ceremony there was Pierce performed "like a man," French thought. The soft-hearted French had been stricken at hearing of Bennie's death. Months later, he still came close to crying when he glimpsed the boy's portrait—"that mild, innocent countenance"—in the White House.[2] French's "AFFECtionate Sone" Ben, as Ben described himself, was seven years old at the time.[3]

As a grieving father, Pierce took office with widespread public sympathy, something of a blessing after a trying contest. Whig campaign fodder had seized on Pierce's obscurity, asking incessantly: Who is Franklin Pierce? They gleefully pointed out that even the Democratic press didn't know who he was; at least one Democratic paper hailed their new candidate as General John A. Pierce, while others showered him with an array of middle initials, though he had no middle name.[4] In response to Pierce's declaration that he knew "no East, no West, no

Franklin Pierce during his
presidential campaign in
1852. One-of-a-kind images
produced without a negative,
daguerreotypes had limited
circulation, but reached a
broad public when reproduced
as engravings. (By Albert S.
Southworth and Josiah J. Hawes.
Courtesy of the National Portrait
Gallery, Smithsonian Institution)

North, no South," the Whig press shot back: "Neither does the East,
West, North or South know Gen. Pierce. The coincidence is truly remarkable!"[5] Pierce's drinking problem also came under attack, as did
his war record, which paled in comparison with the Whig candidate
General Winfield Scott's decades of military service going back as far
as the War of 1812. The Whig press branded Pierce the "hero of many
a well fought Bottle," published a miniature "book" titled *The Military
Service of General Pierce*, and smirked at how he fainted on the battlefield (twice) during the Mexican War, in one case because of a "sense-
taking" groin injury.[6]

But the campaign wasn't purely personal. Whig and Democratic
newspapers harped on each candidate's loyalty to the Compromise of
1850. "Finality" on the issue of slavery was a buzzword of the campaign,
and Pierce had no problem committing to it. His sweeping endorsement
of the Fugitive Slave Act made that fact clear. In a public-minded letter
sent to a friend at the Democratic Convention, Pierce said that the

Union's survival depended on Northern willingness to avoid antagoniz-
ing the South with "unnecessarily offensive" resolutions. He himself
would "never yield to a craven spirit, that from consideration of policy
would endanger the Union."[7] Pierce's use of the word *craven* shows how
complex doughface politicking continued to be. He was declaring himself too brave to back down on supporting the South—the very stance
that many damned as doughface cowardice. His Whig opponent Winfield Scott was more ambivalent on the Compromise, as was his party,
giving Democrats an electoral bludgeon that they used to full effect.

Pierce's South-friendly politics proved particularly problematic for
Southern Whigs and Northern Democrats, who rose to the challenge
with claims that sailed past the bounds of the believable with nary a
look back. While Northern Whigs denounced Pierce as a slave to the
Slave Power, Southern Whigs tarred him as a closet abolitionist who
had denounced the Fugitive Slave Act in a speech in New Hampshire.
("More Yankee Tricks!," screamed the *Richmond Whig*, accusing Pierce
of revealing his abolitionism only in New Hampshire, far removed from
Southern ears.)[8] Northern Democrats took that abolitionist charge and
ran with it, praising Pierce as a comrade in arms with John Quincy Adams in the war against gag rules.[9] Southern Democrats, in turn, cited
Northern Whig anti-Pierce screeds as proof that he was true to the
South. In essence, Northern and Southern allies waged conflicting campaigns, banking on the limited reach of some local papers and the likelihood that the public wouldn't know lie from truth.[10] Neither party had
a single Frank Pierce running for president; they had Northern and
Southern Pierces of opposing politics, an accurate reflection of the state
of the nation and a clear indication of trouble to come.

The Washington *Union* walked a very thin line as the party standard-
bearer, promoting Pierce as "The Man for the Times"—a man for all
sections—singing his praises with vague generalities and countering
Whig accusations.[11] French did a good deal of singing and countering.
Indeed, French played a key role throughout the campaign, even helping to secure Pierce's nomination. As he explained in his diary, his
"whole soul was in the matter."[12] As early as March 1852 he began to
drop Pierce's name into any and every conversation on the coming election, even obtaining from Pierce a vague letter of interest to show around.
As an honorary delegate to the Democratic National Convention, and

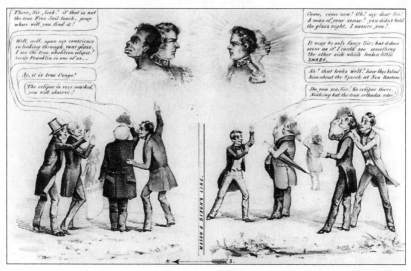

A cartoon from Pierce's presidential run mocking his proslavery *and* antislavery reputation. To the left, pleased abolitionists and Free Soilers see a black man eclipsing Pierce. To the right, equally pleased Southerners see Pierce eclipsing a black man. (*Eclipse & no eclipse or two views of one object* by J. Childs. Courtesy of the Library of Congress)

more important, as its reading secretary—where his famously strong lungs did good work—French lobbied delegates from every state in the Union, even boarding at a hotel that housed key delegates rather than with the New Hampshire delegation. Ultimately, he helped to persuade men from ten state delegations to support Pierce as a last resort.

French's last victory on that count was a vital one. In a remarkable twist of fate, he got Henry Wise, Pierce's former drinking buddy, to commit the Virginia delegation. As mercurial in his politics as in his temperament, Wise had started his career as a Democrat, bucked his party and become a Whig in Congress, and now had returned to the states' rights Democratic fold with the rise of the slavery crisis. To get Wise's support, French had to confront the event that had kept Wise and Pierce at odds for fourteen years: the death of Jonathan Cilley. Pierce hadn't exchanged a friendly word with Wise since 1838, refusing even to shake his hand. Did Wise bear a grudge? French asked. Wise didn't; he understood Pierce's feelings on losing his friend.[13]

In the final push, Virginia led the way to Pierce's nomination. "I do as sincerely believe that I brought about that nomination as I believe

I am alive!" French crowed.[14] Wise gave French due credit in a letter to Pierce, adding that it was "singular" that in 1844 Wise had promoted another man for president who had previously given him the cold shoulder—James K. Polk. (Wise also told Pierce that in response to questions about Pierce's drinking problem, he had regaled delegates with the story of their drunken romp in 1836, declaring it the one and only time that he had seen Pierce drunk. A few months later, while stump-speaking for Pierce, Wise got involved in a scuffle on the podium.[15] Having Wise on your side was a mixed blessing.)

With the nomination in hand, French gave his all to the campaign, even hanging a picture of Pierce next to one of George Washington— "the *first and last Presidents!*"—in his home.[16] As he put it, "I have rode and I have run,—I have written and I have spoken—I have recd. and disbursed lots of cash—I have poured out my own money whenever it has been necessary—in fact I have done all that might become a man, and *some things* that possibly may only become *a partizan.*"[17] Indeed, French wore many hats during the campaign. He was treasurer of the National Democratic Committee, responsible for collecting and dispensing vast sums of money from all over the Union. As chairman of the Executive Committee of Washington's Jackson Democratic Association, he tried to get Democratic associations from around the country to correspond with him in the hope of promoting "mutual action."[18] By his own account, he wrote almost every day for the Washington *Union* as well as its short-term spin-off, *The Campaign*. And because he was known to be Pierce's close friend, he fielded hundreds of queries about the candidate, assuring all that "Pierce is a sure card."[19] The work was never-ending, persisting even beyond Pierce's election when French was bombarded with hundreds of requests for jobs in the Pierce administration. "I am annoyed, bothered, vexed, amused & troubled with the drift-wood of party, which has been set afloat toward Washington, by the rising of the democratic tide," he griped to his half brother Henry after Pierce's inauguration. "[E]very man who ever threw up his beaver [hat] & whoora'd for Frank Pierce" expects to be led on to fortune.[20]

As a core newspaper flack for Pierce's campaign, French had his work cut out for him. The very thing that made Pierce a perfect compromise candidate—his virtually nonexistent public image—made promoting him a challenge. Even the *Union* seemed to damn Pierce with

faint praise. An early campaign biography for the paper, probably written by French, lauds Pierce as a quiet but hardworking congressman
who was well liked for his good sense, good manners, and good temper,
though French cannily added that Pierce had an insider's knowledge of
the fine art of doling out patronage, thereby inviting the hundreds of
letters that would plague him in months to come.[21] A second article
went so far as to praise Pierce's mediocrity, arguing that the "idea that
the presidency is a reward due for eminent or brilliant services in the
council or in the field" was dangerous in a democracy, a backhanded
slap that the Whig press was quick to point out.[22] Pierce's longtime
friend Nathaniel Hawthorne, his official campaign biographer, didn't
relish his job. "It was a hard book to write," Hawthorne admitted, "for
the gist of the matter lay in explaining how it has happened that, with
such extraordinary opportunities for eminent distinction, civil and military, as he has enjoyed, this crisis should have found him so obscure as
he certainly was, in a national point of view. My heart absolutely sank, at
the dearth of available material." To Hawthorne, only a "romancer" could
have managed it.[23] The book ultimately cost him scores of Northern
friends because it defended Pierce's doughface views on slavery.[24]

In the end, Pierce won by a landslide in the Electoral College, but
with a close popular vote, a telling sign of the unsettled state of public
opinion.[25] In free states, 14,000 more votes were cast against Pierce than
for him.[26] The Democracy was losing power in the North. Even so, with
a South-friendly Northerner elected president, national affairs settled
down.

The respite was short-lived. In 1854, the territorial organization of
Kansas and Nebraska unleashed the sectional maelstrom once again.
Senator Stephen Douglas's (D-IL) proposal to allow the two future states
to determine their own slavery status based on popular sovereignty
opened the floodgates of a full-fledged sectional crisis; in effect, Douglas proposed to repeal the Missouri Compromise of 1820, the agree-
ment that had long tamed (though certainly not solved) the slavery
problem by drawing a line across the continent, dividing states into slave
and free. By 1854, the Compromise had achieved the status of a sacred
pact; its proposed repeal suggested that no pact between North and
South, however sacred, could be trusted.[27] This erosion of faith in cross-
sectional bonds would subsume national politics in years to come.

Douglas's proposal stunned many Northerners, including French. Why repeal the Missouri Compromise? And why now? French considered the so-called Nebraska bill both dangerous and unnecessary, a "firebrand that would set the whole Union on fire."[28] In addition, he felt sure that the bill would ravage the ranks of the Democracy by alienating Northerners; Pierce might control Congress, but he couldn't control "the *people* of the Free states."[29] French predicted that "not a single northern man, from President Pierce down to the most insignificant politician who goes for it, will be sustained by the people of the free states!"[30] It was an exaggeration but not by much. In the midterm election, Democrats lost seventy-five seats in the House and only seven of the forty-four Northern Democrats who voted for the bill were reelected; two years later, Pierce wasn't renominated for the presidency.[31]

Outrage at the bill's implications was amply apparent in Congress. With a precedent-setting crisis at hand that could tip the balance of power in the Union, and the South-leaning Democratic majority likely to pass the bill, "anti-Nebraska" Northerners took a strong stand. In 1850, Northerners had defied Southern bullying with a new power. Four years later, they went further, declaring themselves willing to fight.[32]

The press North, South, and West echoed this dynamic, framing the debate as a do-or-die battle against proslavery or antislavery plots to steal the soul of the Union.[33] Anti-Nebraska papers played up Southern bullying, portraying Senator Stephen Douglas as a blustering Slave Power tool who bullied only non-combatants, and damning Pierce as both an iron-fisted Democratic tyrant and a pliant tool of the South. Pierce and Douglas were orchestrating an underhanded plan to spread slavery throughout the Union, these papers argued; the Fugitive Slave Act proved such intentions all too well. "Nebraskite" newspapers returned the favor, denouncing the unruly tactics of anti-Nebraskans who seemed willing to do anything to destroy slavery and the South, and praising the noble Northern Democrats who supported the bill.[34]

The echoes of 1850 were undeniable, but the thrust of the press coverage was far more focused on weaving tales of organized underhanded sectional conspiracies.[35] Framed in this light, congressional violence became more than a parliamentary ploy. It was smoking-gun evidence of a sectional plot in progress: proof of the controlling hand of Pierce, Douglas, and the domineering Slave Power, or proof of how far fanatical antislavery Northerners were willing to go. With the American press fanning the flames of sectionalism, the Kansas-Nebraska crisis moved congressional violence to center stage.[36]

Of course, the American press had a long history of dire predictions about slavery and sectionalism. But by the 1850s, its reach had grown dramatically and news traveled faster than ever before.[37] Steam-powered and then rotary printing presses, railroads, the telegraph, and innovations in paper-making spread news nationally with alarming speed—alarming, that is, for congressmen who were accustomed to shaping their own press narratives. Those same technologies brought more out-of-town reporters to Washington who could say what they liked because they owed nothing to congressmen. Profit-driven New York City newspapers gained nation-shaking influence in this period, displacing Washington's long-standing party organs as major sources of congressional news coverage; New York City editors became power brokers who could make or break congressional careers.

During the sectional crises of the 1850s, the repercussions of this more independent press were severe. By framing those crises for maximum impact, newspapers created an endless loop of sectional strife: congressmen issued rallying cries to their constituents from the floor; the press played up the implications; and the public urged their congressmen to fight for their rights with letters, petitions, and demonstrations as well as with their votes. These extreme emotions were spread throughout the Union with ever-increasing speed and efficiency.[38] Just as the nation's slavery problem intensified because of western expansion, dangerous words and violent actions in the halls of Congress gained greater reach and influence, stoking sectional passions in the process.

The product of this cycle of stridency was pronounced. By portraying Congress as an institution of extremes—extreme rhetoric, extreme policies, extreme belligerence; a den of braggarts and brawlers; a place of sectional conflict waged by sectional champions—the press downplayed the appeal and even the possibility of compromise. Caught in the cross-fire with urgent decisions at hand, congressmen sided with their section more consistently and defiantly than ever before.

The lingering tug of eroding party loyalties only made matters worse, intensifying the pressures of the floor. There were no clean divides between Whig and Democrat, North and South; the crisis advanced man by man, choice by choice. In more ways than one, the halls of Congress became a theater of conflict. The deaths of Daniel Webster and Henry Clay in 1852 seemed to confirm the passing of the spirit of compromise as well as the passing of a generation. Violated pacts and talk of sectional plots pushed cross-sectional trust to an all-time low; as portrayed in the press, neither North nor South was fighting a fair fight.

With newspapers connecting the dots, displaying and deploring congressional threats and violence with full-throated zeal, public opinion of Congress began a downward spiral of doubt that would continue for some time to come.[39] National institutions of all kinds were under fire at precisely the moment when their influence most mattered. Ironically, the workings of a free press enforcing congressional accountability—the very touchstone of democracy—were helping to tear the nation apart. Democracy is an ongoing conversation between the governed and their governors; it should come as no surprise that dramatic changes in the modes of conversation cause dramatic changes in democracies themselves.

The Democracy was hit hard by these changes; doughfaces abandoned the party by the score. French's journey was typical of many; congressional insider and inveterate newsman that he was, even he wasn't immune to the furies of the press and the evolving narrative of sectional warfare. Although in 1852 French promoted Franklin Pierce as a man for all sections, less than three years later he was damning Pierce as a tool of the slavocrats, and damning the slavocrats for their nefarious plot. Somewhat fittingly for a man who devoted so much time to priming the press, newspapers ultimately pushed French to cross the fateful line from defending the Union at any cost to defending the Union as he thought it should be.

A CONGRESS THAT NEVER WAS

In a sense, as a Pierce promoter in the 1852 election, French was as skilled a "romancer" as Hawthorne. Winning a presidential campaign demanded no less, particularly amid rampant sectional distrust. This isn't to say that French openly lied; as he put it, he tried "to keep on the *hither* side of truth." But he didn't tell all that he knew about Pierce, noting that it was better "when the sun is too hot, to travel where it's a *little shady*."[40]

The "hither side of truth" is a good way to describe congressional press coverage during much of the first half of the nineteenth century. As interested as the public was in congressional doings—and judging by the number of column inches devoted to Congress, the public *was* interested—it was difficult, if not impossible, for readers to get an accurate account of what happened on the floor.[41]

This wasn't for lack of coverage. A single issue of a typical newspaper—usually four pages of close type—might contain a lengthy summary of debates in both houses, several articles on congressional politics, and a spicy account of congressional rumors and rumblings framed as a letter to the editor from a reporter on location. Congressmen also published the occasional letter defending themselves or attacking a foe.[42] In addition, they printed and mailed copies of their speeches by the thousands, sometimes by the tens of thousands. There were many avenues of access to Congress.

For a time, congressional press coverage was a largely local enterprise, with two Washington newspapers offering abstracts of debates. The *National Intelligencer* covered Congress beginning in 1800, when the nation's capital moved to Washington; from 1824 to 1837, the editors Joseph Gales, Jr., and William Seaton also published an annual record of congressional coverage called the *Register of Debates*. The daily *Globe* arrived in 1821, founded by the editors Francis Preston Blair and John Cook Rives; beginning in 1833, they also published a weekly record of debate titled—appropriately enough—the *Congressional Globe*, though most people simply called it the *Globe*.[43] Although not official government records, these publications were the period's equivalent of the *Congressional Record*. Reprinted in newspapers around the country, they were also the nation's main access to Congress.[44]

Yet they were hardly objective. For one thing, as party organs, they were unquestionably partisan. The *Intelligencer* began as a Jeffersonian Republican paper and later became Whiggish. The *Globe* was Democratic. Bound to politicians through ties of patronage and woven into the workings of government (congressional printers were sworn officers), the *Globe* and the *Intelligencer* worked for the company in a company town. Not surprisingly, both papers routinely played up friends and played down foes, whose howling protests appeared on their pages, though to preserve their reputations as "journal-like" public records, they couldn't stray *too* far from center. Thus French's liking for the Whig

Intelligencer, which he read first thing every morning. As much as he disliked its politics, he considered it "the Chief Justice Marshall of newspapers"—simple, dignified, and straightforward. The *Globe* had too much "stilted dignity" for his taste.[45]

Both papers also were selective in their coverage. "Leading" speeches were included; lesser attempts were not. Abstracts of debate were exceedingly patchy; the *Globe* promised only "sketches." Legislative proceedings were documented in detail, but most congressional mayhem was missing or glossed over, apart from blowups too big to ignore.

Given the power of threats and violence during debate, their absence is striking—though logical. As official congressional records of a sort, both papers had a certain institutional dignity to uphold. As party organs, they also had to appease their congressional patrons, and as eager as some congressmen were to pose as champions, most of them didn't want to look like thugs. Even bullies wanted their most savage bullying suppressed, as more than one reporter learned the hard way by reporting it. In fact, for the sake of their skin, reporters were well advised to avoid recording insults altogether; it was too easy to become entangled in their impact. As one reporter put it, insults were "dangerous things for Reporters to meddle with."[46] The potential reward for such censorship was mighty: government printing contracts often meant survival for a struggling party press, and Congress was a major source of funding.[47] Until 1861, there was no government printing office, so Washington papers filled the gap and reaped the profits.

Thus the remarkably well-behaved Congress of record. In the *Intelligencer* and the *Globe*, there are few personal insults, though plenty of bravado. Physical clashes—if mentioned at all—are reduced to the barest detail. There are no weapons, unless a congressman mentions having seen one. (French saw "pistols in hand" during an 1836 fight but knew not to mention it.)[48] Personal apologies appear in all their glory, but more often than not the clash that prompted them is nowhere to be found.[49]

Not that there aren't clues. Evidence of violence abounds between the lines. Personal insults are often summed up as "remarks of an unfortunately personal nature." A fistfight might be described as "an altercation of an angry and painfully personal character." A violent uproar might appear as "a sensation." Occasionally there was more detail, particularly when dozens of congressmen rushed toward a fight, alleg-edly to break it up but often to join in; such chaos was hard to hide. But even these episodes were usually glossed over as "indescribable confu-sion and calls to order."[50]

During the rancorous Kansas debate, Washington newspapers would have been hard-pressed to eliminate all of the violence, and in-deed they include plenty of angry exchanges, though almost always with the rough edges smoothed away. Note for example the *Globe*'s account of an 1854 confrontation between two Tennesseans on opposite sides of the aisle. Outraged by Whig William Cullom's speech denouncing the Nebraska bill, the Democrat William Churchwell sneered that abolitionists had applauded it. Cullom had a sharp comeback, but not as sharp as the one that he inserted in the *Globe*'s account of their ex-change. Seeing that account the next day, Churchwell called Cullom a liar. At this, reported the *Globe*, "Mr. CULLOM rose from his seat and rushed towards Mr. CHURCHWELL with threatening gestures," rais-ing "loud shouts of 'Order!' and the greatest confusion." This was spicy stuff for the *Globe* but the truth was spicier: Churchwell pulled a gun on Cullom. *Globe* readers discovered this only when it was discussed during lamentation speeches the next day. As always, little came of the lamentation aside from the burst of laughter and applause that greeted one freshman's suggestion to put a gun rack in the rotunda to keep weapons off the floor. Two years later, that well-meaning freshman—Preston Brooks (D-SC)—showed what harm could be inflicted with-out a gun when he caned Senator Charles Sumner (R-MA).[51]

The appendix to the *Globe* had even fewer rough edges, though it was sometimes more extreme. Published throughout each session, it contained speeches "written out by the members themselves, so that, if the reporters unintentionally make mistakes, these inaccuracies stand corrected."[52] In other words, the appendix included speeches as con-gressmen wished they'd made them. Exceptionally controversial or lengthy speeches often appeared *only* in the appendix. The regular *Globe* is full of meandering oratory, interruptions, questions, and the occa-sional joke or threat. The appendix is a symphony of soliloquies filled with lofty sentiments and bold stands. For example, the *Globe* reported an 1844 argument in the House sparked by the gag rule debate, during which Armistead Burt (D-SC) growled that he'd be responsible for some insults "elsewhere," meaning in a duel or a street fight. In the appendix, Burt states that he is "restrained, no less by [my] own self-esteem than a just respect for my constituents, from entering into any vindication . . . here." The original version was an open threat; the appendix stripped much of the bullying away.[53] Filled with carefully edited showpiece speeches, the appendix truly created a Congress that never was.

If the public knew the truth about Congress they would hold their representatives to account, French thought.[54] There would be less dilly-dallying, less misuse of public funds, less stealing of stationery. But Washington newspapers weren't in the business of truth-telling. Together, Washington newsmen and congressmen created Congress as they needed it to be. Congressional coverage in the Washington papers was as much a record of that partnership as it was a record of Congress.

THE PARTNERSHIP OF THE PRESS

French was part of that partnership for most of his adult life; newspapers were the making and breaking of his political career. His work as a Jacksonian editor in New Hampshire raised him to the national stage, where his yeoman's efforts for the Democratic press promoted both his party and his reputation. By the 1840s, for at least some of the newspaper-reading public, French had a modest national presence. But that presence hurt him during the tumultuous years just before and after the Civil War. In the mid-1850s, newspapers exposed French's wavering Democratic loyalties and drove him to make some hard choices; after the war, they exposed his wavering loyalties once again and lost him a job. It was hard to be moderate in immoderate times. The shaming capabilities of the press made it harder. Even as a member of what he called the "*Press* gang," French was constantly surprised by the power of the press.[55]

That didn't stop him from trying to corral its influence; it would be hard to exaggerate the time and effort that French devoted to the press. In the service of his party, he was tireless; when he wasn't writing for newspapers, he was reading them. During elections, he combed through countless papers from all over the country searching for useful tidbits and a broad national view.[56] During Pierce's presidential campaign, French also kept watch for fires to extinguish, and there were plenty.

(Who *was* Franklin Pierce?) He countered such slurs in the *Union*, which in turn was quoted in other papers.

But the press was more than a political weapon for French. It was his public voice; it gave him a public presence. He needed little if any reason to plunge into print, and his political and editorial connections provided ready outlets. French eulogized men of note in the press. Unusual snowstorm? French would be chirping about snowstorms past in the next day's paper.[57] Inaccurate weather report? French corrected it with ready readings from his own thermometers.[58] He refuted any and every slash at his reputation, often the next day. (His half brother Henry called it "pouncing."[59]) His Masonic writings alone fill hundreds of pages.[60] And of course there were his poems, scores of them. Patriotic, Masonic, commemorative, or melancholy, they were French's way of sharing his feelings with the world and proving himself the man of letters that he yearned to be.

French was doing what many public figures did just as rigorously if not more so: crafting and protecting his image in the press. Congressmen, however, faced special challenges. Not only were their reputations at the mercy of the press, but their jobs depended on it. As representatives, they were accountable to their constituents for their words and actions as they appeared on the pages of newspapers. Thus their compulsive concern with press reports of their speeches.

Only in print were a congressman's words substantiated; only then were they real. Many a man verified harsh words in newspapers before throwing a punch or issuing a challenge. What mattered was what the public saw and heard. Unreported, a speech was "as if it had never been made," complained John Quincy Adams when one of his speeches—a "random shot"—wasn't recorded.[61] Congress revolved around the spoken word; committing those words to paper brought the process of representation to life.

It's no wonder that congressmen devoted long, hard hours to their press coverage.[62] Even such renowned speechifiers as Daniel Webster routinely primed the press, outlining speeches in advance for reporters, testing different wordings while delivering his speeches, then whittling away the excess during editing.[63] Occasionally that excess found its way into print, as it did in the *Globe* in 1850: Webster begins a sentence by stating, "I demur—I hesitate—I doubt—I repel."[64]

Typical are the efforts of John Quincy Adams. On March 6, 1835, he went to the *Intelligencer* office to read notes of a speech he had made four days past, but they weren't available. (While he was there, two other congressmen came to review notes of their speeches.) Three days later Adams got the notes and found them "very imperfect," so he spent the day revising them. He submitted his revisions the next day, then reappeared at the office two days later to review the proof sheets. His speech appeared in print on March 17, two weeks after he delivered it. Adams hated the "double waste of time" so much that he vowed to give fewer speeches.[65] (He failed.) No wonder congressmen often revised one reporter's notes and then referred other papers to the corrected copy, as did Henry Foote in 1850 when he sharpened an anti-Benton screed for the *Union* and then referred the *Intelligencer* to his revised text.[66]

Inserting comebacks into the record was a surefire way to spark a fight, as Foote learned all too well, and it happened all the time. It was also a surefire way to defend your name, and not just for congressmen. Washington newsmen sometimes used the record to have their say. When insulted during debate, they defended themselves in footnotes. In 1840, when William Bond (W-OH) berated a *Globe* reporter for accurately reporting his insults, the reporter insisted in a footnote to his report of Bond's speech that he had *softened* Bond's words.[67] When Waddy Thompson (W-SC) went one step further, throwing the lie at the *Globe* reporters William Curran and Lund Washington, Jr., they too went one step further, denouncing Thompson in a footnote as a bullying coward who attacked men only where they couldn't fight back.[68] Thompson, a man of "alarming" physique according to a fellow reporter, responded as bullies were wont to do: he threatened to beat the reporters, a practice that was all too common and not just in Washington; the *Enquirer* editor Webb suffered his fair share of beatings in New York.[69]

Given that tradition, Curran and Washington immediately armed themselves, one with a knife and the other with a "big stick" (probably a hickory cane), keeping a close eye on Thompson.[70] But they did something more. They stopped reporting him.[71] By erasing him from the record, they effectively erased him from Congress, leaving him no choice but to swallow his pride and apologize, which he did after four weeks of press silence.[72] The Kentuckian William Graves, another member of the Whig anti-*Globe* posse, suffered the same fate and responded the same way.[73] As compromised as it was, the Washington press had the literal last word on Congress, bullying congressional bullies in the process.

Congressmen and newsmen of the independent press had a different sort of partnership. Independent newspapers were not formal party organs.[74] Though many of them were partisan, they were profit-driven and survived by selling papers. And given that nothing sold papers better than spice, scandal, and exaggeration, their rise fostered a new, splashy style of journalism.[75]

Although independent newsmen often worked hand-in-hand with congressmen, they were free to argue and declaim as they saw fit, and with the arrival of the telegraph in the late 1840s, their numbers in Washington grew dramatically. Increasingly, the House and Senate galleries were filled with out-of-town reporters whom congressmen often didn't know and couldn't control. The very things that intensified the nation's sectional slavery crisis—new technologies and national expansion—gave the American press a more fluid and expansive national reach, sapping the power of the Washington press and loosening its grip on congressional coverage. At a peak moment of crisis, Washington's party operatives lost control of national news coverage.[76] As *The New York Herald* declared in 1860, "the only record of what is actually said in the House, is to be found in the independent press, over which the members can have no control."[77]

This doesn't mean that congressmen lost *full* control of their spin. Many became virtual pen pals with influential New York City newsmen; the *New-York Tribune*'s Horace Greeley, *The New York Herald*'s James Gordon Bennett, and *The New York Times*'s Henry Raymond had enormous influence in Congress. Alternately pleading and plotting with independent editors and reporters, congressmen shaped narratives of Congress that were part fact, part fiction, and part aspiration; journalistic objectivity was in its infancy in the 1850s.[78] The press in this period was in the business of projection in every sense of the word: projecting motives and intentions onto foes; projecting the future of the nation; and projecting all of this and more throughout the nation in newsprint.

Such storytelling was in full swing during the Kansas-Nebraska debate, and congressional clashes played a key role in these narratives. To some degree, such combat had always been performative; anyone who bullied an opponent knew that the nation might be watching. Indeed, sometimes that was the point. Bullies were proving themselves champions to their constituents. Extreme rhetoric often followed the same logic. Flame-throwing, fist-waving "Buncombe speeches"—so called because of a North Carolina congressman's claim that his heated diatribes were intended only for the folks back home in Buncombe County—were aimed at a home audience. (It's somehow fitting that the U.S. Congress gave us the word *bunkum*, or *bunk*.) But given their public impact, such diatribes also poisoned politics on the floor and sparked many a fight. David Outlaw hated so called "Buncombe days." They "always produce excitement, and fan the bad feeling of which heaven knows there is enough already."[79]

The independent press didn't hesitate to leap into this fray, urging Northern congressmen to fight. The *New-York Tribune* reporter James Shepherd Pike jumped in with both feet. Even more radically antislavery than the *Tribune* editor Horace Greeley, Pike went to extremes in a letter published on May 10, 1854, eerily echoing the Southern doomsday talk of 1850. "We are in the midst of a revolution," he declared, a struggle that required the "unbending determination" of Northern congressmen to defeat the Kansas-Nebraska bill.

> Better that confusion should ensue—better that discord should reign in the national councils—better that Congress should break up in wild disorder—nay, better that the Capitol itself should blaze by the torch of the incendiary, or fall and bury all its inmates beneath its crumbling ruins—than that this perfidy and wrong should finally be accomplished.[80]

Pike's words resounded in the pro-Nebraska press for weeks thereafter, where they were pilloried as the epitome of Northern aggression.[81] When Pike republished his letter years later, he removed this passage.[82]

The next day, Lewis "Lew" Campbell (KN-OH) put Pike's preaching into practice.[83] When House Democrats attempted to push the Nebraska bill through, Campbell led a campaign of resistance that lasted for a remarkable thirty-six hours, ending only when the House adjourned in exhaustion with no vote taken.

Campbell was fully engaged in this fight, sometimes to the point of howling defiance, though admittedly, howling defiance came naturally to Campbell, an ambitious politico known for storming and sulking.[84] Late at night on May 12, after more than a day of wrangling, his howling reached its peak. When a Democrat tried to force the bill through with the previous question, Campbell jumped to his feet vowing to fight to the bitter end, at which the House erupted. The *Globe* says only that members crowded around Campbell and stood on desks. But as short-tempered as congressmen doubtless were by that point, Campbell's pledge alone wouldn't have caused such an uproar. The crowding was caused by Henry Edmundson (D-VA), who accepted Campbell's challenge and began to remove his jacket in preparation for a fight.[85] As always, a rush of men surged toward the point of conflict; as always, congressmen stood on desks to watch; and as always, bullying and blustering had an impact. Although Edmundson didn't lay a finger on Campbell, the anti-Nebraskan minority got what they wanted: an adjournment and no bill passed.

But Campbell wanted more. A few days later, he wrote to Pike with a request. He had stood firm before the "Nebraskaites's" revolvers and bowie knives and defeated "Edmondson's effort to whip me." Yet there wasn't much of a public response. Could Pike stir people up? Not for himself, Campbell claimed; he needed no encouragement to soldier on. But a few words in the *Tribune* might inspire the public to draft resolves of approbation that would shore up "weak-kneed" anti-Nebraska congressmen by persuading them that the public was on their side—and watching.[86] Israel Washburn (W-ME) seconded this motion, asking Pike to write a column warning Northern congressmen that anyone who chose to "show the white feather will be exposed."[87] Here was the power of the press laid bare on paper: if public approval was a carrot, exposure as a coward was a very big stick.[88]

Such letters show the boomeranging action and reaction between Congress and the public as mediated by the press; the public was a third and all-important part of this partnership. Campbell was using the *Tribune* to shape outcomes in the House, counting on the power of public opinion to keep congressmen in line. That same public opinion might vault the ambitious Campbell to fame and fortune, to the speakership, or even to the presidency, which no one but Campbell saw in his future.[89] In 1854, it earned him fame. Greeted by a crowd of hundreds when he returned to Ohio at the end of the session, he was reelected by a large majority, winning nearly 60 percent of the vote.[90] The press had created an anti-Nebraska hero.

Campbell's victory shows the dynamics of the partnership of the press. Performing before a national audience and hoping to promote their cause and career, congressmen thundered and bellowed with Buncombe speeches. Faced with the blatant affronts of such speeches, their fellow congressmen responded with bellowing and sometimes bruising of their own. Reading about the sectional fury as amplified by the press, and inspired by rising sectional passions, the public urged their congressmen to fight for their rights. And with public opinion behind them and sectional taunts before them, congressmen did as they were told. Congress was trapped in a vicious cycle of sectional outrage.

TELLING TALES OF CONGRESS: THE SLAVE POWER AND NORTHERN AGGRESSION

The *New-York Tribune* had done much of the work in promoting Campbell. When it came to framing narratives, the *Tribune* was a virtuoso. One of the nation's leading newspapers and firmly anti-Nebraska, it pounded away at the Slave Power throughout the Kansas-Nebraska crisis, with the ardent Horace Greeley at its head and equally ardent reporters such as James Shepherd Pike beside him.[91] Pike was a master of one of the period's most powerful journalistic weapons: the "letter." On-the-spot reports framed as letters to the editor and filled with insider information, letters revealed the gritty human reality of politics. Chatty, personal, and irreverent, they had a biting edge that gave them power.[92] In letters, bad speeches looked bad. Controversies looked controversial. And violence sometimes looked violent. The *Globe* routinely suppressed such "gems of . . . brilliant parliamentary display," sniped *The New York Times*.[93] The "congressmen behaving badly" school of journalism, which rose to new heights in the late 1850s (as the next chapter shows), made good use of such letters.[94]

Between roughly 1835 and 1838, French was a letter-writer for the *Chicago Democrat*, edited by the former New Hampshirite, six-foot-six-inch-tall John "Long John" Wentworth (D-IL). Writing as "A Looker

On," "One of the Multitude," and "Nominis in Umbra" (bad Latin for "a name in shadow"), he focused his sights on Congress, offering insider hunches, calculating the rise and fall of reputations, and recounting fights, using his diary entries as fodder. His letters were chatty, good-natured, and staunchly Democratic, much like French himself. They also were "not quite spicy enough," according to at least one reader, and indeed, they lacked a certain gossipy bite; French didn't have a letter-writer's killer instinct. Less than a week after that complaint, the Graves-Cilley duel solved his problem with a vengeance, filling his column with outrage for weeks.[95]

A new sensationalistic style of journalism was springing to life, raising the hackles of congressmen in the process; their vitriol against letter-writers virtually oozes from the pages of the *Intelligencer* and the *Globe*.[96] Fearful to the point of paranoia of being exposed, they sometimes searched for lurking letter-writers in the galleries and under desks before launching closed sessions. One such search in 1859 exposed a cubbyhole housing two black cats; after that, "black cats" became congressional shorthand for suspected leaks.[97] It was for good reason that letters often were written under pseudonyms, particularly given that clerks and even congressmen sometimes wrote them.[98]

As threatening as letters could be, congressmen often benefited. Although Campbell received high praise in a much-reprinted *Tribune* article that singled him out for his "vigilant and determined course in resisting the Nebraska outrage," it was Pike's subsequent letter that sealed the deal.[99] There, Campbell became a heroic freedom fighter against an evil proslavery plot. Senator Stephen Douglas (D-IL) and his cronies had staged a bullying offensive to force the bill through in defiance of all rules, Pike reported. Why else was Douglas in the House issuing orders during the filibuster? Why else had Edmundson threatened not one anti-Nebraskan but three—including French's friend Wentworth, whom the Virginian supposedly drove from the hall? Clearly, Edmundson had been the evening's designated proslavery bully, with Douglas's full approval.[100]

There was truth to this telling. Douglas and other Democrats *were* trying to force the bill through, and bullying played a role in their campaign. But the *Tribune* fit that truth into a conspiratorial narrative of violent barbaric slaveholders engaged in a crafty, clandestine plot to spread slavery throughout the Union. As the *Tribune* told it, Edmundson, drunk and "armed to the teeth"—a virtual caricature of a Southerner—had rushed at Campbell, knife in hand. Campbell, in turn, had bared his chest and dared Edmundson to strike. This stirring bit of melodrama became the stock account of the encounter in the Northern anti-Nebraska press.[101]

More anti-Nebraska lies! charged the eccentric Mike Walsh (D-NY), a rough-and-tumble bravo from the streets of New York with a flair for humorous asides that he used to full effect in mocking the *Tribune*'s account of Campbell's moment of glory. Edmundson was said to have "rushed down . . . armed to the teeth, like Sampson slaying the Philistines," he joked, while Campbell "had his arms thrown behind him in a position similar to that of Ajax defying the lightning. [Great laughter]."[102]

Walsh's jeering received ample press coverage; the anti-Nebraska press wasn't alone in weaving narratives. The pro-Nebraska press told a story of Northern fanatics, Northern violence, and the unholy power of the *Tribune* to dictate orders to Northern congressmen, with Pike's Capitol-razing manifesto standing front and center as "fanaticism . . . openly and boldly avowed."[103] The threats and violence of anti-Nebraska congressmen were "without a parallel . . . in the Legislative history of the country," claimed the *Richmond Whig*—quite a claim for a Southern paper.[104]

Such were the two framing narratives of the Kansas-Nebraska crisis in Congress.[105] Newspapers throughout the country veered toward one or the other of these slavery-centric poles, and the Thirty-third Congress gave them plenty of material to work with, though truth be told, this Congress wasn't exceptionally violent; it just seemed that way in the press—particularly in the Northern press.[106] Representing the underdog in this debate, anti-Nebraska newspapers had every reason to amplify congressional violence in their effort to urge action against a domineering Slave Power. Southern "aggression" in Kansas and in Congress became a byword of this debate.[107]

Given the dire threat and high stakes, Northern fighting men had a powerful appeal: as depicted in the press, they were brave champions fighting the spread of slavery in defense of Northern rights.[108] Francis B. Cutting (D-NY) was one of those fighting Northerners who drew applause. His peak moment of performance took place in March 1854.

Although he supported the Nebraska bill, on March 27, he proposed referring it to the Committee of the Whole for a full discussion, thereby delaying its passage. Democrats in the press and in the House responded by denouncing him as a traitor.

John C. Breckenridge (D-KY) was a loud denouncer. During their harsh exchange—which began when Cutting tried to defend himself against charges in the *Union*—the two men essentially called each other liars, causing a "Great sensation, and cries of 'Order!'" That night, Cutting opened formal duel negotiations with Breckenridge. But with each man claiming to be the insulted party, little happened and an apology on the House floor on March 31 ended the matter.[109]

In and of itself, a near duel between congressmen was guaranteed headline news, so the Cutting-Breckenridge fight produced headlines aplenty. Some newspapers were all sensation. "CUTTING REPORTED KILLED," declared the *Newark Daily Advertiser*, adding in small print that it had no idea if this was true.[110] The *Connecticut Courant* put the power of the telegraph to full use on April 1, printing a 1:30 p.m. report that the two men were in hiding, a 1:45 p.m. report that a bloodless duel had taken place, and an evening report denying any duel. "People have a 'wonderful proclivity' in this country, to the 'spicy,'" stated the *Alexandria Gazette* with marked understatement.[111]

Other papers took a more traditional approach, chiding congressmen for their bad behavior, though with a regional spin. Congress was a place for "gentlemen to exchange ideas," not a place for "passionate bullies to exchange shots," declared the *Massachusetts Spy*, condemning both combatants. The only cure for such barbarities was to "get rid of Slavery." The Baton Rouge *Daily Advocate* blamed the Speaker. Why hadn't he spoken up when insults began to fly? Was he afraid of being challenged to a duel? Given that the Speaker was a Southerner—the Kentucky Democrat Linn Boyd—this was no slight charge.[112]

Such coverage of a congressional sparring match was par for the course. But many anti-Nebraska newspapers went further, fitting the Breckenridge-Cutting episode into a broader Slave Power narrative. The *Tribune* led the charge, declaring the incident "part of a well-considered plan to pursue by intimidation and violence every independent northern Democrat who dares to defy the mandates of the Slaveocracy." The lesson to be learned was clear: "support the Nebraska bill or submit to be bullied or shot."[113] Other newspapers blamed President Pierce, damning him as a bullying truckler to the Slave Power, which had ordered Breckenridge to attack Cutting.[114]

If Pierce was the villain of this story, Cutting was the hero. Southerners had a "dastardly habit" of forcing Northern congressmen to "fight or, be disgraced," wrote the *Albany Evening Journal*. Those "fiery braggarts . . . accustomed to swagger in the House" had met their match. Cutting was not "in the habit of submitting to the lash of a master."[115] Most glorious of all was Cutting's willingness to duel. Cutting "is the best shot in our pistol galleries," crowed the *Portland Weekly Advertiser*. "He will make Mr. Breckenridge rue this quarrel, whether he prefers pistols, rifles, small swords, closed digits, brickbats at twenty paces, or raw hides at two."[116] The Northern press was doing some swaggering of its own, depicting Cutting as a rare and special thing: a Northern "fighting man."[117] Senate freshman William Pitt Fessenden (W-ME) received similar treatment at roughly the same time. As the *Tribune* told it, during his "manly" maiden speech on March 3, he dared Southerners to leave the Union, even as the red-faced Andrew Butler (D-SC) threatened him with clenched fists.[118] The truth was less dramatic. "Poor old Mr. Butler cut very foolish flourishes," Fessenden told his wife, "yet he had no more idea of assaulting or even insulting me than he had of flying." Regardless of the truth, Fessenden became an anti-Nebraska hero.[119]

Fessenden, Cutting, and Campbell hadn't engaged in any fisticuffs, but they were far more confrontational than most of their Northern colleagues had been four years past, and they were roundly applauded for it, particularly given that their resistance was played up in the press. The *National Aegis* thanked Northern fighters, each and every one: "We do hugely like to see the stiffening taken out of the 'chivalry,'" it gloated.[120] As depicted in the press, these stalwart Northerners weren't only fighting the Slave Power; they were defending the fate and spirit of the North with manly bravado. Southerners weren't the only men who knew how to fight.[121]

Not surprisingly, this trend didn't play well in pro-Nebraska papers, which assailed fighting Northerners as violent incendiaries with no respect for the law.[122] *Northerners*, not Southerners, weren't fighting fair, both in Congress and the North, where they routinely violated the Fugitive Slave Act. By flouting the rule of law they surrendered all claim to its protection, declared the *Union* on June 8. "Outlawed enemies to society," they were "like wild beasts of the forest, fair game to be hunted by all whose safety, property, and lives they are perpetually placing in jeopardy."[123] This declaration wasn't on a par with Pike's manifesto, but it came close. That same day in the House, Joshua Giddings (R-OH), referenced by name in the *Union* piece, proposed that its editor, the House printer, A.O.P. Nicholson, be expelled from the hall for encouraging assaults on congressmen. His resolution was tabled, but not before Senator Thomas Clingman (D-NC) declared that Giddings's speeches were far more incendiary than the *Union* article.[124] *Northerners* were the aggressors, not Southerners, who were the soul of moderation throughout the crisis—at least as depicted in the pro-Nebraska press.

The *other* side was plotting illicit plots with wild abandon. The *other* side was forcing its way to power with underhanded assaults. The *other* side was putting sectional interests above the good of the whole. The *other* side wanted to commandeer the Union. The *other* side was violating fundamental rights: the right of free speech, property rights.[125] Pro- and anti-Nebraska newspapers told the same story with the leading roles reversed. Promises were being broken, compromises were being betrayed, parliamentary rules were being violated: each side accused the other of not fighting fair. Sectional conspiracy theories were eroding cross-sectional trust inside and outside of Congress, destroying any hope of a middle ground.

Senator Edward Everett's (W-MA) fate shows how hard it was to avoid taking a stand. Sick at home during the final vote on the Nebraska bill, he was attacked as a coward by anti-Nebraska men and pilloried in the *Tribune*. His timid self-defense and devotion to constructing a compromise drew such abuse that he resigned his Senate seat, a moderate Whig crushed by extremes.[126]

"A PERFECT HELL ON EARTH"

Although a congressional insider, French was as distrustful as anyone. No longer clerking, he was still in Congress's orbit, watching debates from the floor and hobnobbing with congressmen almost every day. In January 1854, he had a fine time at a small dinner with Henry

Edmundson, Laurence Keitt, and Preston Brooks, the trio that would stage the caning of Senator Charles Sumner two years later.[127] French couldn't have been more up close and personal with alleged slaveholding schemers, yet even he came to believe in a nefarious Slave Power plot, a belief that ultimately destroyed his twenty-three-year friendship with Franklin Pierce.

The trouble between the two men began in March 1854. French's half brother Henry had spent the winter in Washington and hadn't been shy about denouncing the Nebraska bill.[128] Outraged by such dissension in the ranks, Pierce scolded French for his brother's sins. Annoyed by the scolding and no fan of the bill, French spouted some Democratic platitudes about popular sovereignty and held his tongue. Pierce responded by asking French to write a letter of support for the bill, to be published in the New England press.

At first, French said yes. But by the end of the day he thought better of it. Convinced that the Nebraska bill was an "unpardonable political blunder" and deeply disappointed in Pierce for supporting it, French decided not to write the letter.[129] It wasn't an easy decision. His lengthy diary entry says as much. He wanted to support Pierce and believed in the principle of popular sovereignty as a good Democrat should. But he could not lend his support to a bill that was a danger to the Union and a threat to the North. Well aware that his decision could have serious consequences, French wrote a carefully worded letter to Pierce, transcribing it in his diary under the title "The Letter." The Kansas-Nebraska controversy had brought French to a turning point, as it had the nation.

French's letter shows how torn he was between his feelings for Pierce, his devotion to the Democracy, his heartfelt desire to keep slavery from spreading, and his fears for both the Union and his political career. His main reason for changing his mind was pragmatic, he explained: a published letter from one of Pierce's close friends would persuade no one and expose Pierce's guiding hand. Treading lightly, French next admitted his doubts about the bill but pledged his firm support; he would stand behind the "great principle of popular rights." French was on the hither side of truth once again. He was hiding his deep dislike of the bill. Even so, he was sending a clear message, admitting his discomfort with the Democratic party line.

French's inability to be frank with his old friend disturbed him, as it had throughout Pierce's presidency. As chummy as the two men were during that time (which wasn't all that difficult for the smooth and charming president), Pierce showed no interest in hearing French's thoughts. Time and again, French offered words of advice or warning, or aired his views, but Pierce wanted none of it. Instead, Pierce wanted his old friend to "toe the mark," French griped. After all that French had sacrificed for Pierce's campaign—committing himself so fully that he drove paying business away—this was a bitter pill. "I Gloried in his election," French grumbled, "and he has treated me as if he deemed me of about as much importance as his bootblack or his coachman."[130] Wounded and disappointed, he began to refer to Pierce as his "former friend."[131]

The passage of the Kansas-Nebraska Act in May 1854 made matters worse, highlighting sectional tensions in national parties. While Southern Democrats and most Southern Whigs supported the bill, Northern Democrats were divided and Northern Whigs voted against it. Pierce signed it into law on May 30. With Kansas's slavery status up for grabs, swarms of free soil and proslavery settlers (branded "border ruffians" by abolitionists and Free Soilers) rushed into the territory to sway the state their way. Within nine months, its white population had increased tenfold.[132] The next year saw outbreaks of man-to-man combat and fraudulent elections, with slaveholders corrupting the electoral process and bludgeoning their way to power, much as slaveholding congressmen had long bullied their way to power in Congress. Only after an extended battle over pro- and antislavery constitutions did Kansas achieve statehood as a free state in 1861.[133]

It wasn't hard to connect the dots. For French—as for many Northerners—the violence in Kansas irrefutably exposed a brutal, underhanded Slave Power plot in progress, propounded by Southerners both in Kansas and in Congress. It was "now perfectly evident that the repeal [of the Missouri Compromise] was for the purpose of establishing more slave territory in this Union," he wrote in 1855. He saw now what he hadn't seen before: "a *determination* among the slaveocracy that the people of that Territory *shall not* make it free if they are ever so much disposed to do so."[134] It was a stunning realization. The South was serving *only* itself. And his old friend had fostered this outrage.

Even so, for a time, French stayed the course, doing his job as commissioner of public buildings, his ultimate reward from Pierce. He even dropped by the White House for the occasional visit, admiring Pierce for his fashion sense if not his common sense. ("No man dresses more appropriately on all occasions than Gen. Pierce.")[135] However much French deplored Pierce's politics, he couldn't deny his fundamental fondness for the man.[136]

Yet French's Democratic loyalties were wavering. And in June 1855, he was forced to make a choice. Annoyed by rumors that French had joined the Know Nothings, a nativist organization and nascent political party that met in secret (thus their name: asked about their meetings, members said that they knew nothing), Pierce demanded an explanation. Was French two-timing the Democrats? French in fact had dabbled in the Know Nothing movement, attracted by its fraternal rituals, its utter devotion to all things American, and—at least in the North—its antislavery drift, though its nativism ultimately drove him away.[137] Like many Northerners, he approached the Know Nothings as a way station to the nascent Republican Party.[138] As Joshua Giddings put it, the Know Nothings acted as "a screen—a dark wall—behind which members of old political organizations could escape unseen from party shackles, and take a position according to the dictates of judgment and conscience."[139] French had taken a step behind that screen, but before he could explain himself, Pierce began to rant about Know Nothing traitors, vowing to remove them all from office. Not until the next day did the two men discuss French's politics in an unusually frank conversation, their longest since Pierce had become president, after which both men declared themselves satisfied. French left their meeting reminded of the good old Frank Pierce of old.[140]

But the following day brought more Democratic accusations about French's politics. True to form, French denied them in the press, declaring himself a member of the "anti Know Nothing party."[141] But in doing so, he angered the Know Nothings, who triumphantly exposed his former loyalties in their press organ, the appropriately named *Daily American Organ*. Their proof was three Know Nothing articles written by French in support of a relative's bid for office; the *Organ* had the originals in his hand. His scribbling impulse had done him in, and now the press was hunting him down, with French unable to take the middle ground because there was no middle ground to take. With a "howling pack of human dogs" on his trail in the press, and "Know Nothings and

Democrats, Catholics & Protestants, great men & little men, & many *very small* would-be-great men" out to get him, French declared his public life "a perfect hell on earth."[142]

Given Pierce's purge of Know Nothings with government jobs, French's fate was clear. On June 4, he resigned his commissionership, grumbling about unfaithful editors and an unreasonable press. The press responded in kind with a parting blow, harping on French's "decapitation" as a way to mock Pierce's ironfisted intolerance of any and all dissent.[143] (Knowing full well French's tendency to pounce into print, his half brother Henry begged him to stay silent.) Ironically, given French's history with the telegraph, wire transmissions mangled the story, nonsensically discussing the "French Commissioner of the Public Buildings."[144]

French's career was crashing down around him. The political ground was shifting beneath his feet. His loyalty to the Democracy had been tried and found wanting; his faith in the Democracy was irreparably shaken. Even so, he was good-natured to the end, titling his account of his ordeal "The diary of a hunted politician!," even managing to express "the kindest feelings of regard" for Pierce in his resignation letter.[145] Yet he bemoaned the tragic impact of Pierce's presidency on his party and the nation. Pierce had done "in two years, what all the enemies of democracy have striven in vain for 50 years to do," French fumed. He had *"broken down the Democratic Party!"* And the Union was at risk as never before.[146]

The time had come for French to make a choice, and he made it. As he explained to Pierce in his letter, in resigning his post, he was withdrawing from the Democratic Party. He was now "a free man, untrammelled by party or personal obligations—ready to do what may seem best for my Country."[147] Thus did French—the man who had made himself "conspicuous and ridiculous" with his "fulsome letters puffing the [Pierce] administration," according to *The New York Herald*—leave the Democracy and break with Pierce.[148] His wrenching transition shows how many a Northern Democrat made that journey.[149]

French was now a man without a party. After a lifetime of electioneering, it was a strange place to be. He knew what he wasn't. He certainly was "no city of Washington, present *administration* Democrat." And he was done with doughface dodging. He wanted "[n]o more time-serving, no more equivocation." Nor could he accept the party's routine sacrifice of

Northern interests and honor; no amount of power was worth that sacrifice. Even the word *Democrat* had ceased to have meaning for him.[150]

French's diary bears witness to what came next; he wasn't untrammeled for long. His ever more frequent references to the "slavocracy's . . . war on Freedom" reveal a man taking sides.[151] By August 1855, he was swearing to stand by the North at any cost.[152] In January 1856 he pledged allegiance to the principles of the nascent Republican Party; impressed by a speech by Joshua Giddings (R-OH) outlining the Republican credo, French declared it his personal "platform."[153] Already busying himself as a Republican activist, he was a nominee for president of the District's Republican Association one month later. That May, he was named a delegate to the Republican National Convention.[154] Not long after, his wife, Bess, was jokingly quoting attacks on "black republicans" in her letters to French "for the fun of the thing."[155] Within a year of his break with Pierce, French had become a Republican.[156]

He was one of many Northerners making that transition, a product of the seeming spread of slavery and the Slave Power through the Fugitive Slave Act and the Kansas-Nebraska Act, and a growing disenchantment with political parties as they were.[157] For many such people, their choice wasn't born of cold calculation. It was a change of mind and heart, a turning away from the South that required a new understanding of the Union and its parts. No longer were these people pinning hopes on pacts and compromises. Southern aggression had to be resisted. Northern rights had to be protected. And the Republican Party was their weapon of choice, the one and only hope for the Union as they felt it should be. Many Southerners faced a similar crisis, turning their backs on Northern allies because the times demanded it but grieving at the parting.[158]

In December 1855, French commemorated his change of heart with a poem, his impulse whenever he felt strong sentiments—and French was a sentimental man living in challenging times. In a speech earlier that year at an antislavery rally, Massachusetts representative Nathaniel Banks, a Know Nothing soon to be a Republican, had made a stunning declaration: If the South persisted in advancing the spread of slavery, then the North should "let the Union slide." (Watching in the audience, the teenaged Thomas B. Reed, later "Czar" Reed of congressional fame, was struck by the burst of applause that greeted Banks's words.)[159]

Although Banks later insisted that he was speaking of a worst-case scenario, his words caused a sensation. Southerners had been threatening
disunion for decades. Here was a Northerner taking that stand. Always
stirred by Northerners who took on the Slave Power, French took Banks's
words to heart. Indeed, he may have intended his poem for Banks,
who was running for Speaker; French was never too proud for self-
promotion. His poem, titled "Then Let the Union Slide," was both a
boast and a dare:

> *Bold words are these, and fearful—*
> *"Then let the Union slide"—*
> *E'en the thought is sad & tearful,*
> *Howe'er it be applied!*
> *There's not a patriot living*
> *Who would not grieve most sore,*
> *At the dread-dark outgiving*
> *"This Union is no more."*
>
> *Is the North to be down-trodden*
> *Beneath the Southern heel*
> *As if their flesh were sodden*
> *And their hearts had ceased to feel?*
> *To all the high toned fancies*
> *Of these lords must they submit,*
> *And receive with slavery Kansas*
> *Because the South saw fit?*
>
> *If o'er that Freedom glorious*
> *For which our fathers died,*
> *Slavery must be victorious,*
> *"Then let the Union slide!"*
> *For 'tis not worth the keeping,*
> *If o'er our Father's graves*
> *Man!—Shackeled man!—is weeping*
> *That half his race are slaves!"*
>
> *"Let it slide" then—this great Union—*
> *Pronounce the compact dead—*

With the South no more communion
If slavery still must spread!
There's land thank God, for Freedom
North of Potomac's tide—
Let the South keep slaves & breed 'em—
But "let the Union slide"

French had come a long way from his doughface dodging of days gone by. With the slavery crisis coming to a head, he was singing a song of disunion, though like Banks, he assumed that the North would cross that final fateful line only if pushed by the South; *if* the South persisted, *then* let the Union slide. When French published his poem in the abolitionist *Liberator* five years later—omitting its conciliatory first stanza—he removed "then" from the title. What had once seemed only possible had become probable by 1860; disunion was at hand.[160]

Banks's rallying cry shows the force and feeling behind the rise of the Republican Party. Antislavery in principle and Northern in orientation, its fuel and fire were born of righteous anger at Southern aggression. In 1855, that aggression was most flagrant in two places: Kansas and Congress. It should thus come as no surprise that the arrival of Republicans in Congress caused a spike in congressional violence. Pledged to fight the Slave Power, Republican congressmen stayed true to that pledge. Face-to-face with slaveholders, they propounded their cause with strong words, bold actions, and—when pushed to extremes—the force of their fists, knives, and guns, and were applauded by Northerners for doing so. Like French, they were prepared to fight for Northern rights if necessary—even to the point of disunion.

7

REPUBLICANS MEET THE SLAVE POWER

CHARLES SUMNER AND BEYOND (1855–61)

rench was a Republican, but a moderate one. As he put it in 1860, he was "an ultra Union man."[1] Even as he championed Northern rights, he desperately wanted to save the Union—at least, the Union as he now understood it, with the North no longer in thrall to the South. As sincerely as he supported the Republican cause, if the party went too far, French wouldn't go with it. "When Republicanism becomes in the least treasonable," he wrote in 1859, "I am no longer a Republican. My Republicanism teaches me to stand by my Country & her Constitution."[2]

French's Republicanism was grounded on a moral balancing act between rights and order. He saw events in Kansas as ample proof of an entrenched Slave Power plot to spread slavery and deny Northern rights, yet he deplored the abolitionist John Brown's extreme actions in fighting that foe. Brown's massacre of proslavery settlers near Pottawatomie Creek, Kansas, in 1856, and his attempt to launch a slave revolt by seizing a federal arsenal in Harpers Ferry, Virginia, in 1859 outraged French. As much as he admired Brown's bravery, he could "feel no admiration for the high qualities of any man who uses those qualities to overturn the Constitution and Laws of my Country!"[3] Along similar lines, although French didn't want slavery "to extend one inch into territory now free," he believed that the Fugitive Slave Act should be enforced in the North because it was the law. Hearing of a violent attempt to free a fugitive slave in Boston in 1854, French poured abuse on the abolitionists Theodore Parker and Wendell Phillips, whose speechifying had helped to rouse an angry crowd. "[O]pposed as I am to hanging people in general," he told his brother, "I really should glory in putting the ropes around their traitor necks—pulling the caps over their traitor eyes, & launching their traitor souls into hell—the only fit place for them!! Savage, aint it?"[4]

In essence, French was a member of the leave-the-South-alone school of thought. As much as he wanted to uphold Northern rights and interests and prevent the spread of slavery into free territory, he didn't want to violate Southern rights under the Constitution by "a single hair's breadth."[5] He was more than willing to let the slave regime solve its own slavery problems, as long as it didn't push beyond the bounded South.[6]

There were many such people in the Republican ranks. People who wanted to quash the Slave Power and champion the North, but who weren't all that eager to stamp out slavery in the South. People who wanted to defend Northern rights without endangering the Union. People who saw the Union as dependent on a pact between North and South that *had* to be upheld. There were other kinds of people in the Republican Party too: racists who wanted to protect free soil for white men; radicals promoting equal rights between the races; nativists suspicious of anti-American influences; working-class and middle-class people who distrusted the "money-power."[7]

The Republican Party was born of this mix, but only gradually. Although the opening of the Thirty-fourth Congress in December 1855 saw the arrival of 108 anti-Nebraska men in the House and 15 in the Senate, there was no single party banner uniting them in a shared cause.[8] Some were Know Nothings; by then, the anti-Catholic, anti-immigrant movement had cohered as the American Party. Some considered themselves Free Soilers. Some called themselves Independent Democrats. Others were ex-Whigs who had broken with their party as it slipped out of existence, fractured by the slavery debate. Still others simply considered themselves an opposition to the Democratic majority. And some had already adopted the Republican label. Regardless of their party name, many of these people were antislavery and anti-administration.

As inchoate as this new party was, the arrival of an explicitly Northern opposition had an enormous impact on Congress. Not only did the number of fights spike precipitously after 1855, but their dynamics fundamentally changed. Republicans promoted themselves as a new kind of Northerner who was willing to fight back, and they were true to their word. They fought to wrest control of Congress and the Union from the Slave Power.[9]

Not surprisingly, the most radical members of this new party were the most confrontational.[10] John Parker Hale, Zachariah Chandler, Benjamin Wade, Elihu Washburne, Henry Wilson, Owen Lovejoy, John Covode, James Lane, Galusha Grow, John Potter, William Fessenden, and, of course, the ever fight-ready Joshua Giddings were essentially Northern fighting men, hoping to radicalize their party and galvanize the public by displaying the emotional power of Northern aggression. They accomplished their purpose with a potent blend of extreme rhetoric and—in some cases—an apparent willingness to defend their principles with their fists. Their bold antislavery talk, the kind that had subjected Giddings to at least seven physical assaults, was virtually guaranteed to provoke a Southern backlash.

These fights served a more complex purpose than past imbroglios sparked by men such as Giddings, Adams, and Hale to denigrate slavery by putting slaveholder savagery on display. Republicans were trying to do something concrete; their numbers were large enough to affect and possibly effect policy and the balance of power in the Union. They also were a nascent party that desperately needed widespread public support. And the core agenda of that party—mentioned in countless petitions and resolves from their constituents—was combating the Slave Power plot to dominate the federal government and spread slavery throughout the Union. Republican aggression in Congress and the Southern belligerence that it provoked served the Republican agenda; in a sense, it was campaigning. By promoting their cause in the face of raging threats, or by provoking those threats, Republicans weren't just proving a point. They were engaging in party politics.

Admittedly, by 1855 the threshold of fight-worthy offenses for congressional slavery supporters was low and getting lower all the time. They, too, believed that they were fighting a powerful foe: Northern aggression was threatening to strangle if not extinguish the South's hold on the Union, and perhaps even to infiltrate the South.[11] By Southern logic, their interests and honor required forceful action, and fight Southerners did. By threatening, insulting, and even assaulting their foes, they, too, were promoting their cause and drumming up support. For both North and South, violence was politics.

Which brings us to the most dramatic innovation in congressional violence after 1855: Northerners fought back.[12] When confronted by screaming slaveholders wielding weapons, Republicans stood firm, often exchanging blow for blow, sometimes with weapons, often with numbers. More than once, when a Republican drove Southerners into a fury, brother Republicans rushed to the rescue, armed and ready to fight.

These men stood their ground deliberately, aggressively, defiantly. They did so knowing that the simple fact of their resistance sent a powerful message. It revealed the presence of a united North willing to fight for its interests and rights. The very act of speaking in the face of howling resistance was a declaration of Northern rights, because it asserted the right of free speech on the floor, a right long violated by Southerners.

The Republican war for free speech wasn't purely symbolic. To promote their party, to get things done, to serve their constituents, to fully represent the North, and to fulfill the pledges that had won them office, Republican congressmen had to say their piece; they had to confront and demand and accuse. Pledged to combat the Slave Power's hold on the federal government, they were pledged to fight bullying Southerners as best they could.

Southerners were equally bound to resist Northern aggression, and Republicans were Northern aggression personified, as well as a fount of dangerous words; to Southern slaveholders, Republican antislavery rhetoric was personally insulting, sectionally degrading, and a threat to the security and stability of the South that had to be silenced. Most congressional clashes between 1855 and 1861 centered on this core dynamic. Republicans propounded their cause; slaveholders tried to gag them with threats and violence; and Republicans fought back. The arrival of a Northern opposition in Congress marked the start of a death struggle over free speech on the floor, which was in truth a fight for control of Congress, and thereby for the fate of the nation.

Free speech was the most powerful weapon in the congressional arsenal.[13] Any words spoken loudly enough to be heard by the press could be heard by the nation. Free speech was also a much heralded sacred right, the essence of democratic representation. A congressman without free speech couldn't fully represent his constituents, as victims of bullying and their supporters said time and again. Cilley said so in the midst of his wrangle. Adams championed that truth as a holy cause for years. Through Adams's persistence and the prodding of the press, the Northern public eventually awoke to this fundamental violation of their rights and rose up in outrage against such degradation to demand their due. Republicans followed in Adams's footsteps, championing the right of free speech on the floor by exercising it often and with feeling, even fighting for it when necessary, sometimes explicitly declaring themselves defenders of that right. They did so with an approving Northern public looking on.[14]

Even as they fought for their rights, Republicans appealed to that public by highlighting their bravery in Congress and its implications. During yet another contentious contest for Speaker in 1859, when Southerners threatened violence if a Republican won the post, the ever sardonic Thaddeus Stevens (R-PA) said that he didn't blame Southerners for their threats, "for they have tried it fifty times, and fifty times they have found weak and recreant tremblers in the North who have been affected by it." When Stevens's quip brought Martin Crawford (D-GA) to his feet uttering threats, Stevens added, "That is right. That is the way that they frightened us before." At this, Crawford headed toward Stevens, fists waving, muttering in an undertone that had clear implications. Within seconds, Republicans and Southern Democrats were rushing down the aisles, several of them reaching for guns. But despite what the *Globe* characteristically called "great confusion," nothing happened, people returned to their seats, and Stevens dismissed the matter as "a momentary breeze," raising a laugh.[15]

Republicans were announcing that they were a different kind of Northerner, and they had to be. Both sides in this battle were playing for the rafters, appealing to their publics to sustain them with support. And their pleas worked. Increasingly, Americans sent their congressmen a clear and consistent message in mass meetings, private letters, petitions, the press, and the ballot box: fight for our rights. Fight.

Thus the fight-filled Thirty-fourth, Thirty-fifth, and Thirty-sixth Congresses, and thus their depiction in the independent press. North and South alike, newspapers emphasized the surge in violence as the ultimate proof of Kansas-fueled sectional conspiracies to dominate the Union—proof of a powerful kind, because it gave those conspiracies names and faces. Many Americans saw their worst fears brought to life on the floor of Congress as congressmen embodied the crisis of the Union, clashing in armed combat over sectional rights. In the process, Americans lost faith in the institution of Congress.

They also lost faith in one another. The full impact of this perfect storm of conspiracy theories, policy conflicts, physical violence, and press coverage was growing distrust between North and South. Not only did the public become ever more distrustful of their sectional foe, but congressmen did too. The fact that large numbers of congressmen armed themselves in this period speaks volumes. These men were prepared for sectional warfare in the halls of Congress. They believed that the driving impact of aggression on aggression could spark a firestorm that would bring the Union down, and if things went that far, they considered it their duty to fight with and for their people. To reverse a much quoted aphorism: politics was becoming war by other means.[16] When congressmen themselves lost faith in the institution of Congress and in one another— when they no longer believed that the institution was powerful enough to prevent sectional bloodshed within the Capitol—a line had been crossed. Resolution would have to come from elsewhere, if not from mediation, then in open war.

In the midst of this sectional strife, French remained moderate, though at a time of violent extremes, the nature of moderation changed. As always, he politicked and paraded on behalf of his cause, organizing mass mailings of Republican pamphlets and campaigning for presidents. As always, he worried about the fate of the nation. As late as 1860, he declared himself "for concession & conciliation."[17] As Grand Master of the Knights Templar of the United States, he even tried to yoke Masonic brotherhood to the cause of Union.

But French was also publishing antislavery poems and protests. He socialized primarily with Republicans, some of them abolitionists. Joshua Giddings remained a favorite; French sometimes stood near Giddings's seat on the floor to hear him speak. Gamaliel Bailey, editor of the abolitionist *National Era*, was also a good friend, as was the New Hampshire antislavery advocate Amos Tuck, one of the founders of the Republican Party, whose daughter Ellen married French's son Frank in 1861. Tuck introduced French to the abolitionist poet John Greenleaf Whittier; after talking about politics and poetry for a while, the two men wandered out to measure an enormous tree stump.[18] And of course, French spent hours with New England Republicans; at times, his social calendar reads like a roster of the New Hampshire delegation, now devoid of Democrats.[19]

Perhaps most striking of all during these years, French began to consider the possibility of disunion. As much as he hoped to avoid that final outcome, he felt that a Union dominated by the Slave Power was no Union at all. If disunion was to come "merely because the South cannot have *all* the old cow's teats to suck," he wrote in 1860, then he could only say, "in John Quincy Adams's words 'Let it come!'" This was the period when French published his ode to Banks without its conditional "Then" in the title.

Like countless others, French now saw the firm assertion of Northern rights against the Slave Power's encroaching grasp as fundamental to the Union. Many people were far more radical than French in demanding those rights. French was more anti–Slave Power than he was antislavery, as were many Northerners.[20] These people experienced these years of crisis as a sectional power struggle more than a battle against an immoral wrong, although a sense of moral rectitude powered their resistance. But however individual Northerners interpreted the crisis, when it came to the balance of power in the Union, for most of them there was no turning back.

Until the firing on Fort Sumter on April 12, 1861—and even beyond—French hoped that the Union would survive this trial as it had survived many trials before. But even as he prayed for peace, he was preparing for war. Events in 1860 pushed even this man of moderation to extremes, compelling him to arm himself to defend the Republican cause.

THE MOST VIOLENT CONGRESS IN OUR HISTORY

In the months before the opening of the Thirty-fourth Congress in December 1855, Americans North, South, and West predicted tough times ahead. The reasons were many. The Kansas-Nebraska Act had divided the nation into two warring factions. Union-rending conspiracies seemed to be afoot. Events in Kansas offered bloody evidence of those plots in action, flooding a watchful national audience with graphic images of slave-state and free-state settlers in open combat. Politicos in Washington were prepared to go to the wall on Kansas's slavery status. A Northern opposition was rising in Congress. And as if this wasn't enough, a presidential election would take place the following fall. After discussing Kansas with "knowing ones" in the summer of 1855, French felt sure that the Union would soon "receive such a shock as it never received before." If so, he was ready "to stand by the North in resisting the unjustifiable attempts now making by the South to add more slave states to this Union."[21]

People throughout the nation echoed French's thoughts. In Massachusetts, Henry Wilson, a Know Nothing on his way to becoming a Republican, had dire predictions for the coming session of Congress. Wilson, a shoemaker, schoolteacher, and newspaper editor who had found his way into politics in the 1840s, had spent a week in June at the national convention of the nascent nativistic American Party, bound and determined to "blow the whole thing to hell and damnation" unless they adopted an anti–Slave Power plank in their platform.[22] When the party refused, Wilson led antislavery Northerners out of the convention, though not without resistance; during one of his speeches, he was threatened by a gun-waving Virginian. "At Philadelphia, for eight days, I met the armed, drunken bullies of the Black Power, without shrinking," he wrote to the abolitionist Theodore Parker in July, "and I hope to do so at the next session of Congress, if it shall be necessary." The South had to understand that threats of disunion, civil war, or personal violence wouldn't carry. "The next Congress will be the most violent one in our history," Wilson predicted. "[I]f violence and bloodshed come, let us not falter, but do our duty, even if we fall upon the floors of Congress."[23] By 1855, this once shocking image of bloody combat in the halls of Congress had become commonplace.

At the other end of the Union, Laurence Keitt (D-SC) drew the same conclusions. Keitt, a self-described man of "nervous irritability" soon to be a congressional frequent fighter, was a fire-eating extremist who was passionately protective of Southern honor.[24] He predicted a "strong struggle" in the pending session, a chance to "marry one's name to mighty events, to mighty measures," and to the South's "immortal future." Writing from London, Keitt's friend Virginian Ambrose Dudley Mann agreed. Because of the Kansas-Nebraska Act, the "time has arrived when the South is compelled to measure strength with the North." If Northerners tried to block slavery from western territories, make Kansas a free state, or repeal the Fugitive Slave Act, "it would be the duty of the South to take possession of the Capitol . . . and expel from it the traitors to the Constitution."[25]

The same rhetoric pervaded the election for Speaker. When slaveholders began to grill candidate Nathaniel Banks (A-MA) about his antislavery views (among other things, pressing him on his "let the Union slide" statement, which had been far more hesitant when he uttered it and was transformed into a rallying cry after the fact), the second-termer Preston Brooks (D-SC) took a stand. Resistance to Northern aggression should begin among the South's appointed leaders in the House, Brooks said. "We are standing upon slave territory, surrounded by slave States, and pride, honor, patriotism, all command us, if a battle is to be fought, to fight it here upon this floor."[26]

Despite such talk, there was no bloodshed during the speakership election, though there were uproars aplenty and two assaults, both against members of the press.[27] On December 21, William "Extra Billy" Smith (D-VA)—so called because of the extra fees he raked in as a government contractor—assaulted the *Evening Star* editor William "Dug" Wallach for calling him a Know Nothing in his paper. The two clinched on the Avenue, and although Wallach routinely carried a "big knife, with which to settle such little controversies," the two men did little more than scratch and claw each other, though one of Wallach's fingers was "catawompously chawed up" by Smith.[28] (Noting the incident, the British foreign minister warned the folks back home that no foreign minister should ever—under any circumstances—go down to the House floor; congressmen were too dangerous.)[29] A few weeks later, when the *New-York Tribune* denounced Albert Rust (D-AR) for trying to disqualify Banks for the speakership, Rust assaulted the *Tribune* editor Horace Greeley twice, first punching him in the head on the Capitol grounds, then hitting him with his cane near the National Hotel a short while later. (Rust must have been contemplating a duel because, before striking a blow, he asked Greeley if he was a non-combatant.) Greeley did as many embattled Republicans would do for years to come, portraying himself as a heroic enemy of the Slave Power. "I came here with a clear understanding that it was about an even chance whether I should or should not be allowed to go home alive," he wrote in the *Tribune*. Even so, he would stay true to the cause, refusing to run "if ruffians waylay and assail me."[30] William Pitt Fessenden believed him. "I do not think he would run to save his life," he concluded after dining with Greeley shortly after the incident.[31] Greeley and a "fighting party of Northern men" went armed thereafter. In private, Greeley let down his fighting-man mask, admitting that he was "too sick to be out of bed, too crazy to sleep, and . . . surrounded by horrors."[32]

It took two months and 132 ballots to resolve the election, but ultimately, something remarkable happened: the House elected an anti-slavery Northern Speaker: Nathaniel Banks of Massachusetts, another Know Nothing on his way to becoming a Republican. Banks's election was a stunning victory for the nascent Republican Party. When it was announced on the evening of February 2, 1856, the Republican side of the House erupted in a shout of triumph followed by hearty handshakes and heartfelt embraces. The stalwart Joshua Giddings, the oldest House member with unbroken service, was given the honor of administering the oath of office. "Our victory is most glorious," he wrote home the next day. "I have reached the highest point of my ambition . . . *I am satisfied*."[33]

Even in victory, the Republican press predicted trials to come. "There *is* a North, thank God; and for once it has asserted its right to be a power under the Constitution," cheered *The New York Times*.[34] "We shall see whether or no the North *can* take care of the Union." Such concern was well founded given the feelings of at least some Southerners, as reflected in a letter to Speaker Banks. Not long after his election, he received a two-page string of insults signed "John Swanson & 40,000 others." Condemning Banks as "a poor Shit ass trator tory Coward," Swanson told him to "Quit the US God damn you and your party if you don't like us." (And in a sentence that raises interesting questions about Swanson's image of hell, he swore that "Hell is full of Such men as You. . . . So full that their feet Stick out at the Window.")[35] Banks must have been amused, or at least struck, because he saved the letter. Doubtless it wasn't his only piece of hate mail. Nor was it Swanson's only commentary on the Thirty-fourth Congress; he had nothing but praise for Preston Brooks (D-SC) for caning "the Damn Rascal liar tory and Traitor Sumner."[36]

From the moment that Brooks inflicted his savage blows, the can-

ing of the abolitionist Senator Charles Sumner (R-MA) on May 22,
1856, has been steeped in meaning. Generations of historians have
plumbed its depths in explaining the coming of the Civil War and ex-
ploring American values at a peak moment of strife.[37] But in the distance of time, its full context has been lost. As violent as it was, Sumner's
caning wasn't shocking *only* because it was violent. It was the nature
of the caning's violence, its timing, and its connection to swirling
conspiracy theories that gave the assault its full sectional punch and
national impact. That impact, in turn, profoundly affected public expectations of congressmen, and in so doing changed the workings of
Congress.

The caning was prompted by Sumner's "Crime Against Kansas"
speech, a monumental effort that took five hours over May 19 and 20,
filling 112 printed pages. Two months past, Sumner had been itching to
confront the "Slave oligarchy."[38] His speech fulfilled that goal and more.

This wasn't Sumner's first oratorical stab at the Slave Power, nor
would it be his last. Like most of his speeches, it was polished to a sheen
before delivery, typeset, and ready for mass mailing as he stood to
speak. As was his habit, Sumner was reaching for a broad national audience, hoping to rouse widespread public support for his cause. In many
ways, given the unlikelihood that persuasion would solve the seemingly irresolvable slavery problem, Sumner wasn't really speaking to the
Senate at all.

With that larger audience in mind, Sumner let loose. He first discussed the brutal "rape" of Kansas by proslavery forces, and condemned
Southern "plantation manners" and his Southern colleagues' habit of
"trampling" congressional rules "under foot"—an echo of John Quincy
Adams's complaint of fifteen years past.[39] The next day, he outlined proposed remedies for the Kansas problem, demanding its admittance to
the Union as a free state. Biting, defiant, and filled with sexual innuendo
about slaveholders and their love of slavery, Sumner's speech was a tour
de force. It also fulfilled the wishes of many of his constituents and supporters, who had been urging him to strike at "Southern bravado" and
"crush these fellows into submission."[40]

Throughout his speech, Sumner took special aim at three senators
who had attacked him during the Kansas-Nebraska debate two years
past—James Mason (D-VA), Stephen Douglas (D-IL), and Andrew But-

Charles Sumner, ca.
1855–65 (Courtesy of the
Library of Congress)

ler (D-SC), a relative of Preston Brooks—insulting them personally as
well as politically. Many Southerners felt the sting. "Mr. Sumner ought
to be knocked down, and his face jumped into," declared Representative
Thomas Rivers (A-TE).[41] Butler's friends felt that he was "compelled to
flog" Sumner.[42] Even as Sumner had been drawing his speech to a close,
Douglas—pacing impatiently in the back of the chamber—had muttered, "That damn fool will get himself killed by some other damn fool."[43]
Given that Sumner wasn't a fighting man, he seemed to be *asking*
Southerners "to kick him as we would a dog in the street."[44] Fearing
that was the case, a few of Sumner's friends asked to walk him home,
but he refused.

The next day, Brooks decided to take action. A newspaper account
of Sumner's speech confirmed that he had insulted Butler, South Carolina, and indeed, the entire South. Considering it his duty as a South
Carolina representative to resent the dishonor, Brooks decided to beat
Sumner rather than challenge him to a duel because he knew that the

New Englander would never accept a challenge *and* because sending a duel challenge "would subject me to legal penalties more severe than would be imposed for a simple assault and battery."[45] Here was the dark logic of the anti-dueling law. Better to beat Sumner than to run the more severe legal risk of challenging him to a duel.

So on May 22, as Sumner sat at his Senate desk franking copies of his Kansas speech for mailing, Brooks entered the Senate, cane in hand. Noticing several women in the chamber, he sat down and impatiently waited for them to leave. (Pointing to the last remaining woman, he asked a Senate secretary, "Can't you manage to get her out?" When the secretary joked that ousting her would be "ungallant" because she was "very pretty," Brooks took a second look and replied, "Yes; she is pretty, but I wish she would go.") Finally, the moment was right. Walking up to Sumner's desk, Brooks declared: "Mr. Sumner, I read your speech with care and as much impartiality as was possible and I felt it was my duty to tell you that you have libeled my state and slandered a relative who is aged and absent and I am come to punish you for it." At that, he

Preston Brooks, ca. 1856, allegedly taken shortly after he caned Sumner (Courtesy of the Library of Congress)

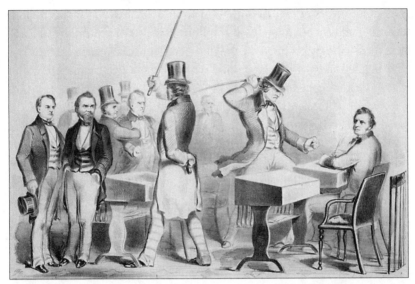

This 1856 print captures Northern outrage at Sumner's caning. Representative Laurence Keitt, hiding a gun behind his back, stands to the left of Brooks and Sumner, preventing intervention. In the background, Senator John J. Crittenden is being held back. (*Arguments of the Chivalry* by Winslow Homer. Courtesy of the Library of Congress)

raised his cane and began to beat Sumner over the head, inflicting more than a dozen brutal blows before his cane shattered, with his friend Laurence Keitt fending off intervention.

Stunned and bloodied, Sumner struggled to get away, but was held fast by his desk, which was bolted to the floor; he ultimately wrenched it free before collapsing. As luck would have it, the elderly Senator John J. Crittenden of Kentucky—who had watched Jonathan Cilley die in 1838—happened to be in the Senate chamber, and he ran toward Brooks yelling, "Don't kill him!" But by the time he reached Sumner, Brooks had stopped. Bloody and barely conscious, Sumner was carried from the chamber.

Although Brooks couldn't possibly have imagined the full impact of his actions before his assault, he made several choices that would amplify its power a thousandfold. Initially intending to obey the rules of congressional combat, he violated them in ways that couldn't be forgiven. His first instinct was good: before attacking, he confirmed the precise wording of Sumner's insults in the press. But from there his decisions went downhill.

Take, for example, his decision to attack Sumner in the Senate chamber. Physical violence on the floor was usually spontaneous; angry words or hostile charges escalated until someone jumped to his feet and headed toward his antagonist with no good intentions. Men who staged violent "collisions" in the House or Senate were usually chastised, as was Foote for arming himself before picking a fight with Benton. As people insisted after the resulting scuffle, deliberate assaults belonged on the street. Sam Houston's 1832 caning of William Stanbery (AJ-OH) on Pennsylvania Avenue was typical of this kind of predetermined clash; before the assault, Houston had hefted his stout hickory cane in the House in full view of Stanbery as an advance warning.[46] Brooks's first impulse was in line with this tradition; he fully intended to attack Sumner out of doors. Only after two fruitless days of watching for Sumner on the Capitol grounds did he decide to confront him in the Senate, and even then he initially planned to ask Sumner to step outside.[47]

The powerful symbolism of a senator beaten to the ground on the Senate floor shows the wisdom of staging such attacks outdoors. Nothing that happened in the Capitol seemed purely personal, and everything that happened there could be played up by the press. This was particularly true in the context of the late 1850s, when a Southern assault against a Northern congressman in the Capitol, inflicted with calm intention, seemed like Slave Power brutality and arrogance personified. Even some Southerners felt that a line had been crossed. "All agree that if Brooks had beaten him anywhere but *on the head & in the Senate*, he would but have served him right," wrote Charlotte Wise, wife of the flame-throwing Henry Wise's cousin Henry.[48] Brooks's friend Henry Edmundson (D-VA) of Campbell-fighting fame, acting as an advisor of sorts, had good reason for questioning the wisdom of staging the confrontation in the Senate, asking a colleague for advice on the matter even as the assault began.[49]

Brooks also failed to make his fight fair. Of course, his most grievous sin along these lines was caning an unarmed man pinioned by his desk. But attacking that man without warning was also foul play. Unlike Houston, Brooks didn't warn his victim of his violent intentions, nor did his confidants Edmundson and Keitt, and Sumner wasn't known to carry weapons for self-defense. The committee report on the caning recommended the House "declare its disapprobation" of both Edmundson and Keitt for this "reprehensible" lapse, as well as recommending that Brooks be expelled for the caning.[50] (A minority report suggested taking no action, claiming that the matter was a case for criminal courts.)

When it came to boosting sectional hostilities, the caning's timing couldn't have been better. One day past, the town of Lawrence, Kansas, founded by antislavery settlers, had been ransacked by proslavery assailants, and the press was rife with bloodshed. Newspapers were also filled with talk of the murder of a waiter at Willard's Hotel by a California congressman. On May 8, the Southern-born Philemon Herbert (D-CA) had shot a waiter dead for refusing to serve him breakfast past the appointed hour (though not before provoking a dish-throwing, chair-tossing brawl). Even before the caning, the Northern press had portrayed the murder as proof of a "systematic" Slave Power reign of violence.[51] Brooks's attack seemed like more of the same but ten times worse. As the *New Hampshire Statesman* put it, the assault on Sumner had created a "hostility against the Slave Power more intense than ever." It was another "link in the chain of flagitious outrages upon the North by which we are debased forever."[52] Violence in Congress and in Kansas were now inseparably linked.

In essence, Sumner's caning was a final, brutal insult that drove home the meaning of a string of violent encounters, and the Northern press was quick to spread that message—very quick; thanks to the telegraph, *The New York Times* received its first news of the caning a mere forty-five minutes after it happened.[53] The *Boston Atlas* heard that message loud and clear, noting: "We understand perfectly well that nothing could give [Southerners] more exquisite pleasure than to kill us all."[54] Linking the beatings of Wallach, Greeley, and Sumner with the murder at Willard's Hotel and events in Kansas, the *New York Courier and Enquirer* editor James Watson Webb—now a Republican—concluded, "No reasonable man should doubt that the Slave power have unalterably determined to extend the area of their now merely *local* institution; and if possible to render it *National*. The bowie-knife, the pistol, and the bludgeon . . . to be used in effecting this result."[55] Webb's column was reprinted widely, in part because, as the *Lowell Daily Citizen* explained, Webb, once a "highly conservative" defender of the slavery status quo, was now preaching resistance to the Slave Power with its own weapons. Webb's conversion was a powerful story in and of itself.[56] His harsh

This print from the presidential election of 1856 attacks the Democratic platform as proslavery, pro-South, and pro-violence, linking "Bleeding Kansas" (in
the left background) with the caning of Sumner (in the left foreground). (Courtesy
of the Library of Congress)

attack on the caning also earned him a letter from Brooks hinting at a
duel.[57]

Republican congressmen were just as quick to stress the caning's
meaning, as was Sumner, who seized on the power of the moment even
as he was carried off the Senate floor; moments later, still bloodied from
the beating, he told William Seward that he hoped it would serve the
antislavery cause.[58] It did. Sumner's speech became a national sensation.
The New York Times printed 40,000 copies and sold out by May 28;
within a month, 90,000 copies had been sold.[59] Caught up in the wellspring of outrage that surrounded the caning, Republican congressmen
voiced their grievances with gusto, raising fears of violent outcomes.

Hannibal Hamlin (R-ME) believed that someone would be shot down before the session closed. "Let it come," he wrote to William Pitt Fessenden. "If we do not stand manfully and fearlessly to the work before us, we ought to be slaves."[60] Fessenden was more optimistic; he thought that violence might subside for a time, but not because of cooler heads. Southerners might think twice before attacking because Northerners had "made up their minds not to be beaten to death without making such an experiment dangerous, and in my judgment such a determination is a duty of the Country, & the cause."[61] This was a severe message indeed: it was the patriotic duty of good Republican congressmen to fight. Brooks heard that message, admitting to his brother that his main risk was "assassination, but this you must not intimate to Mother."[62]

Southerners also were enraged and prepared to take action; by their account, Sumner's speech had been an outrage, Northern aggression was flaming out of control, and Brooks's response was praiseworthy. As Governor Henry Wise of Virginia put it, "How can we stand continual aggression everywhere—in Congress, in the pulpit, in the Press?"[63] Even the mere idea of a Southern conspiracy was insulting; hearing the claim, the ever extreme Thomas Clingman (D-NC) jumped to his feet and declared the Northerner who uttered it a liar. When Lewis Campbell of Kansas fame responded by asking if Clingman meant anything personal—an opening for a duel—the matter fizzled.[64] If Brooks was punished for combatting Southern degradation, the result might be ugly, many claimed. Visiting Washington a week after the caning, Wise's cousin Henry thought the House might "ring with vollies from revolvers" when Brooks's expulsion came up for debate.[65] Laurence Keitt thought that if Northerners fought force with force, the nation's capital would "float with blood."[66]

As Wise predicted, the debate of Brooks's expulsion in July was explosive. The feeling on the floor was made apparent in a letter sent to Speaker Banks on July 10 by a Democratic congressman so fearful of being exposed as a compromiser that he didn't sign his name, identifying himself only as "A Well Wisher." Because of the intense feelings on the floor, the writer feared an "impending calamity."

> Do you know, Sir, that there exists at this time an almost murderous feeling, between certain members of the North and South, and that it is with some difficulty that a few peace-loving

and happily influential associates, can prevent demonstrations upon the floor, which in the present state of excitement, would almost certainly lead to a general melee and perhaps a dozen deaths in the twinkling of an eye.

A number of Southerners were "constantly on the qui vive to prevent the throwing of missiles first from their side." Would Banks do the same among his friends? Would he discourage them from exploiting the crisis with Buncombe speeches full of abuse that would "goad their opponents beyond bearing?"[67] Clearly, as much as congressmen were performing for a national audience, the feelings on the floor were real.[68] Not everyone was ready to throw missiles, but a few missile-throwers could cause chaos.

Despite that warning, one Republican after another condemned Brooks and the "Sumner outrage," and howled defiance at the Slave Power. Brooks saw it coming and swore that "if this is done there will be an exciting time." He stayed true to his word. Although he initially planned to "degrade the most prominent" Republican "to degrade their party too," he went on something of a degradation spree, initiating duels with three Republicans who spoke out against him, insultingly dismissing a fourth Republican as not worth dueling (after allegedly threatening him in the lobby of Willard's Hotel), and trying to bludgeon two Republicans at that same hotel while roistering with friends in a drunken haze.[69] Keitt also nearly fought a duel with a Republican, and Robert Toombs (D-GA) was rumored to have considered one. Alexander Campbell (R-OH), who proposed a House investigation of the caning, was also threatened with violence.[70] All told, the caning spawned at least eight confrontations that session, as well as countless threats.

Brooks's two most notable wrangles were with Massachusetts Republicans Henry Wilson and Anson Burlingame; in response to their speechifying, he challenged both men to duels. Wilson saw trouble coming and armed himself with a revolver. "[H]e is just the man to use it," chirped French, who also predicted trouble for James Watson Webb. Webb's newspaper piece would doubtless "stir up the Chivalry," and as French knew all too well from "Cilley scenes" of years past, "Webb is a man who fights."[71] French was calculating congressional combat, as was most of Washington.

Faced with that eternal conundrum for Northern congressmen—a duel challenge—Wilson and Burlingame took different paths. Wilson denounced the barbarity of the code of honor but upheld "the right of self-defence," essentially making himself available for a street fight, as was widely understood at the time.[72] Burlingame issued a hedgy apology for his words, saying that he meant nothing personal, but then retracted his statement and accepted Brooks's challenge, naming the Canadian side of Niagara Falls as their dueling ground. Burlingame's second claimed to have headed north—far north—because congressional insiders told him that Jonathan Cilley had been disadvantaged by fighting his duel in the South.[73] In both cases, nothing further happened, though Brooks emerged from his non-encounter with Burlingame tainted by a whiff of cowardice for declining to fight, despite his insistence that he had good reason; as he explained in the press, had he traveled north he would have been killed in "the enemy's country."[74] (French was still thinking about the non-duel during a trip to Niagara Falls a year later, quipping *"Burlingame not there!"*)[75] More than one Southerner noted that Brooks clearly didn't want to fight, and that Burlingame and his clueless Yankee friends had missed their cues and almost stumbled into a duel.[76]

Although in the end neither Wilson nor Burlingame did any fighting, they showed what their contemporaries would have called "pluck," and were applauded for it in the North and Northwest, Wilson for spurning a challenge without backing down, and Burlingame for *not* spurning a challenge; as ever, Northerners were conflicted about the code of honor and their congressmen. Although there was a good deal of murmuring about Burlingame's acceptance of a challenge (including on the part of Sumner himself, who deplored Burlingame's surrender to "Southern barbarianism"), in light of the grievous insult of Sumner's caning, the criticism was outweighed by the praise heaped on Burlingame's head for standing tall before the Slave Power.[77] He received reams of fan mail praising his "manly" spirit.[78] Barnstorming out west for the coming elections, he was feted like a hero. In Ohio, Illinois, Indiana, and Michigan, people sang his praises, celebrating him with parades and processions and flocking by the thousands to hear him speak. In Indiana, people traveled in horse teams to see him. One event featured women dressed as states and men as "border ruffians," revealing the close link between the caning and Kansas in the public mind. "It touches my heart Jennie to find how, on account of that Brooks affair, the *people* seem to regard me with tenderness," Burlingame told his wife. The "whole population of the west seems wild to see your naughty husband because he did not run away from Brooks . . . [T]he people like such '*bad*' men as I am."[79] Wilson, too, was heralded with pomp and circumstance. At a massive protest meeting in Faneuil Hall, he was praised as "a gentleman who believed in the defence of freedom, and also in self defence."[80]

Sumner's caning had made heroes of fighting Republicans. Burlingame was right; in the context of a rising Slave Power plot, with the humiliation of Sumner's caning fresh at hand, people in the free states *did* like "bad men." The fist-raised fighting posture of Republicans became so marked that Democrats mocked it in electioneering fodder, as in a campaign song sung to a popular tune titled "Wait for the Wagon," which smacked at swaggering Republicans in its opening lines:

Will you come with me good Democrats,
And rally round our flag,
To fight the black Republicans
Who play the game of brag?[81]

This perfect storm of events—the pull of the Slave Power plot, the chain of events that seemed to prove it, the savvy of Republicans who connected the dots and sold their party as the way to stem the tide, the stunning brutality of Sumner's caning, and the presence of Republican congressmen willing to step up and fight—fueled the Republican Party's rise to power.[82] Although the presidential election of 1856 went to Democrat James Buchanan, the Republicans did remarkably well for a new party, garnering 33.1 percent of the electoral vote.[83] The attack on Sumner and public support of the congressional fighting men who championed him were an inherent part of that telling feat.[84] Congressional violence ushered in the Third Party System.

The fuel that powered the rise of the Republican Party was emotion: fear of Southern dominance, anger at Northern degradation, horror at the brutal realities of slavery.[85] Thus the many heavily attended "indignation meetings" throughout the North after Sumner's caning. As a speaker at a meeting in Cambridge, Massachusetts, put it, Brooks was guilty of an "indignity offered to Massachusetts, a sovereign state, in the person of her Senator." Others considered the assault an insult not only to Massachusetts, "but to New England and all the Free States."[86] For many Northerners, an attack on Sumner was an attack on them all.

Beneath the indignation was a blunt reality, long known but now unavoidably exposed: Northern congressmen were routinely silenced by Southerners. In Northern meetings, demonstrations, and printed resolutions, the same points were made again and again. Northern representatives were being denied freedom of debate on the floor. Their constituents were being denied their representative rights in Congress. As a speech at an indignation meeting at Union College expressed it: the attack on Sumner had been a "blow aimed at the Freedom of debate," a "bold attempt to terrify the representatives of a free people in the exersise of their constitutional rights." A Maine newspaper agreed: "the blows showered upon bleeding Sumner, are blows directed at us, for using rights that we have enjoyed every day of our lives."[87] For this writer, the right of free speech wasn't an abstraction. It was a routine part of everyday life that had to be defended, a thought echoed in dozens of letters to Sumner.

Congressmen had long acted as surrogates for all that they represented, fighting and even dying for the rights and honor of their people, their states, and their sections when duty called. The caning raised awareness of that fact to new heights in both North and South. To countless Americans, Sumner *was* the North suffering at the hand of the South and Brooks *was* the South enforcing its command. As one newspaper put it, the assault was a "representative act."[88] "I have lost my individuality in my representative capacity," Brooks said after the caning. "I am regarded to a great extent as the exponent of the South against which Black Republicanism is war[r]ing in my person."[89] French knew that the caning "*in itself,* was a personal matter." But he also knew that it would create "a feeling throughout the Union that cannot easily be calmed."[90]

The Cilley-Graves duel had touched a similar nerve. Both men fought for the honor of their people, their state, their section, and their party, and the North had responded to Cilley's death with horror and outrage. But national parties had cushioned the blow. Although a Southerner had killed a Northerner using a Southern weapon—the code of honor—the tragedy came to be viewed as an unfortunate moment of excess in an ongoing party struggle. The lesson learned, if any, was that Northerners were at a disadvantage in the sectional middle ground of Congress.

The lessons of Sumner's caning were more severe; Brooks's savage blows hit their mark. Northern audiences learned what Northern degradation felt like; they saw its power in the near-speechless outrage of Northern congressmen as depicted in the press. The all-too-appropriately named Northern indignation meetings show the intensely emotional public response, as did the fleeing of many a man's son to Kansas to champion its admission to the Union as a free state. French calmed his son after the caning, but William Fessenden wasn't as lucky; his son Sam ran away from college to fight in Kansas, though he was tracked down in Illinois and brought home.[91]

Northerners also learned what it felt like when their representatives fought back—and they liked it.[92] Having witnessed Southern bullying in Congress and in Kansas, they found resistance "refreshing."[93] This was a lesson that Northern voters and congressmen would take to heart in years to come. Thus the *Richmond Whig*'s half-joking plea to Southern senators not to cane, kick, or spit on Henry Wilson (R-MA), who seemed "fatally bent" on sparking a fight to ensure his reelection.[94]

Southerners learned equally powerful lessons. Sumner's speech, and to an even greater degree the tirades by Republican congressmen after his caning, schooled Southerners in the emotional power of Northern aggression. Reading the Northern hail of accusations and insults against the South, and seeing in newsprint the red-faced fury of their representatives as they absorbed those blows, they learned what that aggression felt like as never before, and they wanted it put down. Indeed, it *had* to be put down. As a Southern paper put it two years later, in the name of Southern security, interests, and honor, any such aggressors should be "Sumnarized."[95] Had Sumner not been caned, wrote one Southerner, "the impression would have been confirmed, that the fear of our slaves had made us such cowards that we could be kicked with impunity."[96]

Brooks was also of this mind, as his last speech in Congress made clear. Although the House ultimately voted against his expulsion, he resigned his seat and went home—but not before having his say. He had caned Sumner to defend his state and his kinsman, he declared, nothing more. He didn't want to set a precedent that would end in "drenching this Hall in blood." But a blow struck at him by a Northerner could result in revolution, he warned. Sectional tempers were high, and the South would defend him with bloodshed if necessary. (And indeed, at this point in Brooks's speech, Southerners in the visitors' gallery cheered.) Brooks was calling for a cease-fire but issuing a threat. He then left the House and went home, as did Laurence Keitt two days later when he was formally censured. Both men were immediately reelected.[97]

Given the ongoing congressional floor show, public perceptions of Congress became increasingly dark and dire. Writing home from Harvard a few days after the caning, French's son Frank called Congress "a slaughter house."[98] In a letter to Sumner, his fellow Bay State abolitionist Reverend John Turner Sargent described the floor of Congress as a "field of blood." He had fully expected that "blood would flow,—*somebody's* blood, either *yours* or *Wilsons*, or *Hales*, or *Giddings* before the expiration of your present session on that field of blood, the floor of Congress."[99] Former Massachusetts congressman Edward Everett echoed that thought. He had long foreseen that "the crisis in our political relations at home would be brought on by some personal collision at Washington."[100]

Admittedly, such feelings were extreme. In years to come, violence would rise and fall in Congress. The extreme emotion in the wake of the caning didn't—indeed, couldn't—last forever; by the end of July it had passed.[101] But the "Sumner outrage" and the rise of the Republican Party fundamentally changed public expectations of their congressmen, and in so doing, changed the nature of Congress. Violence would be more than a parliamentary ploy in years to come. It would be a declaration of rights, a banner struck for the cause, a battle cry played for the rafters, and Congress would come to seem more like a battleground than ever before.

Given the extreme emotion, it's easy to forget that not everyone shared it. But even in the midst of the uproar, some moderate people remained moderate, at least in private; the din of sectional battle cries silenced most such voices in public. "Nothing but denunciation & defiance seem to be tolerated by the masses," moaned the former Massachusetts congressman Robert Winthrop, commiserating with his former Virginia colleague William Cabell Rives.[102] "Timid men" fear speaking out "for fear of being stigmatised . . . as disloyal to the South," said Virginian Alexander Rives. Edward Everett said much the same. "No one dares speak aloud on the subject except to echo the popular voice." Even failing to be angry enough was dangerous; Everett was assailed in the press when he didn't attend a large indignation meeting in Boston.[103] Ironically, in their fervor to defend free speech, Northerners were stifling it.

French was one such moderate man, but by 1856, the nature of moderation had changed. For many Northerners, preserving the Union meant defending Northern rights. As much as French urged compromise and conciliation, his hunger to champion Northern rights didn't waver. Neither did his commitment to the Republican Party. At its first national convention, in June 1856, French played an active role, just as one would expect of a clerk assisting in the launching of a national organization. He was on the committee that confirmed delegate credentials, and when the convention created a committee composed of a member from each state to draft the party's platform, it was French who reminded the gathering to include someone from Kansas, which was not yet a state.[104]

But even French was getting swept up in the tide of emotions. In January 1857, when thirty-six-year-old Preston Brooks died of suffocation from an acute sore throat—an event that Northerners deemed providential—French thought back to his first encounter with Brooks a few years back. He had liked the man immediately, and liked him more over time. Months before the caning, spotting Brooks seeking votes for a pension for a "poor old soldier friend," French had introduced him to Amos Granger (R-NY), who helped get Brooks's bill passed. French's congratulations were his last words to the South Carolinian. When they next met about ten days before Brooks's death, French and a friend were strolling down the Avenue, but although Brooks chatted with French's friend for several minutes, Brooks and French refused to acknowledge each other.[105] As much as French liked Brooks, in the context of the times he was unable to speak with him, almost despite himself.

In this sense, the crisis of the Union was a crisis of communication. Northerners were waging war against the South with dangerous words; Southerners were trying to stifle those words with force, and the cross-fire was cutting off conversation, particularly in Congress, an institution grounded on open debate and free speech. The Constitution granted congressmen immunity for their words for a reason, though that right had long been violated by bullies inflicting gags and by their victims spurning privilege of debate in honor disputes. The slavery crisis of the 1850s made this gap between ideals and realities glaringly apparent.[106]

For French and countless Northerners, the "fight for freedom," as French called it, was thus fundamentally bound up with the right of free speech.[107] The Northern press celebrated it. Indignation meetings rallied behind it. It was heralded as the pride of Northern democracy, the heart of democratic governance, and the soul of the Union. More than anything else, this was the Northern lesson learned from Sumner's caning. Northern rights, Northern honor, and democratic governance required free speech, and the Slave Power was brutally suppressing it to advance its regime, a violation that called for extreme measures of resistance.

Thus the concern over dangerous words at the national center, where they had the power to tear Congress and the nation in two. The anonymous letter to Nathaniel Banks made this threat clear. The only way to fend off disaster in Congress was to avoid throwing "missiles" of inflammatory words. "Let gentlemen who may choose to take part in this debate, scrupulously avoid the utterance of *unnecessarily harsh language*."[108] Israel Washburn (R-ME) said the same thing when debating Brooks's expulsion: "Let us not irritate each other. Let us avoid disagreeable language to each other."[109] Franklin Pierce echoed that request a few years later from retirement in New Hampshire, pleading for "temperate words" in Congress.[110] During this same period, Thomas Hart Benton was removing dangerous words from the congressional record in the hope of soothing tempers and saving the "brotherly Union." He spent his last years writing an abridgement of congressional debates from 1789 through 1856 with the threats and insults removed, including his infamous 1850 clash with Henry Foote. Sick with cancer and working in intense pain, he died the day after he completed it.[111] As Benton well knew, for Congress and the Union to survive this crisis— for cross-sectional conversation to be even possible—people had to watch their words. The alternative was Union-rending violence.

Free speech and violence were thus dangerously intertwined.[112] For the South, they always had been; to suppress dangerous words was to suppress slave insurrection. In Congress, another kind of insurrection was at hand. Northern congressmen were rising up and their chief weapons were the right of free speech and their willingness to fight for that right. Massachusetts Republican Chauncey Knapp's constituents said as much in June 1856 when they saw him off as he headed back to Washington. Just before Knapp boarded the train, a small assembly of people gave him a parting gift for use in Congress: a revolver inscribed with the words "Free Speech."[113]

"A HELL OF LEGISLATION"

Knapp had been given his marching orders: fight—literally *fight*—for our rights. Such was the legacy of 1856: a heightening of sectional tensions and a spike in congressional violence, as well as an ever more intense emotional investment in the fate of Kansas. Knapp wasn't the only person being presented with weapons by enraged Northerners; this was the period when Northerners began shipping cartons of rifles to free-state settlers in Kansas.[114] Noting the crowded House and Senate galleries in 1858, French thought that the "intense feeling . . . from this political centre has radiated the fever heat to all quarters of the Union." French was doing his part to spread that heat. At the end of January 1857 he became president of the National Republican Association of Washington. Founded in 1855 as a club of roughly twenty-nine members (including the exceedingly clubbable French), within a few years its membership had climbed to several hundred.[115] Its main purpose was to disseminate Republican political tracts and speeches throughout the nation, aided by the inner workings of Congress, congressional clout and mailing lists, and free postage courtesy of the congressional frank. By all accounts, the association did its job admirably; during the 1856 presidential campaign, it claimed to have circulated four million documents.[116]

As president, French set out in earnest to gain Republican seats in the midterm elections of 1858. A newspaper announcement in May showed the association's strategy. First, it needed Republicans around the country to send good Republican cash—"the *freest* offering of a *free people* in the *Free States*." Then, it would produce and disseminate mass mailings. A newspaper announcement a few months later revealed the fruits of its labor: an extensive list of speeches and tracts for sale, ranging in price from 75 cents to $1.75 per hundred copies. With a handful of exceptions, every publication was about Kansas.[117]

By spreading around his name in the press as president, French spread news of his new party loyalties. In June, the *Albany Evening Journal* took notice. "Major B. B. French, an old line democratic politician of New Hampshire, for many years an office-holder at Washington, has become president of the National Republican Association in the capital, which is not agreeable to his old friends."[118] Battle lines were being drawn.

In Congress, that was no mere metaphor. Thinking back to this period after the Civil War, veterans of the Thirty-fifth and Thirty-sixth Congresses remembered the years between 1857 and 1861 as a time of fierce sectional violence on the floor. These were the years that drove Senators Benjamin Wade (R-OH), Simon Cameron (R-PA), and Zachariah Chandler (R-MI) to create their pact to "fight to the coffin" regardless of the consequences. The "gross personal abuse" inflicted by their slave-state colleagues was insulting their manhood and depriving their constituents of their representative rights. Yet, because of Northern anti-dueling sentiment, Northern congressmen held back and were treated like cowards. "I feel it frequently," Wade admitted.[119]

The abuse that produced their pact probably took place during a Senate debate over Kansas's constitution. In 1855, free-state advocates had produced an antislavery constitution in Topeka; two years later, slaveowners drafted a competing proslavery constitution in Lecompton, the state's capital. After a messy and corrupted vote on the two constitutions, Kansans had sent both documents to Washington for congressional approval. During an all-night session on March 15, 1858, hostilities peaked. Eager to push through the Lecompton constitution, Robert Toombs (D-GA) threatened to "crush" the Republican Party, provoking an outburst of Republican outrage.[120]

As a result, Republican nerves were already on edge when later that evening Cameron accused James Green (D-MO) of dictating terms to the Republicans; in the course of the argument that followed, each man threw the lie at the other, Cameron took responsibility for his words, and Green hinted at a duel challenge.[121] Cameron's subsequent consultation with Wade and Chandler led to their decision to put an end to such taunts by challenging future offenders to duels. There seemed to be no other way to counter the "deep humiliation" of the "people of the Free States," and to some degree, their ploy worked. Their willingness to fight checked some abuse. As they later concluded, risking their reputations, their careers, and perhaps even their lives was the price of fighting slavery in Congress.[122]

For Thaddeus Stevens (R-PA), these years marked the start of armed sectional combat in the House. Discussing the imminent return of Southerners to Congress after the Civil War a decade later, he urged colleagues not to be hasty. The new congressmen seated around him had no memory of Congress as a "camp of armed men." They hadn't seen Robert Toombs and his "gang" render the halls of Congress "a hell of legislation" by rushing with knives and guns "as one yelling body" at Northerners who dared to denounce slavery. Bring the Southerners back, but "first re-arm yourself," Stevens counseled, and "wait until I am gone."[123]

Stevens was speaking for effect, but he was very specific about the first instance of full-fledged sectional combat on the floor: the February 6, 1858, House melee caused by a clash between the radical Galusha Grow (R-PA) and the equally radical Lawrence Keitt (D-SC), the first time that a group of Northerners confronted a group of Southerners "force against force."[124] The "battle-royal in the House . . . was the first sectional fight ever had on the floor," wrote former congressman and future vice president of the Confederacy Alexander Stephens, noting that although no blood was shed, there were bad feelings in abundance.[125] The press agreed. "This is the most important and significant of all the fights that ever occurred in Congress," declared the *Charleston Mercury*. It was "a sectional and not a personal quarrel. It was North and South—not Grow and Keitt." Unlike previous fights, "members fought in battalions. They did not go into a corner or a lobby to fight, or entangle themselves as heretofore, between chairs and desks. They took an ample area—the open space before the Speaker's chair."[126]

The reasons for this change were many. Sectional passions were already flaring because of the Supreme Court's landmark Dred Scott decision of 1857, which ruled that enslaved people and their descendants could not be American citizens, and that the federal government could not ban slavery in western territories. Endorsing the spread of slavery and suggesting that the Court was a tool of the Slave Power, it was deeply felt by Northerners.[127]

Lawrence M. Keitt, 1859 (Courtesy of the Library of Congress)

Galusha A. Grow, 1859 (Courtesy of the Library of Congress)

It didn't help matters that the fight took place in the middle of an overnight session, virtually a guarantee of violence. The topic of debate—Kansas's proslavery Lecompton constitution—was also sure to enflame tempers and push people to extremes. Democrats made matters worse by delaying a vote because some Southerners were missing in action and every vote counted. Liquor also played a role, as it almost inevitably did during evening sessions; many of those missing Southerners, boozing at bars, were so dead drunk when dragged into the House that they were kept out of the chamber until it was their turn to vote.[128]

The two men at the heart of the fight were also lightning rods of conflict, though for different reasons; the combative Grow was a leading House Republican with a cut-and-thrust style of debate and strong antislavery views, and Keitt was an almost comically hot-tempered fire-eater who was ever and always defending Southern honor.[129] Their confrontation was the spark that set the congressional tinderbox aflame.

Not surprisingly, Keitt set things off. At about two o'clock in the morning, Grow was conferring with a Pennsylvania Democrat on the Democratic side of the House. As Grow headed back to his seat, someone asked to submit a motion out of order, and Grow objected. Keitt, who by some accounts was dozing and by many accounts was tipsy, was alert enough to yell that Grow should object on his own side of the House. Grow replied that it was a free hall and he could stand where he pleased, at which Keitt (supposedly muttering, "We'll see about that") stalked up to him and demanded to know what Grow meant, perhaps assuming that talk of a "free hall" was a backhanded slap at Southerners, or perhaps—knowing Keitt—assuming nothing at all; it didn't take much to set him off. When Grow repeated his words, Keitt grabbed Grow's throat, vowing to teach the "black republican puppy" a lesson. Knocking Keitt's arm away, Grow declared that he refused to be bullied by a slave driver cracking his whip. Keitt responded by grabbing Grow's throat again, at which Grow slugged him hard enough to knock him flat. And here the trouble began.

A group of Southerners immediately rushed over, some to aid Keitt, some to attack Grow, and some to calm things down, though the latter group ultimately got swept up in the scrimmage. Seeing a pack of Southerners descend on Grow, Republicans rallied to his aid, streaming across the chamber from their side of the hall, jumping on desks and chairs in

A comical view of the Keitt-Grow rumble (Barksdale's toupee is on the ground)
(Courtesy of the American Antiquarian Society)

their haste to save a brother Republican, bringing a rush of Southerners in their wake. The end result was a free fight in the open space in front of the Speaker's platform featuring roughly thirty sweaty, disheveled, mostly middle-aged congressmen in a no-holds-barred brawl, North against South.

Press accounts of the fight vary, but they generally agree that John "Bowie Knife" Potter (R-WI) and the fighting Washburn brothers—Cadwallader (R-WI), Israel (R-ME), and Elihu (R-IL)—stood out in the rumble, with the barrel-chested Potter jogging straight into the scrum, throwing punches as he tried to reach Grow.[130] At one point, he slugged William Barksdale (D-MS), who mistakenly reeled around and socked Elihu Washburne in return. (Elihu liked his Washburn with an *e*.) Potter responded by grabbing Barksdale by the hair to punch him in the face, but to his utter astonishment, Barksdale's hair came off; he wore a toupee. Meanwhile, John Covode (R-PA) had raised a spittoon above his head and was looking for a target, while the ashen-faced Speaker pounded his gavel for all it was worth and ordered the sergeant at arms to grab the mace and do something. Within a few minutes, people had settled back in their seats—thanks, in part, to the hilarity of Barksdale's flipped wig—and the House went back to arguing until its adjournment at 6:30 a.m. With the exception of a few black eyes and some cuts and scrapes, most of the combatants were none the worse for wear; a few men had reached for weapons, but none used them. (The *Globe* summed up the episode as a "violent personal altercation" between Keitt and Grow in which "several members seemed to participate.")[131]

The most notable aspect of the fight was the mass rescue by Republicans, who had rushed over to Grow with fists flying because they thought that Southerners were staging a group assault. This was Slave Power thinking; it was knee-jerk distrust of Southerners as brutal, domineering, determined to cow Northerners, and on the attack. This distrust was no back-of-the-mind matter of speculation. It was immediate; Republicans jumped into action in seconds. They also felt that at long last, they had taught Southerners a lesson. As Grow put it, Southerners had long been "under the delusion that Northern men would not fight." By running "from one side of the Chamber to the other . . . with fists clenched and arms flying," Republicans had taught Southerners that "Northern men will fight in a just cause."[132] In essence, Republicans were a different kind of Northerner. French's friend Daniel Clark (R-NH), boarding with French during this Congress, declared this to Robert Toombs when Toombs threatened to crush the Republican Party. He wouldn't have an easy time of it, Clark warned. "A different class of men now came from the North . . . They are sent not to bow down, but to stand up."[133]

The Republican press echoed Grow, glorying in the show of strength and savoring the vicarious pleasure of slugging Southern blowhards. The *Boston Traveler* listed a string of "comforting reflections" about Northern "pluck." Several newspapers gleefully noted that Reuben Davis (D-MS), who had recently given a rabid speech about conquering the North, got a black eye from Potter. (Davis claimed to have tripped over a chair.)[134] Best of all was the knockdown of the swaggering Keitt. "The great State of South Carolina (in the person of her valorous (!) representative, Mr. Keitt,) lies kicking in the dust," gloated *Frederick Douglass' Paper*, particularly relishing the fact that Grow, a representative of David Wilmot's district, had floored a man who helped Brooks cane Sumner.[135] In this rematch of the caning, the North had won. Many papers thought that after years of bullying Northerners, Southerners had finally learned a lesson. They had been "beaten with their own weapons, in their own way, and on their own ground."[136] "The South is cowed," claimed a *New York Times* letter-writer. "I know what I say—COWED."[137] (Hard-pressed for a comeback, the Democratic *New York Day Book* said that Keitt made a manly apology.)[138]

Judging from the Southern press, the South wasn't cowed. It was angry and defensive. Southern newspapers aimed most of their venom at the "Black Republican" press, so brutal in its accusations that it "cannot fail to be imitated in Congress."[139] The Northern press was full of lies, charged Southern papers. Grow, not Keitt, had started the fight. Grow, not Keitt, was insolent. Grow, not Keitt, had violated rules of order by not objecting from his seat. Nor was this fight anything special; such tussles happened all the time.[140] Equally grating, Northern papers were full of "vulgar boasting."[141] Northerners were entirely too focused on "the mere powers of the pugilism" and Grow's "chance-blow," charged the *Virginia Sentinel*. They didn't understand that honor wasn't a matter of muscle.

In truth, the *Sentinel* cared quite a bit about that blow, as did the many Southern newspapers that went out of their way to prove that

Grow most assuredly had *not* punched Keitt, who had tripped over a desk. Or stubbed his toe. Or been thrown off his feet when pulled away from Grow, who stood by, paralyzed with fear.[142] The *Charleston Mercury* went so far as to admit that Grow *might* have tried to hit Keitt, but he certainly never touched him. A felling blow from a "Black Republican" was not easily swallowed in the South.

This desperate need to prove that Keitt hadn't been punched spawned a cottage industry in jokes, puns, and poetry at Keitt's expense, none of it from the South, which wasn't laughing. Nor was Keitt, who tried to save face, first by claiming that he didn't know if he'd been struck, then by denying it.[143] The British were particularly amused at both the fuss and the rough-and-tumble of American politics. One humorist published a poem titled "How Mr. Keitt of South Carolina Stubbed His Toe."[144] *Punch* magazine outdid itself with an epic poem in the style of Homer's *Iliad*.[145]

> *Sing, O goddess, the wrath, the untamable dander of KEITT—*
> *KEITT of South Carolina, the clear grit, the tall, the*
>   *undaunted—*
> *Him that hath wopped his own niggers till Northerners all unto*
>   *KEITT*
> *Seem but as niggers to wop, and hills of the smallest potatoes.*

The description of Keitt's fall to glory is classic:

> *Prone like a log sank KEITT, his dollars rattled about him.*
> *Forth sprang his friends o'er the body; first, BARKSDALE,*
>   *waving-wig-wearer,*
> *CRAIGE and MACQUEEN and DAVIS, the ra'al hoss of wild*
>   *Mississippi;*
> *Fiercely they gathered round GROW, catawampously up as to*
>   *chaw him.*

Americans also tried their hand at poetry. In "Grow vs. Keitt," the *New London Chronicle* had this to say about Keitt's moment of glory:

> *Just then came a stunner beneath his left ear;*
> *And "the gentleman from South Carolina" felt queer;*

('Tis whispered that "stunner" was "planted" by Grow,
But "Chivalry" fancies he just "stubbed his toe.")

Keitt "stubbed his head against Grow's fist and fell down," charged one newspaper.[146] There was punning: "According to one Washington correspondent, Grow struck Keitt twice in the face. First the *eyes* had it, and then the *nose*."[147] During a theater performance a few days after the brawl, an actor even referenced the fight with an impromptu quip.[148]

Keitt's stubbed toe was an international sensation, though it was hardly the only fun poked at Congress in this period. The rise of congressional violence saw the rise of Congress-bashing in popular culture, and with it a healthy sampling of boxing culture, as countless references to "side licks, back handers, and stomach winders" attest.[149] Mocking do-nothing Congresses and congressmen was nothing new. There was a long and storied history of ridiculing the People's Branch that went back to the dawn of the republic. What changed in the 1850s was the amount of ridicule, its cutting edge, and its focus on violence.

A SCENE IN CONGRESS—SPECTATOR'S GALLERY.

FIRST PROFESSOR OF THE NOBLE ART OF SELF-DEFENSE. "I tell yer, Bill, them Republicans is the chaps to strike out with their left."

SECOND PROFESSOR OF DITTO. "Vell, Jim, I von't contradict yer; but if ever I seed better play of the Maulies nor them Car'lina chaps is making, vy, I'm an oyster."

A cartoon depicting a congressional rumble as a boxing match. A "mauly" is a fist. (*Harper's Weekly*, February 20, 1858. Courtesy of HarpWeek)

By far the best practitioner of this new school of journalism was *Vanity Fair*, a New York–based humor magazine that had the good fortune to publish its first issue in December 1859, at the start of the months-long struggle to organize the Thirty-sixth Congress, a stalemate that guaranteed more material than any one humor magazine could handle.[150] For a time, almost every issue spoofed brawling congressmen, making the journal a kind of *Congressional Fights Quarterly*. An article called "A Day in the House" was typical of the genre. Mimicking the style of conventional congressional press coverage, it reported a day's proceedings, consisting largely of an extended exchange of insults, Congress-style ("Without calling in question the integrity of Mr. Sherman, he would say that gentleman was not fit, politically, to iron shirts in a third class laundry"), and climaxed with a fight:

> Some evil-disposed person here cried "Order." This was the signal for instantaneous uproar. . . . Then ensued rare pegging and stepping, unexceptionable clinching, feinting, and planting of one twos on pimple and in wind. The Sergeant-at-Arms, having at length detected a foul blow on the part of an inexperienced new member, interposed, and said that if the disturbance continued he should be compelled to exclude the reporters.

The following week an article depicted Congress as "The Great National Circus," complete with knife-throwers, fire-eaters, and an equestrian who rides two horses going in different directions. A later issue included an advertisement for "The Congressman's Guide to Fame; or, The True Vocabulary of Vituperation," an alphabetical catalog of insults, including an example of the book in use: "Do we not know him for a Babbler,—for a Blasted Blattering, Blustering, Brawling, Blower?" Still another issue offered a skit in which a Democrat and a Republican, insulting each other in front of that perennial favorite of congressional combatants, Willard's Hotel, agree to postpone their duel until after the organization of Congress—meaning, forever. One issue even featured a fight on the cover, complete with a bowie knife and a revolver flying through the air.[151]

Of course, there was plenty to ridicule in Congress aside from violence. A mock letter from a Washington correspondent made fun of the perpetual struggle to avoid talk of slavery:

> Mr. SNOOKS (Dem.) of Coney Island, rose to introduce some resolution—concerning the state of the Union.
>
> Mr. GRIMES (Rep.) of Kennebec, said he hoped no member would discuss such exciting matters in these times.
>
> Mr. JONES (Opp.) of South Amboy, wished to present a bill for the better preservation of the Confederacy.
>
> Mr. ROBINSON (Rep.) of Sconsett, expressed great sorrow that gentlemen should introduce such disturbing subjects now.

Precisely mimicking such excuses as they appeared in the press, the article implied that in their efforts to avoid controversy (and thereby the fights that studded *Vanity Fair*'s pages), congressmen were doing nothing at all.[152]

Vanity Fair specialized in congressional violence, but images of brawling congressmen appeared everywhere: in poetry, in literature, in cartoons, even in plays.[153] In 1857, the government clerk Henry Clay Preuss published *Fashions and Follies of Washington Life*, a play that centers on a Northern congressman in love with a boardinghouse owner's daughter, and a government clerk and newspaper correspondent who loves the same woman and uses his column in a New York City newspaper to provoke a Southern congressman into challenging the Northerner to a duel and killing him. ("Sent off a slashing letter to New-York yesterday—fell like a bomb-shell in the House to-day!") The clerk's evil plot—to mention a recent congressional spat between the two congressmen and hint at "Southern chivalry and Southern aggression—and lament, most pathetically, a want of Northern pluck"—is remarkably true to life, as is his concern that the Northerner might not bite because he is "a Yankee—and these Yankees are hard to get in the ring." The Northern congressman's fear that he'll be ostracized back home for dueling is just as searingly true, as are his friend's urgings that the peculiarities of being a member of Congress leave him no choice but to fight. All in all, *Fashions and Follies* does a fine job of portraying the Northern congressman's dilemma as well as the boomerang-like nature of congressional threats and violence, which influenced the public through the vehicle of the press and rebounded back to influence Congress.[154]

Popular culture offered the public an image of Congress as a bull-pen of bravado, full of hot air and signifying nothing, and in so doing, made Washington a laughingstock as well, as in this quip from *The New York Times*:

> Judge Kellogg, a venerable citizen of Michigan, arrived in this city on Saturday evening. It was his first visit to the Federal Capital, and when the cars stopped, he was a little uncertain where he was. . . . As he entered the main hall of the depot, he saw a man engaged in caning another ferociously, all over the room. "When I saw this," says the Judge, "*I knew I was in Washington.*"[155]

Willard's Hotel didn't fare much better. A much-mentioned *Punch* cartoon showed an alarmed diner seated at a table in an "American hotel" with a gun pointed at his head. The caption? "Pass the mustard!"[156]

The rise of Congress-bashing and the rise of violence were in sync for good reason. First of all, there was a lot to bash. The image of staid congressmen throwing sidewinders and tossing spittoons was a near ir-resistible target of ridicule. But more than that, the humor served a purpose. For one thing, it defused tension, and there was plenty of ten-sion to defuse. If Congress's seemingly self-destructive chaos could be ridiculed, maybe it wasn't so threatening after all.

Humor was also a prod—a kinder, gentler way of urging congress-men to do better.[157] No one wanted to be laughed at, particularly self-important congressmen. Nor did they want to feel that they deserved ridicule; congressmen were all too familiar with the crushing weight of public opinion. (Keitt must have suffered agonies in 1858, though given that he started the fight, he deserved it.)

But perhaps most of all, humor was a way to vent public frustra-tion. A fistfight between a Northerner and a Southerner was the ulti-mate demonstration of an overwhelmed Congress succumbing to the temper of the times at the precise moment when congressional inter-vention was urgently needed. Even worse, clusters of brawling North-erners and Southerners were playacting the very thing that they were

This cartoon from British *Punch* magazine, published not long after California's Representative Philemon Herbert shot a waiter at Willard's Hotel, mocks America's routine violence. ("Life in an American Hotel?" by John Leech, 1856. Reproduced with permission of Punch Ltd., www.punch.co.uk)

supposed to prevent: civil warfare. It was more than irresponsible. It was disgraceful, as many tsk-tsking newspaper commentators said.

This isn't to say that congressmen were blunderers. They were fighting for good reasons: to win political power, to impress constituents, to support a cause, to defend sectional interests, to shape the nation. When literal push came to literal shove, the voting public *wanted* their congressmen to fight for their rights at this moment of crisis. In fighting one another with fists, knives, and guns, congressmen were doing their job. Of course, not all congressmen turned to violence. Behind the scenes, out of the public eye, peace-loving congressmen were struggling to bind sectional ties. The ultimate example of such negotiations was the "Peace Conference" held at Willard's Hotel in 1861 as a last-ditch effort to avoid disaster.

But regardless of the counterforce, the fighting's impact was severe. The image of Congress as filtered through the press and popular culture was hardly reassuring. In mocking violence so enthusiastically, humorists suggested that it was pervasive, even unstoppable. The sensationalistic penny press sent a similar message: Congress was a brawling den of thieves, a "bear garden," to use a favorite phrase of the time. It was a place where people of contending politics clashed but didn't compromise. A place where underhanded plots to seize control of the Union were effected, step by step. A place of argument, not conversation. A place corroded by mutual distrust.

By the late 1850s, much of this was true; Congress wasn't doing much to earn the public's trust. And the violence reflected a very real problem: the inability of Congress to legislate, or for that matter, even to discuss, the issue of slavery. But in ironing out subtleties and highlighting the tempers and tempests of the floor, the press and popular culture filtered the public view of Congress so effectively that even today it's hard to tell truth from lie.[158]

The end result was pervasive distrust of Congress, and not just for the public. The hotheads who plunged into collisions at a moment's notice; the Buncombe speeches and banner-waving that provoked those fights; the waves of anger and violence that those fights produced; and the very real presence of a sectional foe that was desperate to have its way, perhaps at the expense of the Union: together these things taught congressmen to distrust one another. However moderate some congressmen were, however disposed they were to compromise, however much they got along in private, in the political climate of the late 1850s they would not—could not—compromise their section's honor, interests, and rights, and they knew all too well that their opponents felt the same. There couldn't be much give and take in a battle for the soul of the republic. Desperate measures were always on the table, breeding mutual distrust. The ultimate sign of this distrust was the decision of many congressmen to arm themselves in the late 1850s, not because they wanted to fight, but because they were afraid that they might have to.

DISTRUST AND DISUNION

In June 1860, French bought a gun.[159] Not for hunting, which he loved to do on weekends. Not for his sons, whom he taught to hunt as boys. Not to guard his home, where he kept a loaded gun in case of burglary.[160]

Not even to shoot the irritatingly loud rooster next door, which French accidentally killed with a warning shot from his window.[161] French bought a gun to defend himself from Southerners. He didn't want to shoot them. But he feared that he might have to.

The chain of events that led to this decision and the circumstances that surround it reveal a lot about the congressional community in 1859–60. French wasn't the only person who decided to wear a gun. Many congressmen strapped on knives and guns each morning as they headed off to Congress, and their number was growing; Northerners had been urging their representatives to arm since Sumner's caning.[162] At times, the distrust and simmering resentment on the floor was palpable.

Momentum had been building to this point for years, but in the Thirty-sixth Congress, violence intensified. What had first been parliamentary power plays, and then declarations of sectional rights and honor, had now become something different. For at least some congressmen, fighting had become a matter of life and death.

The change in the air was partly a product of circumstance and timing; several game-changing events happened just before Congress opened in December 1859. Conspiracy theories did their worst as well. A confluence of events and evidence increasingly convinced people on all sides that their darkest fears about their sectional foe were true. Considered in the light of an evil plot, simply wearing a gun seemed threatening. Why were Republicans armed?, asked *The New York Herald* in January 1860. "Is the republican party prepared to resort to violence and bloodshed on the floor of Congress as well as on the soil of the South?"[163] Even self-defense could seem aggressive in a climate of extremes.

Even without game-changing events, the Thirty-sixth Congress was destined to be plagued with problems, particularly in the House, where no party had a controlling majority; there were 109 Republicans, 101 Democrats (some of them Anti-Lecompton Democrats), and 27 Americans. As in 1856, the possibility of a Republican Speaker enraged Southerners. As in 1856, the high stakes of a pending presidential contest heightened tensions—though in this case, with the very real possibility that a tied presidential election would be resolved by the House. As in 1850, Southerners threatened to raze the Capitol and destroy the Union. But in 1859, for the first time they took action.[164]

Two recent episodes had especially stoked their fury. One month before the opening of Congress, the abolitionist John Brown had made his infamous raid on a federal arsenal in Harpers Ferry, Virginia, setting the nation on edge and terrifying Southerners. Brown was hanged on December 2, 1859. Congress opened three days later. Even as the House struggled to organize, the Senate was debating and investigating Brown's actions.

Even more productive of turmoil in the House was Hinton Rowan Helper's controversial antislavery tract, *The Impending Crisis—How to Meet It*, published in 1857, and then in a compendium edition in 1859 at the encouragement of Republicans with fall elections in mind. A North Carolina abolitionist, Helper was a rare and special thing for Republicans: a Southerner attacking slavery for the sake of the South. His argument was straightforward: slavery was harmful to the economic and cultural prosperity of the South, and detrimental to poor whites who didn't own slaves. Among Helper's many inflammatory suggestions was his plea for those whites to join with slaves in fighting domineering slaveholders and abolishing slavery; Helper's attack on tyrannical slaveholders was particularly severe. Essentially propounding class warfare and slave rebellion, the book was banned throughout the South.[165] In 1858, Southern congressmen disparaged the first edition so caustically that Helper went to the House to assault his attackers in defense of his honor (thereby proving himself a Southerner at heart).[166]

When Congress opened in December 1859, Helper's book dropped on the House like a bombshell because of a revelation only a few weeks before. As reported in the *Herald*, sixty-eight Republicans had signed a circular letter endorsing the compendium edition of Helper's book, including sixty House members and the two leading Republican candidates for Speaker, Galusha Grow (R-PA) and John Sherman (R-OH). So on December 5, when John Clark (D-MO) proposed a resolution stating that anyone who endorsed the "insurrectionary" book would be banned from being Speaker, and then had the circular listing its endorsers read aloud, the House exploded.[167]

Southerners were outraged. Harpers Ferry threatened the security of the South. Helper's book put such threats in print and promoted them. The endorsement of such a work by leading Republicans seemed to validate the South's nightmare vision of the Republican Party's true intentions. How could anyone who endorsed this book deny that he wanted to infiltrate and subjugate the South? To Southerners, the proof was on the printed page. To put a supporter of such a book in charge of the House—to submit to being governed by a declared enemy of the South: for many if not most Southerners, the dishonor not to mention the danger of such an outcome was too much to bear.

Thus the extreme Southern actions and reactions during the speakership contest.[168] Of course, for many Republicans, the threats and bluster were all too familiar. Virginian Roger Pryor's complaints about Southern degradation; Laurence Keitt's vow to "shatter this Republic from turret to foundation stone" in defense of Southern rights and honor: Northerners had heard it all before.[169] The Southern disunion song had been sung for so long that it had become meaningless. It was a kind of "tragic strut," said Henry Wilson in the Senate in January 1860, a Slave Power ploy "intended to startle and appall the timid, make the servility of the servile still more abject . . . and so retain their grasp on power."[170] Thaddeus Stevens spoke for many when he dismissed Southern threats as "barren thunders."[171]

But in truth, the Southern fulminations weren't more of the same. Southerners felt threatened and insulted as never before.[172] During the first eight weeks of the first session alone there were nine fights and numerous "scenes" (nonviolent confrontations); six of the fights pitted a Republican against a Southern Democrat.[173] Notable among that number was the assault of John Hickman (R-PA) by Henry Edmundson (D-VA), clearly a frequent fighter. During the speakership kerfuffle, Hickman belittled Southern fears and threats, scoffing that John Brown had terrified the entire state of Virginia with a handful of men. This was Republican bravado with a vengeance, and not surprisingly, Edmundson defended Virginia's honor by striking Hickman during a chance encounter on the street. Laurence Keitt, of all people, grabbed Edmundson's arm and pulled him away. The *Richmond Whig* half-joked that Keitt had been trying to avoid the talk of murderous Slave Power plots that were sure to appear in the *Tribune* the next day.[174]

The Senate wasn't immune to uproars. During a closed session on January 17, Republican objections against a Southern diplomatic nominee launched a heated argument and almost caused a duel. Republicans complained that the nominee had vowed to destroy the Union in defense

of the South, outraging Southerners who insisted that *all* loyal Southerners felt that way, and in the angry exchange that followed, Robert Toombs
(D-GA) and James Doolittle (R-WI) each threw the lie at the other.
Started and settled behind closed doors, this spat wasn't mere theater; it
was testimony to bad feelings on all sides.[175]

Even more alarming were the actions of Southerners off the floor.
In December, Governor William Gist of South Carolina told his state's
congressional delegation that if a Republican was elected Speaker he
should be ejected by force if necessary, and if it came to that, he would
send armed forces to Washington. He was prepared "to wade in blood
rather than submit to inequality & degradation."[176] But a governor couldn't
cross this line, Gist explained. The ultimate decision to bloody the
House would have to come from congressmen.

Gist's letter helps to explain Keitt's actions during the speakership
contest as witnessed by his wife, Susanna. In December, she wrote to
her brother in a panic. Her husband, Thomas Clingman (W-NC), Roger
Pryor (D-VA), and Virginian Ambrose Dudley Mann had just left
her parlor—all of them armed—ranting about a Black Republican
Speaker and swearing to "fight to the knife there on the floor of Congress. And either take possession of the Capitol or fall." And they weren't
alone. "Bowie knives and revolvers are the companions of every Southern Member," Susanna Keitt fretted, and Governor Wise was said to
have 10,000 men armed and ready to march on Washington at the first
sign of trouble. The tension was unbearable. "I am nervous and excited
so I can hardly keep my seat," she confessed. "Heaven help us all."[177]

Republicans weren't sitting silent during the crisis.[178] They swore
up and down that they had no desire to invade or harm the South; a
few even withdrew their endorsement of Helper's book. They had endorsed it only after being told that he would cut the most objectionable
passages, which—clearly—he hadn't done.[179] But Southerners didn't believe them, just as Northerners refused to believe Southern threats of
disunion. By 1859, there was little faith between North and South, and
for some men of extreme feelings on both sides, little liking.

Even so, in the end nothing happened, even when freshman William Pennington (R-NJ) won the speakership on February 1. A conservative Whig who had only recently become a Republican, Pennington
became Speaker during his first term because he was moderate on slav-

ery, opposing the Lecompton constitution and slavery extension but up-holding the Fugitive Slave Act as the law of the land, much like French.[180] The immediate crisis of the moment had passed, though the Speaker-ship vote set the tone for the session: every Northerner in the House voted for Pennington, and every Southerner but one—Henry Winter Davis (A-MD)—voted against him. A few weeks later, when the Ameri-can flag in the House chamber was accidentally hoisted upside down—or "Union down," as French put it—he took it as an omen.[181]

For the next few months, Congress rumbled along, erupting into violent outbreaks every few weeks, sometimes more often. All told, there were more than a dozen fights in the Thirty-sixth Congress as well as many near misses. Prominent among these was a near duel between Roger Pryor (D-VA) and John "Bowie Knife" Potter (R-WI), the clash that earned Potter his nickname.[182] Pryor was a bully of the first order, involving himself in at least five confrontations that session.[183] The Maine native Potter was likewise "a most uncomfortable antagonist to run against in a conflict," noted a friend.[184] The two came head-to-head in the wake of a near melee sparked by Owen Lovejoy (R-IL), brother of the antislavery newspaper editor Elijah Lovejoy, who had been mur-dered by proslavery forces in 1837. When Lovejoy, warming to his sub-ject ("The Barbarism of Slavery"), strayed too close to the Democratic side of the House, waving his fists, Democrats leaped to their feet, hurl-ing insults, and streamed toward Lovejoy, bringing a wave of Republi-cans in their wake. When Pryor threatened to silence Lovejoy, Potter insisted that Republicans would be heard, "let the consequences be what they may." This was a virtual invitation to fight, and so Pryor took it, initiating formal duel negotiations.

Potter immediately consulted the fighting Republicans Cadwallader and Israel Washburn, Galusha Grow, Zachariah Chandler, and Ben Wade. Determined to show the South that they "were not to be bullied any longer," Potter then accepted Pryor's challenge and chose bowie knives as weapons. When Pryor refused to fight with such "vulgar" weap-ons, Republicans rejoiced, celebrating Potter's fighting-man gumption. At the Republican national convention one month later, Potter was awarded a seven-foot-long "monster Bowie knife" inscribed with the words "Will Always Meet a Pryor Engagement."[185] Potter's second, Frederick Lander, who offered to duel Pryor with pistols in Potter's place, was likewise celebrated. When the surprised Lander asked a gathered crowd why they were honoring him, someone yelled back, "Because you've got pluck!"[186] Democrats who claimed that Potter's posturing was aimed at upcoming elections weren't far from the truth; he was easily reelected that fall, with his fighting-man status front and center.[187]

Fighting man Galusha Grow (R-PA) was also challenged to a duel during this Congress—and reelected. During an argument in the House, Grow accused Lawrence O'Bryan Branch (D-NC) of violating the "gentlemanly courtesies" of deliberative bodies. Branch took offense and sent Grow a letter of inquiry regarding a duel. Refusing to accept a challenge, Grow made himself available for a street fight, vowing to prove to Southern men that Northern men would fight. But for once, the antidueling law worked. Branch was arrested, and closed the matter by publishing their correspondence in the press.[188] (*Vanity Fair*, resorting to the tried-and-true cliché about the fighting Irish, summed up the incident as a fight between Galellshy A. Grow and O'Blarney J. Branch.)[189]

North and South, fighting men were in the limelight. Although the vast majority of congressmen hoped to avoid conflict, in the charged atmosphere, it didn't take much to spark it. French experienced the temper of the times firsthand in May 1860 when the Washington Republican Association celebrated the nomination of Abraham Lincoln and Hannibal Hamlin for the 1860 Republican presidential ticket. As president of the association, French was the master of ceremonies. Lincoln wasn't in Washington, but Hamlin was, so on the evening of May 19, a crowd of about two hundred Republicans marched to Hamlin's lodgings as the Marine Band played "The Star-Spangled Banner" and "Hail to the Chief." After an introduction by French, Hamlin thanked the party and praised Lincoln in a brief speech. By this time, the crowd had at least doubled; French thought that there were thousands of people present "of all sorts of politics." The procession next moved to the lodgings of Senator Lyman Trumbull (R-IL). But during Trumbull's speech, "uneasy spirits," as French called them, began to heckle, cheering for Stephen Douglas and asking where John Brown was. Elihu Washburne (R-IL) had just begun to speak when a swarm of people ("drunken rowdies," French thought) descended on the crowd throwing rocks, starting a general stampede with the band leading the way. Enough people stood their ground for Washburne to finish his speech, and after a rousing three cheers, everyone went home.[190] But a point had been made; the Republican Party's ratification meeting nine days later had police protection.[191] Washington was a Southern city, and Republicans had to take care.

This was particularly true of the most aggressive Republicans, men such as Charles Sumner, who returned to the Senate in December 1859, a little more than three years after his caning. On June 4, 1860, he showed just how aggressive he was by delivering a savage four-hour antislavery speech. Titled "The Barbarism of Slavery"—like Owen Lovejoy's speech—it fulfilled the promise of its title, arguing with carefully documented statistics as well as stunningly powerful rhetoric that slavery had made the South an inferior civilization: "Barbarous in origin; barbarous in its law; barbarous in all its pretensions; barbarous in the instruments it employs; barbarous in consequences; barbarous in spirit; barbarous wherever it shows itself, Slavery must breed Barbarians."

For Sumner's Southern colleagues, one portion of his speech hit particularly close to home: the section on "Slave-masters in Congressional history." Beginning with Henry Wise's and Bailie Peyton's near-shooting of Reuben Whitney in a committee-room in 1837, Sumner marched his listeners through a congressional chamber of horrors, quoting Southern threats from the *Globe*, often with volume, page, and date citations. He talked of John Dawson of throat-cutting fame; of John Quincy Adams's years of abuse; of Joshua Giddings's sufferings and censure; of Henry Foote's threat to hang John Parker Hale, and Foote's later attack on Thomas Hart Benton, complete with its dramatic denouement in the Senate. Nor did he stop there. He read some of the insults thrown at Owen Lovejoy two months past. He said nothing about his own attack, but of course, he didn't have to. Such examples could be "multiplied indefinitely," he concluded. Every one of them, "every appeal, whether to the Duel, the bludgeon, or the revolver—every menace of personal violence, and every outrage of language, besides disclosing a hideous Barbarism, also discloses the fevered nervousness of a cause already humbled in debate."[192] By blasting slaveholders as barbarians, Sumner put into words what antislavery toreadors had been implying for decades. When he concluded, James Chestnut (D-SC) rose to explain why Southerners had quietly submitted to such abuse: after watching Sumner whine and cringe his cowardly way through Europe, they didn't want to send him "howling through the world" again in martyrdom. Sumner responded by promising to include Chestnut's words in an appendix in the printed edition of his speech "as an additional illustration" of slave-holder barbarism, and he kept his word.[193]

Sumner's words were explosively powerful, so powerful that French worried about how his son Frank would respond. Writing to his wife in New Hampshire, where his family was visiting, French asked her to tell Frank that the speech was a personal matter, not a matter of party. The speech was "terribly, vindictively, savagely severe," thought French, "a mortal tongue stab at the South, for every blow Brooks gave." The Republican Party didn't endorse its severity, he noted, but it admitted its truth and understood its personal logic for Sumner: "Heaven avenged him first and now he has avenged himself."[194]

Two days later, French met his fellow Republican Association member Lewis Clephane and some strangers on the street, clearly upset about something. One of the strangers, a visitor from Kansas, asked French if he could borrow a gun. When French asked why, Clephane took him aside and explained what had happened the night before: some Southerners had tried to assassinate Sumner, forcing their way into his room, demanding to speak to him privately, and running off when refused. Clephane had been there when it happened and had stayed by Sumner's side until 2:00 in the morning, when Sumner finally went to bed. Because Sumner was a non-combatant on principle, he refused to wear a gun, Clephane explained. So the men who French had just encountered on the street had decided to act as bodyguards, accompanying Sumner wherever he went, sometimes staying by his side, sometimes hanging back and watching for trouble. French loaned them a revolver, hoping that if someone attacked Sumner, it would fire true.[195]

French's chance encounter bothered him for hours, upsetting him, angering him, even frightening him. By the afternoon, he was so disturbed that he decided to arm himself and headed straight downtown to buy a small pistol that he could carry in his pocket every day. Explaining his decision to his wife, French said that he was arming himself in self-defense, "for if we are to be bullied for our republican principles, I think we ought to be prepared to defend ourselves."[196] French was preparing for the possibility of armed conflict with Southerners on the streets of Washington.

It was a telling decision, yet in explaining it, French didn't act as though he'd crossed a line. In his letter, a gun was one of several purchases he made that day. He also bought two pairs of underwear. He had a pair on even as he wrote, and he declared them very comfortable. The purchase of underwear and the purchase of a gun: the routine dailiness of French's decision is striking. Although he hadn't worn arms for protection before, he didn't feel like he was going to extremes. It was Southerners who had him worried. French was wearing a gun in case *they* crossed a line.

This was the logic of many weapon-wearing congressmen in 1860. They didn't arm themselves every morning and head off for the Capitol hoping to gun people down. They were defending themselves against an unpredictable foe. That's how Senator James Henry Hammond (D-SC) explained his decision to arm himself in April 1860 after the "Lovejoy explosion" had blown over. Convinced that almost every member of both houses was armed, and seeing even the oldest and most conservative senators with revolvers, Hammond "most reluctantly" got one for himself and kept it fully loaded in his Senate desk. "I can't carry it," he admitted to a friend. Twice in his life he had worn a pistol, and both times he'd gotten so unnerved that he'd put it aside. But now he had a loaded pistol in his desk because there was no telling what Republicans might say or do. They had the power to provoke a fight whose bloodiness would "shock the world and dissolve the government," he thought. If that happened, as much as he hoped to avert it, he would stand by his fellow Southerners to the end. Hammond was armed "as a matter of duty to my section," ready to fight and die with his countrymen on the Senate floor. And he wasn't alone.[197]

John Haskin (R-NY) had a similar reason for wearing a gun, which became national news during the speakership debate in January 1860. During an angry exchange over John Clark's (D-MO) anti-Helper resolution, Haskin accused his fellow New Yorker Horace Clark—an Anti-Lecompton Democrat—of both supporting and opposing slavery in Kansas, vowing to reveal to the world "in what a circus-riding aspect that colleague stands." (This is doubtless what inspired *Vanity Fair*'s "Great National Circus.") Haskin's remark caused an uproar during which he pulled a gun on Horace Clark. In the crowding, pushing, and shoving that followed, Haskin's gun went clattering to the floor, though not before Laurence Keitt, again playing against type, said that personal fights should be taken outside. (In its account, the *Globe* mentions only "confusion" and "crowding.")

After some strategic mace-wielding by the sergeant at arms, the House went back to work—or at least, it tried to. There was some joking (Thomas Davidson [D-LA] said that "if these things are to continue in the future, I must bring a double-barreled shot-gun into the House") and some scolding, with no one citing names or details, until Sherrard Clemens (D-VA) said that he had seen Haskin pull his gun on Clark, and felt that the New Yorker owed his constituents an explanation. (Clemens's statement that he was shocked—*shocked*—to see a weapon in the House didn't get any laughter, but it should have.) The House immediately silenced Clemens with roars of order and objections; such things were not to be mentioned on the floor, and any such discussion was bound to make matters worse.

But a few minutes later, Haskin made a personal explanation. Never in his life had he been armed before coming to Washington, he said. Now he wore a gun because he feared being attacked; in this session and the session before, a number of Northern congressmen had been assaulted, and he had to protect himself. Of course, he would *never* use his pistol in the House, he insisted—*unless* he was "unjustly assaulted and had to do it in my own self-defense."[198] Like Hammond and French, Haskin was protecting himself against a desperate and unpredictable foe: his fellow congressmen. And like Hammond, he was fully prepared to use his gun in the halls of Congress, however much he hoped he wouldn't have to. So was "Bowie Knife" Potter. As he explained to a friend as he strapped on a pistol and a knife before heading to the House, there was no telling what would happen, particularly if Southerners in the galleries took action.[199]

And so did the United States Congress become an armed camp, just as Thaddeus Stevens said (though *Vanity Fair* urged congressmen to follow Haskin's example and drop their weapons).[200] Also, as Stevens said, at least a few dwellers in that camp were prepared to gun people down. A few days after the Lovejoy scuffle, Martin Crawford (D-GA) admitted that in the midst of the melee, he had cocked his revolver in his pocket and taken a position "in the midst of the mob," fully prepared to fight and die.[201] "We have the men of sufficient nerve to bring this matter to a bloody issue" with armed combat in the House, he assured

former congressman Alexander Stephens (D-GA). The only thing holding them back was fear of public opinion back home. Launching a shoot-
out in the Capitol required a respected champion who could justify the
bloodshed and "inaugurate the movement." Too bad Henry Wise was
no longer in Congress, Crawford thought. Without such a man, he feared
"that the people would be disgusted and we should be disgraced."[202]
Here was a grand irony. After years of intimidating Northerners with
threats and duel challenges, knowing full well that Northern public
opinion kept them from fighting back, Southerners now faced the same
dilemma. Events in Congress were driving them beyond where their
constituents might go.

Men such as Miles, Keitt, Crawford, Pryor, and Clingman were
ready for open combat—in Keitt's case, regardless of what his people
thought.[203] Yet even such extremists framed their violence as defensive.
Governor Gist of South Carolina was fully prepared for "war to begin
at Washington," but he wanted it to "begin in sudden heat & with good
provocation, rather than a deliberate determination to perform an act
of violence which might prejudice us in the eyes of the world."[204]

In a sense, America was backing its way into civil warfare. The fire-
eating rhetoric, the threats and dares, the talk of bloodying the Capitol, the pervasive guns and knives, and now the group fights on the floor:
they were clear signs of a nation being torn in two. They were also blunt
reminders of a lack of faith in the institution of Congress, even on the
part of congressmen; a body of armed legislators is a body of men with
no confidence in the power or practices of their own institution. The
implications of this loss of faith were profound. If the nation's representative body couldn't function, could the nation long survive? Where
else but in Congress could the interests of America's many regions and
constituencies be addressed through debate and compromise? As Illinois Republican E. W. Hazard wrote shortly after Sumner's caning, "If
we can no longer look to Congress . . . what remains to us but a resort to
the means given us by the God of nature for self-defence?"[205]

Self-defense: Hazard's wording is noteworthy. In truth, most congressmen didn't want to dissolve the Union; they were taking up arms
in defense of their people, their state, their section, and themselves. Republicans urged their congressmen to fight—in self-defense. Southerners would start a war in Washington—in self-defense. Conspiracy

theories encouraged this kind of magical thinking. If there really was a brewing plot to subjugate the North or South, if the security of a people and the stability of their society were under attack, then any and all extreme measures were justifiable as self-defense.[206] Indeed, the situation *demanded* such measures. Yet even now, there wasn't total mayhem in Congress. People weren't itching to fight. They were afraid that they might have to.

This ethos of "aggressive defensiveness" pervaded the presidential election of 1860.[207] Many Northerners campaigned on that idea, citing the Kansas-Nebraska bill, the battle over the proslavery Lecompton constitution, and the Dred Scott ruling as a holy trinity of Southern aggression that proved their intentions to swallow up the Union and had to be repulsed. Southerners, in turn, told horror stories about the Republican Party infiltrating the South and destroying it from within. Former representative William Lowndes Yancey of Alabama told such tales in a rip-roaring speech before hundreds in New Orleans. With Lincoln in power, Southern federal officers were bound to be Republicans, he argued. As a result, in the South, "there will be free speech, as they call it, everywhere for the propagation of Abolition opinions. There will be a free press, as they call it, for the circulation of Abolition documents." And once there were more free states in the Union—which there most assuredly would be, with Republicans in power—their antislavery regime would abolish slavery throughout the Union, their unwavering goal. To Laurence Keitt, the future was clear: slave insurrections, slaveholders poisoned, and plantations put to the torch.[208] His wife, Susanna, was of like mind. "Submission to Lincoln" meant "sectional disgrace, sectional subjugation, poverty, exile and ruined homesteads."[209]

For North and South alike, the election of 1860 seemed like a mandate on the future of slavery, and the outcome of that mandate was clear. Not only was Lincoln elected president, but Republicans took both houses of Congress, taking 49.1 percent of the House and 55.5 percent of the Senate. At the opening of the next session of Congress in December, the election's emotional impact was apparent. Senator Albert Gallatin Brown (D-MS) condemned the "triumph of principles, to submit to which would be the deepest degradation that a free people ever submitted to."[210] Thomas Clingman (D-NC)—who had threatened to bloody the Capitol in 1850, and was now a senator—swore that the outcome would be secession. Senator Alfred Iverson, Sr. (D-GA), saw the first signs of secession even as he spoke. Seated before him were "two hostile bodies," he told Republicans. "You sit upon your side, silent and gloomy; and we sit upon ours with knit brows and portentous scowls. Yesterday, I observed that there was not a solitary man on that side of the Chamber came over here even to extend the civilities and courtesies of life; nor did any of us go over there."[211]

Distrust, defensiveness, and degradation. Years of conflict had brought both Congress and the nation to this point. Given that long history, what came next? After decades of defending the South's rights, honor, and interests with their words, deeds, and fists, and years of raging against Northern degradation, could Southerners succumb to being governed by the enemy? Could Southern congressmen or their constituents stomach such disgrace? For many Southerners, the answer was no.

Congressional violence didn't cause this sectional standoff, but it intensified it. By performing sectional warfare in the halls of Congress during a crisis of the Union, congressmen exposed the emotional power of sectional degradation to a watchful national audience, giving human form to the fraying of national bonds. In the process, they stoked the flames of disunion.

That same long history of bullying and violence encouraged Northerners to downplay Southern threats of secession, even as late as 1860. French was typical of many in suspecting that they were a mere opening gambit—a ploy for Southerners to get their way. Threats had long served slaveholders well. Perhaps this was more of the same. "They will all come to their senses by & by," he thought.[212] Others agreed. "Maryland and Virginia have no idea of breaking up the Union," wrote the *New-York Tribune*, "but they would both dearly like to bully the North into a compromise."[213] Here is a rich irony. Southerners themselves had taught Northerners to dismiss Southern disunion threats as crying wolf.[214]

But Southerners stayed true to their word. Between December 20, 1860, and June 1861, the *fact* of disunion was performed in human form in the House and Senate. As one Southern legislature after another resolved their state out of the Union, Southern congressmen rose to their feet one by one and bade farewell to the Union and their colleagues, some of them in tears.[215] When three state delegations withdrew in one day,

Senator James Mason (D-VA) stated the obvious in terms so bald that they silenced the chamber. Pointing to the now empty seats surrounding him, he declared: "The Union was now dissolved." A reporter for *The New York Herald* witnessed the impact: with those five words, the "momentous events now daily occurring—the dissolution of the Union, the breaking up of the government, and the awful imminence of civil war" seemed unavoidably at hand.[216]

French was as stunned as any, but he remained convinced that soon enough, the seceded states would be in ruins, begging to return. If not, so much the better. The North would thrive without them. In the meantime, he wished those states well, but he wished them gone.[217]

Yet even as he minimized the crisis, French was preparing for disaster. On the home front, in the midst of the political chaos, his wife, Bess, took ill. After months of failing health, she was diagnosed with breast cancer and underwent a mastectomy, leaving her weak and languid.[218] Suddenly, French faced the terrifying possibility of losing his life's love after thirty-five years of marriage.

Matters on the political front were also rocky. In January 1861, French heard rumors that "some misguided scoundrels" intended to prevent Lincoln's inauguration "by force," perhaps by assassination. Though he declared in his diary that he couldn't believe it, he held himself ready "at a minute's warning" to repel an attack—particularly after hearing whispers about a plot in Baltimore.[219] French breathed a huge sigh of relief when Lincoln arrived in Washington on February 23 and was whisked away to safety at Willard's Hotel.[220] Three days later, when Lincoln visited the House and Senate, French was watching. Fellow Republicans crowded around the president-elect, shaking his hand with more enthusiasm than French had ever seen. Democrats were less enthusiastic, but cordial. A week later, on March 4, Lincoln's inauguration went off without a hitch, with Marshal-in-Chief French presiding.[221]

The Southern violence feared by French took another month to surface. Although South Carolina had been the first state to leave the Union in December 1860, Fort Sumter in Charleston Harbor was still in Union hands four months later, though in dire need of supplies. On April 12, 1861, knowing that supply ships were on their way, Confederate troops took action. At 4:30 in the morning, they launched a cannonade against the fort that continued for thirty-four hours. The sound and fury were dramatic; people in Charleston sat on their roofs and watched. Two days later, on April 14, Fort Sumter was surrendered and evacuated. Civil war had begun.

Hearing the news, French made one final, desperate attempt to stay the crisis. As a Mason, he considered it his "solemn duty" to do everything in his power to prevent civil warfare, and as Grand Master of the Knights Templar of the United States, he actually possessed some power. So on April 16, he put pen to paper in defense of the Union, as he had so many times before, addressing a circular to "all True and Patriotic Templars," pleading with them to use their influence to fend off civil war.[222] There were tens of thousands of Templars in America, he argued; if every one did his part within his circle to encourage peace, they might just have an influence. If ever there was a moment to wield the power of Masonic brotherhood, that moment was now. French wasn't asking people to surrender their principles, he assured his readers; he was asking them to cast politics aside. With the Union in the balance, French was trying to get the Masons to do what Congress seemed unable to do: prove that national bonds of sentiment crossed sectional lines.

Less than two weeks later, French received a response from E. H. Gill, Grand Commander of Virginia. Why was French preaching peace and brotherhood to Virginians? Gill asked. Southerners had already tried every honorable means of avoiding war, casting aside politics and working for peace. And yet the North had trampled the South's constitutional rights and was now "about to invade their soil, their homes and their fire-sides." Northerners were the problem. Southerners were only acting in self-defense. The "God of Battles" would sustain Virginians in their fight against "this Cain-like and marauding attack of the Vandals of the North," Gill felt sure. He and his fellow Virginians were only too happy to help Northerners into their graves. And with that, Gill declared that the Grand Encampment of Knights Templar of the State of Virginia was no longer under the jurisdiction of the Grand Encampment of the United States. Virginia had seceded from the Masonic union. As Grand Master, French was suffering a secession crisis of his own.[223]

A few weeks later, French got a letter from a commander in western Virginia saying that his commandery refused to secede. Deeply moved, French replied with grateful thanks. Gill's letter had astonished him, he admitted. Gill seemed to have gone out of his way to stab at

French's feelings. If he had known when and where French wrote his circular, Gill might well have held his tongue, French thought; French had written it at midnight at Bess's sickbed, hoping that this one last desperate effort might slow, if not stop, the nation's march toward civil war. But Gill hadn't heard French's heartfelt words of brotherhood. Gill didn't seem to have heard French at all. Unwilling to respond in anger and knowing that words of peace would fall on deaf ears, French left Gill's letter unanswered.[224]

For French, this was a turning point; the nation's crisis of communication had come to a head. Viewed through the distorting haze of conspiracy thinking, even a call for peace became a call for war. The pull of that thinking was so powerful that even French couldn't escape it. Even as he wrote his circular, grasping at straws for the sake of the Union, he was ranting about "Southern hotspurs" and invoking the "God of Battles" in his diary. "The United States is no longer to be triumphed over as if it were a coward and dared not protect himself!," he ranted, an eerie echo of his praise for Northern fighters in years past, now a rallying cry for the nation.[225] Given a choice between fighting and submitting to a domineering South, French wanted to fight.

And so French watched Virginia secede from the Masonic union, much as he had watched Southern states leave the national Union, one by one. Beginning the eighth volume of his diary on January 1, 1861, he put pen to paper with a sense of foreboding. "I commence this Journal at what still continues to be the seat of Government of 'The United States of America,'" he wrote, envisioning a future when that might not be true. Twenty-seven years ago as a newcomer to Washington, French had gazed at the Capitol and wondered if it would "always be the capitol of my happy country." He had never stopped wondering. Now the fight to answer that question was at hand, and French welcomed that fight. After a lifetime of compromising, politicking, singing, rhyming, denying, dodging, and ultimately fighting to save the Union, French was ready to let the Union slide.

EPILOGUE

"I WITNESSED IT ALL"

French's life during the secession crisis echoed the state of the nation. For months, his diary entries were divided between his fears for the Union and his fears for his wife, and all of his worst fears came true. Between December 1860 and June 1861, eleven states left the Union. And on May 6, 1861, Bess died. Although friends flocked to his side that day, he spent most of its long, lingering hours by her side or with his diary. He wrote in it more than once that afternoon, concluding his last entry with a moan: "Oh how lonely—lonely—lonely."[1]

His workday offered no escape. Appointed clerk of the House Committee of Claims in 1860, French was charged with evaluating 487 claims for damages by citizens of Kansas. For two months, he reviewed a veritable litany of destruction: homes and stores plundered and burned, crops destroyed, horses stolen. Pressman that he was, he took special note of the destruction of the Lawrence *Herald of Freedom*; witnesses described a band of roughly seventy armed men riding from the scene waving bayoneted books above their heads as war trophies. He was particularly generous to the free-state governor Charles Robinson, who claimed to have lost a six-hundred-page manuscript history of California when his house burned down. French granted Robinson damages for his lost work as well as his home, assigning him almost $24,000 out of a grand total of roughly $450,000.[2]

The one ray of hope in French's diary throughout this period was

Benjamin Brown French,
ca. 1855–65. The statue
of Charlemagne, king of
the Franks, is a not-so-
subtle reference to
French's name. (Courtesy of
the Library of Congress)

Abraham Lincoln. French liked the unassuming president virtually from
the moment that he met him. When Lincoln—drafting a letter in a room
full of visitors—asked aloud how to spell the word *missile*, French was
charmed. "Is there another man in this whole union who, being President, would have done that? It shows his perfect honesty and simplicity, &
that he is truly a great man."[3] The liking seems to have gone both ways.
Lincoln reappointed French commissioner of public buildings in September 1861, a position that ensured French close and frequent contact
with the president, particularly given the city's wartime disruptions.[4]

French's relationship with Mary Todd Lincoln was more complex;
he admired her independence but as commissioner he had to reckon
with it. One of his duties was to present visitors to her at White House
receptions, and he was both bemused and put off by her "Queenly" manners.[5] He had the same mixed response when she outspent the $20,000
budget for White House furnishings and asked French to appease her
husband; by law, the president had to approve the expenditures.[6] When
French undertook his "mission," Lincoln exploded. "[I]t would stink in the

land" to spend such money at a time when freezing soldiers went without blankets, he roared, vowing not to approve any bills for *"flub dubs for that damned old house!"*[7] "Not very pleasant," French wrote in his diary that night, "but a portion of it very amusing." In later years, when asked to write a book of reminiscences of Lincoln, he demurred. It would be impossible to do so without mentioning "Mrs. Abraham . . . in an unpleasant way."[8]

With the firing on Fort Sumter, Washington braced for conflict. In April 1861, French watched Union troops pour into the city as Maryland secessionists tore up railroad tracks and cut telegraph lines, cutting off the District from the outside world. Even Lincoln was uninformed of doings outside Washington, French noted with alarm.[9] With Congress out of session, thousands of soldiers were barracked in the Capitol and on its grounds.[10]

At a flag-raising ceremony in June, French saw what he took to be an omen. When the president grabbed the halyard and began to pull, the flag got caught. Lincoln responded by tugging *"with a will,"* tearing the

Union troops in front of the Capitol at the opening of the Civil War, May 13, 1861. From a photo album French created for his son Frank. (Courtesy of the Library of Congress)

flag in two. "I felt a sorrow that I cannot describe, at seeing *the torn flag*," French confessed. His only consolation was Lincoln's utter determination to get the job done. Whatever challenges were to come, he trusted Lincoln to "meet them *with the same energy*, and bring us out of the war, if with a tattered flag, still it will *all* be there!"[11]

In July 1861, the dam broke in Washington: the war came to Congress and Congress went to war. Lincoln called a special session of Congress to begin on July 4; on July 21, Union and Confederate forces met at the First Battle of Bull Run, less than a day's march from Washington. Excited congressmen rushed to the battleground, some to witness a Union victory, others to take part in it. Some of these would-be soldiers were proven fighting men shifting their skills to a new field of battle; Wade, Chandler, and Secretary of War Cameron were present, as was one of the fighting Washburn brothers, and at least fifteen others.[12] Their presence is a reminder that battlefield violence wasn't a break from politics as normal; the outbreak of warfare wasn't a thing apart from the coming of the war. Congressmen had been rehearsing civil warfare for years. Congressional violence framed the opening of the war.

But for congressional fighting men, there wasn't much cheering at Bull Run. When congressmen got near the point of battle, they found the Union army in a frantic full retreat. Upon seeing the flood of panicked soldiers headed their way, Wade and Chandler jumped out of their carriage and threatened to shoot any soldier who passed them by—the sixty-year-old Wade, his hat askew, waving the rifle that he had brought from home when he entered Congress.[13] But they were brushed aside. The only congressional casualty was Alfred Ely (R-NY), who strayed too close to the battleground and became a prisoner of war for six months.[14] In the Capitol that afternoon, the gloom was palpable to French as soldiers straggled into the city "in all sorts of *shapes*. Some without guns— some with two. Some barefooted, some bareheaded, & all with a doleful story of defeat."[15]

As violence descended on wartime battlefields, it retreated from the floor of Congress, though not before a cluster of clashes during the secession crisis early in 1861. Even as Southern congressmen were leaving Congress and the Union, there were six sectional wrangles, though only a few were violent. Fire-eater Louis Wigfall (D-TX), who remained in the Senate even after his election to the Provisional Confederate

Congress, provoked two nasty exchanges, one of them with the future president Andrew Johnson (D-TN), the other outside of the Senate with James Jackson (W-KY), who slapped Wigfall for insulting the former senator John Crittenden of Kentucky. Lingering in Washington largely to cause trouble, Wigfall was wildly successful.[16] Another off-the-floor wrangle took place at a dinner party when Robert Toombs (D-GA) said that he hoped the U.S.-government-hired steamship *Star of the West*—sent to supply Fort Sumter in January 1861—would sink; seventy-four-year-old General Winfield Scott responded by rushing at Toombs but the men were pulled apart.[17] When Albert Rust (D-AR), of Greeley assault fame, charged Republicans with supporting John Brown, William Dunn (R-IN) threw the lie; friends negotiated apologies.[18]

There were also two assaults, one more dramatic than the other. William Kellogg (R-IL) assaulted the *Chicago Tribune* editor Joseph Medill for denouncing Kellogg's compromise position on slavery.[19] But Charles Van Wyck (R-NY) suffered the more serious attack. In the previous session of Congress, Van Wyck had given a rousing antislavery speech that provoked threats of a duel challenge on the House floor and death threats for months thereafter.[20] He repeated the insult in a speech on January 29, 1861. A few weeks later, three men with knives attacked him on the Capitol grounds. Van Wyck pulled a gun and shot one of his assailants; a folded copy of the *Globe* kept a knife from piercing his heart. Although the Republican press deemed the attack a foiled assassination, the attackers were never identified.[21] This burst of passions marked the last physical violence for some time to come.[22]

The dynamics of Congress were changing again. With Republicans in power and secessionists departing, bullying lost much of its power, in part because the decidedly Southern custom of dueling had lost much of its cachet. During a heated debate about forts in seceded states in March 1861, William Fessenden (R-ME) scoffed when Stephen Douglas (D-IL) hinted at a duel challenge. Men who bullied men with a "code" different from their own were cowards, Fessenden declared.[23] It was cowardly to insult a man who you knew full well wouldn't fight back on your terms. Such bravado was possible with a Northern majority and the prospect of Union forces preparing to fight. Just as French said, Union men were no longer cowards. The North was prepared to do some bullying of its own.

Not every Northern congressman was as bold as Fessenden or as disdainful of dueling. Even after secession, a few hinted darkly at duel challenges when embroiled in a fight. But little came of it. Press coverage of such spats was equally laconic; what little there was focused on juicy details rather than broad implications.[24] Times had changed. With the outbreak of war, the Southern reign of violence in Washington ended.

And people noticed. "The change in a short six months is most striking," noted *The New York Times* early in 1862. On the street, congressmen no longer "throw hasty glances on either side, to see that no fellow-member has put himself in ambush. . . . A short time since it was a constant practice to carry concealed weapons—or rather, to carry them in a most ostentatious manner." The war had changed all that. "[T]he great rebellion suddenly freed Washington from barbarians" who would now be forced "to submit, by main force, to the civilization of the North . . . [H]ow inexpressible the sense of relief when the yoke of an intolerable bondage is thrown off."[25] The reporter was speaking for effect. And the supposedly civilized North wasn't always civilized, as violent outbursts such as the New York City draft riots in 1863 show all too well. But after decades of kowtowing to Southerners in Washington, the release of open warfare was sweet.

Of course, the departure of the Slave Power alone didn't quash congressional violence. The onset of bloody civil warfare likely played a role. Internecine clashing may have seemed unpatriotic or even dangerous during a war of brother against brother, and probably wouldn't have won plaudits from a war-weary public. It's also worth noting that a nonviolent Congress wasn't necessarily well behaved. Quite the opposite: with the drop in violence, verbal abuse soared. "Nothing can palliate the brutality of old," one reporter observed in 1864, "the faction-fights, the duels, the assassinations; but the personal insults that stain the air of the Capitol today are louder than then, and the reply they seem to call forth is not cleansing blood, but responsive blackguardism."[26] *Coward, liar, scoundrel, drunkard, traitor*: the halls of Congress rang with words that would have drawn blood (or at least fists) in the Congress of old.[27] "[T]he barbarism of anti-slavery" had transformed Congress into a den of "verbal bullies," sniped *The New York Herald* in 1866.[28] Ironically, a Slave Power–less

Congress confirmed a long-held truism about the code of honor: it did indeed force men to watch their words.

But regardless of the verbal fireworks in the wartime Congress, its lack of physical violence is striking, particularly in comparison with the Confederate Congress, which most decidedly was *not* violence free.[29] Notably, some fighters in the U.S. Congress remained fighters in its Confederate equivalent. Among its moments of glory was a scramble between Senators Benjamin Hill of Georgia and the former congressional duelist William Lowndes Yancey of Alabama; after exchanging insults over loyalty to the Confederacy, Hill threw an inkwell at Yancey and then rushed him with a chair.

And then there was Henry Foote, who continued to be Henry Foote. He "does not seem to have changed his habits one whit by going to Richmond," noted *The New York Times* in 1864. Unquestionably the Confederate Congress's most frequent fighter, he almost shot a Tennessee colleague and, during one particularly eventful committee meeting, knocked a witness into a corner and tore a member's shirt. He was also attacked with a bowie knife on the House floor, beaten in a committee-room, and clubbed with an umbrella.[30] He took a remarkably Bentonian stance during the knife attack: once his attacker was safely pinned to the floor by several congressmen, Foote melodramatically bared his chest and declared, "I defy the steel of the assassin!"[31] When it came to congressional clashes, he was a quick study. Somewhat predictably, by the end of the war Foote had been banished by both South and North. Exiled after fleeing the Confederacy in the middle of the war, he was then cast out of the North for being generally troublesome. He lived briefly in England and then Montreal, where he earned a pardon from the U.S. government by preventing a group of Confederate refugees from mobbing the American consulate and tearing down its flag.[32]

Clearly, battlefield bloodshed and concerns about patriotism didn't stem the tide of violence in the Confederate Congress, and seceded Southerners brought brawling back to Washington when they returned. This was true even of the first states readmitted to the Union.[33] When Union troops captured New Orleans in 1862, Lincoln decided to use Louisiana as a showcase for his plan of reconstruction; for readmission to the Union, one-tenth of the state's voting population had to take a prescribed oath of loyalty to the Union, and the state needed to organize a government that abolished slavery. Radical Republicans in Congress wanted stronger terms, including black suffrage. Unfortunately for the Louisiana delegates who arrived in Washington in 1864 seeking their seats in Congress, this standoff kept them in limbo for months. On January 22, 1865, the would-be Louisiana representative Alexander P. Field snapped. Spotting the radical Republican William Kelley of Pennsylvania in the dining room of Willard's Hotel—that perennial fighting-man favorite—he asked why Louisiana was being kept "out in the cold." After a brief heated exchange, Field stormed off. A short while later, after lying in wait for Kelley in a hallway, Field attacked him with a knife, stabbing him in the hand he raised in self-defense, then swaggering around the hotel bragging about it, a jolting reminder to congressional onlookers to consider carefully the South's reentry to the Union.[34]

The next violent incident—yet another Southern attack on a Northerner—was even more dramatic. During a February 1866 debate over the Freedmen's Bureau, a government agency established to help freed slaves, Lovell Rousseau (UU-KY) sneered that he would kill any man who arrested him based on a black man's testimony. The radical Republican Josiah Grinnell of Iowa returned the sneer, blasting Rousseau's loyalty to the Union. The two continued to toss insults back and forth over the next few months, until June 11, when they hit their peak. During a debate about seating Southern delegates, Grinnell ridiculed the Kentuckian's Civil War record. A few days later, Rousseau confronted Grinnell in the Capitol's east portico and demanded an apology. When Grinnell refused, Rousseau caned him, raining down blows on Grinnell's head and shoulders with an iron-topped rattan cane, stopping only when it shattered.[35] Grinnell, having blocked most of the blows with his arms, suffered only minor injuries, and immediately stalked off to buy a gun and seek revenge. But he was dissuaded from taking violent action by two caning experts who were waiting at his lodgings when he got home that night: Senators Henry Wilson and Charles Sumner.[36]

Sumner's involvement signals perhaps the most noteworthy aspect of Grinnell's caning; it was a virtual reenactment of Sumner's caning ten years past. Like Preston Brooks, Rousseau felt that he was defending his state's honor. Like Brooks, he staged his attack in the Capitol, though he deliberately avoided disgracing the House floor. Like Brooks, he bore down on his victim until his cane shattered. And like Brooks, he had friends at hand to fend off interference and promote a "fair fight," though here Rousseau outdid his illustrious forebear. Lawrence Keitt used a cane as his weapon of defense; Rousseau's three friends had guns.[37]

The congressional response also mirrored events of 1856. As before, the House appointed a committee that delivered a split decision, the majority recommending expulsion for Rousseau, the minority proposing a reprimand. As before, the report sparked a heated debate about the caning's congressional implications, with moderate Republicans arguing that expulsion was too severe given the severity of Grinnell's insults. In its long history of brawling and bullying, the House had never expelled anyone for violence, argued Henry Raymond (R-NY), offering as evidence a roll call of congressional combatants who kept their seats, including Preston Brooks. Brooks escaped expulsion "because there were enough bullies in the House to keep him in his seat," countered James Garfield (R-OH). At the dawning of a new era, Congress had to take strong action "to show that no man shall hereafter hope to gain any glory by becoming a bully."[38] Keep Rousseau in his seat and he would be feted with gifts of canes, Garfield warned. He was right. Like Brooks, Rousseau was reprimanded, resigned his seat, received trophy canes (though only a few), and was reelected.[39] In some ways, little had changed. Congress sanctioned rule-bound violence and a violent congressman won popular acclaim.

But some things *had* changed, and nowhere was this more apparent than in the press. A Southerner had caned a Northerner within the walls of the Capitol: the offense was mighty. But the press response was minimal. In Northern papers, there was some ranting about the revival of "plantation manners" and the "spirit of slavery," and some crowing about how Congress had "reconstructed" its decorum once the Slave Power left. In Southern papers there was some snickering at Grinnell's alleged cowardice.[40] But there was little indignation and few dire predictions. The same was true of the muted response to Field's attack, which included some offhand references to the "old bowie-knife rule of the slavery programme," but little more.[41] Equally striking, there was less Northern support for Northern non-combatants; Grinnell was disparaged in the North for not fighting back.[42]

The war had made fighting men of people North, South, and West, but the furies of sectional combat no longer centered on the halls of

Congress. Defeated in war and politically disempowered, Southern whites vented their outrage and asserted their control in a new arena, inflicting a reign of violence on the Reconstruction South and once again bullying their way to power, using terrorism and Black Codes to assert white supremacy.[43] The Ku Klux Klan was born in this period; a secret vigilante group founded in Tennessee in 1865, it spread rapidly throughout the South.

Not all white Southerners followed that path. Ever the contrarian, Henry Wise veered toward becoming a Republican in his final years, sensing the possibility of reconciliation in their rule. Even so, too stubborn to apply for a pardon (or even admit that he needed one), he remained unreconstructed. He died in 1876, fending off Cilley-Graves accusations until the end.[44]

French certainly became more of a fighting man during the war. Reviewing his past year's diary entries in 1862, he saw the change. "Up to 'Sumter' I was in favor of letting the Southerners, who desired it, go. I was for peace. I dreaded the terrible issue of war & bloodshed." But now? Characteristically, he put his changed feelings in verse:

If they still advance,
Friendly caution slighting,
They may get, by chance,
A belly full of fighting![45]

Taken from a song written during the War of 1812 which itself hearkened back to the American Revolution, these warmongering lines show how far French had come. His feelings about Frank Pierce had progressed as well. Hearing in 1863 that Pierce had given a Fourth of July speech denouncing Lincoln and the war, French gave Pierce "over to Secesh & Rebeldom." His old friend had "disgraced himself and the name he bears."[46]

For French, the war years were busy. As commissioner of public buildings, he had to tend to railroad tracks and bridges as well as oversee the extension of the Capitol. One month into his commissionership, he was surprised to learn that he also supervised the "Old Capitol Prison," occupied by Congress after the burning of the Capitol during the War of 1812 and now used for prisoners of war. An executive appointee,

French was in and out of the White House on an almost daily basis and became friendly with Lincoln, on one occasion handing him a pair of socks knitted by a friend that placed the Confederate flag beneath each foot; Lincoln was amused.[47]

With the city filled with the trappings of war, French longed for Washington to "once more be *a civil* city," but he enjoyed mingling with New England soldiers encamped in and around Washington. The feelings must have been mutual: when the 34th Regt. Massachusetts headed to the train station to leave town, two companies gave three cheers for French.[48] When the Confederate capital, Richmond, fell in April 1865, Commissioner French posted his feelings for all to see on an enormous transparency hung on the Capitol's west portico. Its motto—"This is the Lord's doing; it is marvellous in our eyes"—could be seen well up Pennsylvania Avenue.[49] A few days later he gloried in the victory during a visit to Richmond with the Joint Committee on the Conduct of the War, asking someone to play "Yankee Doodle" on Confederate president Jefferson Davis's piano.[50]

French enjoyed some personal victories during wartime as well. In 1862, he married Mary Ellen Brady, his brother Edmund's sister-in-law. Thirty-one years French's junior, Mary Ellen had gotten to know French while nursing Bess through her final illness and keeping house for French for months thereafter. Tall, stately, and gentle, she was a calming influence on French's life.[51] By April 1862, he felt that he couldn't live without her. After their marriage on September 9, he didn't have to.

A second moment of glory took place on November 19, 1863, at the dedication of a national soldier's cemetery in Gettysburg, Pennsylvania, an event that French helped organize. Told during a planning session a few days earlier that Henry Wadsworth Longfellow, John Greenleaf Whittier, and William Cullen Bryant had declined to write a hymn for the occasion, French decided to try his hand at it. By breakfast the next morning he had written a five-stanza elegy that concluded with a plea to God to "save a people's freedom from its grave."[52] Seeing it sung before the crowd of roughly 20,000 spectators and dignitaries was a proud moment for French. Indeed, he was moved by the entire ceremony. Standing beside the orator Edward Everett as Everett delivered a two-hour speech (after which Lincoln delivered a remarkably powerful 272-word, three-minute address), French thought back to another

LINCOLN   B. B. FRENCH

Detail of a photograph of the crowd gathered before the speaking platform on the day of Abraham Lincoln's Gettysburg Address in 1863. Lincoln can be seen seated to the left. French is standing to the right. (Courtesy of the Library of Congress)

great speech by a great man long dead. In 1834, French had stood beside John Quincy Adams in the House when Adams delivered a eulogy for the Marquis de Lafayette. If Adams were here today, French thought, his "heart would swell with the patriotism that has followed his own great efforts to bring about that emancipation of the negro race which is so rapidly approaching."[53] The change in French's politics was profound.

As suggested by French's presence at Gettysburg, he continued to be a history stalker of the first order, particularly when it came to Lincoln. In 1861, French had welcomed Lincoln to Washington by conducting his inaugural ceremonies. At Lincoln's second inauguration, French probably saved Lincoln's life. As French explained to his son, as the president's procession passed through the rotunda, a man jumped out of the crowd and ran behind Lincoln. French ordered a policeman to grab the intruder, who insisted so strenuously that he had a right to be there that French thought he must be a new member of Congress and let him go.

By that time, the procession had passed. Later shown a photograph of John Wilkes Booth, the stunned French felt sure that he had waylaid the assassin.[54]

Even the Lincoln Memorial has ties to French; in 1920, his nephew Daniel Chester French—his half brother Henry's son—sculpted the colossal Lincoln statue at its center. (*"Dan is a sculptor.* I mean it," French wrote in his diary after seeing an early example of his young nephew's work.)[55] To Daniel, French was "Uncle Major."[56]

But French's history stalking reached its height of intensity on April 15, 1865. Puzzled that the streetlamps were still lit when he rose that morning, he went down to the street and heard about the night's grisly events: Lincoln had been shot and Secretary of State William Seward had been slashed, perhaps fatally.[57] Worried about security, French immediately began to shut down government buildings, first closing the Capitol. He then rushed to Lincoln's bedside. Seeing that Lincoln was beyond help, he sat with Mary Lincoln for a time, then fetched some of her friends. He next raced to close the White House. He was there when Lincoln was taken inside, and for a time he stayed by Lincoln's side, watching as his body—"all limp and warm"—was laid upon a cooling board.[58] He then began arranging Lincoln's funeral. The Capitol needed to be clothed in mourning. A catafalque had to be built for Lincoln's coffin in the rotunda. French had his son Benjamin design it.[59]

An intimate of every president since Andrew Jackson, French welcomed Andrew Johnson into office, pleased that "Andrew the energetic" had succeeded "Abraham the good."[60] French had been friendly with Johnson for years, probably dating back to Johnson's early years in Congress, and he liked the man, in part because Johnson was an active Mason. Seeing Johnson in full regalia at a Masonic ceremony in 1866, French was struck: Johnson was "the first President I ever saw so clothed."[61] He hadn't supported Johnson's nomination as vice president and didn't agree with all of his views, but he agreed with enough of them to become a target in the raging dispute between Johnson and radical Republicans in Congress.[62]

In truth, French was on neither side of this debate; as ever, he was a moderate. Radical Republicans had an egalitarian agenda of racial reform, Johnson vehemently opposed it, and French fell somewhere in the middle. He supported bettering the rights and lives of black Americans, but not to the point of racial equality; he considered the white race superior. He wanted Confederates punished heartily for their sins, but only those who had taken arms against the Union; he worried that Reconstruction measures were violating the constitutional rights of white Southerners, or as French put it, "enslaving" them.[63] Although he remained firmly Republican, fearful that Johnson would oppose Republican policies, he was no fan of what he called Republican "ultradom."[64]

At a time of tangled and polarized politics, it almost goes without saying that French's scribbling habit was his downfall; a typically effusive poem praising Johnson planted him firmly on one side of this debate. At the advanced age of sixty-six, French still hadn't learned his lesson about putting things in print. In this case, he was partly driven by crass practicalities; as a professional officeholder of sorts, he had good reason to curry favor with men in power. Thus his custom of writing a poem of tribute for every president from Jackson to Grant. And thus his trouble with the radical Republican-controlled Congress.

The title of French's poem for Johnson says it all: "Andrew Jackson and Andrew Johnson." A lengthy string of couplets lauding Johnson as a "second Andrew," the poem was over the top even by French's standards. He printed it in broadside form in 1866. Eight months later, it cost him his job. During a debate over a House appropriations bill in February 1867, the office of commissioner of public buildings came up, and radicals leaped at the chance to smack at Johnson by attacking French. Mocking French as the "poet-laureate of the Administration," they laughingly read his poem aloud. William Kelley (R-PA) bragged that he had ridiculed the poem to French's face, telling French that "some scoundrel" had signed French's name to a terrible poem. "He seemed very much confused," Kelley reported to the great amusement of the hall. Josiah Grinnell (R-IA) then piped up with a second French poem to ridicule. Titled "Orgies in Hell, over Secession," it made an easy target for its style if not its subject. (Its opening line is "Hark! hark! to the Fiend—'ha! ha! ha! ha! ha! ha!'") It described a Satanic board meeting of sorts in which Satan rejoiced at the services of Jefferson Davis, Alexander Stephens, William Lowndes Yancey, and a host of other Confederates.[65] The grand finale of French's roasting was the abolishment of his office and the granting of its rights and duties to the chief engineer of the army, a congressional appointment.[66]

French was both mortified and angry. "Dignified work for the House of Representatives of a great Nation! To snub poor modest me, just because I dared speak well of Andrew Johnson."[67] Although he pleaded with Johnson to intervene, the president could (or would) do nothing. "I sincerely wish them Hell on earth, & everlasting damnation hereafter," he wrote of his tormentors. "Oh how I despise and hate them. I hope none of them are Freemasons!"[68] This was strong stuff for French, and he meant it. In time, he grew to dislike Johnson, too; the president had promised to find him a job but never did.[69] Though French himself may not have realized it, his downfall had an upside: he seems finally to have learned his lesson. "I wrote some rhymes applauding Grant," he wrote in January 1868. "I *shall not publish them now*."[70]

As always, French tried to make the most of the waxing and waning of his political fortunes. Relieved at giving up his government responsibilities, he set out on his own, hoping to support himself with a claims agency like the one he had before, but his partners were shirkers and he didn't get much business.[71] His reelection as Grand Master of the Masons late in 1867 soothed his pride but didn't fill his wallet.[72] So in February 1868 he took a minor clerkship in the Treasury Department, feeling "as humble as a whipped spaniel to think that after holding the offices I have, I should humiliate myself so much as to accept a 4th class Clerkship!"[73] But he needed the money so he sacrificed his pride and went to work.

From this point on, French's center of gravity shifted. Although he kept up with the politics of the day, he didn't take part in them. He played no role in the 1868 presidential contest that elected Grant. "I ask no political favors from him or anybody else," he wrote in November 1868. "My political life is over."[74] His diary pages increasingly were filled with friends and family. His new priorities were apparent when Thaddeus Stevens died in August 1868. French loved Stevens, who had been loyal to French throughout his recent trials. Seeing Stevens's body being borne to the Capitol, French longed to see him one last time but decided against it. He had too much to do.[75]

One of the things keeping him busy that day was preparing for a lengthy vacation; with more time on his hands, French headed north more often. During his trip in 1868 he settled a score: he called on Franklin Pierce. It was the first time French had seen Pierce since his presidency. Though sick in bed, Pierce immediately beckoned French into his bedroom for a chat. It was their last meeting. A little more than a year later, Pierce died. "No living man knew Franklin Pierce from his young manhood to the day when he left Washington the last time, better than I did," French mused on hearing the news. "He had many of the best qualities that adorn human nature. 'De mortuis nil nisi bonum' [Of the dead say nothing but good]."[76]

A chapter of French's life had closed and he knew it. At sixty-nine years of age he began to take stock of his life, relying on his diary to fill the gaps. It was "the duty of every man who is in any wise mixed up with the great rush of national events, and with national men, as I have been, to keep a constant and faithful journal of what he sees and how he hears," he mused as he paged through the thoughts, feelings, and events of a lifetime, glad to see what he had chronicled, sad to see what he'd left out.[77]

Hardy and active to the end, French didn't die easily. "I am sick," he wrote in his diary on July 31, 1870, after a week of sporadic chest pains and shortness of breath. "Unless I get better must soon give up."[78] French's heart and famously strong lungs were giving out. Nine days later, he telegrammed his son Frank in Boston, who arrived late the next day. Taking after his father, Frank chronicled the next few days in his own diary, noting that French looked thin and anxious but seemed like himself, curious about everything as always.

The morning of August 11, French rallied. After dressing and eating breakfast, he suggested a game of cribbage. He and Frank played several hands, French "taking the usual zest" in winning, Frank noted. French had plans, he told his son. He was going to sell his house and move north to be near Frank and his family.

But at 11:00 a.m., something changed. "There is that pain again," French said, assuring Frank that it would pass. Frank knew better and ran for the doctor. For the next fourteen hours, French suffered so intensely that his moans were heard by passersby on the street below. At 1:00 in the morning on Friday, August 12, he died, just short of his seventieth birthday. "Tell the children and give them some idea of his beautiful affection for all that came within his circle," Frank wrote in a hastily dashed-off note to his wife.[79] The last words in French's diary were a tribute of sorts to a member of that circle. "Mrs. French has come up and says I must not write any more," he penned. "I *obey*."[80]

That night, the Masons arrived at the French household in force to plan a full Masonic funeral. Though initially bothered by the commotion, Frank found himself moved by their concern and care, much as his father had been moved fifty years past upon witnessing the funeral that had drawn him to the order. Two days later, on Sunday, August 14, a parade of Masonic rites and rituals played out. After a brief service in French's parlor, complete with an impressive wreath sent from the Capitol, his remains were carried to a nearby church for his funeral. When something went awry amid the pomp and circumstance, French's sister-in-law Sarita Brady half expected him to leap to his feet to put things right. The service was followed by a procession down Pennsylvania Avenue to the Congressional Cemetery, with the Marine Band and the Masons leading the way and the District's own B. B. French Lodge No. 15 in a place of honor. Crowds lined the streets in "an impenetrable barrier of people," Brady reported. "Since the day of Lincoln there has been no such funeral."[81] As French's coffin passed the Capitol, the Columbia Fire Company bell began to toll in tribute; French had lobbied Congress for money to rebuild the firehouse after it burned down and had been made an honorary member of the Company in thanks—one of the countless civic services that filled his life.[82]

By dusk the procession had reached the cemetery, where French was laid to rest at Bess's side, accompanied by the mournful strains of a Masonic choir, with Knights in full regalia bathing the scene in candlelight. The scene was "beautiful beyond description," Brady thought.[83] Ten days later, the Masons held a formal Lodge of Sorrow in French's honor, attended by scores of Masons from Pennsylvania, Maryland, Virginia, and the District. More than 1,500 people attended the ceremony.[84]

French had come a long way from the knockabout days of his New Hampshire youth. He lived most of his life in the corridors of power, an insider's insider, an intimate of presidents who socialized with congressmen. For a time, he even had a modest national presence in the press. He achieved his greatest glory among the Masons, becoming a national leader of the highest rank. His death made the front page of *The New York Times*.[85]

Since then, French has been almost totally forgotten, perhaps for good reason. Although he lived his life amid the nation's ruling elite, he held little power of his own. He was the man behind the scenes par excellence, the one who made things go, the instigator, organizer, and promoter all in one. Such a man doesn't often make the history books, as French well knew. It was one of the many reasons he valued his diary. Future generations would see only what appeared in public documents, he worried. Diaries offered a different truth. Filled with the minutiae of life, they captured something of the past's human reality, the commonplace people and everyday events that form the backbone of a time. As a newspaper clipping pasted in his diary put it: a diary "is the soul of days long ago."[86]

And what of Congress? What of its real history would survive? French had his doubts. A few months before he died, he addressed this theme in a speech before the Association of Oldest Inhabitants of the District, an organization that had welcomed him into its ranks several years past. Speaking of the "Old Capitol Prison," he feared that the truth would be forgotten. Future "romancers" would tell tall tales about the prison's horrors at the expense of its reality and truth. "I now predict, that the time will come when some fruitful but distempered imagination . . . will produce a 'Myth of the Old Capitol' that will blanch the ruddiest cheek, and make the darkness of midnight awful."[87] He knew whereof he spoke, he insisted. In some distant future, someone would read his speech and declare him a prophet.

French was talking about the construction of history, and he was indeed prophetic; he knew that past events are stripped of subtleties at the expense of truths in the progress of time. In the case of Congress, later generations overlooked its ugly undertow, envisioning its history as a succession of great issues discussed by great men speaking great words, with nary a trace of the tobacco-stained rugs. French preferred a history of light and shadows: the majestic vista of a candlelit night session peopled by bleary-eyed, cranky, unshaven congressmen. His attempt at a memoir in 1856 put his ideas into practice. Characteristically, it opens with a few lines of verse, though not his own. Quoting Robert Burns, French wrote:

But how the subject-theme may gang,
Let time and chance determine;
Perhaps it may turn out a song,
Perhaps turn out a sermon.[88]

The end result was part song, part sermon. French lauded great men of the past while detailing the House's howling fury, including some of its fights and its one death by duel. As he himself put it, "I witnessed it all."[89]

French knew what later generations sometimes forgot: Congress was an institution with a checkered story to tell. Its trials are the nation's trials. Its flashpoints are the nation's flashpoints. Its strengths and accomplishments are the ultimate proof of powerful bonds of Union. Its flaws reveal the human realities underlying the process of national governance. And its failings are vital reminders that even the strongest of nations can fall.

But responsibility for these failings doesn't rest solely on Congress. As a representative institution, the U.S. Congress embodies the temper of its time. When the nation is polarized and civic commonality dwindles, Congress reflects that image back to the American people. The give-and-take of deliberative politics breaks down, bringing accusations, personal abuse, and even violence in its wake. National political parties fracture. Trust in the institution of Congress lapses, as does trust in national institutions of all kinds, and indeed, the trust of Americans in one another.[90] At such times, they are forced to reckon with what their nation is, and what it should be. During such periods of national moment, the failures of the People's Branch are profound failures indeed.

French saw many such lapses during his congressional career. Then, as ever, Congress was a barometer of the times, which were divisive and violent. He saw the failure of gag rules to stifle debate over slavery; the failure of Democrats to fulfill his party's promise as he envisioned it; the failure of Northerners to subdue the Slave Power. Yet, as flawed as Congress was, French had high expectations. He believed in its power to negotiate national compromises. When it failed, he had a front-row seat to the disastrous consequences.

That front-row seat revealed Congress as the exceedingly human institution that it was and always has been. French's Congress was flawed, raucous, funny, frustrating, occasionally unstable, often unpredictable, sometimes dangerous. It was a place of conflict and passions as well as compromise, housed within a symbol made of mortar and brick. French wandered that building's passages for decades, sometimes happily, sometimes not, always hopeful that the clash of interests in the

This view of Washington from 1861, taken from the same vantage point as the view on page 22, shows the city's remarkable growth in the twenty-eight years since French's arrival. Pennsylvania Avenue is to the left. From a photo album French created for his son Frank (Courtesy of the Library of Congress)

House and Senate chambers would solve more problems than it caused. Sometimes it did. More often, it didn't. Either way, for better and worse, French saw Congress as the nation's beating heart.

In 1869, thirty-six years after he arrived in Washington and first gazed at the Capitol in wonderment and worry, he wrote a poem commemorating all that he believed the Capitol and Congress to be. It was a celebratory poem of sorts, infused with a knowing sadness of suffering but born of comfort and relief. Titled "A Vision," it opened with a description of the Capitol as French saw it from his window at home: "a grand old pile and massive dome / High looming in the air." But the building meant far more than that to French, and after a lifetime within its walls he said so. He felt as if it were "My dwelling and my home."[91]

The crux of the piece was a vision that his poem-persona had while roaming the building on a—literally—dark and stormy night. As he passed through the crypt, a bolt of lightning knocked him flat, and in his senseless state he saw a group of men take form. Washington, Hamilton, Franklin, Adams, Jay, and hundreds more: standing before him were the men who he believed had brought the Union to life. Together, they gave thanks for the end of civil warfare. Never again would "rebel hand / Seek the Republic's life." Forevermore the Capitol would be the Union's home. The emotional power of this message for French is contained in the poem's closing lines:

And while I live, to the Great Power
Who rules above the sky
My thanks shall rise, in firm belief,
My Country cannot die!

My country cannot die: it was a striking thought, beyond imagination before the war. Having suffered through a titanic clash of arms with the South, the North had emerged victorious, to be bullied no more, the Union formed anew. As violent and strife-ridden as the nation and its politics continued to be, a new day was at hand.

So French believed. He published the poem a month after writing it, compelled to proclaim his politics to the world almost literally until his dying day. And on that day, he died at peace. The Union had survived.

APPENDIX A

A WORD ABOUT WORDS
PARTY ABBREVIATIONS AND
SECTIONAL LOYALTIES

Sorting out party labels at such a politically volatile time presents challenges. Political parties came and went in the 1830s, 1840s, and 1850s, sometimes in the space of a few elections. Even so-called party systems rose and fell. Given this ever-shifting roster, this book identifies politicians by their political allegiance at precise moments in time, using the *Biographical Directory of the United States Congress* (bioguide .congress.gov) and the Roster of Congressional Officeholders and Biographical Characteristics (ICPSR 7803) as a guide, with several reservations. Neither source is entirely consistent with party labels; both sometimes mistake the timing of a congressman's shift from party to party. Any divergences from the *Directory* and the *Roster* within these pages are grounded on historical evidence. Party abbreviations can be found below.

Finding the right words for sectional loyalties poses fewer challenges, though the period's aggressive national expansion complicates matters. People at the time often divided Westerners into two categories: "Southern-born Westerners" and "Northern-born Westerners"—a clear indication of the period's pervasive sense of an ongoing battle between a free North and a slaveholding South. At various points, I've used these designations; at other points, I refer only to "Westerners"; at still other points, "Southern" or "Northern" encompasses the West. As with political parties, when pinning down sectional identities I've tried to be true to place, time, and circumstance, as well as to the phrasing of the people doing the talking.

A   American Party
AJ   Anti-Jacksonian Party
D   Democratic Party
FS   Free Soil Party
ID   Independent Democratic Party
J   Jacksonian Party
KN   Know Nothing Party

L   Liberty Party
N   Nullifier
NR   National Republican (or Adams-Clay Republican)
O   Opposition Party
R   Republican Party
SRD   State's Rights Democrat
UU   Unconditional Unionist
W   Whig Party

APPENDIX B

A NOTE ON METHOD
CONSTRUCTING FIGHTS AND
DECONSTRUCTING EMOTIONS

Much of the fighting at the core of *The Field of Blood* is hidden between the lines of public records or scattered in personal correspondence and diaries. Finding and confirming it raised interesting questions about the trustworthiness of evidence. Of course, the craft of history relies on finding, interpreting, and evaluating things long hidden; that's nothing new. But from the outset of this project, the rich vein of congressional violence that I was uncovering raised an obvious question: How could I track and confirm the pieces of a deliberately suppressed story?

I stumbled across that story almost by accident. Thinking of my first book—*Affairs of Honor: National Politics in the New Republic*—and curious about the fate of honor culture after the 1790s, I investigated a political honor dispute from a few decades later—the Cilley-Graves duel of 1838—in the hope of sensing a shift of tone or logic. I started with the letters of Cilley's Maine colleague Representative John Fairfield. As luck would have it, Fairfield wrote to his wife frequently, sometimes daily, and many of his letters mentioned congressional violence. Congressmen rolling up their sleeves to throw a punch. Full-fledged fistfights. Henry Wise behaving like Henry Wise, often and with vigor. (Fairfield described him as "one of those men who would as soon fight as eat.")[1] Intrigued, I turned to the correspondence of other congressmen. In three months of research at the Library of Congress, I never opened a congressman's papers without finding at least one fight or confrontation. Clearly, there was a story to tell.

Personal letters and diary entries were vital points of entry. Not only did they reveal congressional clashes, but they discussed the details: their causes, tone, and temper, their personal and political implications. Some congressmen even confessed their feelings about a clash, often in letters to their wives. Such personal insights are invaluable in trying to understand the culture of a people or an institution. It's one thing to note a pattern of behavior in the past and quite another to grasp how people understood and experienced it.

But the very thing that gave such evidence its value—its subjectivity—presented challenges. How could I judge its truthfulness? Was Fairfield inventing stories to amuse his wife? (The thought did cross my mind.) Was he playing up or playing down what happened? The fragmentary nature of personal letters and diary entries was also problematic. They represent part of a conversation—with another person or with oneself—that relies on context and background for meaning. "It is said here that Fremont is 'going' to challenge Toombs" is a tantalizing bit of evidence, particularly tacked on to a letter (by Henry Wise!) as a juicy piece of gossip in a postscript. But it suggests very little in and of itself. Years later, I stumbled across its context in some letters to the *New-York Evening Post* editor John Bigelow. Writing to Bigelow, Ohio congressman Timothy Day urged him to convince the renowned explorer and leading Republican John C. Fremont to challenge Toombs to a duel. Toombs had insulted Fremont, who was deciding how to respond. It would "be the making" of Fremont, Day insisted, "and he cannot avoid it with honor. He must not listen to such chuckleheads as Greeley, or such pious men as Beecher. The masses like a brave man."[2] Day was focused on the masses because Fremont had just lost the presidential election of 1856 with no support from the slave states. A duelist might play well in the South; Day was thinking of Fremont's future. The Fremont-Toombs affair (which seems to have sputtered) was bound up with electoral politics.

Given the subjectivity, incompleteness, and needle-in-a-haystack randomness of my evidence, I had to go further. The *Congressional Globe* was my next step. Most of the clashes underlying this book are not detailed in the *Globe*. Those that are there are often masked as "sudden sensations" or "unpleasantly personal" discussions. Add the enormous size of the *Globe*—each session of Congress produced some six thousand poorly indexed, three-columned pages of close text—and it's easy to see how the violence has remained undercover. You have to know to look for it, you need to dig to find it, and a lot of what you're seeking isn't there.

My research in letters and diaries solved this problem. When I cross-checked dates and names gleaned from that evidence against the *Globe*, I found "unpleasantly personal" confrontations hidden in plain view. I also discovered how to scan the *Globe* for conflicts, which was essential given the sheer volume of text. Interspersed between lengthy speeches were occasional rapid-fire exchanges: A sentence. A very brief response. An equally brief rejoinder. Some of these exchanges proved to be moments of conflict. In time, I became so good at sight-scanning clashes that I spotted one while glancing at a record of the mid-nineteenth-century French Assembly in a Paris museum; when I translated the text, it was indeed some name-calling.

Such searching taught me how revealing a cultural document the congressional record can be. Historians don't often mine the *Globe* or *National Intelligencer* for cultural input. They use it to track the ins and outs of specific debates; to judge the politics and politicking of individuals; to track the course of national politics; to study the institutional workings of Congress. But much like congressional violence, the culture of Congress was hiding in plain sight. What words drew objections? What actions garnered protests? How did congressmen talk to one another between their speechifying and voting? What was the tone of their conversational exchanges, and how did it vary? How did they discuss their constituents? And what about the press? When and how were individual reporters mentioned, and why? What kind of press coverage upset congressmen? What kind pleased them? How did they interact with editors and reporters? All this and more lies within the pages of the *Globe*, revealing the character, customs, tempo, and temper of the antebellum Congress, and offering a window into the culture of the period's politics.

Newspapers offered similar evidence of congressional culture, but with important differences. Given the rise of a spicier style of political press coverage in this period (as well as the rise of the slavery crisis), newspapers increasingly offered evidence of personal exchanges and personalities, highlighting lines crossed and amends made. Even better, they offered editorial opinions to weigh in the balance. Sometimes newspapers even judged themselves. But how could I evaluate their truthfulness? More than once, an incident played up in the press was explicitly denied in Congress. Did John Wright (D-TN) really kick John "Bowie Knife" Potter (R-WI) in March 1858, as the *Southern Argus* suggested? (The *Argus* claimed that Wright "made a very brisk application of his pedal extremity.") On the House floor, Potter vehemently denied it in a personal explanation. So did it happen?[3] I still don't know.

Thus the process of triangulation that I used in my research. For the most part, the incidents in this book appear in at least two of my three main forms of evidence: newspapers, the congressional record, and personal letters and diaries; or they are extensively covered in one of them. (For this very reason, the Wright-Potter kick-fest didn't make the cut.)

The burden of proof becomes particularly challenging when detecting emotions in the historical past. How do you prove the existence of an emotion? How do you explore it in the context of its time? How do you evaluate its impact? And how do you weave that impact into a historical narrative? This was one of my foremost challenges in writing *The Field of Blood*. Emotions gave congressional bullying and violence their power. Humiliation, fear, shame, degradation: displayed before colleagues, friends, constituents, and a broader public, such feelings could wound a person to the core. This was particularly true in the case of congressmen whose livelihood rested on their reputation, and whose honor was bound up with the honor of all that they represented. Emotions were also contagious, boomeranging between the national center and the public through the vehicle of the press, a product of events as much as a cause of them. Then as now, strong emotions were a shaping influence on the People's Branch, and indeed, on politics as a whole.

But they weren't the *only* shaping influence. Some revisionist historians in the mid-twentieth century suggested as much, arguing that the Civil War was caused by the "emotionalism" of antebellum politics, and blaming those emotions on a "blundering generation" of politicians and politicos.[4] This book makes no such claim. Emotions are only part of the story told on these pages. The degradation of violated rights did indeed cause a stream of emotions that ran powerfully and deep. But these feelings didn't cause the war. Rather, they framed the period's sectional crises, giving the growing rift between national sensibilities and sectional loyalties a profoundly personal impact that had political consequences. French and his contemporaries weren't pushed into civil warfare through blind emotion. But strong emotions highlighted and shaped sectional conflicts in ways that eroded the mutual trust that bound the Union as one.

This isn't the first time that I've deployed emotions in my scholarship. In *Affairs of Honor*, they were a vital source of evidence in tracking the cultural norms of politics at the national center in the 1790s.[5] But in *The Field of Blood*, emotions are more than tools. They are a fundamental part of the story. They reveal the emotional logic of disunion among national lawmakers, or rather, the emotional logic of dis-Union, the wrenching experience of plotting a political path in a nation being torn in two.

Disunion is a political condition. Dis-Union is the lived experience of reaching that condition, and the close consideration of shifting emotions helps to tell that story.

Benjamin Brown French was an essential starting point in my search for such evidence. Finding an eyewitness to the story that I was telling was invaluable. Finding an eyewitness who so readily expressed his thoughts and feelings on paper was providential. Of course, one person's experience of events isn't representative. But it can show the personal impact of change over time with powerful specificity. Sensing the lived reality of historical change requires a kind of double vision, joining an awareness of contingencies with knowledge born of hindsight. French's feelings as portrayed in his writings helped me gain that perspective. Properly contextualized in the historical past and taken beyond the merely anecdotal, the study of emotions shows people reacting to events in a specific place and time, offering insight into how they understood and experienced those events.[6] Particularly when studying a period that lies in the shadow of the Civil War, the immediacy and power of emotions is an invaluable pathway to the sense of contingency that shaped events for people living through them.

Although congressmen threatened, feared, and sometimes even expected disunion, they didn't see war as inevitable. They fought to effect outcomes. The contingencies of the moment fueled their fires. (The word *antebellum*—literally "before the war"—is problematic for just this reason, though it's hard to discuss the 1830s, 1840s, and 1850s without it.) To fully grasp the logic of their decisions, we need to understand their process of discovery. We need to see events unfolding as they were lived.[7] We need to join the nation on the road to civil war, a long and winding trail with no clear destination.

NOTES

ABBREVIATIONS

BBFFP   Benjamin Brown French Family Papers, Library of Congress
DOP   David Outlaw Papers, UNC
GPO   Government Printing Office
JER   *Journal of the Early Republic*
LC   Library of Congress
LSU   Louisiana State University
MHS   Massachusetts Historical Society
NHHS   New Hampshire Historical Society
NYPL   New York Public Library
NYT   *The New York Times*
UNC   University of North Carolina
UVA   University of Virginia

AUTHOR'S NOTE

1. Tim Alberta, "John Boehner Unchained," *Politico*, November–December 2017, www.politico.com/magazine/story/2017/10/29/john-boehner-trump-house -republican-party-retirement-profile-feature-215741; Jacqueline Thomsen, "GOP Lawmaker Once Held a Knife to Boehner's Throat," *The Hill*, October 29, 2017, thehill.com/blogs/in-the-know/in-the-know/357743-gop-lawmaker-once-held-a -knife-to-boehners-throat; Martha Brant, "The Alaskan Assault," *Newsweek*, October 1, 1995, www.newsweek.com/alaskan-assault-184084, accessed on December 14, 2017. For video of Young twisting the arm of a staffer who tried to keep him from entering a room, see www.youtube.com/watch?v=VmSXqn2xxS4.

2. On the sweeping cultural and political impact of collapsing political structures in the 1850s, see John L. Brooke, "Party, Nation, and Cultural Rupture: The Crisis of the American Civil War," in *Practicing Democracy: Popular Politics in the*

United States from the Constitution to the Civil War, ed. Daniel Pearl and Adam I. P. Smith (Charlottesville: UVA Press, 2015). Selinger argues that a permanent settled two-party system provided an alternative to violence. Jeffrey S. Selinger, *Embracing Dissent: Political Violence and Party Development in the United States* (Philadelphia: University of Pennsylvania, 2016).

3. This book begins in the 1830s because violence took an upswing in that decade. The congressional record supports this observation; 40 percent of all recorded breaches of comity between 1789 and 1956 took place between 1831 and 1860. Eric M. Uslaner, *The Decline of Comity in Congress* (Ann Arbor: University of Michigan, 1993), 40. This shift was partly a product of the rise of the divisiveness of the Second Party System, partly a product of the ongoing slavery crisis, and partly due to the expanding growth and reach of the press. Close study of both the *Globe* and congressional correspondence shows growing interest in the exposure and impact of the press beginning in that decade. Also note: the *Register of Debates in Congress* began in 1824, the *Congressional Globe* began in 1833, and the *Annals of Congress* began in 1834. Mildred L. Amer, "The Congressional Record: Content, History and Issues," January 14, 1993, CRS Report for Congress (93–60 GOV). For a handy look at the burst of new newspapers in the 1830s and 1840s, see Judith R. Blau and Cheryl Elman, "The Institutionalization of U.S. Political Parties: Patronage Newspapers," *Sociological Inquiry* (Fall 2002): 576–99, figure on 590.

4. The phenomenon is sometimes called "Fenno's Paradox." Richard F. Fenno, "If, as Ralph Nader Says, Congress Is the 'Broken Branch,' How Come We Love Our Congressmen So Much?," in *Congress in Change: Evolution and Reform,* ed. Norman J. Ornstein (New York: Praeger, 1979); idem., *Home Style: House Members in Their Districts* (Boston: Little, Brown, 1978).

5. On the importance of institutional trust to the functioning of government, see Josh Chafetz, *Congress's Constitution: Legislative Authority and the Separation of Powers* (New Haven: Yale University Press, 2017), esp. chapter 1.

6. On competing ideas of "exclusionary nationalism," see Michael E. Woods, "What Twenty-first Century Historians Have Said about the Causes of Disunion: A Civil War Sesquicentennial Review of the Recent Literature," *JAH* (September 2012): 415–39, quote on 427; Robert E. Bonner, *Mastering America: Southern Slaveholders and the Crisis of American Nationhood* (New York: Cambridge University Press, 2009). Bonner notes that Southerners were true to national values in joining slavery with nationalism; slavery had been baked into America's national identity since the founding. On Americanism, un-Americanism, and conflicting views of American democracy, see Shearer Davis Bowman, *At the Precipice: Americans North and South During the Secession Crisis* (Chapel Hill: UNC Press, 2010); Sean Wilentz, *The Rise of American Democracy: Jefferson to Lincoln* (New York: Norton, 2005).

7. For the 1874 memorandum, see Simon Cameron Papers, LC. The three men were probably inspired to write their statement by the recent failure of a bill promoting black civil rights. In the final tally, only 45 of 79 senators voted; neither Chandler nor Cameron voted, because their constituents wanted them to vote against it. William Gillette, *Retreat from Reconstruction, 1869–1879* (Baton Rouge: LSU Press, 1982), 193–94, 204–207; *Journal of the Senate of the USA,* 43rd Cong., 1st Sess., May 22, 1874, vol. 69, 605–609.

8. The three men each put a copy of the statement in their confidential papers for future eyes to read. For passing references to the statement, see Albert T. Voll-weiler, "The Nature of Life in Congress (1850–1861)," *Quarterly Journal of the University of North Dakota* 6, no. 1 (October 1915), 145–58; Wilmer C. Harris, *The Public Life of Zachariah Chandler, 1851–1875* (Lansing: Michigan Historical Publications, 1917), 48; Lately Thomas, *The First President Johnson: The Three Lives of the Seventeenth President of the United States of America* (New York: William Morrow, 1968), 126; William Parker, *The Life and Public Services of Justin Smith Morrill* (Boston: Houghton Mifflin, 1924), 92; Albert Gallatin Riddle, *Life of Benjamin Franklin Wade* (Cleveland: Williams, 1888), 250–51; Arthur Tappan Pierson, *Zachariah Chandler: An Outline Sketch of His Life and Public Services* (Detroit: Post and Tribune, 1880), 146; Hans L. Trefousse, *The Radical Republicans: Lincoln's Vanguard for Racial Justice* (New York: Knopf, 1969), 116–17; Eric Foner, *Free Soil, Free Labor, Free Men: The Ideology of the Republican Party Before the Civil War* (New York: Oxford University Press, 1995), 146.

9. See esp. Norman Ornstein and Thomas E. Mann, *The Broken Branch: How Congress Is Failing America and How to Get It Back on Track* (New York: Oxford University Press, 2008), which argues that the spurning of norms and a lack of respect for the institution of Congress from congressmen themselves, dating back to the 1990s—including the disappearance of oversight, indifference to reform, the weakening of institutional identity, tolerance of executive secrecy, and the so-called nuclear option—have contributed to Congress's decline. See also Juliet Eilperin, *Fight Club Politics: How Partisanship Is Poisoning the House of Representatives* (New York: Rowman & Littlefield, 2006); Burdett A. Loomis, ed., *Esteemed Colleagues: Civility and Deliberation in the U.S. Senate* (Washington, D.C.: Brookings Institution, 2000); Sunil Ahuja, *Congress Behaving Badly: The Rise of Partisanship and Incivility and the Death of Public Trust* (Westport, Conn.: Praeger, 2008); Uslaner, *Decline of Comity in Congress.*

INTRODUCTIONS

1. Charles Dickens, *American Notes for General Circulation*, 2 vols. (London: Chapman and Hall, 1842), 1: 272.

2. Ibid., 1:294–95. On Dickens's seat of honor on the floor, see French, diary entry, March 13, 1842, in *Witness to the Young Republic: A Yankee's Journal, 1828–1870*, ed. Donald B. Cole and John J. McDonough (Hanover, N.H.: University Press of New England, 1989), 138 (hereafter cited as *Witness*).

3. For a sampling of comments on tobacco spitting—and there were plenty, particularly among the British—see N. A. Woods, *The Prince of Wales in Canada and the United States* (London: Bradbury & Evans, 1861), 342; Frederick Marryat, *A Diary in America: With Remarks on Its Institutions* (New York: William H. Colyer, 1839), 91; Adam Hodgson, *Remarks During a Journey Through North America in the Years 1819, 1820, and 1821,* 91; Rubio [Thomas Horton James], *Ramble in the United States and Canada During the Year 1845, With a Short Account of Oregon* (London: Samuel Clarke, 1846), 117; Frances Trollope, *Domestic Manners of the Americans,* 30–31; William Howard Russell, *My Diary North and South* (New York: Harper & Brothers, 1863), 144–45; George Combe,

Notes on the United States of North America, During a Phrenological Visit in 1838–39–40, 2 vols. (Edinburgh: Maclachlan, Stewart, 1841), 2:95. See also Ella Dzelzainis, "Dickens, Democracy, and Spit," in *The American Experiment and the Idea of Democracy in British Culture, 1776–1914*, ed. Ella Dzelzainis and Ruth Livesey (London: Routledge, 2013), 45–60.

4. Christian F. Eckloff, *Memoirs of a Senate Page, 1855–1859* (New York: Broadway Publishing Company, 1909), 19–20. See also Grace Greenwood, *Greenwood Leaves: A Collection of Sketches and Letters* (Boston: Ticknor, Reed, and Fields, 1852), 307.

5. In 1871, there were 148 spittoons in the House and 43 in the Senate. "Inventory of Public Property. Letter from the Architect of the United States Capitol," December 18, 1871 (Washington: GPO, 1871), 6, 18.

6. David Outlaw to Emily Outlaw, May 28, 1850, DOP.

7. David Outlaw to Emily Outlaw, February 20, 1848, DOP.

8. Benjamin Brown French to Harriette French, January 31, 1839, BBFFP. See also William Cabell Rives to his wife, June 2, 1838, William Cabell Rives Papers, LC.

9. David Grimsted, *American Mobbing, 1828–1861: Toward the Civil War* (New York: Oxford University Press, 1998), 4.

10. For an evocative look at violence and the Second Party System, see Mark E. Neely, Jr., "Apotheosis of a Ruffian: The Murder of Bill Pool and American Political Culture," in *A Political Nation: New Directions in Mid-Nineteenth Century American Political History*, ed. Gary W. Gallagher and Rachel A. Shelden (Charlottesville: UVA Press, 2012), 36–63.

11. The Plug Uglies were a Baltimore gang that joined the Chunkers and Rip-Raps in Washington for the riot; the Marines were called in by President Buchanan at the mayor's urging. *Baltimore Sun*, June 2 and 5, 1857; Constance McLaughlin Green, *Washington: Village and Capital, 1800–1878*, 2 vols. (Princeton, N.J.: Princeton University Press, 1962), 1:216–17. See also ibid., 159–61, 215; French, diary entry, June 9, 1857, BBFFP. On 1858, see French, diary entry, June 13, 1858, *Witness*, 293.

12. *New York Daily Times*, January 13, 1857.

13. *NYT*, March 20, April 2, 1858. For a scuffle in the Maine legislature, see *Charleston Mercury*, March 10, 1841, which calls it "almost as bad as Congress."

14. Ted R. Worley, "The Control of the Real Estate Bank of the State of Arkansas, 1836–1855," *Mississippi Valley Historical Review* 37, no. 3 (December 1950): 403–26, 410–11; Jeannie M. Whayne, Thomas A. Deblack, George Saba III, Morris S. Arnold, *Arkansas: A Narrative History* (Fayetteville: University of Arkansas, 2002), 113.

15. Given the lack of knowledge about the scale of violence in the antebellum Congress, acknowledgments of *patterns* of violence are rare; most studies focus on the caning of Sumner and note in passing that violence increased in the 1850s. On congressional violence generally, see Ollinger Crenshaw, "The Speakership Contest of 1859–1860: John Sherman's Election as a Cause of Disruption?," *Mississippi Valley Historical Review* 29 (December 1942): 323–38; Rachel A. Shelden, *Washington Brotherhood: Politics, Social Life, and the Coming of the Civil War* (Chapel Hill: UNC, 2013), 120–43; James B. Stewart, "Christian Statesmanship, Codes of Honor, and Congressional Violence: The Antislavery Travails and Triumphs of

Joshua Giddings," in Finkelman and Kennon, *In the Shadow of Freedom*, 36–57; Eric M. Uslaner, "Comity in Context: Confrontation in Historical Perspective," *British Journal of Political Science* 21 (1991): 45–77; Katherine A. Pierce, "Murder and Mayhem: Violence, Press Coverage, and the Mobilization of the Republican Party in 1856," in *Words at War: The Civil War and American Journalism*, ed. David B. Sachsman, S. Kittrell Rushing, Roy Morris Jr. (West Lafayette, Ind.: Purdue University Press, 2008): 85–100; Donald C. Bacon, "Violence in Congress," in *The Encyclopedia of the United States Congress*, ed. Donald C. Bacon, Roger H. Davidson, and Morton Keller (New York: Simon and Schuster, 1995): 2062–66; R. Eric Petersen, Jennifer E. Manning, and Erin Hemlin, "Violence Against Members of Congress and Their Staff: Selected Examples and Congressional Responses," CRS Report, 7–5700, R41609 (January 25, 2011); Nancy E. Marion and Willard M. Oliver, *Killing Congress: Assassinations, Attempted Assassinations, and Other Violence Against Members of Congress* (London: Lexington Books, 2014). Corey M. Brooks's *Liberty Power: Antislavery Third Parties and the Transformation of American Politics* (Chicago: University of Chicago, 2016) is one of very few books that notes the deliberate and politically strategic provocation of violence in Congress.

16. A word on the word *fight* as used in this volume: the more than seventy altercations at the heart of this book involved physical action—punching, slapping, caning, lunging, shoving, duel negotiations, dueling, wielding weapons, flipping desks, breaking windows, and the like. They took place within the walls of the Capitol and on its grounds, or out and about in Washington and its immediate environs when Congress was in session. Most fights are also referenced in more than one form of evidence. (Verifying fights is trickier than it may seem; for more on this process of evidentiary triangulation, see Appendix B, "A Note on Method.")

17. Caroline Healey Dall, diary entry, December 26, 1842, in Helen R. Deese, ed., *Daughter of Boston: The Extraordinary Diary of a Nineteenth-Century Woman: Caroline Healey Dall* (Boston: Beacon Press, 2005), 67–68. See also *The Huntress*, December 7, 1839, September 18, 1847. On French and his diary, see Cole and McDonough, *Witness*, 1–11 and passim; "The Biography of Benjamin Brown French," in Ralph H. Gauker, *History of the Scottish Rite Bodies in the District of Columbia* (Washington, D.C.: Mithras Lodge of Perfection, 1970), 5. My thanks to Peter S. French for bringing the previous work to my attention.

18. French, diary entry, November 27, 1836, *Witness*, 65.

19. Ibid., September 13, 1841, 124–25.

20. Ibid., May 1, 1829, 18.

21. Ibid., December 21, 1833, 35.

22. Ibid., September 10, 1835, 45.

23. Ibid., October 18, 1835, 52.

24. Francis O. French, diary entry, February 7, 1850, ed. John J. McDonough, *Growing Up on Capitol Hill: A Young Washingtonian's Journal, 1850–1852* (Washington, D.C.: LC, 1997), 7.

25. French, diary entry, January 1, 1854; December 12, 1858; January 1, 1859; June 1, 1860, BBFFP. French and his wife rented a house beginning in 1838; in 1842 they built a house of their own.

26. For example, French's friend F.O.J. Smith (D-ME) stayed with him for a few extended visits, and at the close of Caleb Cushing's (W-MA) congressional career,

when his changing politics got him thrown out of his boardinghouse, he stayed with French for a time. French, diary entries, February 25, 1842; July 16, 19, 30, 31, 1843; *Witness*, 137, 151–52.

27. French to Henry Flagg French, April 9, 1853, BBFFP. French was a clerk in the House (1833–45); the Clerk of the House (1845–47); and clerk of the House Committee of Claims (1860–61). He was a lobbyist in the 1850s and again briefly in the 1860s. On his failed lobbying career, see French, diary entry, December 21, 1850; French to Bessie French, August 1, 15, 20, 21, 1852; French to Henry Flagg French, January 17, 1853, BBFFP; Kathryn Allamong Jacob, *King of the Lobby: The Life and Times of Sam Ward, Man-About-Washington in the Gilded Age* (Baltimore: Johns Hopkins, 2010), 19–20; and Margaret Susan Thompson, *The "Spider Web": Congress and Lobbying in the Age of Grant* (Ithaca: Cornell, 1985). For an example of French as substitute clerk, see French to Bessie French, August 17, 1856, BBFFP.

28. A burst of recent scholarship highlights the power and extent of the Southern grip on the national government. On the reality of a Slave Power in Congress, see Alice Elizabeth Malavasic, *The F Street Mess: How Southern Senators Rewrote the Kansas-Nebraska Act* (Chapel Hill: UNC Press, 2017). On Southern control of the federal government more generally, see esp. Don E. Fehrenbacher, *The Slaveholding Republic: An Account of the United States Government's Relations to Slavery* (New York: Oxford University Press, 2001); George William Van Cleve, *A Slaveholders' Union: Slavery, Politics, and the Constitution in the Early Republic* (Chicago: University of Chicago Press, 2010); Matthew Karp, *This Vast Southern Empire: Slaveholders at the Helm of American Foreign Policy* (Cambridge, Mass.: Harvard University Press, 2016).

29. I am not arguing that the Civil War was grounded on irrational behavior or suggesting that emotions are the primary reason for the coming of the war. But as a genre of evidence, emotions—grounded in very real causes with longstanding histories—are vital to understanding the actions and mentalities that fueled the crisis of the Union. For an introduction to the use of emotions as evidence in the study of honor and violence, see Carolyn Strange, Robert Cribb, and Christopher E. Forth, eds., *Honour, Violence and Emotions in History,* (London: Bloomsbury, 2014); and the seminal William M. Reddy, *The Navigation of Feeling: A Framework for the History of Emotions* (New York: Cambridge University Press, 2001). For a model application of the study of emotion to the coming of the war, see Michael E. Woods, *Emotional and Sectional Conflict in the Antebellum United States* (New York: Cambridge University Press, 2014); Woods's introduction (1–20) does a superb job of explaining the historiography of the study of emotions, politics, and the Civil War. See also Anna Koivusalo, "'He Ordered the First Gun Fired & He Resigned First': James Chesnut, Southern Honor, and Emotion," in *The Field of Honor: Essays on Southern Character and American Identity*, ed. John Mayfield and Todd Hagstette (Columbia: University of South Carolina, 2017), 196–212; Stephen W. Berry II, *All That Makes a Man: Love and Ambition in the Civil War South* (New York: Oxford University Press, 2003); Bertram Wyatt-Brown, *The Shaping of Southern Culture: Honor, Grace, and War, 1760s–1880s* (Chapel Hill: UNC Press, 2001), 177–202; William W. Freehling, *The Road to Disunion* (New York: Oxford University Press, 2007), 2 vols.

30. See for example Stanley Harrold, *Border War: Fighting over Slavery Before the Civil War* (Chapel Hill: UNC Press, 2010).

31. On Southern nationalism, see esp. Bonner, *Mastering America*. On "Union" as antebellum shorthand, see Gary W. Gallagher, *The Union War* (New York: Cambridge University Press, 2011).

32. Joel H. Silbey, *The American Political Nation, 1838–1893* (Stanford, Calif.: Stanford University Press, 1991), passim.

33. On the idea that political ambitions and the stoking of popular passions—a "blundering generation" of politicos—led to the Civil War, see for example J. G. Randall, "The Blundering Generation," *Mississippi Valley Historical Review* 27, no. 1 (June 1940): 3–28; Avery Craven, *The Coming of the Civil War* (Chicago: University of Chicago Press, 1957). For arguments on the other end of the historiographical spectrum about the war's inevitability, see Kenneth M. Stampp, "The Irrepressible Conflict," in *The Imperiled Union: Essays on the Background of the Civil War* (New York: Oxford University Press, 1980), 191–245. For skilled discussions of this debate overall, see esp. Edward L. Ayers, *What Caused the Civil War? Reflections on the South and Southern History* (New York: Norton, 2005); Woods, "What Twenty-first Century Historians Have Said About the Causes of Disunion."

34. See for example *Chicago Press and Tribune*, March 31, 1860; *Lowell Daily Citizen*, June 6, 1856; *Salem Register*, June 9, 1856. A friend sent French a revolver for his safety in 1863; Samuel Strong to French, September 17, 1863, BBFFP.

35. See for example *Charleston Mercury*, February 11, 1858; *NYT*, February 8, 1858.

36. Edward L. Ayers, *The Thin Light of Freedom: The Civil War and Emancipation in the Heart of America* (New York: Norton, 2017), xxi. Other noteworthy examples of this approach include David M. Potter, *The Impending Crisis: 1848–1861* (New York: Harper, 1976); Freehling, *Road to Disunion*.

37. French to Bess French, April 25, 1838, BBFFP.

38. French, diary entry, June 21, 1831, *Witness*, 23.

39. French lived in Chester, Sutton, Newport, and Concord. French to Henry Flagg French, September 28, 1829, and March 3, 1833, BBFFP.

40. French, diary entry, June 5, 1833, *Witness*, 26–27.

41. Martha Derthick, ed., *Dilemmas of Scale in America's Federal Democracy* (New York: Cambridge University Press, 1999), esp. 2–3; Brian Balogh, *A Government Out of Sight: The Mystery of National Authority in Nineteenth-Century America* (New York: Cambridge University Press, 2009).

42. Timothy Dwight, *Travels in New-England and New-York*, 4 vols. (New Haven: Published by author, S. Converse, Printer), 2:247.

43. *Witness*, 1; Benjamin Chase, *History of Old Chester from 1719 to 1869* (Auburn, N.H.: Published by author, 1869), 247, 412, 527; *The Farmer's Monthly Visitor* (Concord), November 30, 1840, 174.

44. For an obituary, see *United States Oracle* (Portsmouth, N.H.), March 20, 1802.

45. John Carroll Chase, *History of Chester New Hampshire Including Auburn* (Derry, N.H., 1926), 444–45; Charles H. Bell, *The Bench and Bar of New Hampshire* (Boston: Houghton, Mifflin, 1894), 383. The quote comes from Charles Bell, U.S. senator and governor of New Hampshire.

46. French, diary entry, October 9, 1866, *Witness*, 520–21. French was helping to move an outbuilding closer to a house, and the householder treated his helpers to "the best of gin" doled out from a copper teakettle.

47. French, diary entry, February 17, 1867, *Witness*, 530. On French's life, see ibid., 1–11.

48. French, diary entry, October 25, 1840, ibid., 103.

49. John Adams Vinton, *The Richardson Memorial: Comprising a Full History and Genealogy of the Posterity of the Three Brothers, Ezekiel, Samuel, and Thomas Richardson* (Portland, Maine: Brown, Thurston & Co., 1876), 114–17; French, diary entry, March 29, 1838, *Witness*, 77.

50. Margaret French Cresson, *Journey into Fame: The Life of Daniel Chester French* (Cambridge, Mass.: Harvard University Press, 1947), 17.

51. Ibid., 15–17; August Harvey Worthen, *The History of Sutton, New Hampshire*, 2 vols. (Concord, N.H.: Republican Press Association, 1890), 1:236.

52. The *Spectator*, founded in 1825, was Newport's first and only newspaper until 1831. On the New Hampshire press in this period, see Jacob B. Moore, "History of Newspapers Published in New Hampshire, from 1756 to 1840," *American Quarterly Register* 13 (1841); Simeon Ide, "History of New Hampshire Newspaper Press, Sullivan County," *Proceedings of the Annual Meeting of the New Hampshire Press Association* (January 1874), 56–64; H. G. Carleton, "The Newspaper Press in Newport," in Edmund Wheeler, *The History of Newport, New Hampshire: From 1766 to 1878* (Concord, N.H.: Republican Press Association, 1879).

53. The best extended account of Hill's New Hampshire political activities, as well as antebellum New Hampshire politics generally, is Donald B. Cole, *Jacksonian Democracy in New Hampshire* (Cambridge, Mass.: Harvard University Press, 1970). See also Cyrus P. Bradley, *Biography of Isaac Hill* (Concord, N.H.: Published by John Brown, 1835). On antebellum New Hampshire politics, see also Richard H. Sewell, *John P. Hale and the Politics of Abolition* (Cambridge, Mass.: Harvard University Press, 1965); Jonathan H. Earle, *Jacksonian Antislavery & the Politics of Free Soil, 1824–1854* (Chapel Hill: UNC Press, 2004), 78–102; Richard P. McCormick, *The Second American Party System: Party Formation in the Jacksonian Era* (New York: Norton, 1966), 54–62.

54. French, draft of memoir, BBFFP.

55. French, diary entry, February 17, 1834, *Witness*, 38.

56. Cole, *Jacksonian Democracy*, 60–61.

57. Ibid., 3–6, 69.

58. Ibid., 61. See also Richard R. John, *Spreading the News: The American Postal System from Franklin to Morse* (Cambridge, Mass.: Harvard University Press, 1995), esp. 208–13; Steven P. McGiffen, "Ideology and the Failure of the Whig Party in New Hampshire, 1834–1841," *New England Quarterly* 59 (September 1986): 387–401.

59. On politics and the press in this period, see esp. Michael Schudson, *Discovering the News: A Social History of American Newspapers* (New York: Basic Books, 1981); Katherine A. Pierce, "Networks of Disunion: Politics, Print Culture, and the Coming of the Civil War" (Ph.D. dissertation, University of Virginia, 2006); Thomas C. Leonard, *The Power of the Press: The Birth of American Political Reporting* (New

York: Oxford University Press, 1986); Lorman A. Ratner and Dwight L. Teeter, Jr., *Fanatics and Fire-Eaters: Newspapers and the Coming of the Civil War* (Urbana: University of Illinois, 2003); Craig Miner, *Seeding Civil War: Kansas in the National News, 1854–1858* (Lawrence: University of Kansas, 2008); Richard B. Kielbowicz, *News in the Mail: The Press, Post Office, and Public Information, 1700–1860s* (Westport, Conn.: Greenwood, 1989); or Sachsman, Rushing, and Morris Jr., eds., *Words at War.*

60. Jefferson to James Madison, February 5, 1799, founders.archives.gov/documents/Jefferson/01-31-02-0005, accessed June 8, 2015.

61. Jeffrey Pasley, "Printers, Editors, and Publishers of Political Journals Elected to the U.S. Congress, 1789–1861," pasleybrothers.com/newspols/congress.htm, accessed June 8, 2015.

62. "Biography of Benjamin Brown French," in Gauther, *History of the Scottish Rite Bodies*, 35. For a listing of his Masonic activities, see ibid., 73–74.

63. French, diary, *Witness*, June 10, 1831, 21.

64. Ibid., April 24, 1853, 238–39. On Pierce, see Roy Franklin Nichols, *Franklin Pierce: Young Hickory of the Granite Hills* (Philadelphia: University of Pennsylvania Press, 1931); Michael F. Holt, *Franklin Pierce* (New York: Henry Holt, 2010); Peter A. Wallner, *Franklin Pierce: New Hampshire's Favorite Son* (Concord, N.H.: Plaidswede, 2004); idem., *Franklin Pierce: Martyr for the Union* (Concord, N.H.: Plaidswede, 2007); Larry Gara, *The Presidency of Franklin Pierce* (Lawrence: University Press of Kansas, 1991).

65. Horatio Bridge to Nathaniel Hawthorne, December 25, 1836, in Julian Hawthorne, *Nathaniel Hawthorne and His Wife: A Biography*, 2 vols. (New York: Houghton, Mifflin, 1884), 1:148.

66. French, diary entry, June 18, 1831, *Witness*, 23.

67. *New Hampshire Sentinel*, June 27, 1833. See also French, diary entry, June 10, 1831.

68. French, diary entry, June 18, 1831, *Witness*, 23.

69. Ibid., June 3, 1831, 20.

70. Ibid., June 2, 1831, 19.

71. Ibid., December 18, 1843, 157.

72. Steven C. Bullock, *Revolutionary Brotherhood: Freemasonry and the Transformation of the American Social Order, 1730–1840* (Chapel Hill: UNC Press, 1996); Mark C. Carnes, *Secret Ritual and Manhood in Victorian America* (New Haven: Yale University Press, 1989); idem., "Middle-Class Men and the Solace of Fraternal Ritual," in *Meanings for Manhood: Constructions of Masculinity in Victorian America*, ed. Marc C. Carnes and Clyde Griffen (Chicago: University of Chicago Press, 1990), 37–52.

73. French, diary entry, September 15, 1828, *Witness*, 16. For an excellent account of politics and Congress in this period, see Joel H. Silbey, "Congress in a Partisan Political Era," in *The American Congress: The Building of Democracy*, ed. Julian Zelizer (New York: Houghton Mifflin, 2004), 139–51.

74. French, diary entry, September 15, 1828, *Witness*, 16.

75. French to Henry Flagg French, May 22, 1832, BBFFP. Emphasis in original.

76. French was referring to Houston's caning of William Stanbery (AJ-OH) on April 13; an assassination attempt by Major Morgan A. Heard against Thomas

Arnold (AJ-TE); and a near duel between E. S. Davis and Eleutheros Cooke (AJ-OH).

77. Isaac Hill probably facilitated French's rise; he routinely drew young blood into the Jacksonian fold by dangling jobs. Cole, *Jacksonian Democracy*, 165.

78. French, diary entry, July 20, 1833, *Witness*, 29–34. The next few paragraphs are based on ibid.

79. Ibid.; *New Hampshire Sentinel*, July 18, 1833. For accounts of the Concord celebration, see chapter 35 in the unpublished Grace P. Amsden, "A Capital for New Hampshire," NHHS, www.concordnh.gov/Library/concordhistory/concordv2.asp?siteindx=L20,08,05, accessed August 18, 2012.

80. French to Daniel French, January 30, 1835, BBFFP.

81. On Jackson's image, see esp. John William Ward, *Andrew Jackson: Symbol for an Age* (New York: Oxford University Press, 1955); Thomas Brown, "From Old Hickory to Sly Fox: The Routinization of Charisma in the Early Democratic Party," *JER* 3 (Autumn 1991): 339–69; Andrew Burstein, *The Passions of Andrew Jackson* (New York: Random House, 2007); James C. Curtis, *Andrew Jackson and the Search for Vindication* (Boston: Little, Brown, 1976).

82. French, diary entries, December 13, 1836, and January 9, 1844, *Witness*, 69, 158.

83. Cole, *Jacksonian Democracy*, 167. On increased voter participation in this election, see John H. Aldrich, *Why Parties? A Second Look* (Chicago University of Chicago Press), 122–26. On Van Buren's pitch for the party, see ibid., 113–14; and more generally, Donald B. Cole, *Martin Van Buren and the American Political System* (Princeton, N.J.: Princeton University Press, 1984); Robert V. Remini, *Martin Van Buren and the Making of the Democratic Party* (New York: Columbia University Press, 1959); Joel H. Silbey, *Martin Van Buren and the Emergence of American Popular Politics* (Lanham, Md.: Rowman & Littlefield, 2002). On the election of 1828 and the organizational origins of the Jacksonian Democrats, in addition to the above, see Ralph M. Goldman, *The National Party Chairmen and Committees: Factionalism at the Top* (Armonk, N.Y.: M. E. Sharpe, 1990); Donald B. Cole, *Vindicating Andrew Jackson: The 1828 Election and the Rise of the Two-Party System* (Lawrence: University Press of Kansas, 2009); Robert Remini, *The Election of Andrew Jackson* (New York: J. B. Lippincott, 1963); idem., "Election of 1828," in Arthur M. Schlesinger and Fred L. Israel, *History of American Presidential Elections* (New York: Chelsea House, 1971), 1:413–92; Lynn Hudson Parsons, *The Birth of Modern Politics: Andrew Jackson, John Quincy Adams, and the Election of 1828* (New York: Oxford University Press, 2009).

1. THE UNION INCARNATE FOR BETTER AND WORSE

1. French, diary entry, December 21, 1833, and September 10, 1835, *Witness*, 34, 45. In November 1835, French made this trip again by stagecoach, boat, and—for the first time—train.

2. French to Bess French, January 1834, in Gauker, *History of the Scottish Rite Bodies in the District of Columbia*, 7.

3. French, diary entry, December 21, 1833, *Witness*, 34.

4. Edmund Morris, ed., *The Education of Henry Adams* (New York: Modern Library, 1996), 44; Seward, *Reminiscences*, 68–69; J. S. Buckingham, *America, Historical, Statistic, and Descriptive*, 3 vols. (London: Fisher, Son, & Co., 1841) 1:293–94, 319, 321; George Augustus Sala, *My Diary in America in the Midst of War*, 2 vols. (London: Tinsley Brothers, 1865), 2:68. For older accounts of antebellum Washington, see Wilhelmus B. Bryan, *A History of the National Capital from Its Foundation Through the Period of the Adoption of the Organic Act*, 2 vols. (New York: Macmillan, 1914); John C. Proctor, *Washington Past and Present: A History*, 5 vols. (New York: Lewis Historical Publishing, 1930). Particularly useful in this study were Barbara G. Carson, *Ambitious Appetites: Dining, Behavior, and Patterns of Consumption in Federal Washington* (Washington: American Institute of Architects, 1990), 1–23; Young, *Washington Community*; Howard Gillette, Jr., ed., *Southern City, National Ambition: The Growth of Early Washington, D.C., 1800–1860* (Washington, D.C.: George Washington University Center for Washington Area Studies, 1995); Carl Abbott, *Political Terrain: Washington, D.C., from the Tidewater to Global Metropolis* (Chapel Hill: UNC Press, 1999); David C. Mearns, "A View of Washington in 1863," *Records of the Columbia Historical Society, Washington, D.C.*, 63/65 (1963–1965): 210–20; Kenneth J. Winkle, *Lincoln's Citadel: The Civil War in Washington, D.C.* (New York: Norton, 2014); Guy Gugliotta, *Freedom's Cap: The United States Capitol and the Coming of the Civil War* (New York: Hill and Wang, 2013); and Constance McLaughlin Green, *Washington: Village and Capital, 1800–1878*, 2 vols. (Princeton, N.J.: Princeton University Press, 1962), 1:23–229.

5. Seward, *Reminiscences*, 69. In 1851, the government was accepting bids to light Pennsylvania Avenue, the Capitol, the President's House, and "other public grounds." The first contract was granted in 1852. In 1854, lamps went up on Pennsylvania Avenue at a cost of almost $2,000. "Report of the Commissioner of Public Buildings," October 5, 1854, 599.

6. Green, *Washington*, 1:255. On the "National Hotel Disease," see Jean H. Baker, *James Buchanan* (New York: Henry Holt, 2004), 78; Eric H. Walther, *The Shattering of the Union: America in the 1850s* (Lanham, Md.: Rowman & Littlefield, 2004), 118; M. C. Meigs, diary entry, March 7, 1857, in Senate Document 106–20, "Capitol Builder: The Shorthand Journals of Montgomery C. Meigs, 1853–1859, 1861," ed. Wendy Wolff (Washington, D.C.: GPO, 2000), 496. See also Michael A. Cooke, "Physical Environment and Sanitation in the District of Columbia, 1860–1868," *Records of the Columbia Historical Society, Washington, D.C.*, 52 (1989): 289–303.

7. French, diary entry, May 11, 1838, August 24, 1844, *Witness*, 82, 162.

8. Green, *Washington*, 1:354. Washington was 54 percent streets and alleys as compared with New York at 35 percent and Philadelphia at 29 percent. Goldfield notes that the poor streets and lack of city services reflected the sensibilities of a Southern city more than a Northern or even a Western one. David R. Goldfield, "Antebellum Washington in Context: The Pursuit of Prosperity and Identity," *Southern City, National Ambition: The Growth of Early Washington, D.C., 1800–1860*, ed. Howard Gillette, Jr. (Washington, D.C.: George Washington University Center for Washington Area Studies), 16.

9. Green, *Washington*, 1:211; Charles Billinghurst to his wife, December 15, 1855, ibid. See also French, diary entry, June 18 and November 6, 1863, *Witness*, 423, 431; Mary Jane Windle, *Life in Washington: and Life Here and There* (Philadelphia: J. B. Lippincott, 1859), 158. Consumer Price Index calculated on www .measuringworth.com, May 12, 2011.

10. Nicholas Trist to Virginia Jefferson Randolph Trist, May 8, 1829, Nicholas P. Trist Papers, UNC. Trist was a clerk in the State Department.

11. "Population of States and Counties of the United States: 1790–1990," compiled and edited by Richard L. Forstall (Department of Commerce, U.S. Bureau of the Census), 4.

12. "The Metropolis," *Yale Literary Magazine, Conducted by the Students of Yale University* 3 (February 1838): 139–43. See also Harriet Martineau, *Retrospect of Western Travel* (New York: Harper and Brothers, 1838), 1:238; Susan Keitt to Carrie, February 2 [ca. 1860], Laurence Massillon Keitt Papers, Duke University.

13. *Globe*, 28th Cong., 1st Sess., February 6, 1844, 231.

14. French, diary entry, May 30, 1841, *Witness*, 116.

15. Ibid., December 21, 1833, 35. Henry Hubbard (J-NH) was French's other guide.

16. Ibid., 34–35.

17. Ibid., December 21 and 30, 1833, 35. Emphasis in original.

18. Within the large body of scholarship on the art and architecture of the Capitol, particularly useful for this study were Donald R. Kennon, *American Pantheon: Sculptural and Artistic Decoration of the United States Capitol* (Athens: Ohio University, 2004); idem., *The United States Capitol: Designing and Decorating a National Icon* (Athens: Ohio University, 2000); idem., ed. *A Republic for the Ages: The United States Capitol and the Political Culture of the Early Republic* (Charlottesville: UVA Press, 1999); Henry Hope Reed, *The United States Capitol: Its Architecture and Decoration* (New York: Norton, 2005); Pamela Scott, *Temple of Liberty: Building the Capitol for a New Nation* (New York: Oxford University Press, 1995); House Document 108–240, 108th Cong., 2nd Sess., January 18, 2008, *Glenn Brown's History of the United States Capitol*; William C. Allen, *History of the United States Capitol: A Chronicle of Design, Construction, and Politics* (Washington, D.C.: GPO, 2001).

19. George Watterston, *New Guide to Washington* (Washington: Robert Farnham; New York: Samuel Colman, 1842), 20–22. Watterston's popular guide series was reprinted many times; a copy was even deposited for posterity in the cornerstone of the Washington Monument. National Monument Society, *Oration Pronounced by the Honorable Robert C. Winthrop, Speaker of the House of Representatives of the United States . . . on the Occasion of Laying the Corner-Stone of the National Monument to the Memory of Washington* (Washington, D.C.: J. & G. S. Gideon, 1848). Watterston's observations were first collected and published by William Elliott under the title *The Washington Guide* (Washington City: Franck Taylor, 1837). After Elliott died in 1840, Watterston came out with his own publication, *A Picture of Washington* (Washington: William M. Morrison, 1840). For his account of his various publications, see Watterson, *Picture of Washington*, introduction.

20. On the history of paintings in the Capitol, see Kent Ahrens, "Nineteenth Century History Painting and the United States Capitol," *Records of the Columbia Historical Society, Washington, D.C.*, 50 (1980): 191–222; Vivien Green Fryd, "Representating the Constitution in the US Capitol Building: Justice, Freedom, and Slavery," in *Constitutional Cultures: On the Concept and Representation of Constitutions in the Atlantic World*, ed. Silke Hensel, Ulrike Bock, Katrin Dircksen, and Hans-Ulrich Thamer (New York: Cambridge University Press, 2012), 227–50; Vivien Green Fryd, *Art and Empire: The Politics of Ethnicity in the United States Capitol, 1815–1860* (Athens: Ohio University Press, 2001); Ann Uhry Abrams, "National Paintings and American Character: Historical Murals in the Capitol's Rotunda," in *Picturing History: American Painting, 1770–1930*, ed. William Ayres (New York: Rizzoli, 1993), 65–78. For House discussion of paintings in addition to those of Trumbull, see *Globe*, 23rd Cong., 2nd Sess., December 15, 1834, 37–40.

21. Margaret B. Klapthor, "Furniture in the Capitol: Desks and Chairs Used in the Chamber of the House of Representatives, 1819–1857," *Records of the Columbia Historical Society, Washington, D.C.*, 69/70 (1969–70): 192–93.

22. On the House and Senate chambers in this period, see esp. House Document No. 108–240, *Glenn Brown's History of the United States Capitol*, 183–213; Robert Mills, *Guide to the Capital of the United States Embracing Every Information Useful to the Visiter* [sic], *Whether on Business or Pleasure* (Washington: n.p., 1834), 31–38, 43–45.

23. French to Catherine French Wells, March 13, 1834, BBFFP.

24. French, diary entry, April 2, 1837, *Witness*, 71–72.

25. Samuel Kernell and Gray C. Jacobson, "Congress and the Presidency as News in the Nineteenth Century," *Journal of Politics* 49 (November 1987): 1016–35. According to Elaine Swift, in the second session of the Seventeenth Congress (1822–23), Washington's *Intelligencer* devoted 33 percent of its column inches to the House and 10 percent to the Senate, while Baltimore's *Niles' Weekly Register* devoted 32 percent and 8 percent, respectively. The numbers were similar in the second session of the Twentieth Congress (1828–29) and the second session of the Twenty-third Congress (1834–35), though eventually coverage of the House and Senate evened out. Swift, *The Making of an American Senate: Reconstitutive Change in Congress, 1787–1841* (Ann Arbor: University of Michigan, 1996), 193–94.

26. Alexander Stephens to Linton Stephens, January 19, 1848, in *Life of Alexander H. Stephens*, ed. Richard Malcolm Johnston and William Hand Browne (Philadelphia: J. B. Lippincott, 1878), 183–84. Johnston and Browne misdate this letter to 1845. For accounts of the speech, see the *Baltimore Sun*, January 19, 1848, and a particularly lively account in *The New York Herald*, January 21, 1848.

27. Newspaper clipping in scrapbook, Fisher Family Papers, UNC. On antebellum oratory, see Kenneth Cmiel, *Democratic Eloquence: The Fight over Popular Speech in Nineteenth-Century America* (Berkeley: University of California, 1990); Barnet Baskerville, "19th Century Burlesque of Oratory," *American Quarterly* 20, no. 4 (Winter 1968): 726–43; Edward G. Parker, *The Golden Age of American Oratory* (Boston: Whittemore, Niles, and Hall, 1857); James Perrin Warren,

Culture of Eloquence: Oratory and Reform in Antebellum America (University Park: Pennsylvania State University Press, 1999).

28. French, diary entry, May 11, 1838, *Witness*, 82.

29. Ibid., December 2, 1836, 68; French, "Congressional Reminiscences," *National Freemason* (Washington) 2 (July 1863), 23. See also French, diary entry, December 30, 1833, *Witness*, 35.

30. Hale to Lucy Hale, January 8, 1844, John Parker Hale Papers, NHHS.

31. *Globe*, 27th Cong., 3rd Sess., February 27, 1843, 357, 359. Benton was refuting a request to adjourn. For couch-sleeping in the House, see for example Adams, diary entry, May 31, 1838, *Memoirs*, 9:551.

32. French, diary entry, April 2, 1837, *Witness*, 72. See also French's almost identical *Chicago Democrat* column, dated September 29, 1837. For an evening session that follows this precise script, see Adams, diary entry, June 7, 1836, *Memoirs*, 294–95.

33. For a sense of the comings and goings, see the House Journal, 23rd Cong., 2nd Sess., March 3, 1835, 516–32 passim. At the start of the evening, roughly 200 men were voting; when the Democratic power play began, roughly 110 men were voting.

34. French to Harriette French, March 8, 1835, BBFFP.

35. *Globe*, 23rd Cong., 2nd Sess., March 3, 1835, 332.

36. Longtime Senate staffer Isaac Bassett noted that "an all night session is never a veary [sic] creditable affair." Isaac Bassett Papers, Office of the Curator of the United States Senate, 5c134–37. My thanks to Scott Strong for this document.

37. *Globe*, 23rd Cong., 2nd Sess., March 3, 1835, 331–32.

38. *National Era*, January 28, 1847; *The Huntress*, August 8, 1846.

39. *National Era*, January 7, 1847.

40. Darryl Gonzalez, *The Children Who Ran for Congress: A History of Congressional Pages* (Santa Barbara, Calif.: Praeger, 2010), 15. See also Harriet Prescott Spofford, "The Messenger Boys at the Capitol," *Harper's Young People* 63 (January 11, 1881), 162–63.

41. French, diary entry, November 18, 1841, *Witness*, 129.

42. The seating was changed in 1832 and changed back in 1838. A cloth ceiling was put up to discourage echoes, but it blocked out light and was removed. William Charles Allen, *History of the United States Capitol: A Chronicle of Design, Construction, and Politics* (Washington, D.C.: GPO, 2000), 180. On the acoustics, see John Morrill Bryan, *Robert Mills: America's First Architect* (Princeton, N.J.: Princeton Architectural Press, 2001), 217; H. Doc. 108–240, *Glenn Brown's History of the United States Capitol*, 210–13.

43. *The Western Literary Messenger: A Family Magazine of Literature, Science, Art, Morality and General Intelligence* (Buffalo, NY) 12 (1849), 223. John Wentworth (D-IL) wrote this piece.

44. French to Harriette French, April 6, 1840, BBFFP.

45. House Report No. 1980, "Sanitary Condition of the Capitol Building," 53rd Cong., 3rd Sess., March 2, 1895, 16. For a similar (but less juicy) earlier description, see House Report No. 65, "Ventilation of the Hall of the House of Representatives," 40th Cong., 2nd Sess., June 20, 1868, 2.

46. Ibid., 1; Forrest Maltzman, Lee Sigelman, and Sarah Binder, "Leaving Office Feet

First: Death in Congress," *Political Science and Politics* 29 (December 1996): 665–71, 670, note 7. (This article contains more puns and euphemisms about death than I knew existed.)

47. House Report No. 116, "Ventilation of the Hall of the House of Representatives," 45th Cong., 3d Sess., February 21, 1879, 3, 8, 18.

48. French to Henry Flagg French, December 18, 1857, BBFFP.

49. House Report No. 1970, "Method of Heating, Lighting, and Ventilating the Hall of the House of Representatives," 48th Cong., 1st Sess., June 24, 1884, 11.

50. *Globe*, 26th Cong., 1st Sess., March 14, 1840, 268.

51. Adams, diary entry, January 3, 1840, *Memoirs*, 10:183. For a similar incident, see "Report . . . Foote Benton," 119.

52. Adams, *Memoirs*, December 13, 1837, 9:450–51. In a speech in Massachusetts, Fletcher had suggested that the Democrats were under the influence of President Jackson. Adams explained that to defend himself, Fletcher would have had to declare his attackers liars (given them the "lie direct"), almost certainly resulting in violence. The *Globe* doesn't include the "coarse and abusive" language that upset Fletcher. *Globe*, 25th Cong., 2nd Sess., December 13, 1837, 21–24. See also "Mr. Fletcher's Address to His Constituents, Relative to the Speech Delivered by Him in Faneuil Hall," December 23, 1837; Charles Francis Adams, diary entry, December 18 and 19, 1837, in Marc Friedlaender et al., *Diary of Charles Francis Adams* (Cambridge, Mass.: Harvard University Press, 1986), 7:363–64.

53. French, diary entry, November 23, 1835, *Witness*, 61. For accounts of the activities of senators on the floor, see Grace Greenwood, *Greenwood Leaves: A Collection of Sketches and Letters* (Boston: Ticknor, Reed, and Fields, 1852), 314; Windle, *Life in Washington*, 31.

54. Anson Burlingame to his wife, July 13, 1856, Anson Burlingame and Family Papers, LC; *Globe*, 36th Cong., 1st Sess., January 21, 1859, 507.

55. Susan Hill to her children, February 28[?], 1832, Isaac Hill Papers, NHHS.

56. Adams, *Memoirs*, February 20, 1832, 8:476–77. See also Robert Remini, *Henry Clay: Statesman for the Union* (New York: Norton, 1991), 383; *Register of Debates*, 22nd Cong., 1st Sess., February 6, 1832, 296–97.

57. There were occasional senatorial slugfests, as in 1860, when Thomas Clingman (D-NC) and Clement Claiborne Clay (D-AL) exchanged blows in the chamber over charges surrounding the presidential campaign of Stephen Douglas (D-IL); Clingman ended up with a black eye. *Chicago Press and Tribune*, March 31, April 6, 1860; *NYT*, April 5, 1860.

58. See esp. Jacob, *King of the Lobby*, 19–20.

59. See esp. George B. Galloway, *History of the House of Representatives* (New York: Thomas Y. Crowell, 1961), 64–67; Nelson W. Polsby, "The Institutionalization of the House of Representatives," *American Political Science Review* 62 (March 1968): 144–68. On the impact of committees, see Joseph Cooper, *Congress and Its Committees: A Historical Approach to the Role of Committees in the Legislative Process* (New York: Garland, 1988); idem., "The Origins of Standing Committees and the Development of the Modern House," (Houston, Tex.: Rice University Press, 1970); Gerald Gamm and Kenneth Shepsle, "Emergence of Legislative Institutions: Standing Committees in the House and Senate, 1810–1825,"

Legislative Studies Quarterly 14, no. 1 (February 1989): 39–66; Thompson, *The "Spider Web,"* 93–96.

60. *Globe*, 23rd Cong., 1st Sess., December 10, 1833, 19. On antebellum versus modern committees, see Jeffrey A. Jenkins and Charles Stewart III, *Fighting for the Speakership: The House and the Rise of Party Government* (Princeton, N.J.: Princeton University Press, 2013), 38–39.

61. Senate Doc. 100–20, 100th Cong., 1st Sess., Wendy Wolff, ed., Robert C. Byrd, *The Senate, 1789–1989: Addresses on the History of the United States Senate*, 2 vols. (Washington: GPO, 1991), 2:220–37; French, diary entry, December 25, 1851, *Witness*, 224. When Charles Sumner took over the Senate Foreign Relations Committee in 1861, he had the liquor removed. My thanks to James Shinn for this information.

62. *Globe*, 26th Cong., 2nd Sess., February 13, 1841, 173.

63. There were many controversies about minority members in committees being unable to influence the final version of a report as doctored by the majority. See for example ibid., 26th Cong., 1st Sess., March 14, 1840, 268–69.

64. Ibid., 26th Cong., 1st Sess., May 14, 1840, 397.

65. Ibid., March 11 and 14, 1840, 260–61, 268. Daniel Jenifer (W-MD) ranted about Democratic bullying on March 11, 12, 13, and 14; see ibid., 260, 263, 267–68. The two bullied Whigs were Millard Fillmore of New York and Truman Smith of Connecticut. The committee had been investigating the outcome of a contested New Jersey election; Democrats forced through their preferences in committee, then silenced Whig objectors on the floor by calling for an immediate vote. See also "Address and Suppressed Report of the Minority of the Committee on Elections on the New Jersey Case" (Washington: Madisonian Office, 1840); *Baltimore Sun*, March 13, 1840.

66. *Globe*, 26th Cong., 1st session, March 11 and 14, 1840, 260–61, 268.

67. Ibid., 25th Cong., 1st Sess., September 21 and 22, 1837, 46–78, 52, 56. Wise mentioned the episode to encourage the appointment of a select committee by ballot rather than by the Democratic Speaker James K. Polk. Outraged at a lie-filled majority report, a minority committee member had threatened to pummel whoever dared present the report to the House. The committee in question was to investigate the cause and conduct of the Florida War.

68. *The New World* (N.Y.), January 8, 1842, 29. Whitney denied that his hand was in his pocket, claiming that he needed both hands to defend himself. See ["The affair between Mr. Peyton, and myself"], undated, HR 24A-D24.1, National Archives, Washington, D.C. The same file contains a journal with Whitney's answers to the committee's interrogatories pasted inside; not allowed to speak during part of his testimony (because Peyton was so disgusted with him), he had to record his testimony on pieces of paper. On the Whitney affair generally, see John M. McFaul and Frank Otto Gatell, "The Outcast Insider: Reuben M. Whitney and the Bank War," *Pennsylvania Magazine of History and Biography* 91 (April 1967): 115–44. For the House investigation that exposed the Whitney affair, see *Register of Debates*, 24th Cong., 1st Sess., February 15–20, 1837, 1767–1878, 157–89 appendix; *Globe*, 24th Cong., 2nd Sess., February 15–20, 1837, 184–91, 222–39.

69. French to Henry Flagg French, January 31, 1839, BBFFP.

70. *Globe*, 25th Cong., 1st Sess., September 22, 1837, 56.

71. Ibid., 40th Cong., 1st Sess., March 8, 1867, 30.

72. Ibid., 30–31; "The National Metropolis," *De Bow's Review* 1 (April 1859): 389.

73. *Hinds' Precedents of the House of Representatives of the United States,* 5 vols. (Washington, D.C.: GPO, 1907), vol. 5, chapter 147, section 7244, note 4. By 1867, both "holes" had vanished and there was seemingly less liquor in committee-rooms—or so congressmen claimed while speaking on the floor before the press. See *Globe,* 40th Cong., 1st Sess., March 8, 1867, 30–32.

74. Marryat, *A Diary in America,* 1:166.

75. Robert V. Remini, *Daniel Webster: The Man and His Times* (New York: Norton, 1997), 287.

76. *Globe,* 40th Cong., 1st Sess., March 8, 1867, 30.

77. Senate Report 475, 43rd Cong., 1st Sess., "Report of the Committee to Audit and Control the Contingent Expenses of the Senate," June 22, 1874, 3. The "syrup" was bought with contingent funds in 1809–10.

78. *Alexandria Herald,* July 27, 1818; *City of Washington Gazette,* February 6, 1821. The *Herald* article blends material from Benjamin Franklin's "Poor Richard" (January 13, 1737, *Pennsylvania Gazette*) and Mason Locke Weems's *The Drunkard's Looking Glass* (printed for the author, 1818).

79. See generally Ian R. Tyrell, *Sobering Up: From Temperance to Prohibition in Antebellum America, 1800–1860* (Westport, Conn.: Greenwood Press, 1979); W. J. Rorabaugh, *The Alcoholic Republic: An American Tradition* (New York: Oxford University Press, 1979).

80. The antebellum Congressional Temperance Society was formed in 1833, faltered in 1834, and had a brief revival in 1842. "Congressional Temperance Society," in *Alcohol and Temperance in Modern History: A Global Encyclopedia,* ed. Jack S. Blocker, David M. Fahey, and Ian R. Tyrrell, 2 vols. (Santa Barbara, Calif.: ABC-Clio, 2003), 1:171–72; Keith L. Springer, "Cold Water Congressmen: The Congressional Temperance Society Before the Civil War," *Historian* 27, no. 4 (1965): 498–515.

81. In 1837, both houses passed Joint Rule 19: "No spirituous liquors shall be offered for sale, or exhibited within the Capitol, or on the public grounds adjacent thereto." In 1844 in the House and 1867 in the Senate, attempts were made to strengthen it by precisely defining "spirituous liquors" and listing *every* Capitol space where drinking was banned. See *Hinds' Precedents,* vol. 5, chapter 147, section 7244, note 4 (Washington, D.C.: GPO, 1907), 5:1090–91, note 3. See also *Cincinnati Weekly Herald and Philanthropist,* March 6, 1844, which approved of the amendment banning *all* intoxicating liquors (rather than "only *spirituous* liquors," meaning hard liquor).

82. *Hinds' Precedents,* vol. 5, chapter 147, section 7244, note 4.

83. Republicans tried to dry out the Capitol in the 1860s but weren't entirely successful, and the booze flowed on. For twentieth-century commentary on drunken congressmen, see *Watson's Magazine* 5 (September 1906): 341–42; Raymond Clapper, "Happy Days," *American Mercury Magazine* (January 1927): 25–29; "The Committee Era: 1910s–1960s," introduction, *American Congress,* ed. Zelizer, 313; Robert T. Mann, *Legacy to Power: Senator Russell Long of Louisiana* (New York: Paragon House, 2003 ed.), 287–88; Ron F. Smith, *Groping for Ethics in Journalism* (Ames: Iowa State University, 2003), 226–29.

84. *Globe*, 40th Cong., 1st Sess., March 8, 1867, 30.

85. Ibid., 24th Cong., 1st Sess., January 22, 1836, 761 appendix.

86. Ibid., 25th Cong., 2nd Sess., April 5, 1838, 284. The topic of debate was dueling in Congress, sparked by the death of Representative Jonathan Cilley (D-ME) in a duel at the hands of Representative William Graves (W-KY). On this duel generally, see chapter 3.

87. In the new House chamber that opened in 1857, a maximum of 1,250 people could fit into the galleries. 48th Cong., 1st Sess., Report No. 1970, "Method of Heating, Lighting, and Ventilating the Hall of the House of Representatives," June 24, 1884, 18.

88. John Parker Hale to Lucy Hale, January 2, 1845, John Parker Hale Papers, NHHS.

89. French, diary entry, May 24, 1838, *Witness*, 86.

90. Harriet Martineau, *Retrospect of Western Travel*, 3 vols. (London: Saunders and Otley, 1838), 1:300.

91. "Scenic and Characteristic Outlines of Congress, I," *The National Magazine and Republican Review* 1 (January 1839): 83–84. For more head-shots, see "A Peep at Washington," *The Knickerbocker; or New York Monthly Magazine*, June 1834, 443; Greenwood, *Greenwood Leaves*, 326; and the ultimate head-ography, George Combe, *Notes on the United States of North America, During a Phrenological Visit in 1838–39–40*, 2 vols. (Edinburgh: Maclachlan, Stewart, 1841), 2:95–98.

92. "A Peep at Washington," *The Knickerbocker*, June 1834, 443.

93. "The Desultory Speculator No. IV. Sketches," *Southern Literary Messenger* 5 (May 1839): 316–18.

94. Dickens, *American Notes*, 286–93.

95. On phrenology generally, see Charles Colbert, *A Measure of Perfection: Phrenology and the Fine Arts in America* (Chapel Hill: UNC Press, 1998).

96. French, diary entry, November 18, 1841, *Witness*, 128–29. He described himself as "portly" when he was in his sixties; ibid., June 11, 1861, 360; and Caroline Dall called him "large and fat." Dall, diary entry, December 26, 1842, Deese, *Daughter of Boston*, 67–68.

97. George R. McFarlane [?] to Robert Barnwell Rhett, June 6, 1841, Robert Barnwell Rhett Papers, UNC.

98. Particularly useful studies of the Washington press and the antebellum Congress include Donald A. Ritchie, *Press Gallery: Congress and the Washington Correspondents* (Cambridge, Mass.: Harvard University Press, 1991); Culver H. Smith, *The Press, Politics, and Patronage: The American Government's Use of Newspapers, 1789–1875* (Athens: University of Georgia, 1977); William E. Ames, *A History of the National Intelligencer* (Chapel Hill: UNC Press, 1972); Elizabeth G. McPherson, "Major Publications of Gales and Seaton," *Quarterly Journal of Speech* 31 (December 1945): 430–39; idem., "Reporting the Debates of Congress," *Quarterly Journal of Speech* 28 (April 1942): 141–48; F. B. Marbut, *News from the Capital: The Story of Washington Reporting* (Carbondale: Southern Illinois University, 1971); J. Frederick Essary, *Covering Washington: Government Reflected to the Public in the Press, 1822–1926* (Boston: Houghton Mifflin, 1927); Leonard, *Power of the Press*, esp. chapter 3; and for a slightly later period, Mark W. Summers, *The Press Gang: Newspapers and Politics, 1865–1878* (Chapel Hill: UNC Press, 1994). On the press and Congress generally, see chapter 6.

99. *Globe*, 26th Cong., 1st Sess., March 14, 1840, 268.

100. Ibid., 23rd Cong., 1st Sess., April 18, 1834, 328. The Senate had been discussing President Jackson's protest against the Senate's motion to censure him; people were cheering and booing at mentions of Jackson and Henry Clay.

101. A Traveller [Henry Cook Todd], *Notes upon Canada and the United States from 1832 to 1840* (Toronto: Rogers and Thompson, 1840), 33, 471. See also Edward T. Coke, *A Subaltern's Furlough, descriptive of Scenes in various parts of the United States, Upper and Lower Canada, New Brunswick, and Nova Scotia, during the Summer and Autumn of 1832* (London: Saunders and Otley, 1833), 89.

102. See generally, McDonough, *Growing Up on Capitol Hill*.

103. See United States Senate Commission on Art and Antiquities, "Manners in the Senate Chamber: 19th Century Women's Views" (Washington, D.C.: GPO, 1985); Ritchie, *Press Gallery*, 146.

104. Francis Lieber, *Letters to a Gentleman in Germany: Written After a Trip from Philadelphia to Niagara* (Philadelphia: Carey, Lea & Blanchard, 1834), 75. On the political influence of women in Washington through Jackson's presidency, see Catherine Allgor, *Parlor Politics: In Which the Ladies of Washington Help Build a City and a Government* (Charlottesville: UVA Press, 2000).

105. Randolph was attacking Daniel Webster (W-MA), who was then in the House. He next attacked Speaker John W. Taylor; when he finished, he sarcastically asked if Taylor's wife was also in the gallery. Benjamin Perley Poore, *Perley's Reminiscences of Sixty Years in the National Metropolis*, 2 vols. (Philadelphia: Hubbard Brothers, 1886), 1:69.

106. Women influenced Washington politics in countless ways, but their influence was less immediate in the realm of congressional violence. They sometimes witnessed it, occasionally discouraged it, and, by the late 1850s, routinely recorded it for the press as reporters. But congressional bullying and violence was largely a man-to-man affair, imposed by murmured insults and backroom threats as well as by grand displays on the House and Senate floor, and negotiated by groups of men out of the public eye or on the field of honor. Even so, the influence of women appears throughout this volume. Not only were they active observers, confidants, influencers, lobbyists, and petitioners, but letters exchanged between congressmen and their wives offer by far the most emotionally expressive views of congressional mayhem and its impact. It would be impossible to fully grasp the emotional impact of bullying without those letters—and its emotional impact was its power. On women and party politics in this period, see Melanie Susan Gustafson, *Women and the Republican Party, 1854–1924* (Chicago: University of Illinois, 2001); Elizabeth R. Varon, *We Mean to Be Counted: White Women and Politics in Antebellum Virginia* (Chapel Hill: UNC Press, 1998); Jean Harvey Baker, "Public Women and Partisan Politics, 1840–1860," *A Political Nation*, 64–81; Allgor, *Parlor Politics*. Allgor posits that women became more removed from the doings of politics with the rise of Jacksonian democracy.

107. Senate Journal, December 7, 1835, 5. The Senate gained a ladies' gallery in 1835, the House in 1833.

108. French to Henry Flagg French, September 12, 1841, BBFFP. Emphasis in original. See also French, diary entry, September 13, 1841, *Witness*, 124–25; House Journal, September 9, 1841, 488.

109. Jean H. Baker, *Affairs of Party: The Political Culture of Northern Democrats in the Mid-Nineteenth Century* (Ithaca: Cornell University Press, 1983), 287–306. See also Robert W. Johannsen, *To the Halls of the Montezumas: The Mexican War in the American Imagination* (New York: Oxford University Press, 1985); Marcus Cunliffe, *Soldiers and Civilians: The Martial Spirit in America, 1775–1865* (Boston: Little, Brown, 1968); Albrecht Koschnik, *"Let a Common Interest Bind Us Together": Associations, Partisanship, and Culture in Philadelphia, 1775–1840* (Philadelphia: University Press of Virginia, 2007), esp. 90–152; and more generally, Glenn C. Altschuler and Stuart M. Blumin, *Rude Republic: Americans and Their Politics in the Nineteenth Century* (Princeton, N.J.: Princeton University Press, 2000); Silbey, *The American Political Nation*, esp. 90–108; Mary Ryan, *Civic Wars: Democracy and Public Life in the American City During the Nineteenth Century* (Berkeley: University of California, 1997), 94–131; Mark W. Brewin, *Celebrating Democracy: The Mass-Mediated Ritual of Election Day* (New York: Peter Lang, 2008); Mark E. Neely, Jr., *The Boundaries of American Political Culture in the Civil War Era* (Chapel Hill: UNC Press, 2005); Michael Feldberg, *The Turbulent Era: Riot and Disorder in Jacksonian America* (New York: Oxford University Press, 1980), 56–57; Grimsted, *American Mobbing*, 181–217; Paul A. Gilje, *The Road to Mobocracy: Popular Disorder in New York City, 1763–1834* (Chapel Hill: UNC, 1987), passim.
110. Michael E. McGerr, *The Decline of Popular Politics: The American North, 1865–1928* (New York: Oxford University Press, 1988), 24–25; Altschuler and Blumin, *Rude Republic*, 63.
111. French to Harriette French, December 10, 1839, BBFFP.
112. Ibid.

2. THE MIX OF MEN IN CONGRESS

1. On the local lives of most Americans, see Franklin, *Southern Odyssey*, 1–44, 58–75; Richard H. Gassan, *The Birth of American Tourism: New York, the Hudson Valley, and American Culture, 1790–1830* (Amherst: University of Massachusetts Press, 2008).
2. On the nexus of party and Union, see Jeffrey J. Selinger, *Embracing Dissent: Political Violence and Party Development in the United States* (Philadelphia: University of Pennsylvania Press, 2016).
3. See note 7 for sources of demographic information on the antebellum Congress. On turnover, see also Rosemarie Zagarri, "The Family Factor: Congressmen, Turnover, and the Burden of Public Service in the Early American Republic," *JER* 2 (Summer 2013): 283–316; Morris P. Fiorina, David W. Rohde, and Peter Wissel, "Historical Change in House Turnover," *Congress in Change: Evolution and Reform*, ed. Norman J. Ornstein (New York: Praeger, 1975), 24–46; Stephen Erickson, "The Entrenching of Incumbency: Reflections in the U.S. House of Representatives, 1790–1994," *Cato Journal* 3 (Winter 1995): 397–420 (see esp. 404–407); Robert Struble, Jr., "House Turnover and the Principle of Rotation," *Political Science Quarterly* 4 (Winter 1979–80): 649–67; Ronald P. Formisano, *The Transformation of Political Culture: Massachusetts Parties, 1790s–1840s* (New York: Oxford University Press, 1983), 41–54; H. Douglas Price, "Careers

and Committees in the American Congress: The Problem of Structural Change," in *The History of Parliamentary Behavior*, ed. William O. Ayedelotte (Princeton, N.J.: Princeton Legacy Library, 2015: orig. pub. 1977), 3–27.

4. Samuel Kernell, "Toward Understanding 19th Century Congressional Careers: Ambition, Competition, and Rotation," *American Journal of Political Science* 21 (November 1977): 673.

5. French, diary entry, December 29, 1842, February 11, 1848, *Witness*, 198–99. French's musings in 1848 were inspired by an address by Representative George P. Marsh (W-VT) arguing that historians should go beyond "the great, prominent public actions of a nation." Marsh, "The American Historical School: A Discourse Delivered Before the Literary Societies of Union College" (Troy, N.Y.: Steam Press, 1847). On the impact of daguerreotypes in antebellum America, see Alan Trachtenberg, *Lincoln's Smile and Other Enigmas* (New York: Hill and Wang, 2007); Stephen John Hartnett, *Democratic Dissent & the Cultural Fictions of Antebellum America* (Chicago: University of Illinois Press, 2002), 132–72.

6. Frederic Hudson, *Journalism in the United States from 1690 to 1872* (New York: Harper & Brothers, 1873), 252.

7. For House statistics, see Allan G. Bogue, Jerome M. Clubb, Carroll R. McKibbin, and Santa A. Traugott, "Members of the House of Representatives and the Process of Modernization, 1789–1960," *Journal of American History* 63 (September 1976): 275–302; Kernell, "Toward Understanding 19th Century Congressional Careers: 669–93; Nelson W. Polsby, "The Institutionalization of the U.S. House of Representatives," *American Political Science Review* 62 (March 1968): 144–68. For the Senate, see Allan G. Bogue, *The Congressman's Civil War* (New York: Cambridge University Press, 1989), 1–28; Susan Radomsky, "The Social Life of Politics: Washington's Official Society and the Emergence of a National Political Elite, 1800–1876," 2 vols. (Ph.D. dissertation, University of Chicago, 2005), esp. vol. 2; Elaine K. Swift, *The Making of an American Senate: Reconstitutive Change in Congress, 1787–1841* (University of Michigan Press, 2002). See also Matthew Eric Glassman, Erin Hemlin, and Amber Hope Wilhelm, "Congressional Careers: Service Tenure and Patterns of Member Service, 1789–2011," CRS Report R41545, Congressional Research Service, January 7, 2011; H. Douglas Price, "Congress and the Evolution of Legislative 'Professionalism,'" *Congress in Change*, 14–27; Silbey, *American Political Nation*, 185; Congressional Biographical Directory (H. Doc. 108–222); Roster of Congressional Officeholders and Biographical Characteristics (ICPSR 7803). Some of this data is slippery because the Congressional Biographical Directory doesn't consistently list the same kinds of information for every congressman, and ICPSR 7803 contained some errors.

8. Haskell M. Monroe, Jr., and James T. McIntosh, eds., *The Papers of Jefferson Davis: Volume 1, 1808–1840* (Baton Rouge: LSU Press, 1991 rev. ed.), 1:327 footnote.

9. Between 1789 and 1810, most college-educated congressmen had attended Ivy League schools because there were few other options. Between 1811 and 1860, the number of congressmen who attended other private colleges increased dramatically, partly because of the democratization of Congress and partly because of the founding of more private colleges. During that same period, the number

of congressmen attending state schools increased from 3.8 percent to 7.1 percent. Bogue et al., "Members of the House," 282. In the House in the 1830s, 61.1 percent hadn't attended college; in the 1840s, 55.9 percent; and in the 1850s, 48.5 percent. Fifteen percent of the House had Ivy League educations, a number that remained relatively constant for several decades. In the late 1830s and early 1840s roughly 65 percent of the Senate had college educations. Bogue et al., "Members of the House," 282; Daniel Wirls, "The 'Golden Age' Senate and Floor Debate in the Antebellum Congress," *Legislative Studies Quarterly* 2 (May 2007): 193–222, cited at 207. On common schools generally, see Donald H. Parkerson and Jo Ann Parkerson, *The Emergence of the Common School in the U.S. Countryside* (Lewiston, N.Y.: Edwin Mellen Press, 1998); Carl F. Kaestle, *Pillars of the Republic: Common Schools and American Society, 1780–1860* (New York: Hill and Wang, 1983); and more generally, Gerald F. Moran and Maris A. Vinovskis, "Schools," in *An Extensive Republic: Print, Culture, and Society in the New Nation, 1790–1840*, ed. Robert A. Gross and Mary Kelley, vol. 2 in *A History of the Book in America* (Chapel Hill: UNC Press, 2010), 286–303.

10. French, diary entry, February 17, 1867, *Witness*, 530–31.

11. In the pre–Civil War South, only North Carolina and Kentucky had reasonably well established statewide systems of public education. John Hope Franklin, *A Southern Odyssey: Travelers in the Antebellum North* (Baton Rouge: LSU Press, 1976; 1991 printing), 53.

12. Categories are taken from Bogue et al., "Members of the House," 284. The study's other options for professions include "Education," "Other," and "Unknown."

13. See Jeffrey Pasley's "Printers, Editors, and Publishers in Congress, 1789–1861," pasleybrothers.com/newspols/congress.htm. Recruiting young men to edit party papers was relatively common. For example, in 1835, at the request of Alabama Democrats who desperately wanted a party paper, the Tennessee editor Samuel Laughlin put out a search for "a young man to take charge of a press . . . which will be bought for him." Laughlin to James K. Polk, December 16, 1835, *Correspondence of James K. Polk*, ed. Herbert Weaver and Kermit L. Hall (Kingsport, Tenn.: Vanderbilt University, 1975), 3:397.

14. Alfred Zantzinger Reed, *Training for the Public Profession of the Law: Historical Development and Principal Contemporary Problems of Legal Education in the United States with Some Account of Conditions in England and Canada* (Boston: Merrymount Press, 1921), 87. By 1860, only nine out of thirty-nine states required a definite period of legal study. Ibid., 86. See also Gary B. Nash, "The Philadelphia Bench and Bar, 1800–1861," *Comparative Studies in Society and History* 7, no. 2 (January 1965): 203–220; Charles Warren, *A History of the American Bar* (Boston: Little, Brown, 1911); Maxwell Bloomfield, *American Lawyers in a Changing Society, 1776–1876* (New York: Cambridge University Press, 1976); Gerald W. Gawalt, *The Promise of Power: The Emergence of the Legal Profession in Massachusetts, 1760–1840* (Westport, Conn.: Greenwood Press, 1979); Anton-Hermann Chroust, *The Rise of the Legal Profession in America: The Revolution and the Post-Revolutionary Era* (Norman: University of Oklahoma Press, 1965); Michael Grossberg and Christopher Tomlins, eds., *The Cambridge History of Law in America: The Long Nineteenth Century (1789–1920)* (New York: Cambridge

University Press, 2008); Steve Sheppard, ed., *The History of Legal Education in the United States: Commentaries and Primary Sources*, 2 vols. (Pasadena, Calif.: Salem Press, 1999).

15. In the 1830s, 63.5 percent of the House were lawyers; in the 1840s, 66.9 percent; in the 1850s, 66.1 percent. During the Twenty-third Congress, 176 of the 263 House members were lawyers; 43 of the 52 senators were lawyers. These numbers include replacements for men who left office midterm or died in office. On lawyers as political leaders, see also Altschuler and Blumin, *Rude Republic*, 97–105; Bogue et al., "Members of the House," 284–85.

16. French, diary entry, February 17, 1833, *Witness*, 38.

17. In addition to the Congressional Biographical Directory, see Benjamin Franklin Morris, ed., *The Life of Thomas Morris: Pioneer and Long a Legislator of Ohio, and U.S. Senator from 1833 to 1839* (Cincinnati: Moore, Wilstach, Keys & Overend, 1856), 15; Earle, *Jacksonian Antislavery*, 37–44.

18. Lynch, "Washington City Forty Years Ago," *Memoirs of Anne C. L. Botta Written by Her Friends* (New York: J. Selwin Tait & Sons, 1894), 438.

19. George P. Marsh, *Lectures on the English Language* (New York: Charles Scribner, 1863), 671. Marsh delivered the lectures at Columbia College in 1858–59.

20. After devising this term, I discovered Roy F. Nichols's argument that cultural federalism—a Union of people with fundamentally different cultural outlooks—was the fundamental cause of the Civil War, though his cultural clusters are not necessarily sectional; "southernism," "New Englandism," and "antislaveryism" are among ten different "attitudes" that composed cultural federalism. Nichols, *The Disruption of American Democracy* (New York: Collier Books Edition, 1962; orig. pub. 1948), 34–53. See also James C. Malin, *The Nebraska Question, 1852–54* (Michigan: Edwards Brothers, 1953), 426. On the city's licentiousness, see for example Daniel Dickinson to Lydia Dickinson, February 12, 1858, in *Speeches, Correspondence, Etc., of the Late Daniel S. Dickinson of New York*, John R. Dickinson, ed., 2 vols. (New York: G. P. Putnam & Son, 1867), 509; Dickinson to Mary Dickinson, February 12, 1858, ibid.; John Parker Hale to Lucy Hale, 1837, in Sewell, *John P. Hale*, 36; Duncan McArthur (NR-OH) to Mrs. McArthur, February 6, 1824, in Cynthia D. Earman, "Boardinghouses," 105; David Outlaw to Emily Outlaw, January 30, 1848, DOP.

21. On drunkenness and politics, see also Rachel A. Shelden, *Washington Brotherhood: Politics, Social Life, and the Coming of the Civil War* (Chapel Hill: UNC Press, 2013), 125–30.

22. An American Temperance Society report notes that in 1830 alone, the city of Washington granted 60 tavern licenses, 34 grog-shop licenses, 4 confectionary licenses, and 126 licenses to sell "spirits in quantities not less than a pint." *Permanent Documents of the American Temperance Society*, 2 vols. (Boston: Seth Bliss, 1835), 1:76.

23. French to Henry Flagg French, December 1, 1855, BBFFP, LC. "Villainous smells" is a reference to a quote by Falstaff in Shakespeare's *The Merry Wives of Windsor*, act 3, scene 5.

24. "Temperance," *The Independent*, January 7, 1869, 21; Robert McClelland to John Parker Hale, January 20, 1844, John Parker Hale Papers, NHHS. (My thanks to

Bill Copeley of the NHHS for helping me track down the writer.) Jenkins's grocery on Pennsylvania Avenue between Third and Four-and-a-half Streets, just a few blocks from the Capitol, saw a lot of politicking. Lucius Elmer (D-NJ) was taken there when he seemed likely to deny John Parker Hale (D-NH) his House seat. *Boyd's Directory* for 1850 lists eight "porter houses" at 253, 369, 391, 420, 460, 490, 528, and 538 Pennsylvania Avenue, but doesn't include listings for other types of drinking establishments. According to the *OED*, porter houses sold porter and other malt liquors; saloons served liquors of all kinds; and dram shops and groceries served liquor in small quantities.

25. French, diary entry, December 15, 1835, *Witness*, 64.

26. Daniel French to French, December 31, 1833, BBFFP.

27. See for example Buckingham, *America*, 1:358.

28. Robert McClelland to John Parker Hale, January 20, 1844, John Parker Hale Papers, NHHS.

29. Ibid.; Henry Watterson, *Marse Henry: An Autobiography*, 2 vols. (New York: George H. Doran Company, 1919), 1:40; French, diary entry, February 15, 1846, *Witness*, 184–85. See also McConnell's behavior in 1846 when he was called a "drunken blackguard" by Garrett Davis (W-KY). Adams, diary entry, *Memoirs*, January 10, 1846, 12:234–35. The following (very bad) pun is attributed to a McConnell contemporary, the journalist George Prentice: "A Washington letter-writer says that Mr. McConnell was once a schoolmaster. If he taught his pupils to imitate his own drunken habits, it must have been a *high school*." (Emphasis in original). G. W. Griffin, ed., *Prenticeana: or, Wit and Humor in Paragraphs* (Philadelphia: Claxton, Remsen & Haffelfinger, 1871), 133.

30. Robert McClelland to John Parker Hale, January 20, 1844, John Parker Hale Papers, NHHS.

31. Peter A. Wallner, *Franklin Pierce: New Hampshire's Favorite Son* (Concord, N.H.: Plaidswede, 2004), 62–63; Nichols, *Franklin Pierce*, 86–87.

32. David Outlaw to Emily Outlaw, February 20, 1848, DOP. See also Edwin Morgan to his brothers, January 10, 1856, "A Congressman's Letters on the Speaker Election in the Thirty-fourth Congress," Temple R. Hollcroft, *Mississippi Valley Historical Review* 43, no. 3 (December 1956): 444–58, quote on 454.

33. Adams, diary entry, December 26, 1843, *Memoirs*, 11:461. For more on drunken congressmen, see diary entry, March 1849, *Joshua R. Giddings: A Sketch*, ed. Walter Buell (Cleveland: William W. Williams, 1882), 190; "Temperance in High Places," *Saturday Evening Post*, March 23, 1850.

34. "Proceedings of the Congressional Total Abstinence Society" (New York: Office of the American Temperance Union, 1842), 28.

35. French, diary entry, August 29, 1841, *Witness*, 121–22; Adams, diary entry, August 23 and 25, 1841, *Memoirs*, 10:539, 542. On Marshall's sad state of drunkenness in later years and his "curious half-abandoned mode of life," see John Wilson Townsend, *Kentucky in American Letters, 1784–1912*, 2 vols. (Cedar Rapids, Iowa: Torch Press, 1913), 1:339–41.

36. *Globe*, 27th Cong., 1st Sess., August 25, 1841, 387.

37. Adams, diary entry, July 17, 1840, and September 13, 1841, *Memoirs*, 10:337, 11:17–18.

38. Samuel Cox, *Eight Years in Congress*, 19–20. On Wigfall's allegedly drunken (but certainly wandering) speech of March 1860, see Beman Brockway, *Fifty Years in Journalism: Embracing Recollections and Personal Experiences with an Autobiography* (Watertown, N.Y.: Daily Times Printing and Publishing House, 1891), 223–24; *NYT*, March 28, 1860.

39. Adams, diary entry, September 13, 1841, *Memoirs*, 11:17–18. See also French, diary entry, August 19 and 29, 1841, *Witness*, 86, 122.

40. Oscar Fitzgerald, *California Sketches* (California: Southern Methodist Publishing House, 1882), 106–107. See also "Manhood Suffrage and the Ballot in America," *Blackwood's Edinburgh Magazine* 101 (April 1867): 461–78, quote at 470; George Rothwell Brown, ed., *Reminiscences of Senator William M. Stewart, of Nevada* (New York: Neale Publishing Company, 1908), 207–12; Russell Buchanan, "James A. McDougall: A Forgotten Senator," *California Historical Society Quarterly* 15 (September 1936): 199–212.

41. Quoted in John B. Gough, *Sunlight and Shadow or, Gleanings from My Life Work* (London: R. D. Dickinson, 1881), 272. See also *History of St. Joseph County, Indiana* (Chicago: Chas. C. Chapman & Co., 1880), 314–15; Federal Writers Project, *Indiana: A Guide to the Hoosier State* (New York: Oxford University Press, 1941), 353–54; John Wesley Whicker, "Edward A. Hannegan," *Indiana Magazine of History* 14 (December 1918): 368–75. Hannegan allegedly killed his brother-in-law while drunk and died of a morphine overdose. Two problem drinkers were evicted from their boardinghouses: Vice President Daniel Tompkins and Attorney Luther Martin. Earman, "Boardinghouses," 55.

42. Adams, *Memoirs*, April 2, 1834, 9:118–19. See also J. Marion Sims, *The Story of My Life*, ed. H. Marion Sims (New York: D. Appleton, 1894), 95–96.

43. Diary entries, September 8 and 10, 1846, in *The Diary of James K. Polk During His Presidency, 1845 to 1849*, ed. Milo Milton Quaife, 4 vols. (Chicago: A. C. McClurg, 1910), 2:123, 130–33. See also Perley Poore, *Perley's Reminiscences*, 1:300.

44. *Merchant's Magazine* (1848), 373.

45. Article 1, Section 6 of the Constitution states that senators and representatives "shall in all cases, except treason, felony, and breach of the peace, be privileged from arrest during their attendance at the session of their respective Houses, and in going to and returning from the same; and for any speech or debate in either House, they shall not be questioned in any other place." See also Thomas Jefferson, *A Manual of Parliamentary Practice for the Use of the Senate of the United States* (Georgetown: Joseph Milligan, 1812), in *Jefferson's Parliamentary Writings: "Parliamentary Pocket-Book" and A Manual of Parliamentary Practice*," ed. Wilbur Samuel Howell (Princeton, N.J.: Princeton University Press, 1988), 358–63.

46. French, diary entry, April 27, 1838, *Witness*, 79–80.

47. See Radomsky, "The Social Life of Politics"; Shelden, *Washington Brotherhood*; Earman, "Boardinghouses"; and for an earlier period, Allgor, *Parlor Politics*.

48. Robert McClelland to John Parker Hale, January 20, 1844, John Parker Hale Papers, NHHS.

49. Anne C. Lynch, "Washington City Forty Years Ago," 437–38; Annie C. Lynch to Lydia and Daniel Dickinson, January 7, 1853, *Speeches, Correspondence, Etc., of the Late Daniel S. Dickinson of New York*, ed. John R. Dickinson, 2 vols. (New York: G. P. Putnam & Son, 1867), 2:473. On Lynch, see also Edward T. James, Janet Wilson James, and Paul S. Boyer, eds., *Notable American Women: A Biographical Dictionary* (Cambridge, Mass.: Radcliffe College, 1971), 212–14; *NYT*, December 31, 1893.

50. French, diary entry, December 15, 1835, *Witness*, 64. For more talk of dissipation, see Daniel Dickinson to Mary Dickinson, February 12, 1858, in *Speeches, Correspondence, Etc., of the Late Daniel S. Dickinson*, 2:509; John Parker Hale to Lucy Hale, March 6, 1837, in Sewell, *John P. Hale*, 36; Duncan McArthur (NR-OH) in Earman, "Boardinghouses," 105.

51. Francis J. Grund, "Society in the American Metropolis," *Sartain's Union Magazine of Literature and Art* (Philadelphia), vol. 6 (January–June 1850), 17–18.

52. French to Harriette French, May 12, 1834, BBFFP.

53. French, diary entry, December 15, 1836, ibid.

54. French, diary entry, May 7, 1838, *Witness*, 81.

55. Albert Gallatin Riddle, *Recollections of War Times* (New York: G. Putnam's Sons, 1895), 9. Riddle (R-OH) was in the House from 1861 to 1862. On Washington's Southern social spirit, see also [Address at dedication of a monument to Joshua Giddings], July 25, 1870, *The Works of James Abram Garfield*, ed. Burke A. Hinsdale (Boston: James Osgood, 1882), 1:606.

56. Roughly 17 percent of the city's population was free black and 12 percent were enslaved. William Darby and Theodore Dwight, Jr., *A New Gazetteer of the United States of America* (Hartford: Edward Hopkins, 1833), 112; 22nd Cong. 1st Sess., H. Doc. No. 269, Abstract of the Returns of the Fifth Census (Washington: Duff Green, 1832); Goldfield, "Antebellum Washington in Context," 9. On Washington as a border city, see Robert Harrison, *Washington During the Civil War and Reconstruction: Race and Radicalism* (New York: Cambridge University Press, 2011), 6–12; Carl Abbott, *Political Terrain*, 57–92; Stanley Harrold, *Subversives: Antislavery Community in Washington, D.C., 1828–1865* (Baton Rouge: LSU Press, 2003), 1–12; Goldfield, "Antebellum Washington in Context," 1–20.

57. Bernard L. Herman, "Southern City, National Ambition: Washington's Early Town Houses," *Southern City, National Ambition*, 21–46. Herman calls them "urban plantations."

58. See for example Henry Adams, *The Education of Henry Adams*, 44; Seward, *Reminiscences*, 69. Abraham Lincoln (R-IL) and Joshua Giddings (FS-OH) both noticed the slave pen during their time in the House. Lincoln, Speech on Kansas-Nebraska Act at Peoria, Illinois, October 16, 1854, *Speeches and Writings: Abraham Lincoln*, ed. Don E. Fehrenbacher (New York: Library of America, 1989), 313; Giddings, Speech on Relation of the Federal Government to Slavery, in Giddings, *Speeches in Congress* (Boston: John P. Jewett, 1853), 348. See also Paul Finkelman and Kennon, *In the Shadow of Freedom*; Walter C. Clephane, "The Local Aspect of Slavery in the District of Columbia," March 6, 1899, in *Records of the Columbia Historical Society* 3 (1900): 224–25; Letitia W. Brown, *Free Negroes in the District of Columbia, 1790–1846* (New York: Oxford Univer-

sity Press, 1972); Constance M. Green, *The Secret City: A History of Race Relations in the Nation's Capital* (Princeton, N.J.: Princeton University Press, 1967); Harrold, *Subversives*; Harrison, *Washington During the Civil War*, 6–12; Goldfield, "Antebellum Washington in Context"; Fehrenbacher, *The Slaveholding Republic*, 49–88.

59. Horace Mann to Reverend A. Craig [?], December 5, 1852, *Life of Horace Mann by His Wife*, ed. Mary T. P. Mann (Boston: Lee & Shepard, 1904), 389.

60. James Brewer Stewart, *Joshua R. Giddings and the Tactics of Radical Politics* (Cleveland: Press of Case Western Reserve University, 1970), 41.

61. "Abstract of the Returns of the Fifth Census," 4. Slavery lingered in New Hampshire as it did in several New England states; New Hampshire didn't pass a final abolition bill until 1857. Joanne P. Melish, *Disowning Slavery: Gradual Emancipation and Race in New England, 1780–1860* (Ithaca, N.Y.: Cornell University Press, 1998), 76. Melish notes that New Hampshirites were divided over whether the state constitution's "Declaration of Rights" declaring all men free and equal ended slavery. Ibid., 66. See also Leon Litwack, *North of Slavery: The Negro in the Free States, 1790–1860* (Chicago: University of Chicago Press, 1961), 91–92; Sewell, *John P. Hale*, 28–31; Cole, *Jacksonian Democracy in New Hampshire*, 178–80; Earle, *Jacksonian Antislavery*, 82–83.

62. French to Bess French, in Gauker, *History of the Scottish Rite Bodies in the District of Columbia*, 5. Emphasis in the original. The quote is probably from a letter of December 26, 1833. See also Hale to Lucy Hale, December 24, 1843, in Sewell, *John P. Hale*, 38.

63. Melish, *Disowning Slavery*, 22–23.

64. On slavery in New England and its erasure, see esp. Melish, *Disowning Slavery*. On New Hampshire, see Earle, *Jacksonian Antislavery*, 78–102. On the foundations of slavery in colonial New England, see Wendy Warren, *New England Bound* (New York: Liveright, 2016).

65. *Globe*, 34th Cong., 1st Sess., June 12, 1856, 34:1, 626 app. See also James L. Huston, "The Experiential Basis of the Northern Antislavery Impulse," *Journal of Southern History* 4 (November 1990): 609–40; Horace Mann to E. W. Clap, January 28, 1850, Mann, ed., *Life of Horace Mann*, 287–88.

66. Maria Weston Chapman, ed., *Harriet Martineau's Autobiography*, 3 vols. (Boston: Houghton, Mifflin, 1877), 1:342–43.

67. Hale to Lucy Hale, January 8, December 6 and 12, 1844, John Parker Hale Papers, NHHS. Hale spoke with Richard Simpson (D-SC) and David Levy (D-FL), the first Jewish senator, who changed his name to Yulee in 1846.

68. Sewell, *John P. Hale*, 120.

69. See for example the comments of Henry Hubbard (D-NH) about his frequent visits to nearby plantations, or William Seward's (R-NY) visit in 1857. *Globe*, 24th Cong., 1st Sess., March 7, 1836, 168 app.; Frederick William Seward, *Autobiography: Seward at Washington, as Senator and Secretary of State* (New York: Derby and Miller, 1891), 331.

70. On Carroll's Masonic ties, see Edward T. Schultz, *History of Freemasonry in Maryland of All the Rites Introduced into Maryland from the Earliest Time to the Present*, 2 vols. (Baltimore: J. H. Medairy, 1885), 528.

71. French, diary entry, July 27, 1851, *Witness*, 220–21.
72. Ibid., September 4, 1851, 221; *National Intelligencer*, September 5, 1851.
73. *Chicago Democrat*, dateline January 12, 1838, BBFFP. (French clipped his "letters" and pasted them in a scrapbook without listing the date of the *Democrat* that contained them.)
74. French, diary entry, January 21, 1849, *Witness*, 207–208.
75. French, "To the Hon. J. R. Giddings, upon reading his great speech in the H of Reps U.S. on Presidential nominations," July 11, 1852, BBFFP. Giddings gave his speech on June 23, 1852; see Stewart, *Joshua Giddings*, 211–13.
76. For an example of the coaching efforts of the Washington Democratic Association, see "Circular from the Executive Committee of the Democratic Association of Washington City," September 1844, memory.loc.gov/cgi-bin/query/h?ammem /rbpebib:@field%28NUMBER+@band%28rbpe+1970400a%29%29, accessed July 29, 2013. On the localized nature of party politics, see Daniel Klinghard, *The Nationalization of American Political Parties, 1880–1896* (New York: Cambridge University Press, 2010), 25–32; John H. Aldrich, *Why Parties? A Second Look* (Chicago: University of Chicago Press, 2011), 119–29; William E. Gienapp, "'Politics Seem to Enter into Everything': Political Culture in the North, 1840–1860," in *Essays on American Antebellum Politics, 1840–1860*, ed. Stephen E. Maizlish and John J. Kushma (College Station: University of Texas at Arlington, 1982), 15–69, cited at 48–50; Formisano, *Transformation of Political Culture*; Silbey, *American Political Nation*.
77. Silbey, *American Political Nation*, 59–70; Formisano, *Transformation of Political Culture*, 258–60; James S. Chase, *Emergence of the Presidential Nominating Convention, 1789–1832* (Urbana: University of Illinois Press, 1973). On party politics displacing violence, see Selinger, *Embracing Dissent*.
78. On slang-whanging, see John Russell Bartlett, *Dictionary of Americanisms: A Glossary of Words and Phrases Usually Regarded as Peculiar to the United States* (Boston: Little, Brown, 1977), 602.
79. French seems to have begun writing for the *Chicago Democrat* in 1834; the first newspaper in Chicago, it began publication in 1833. Horatio Hill co-owned the *Democrat* with John "Long John" Wentworth, also from New Hampshire. French knew them both. Wentworth later represented Illinois in the House.
80. Holt, *Rise and Fall of the Whig Party*, xiii; Howe, *Political Culture of the American Whigs*, passim. Scholarship on the persistence of antiparty sentiment is vast and deep. Particularly useful in a congressional context are Edward L. Mayo, "Republicanism, Antipartyism, and Jacksonian Party Politics: A View from the Nation's Capital" *American Quarterly* 31 (Spring 1979): 3–20; Silbey, *American Political Nation*; Formisano, *Transformation of Political Culture*; idem., "Political Character, Antipartyism and the Second Party System," *American Quarterly* 21 (Winter 1969): 683–709; William Shade, "Political Pluralism and Party Development: The Creation of a Modern Party System, 1815–1852," in *The Evolution of American Electoral Systems*, ed. Paul Kleppner, Walter Dean Burnham, Ronald P. Formisano, Samuel P. Hays, Richard Jensen, and William G. Shade (Westport, Conn.: Greenwood Press, 1981), 77–111; Richard McCormick, *The Second American Party System: Party Formation in the Jacksonian Era* (Chapel Hill: UNC

Press, 1966); Christopher J. Olsen, *Political Culture and Secession in Mississippi: Masculinity, Honor, and the Antiparty Tradition, 1830–1860* (New York: Oxford University Press, 2000), 55–69. On Whigs and antipartyism, see esp. Daniel Walker Howe, *The Political Culture of the American Whigs* (Chicago: University of Chicago Press, 1979), 51–54; Gerald Leonard, *The Invention of Party Politics: Federalism, Popular Sovereignty, and Constitutional Development in Jacksonian Illinois* (Chapel Hill: UNC Press, 2002).

81. Chicago *Democrat*, dateline December 11, 1834, BBFFP; French, diary entry, September 15, 1828; November 16, 1840; August 15, 1841, *Witness*, 16, 105, 121. In the later entries, French was peeved about the presidential election of 1840. Michael Holt notes that although the Whigs were a diverse group brought together by their hatred of Jackson and what he represented, they shared broader ideological bonds: their hatred of "executive tyranny was based on principle." Holt, *The Rise and Fall of the American Whig Party: Jacksonian Politics and the Onset of the Civil War* (New York: Oxford University Press, 1999), 28–29. The first appearance of "Whig" to describe anti-Jacksonians seems to date to 1834. Howe, *Political Culture of the American Whigs*, 88, 332, note 73; Steven P. McGiffen, "Ideology and the Failure of the Whig Party in New Hampshire, 1834–1841," *New England Quarterly* 3 (September 1986): 387–401, cited at 390. See also Holt, *Rise and Fall of the Whig Party*, 20.

82. See for example French, diary entry, January 9, 1844, *Witness*, 158.

83. French wrote countless electioneering songs. On his songwriting generally, see French, diary entry, January 9, 1844, *Witness*, 158.

84. *Baltimore Sun*, June 16, 1842; French, diary entry, January 10, 1852, *Witness*, 226. For a full account of the banquet and a copy of the invitation, see "Proceedings at the Banquet of the Jackson Democratic Association, Washington, Eighth of January, 1852" (Washington, D.C., 1852). For another such dinner, see *New Hampshire Sentinel*, January 29, 1835; *New York Evening Post*, January 16, 1835; Franklin Pierce to his brother, January 9, 1835, Franklin Pierce Papers, LC.

85. *Salem Gazette*, January 8, 1828; *Salem Register*, March 30, 1833. Published anonymously, the piece was probably written by the future congressman Robert Rantoul, Jr. (D-MA). *Globe*, 32nd Cong., 1st Sess., March 6, 1852, 248 app.; ibid., March 9, 1852, 293 app. Ultimately becoming a cliché for empty pomp, this line morphed into countless variations over the decades; for example, "tunjo," became "tonjon," "tonton," "tomjohn," and "tom-tom." As late as 1916, a novelist put the phrase in the mouth of a happy coal miner: "Get ready to blow the hewgag and beat the tom-tom. We're in it, this time!" Francis Lynde, *After the Manner of Men* (New York: Charles Scribner's Sons, 1916), 252.

86. Joel Mitchell Chapple, "Affairs at Washington," *National Magazine* (October 1903), 20.

87. For a list of some of French's activities, see *Witness*, xv–xvi; *Rural Repository* (Hudson, N.Y.), March 31, 1849; and his obituary in the *NYT*, August 14, 1870. French co-founded the Guardian Society to reform the city's juvenile delinquents. Charles Moore, ed. and comp., *Joint Select Committee to Investigate the Charities and Reformatory Institutions in the District of Columbia* (Washington: GPO, 1898),

154; French, diary entry, August 24, 1862, *Witness*, 405. For the school for girls, see French, diary entry, January 10, 1852, *Witness*, 226.

88. French, diary entry, June 23, 1840. *Witness*, 101. French went to Bladensburg with George M. Phillips of Pennsylvania, a clerk in the solicitor's office of the Treasury Department, and two House clerks, Horatio N. Crabb of Pennsylvania and Simon Brown of Massachusetts.

89. See for example *Alexandria Gazette*, October 3, 1844, which describes Western competition over the height of Whig and Democratic flagpoles.

90. French to M. P. Wilder, October 29, 1849, in *Festival of the Sons of New Hampshire . . . Celebrated in Boston, November 7, 1849* (Boston: James French, 1850), 134.

91. French, "A Song," in *Festival of the Sons of New Hampshire*, 108–10.

92. *Daily National Intelligencer*, March 29, 1843.

93. French, diary entry, November 6, 1841, *Witness*, 127–28. See also his speech at the laying of the cornerstone of a new Masonic temple on October 14, 1864. *Freemason's Monthly Magazine* 24 (November 1, 1864): 23–25.

94. French, diary entry, March 13, 1842, *Witness*, 138.

95. See generally Cephas Brainerd and Eveline Warner Brainerd, eds., *The New England Society Orations: Addresses, Sermons, and Poems Delivered Before the New England Society in the City of New York, 1820–1885*, 2 vols. (New York: Century Co., 1901), 1:6; New England Society in the City of New York, www .nesnyc.org/about-us/history, accessed June 14, 2013.

96. Dall, diary entry, December 26, 1842, *Daughter of Boston*, 67–68.

97. *Rural Repository* (Hudson, N.Y.), March 31, 1849.

98. See generally Susan-Mary Grant, *North over South: Northern Nationalism and American Identity in the Antebellum Era* (Lawrence: University Press of Kansas, 2000), passim (esp. 64–65).

99. Martin F. Tupper, "On the Union," *Littell's Living Age*, March 22, 1851, 575.

100. David Outlaw to Emily Outlaw, January 30, 1848; July 27 and February 14, 1850, DOP. Outlaw found the Northern "he-woman" Anne Lynch unattractive and "as hard favoured as could be desired." Ibid., July 3, 1850. On Outlaw and women, see also Berry, *All That Makes a Man*, 118–36, 158–60.

101. Notes for a speech, ca. 1844–45, Fisher Family Papers, UNC. Fisher was in Congress from 1817 to 1820 and 1839 to 1840.

102. George C. Rable, *Damn Yankees!: Demonization and Defiance in the Confederate South* (Baton Rouge: LSU Press, 2015).

103. On Northern ignorance about the South, see esp. Grant, *North over South*. On the intellectual erasure of Northern slavery, see Melish, *Disowning Slavery*. On the small cohort of Northern antislavery Democrats, see esp. Earle, *Jacksonian Antislavery*.

104. See for example French to Henry Flagg French, November 1846, BBFFP.

105. French, diary entry, July 1, 1855, *Witness*, 260.

106. John Russell Bartlett, *Dictionary of Americanisms: A Glossary of Words and Phrases Usually Regarded as Peculiar to the United States* (Boston: Little, Brown, 1848), 128. The dictionary's 1860 third edition had a new term, "doughfacism," defined as "truckling to the slave power." Ibid., 128. Bartlett turned to

John Inman, editor of the *New York Commercial Advertiser,* for some political definitions; Inman refined Bartlett's definition of *doughface* in an appendix. Ibid., 397.

107. William Plumer, Jr., "Reminiscences of Daniel Webster," in *The Writings and Speeches of Daniel Webster,* National Edition, 18 vols. (Boston: Little, Brown, 1903), 17:553–55. Plumer (R-NH) noticed Benton's formal manner, guessed what was happening, and later confirmed it with Webster. His assumption, based on nothing other than Benton's body language, says a lot about the routine nature of honor disputes in Congress.

108. *Connecticut Courant,* March 15, 1809.

109. *New-Hampshire Sentinel* (Keene), April 1, 1820. On doughfaces and Northern Democrats, see esp. Landis, *Northern Men with Southern Loyalties;* Leonard L. Richards, *The Slave Power: The Free North and Southern Domination, 1780– 1860* (Baton Rouge: LSU Press, 2000), 85–88, 109–16; Joshua A. Lynn, "Half-Baked Men: Doughface Masculinity and the Antebellum Politics of Household," M.A. thesis, UNC, Chapel Hill, 2010; Earle, *Jacksonian Antislavery;* Nicholas Wood, "John Randolph of Roanoke and the Politics of Slavery in the Early Republic," *Virginia Magazine of History and Biography* 2 (Summer 2012): 106–43 (esp. 129–30). Wood argues that Randolph was mocking Northerners who advocated restricting slavery for purely mercenary (as opposed to moral) reasons; others argue that he was mocking Northern allies. For discussion of the origins and meaning of the word, see Lynn, "Half-Baked Men," 15–18; Hans Sperber and James N. Tidwell, "Words and Phrases in American Politics," *American Speech* 2 (May 1950): 91–100 (esp. 95–100). For a lengthy (angry) opinion written not long after Charles Sumner's caning, see "A Former Resident of the South" [Darius Lyman], *Leaven for Doughfaces; or Threescore and Ten Parables Touching Slavery* (Cincinnati: Bangs and Company, 1856).

110. Whitman, "Song for Certain Congressmen," 1850, in *Whitman: Complete Poetry and Collected Prose* (New York: Library of America, 1982), 1076. See also Betsy Erkkila, *Whitman the Political Poet* (New York: Oxford University Press, 1989); Martin Klammer, *Whitman, Slavery, and the Emergence of Leaves of Grass* (University Park: Pennsylvania State University Press, 1995); Edward L. Widmer, *Young America: The Flowering of Democracy in New York City* (New York: Oxford University Press, 1999), 81–85. On doughfaces as cowards, see Lynn, "Half-Baked Men," esp. 15–18.

111. Seward, *Reminiscences,* 83. See also Henry Wilson, *History of the Rise and Fall of the Slave Power in America* (Boston: Houghton Mifflin, 1874), 2:295. During voting on slavery in the District of Columbia in 1848, Joshua Giddings (W-OH) saw dodgers vanish for that vote and return for the next one. Giddings to Charles Sumner, December 1848, in George Washington Julian, *The Life of Joshua R. Giddings* (Chicago: A. C. McClurg, 1892), 260. See also Landis, *Northern Men,* 312.

112. *Globe,* 31st Cong., 1st Sess., September 12, 1850, 1807. Twenty-one senators didn't vote for the Fugitive Slave Act. No Northern Whigs voted for it; eight voted against it and five were absent. Three Northern Democrats voted against it, three voted for it, and nine were absent. Sean M. Theriault and Barry R. Weingast,

"Agenda Manipulation, Strategic Voting, and Legislative Details in the Compromise of 1850," in *Party, Process, and Political Change in Congress*, ed. David Brady and Matthew McCubbins, 2 vols. (Stanford, Calif.: Stanford University, 2002), 1:375; James L. Sundquist, *Dynamics of the Party System: Alignment and Realignment of Political Parties in the United States* (Washington, D.C.: Brookings Institute, 1983), 69 footnote; Holman Hamilton, *Prologue to Conflict: The Crisis and Compromise of 1850* (Lawrence: University of Kansas Press, 1964), 161–64; Landis, *Northern Men*, 31–32.

113. Jeffrey A. Jenkins and Charles Stewart III, "The Gag Rule, Congressional Politics, and the Growth of Anti-Slavery Popular Politics," paper presented at "Congress and History" conference, MIT, May 30–31, 2003, 27–28.

114. Fessenden to Ellen Fessenden, June 15, 1841, William P. Fessenden Papers, Bowdoin College. Giddings said much the same thing, complaining during debate that free-state men had been silent when insulted because they wanted to get down to business (and past the adoption of rules). *Globe*, 27th Cong., 1st Sess., June 15, 1841, 54.

115. Fessenden to Samuel Fessenden, July 29, 1841, William P. Fessenden Papers, Bowdoin College.

116. *Globe*, 27th Cong., 3rd Sess., February 13, 1843, 195 appendix; Giddings, diary entry, December 14, 1838, in Julian, *Life of Joshua R. Giddings*, 52.

117. Hale to Lucy Hale, June 10, 1844, John Parker Hale Papers, NHHS. See also Amos Tuck to John Parker Hale, January 15, 1845, ibid.; Charles D. Cleveland to Hale, March 24, 1844; S. Hale to Hale, April 12, 1850; W. Claggett to Hale, March 7, 1844, ibid.; Giddings, diary entry, December 14, 1838, in Julian, *Life of Joshua Giddings*, 52.

118. *Globe*, 25th Cong., 2nd Sess., January 11, 1838, 71 app. Discussing slavery in Florida, John C. Calhoun praised Randolph's unyielding opposition to abolitionism; Clay was urging Calhoun to "deal more calmly with all parts of the Union."

119. Ibid., 27th Cong., 3rd Sess., February 13, 1843, 195 app.

120. Hale to Lucy Hale, June 10, 1844, John Parker Hale Papers, NHHS.

121. Joseph Root (W-OH) made the comment. *Globe*, 29th Cong., 2nd Sess., February 5, 1847, 333; Hale to Lucy Hale, June 10, 1844, John Parker Hale Papers, NHHS.

122. "Northern Truckling," *Philanthropist* (Cincinnati), March 1, 1843. See also ibid., February 8, 1843. Fillmore's attacker was Henry Wise (W-VA).

123. See also Brie Anna Swenson Arnold, "'Competition for the Virgin Soil of Kansas': Gendered and Sexualized Discourse About the Kansas Crisis in Northern Popular Print and Political Culture, 1854–1860" (Ph.D. dissertation, University of Minnesota, 2008), 194–243; Lynn, "Half-Baked Men; Thomas J. Balcerski, "Intimate Contests: Manhood, Friendship, and the Coming of the Civil War" (Ph.D. dissertation, Cornell University, 2014).

124. Benton, *Thirty Years' View*, 2:618; *Globe*, 24th Cong., 1st Sess., February 12, 1836, 89–93 app.; ibid., February 29, 1836, 149 app. King was talking about both Calhoun's gaffe and a similar one made by John Black (AJ-MS) a few days later.

125. On women petitioners in the period, see esp. Zaeske, "'The South Arose as One Man'"; idem., *Signatures of Citizenship: Petitioning, Antislavery, and Women's*

Political Identity (Chapel Hill: UNC Press, 2003); Jennifer Rose Mercieca, "The Culture of Honor: How Slaveholders Responded to the Abolitionist Mail Crisis of 1835," *Rhetoric and Public Affairs* 10, no. 1 (2007): 51–76.

126. *Globe*, 24th Cong., 1st Sess., February 12, 1836, 89–93 app.; ibid., February 15, 1836, 185–86. The article was in the *Herald of Freedom* (Concord). Holt, *Franklin Pierce*, 18–19; Cole, *Jacksonian Democracy in New Hampshire*, 180–82; Nichols, *Franklin Pierce*, 83–86; Benton, *Thirty Years' View*, 2:615–18.

127. John Fairfield to Ann Fairfield, February 15, 1836, John Fairfield Papers, LC. Unfortunately, French didn't "journalize" from January through March of 1836. French, diary entry, March 20, 1836, *Witness*, 64. On Pierce's "excited" harangue, see also *New-Bedford Mercury* (Massachusetts), February 26, 1836.

128. *Connecticut Courant*, February 22, 1836.

129. *New Hampshire Patriot*, March 14, 1836.

130. French to Henry Flagg French, June 8, 1834, BBFFP.

131. French, *Chicago Democrat*, dateline January 4, 1837, BBFFP.

132. See for example the comments of Andrew Stewart (W-PA), *Globe*, 28th Cong., 1st Sess., January 20, 1844, 173; David Outlaw to Emily Outlaw, March 20, 1848, DOP.

133. Dawson to William S. Hamilton, June 29, 1824, in Joseph G. Dawson, III, *The Louisiana Governors, from Iberville to Edwards* (Baton Rouge: LSU Press, 1990), 114; Elrie Robinson, *Early Feliciana Politics* (St. Francisville, La.: *St. Francisville Democrat*, 1936), 29. On Dawson, see ibid., 12–32, 57–64. Dawson almost fought a duel using a cut-and-thrust sword, described by his pistol-preferring opponent as a three-foot-long blade. Ibid., 29.

134. *Globe*, 27th Cong., 2nd Sess., January 28, 1842, 183–83. See also *The New World* (N.Y.), January 29, 1842; *Liberator* (Boston), February 14, 1845; *Globe*, 27th Cong., 3rd Sess., February 13, 1843, 277.

135. *Globe*, 29th Cong., 1st Sess., December 10 and 11, 1845, 41–42.

136. Ibid., 27th Cong., 3rd Sess., February 13, 1843, 277.

137. Standing by Giddings were John Causin (W-MD), Solomon Foot (W-VT), Kenneth Rayner (W-NC), and Charles Hudson (W-MA); Giddings said that Causin and Rayner—the two Southerners—were armed. Standing by Dawson were John Slidell (D-LA), William Henry Stiles (D-GA), and two unnamed Democrats. Giddings says that Dawson and Causin stayed standing until he finished speaking. Giddings, *History of the Rebellion*, 241; George Washington Julian, *The Life of Joshua R. Giddings* (Chicago: A. C. McClurg, 1892), 174; *Commercial Advertiser* (N.Y.), February 8, 1845; *Salem Register*, February 10, 1845; *Huron Reflector* (Norwalk, Ohio), February 25, 1845.

138. Mercieca shows the link between the mail crisis and the culture of honor in "The Culture of Honor." See also Bertram Wyatt-Brown, "The Abolitionists' Postal Campaign of 1835," *Journal of Negro History* 50 (October 1965): 227–38; idem., *Lewis Tappan and the Evangelical War Against Slavery* (Cleveland: Case Western 1969), 149–66; Leonard Richards, *"Gentlemen of Property and Standing": Anti-Abolition Mobs in Jacksonian America* (New York: Oxford University Press, 1970); Susan Wyly-Jones, "The 1835 Anti-Abolition Meetings in the South: A New Look at the Controversy over the Abolition Postal Campaign," *Civil War*

History 47 (2001): 289–309; Lacy K. Ford, *Deliver Us from Evil: The Slavery Question in the Old South* (New York: Oxford University Press, 2009), 481–504; Mitchell Snay, *Gospel of Disunion: Religion and Separatism in the Antebellum South* (Chapel Hill: UNC Press, 1997).

139. *Globe*, 24th Cong., 1st Sess., January 7, 1836, 81.
140. Grimsted, *American Mobbing*, passim.
141. Ibid., 15, 133–34. Scholarship on the link between Southern honor and violence is vast; particularly useful in a comparative or congressional context are Dickson D. Bruce, Jr., *Violence and Culture in the Antebellum South* (Austin: University of Texas, 1979); "'Let Us Manufacture Men': Educating Elite Boys in the Early National South," in *Southern Manhood: Perspectives on Masculinity in the Old South* (Athens: University of Georgia, 2004), 22–48; Nisbett and Cohen, *Culture of Honor*; Bowman, *At the Precipice*, chapter 3; Edward L. Ayers, *Vengeance and Justice: Crime and Punishment in the 19th-Century American South* (New York: Oxford University Press, 1984); Franklin, *Militant South*.
142. William S. Powell, ed., *Dictionary of North Carolina Biography* (Chapel Hill: UNC Press, 1994), 5:133; Ernest G. Fischer, *Robert Potter: Founder of the Texas Navy* (Gretna, La.: Pelican Publishing, 1976), 22–25; Eric H. Walther, *William Lowndes Yancey and the Coming of the Civil War* (Chapel Hill: UNC Press, 2006), 47–48; Grimsted, *American Mobbing*, 90, 93.
143. Grimsted, *American Mobbing*, 99.
144. On the ethic of Southern honor overall, see esp. Bertram Wyatt-Brown, *Southern Honor: Ethics and Behavior in the Old South* (New York: Oxford University Press, 1982); Greenberg, *Honor and Slavery*; Ayers, *Vengeance and Justice*.
145. On the importance of proving bravery rather than shedding blood in dueling, see esp. Joanne B. Freeman, *Affairs of Honor: National Politics in the New Republic* (New Haven: Yale, 2001), 159–198.
146. On Northern honor, see Lorien Foote, *The Gentlemen and the Roughs: Manhood, Honor, and Violence in the Union Army* (New York: NYU, 2010), 96 and passim; Kanisom Wongsrichanalai, *Northern Character: College-Educated New Englanders, Honor, Nationalism, and Leadership in the Civil War* (New York: Fordham, 2016); Robert S. Levine, "'The Honor of New England': Nathaniel Hawthorne and the Cilley-Graves Duel of 1838," in Mayfield and Hagstette, *The Field of Honor*, 158–59; Freeman, *Affairs of Honor*.
147. "A Looker On" [French], *Chicago Democrat*, dateline February 13, 1835, BBFFP.
148. "Letter of Leonard Jarvis to his constituents of the Hancock and Washington District, in Maine" (n.p.), 15. See also H. W. Greene, "Letters Addressed to Francis O. J. Smith, Representative in Congress from Cumberland District (Me.), Being a Defence of the Writer Against the Attacks Made on Him by That Individual—And a Sketch of Mr. Smith's Political Life" (n.p., 1839), 13–14; *History of Penobscot County, Maine, with Illustrations and Biographical Sketches* (Cleveland: Williams, Chase & Co., 1882), 673–74; William Leo Lucey, *Edward Kavanagh: Catholic, Statesman, Diplomat from Maine, 1795–1844* (Worcester, Mass.: College of the Holy Cross, 1946), 114–15; "Mr. Smith's Review of the Letter of Leonard Jarvis, to his Constituents" (n.p.); *Daily Pittsburgh Gazette*, February 27, 1835, news.google.com/newspapers?nid=1125&dat=18350227&id

=JzYPAAAAIBAJ&sjid=04UDAAAAIBAJ&pg=4187,6604027, accessed June 13, 2012. See also Thomas Todd to F.O.J. Smith, January 17, 1835, F.O.J. Smith Papers, NYPL.

149. Grimsted, *American Mobbing*, 86, 13.
150. Adams, *Memoirs*, April 21, 1840, 10:271.
151. On sectional patterns or "systems" of violence, see Grimsted, *American Mobbing*; Ayers, *Vengeance and Justice*. Much scholarship on sectional modes of manhood agrees with Amy Greenberg's seminal *Manifest Manhood*, which delineates two prevailing modes of antebellum manhood, restrained and martial, the former more common among Northerners, the latter more common among Southerners. Congressional combat confirms but complicates this idea. In the national arena of Congress, comfort with personal combat gave Southerners a literal fighting advantage over Northerners that they used to full effect. But over time, Northerners became more violent, adapting their sense of manhood to the demands of the moment—a reminder of manhood's fluid and contested nature. Greenberg, *Manifest Manhood and the Antebellum American Empire* (New York: Cambridge University Press, 2005), esp. 11–14, 272–75. On sectional patterns of emotion, see Woods, *Emotional and Sectional Conflict*.
152. Grimsted, *American Mobbing*, ix. On fighting men, see for example comments of Andrew Stewart (W-PA), *Globe*, 28th Cong., 1st Sess., January 20, 1844, 173; David Outlaw to Emily Outlaw, March 20, 1848, DOP.
153. Harriet Martineau, *Retrospect of Western Travel*, 2 vols. (London: Saunders and Otley, 1838), 1:145. Her comments should be taken with a grain of salt since she was likely venting antislavery frustration at doughfaces.
154. Harriet Martineau, *Society in America* (Paris: Baudry's European Library, 1837), 2:92. See esp. Ayers, *Vengeance and Justice*. Grimsted aptly sums up the Southern mode of justice: "Being a Southern rioter meant seldom having to say you were sorry." Grimsted, *American Mobbing*, 13–16. On Southern violence in a political context, see Dickson Bruce, *Violence and Culture in the Antebellum South* (Austin: University of Texas Press, 1979); John Hope Franklin, *The Militant South, 1800–1861* (Cambridge, Mass.: Harvard University Press, 1956); Sheldon Hackney, "Southern Violence," *American Historical Review* 74 (1969): 906–25; John S. Reed, "Below the Smith and Wesson Line: Southern Violence," in *One South: An Ethnic Approach to Regional Culture* (Baton Rouge: LSU Press, 1982), 139–53; Kenneth Greenberg, *Masters and Statesmen: The Political Culture of American Slavery* (Baltimore: Johns Hopkins, 1985); Olsen, *Political Culture and Secession in Mississippi*; Woods, *Emotional and Sectional Conflict*; as well as Wyatt-Brown's seminal *Southern Honor*; idem., *Shaping of Southern Culture*. On Northern collective violence and institutional solutions, see Weinbaum, *Mobs and Demagogues*.
155. *Globe*, 30th Cong., 1st Sess., March 10, 1848, 454–55; *National Era*, March 16, 1848, 43. The two publications have identical accounts of Wick's speech, but only the *National Era* gives a full account of the fight. George Jones (D-TN) and Hugh Haralson (D-GA) were the two combatants.
156. My thanks to Tony Rotundo for suggesting this pattern.
157. On the eve of the Civil War, slaves were 12.7 percent of the population in border

states; 30 percent in the middle South; and 58.5 percent in the lower South. Of border-state blacks 21.2 percent were free, as opposed to only 1.5 percent of lower-South blacks. Freehling, *South Against the South*, 18–19, 24; idem., *Road to Disunion*, 33–35.

158. This section is particularly indebted to Freehling, *South Against the South*, 23.

159. On Whigs and violence, see also Howe, *Whigs*, 128. Delaware and Kentucky were Whig-dominated and Maryland was consistently mixed.

160. Compromisers included John Crittenden (W-KY), Cost Johnson (W-MD), Louis McLane (J-DE), "Great Pacificator" Charles Fenton Mercer (W-VA), and "Great Compromiser" Henry Clay (W-KY). On Clay, compromise, and culture, see also Howe, *Whigs*, 123–49. To see him in action as the "universal pacificator," see *Brattleboro Messenger*, March 7, 1834, and *Connecticut Gazette*, March 12, 1834, describing a near duel between George Poindexter (AJ-MS) and John Forsyth (J-GA). Mercer lived in Loudon County, not far from Washington. For "the great pacificator," see *The Liberator*, May 13, 1836; "Funeral Oration Delivered at the Capitol in Washington over the Body of Hon. Jonathan Cilley, With a Full Account of the Late Duel, Containing Many Facts Never Before Published" (New York: Wiley & Putnam, 1838), 24; and "Nominis in Umbra" [French], *Chicago Democrat*, dateline February 23, 1838, BBFFP, which notes that Mercer is the "general peace maker in the House" during disputes that seem "likely to end in a duel." On Johnson, see "The Polite Duel," Thomas William and Folger McKinsey, *History of Frederick County Maryland*, 2 vols. (Baltimore: Genealogical Publishing Co., 1979), 1:308–309. On "border pacifiers," see also Freehling, *Road to Disunion*, 432.

161. See for example French, diary entry, January 22, 1838, *Witness*, 74.

162. French to Henry Flagg French, March 9, 1834, BBFFP; *Journal of the Senate*, 23rd Cong., 1st Sess., February 28, 1834, 163; *Globe*, 23rd Cong., 1st Sess., February 28, 1834, 208; *Salem Gazette*, March 7, 1834; *Pittsfield Sun*, March 13, 1834. Poindexter was objecting to Jackson's removal of funds from a Mississippi bank.

163. "Nominis in Umbra" [French], "Washington Correspondence, No. 4," *Chicago Democrat*, dateline January 19, 1838, clipping in BBFFP. Jonathan Cilley told his wife that people expected a duel; Cilley to Deborah Cilley, January 16, 1838, in Eve Anderson, *A Breach of Privilege: Cilley Family Letters, 1820–1867* (Spruce Head, Maine: Seven Coin Press, 2002), 146.

164. On parties as a counterbalance, see esp. Michael F. Holt, *The Political Crisis of the 1850s* (New York: Norton, 1978).

3. THE PULL AND POWER OF VIOLENCE

1. John Wentworth, *Congressional Reminiscences: Adams, Benton, Calhoun, Clay, and Webster* (Chicago: Fergus Printing Company, 1882), 13.

2. French to Henry Flagg French, April 24, 1844, BBFFP. Emphasis in original. The gun was fired during a fight between John White (W-KY) and George Rathbun (D-NY), who were arguing about the presidential contender Henry Clay. *Globe*, 28th Cong., 1st Sess., April 23, 1844, 551–54, 577–80; 28th Cong., 1st Sess., H. Rpt. 470, May 6, 1844, "Rencounter Between Messrs. White and Rathbun." The

House voted to give Wirt $150 in compensation, but he never fully recovered from the wound. 34th Cong., 3rd Sess., H. Rpt. 29, December 19, 1856, "John L. Wirt."

3. For contemporary accounts of the Graves-Cilley duel, in addition to French's various writings and H. Rpt. 825 (mentioned below), see *Niles' National Register*, July 27, 1839; "Funeral Oration Delivered . . . Over the Body of Hon. Jonathan Cilley"; "Autobiography," in John Carl Parish, *George Wallace Jones* (Iowa City: State Historical Society of Iowa, 1912), 157–70; E. M. Boyle, "Jonathan Cilley of Maine and William J. Graves of Kentucky, Representatives in Congress. An Historical Duel, 1838, as Narrated by Gen. Geo. W. Jones, Cilley's Second," *Maine Historical and Genealogical Recorder* 6 (1889), 392. For accounts of Cilley's college friend Horatio King, see "History of the Duel Between Jonathan Cilley and William J. Graves," *Collections and Proceedings of the Maine Historical Society* 2 (April 1892): 127–48; King, *Turning on the Light: A Dispassionate Survey of President Buchanan's Administration, from 1860 to Its Close* (Philadelphia: J. B. Lippincott, 1895), 287–316; "Death of Cilley," *United States Magazine and Democratic Review* 4 (November–December 1840): 196–200. See also Bruce R. Kirby's excellent "The Limits of Honor: Party, Section, and Dueling in the Jacksonian Congress" (M.A. thesis, George Mason University, 1997), 133–84; Don C. Seitz, *Famous American Duels* (New York: Thomas Y. Crowell, 1929), 251–83; Myra L. Spaulding, "Dueling in the District of Columbia," *Records of the Columbia Historical Society* 29–30 (1928): 186–210; Lorenzo Sabine, *Notes on Duels and Duelling* (Boston: Crosby, Nichols, and Co., 1855), 89–108; Eve Anderson, *A Breach of Privilege: Cilley Family Letters, 1820–1867* (Spruce Head, Maine: Seven Coin Press, 2002); Jeffrey L. Pasley, "Minnows, Spies, and Aristocrats: The Social Crisis in Congress in the Age of Martin Van Buren," *JER* 27 (Winter 2007): 599–653; Ryan Chamberlain, *Pistols, Politics and the Press: Dueling in 19th-Century American Journalism* (Jefferson, N.C.: McFarland, 2009), 55–62; Robert S. Levine, "'The Honor of New England': Nathaniel Hawthorne and the Cilley-Graves Duel of 1838," in *The Field of Honor: Essays on Southern Character and American Identity*, John Mayfield and Todd Hagstette, eds. (Columbia: University of South Carolina Press, 2017), 147–62; Roger Ginn, *New England Must Not Be Trampled On: The Tragic Death of Jonathan Cilley* (Camden, Maine: DownEast Books, 2016). My thanks to Mr. Ginn for sending me his book.

4. French, diary entry, February 28, March 10 and 12, April 4 and 27, 1838, *Witness*, 75–80. His drawing appears in his diary entry of April 4, BBFFP.

5. *National Freemason* 2, no. 6 (November 1864); ibid., 8 (February 1865).

6. On "rough play," see Richard Stott, *Jolly Fellows: Male Milieus in Nineteenth-Century America* (Baltimore: Johns Hopkins, 2009).

7. 25th Cong., 2nd Sess., H. Rpt. 825, April 21, 1838, "Death of Mr. Cilley—Duel" (hereafter cited as H. Rpt. 825).

8. French, diary entry, February 28, 1838, *Witness*, 75.

9. French to Daniel French, January 30, 1835, BBFFP.

10. French, diary entry, March 18, 1842, *Witness*, 139.

11. Ibid., February 22, 1848, 199.

12. Ibid., April 15, 1865, 469–71. Also ibid., April 15, 1866, 507.

13. French thought that he had witnessed Cilley's acceptance of Graves's challenge, but Cilley received it at his boardinghouse. French, "Congressional Reminiscences," *National Freemason* 2, no. 6 (November 1864).

14. Most details in this paragraph are from ibid.; ibid., 8 (February 1865); French, diary entry, February 28, March 10, April 4, 1838, *Witness*, 75–76, 78–79; "Nominis in Umbra" [French], Washington Correspondent No. 10 and No. 12, dateline February 23, 1838, and undated, *Chicago Democrat*, BBFFP.

15. French, "Congressional Reminiscences," *National Freemason* 2, no. 6 (November 1864); Caleb Cushing to John Cushing, July 7, 1836, in John M. Belohlavek, *Broken Glass: Caleb Cushing and the Shattering of the Union* (Kent, Ohio: Kent State University, 2005), 92.

16. "Washington Correspondence No. 12," *Chicago Democrat*, [April 1838], BBFFP; French, "Congressional Reminiscences," *National Freemason* 2, no. 6 (November 1864).

17. Cilley served from September 4 to October 16, 1837, and December 4, 1837, to February 24, 1838. French, "Congressional Reminiscences," *National Freemason* 2, no. 6 (November 1864); ibid., 8 (February 1865); Cilley to Deborah Cilley, September 24, 1837, in Anderson, *Breach of Privilege*, 120. On Cilley, see Anderson, *Breach of Privilege*; Nathaniel Hawthorne, "Biographical Sketch of Jonathan Cilley," *The United States Magazine and Democratic Review* 3 (September 1838): 69–77; King, *Turning On the Light*, 287–316; Cyrus Eaton, *History of Thomaston, Rockland, and South Thomaston, Maine, from Their First Exploration A.D. 1605; With Family Genealogies*, 2 vols. (Hallowell: Masters, Smith, 1865), 1: passim (esp. 391–93); *Memoirs and Services of Three Generations* (Rockland, Maine: reprint from *Courier-Gazette*, 1909). On his fighting temper, see also John Ruggles to F.O.J. Smith, August 17, 1833, F.O.J. Smith Papers, NYPL (which notes the "violence" and "bitterness of his invective"); and an anonymous contemporary biographical sketch in the Cilley Biographical File at Bowdoin College Library, which mentions his "harsher traits" and "almost terrible energy."

18. General Joseph Cilley appears in Trumbull's "The Surrender of General Burgoyne." On the portrait, see Cilley to Deborah Cilley, January 16, 1838, in Anderson, *Breach of Privilege*, 144. Bradbury Cilley (F-NH) was a representative from 1813 to 1815; Jonathan's older brother Joseph (Liberty-NH) was a senator from June 13, 1846, to March 3, 1847, filling the vacancy caused by the resignation of Levi Woodbury. See also *Memoirs and Services of Three Generations*.

19. Cilley to Deborah Cilley, January 13, 1833, in Anderson, *Breach of Privilege*, 84.

20. Hawthorne, journal entry, July 28, 1837, *Passages from the American Note-Books of Nathaniel Hawthorne, vol. 9 of The Works of Nathaniel Hawthorne*, 12 vols. (Boston: Houghton, Mifflin, 1883), 9:75–77. Along similar lines, after the duel, Cilley's brother-in-law Hezekiah Prince, Jr., described him as "prompt, independent, and even obstinate," noting that the only way to understand his actions was to understand his character. Prince to Franklin Pierce, undated, in F. B. Wilkie, "Geo. W. Jones," *Iowa Historical Record* 2 (April 1887), 446.

21. French, "Congressional Reminiscences," *National Freemason*, vol. 2, no. 6 (November 1864).

22. Cilley to Deborah Cilley, September 24, 1837, in Anderson, *Breach of Privilege*, 120.

23. Cilley to Deborah Cilley, January 12, 1838, ibid., 143.

24. On Wise, see Simpson, *A Good Southerner*; Barton H. Wise, *The Life of Henry A. Wise of Virginia, 1806–1876* (New York: Macmillan, 1899); James Pinkney Hambleton, "A Biographical Sketch of Henry A. Wise, with a History of the Political Campaign in Virginia in 1855" (Richmond, Va.: J. W. Randolph, 1856); Clement Eaton, "Henry A. Wise, a Liberal of the Old South," *Journal of Southern History* 7, no. 4 (November 1941): 482–94; Clement Eaton, "Henry A. Wise and the Virginia Fire Eaters of 1856," *Mississippi Valley Historical Review* 21, no. 4 (March 1935): 495–512; Henry A. Wise, *Seven Decades of the Union* (Philadelphia: J. B. Lippincott, 1872); William A. Link, *Roots of Secession: Slavery and Politics in Antebellum Virginia*, passim. For a different side of Wise, see Clayton Torrence, ed., "From the Society's Collections: Letters of Mrs. Ann (Jennings) Wise to Her Husband, Henry A. Wise," *Virginia Magazine of History and Biography* 58, no. 4 (October 1950): 492–515; John Sergeant Wise (Wise's son), *The End of an Era* (New York: Houghton, Mifflin, 1902).

25. French, diary entry, July 12, 1838, *Witness*, 90.

26. Wise, *Life of Henry Wise*, 13.

27. Ann Jennings Wise to Wise, January 4(?), 1836, in Torrence, ed., "Letters of Mrs. Ann (Jennings) Wise to Her Husband, Henry A. Wise," 512.

28. Buckingham, *America*, 2:324; [Memorandum of life in Washington], 21, Daniel R. Goodloe Papers, UNC.

29. *Globe*, 26th Cong., 2nd Sess., February 24, 1841, 206.

30. French, diary entry, March 12, 1838, *Witness*, 77.

31. Cilley to Deborah Cilley, January 16, 1838, in Anderson, *Breach of Privilege*, 146.

32. Dickens to Albany Fonblanque, March 12, 1842, *The Pilgrim Edition of the Letters of Charles Dickens*, 12 vols. (Oxford, U.K.: Clarendon Press, 1974), 3:118.

33. "Address of Mr. Wise, Representative in Congress from the State of Virginia, to His Constituents," in *Washington Intelligencer*, March 16, 1838.

34. *Daily National Intelligencer*, March 9, 1839, reporting Wise's speech of February 21.

35. *Daily National Intelligencer* (Washington), January 25, 1838; *Globe*, 25th Cong., 1st Sess., January 23, 1838, 127; Adams, *Memoirs*, January 23, 1838, 9:475.

36. *Globe*, 25th Cong., 2nd Sess., February 12, 1838, 173. This turned out to be Senator John Ruggles (D-ME), Cilley's former patron and next-door neighbor turned enemy back in Maine. Convinced that Cilley didn't support Ruggles's run for the Senate in 1832, Ruggles and his supporters had dedicated themselves to destroying Cilley's career. Now Ruggles was charged with using his influence to help a friend get a patent in exchange for a cut of the profits. On the Ruggles dispute, see Ginn, *New England Must Not Be Trampled On*, 65–74, 140–45; Senate Report No. 377, "Report on the Investigation of John Ruggles, Senator from Maine," 25th Cong., 2nd Sess., April 12, 1838.

37. *Globe*, 25th Cong., 2nd Sess., February 12, 1838, 174–75.

38. Ibid., 176.

39. "Nominis in Umbra" [French], "Washington Correspondence," *Chicago Democrat*, dateline February 12, 1838, clipping in BBFFP.

40. Silbey, *American Political Nation*.

41. Greenleaf Cilley to Jonathan Cilley, January 21, 1838; Jonathan Cilley to Greenleaf Cilley, January 26, 1838, in Anderson, *Breach of Privilege*, 107–108.
42. French, diary entry, January 10, 1842, *Witness*, 135. Although a Whig, Tyler had vetoed a bank bill because it violated his sense of states' rights. On "heading Captain Tyler," see Dan Monroe, *The Republican Vision of John Tyler* (College Station: Texas A&M, 2003), 101–106.
43. *Niles' National Register* (Washington, D.C.), August 4, 1838; *Extra Globe* (Washington, D.C.), July 16, 1838.
44. Ibid., *The Times* (Hartford); *New Hampshire Gazette* (Portsmouth), July 24, 1838.
45. *Globe*, 26th Cong., 1st Sess., April 27, 1840, 362–63. Black had attacked Whigs for insisting on reduction, reform, and less government spending, and then squawking when a Whig committee chair's salary would be reduced as a result.
46. On the hold of manliness, loyalty, and "in-group honor," see Patricia Roberts-Miller, *Fanatical Schemes: Proslavery Rhetoric and the Tragedy of Consensus* (Tuscaloosa: University of Alabama Press, 2009), 194.
47. John Fairfield to Anna Fairfield, June 1, 1838, John Fairfield Papers, LC. On their fight generally, see *Globe*, 25th Congress, 2nd Sess., June 1, 1838, 422–23; William Cabell Rives to his wife, June 2, 1838, William Cabell Rives Papers, LC; Isaac Fletcher to General E. B. Chase, June 5, 1838, MSS 838355, Dartmouth College; Kirby, "Limits of Honor," 199–200.
48. Balie Peyton to Henry Wise, June 17, 1838, in *The Collector: A Magazine for Autograph and Historical Collectors* 20 (January 1907): 26–27.
49. This isn't to say that manly honor was a Southern construct or that non-Southerners were unmanly, oblivious to honor culture, or nonviolent by nature. Rather, modes of fighting and ideas of manhood differed in North, South, and West, and the *code duello*—a defined set of rites and rituals centered on the practice of dueling—was seen as explicitly and defiantly Southern for much of the nineteenth century. During that same period, Northerners increasingly found the code both alien and extreme, though not entirely unfamiliar; indeed, Northern moral and sectional discomfort with dueling, joined with their understanding of dueling's implications, was precisely what gave the code of honor its power in the national arena of Congress. See notes 141, 146, and 151 in chapter 2.
50. *Daily National Intelligencer* (Washington), February 16, 1838; "Washington Correspondent," *Chicago Democrat*, undated [April 1838], BBFFP.
51. On the importance of manliness in Southern rhetoric, see Roberts-Miller, *Fanatical Schemes*, 103–26; on Wise as a manly champion of the South, see ibid., 203.
52. Jones told the investigative committee that Cilley had been handed an article from a Baltimore paper dated February 22 or 23. Based on his summary, this one seems likely. *Baltimore Sun*, February 22, 1838; H. Rpt. 825, 49. See also *Baltimore Sun*, February 23, 1838.
53. *Register of Debates*, 25th Cong., 1st Sess., September 23, 1837, 766.
54. *Globe*, 25th Cong., 2nd Sess., December 4, 1837, 284.

55. H. Rpt. 825, testimony of Duncan (quoting Pierce), 102–103; ibid., testimony of Pierce, 121. On Northern ambivalence about dueling in this period, see Foote, *Gentlemen and the Roughs*, 93–118.

56. For example, William Duer (W-NY) had Charles Conrad (W-LA) by his side after Richard Kidder Meade (D-VA) challenged him in 1849; Jonathan Cilley was advised by Jesse Bynum (D-NC) among others when William Graves (W-KY) challenged him in 1838; George Kremer (J-PA) was advised by George McDuffie (D-SC) among others during his 1825 honor dispute with Henry Clay (W-KY); Leonard Jarvis (J-ME) chose Robert Lytle (J-OH)—who spent his young adulthood in Kentucky—as his second when he challenged F.O.J. Smith (J-ME) to a duel in 1835, and Smith chose James Love (AJ-KY) as his second; and Kentucky-born Francis Blair (R-MO) advised New York–born Charles James, Anson Burlingame's second, in his near-duel with Preston Brooks in 1856. James almost refused the job because he knew "almost nothing of the code." "Passing of a Remarkable Man," *Washington Post*, October 27, 1901, 29.

57. Bertram Wyatt-Brown, "Andrew Jackson's Honor," in Wyatt-Brown, *Shaping of Southern Culture*, 56–80; John William Ward, *Andrew Jackson: Symbol for an Age* (New York: Oxford University Press, 1955). On the nonenforcement of anti-dueling laws, see esp. Matthew A. Byron, "Crime and Punishment: The Impotency of Dueling Laws in the United States" (Ph.D. dissertation, University of Arkansas, 2008); Harwell Wells, "The End of the Affair? Anti-Dueling Laws and Social Norms in Antebellum America," *Vanderbilt Law Review* 54, 1805–47 (see esp. 1831–37).

58. *Globe*, 25th Cong., 2nd Sess., April 5, 1838, 282. On dueling as a civilizing force, see John Hope Franklin, *The Militant South: 1800–1861* (Chicago: University of Illinois, 2002; orig. ed. 1956), 59–62; Wyatt-Brown, *Southern Honor*, 353.

59. *Daily National Intelligencer*, March 9, 1839, reporting February 21, 1839, speech of Wise.

60. Franklin, *Militant South*, 61.

61. Frederic Hudson, *Journalism in the United States, from 1690 to 1872* (New York: Harper & Brothers, 1873), 353–54; W. Stephen Belko, *The Invincible Duff Green: Whig of the West* (Columbia: University of Missouri Press, 2006), 245–46. Green raised the matter in his paper two years later when he published (and sneered at) Webb's private letter discussing the incident. Webb tried to challenge Green to a duel, but when Green cowhided Webb's second, Webb posted Green as a "SCOUNDREL and a COWARD" in broadsides pasted all over Washington. See Webb, "To the Public" (Washington, D.C., 1832), American Broadsides and Ephemera, infoweb.newsbank.com/iw-search/we/HistArchive/?p_product=ABEA&p_theme =abea&p_nbid=C4AB50NEMTMyMDUwODM2OS40MzY1MTE6MToxMzo xMzAuMTMyLjIxLjc3&p_action=doc&p_queryname=4412&p_docref =v2:0F2B1FCB879B099B@ABEA-10F453EC151070D8@4412-10DEEFA 6F1F28B78@1, accessed November 5, 2011.

62. *Daily National Intelligencer*, September 12 and 13, 1837; *Globe*, September 13, 1837; *Morning Herald* (N.Y.), September 13, 1837; *Pennsylvania Inquirer and Daily Courier*, September 14, 1837.

63. Report, testimony of Schaumburg, 86. Emphasis in original.

64. "The Cilley Duel," *Niles' National Register*, July 27, 1839. The quote comes from a speech by Graves to his constituents in the wake of the duel.
65. H. Rpt. 825, testimony of Wise, 55.
66. Ibid., testimony of Bynum, 66.
67. Ibid., testimony of Graves, 127; *Niles' National Register*, July 27, 1839. For the note, see H. Rpt. 825, 40; Graves presented the committee with the letter, which Wise endorsed on the back as Graves's second, noting that he hadn't known that Graves had borne the letter until after he had tried to deliver it to Cilley.
68. Details in these paragraphs are from H. Rpt. 825. See chapter 5 for more on street fights as northern duels.
69. Adams, diary entry, June 29, 1840, *Memoirs*, 10:324.
70. H. Rpt. 825, 126–27.
71. Shelden, *Washington Brotherhood*, discusses this extensively.
72. Ibid., 105; Thomas Hart Benton to Editor of *Globe*, March 6, 1838, *Washington Globe*, March 7, 1838; *Niles' Weekly Register*, March 10, 1838; *Farmer's Cabinet* (Amherst, N.H.), March 16, 1836. Three of Cilley's advisors—George Jones (delegate-WI), Alexander Duncan (D-OH), and Jesse Bynum (D-NC)—sought Benton's advice on their way to the dueling ground; Benton thought that because Cilley and Graves were family men with no ill will between them, the matter should be settled without gunplay or at most with one exchange of fire. H. Rpt. 825, 105.
73. On Clay's involvement, see Melba Porter Hay, "Henry Clay and the Graves-Cilley Duel," in *A Mythic Land Apart: Reassessing Southerners and Their History*, ed. John David Smith, Thomas H. Appleton, and Charles Pierce Roland (Westport, Conn.: Greenwood Press, 1997), 57–80; as well as Wise's later statement and the resulting correspondence. See chapter 4 for details.
74. Jones, "Autobiography," in Parish, *George Wallace Jones*, 158.
75. Graves to Henry Clay, February 16, 1842, *The Papers of Henry Clay: The Whig Leader, January 1, 1837–December 31, 1843*, ed. Robert Seager II (Lexington: University Press of Kentucky, 1988), 9:657.
76. On privilege of debate, see Joseph Story, *Commentaries on the Constitution of the United States*, ed. Thomas M. Cooley, 2 vols. (Clark, N.J.: Lawbook Exchange, 2008: orig. ed. 1833), 1:610–12.
77. For their correspondence, see *Daily National Intelligencer*, September 13, 1837, and the *Globe* of the same day.
78. H. Rpt. 825, 10; ibid., testimony of Wise, 59, 64; ibid., testimony of Jones, 46–47.
79. Ibid.
80. Webb to unknown, February 28, 1836, *Niles' National Register*, March 10, 1838. Emphasis in original.
81. On the complications of dishonoring Graves, see Chamberlain, *Pistols, Politics and the Press*, 57–58.
82. H. Rpt. 825, testimony of Duncan, 103.
83. Ibid., testimony of Schaumburg, 87.
84. Boyle, "Jonathan Cilley of Maine and William J. Graves of Kentucky," *Maine Historical and Genealogical Recorder* 6 (1889): 391.

85. Cilley to Deborah Cilley, February 22, 1838, in Anderson, *Breach of Privilege*, 154.
86. Graves to Cilley, February 23, 1838; Cilley to Graves, February 23, 1838, *Congressional Globe*, 25th Cong., 2nd Sess., 330.
87. Calhoon and Hawes testified that Crittenden was chosen because he was "known to the nation"; because "his efforts to compromise the matter would be more likely than ours to prove successful"; and because if no compromise was reached, his presence would suggest that everything had been done to preserve Graves's life. H. Rpt. 825, testimony of Calhoon and Hawes, 131–32.
88. Graves to Henry Clay, February 16, 1842, *Papers of Henry Clay*, 9:656–57.
89. On Jones's duels, see his obituary in the *Daily Picayune* (New Orleans), July 27, 1896. On Schaumburg's status as a notorious duelist, see H. Rpt. 825, 170; "Ye Ancient Chivalry," *Macon Telegraph and Messenger*, June 14, 1882; John Augustin, "The Oaks. The Old Duelling-Grounds of New Orleans" (1887), in *The Louisiana Book: Selection from the Literature of the State*, ed. Thomas M'Caleb (New Orleans: R. F. Straughan, 1894), 80. On Pierce noticing him on the street, see H. Rpt. 825, testimony of Pierce, 122. According to Jones, Lewis Linn (D-MO) recommended Jones as Cilley's second; Jones's autobiography, Parish, *George Wallace Jones*, 160.
90. [William Graves's address to his constituents], *Niles' National Register*, July 27, 1839.
91. George W. Jones to H. Prince, March 17, 1838, in Anderson, *Breach of Privilege*, 178.
92. The next few pages draw on testimony of various duel participants in H. Rpt. 825.
93. Ibid., testimony of Menefee, 79.
94. Ibid., 58, 79.
95. Ibid., testimony of Wise, 60.
96. Ibid., 9.
97. Ibid., testimony of Bynum, March 11, 1838, 71.
98. Ibid., testimony of Duncan, 107.
99. Ibid.
100. Wise to Pierce, June 22, 1852, Franklin Pierce Papers, LC; John C. Wise, *Recollections of Thirteen Presidents* (New York: Doubleday, Page, 1906), 35–39.
101. Nominis in Umbra [French], "Washington Correspondence," dateline February 23, 1838, *Chicago Democrat*, BBFFP.
102. Adams to Charles Francis Adams, March 19, 1838, *Proceedings of the Massachusetts Historical Society* (Boston, 1899), June Meeting, 1898, 288–92, quote on 289.
103. H. Rpt. 825, testimony of Fairfield, 144.
104. French, "Congressional Reminiscences," *National Freemason* 2, no. 8 (February 1865).
105. The friends were Charles King and Reverdy Johnson. Statement of Charles King, February 4, 1842, in *Clay Papers*, 9:644 footnote; also Clay to Webb, January 30, 1842, ibid., 9:643–44; Clay to Wise, February 28, 1842, ibid., 9:662–63. Some of Graves's advisors slowed down his search for a rifle in the hope of devising a compromise; sadly, Jones's helpful offer of a rifle foiled this plan. H. Rpt. 825, testimony of Wise, 57.

106. Most details in this paragraph are from "Congressional Reminiscences," 8 (February 1865); French, diary entry, February 28, March 10, April 4, 1838, *Witness*, 75–76, 78–79; "Nominis in Umbra" [French], Washington Correspondent No. 10 and No. 12, dateline February 23, 1838, and undated, *Chicago Democrat*, BBFFP.
107. "Funeral Oration Delivered at the Capitol," 13.
108. French, diary entry, February 28, 1838, *Witness*, 75.
109. Condemning the hypocrisy of Cilley's funeral a year later, Wise said, "[I]f I ever fall on the field of honor whilst a member of this House, I now beseech my friends . . . not to permit a *political parade* to be made over my dead body." Speech of February 21, 1839, *Daily National Intelligencer*, March 9, 1839. Emphasis in original.
110. [Washington] *Niles' National Register*, March 24, 1838. My thanks to R. B. Bernstein for bringing this to my attention. See also John Quincy Adams to Charles Francis Adams, March 19, 1838, *Proceedings of the Massachusetts Historical Society*, 291.
111. John Quincy Adams to Charles Francis Adams, March 19, 1838, *Proceedings of the Massachusetts Historical Society*, 290.
112. "Nominis in Umbra" [French], "Washington Correspondent," dateline March 3, 1838, *Chicago Democrat*, March 21, 1838, clipping in BBFFP.
113. Dolley Madison to Elizabeth Coles, February 21 and 26, 1838, *The Papers of Dolley Madison Digital Edition*, ed. Holly C. Shulman (Charlottesville: UVA Press, 2008), rotunda.upress.virginia.edu/founders/DYMN-01-05-02-0344, accessed October 5, 2011.
114. *New York Courier and Enquirer*, February 26, 1838; *Waldo Patriot* (Belfast, Maine), March 9, 1838.
115. They fought in Delaware. New York's anti-dueling law applied to New Yorkers who left the state. According to Byron, there had been only two previous indictments under that law, which dated back to 1817; both offenders were pardoned. Byron, "Crime and Punishment," 86–88. On the duel, see also Seitz, *Famous American Duels*, 283–309; James L. Crouthamel, *James Watson Webb: A Biography* (Middletown, Conn.: Wesleyan, 1969), 74–76; Henry Clay to James Watson Webb, February 7, 1842, *Papers of Henry Clay*, 9:648; correspondence in the Webb Papers; and a remarkable commemorative volume given to Webb by Governor William Seward, containing accounts of Webb's trial and petitions for his release. James Watson Webb Papers, Sterling Memorial Library, Yale University.
116. Frederick Marryat, *A Diary in America, with Remarks on Its Institutions*, 3 vols. (London: Longman, Orme, Brown, Green, & Longman's, 1839), 2:16.
117. In February 1841, William King (D-AL) challenged Henry Clay (W-KY) to a duel and Clay accepted, but the matter was mediated behind closed doors, though not before both men were arrested and released on bond. *The New Yorker*, March 13, 1841; Adams, diary entry, March 9, 1841, *Memoirs*, 10:441–42; Gobright, *Recollection of Men and Things*, 44–49; Forney, *Anecdotes*, 300; Perley, *Reminiscences*, 1:259–60; *The New World* (N.Y.), March 13, 1841; and for the bond posted against Clay, see *Churchman's Weekly Herald and Philanthropist*, September 4, 1844. The *Globe* mentions only a "very unpleasant collision." *Globe*, 26th Cong., 2nd Sess., March 14, 1841, 256–57; for the collision, see ibid., March 9, 1841,

248. The next duel was in spring 1842, when Thomas Marshall (W-KY) challenged James Watson Webb. The next fistfight, on June 1, 1838, pitted Hopkins Turney (D-TN) against John Bell (W-TN).

118. Henry Flagg French to Benjamin Brown French, March 4, 1838, BBFFP.

119. J. Emery to John Fairfield, March 19, 1838, John Fairfield Papers, LC.

120. For a sampling of the petitions, see H. Rpt. 825, 161–62, 174–75.

121. *New-Hampshire Patriot and State Gazette* (Concord), March 5, 1838.

122. *United States Magazine and Democratic Review* 1 (March 1838): 493–508. See also Robert Sampson, *John L. O'Sullivan and His Times* (Kent, Ohio: Kent State University Press, 2003), 54–57.

123. *New Hampshire Patriot and State Gazette* (Concord), March 5, 1838; *Waldo Patriot* (Belfast, Maine), March 9, 1838; *Portsmouth* (N.H.) *Journal of Literature and Politics*, March 10, 1838.

124. Crittenden to Leslie L. Coombs, March 20, 1838, in *The Life of John J. Crittenden, with Selections from His Correspondence and Speeches*, ed. Chapman Coleman, 2 vols. (Philadelphia: J. B. Lippincott, 1871), 1:107–8.

125. Franklin, *Militant South*, 61–62.

126. Wise insisted that he had done all he could to prevent a fight; he thought Cilley's Democratic friends had prevented him from putting in writing what he'd said to Graves in person.

127. Thomas Hart Benton to Editor of the *Globe*, March 6, 1838, *Washington Globe*, March 7, 1838; *Niles' Weekly Register*, March 10, 1838; *Farmer's Cabinet* (Amherst, N.H.), March 16, 1836. See also H. Rpt. 825, 105. Benton may have been more involved than he admitted. In his autobiography written years later, Jones recalled seeing Pierce and Benton conferring in the room of Lewis Linn (D-MO), and hearing Benton say, "They can't object to the rifle and you can refer them to the cases of Moore and Letcher, of Kentucky, and others." Linn and Jones were messmates. Jones's autobiography, in Parish, *George Wallace Jones*, 160.

128. "Address of Mr. Wise," *National Intelligencer*, March 16, 1838; "The Cilley Duel," *Niles' National Register*, July 27, 1839; "Letter from Col. Webb," February 28, 1838, *Niles' National Register*, March 3, 1838; Pierce to Isaac Toucey, March 12, 1838, published as "Mr. Pierce's Letter," *New Hampshire Statesman and State Journal*, March 31, 1838; and *Niles' National Register*, March 24, 1838 (among other places).

129. "Address of Mr. Wise," *National Intelligencer*, March 16, 1838; "The Cilley Duel," *Niles' National Register*, July 27, 1839.

130. Crittenden to Leslie L. Coombs, March 20, 1838, in Coleman, *Life of John J. Crittenden*, 108. Emphasis in original.

131. My reasoning here was inspired by Hanna F. Pitkin, *The Concept of Representation* (Berkeley: University of California Press, 1972).

132. H. Rpt. 825, testimony of Pierce, 121–22; ibid., testimony of Schaumburg, 86–87; ibid., testimony of Williams, 142.

133. "Nominis in Umbra" [French], "Washington Correspondence" [ca. February 1838], *Chicago Democrat*, BBFFP; French, diary entry, February 28, 1838, *Witness*, 75; "Washington Correspondent," dateline February 12 and 23, 1838, *Chicago Democrat* clipping in BBFFP; *Baltimore Age*, February 24, 1838.

134. French to unknown correspondent, January 29, 1837, BBFFP. See also *Globe*, 24th Cong., 2nd Sess., January 27, 1837, 135. Emphasis in original.
135. French, diary entry, March 10, 1838, *Witness*, 76.
136. Adams to Charles Francis Adams, February 12, 1838, in Kirby, "Limits of Honor," 145. Adams was praising Maine-born Seargent Smith Prentiss (W-MS).
137. Francis Pickens to James Henry Hammond, March 5, 1838, in Kirby, "Limits of Honor," 175. Franklin Elmore (SRD-SC) likewise praised Cilley as "a true friend of the South." Elmore to James Henry Hammond, April 2, 1838, ibid., 147.
138. See for example J. Emery to John Fairfield, March 19, 1838, John Fairfield Papers, LC. See also Levine, "Honor of New England," 153–60.
139. *Globe*, 25th Cong., 2nd Sess., February 26, 1838, 199, 200. John Fairfield (D-ME) announced Cilley's death in the House; Reuel Williams (D-ME) announced it in the Senate.
140. Adams to Charles Francis Adams, March 19, 1838, *Proceedings of the Massachusetts Historical Society* (Boston, 1899), June Meeting, 1898, 288–92, quote on 292.
141. "Nominis in Umbra" [French], "Washington Correspondence," dateline March 15, 1838, clipping in BBFFP; *New Hampshire Patriot* (Concord), April 9, 1838.
142. [French], dateline March 15, 1838, clipping in BBFFP.
143. See photo at www.findagrave.com/cgi-bin/fg.cgi?page=gr&GRid=39386650, accessed October 2, 2011.
144. *Globe*, 25th Cong., 2nd Sess., February 28, 1838, 200–202.
145. The lone Rhode Island Whig was Robert B. Cranston. Of the forty-nine negative votes, five were from Northerners (in addition to Cranston, three from New York and one from New Jersey), seven were from Northwestern states (Illinois and Indiana), and eight Southern votes were Democratic. *Journal of the House*, vol. 32, February 28, 1838, 506–507.
146. Intriguingly, modern Southerners are more likely than Northerners to approve of violence when used as a tool. Nisbett and Cohen, *Culture of Honor*, 28, 38.
147. In addition to the committee members, Graves, Wise, Jones, Menefee, and Pierce attended and were permitted to cross-examine witnesses. H. Rpt. 825, 2.
148. The four congressmen were Isaac Toucey (D-CT), William Potter (D-PA), Andrew D. W. Bruyn (D-NY), and Seaton Grantland (W-GA).
149. George Grennell (W-MA) and James Rariden (W-IN).
150. Franklin H. Elmore (D-SC).
151. This was the optimum outcome to Adams, who was outraged that the Democratic committee majority had taken sides. Adams, diary entry, May 10, 1838, *Memoir*, 10:527; for an account of the committee debate and the decision to table punishment, see *Hinds' Precedents*, chapter LII, "Punishment of Members for Contempt," no. 1644, 2:1116–19.
152. The Senate passed the bill on April 6, 1838; the House on February 13, 1839. See also Wells, "End of the Affair," esp. 1805–808.
153. *Globe*, 25th Cong., 2nd Sess., March 30, 1838, 278.
154. Ibid., April 5, 1838, 284.

155. House Journal, February 13, 1839, 539. The bill passed with 110 yeas, 16 nays (virtually all Southerners), and 93 men in town but absent, only 23 of them offering a formal excuse.
156. French, diary entry, April 27, 1838, *Witness*, 79–80; French, diary entry, April 28, 1838, BBFFP. The marginal addition is dated 1847.
157. Parish, *George Wallace Jones*, 27; Joseph Schafer, "Sectional and Personal Politics in Early Wisconsin," *Wisconsin Magazine of History* 4 (June 1935): 456–57; Shelly A. Thayer, "The Delegate and the Duel: The Early Political Career of George Wallace Jones," *Palimpsest* 5 (September–October 1984): 178–88. Menefee didn't run for reelection.

4. RULES OF ORDER AND THE RULE OF FORCE

1. *Festival of the Sons of New Hampshire*, 108–110. French told the organizers that if they didn't like the song, it would "make very good cigar lights." French to M. P. Wilder, October 29, 1849, ibid., 134.
2. French, "Congressional Reminiscences," *National Freemason* 6 (November 1864), 93.
3. On the gag rule controversy, see William Lee Miller, *Arguing About Slavery: The Great Battle in the United States Congress* (New York: Knopf, 1996); Freehling, *Road to Disunion*, 1:287–352; James McPherson, "The Fight Against the Gag Rule: Joshua Levitt and Antislavery Insurgency in the Whig Party, 1839–1842," *Journal of Negro History* 48 (1963):177–95; Robert Ludlum, "The Antislavery 'Gag-rule': History and Argument," *Journal of Negro History* 26 (1941): 203–43; George C. Rable, "Slavery, Politics, and the South: The Gag Rule as a Case Study," *Capitol Studies* 3 (1975), 69–87; Scott Meinke, "Slavery, Partisanship, and Procedure: The Gag Rule, 1836–1845," *Legislative Studies Quarterly* 1 (February 2007): 33–58; Jeffrey A. Jenkins, Charles Stewart III, "The Gag Rule, Congressional Politics, and the Growth of Anti-Slavery Popular Politics," paper presented at Congress and History Conference, MIT, May 30–31, 2002; Russell B. Nye, *Fettered Freedom: Civil Liberties and the Slavery Controversy, 1830–1860* (East Lansing: Michigan State, 1963); Samuel Flagg Bemis, *John Quincy Adams and the Union* (New York: Knopf, 1956), 326–51; Leonard L. Richards, *The Life and Times of Congressman John Quincy Adams* (New York: Oxford University Press, 1986), 115–31; David C. Frederick, "John Quincy Adams, Slavery, and the Disappearance of the Right of Petition," *Law and History Review* 9, no. 1 (Spring 1991): 115–55; Stephen Holmes, "Gag Rules, or the Politics of Omission," in *Constitutionalism and Democracy*, ed. Jon Elster and Rune Slagstad (New York: Cambridge University Press, 1988), 19–58; Stewart, *Joshua R. Giddings*, 39–42, 69–78. For a skilled analysis of how public opinion shaped the debate, see Edward B. Rugemer, "Caribbean Slave Revolt and the Origins of the Gag Rule: A Contest Between Abolitionism and Democracy, 1797–1835," in *Contesting Slavery: The Politics of Slavery in the New American Nation*, ed. John Craig Hammond and Matthew Mason (Charlottesville: UVA Press, 2011), 94–113; Zaeske, *Signatures of Citizenship*, 71–104. For a handy time line of gag rule votes, see Jenkins and Stewart, "Gag Rule," 34.

4. In 1837–38, the House received roughly 130,200 petitions protesting against slavery in the District of Columbia, 32,000 petitions against the gag rule, 21,200 petitions against slavery in the territories, 23,160 petitions against the slave trade, and 22,160 petitions against new slave states. Nye, *Fettered Freedom*, 46; Bemis, *John Quincy Adams and the Union*, 340. See also Owen W. Muelder, *Theodore Dwight Weld and the American Anti-Slavery Society* (Jefferson, N.C.: McFarland, 2011). Far fewer petitions were presented on the floor. Jenkins and Stewart, "Gag Rule," 39.

5. Adams, diary entry, February 14, 1838, *Memoirs*, 9:496; *Globe*, 25th Cong., 2nd Sess., February 14, 1838, 180.

6. French, *Chicago Democrat*, April 11, 1838, BBFFP.

7. Dale W. Tomich, ed., *The Politics of the Second Slavery* (Albany: State University of New York, 2016); idem., *Through the Prism of Slavery: Labor, Capital, and World Economy* (Lanham, Md.: Rowman & Littlefield, 2004), chapter 3. On the noninevitability of abolition in the 1850s, see esp. James Oakes, *The Scorpion's Sting: Antislavery and the Coming of the Civil War* (New York: Norton, 2014).

8. Corey Brooks, "Stoking the 'Abolition Fire in the Capitol': Liberty Party Lobbying and Antislavery in Congress," *JER* (Fall 2013): 523–47; idem., *Liberty Power*, chapter 2.

9. "Nominis in Umbra" [French], dateline January 12, 1838, *Chicago Democrat*, BBFFP.

10. Fairfield to Ann Fairfield, December 20 and 22, 1837, John Fairfield Papers, LC. Present at the meeting were the full Georgia, South Carolina, and Virginia delegations, as well as large numbers of men from Maryland, North Carolina, Tennessee, and Kentucky. Several senators also attended, including John C. Calhoun and John C. Crittenden.

11. On gag rules as attempts to salvage the functionality of Congress, see Douglas Dion, *Turning the Legislative Thumbscrew: Minority Rights and Procedural Change in Legislative Politics* (East Lansing: University of Michigan, 1997), 81; Holmes, "Gag Rules or the Politics of Omission."

12. For party percentages on gag rule votes from 1836 to 1844, see Jenkins and Stewart, "Gag Rule," 41, 43. In 1836, 82 percent of the Northern Democrats and 28 percent of the Northern Whigs supported the gag; by 1841, those numbers had dropped to 53 percent and 14 percent; and in 1844, 35 percent of the Northern Democrats and 16 percent of the Northern Whigs supported Rule 21.

13. French, ca. December 1837, *Chicago Democrat*, BBFFP.

14. *Globe*, 27th Cong., 2nd Sess., July 22, 1842, 780. See also ibid., 26th Cong., 2nd Sess., February 4, 1841, 324 appendix.

15. Adams, diary entry, July 22, 1842, *Memoirs*, 11:216; also www.masshist.org /jqadiaries/php/doc?id=jqad43_212&year=1842&month=07&day=22&entry =entry&start=0.

16. Giddings to Laura Giddings, February 13, 1843, in Stewart, "Joshua Giddings," 185. On Giddings, see esp. Stewart, *Joshua R. Giddings*; and idem., "Joshua Giddings."

17. On the usefulness of congressional chaos to abolitionism, see Brooks, "Stoking the 'Abolition Fire'"; idem., *Liberty Power*, chapter 2.

18. French, *Chicago Democrat*, dateline January 12, 1838, BBFFP. On the right of petition, see esp. Ronald J. Krotoszynsi, *Reclaiming the Petition Clause: Seditious Libel, "Offensive" Protest, and the Right to Petition the Government for a Redress of Grievances* (New Haven: Yale University Press, 2012), 81–123; Zaeske, *Signatures of Citizenship*.

19. *Register of Debates*, 24th Cong., 2nd Sess., February 7, 1837, 1628–39.

20. *Globe*, 33rd Cong., 1st Sess., May 10, 1854, 976 app., in Foner, *Free Soil*, 101.

21. Ibid., 24th Cong., 2nd Sess., February 6, 1837, 162.

22. Daniel Wirls, "'The Only Mode of Avoiding Everlasting Debate': The Overlooked Senate Gag Rule for Antislavery Petitions," *JER* (Spring 2007): 115–38; Earle, *Jacksonian Antislavery*, 44. Henry Clay favored a gag rule like the House's. *Globe*, 27th Cong., 1st Sess., August 7, 1841, 188 app.

23. Mary M. Cronin, ed. *An Indispensable Liberty: The Fight for Free Speech in Nineteenth-Century America* (Carbondale, Ill.: Southern Illinois University Press, 2016). Michael Ken Curtis, *Free Speech, "The People's Darling Privilege": Struggles for Freedom of Expression in American History* (Durham, N.C.: Duke University Press, 2000), 55–181.

24. Wirls, "'The Only Mode of Avoiding Everlasting Debate,'" 133.

25. French, diary entry, February 6, 1842, *Witness*, 136.

26. See for example the debate of December 21, 1843, when Southerners claimed there had been a motion to table an antislavery petition and Adams yelled back, "Look to your Journal! That tells the truth!" *Portsmouth Journal of Literature and Politics*, December 30, 1843; *Globe*, 28th Cong., 1st Sess., December 21, 1843, 59.

27. The resolution was tabled. 31st Cong., 1st Sess., Journal of the House of Representatives, September 3, 1850, 1363. French set this proceeding in motion. French to Henry Flagg French, August 21, 1850, BBFFP.

28. *Rural Repository* (Hudson, N.Y.) (March 1849), 106. The *Repository* editor William B. Stoddard quizzed French on parliamentary questions.

29. See for example French, *Chicago Democrat*, February 22, 1837, BBFFP.

30. Emerson, journal entry, 1843, in *Journals of Ralph Waldo Emerson with Annotations*, ed. Edward Waldo Emerson and Waldo Emerson Forbes, 10 vols. (New York: Houghton Mifflin, 1910–14), 6:349. On Adams in Congress, see esp. Richards, *Life and Times of Congressman Adams*; Bemis, *Adams and the Union*; Daniel Walker Howe, *The Political Culture of the American Whigs* (Chicago: University of Chicago Press, 1979), 43–68; Miller, *Arguing About Slavery*; Charles N. Edel, *Nation Builder: John Quincy Adams and the Grand Strategy of the Republic* (Cambridge: Harvard University Press, 2014), chapter 5.

31. Giddings, diary entry, February 12, 1839, in Miller, *Arguing About Slavery*, 347. Also Julian, *Life of Giddings*, 70.

32. Giddings, diary entry, December 13, 1838, in Julian, *Life of Giddings*, 52. Giddings adds that Waddy Thompson (W-SC), "possessing much ready wit, and being himself willing to raise a laugh at the expense of the Speaker," stepped up to Adams after the Speaker's call for help and said, with great earnestness, "I am here, Mr. Speaker; I am ready to help. What shall I do?"—producing a roar of laughter. Adams caused the uproar by stating that he refused to vote because he deemed the House proceedings unconstitutional. See also Adams, diary entry,

December 14, 1838, *Memoirs*, 10:65; see also www.masshist.org/jqadiaries/php
/doc?id=jqad33_689.

33. *Globe*, 28th Cong., 2nd Sess., February 6, 1845, 255.

34. Adams, diary entry, December 22, 1836; May 2, 1838; *Memoirs*, 9:331, 521–23;
see also www.masshist.org/jqadiaries/php/doc?id=jqad33_470&year=1838&
month=05&day=02&entry=entry&start=0.

35. Richards, *Congressman John Quincy Adams*, 131. On abolitionist lobbying, see
Brooks, "Stoking the 'Abolition Fire in the Capitol.'"

36. According to chapter 5 of the book of Daniel, God wrote those words on the
wall of Belshazzar's palace to predict his downfall.

37. *Globe*, 27th Cong., 2nd Sess., January 25 and February 19, 1842, 168, 209; Adams, diary entry, May 21, 1842; May 2, 1838; *Memoirs*, 11:159, 9:523.

38. Adams, diary entry, December 25, 1839; *Memoirs*, 10:175–76; see also www
.masshist.org/jqadiaries/php/doc?id=jqad42_312&year=1839&month=12&day
=25&entry=entry&start=0.

39. On the existence of a slave power dominating the federal government, see esp.
Fehrenbacher, *The Slaveholding Republic*; Richards, *Slave Power*; Van Cleve, *A
Slaveholders' Union*. See also Introductions, note 28; chapter 6, note 108.

40. This is the so-called Haverhill petition.

41. *Globe*, 27th Cong., 2nd Sess., January 25, 1842, 168.

42. Fessenden to unknown correspondent, January 23, 1843, Fessenden, *Life and
Public Service of W. P. Fessenden*, 24. Fessenden was speaking generally about
the debate as it unfolded over the course of a few days. Adams was a bit extreme,
but given the provocation, it was justified, he thought.

43. French, diary entry, February 6, 1842, *Witness*, 136.

44. *Globe*, 27th Cong., 2nd Sess., January 25 and 26, 1842, 170, 176.

45. Joshua Giddings heard Marshall say this to John Campbell (D-SC) sitting
nearby. Giddings, *History of the Rebellion: Its Authors and Cases* (New York: Follet, Foster, 1864), 167; *Harper's New Monthly Magazine* (November 1885), 970.

46. *Harper's New Monthly Magazine* (November 1885), 970. A few days after the incident, Marshall swore never to go up against "the damned old bull" again. Hugh
McCulloch, "Memories of Some Contemporaries," *Scribner's Magazine* 3 (September 1888): 280.

47. *Globe*, 27th Cong., 2nd Sess., January 26, 1842, 176; Henry Wise to William
Graves, January 31, 1842, Henry A. Wise Papers, UNC. Wise said there was
never a proposal to try him for murder, but rather for breach of privilege. He sent
Graves a draft of a lengthy defense against Adams's charges that was published
in several newspapers, including the *National Intelligencer*. Wise's papers include numerous letters and essay drafts refuting Adams's charges in later years.

48. *Globe*, 29th Cong., 1st Sess., January 7, 1846, 157.

49. Adams, diary entry, January 1, 1844; *Memoirs*, 11:467; Wentworth, *Congressional Reminiscences*, 12.

50. "Impious Scene in Congress," *Zion's Herald*, April 6, 1836. Wise's quote isn't in
the *Globe*, but the *Herald*'s account follows the *Globe*'s version closely. *Globe*,
24th Cong., 1st Sess., March 26, 1836, 298.

51. Adams, *Memoirs*, June 11, 1841, 10:478; Leverett Saltonstall to Mary Eliza-

beth Sanders Saltonstall, June 11, 1841, *The Papers of Leverett Saltonstall, 1816–1845*, ed. Robert E. Moody, 5 vols. (Boston: Massachusetts Historical Society, 1984), 3:108; see also www.masshist.org/jqadiaries/php/doc?id=jqad41_366&year=1841&month=06&day=11&entry=entrycont&start=0.

52. *Globe*, 26th Cong., 1st Sess., July 15, 1840, 528.

53. Ibid., 27th Cong., 2nd Sess., January 27, 1842, 183. See also ibid., 27th Cong., 1st Sess., June 16, 1841, 62.

54. B. B. French, "Application of Parliamentary Law to the Government of Masonic Bodies," *American Quarterly Review of Freemasonry and Its Kindred Sciences* 3 (January 5858 [i.e., 1857]): 320–25.

55. John W. Simons, *A Familiar Treatise on the Principles and Practice of Masonic Jurisprudence* (New York: Masonic Publishing and Manufacturing Co., 1869), 158–65.

56. The *Manual* was written for the Senate but only the House adopted it as rules of practice, beginning in 1837. Jefferson, "Manual of Parliamentary Practice," preface, *Jefferson's Parliamentary Writings: "Parliamentary Pocket-Book" and a Manual of Parliamentary Practice*, ed. Wilbur Samuel Howell, *The Papers of Thomas Jefferson*, Second Series (Princeton, N.J.: Princeton, 1988), 356; DeAlva Stanwood Alexander, *History and Procedure of the House of Representatives* (Boston: Riverside Press, 1916), 180–82. On Jefferson's *Manual*, see *Jefferson's Parliamentary Writings*, 3–38, 339–48.

57. Jefferson, "Manual," in *Jefferson's Parliamentary Writings*, 374–76. The Constitution deals with misconduct only cursorily: each house can punish members for disorderly behavior and expel members with a two-thirds majority. U.S. Constitution, Article 1, section 5. For the link with dueling, see Jefferson's source material: Anchitell Grey, ed., *Debates of the House of Commons*, 10 vols. (London: D. Henry and R. Cave, 1763), 3:293, 316.

58. *Globe*, 26th Cong., 1st Sess., April 1, 1840, 301.

59. Jefferson, "Manual," in *Jefferson's Parliamentary Writings*, 357.

60. Sarah A. Binder, *Minority Rights, Majority Rule: Partisanship and the Development of Congress* (New York: Cambridge University Press, 1997), 84–85, 178–83.

61. This kind of obstruction emerged as a strategic weapon of debate in the 1830s and came to an end with the institution of Speaker Thomas Brackett Reed's rules (the so-called Reed Rules) in 1889. Jeffrey A. Jenkins and Charles Stewart III, *Fighting for the Speakership: The House and the Rise of Party Government* (Princeton, N.J.: Princeton, 2013), 41.

62. Gregory J. Wawro and Eric Schickler, *Filibuster: Obstruction and Lawmaking in the U.S. Senate* (Princeton, N.J.: Princeton, 2006); Sarah A. Binder and Steven S. Smith, *Politics or Principle? Filibustering in the United States Senate* (Washington, D.C.: Brookings Institution Press, 1997); Sarah A. Binder and Steven S. Smith, "Political Goals and Procedural Choice in the Senate," *Journal of Politics* 60, no. 2 (May 1998): 396–416. Wawro and Schickler note that many Senate privileges of debate resulted from the absence of rules to curtail them; they also point out—as do Binder and Smith—that filibustering in the modern sense began later in the nineteenth century.

63. This became truer over time. Initially the Senate and House shared rules regarding the previous question, but the Senate came to view itself as a body constitutionally grounded on unlimited debate. Binder, *Minority Rights*, 39–40.
64. *Globe*, 31st Cong., 1st Sess., April 3, 1850, 632. Fillmore was discussing the need to strengthen the power of the vice president to call senators to order; he had avoided the discussion until it was necessary, but "that time has now arrived." See George P. Furber, *Precedents Relating to the Privileges of the Senate of the United States* (Washington, D.C.: GPO, 1893), 122.
65. *Globe*, 27th Cong., 2nd Sess., February 8, 1842, 217. Linn was discussing the proper response to a rude exchange between Nathaniel Tallmadge (W-NY) and Thomas Hart Benton (D-MO).
66. Adams, *Memoirs*, February 13, 1843, 11:318; *Globe*, 27th Cong., 2nd Sess., January 27, 1842, 182–83.
67. *Globe*, 27th Cong., 2nd Sess., January 28, 1842, 183–84. See also *New World* (N.Y.), January 29, 1842. Arnold had called Kenneth Rayner (W-NC) to order. The other Southerner who came to Arnold's seat was William Payne (D-AL).
68. James F. Hopkins, ed., *The Papers of Henry Clay*, 8:513; *Niles Weekly Register*, May 19, 1832. During a House debate in 1832, Arnold had insulted Jackson's friend and ally Sam Houston. Houston's friend Major Morgan Heard defended him—and Jackson—by attacking Arnold, hitting him with a club and then trying to shoot him; Arnold bested him with a sword cane.
69. Ibid., 14; Dion, *Turning the Legislative Thumbscrew*, 11. For a disappearing quorum in action, see French to Harriette French, March 8, 1836, BBFFP. A demand for the previous question was the equivalent of asking "Shall the main question be not now put?" Regardless of how it was decided, a call for the previous question brought debate to a halt and usually required a full vote. See Alexander, *History and Procedure of the House of Representatives*, 180–81.
70. For example, see David Outlaw to Emily Outlaw, December 1849, DOP; William Cabell Rives, Jr., to William Cabell Rives, May 26, 1856, William Cabell Rives Papers, LC. See also Eric M. Uslaner, "Is the Senate More Civil Than the House?," in Burdett A. Loomis, ed., *Esteemed Colleagues: Civility and Deliberation in the U.S. Senate* (Washington, D.C.: Brookings Institution, 2000), 32–55. According to the *OED*, a "bear garden" is "a place originally set apart for the baiting of bears, and used for the exhibition of other rough sports," or more generally, "a scene of strife and tumult."
71. Adams, diary entry, March 28, 1842, *Memoirs*, 11:101–102.
72. French, memoir, BBFFP.
73. *Globe*, 28th Cong., 1st Sess., December 21, 1843, 62.
74. Ibid., 27th Cong., 2nd Sess., January 21 and 22, 1841, 158, 162.
75. Ibid., January 22, 1841, 163.
76. Ibid., 27th Cong., 1st Sess., June 15 and 16, 1841, 54, 58. The previous question was often described as a "gag." See for example *Portland Weekly Advertiser*, February 16 and 23, and October 24, 1837; *New Hampshire Patriot* (Concord), May 2, 1836.
77. Binder, *Minority Rights*, 43–67, 92–99. The Senate abandoned the practice in 1806, partly because it was rarely if ever used. Richard R. Beeman, "Unlimited

Debate in the Senate: The First Phase," *Political Science Quarterly* 83, no. 3 (September 1968): 419–34.

78. *Globe*, 26th Cong., 1st Sess., April 2, 1840, 301.

79. Ibid., 27th Cong., 1st Sess., June 14, 1841, 51.

80. Theodore Weld to Angelina Grimke Weld and Sarah Grimke, January 22, 1842, *Letters of Theodore Dwight Weld, Angelina Grimke Weld and Sarah Grimke, 1822–1844*, 2 vols. (New York: D. Appleton-Century Company, 1934), 999.

81. *Globe*, 27th Cong., 2nd Sess., January 22, 1842, 163.

82. French to Henry Flagg French, January 25, 1842, BBFFP.

83. *Register of Debates*, 23rd Cong., 2nd Sess., December 16, 1834, 795.

84. On the mace, see Silvio A. Bedini, "The Mace and the Gavel: Symbols of Government in America," *Transactions of the American Philosophical Society* 87, no. 4 (1997): 1–84.

85. French, diary entry, September 13, 1841, *Witness*, 124.

86. Particularly helpful on the speakership in the nineteenth century is Jenkins and Stewart, *Fighting for the Speakership*, which shows the evolution of the post as a party office.

87. *Globe*, 26 Cong., 2nd sess., January 25, 1841, 126.

88. On the antislavery implications of speakership elections, see Brooks, *Liberty Power*.

89. Horace Mann to E. W. Clap, December 23, 1849, January 7, 1850, Mann, ed., *Life of Horace Mann*, 284. See also Mann to E. W. Clap, February 7, 1850, ibid., 286.

90. *Globe*, 27th Cong., 1st Sess., June 16, 1841, 58. On the link between violence and a lax Speaker, see ibid., 26th Cong., 1st Sess., May 14, 1840, 396; ibid., 28th Cong., 1st Sess., January 26, 1844, 196.

91. Jefferson, "Manual of Parliamentary Practice," section 34, in *Jefferson's Parliamentary Writings*, 395.

92. "Nominis in Umbra" [French], dateline January 1, 1838, *Chicago Democrat*, January 24, 1838, BBFFP.

93. S. Rpt. 170, 31st Cong., 1st Sess., July 30, 1850, on the investigation of the clash between Henry Foote (D-MI) and Thomas Hart Benton (D-MO) on April 17, 1850.

94. *Globe*, 24th Cong., 2nd Sess., February 17, 1837, 222.

95. Adams, diary entry, April 9, 1840, *Memoirs*, 5:258.

96. *Niles' National Register*, July 10, 1824, vol. 26, 298. In the Committee on Public Lands, Barton had presented documents reflecting badly on the Arkansas delegate Henry W. Conway, who challenged Barton. For "bully" as "political champion," see Adams, diary entry, January 3, 1840, *Memoirs*, 10:183.

97. Wyatt-Brown, *Southern Honor*, 358. The *OED* defines a "bully" as "a 'blustering gallant'; a bravo, hector, or 'swash-buckler'; now, *esp.* a tyrannical coward who makes himself a terror to the weak."

98. Other House bullies included Edward Stanly (W-NC), Daniel Jenifer (W-MD), John Dawson (D-LA), James Belser (D-AL), John B. Weller (D-OH), Balie Peyton (W-TN), John Bell (J/W-TN), Hopkins L. Turney (D-TN), Charles Downing (D-FL delegate), William B. Campbell (W-TN), George McDuffie (D-SC), Felix

Grundy McConnell (D-AL), William Cost Johnson (W-MD), Samuel Gholson (D-MS), Roger Pryor (D-VA), Laurence Keitt (D-SC), and Alexander Duncan (D-OH). On Stanly: Norman D. Brown, *Edward Stanly: Whiggery's Tarheel "Conquerer"* (Tuscaloosa: University of Alabama Press, 1974), 45 and passim; John H. Wheeler, *Reminiscences and Memoirs of North Carolina and Eminent North Carolinians* (Columbus, N.C.: Columbus Printing Works, 1884), 17; "The Campaigns of a 'Conqueror'; or, The Man 'Who Bragged High for a Fight,'" undated, UNC. On Bell and Turney: Balie Peyton to Henry Wise, June 17, 1838, in *The Collector: A Magazine for Autograph and Historical Collectors* 3 (January 1907): 26–27. Turney—"a wolfish, Snakey looking ruffian"—electioneered on the idea that he would cause "all sorts of Hell in the House, & out of it too," and craved "the eclat, & distinction of a quarrel" with Wise. Peyton to Wise, August 15, 1837, Henry A. Wise Papers, UNC. On McDuffie: Louis McLane to unknown recipient, December 23, 1821, Louis McLane Papers, LC; William Greenhow to Henry Wise, February 5, 1844, Henry A. Wise Papers, UNC. On Pryor and Keitt: Samuel S. Cox, *Eight Years in Congress, from 1857–1865: Memoir and Speeches* (New York: Appleton, 1865), 23–25. On Duncan: Adams, diary entry, June 29, 1840, *Memoirs*, 10:323.

Senate bullies included Henry Clay (W-KY), Thomas Hart Benton (D-MO), Henry Foote (D-MS), Lewis Wigfall (D-TX), and Robert Augustus Toombs (W-GA), among others. Wise dated Clay's worst bullying to his loss of the presidential nomination in 1839, when he became "excessively intemperate in his habits, and more intemperate in exacerbation of temper and in his political conduct." Wise, *Seven Decades*, 172. On Slidell: Cox, *Eight Years*, 20. On Toombs: John Bell to W. B. Campbell, August 10, 1854, *Tennessee Historical Magazine* 3 (September 1917): 223–24. Toombs was a notorious "college bully" in the 1820s. James H. Justus, *Fetching the Old Southwest: Humorous Writing from Longstreet to Twain*, 439. All of these House and Senate bullies were noted as such in the press.

99. *Globe*, 24th Cong., 1st Sess., 298; "Riots in Congress," *Niles' Weekly Register*, April 2, 1836; French, diary entry, April 10, 1836, *Witness*, 64; "A Night in the House of Representatives," *New-Yorker*, April 2, 1836.

100. See for example how James Belser (D-AL) responded to being called a bully in 1844; had his accuser been present, Belser "would have made an example of him which he would long have remembered." *Globe*, 28th Cong., 1st Sess., February 3, 1844, 224. I classify men as bullies based on patterns of bullying behavior joined with charges of being a bully. Shields's division of congressmen between 1836 and 1860 into "mavericks" and "conformists" is provocative, but largely based on voting patterns and eulogies, so some of my bullies weren't mavericks, and many of her mavericks weren't bullies. Johanna Nicol Shields, *The Line of Duty: Maverick Congressmen and the Development of American Political Culture, 1836–1860* (Westport, Conn.: Greenwood Press, 1985).

101. Adams, diary entry, January 16, 1845, *Memoirs*, 12:148. The debate concerned appointing a committee to investigate a congressional duel.

102. Scholars generally downplay Whig bullyism. See for example Howe's seminal *Political Culture of the American Whigs*, esp. 128–29.

103. Adams, diary entry, July 22, 1841, *Memoirs*, 10:512.

104. On Peyton's efforts, see Powell Moore, "James K. Polk: Tennessee Politician," *Journal of Southern History* 17 (November 1951): 497; Walter T. Durham, *Balie Peyton of Tennessee: Nineteenth Century Politics and Thoroughbreds* (Franklin, Tenn.: Hillsboro Press, 2004). Polk thought that his attackers were aiming at "the Tennessee market." Polk to William R. Rucker, February 22, 1836, *Correspondence of James K. Polk*, 513. On Polk in the context of Tennessee politics, see also Jonathan M. Atkins, *Parties, Politics, and the Sectional Conflict in Tennessee, 1832–1861* (Knoxville: University of Tennessee, 1997). Wise later said that he attacked Polk the Speaker—not the man—for impinging on his representative rights. Wise to unknown, December 2, 1846, Henry A. Wise Papers, UNC. See also Henry A. Wise, "Opinions of Hon. Henry A. Wise, Upon the Conduct and Character of James K. Polk, Speaker of the House of Representatives, with Other 'Democratic' Illustrations" (Washington, D.C., 1844).

105. Jenkins and Stewart, *Fighting for the Speakership*, 41, note 12. For an example of one such challenge, see *Globe*, 24th Cong., 1st Sess., February 29, 1836, 214.

106. Charles G. Sellers, *James K. Polk: Jacksonian, 1795–1843* (Norwalk, Conn.: Easton Press, 1987), 307–10, from an 1836 letter from Balie Peyton. See also Polk, diary entry, October 14, 1847, in *The Diary of James K. Polk During His Presidency, 1845–1849*, ed. Milo Milton Quaife, 4 vols. (Chicago: A. C. McClurg, 1910), 3:191. Polk noted that during his presidency, a "somewhat embarrassed" Wise called on him but made "[n]o allusion . . . to his former hostility to me, and his unprovoked and unjustifiable assaults upon me when I was speaker of the Ho. Repts. in 1836 & 37."

107. See for example "A Coward" in *Louisville Daily Journal*, June 5, 1844; ibid., September 11, 1844. See also Kirby, "Limits of Honor," 121–22, 130.

108. "True-Hearted Statesman," in *Early Songs of Uncle Sam*, George S. Jackson, (Boston: Bruce Humphries, Publishers, 1962), 115.

109. *Globe*, 24th Cong., 2nd Sess., February 20, 1837, 239; ibid., 25th Cong., 1st Sess., October 13, 1837, 326 app. See also Thornton, *An American Glossary*, 456. Jackson coined the word in 1832, the year of the caning. See Jackson to Francis Preston Blair, May 26, 1832, *Jackson Papers*, 10:487–88. My thanks to Dan Feller for pointing this out and sharing his materials on it.

110. *Globe*, 26th Cong., 2nd Sess., February 4, 1841, 321 app.

111. Adams, "Address of John Quincy Adams to Constituents" (Boston: J. H. Eastburn, 1842), 55. Zaeske offers a fascinating study of the gendered aspects of the congressional petition furor but concludes that oratorical duels were replacements for duels with gunplay, which—she mistakenly claims—were no longer possible. Susan Zaeske, "'The South Arose as One Man': Gender and Sectionalism in Antislavery Petition Debates, 1835–1845," *Rhetoric and Public Affairs* 12 (2009): 341–68.

112. Giddings, diary entry, December 14, 1838, in Julian, *Life of Giddings*, 52.

113. *Liberator*, February 14, 1845; *Salem Register*, February 10, 1845; *Bellows Falls Gazette* (Vermont), February 15, 1845.

114. *Globe*, 28th Cong., 2nd Sess., February 6, 1845, 256.

115. *Commercial Advertiser* (N.Y.), February 8, 1845.

116. Giddings, *History of the Rebellion*, 210; Julian, *Life of Giddings*, 174; *Commercial Advertiser* (N.Y.), February 8, 1845; Adams, diary entry, February 6, 1845, *Memoirs*, 12:162; *Globe*, 34th Cong., 1st Sess., July 11, 1856, 1121 app.; *Huron Reflector* (Norwalk), February 25, 1845. See also chapter 2.

117. *Huron Reflector* (Norwalk, Ohio), February 25, 1845.

118. Jacob Collamer (W-VT) to Mary Collamer, February 4, 1844, University of Vermont Libraries' Center for Digital Initiatives, cdi3.uvm.edu/collections/item /collamerC01f015i002&view=transcript.

119. Giddings to Laura Giddings, January 23, 1842, in Stewart, *Joshua R. Giddings*, 71.

120. French, diary entry, December 9, 1836, *Witness*, 69.

121. Ibid.

122. Ibid., January 6, 1843, *Witness*, 146.

123. Adams, diary entry, January 2, 1843, *Memoirs*, 11:285.

124. Ibid., June 18, 1842, 11:180.

125. Ibid., February 22, 1844, 11:516–17.

126. *Globe*, 26th Cong., 2nd Sess., February 4, 1841, 322 app. For an insightful analysis of the rhetoric of this speech, see Patricia Roberts-Miller, "Agonism, Wrangling, and John Quincy Adams," *Rhetoric Review* 25, no. 2 (2006): 141–61. As Roberts-Miller notes, scholars who dismiss this speech as "irrational and uncalculated" entirely miss the validity of Adams's comments about violence and its congressional implications. Ibid., 143. Richards notes the anti-dueling law as a moral victory for the North in the midst of the gag rule furor. *Congressman John Quincy Adams*, 131–35.

127. See for example *New Hampshire Sentinel*, February 28, 1844, which states that Southerners challenge Northerners because they know they can't accept a challenge without destroying their reputations.

128. Giddings, diary entry, December 14, 1838, in Julian, *Life of Giddings*, 52

129. *Globe*, 28th Cong., 2nd Sess., February 6, 1845, 256. On the insult inherent in antislavery petitions by women, see Zaeske, "'The South Arose as One Man'"; Jennifer Rose Mercieca, "The Culture of Honor: How Slaveholders Responded to the Abolitionist Mail Crisis of 1835," *Rhetoric and Public Affairs* 10, no. 1 (2007): 51–76.

130. "Address of John Quincy Adams," 58–59.

131. Shelden argues that bullying and bravado were just for show, but a watchful national audience was precisely what gave such displays their power. Humiliation before a widespread public could destroy a reputation and damage a career. In addition, often there was very real fear of bloodshed. *Washington Brotherhood*, 39–40 and passim.

132. Washington Greenhow to Wise, February 5, 1844, Henry A. Wise Papers, UNC. See also G. S. Henry to Robert L. Caruthers, August 5, 1841, Robert L. Caruthers Papers, UNC.

133. Doctrine Davenport to Ebenezer Pettigrew, August 10, 1843, in Brown, *Edward Stanly*, 91; Thomas S. Hoskins to William Graham, May 9, 1842, ibid., 83. For electioneering fodder accusing Stanly of cowardice, see ibid., 90; "The Campaigns of a 'Conqueror,'" undated, UNC. For the carefully worded apology: *Huron Reflector* (Norwalk, Ohio), May 31, 1842. Stanly and Wise had an ongo-

ing grudge match, brawling at least twice and nearly dueling three times. In 1841 their fisticuffs sparked a House brawl and nearly led to a duel. Eight months later, harsh words (Coward! Cur!) led to talk of another duel. The caning incident that sparked talk of *another* duel happened days later. Fight #1: *Globe*, 27th Cong., 1st Sess., September 9–11, 1841, 444–45, 447, 451; French, diary entry, September 13, 1841, *Witness*, 124–25; Adams, diary entry September 9, 1841, *Memoirs*, 11:11; House Journal, 27th Cong., 1st Sess., 513–14. Fight #2: *Globe*, 27th Cong., 2nd Sess., May 4, 1842, 476–78; Adams, diary entry, May 4, 1842, *Memoirs*, 11:148; French to Henry Flagg French, May 13, 1842, BBFFP. Fight #3: Adams, diary entry, May 7, 1842, *Memoirs*, 11:151; Brown, *Edward Stanly*, 83–86.

134. *Globe*, 34th Cong., 1st Sess., June 26, 1856, 1476. On Hale, see esp. Sewell, *John P. Hale*; Earle, *Jacksonian Antislavery*, 78–102. Earle's discussion of Hale's conversion from loyal Democrat to antislavery advocate is particularly good.

135. On abolitionists and manhood: Amy S. Greenberg, *Manifest Manhood*; Stanley Harrold, *American Abolitionists* (London and New York: Routledge, 2001), 44–46; Donald Yacovone, "Abolitionists and the 'Language of Fraternal Love,'" in *Meanings for Manhood*, ed. Mark C. Carnes and Clyde Griffen (Chicago: University of Chicago Press, 1990), 85–95.

136. W. Claggett to Hale, March 7, 1844; Charles D. Cleveland to Hale, March 24, 1844; Amos Tuck to Hale, January 15, 1845; James Peverly to Hale, January 16, 1845, in John Parker Hale Papers, NHHS.

137. The meeting passed the resolutions before adjourning in an uproar; the antislavery editor Nathaniel Rogers insulted Pierce. *Boston Courier*, March 21, 1844; "Proceedings of the Annual Town Meeting in Concord, March 12, 13, 14, 15, 1844," 21–22, accessed August 18, 2012, at www.onconcord.com/books/2histcity_reports /1844.pdf; *History of Concord, New Hampshire*, 1:415; Nichols, *Franklin Pierce*, 125–29; Cole, *Jacksonian Democracy*, 217. For other doughface self-defenses, see the speeches of Charles Atherton (D-NH), *Globe*, 27th Cong., 2nd Sess., December 23, 1841, 36 app.; and Jacob Thompson (D-MI), ibid., 31st Cong., 1st Sess., June 5, 1850, 661 app.

138. Cole, *Jacksonian Democracy*, 230; Wallner, *New Hampshire's Favorite Son*, 128; *New Hampshire Patriot and State Gazette* (Concord), October 22, 1846.

139. On slavery and the New Hampshire Democracy, see Cole, *Jacksonian Democracy*, 216–33.

140. Giddings's resolutions concerned a rebellion on the *Creole*. John Botts (W-VA) first proposed resolutions punishing Giddings, but when people objected, Weller rephrased the resolutions as his own and then moved the previous question. *Globe*, 27th Cong., 2nd Sess., March 21, 1842, 343.

141. Adams, diary entry, March 22, 1842, *Memoirs*, 11:114. On censure, see Jack Maskell, "Expulsion, Censure, Reprimand, and Fine: Legislative Discipline in the House of Representatives," CRS Report No. RL31382 (Washington, D.C.: Congressional Research Service, June 27, 2016), 12, fas.org/sgp/crs/misc /RL31382.pdf, accessed May 15, 2017.

142. Giddings, diary entry, February 12, 1839, in Miller, *Arguing About Slavery*, 347; Julian, *Life of Giddings*, 70.

143. On the joint efforts of Giddings, William Slade, Seth Gates, and others—many of them staying at Ann Sprigg's boardinghouse, nicknamed "abolition house"— see Brooks, "Stoking the 'Abolition Fire in the Capitol,'" 541; idem., *Liberty Power*, chapter 2; Gilbert Hobbs Barnes, *The Antislavery Impulse, 1830–1844* (New York: Harbinger, 1933), 179–80. On networks of influence, see also James B. Stewart, *Joshua R. Giddings and the Tactics of Radical Politics, 1795–1864* (Cleveland, Ohio: Case Western Reserve, 1970).

144. In *Liberty Power*, Brooks reveals how Liberty Party lobbyists prompted congressmen to make antislavery trouble on the floor to spread a Slave Power message.

145. Adams, diary entry, March 22, 1842, *Memoirs*, 11:114.

146. See for example *Painesville Telegraph*, April 13, 1842; *Weekly Ohio State Journal*, April 20 and 27, 1842.

147. Giddings to Joseph Addison Giddings, May 19, 1842, in Stewart, *Giddings*, 76.

148. Jenkins and Stewart, "Gag Rule," 29–31.

149. *Chicago Democrat* [undated], BBFFP.

150. Not every fight between 1836 and 1844 was explicitly caused by the gag rule debate, but it poisoned the atmosphere enough to have an impact. The top five fighting Congresses were (in order): the Thirty-fourth, Thirty-fifth, Thirty-sixth, Twenty-sixth, and Twenty-seventh.

151. Wise to unknown, December 2, 1846, Henry A. Wise Papers, UNC. Wise was talking about his congressional sparring generally.

152. Adams, *Memoirs*, February 5, 1841, 10:413–14; see also www.masshist.org /jqadiaries/php/doc?id=jqad41_240&year=1841&month=02&day=05&entry =entrycont&start=0.

153. *Globe*, 28th Cong., 1st Sess., December 21, 1843, 62; Adams, diary entry, December 21, 1843, *Memoirs*, 11:455, 457.

154. Jenkins and Stewart, "Gag Rule," 22, 27–28.

155. Adams, diary entry, December 3, 1844, *Memoirs*, 116. The Senate's far more indirect gag rule lasted six more years. Wirls, "Overlooked Senate Gag Rule," 133.

156. Adams, "Address to Constituents," 57; Thomas F. Marshall, "Speeches of Thomas F. Marshall of Kentucky on the Resolutions to Censure John Q. Adams" (Washington: Blair & Rives, 1842), 5. Marshall wrote a preface explaining his speeches' significance.

5. FIGHTING FOR THE UNION

1. Cresson, *Journey into Fame*, 17–18, 107.

2. On the importance of Texas to Southerners as a slaveholding republic in the western hemisphere, see Karp, *Vast Southern Empire*, 82.

3. On Texas, see ibid., 82–102; Joel H. Silbey, *Storm over Texas: The Annexation Controversy and the Road to Civil War* (New York: Oxford University Press, 2005); Mark J. Stegmaier, *Texas, New Mexico, and the Compromise of 1850: Boundary Dispute and Sectional Crisis* (Kent, Ohio: Kent State University, 1996); Morrison, *Slavery and the American West*; and Potter, *Impending Crisis*, passim.

4. Whig newspapers predicted that the well-liked French might keep his job; Demo-

cratic papers taunted Whigs—who claimed to be above party—for their eager-ness to oust the hyperqualified French in favor of a Whig. See for example *Richmond Whig*, May 28, 1847; *Albany Evening Journal*, May 29, 1847.

5. E. C. Cabell to the editors of the *Daily National Intelligencer*, January 15, 1848; French to the editors of the *Daily National Intelligencer*, January 24 and 26, 1848. Particularly helpful on the proviso in a congressional context is Mi-chael F. Holt, *The Fate of Their Country: Politicians, Slavery Extension, and the Coming of the Civil War* (New York: Hill and Wang, 2004).

6. French to Henry Flagg French, December 12, 1847, BBFFP; French, diary entry, December 16, 1847, *Witness*, 197.

7. French, diary entry, November 27 and December 30, 1849, *Witness*, 210–12.

8. French, diary entry, May 23, 1848, *Witness*, 202. French gave a eulogy for Adams at a meeting of the Board of Aldermen on February 25, 1848. "Proceedings in the Board of Aldermen and Board of Common Council, of the City of Washington, on the Occasion of the Death of John Quincy Adams" (Washington: John T. Towers, 1848), 5–8, www.mocavo.com/Proceedings-of-the-Corporation-and-Citizens -of-Washington-on-the-Occasion-of-the-Death-of-John-Quincy-Adams-Who -Died-in-the-Capitol-on-Wednesday-Evening-February-23-1848-Volume-2 /269014/13#13, accessed February 23, 2014.

9. French, diary entry, February 22, 1848, *Witness*, 199.

10. Richards, *Life and Times of Congressman John Quincy Adams*, 202–203.

11. French to unknown correspondent, 1847, in Robert R. Hershman, "Gas in Wash-ington," *Columbia Historical Society* 50 (1948–50): 146. In the fall of 1847, French visited Professor Joseph Henry of Princeton, a noted expert on electricity, on tele-graph business, but discussed the mast with him as well. It was taken down on June 18, 1848. See also William Charles Allen, *History of the United States Capitol: A Chronicle of Design, Construction, and Politics* (Washington, D.C.: GPO, 2000), 179–80.

12. It took sixty-three ballots and nearly three weeks to elect a Speaker, and another week and twenty ballots to elect a clerk. For a detailed account, see Jenkins and Stewart, *Fighting for the Speakership*, 155–74. On the fight, see *Globe*, 31st Cong., 1st Sess., December 13, 1849, 27; Nathan Sargent, *Public Men and Events from the Commencement of Mr. Monroe's Administration, in 1817, to the Close of Mr. Fillmore's Administration, in 1853*, 2 vols. (Philadelphia: J. B. Lippincott, 1875), 2:351; David Outlaw to Emily Outlaw, December 13 and 16, 1849, DOP; *Huron Reflector* (Norwalk, Ohio), January 1, 1850; *National Era* (Washington), December 20, 1849.

13. The House hadn't yet elected its new sergeant at arms. Ultimately, Nathan Sar-gent, who had held the post in the previous Congress, kept it for the Thirty-first Congress, when the exhausted House voted to keep several officers from the previous Congress rather than spend more weeks organizing. Sargent, *Public Men and Events*, 2:351; *Globe*, 31st Cong., 1st Sess., December 13, 1849, 27.

14. *Globe*, 31st Cong., 1st Sess., December 13, 1850, 28. Emphasis in original.

15. David Outlaw to Emily Outlaw, December 13, 1850, DOP.

16. *Globe*, 31st Cong., 1st Sess., December 13, 1850, 28–29.

17. Ibid., 29.

18. Ibid., 26.
19. Cobb to Amelie Cobb, December 20, 1849, *The Correspondence of Robert Toombs, Alexander H. Stephens, and Howell Cobb*, 2 vols., ed. Ulrich B. Phillips, (Washington, D.C.: GPO, 1913), 2:179, in *Annual Report of the American Historical Association for 1911*.
20. *New York Evening Post*, January 8, 1850.
21. French, diary entry, January 6, 1850, *Witness*, 213. Forney was a strong James Buchanan supporter. On Forney's Southern leanings, see *New York Evening Post*, January 8, 1850; George W. Julian, *Political Recollections 1840 to 1872* (Chicago: Jansen, McClurg, 1884), 78. Julian voted for French.
22. French, diary entry, January 6, 1850, *Witness*, 213; idem., "To the Editors," January 14, 1850, in *Daily Union* (Washington), January 15, 1850; Forney, "To the Editors," *Daily Union*, January 19, 1850.
23. Forney, "To the Editors," *Daily Union*, January 19, 1850. When Campbell died the following year, Forney became Clerk and gave government printing contracts to his *Daily Union* partner A. Boyd Hamilton, thereby keeping the paper from going under. Elwyn Burns Robinson, "The 'Pennsylvanian': Organ of the Democracy," *Pennsylvania Magazine of History and Biography* 3 (1938): 350–60; cited on 350.
24. French received a cluster of votes from Western Democrats, a few Northern Whigs, and three of the House's six Free Soilers, receiving at most eighteen votes. See chapter 6.
25. Defecting Democrats included South Carolinians William Colcock, John McQueen, Joseph Woodward, James Orr, and Daniel Wallace; Andrew Ewing (TN); David Hubbard (AL); and Abraham Venable (NC). Venable said they supported Campbell because they didn't think Forney could get enough votes to win, and they wanted to get down to business. Letter to the editor, *Daily Union*, January 13, 1850. Forney's chief supporter, James Buchanan, was "deeply mortified" at Forney's loss, and stunned at the "defection" of Southern Democrats. Buchanan to A. Boyd Hamilton, January 12, 1850, www.historyforsale.com/html/printfriendly .asp?documentid=5234.
26. On antislavery Democrats, many of whom bolted the party, see esp. Earle, *Jacksonian Antislavery*.
27. French to Henry Flagg French, January 20, 1850, BBFFP.
28. Ibid.
29. Particularly useful studies of the Compromise of 1850 include Holman Hamilton, *Prologue to Conflict: The Crisis and Compromise of 1850* (Lexington: University Press of Kentucky, 1964); Holt, *Political Crisis of the 1850s*; Stegmaier, *Texas, New Mexico, and the Compromise of 1850*; Landis, *Northern Men*, chapter 1; Paul Finkelman and Donald R. Kennon, eds., *Congress and the Crisis of the 1850s* (Athens: Ohio University, 2012); Freehling, *Road to Disunion*, 1:487–510; Michael A. Morrison, *Slavery and the American West: The Eclipse of Manifest Destiny and the Coming of the Civil War* (Chapel Hill: UNC, 1997), 96–125; Varon, *Disunion!*, 199–231.
30. On the link between sectional honor, degradation, and the Civil War, see esp. Bertram Wyatt-Brown, "Honor, Humiliation, and the American Civil War," in

A *Warring Nation: Honor, Race, and Humiliation in America and Abroad* (Charlottesville: UVA Press, 2014), 80–105; idem., "Shameful Submission and Honorable Secession," in *The Shaping of Southern Culture: Honor, Grace, and War, 1760s–1880s* (Chapel Hill: UNC, 2001), 177–202; Varon, *Disunion!*; and Olsen, *Political Culture and Secession in Mississippi*; Bowman, *At the Precipice*, chapter 3.

31. These threats mesh with Varon's account of the rise of disunion talk as "a process" in the early 1850s. Varon, *Disunion!*

32. For similar logic in the clash of proslavery and antislavery settlers in Kansas, see Kristen T. Oertel, *Bleeding Borders: Race, Gender, and Violence in Pre–Civil War Kansas* (Baton Rouge: LSU Press, 2009), 87–108.

33. Only 48 of the 124 Southern congressmen signed the "Southern Address." Holt, *Rise and Fall of the Whig Party*, 386–87. On the address's impact on the sectional crisis and Southern rights, see esp. Silbey, *Storm over Texas*, 144–46; Holt, *Fate of Their Country*, 51–55; Freehling, *The Road to Disunion*, passim, esp. 473–86. On the Missouri resolutions—known as the Jackson Resolutions, after Claiborne Fox Jackson, who proposed them—see Chambers, *Old Bullion Benton*, 340–43.

34. Benton denounced Calhoun, the "Address," and the resolutions in a speech in Jefferson City, Missouri, on May 26, 1849. Foote responded in a letter addressed to Wise, dated June 23, 1849, that appeared in several newspapers. See for example the *Washington Union*, June 24, 1849; *Richmond Enquirer*, July 3, 1849; *Baltimore Sun*, June 25, 1849. For more on the Benton-Calhoun clash, see Joseph M. Hernon, *Profiles in Character: Hubris and Heroism in the U.S. Senate, 1789–1990* (New York: M. E. Sharpe, 1997), esp. chapter 2, "Thomas Hart Benton vs. John C. Calhoun"; Clyde N. Wilson, Shirley Bright Cook, and Alexander Moore, eds., *The Papers of John C. Calhoun: 1848–1849* (Columbia: University of South Carolina Press, 2001), vol. 26. On the blend of electioneering and political principles that motivated Benton, see John D. Morton, "'A High Wall and a Deep Ditch': Thomas Hart Benton and the Compromise of 1850," *Missouri Historical Review* 94 (October 1999): 1–24; Benjamin C. Merkel, "The Slavery Issue and the Political Decline of Thomas Hart Benton, 1846–1856," *Missouri Historical Review* 38 (July 1944): 3–88; Clarence McClure, *Opposition in Missouri to Thomas Hart Benton* (Warrensburg: Central Missouri State Teachers College, 1926); Robert E. Shalhope, "Thomas Hart Benton and Missouri State Politics: A Re-Examination," *Bulletin of the Missouri Historical Society* 25 (April 1969): 171–91.

35. *Globe*, 31st Cong., 1st Sess., July 30, 1850, 1480.

36. 31st Cong., 1st Sess., S. Rpt. No. 170, July 30, 1850, "Thomas H. Benton of Missouri and Henry S. Foote of Mississippi," 93–113, quote on 99. For Wise's role in egging Foote on, see A.Y.P. Garnett to Muscoe Russell Hunter Garnett, June 29, 1849, Papers of the Hunter-Garnett Family, UVA. Outraged at Benton's attack on Calhoun and the South, A.Y.P. Garnett (Wise's son-in-law) asked Foote to "come out against Benton" and then asked Wise to urge Foote "to come out and address his letter to Wise," so that Wise might also have an excuse to publicly attack Benton. Some people at the time believed—rightly—that Foote had been chosen by Southerners to attack Benton. See Meigs, *Life of Thomas Hart Benton*, 401; Meigs says that he learned of this allegation from James Bradbury (D-ME), one of Benton's colleagues in the Senate.

37. *Globe*, 31st Cong., 1st Sess., April 18, 1850, 773.
38. French, diary entry, December 21–22, 1850, *Witness*, 215.
39. Bess to French, August 11, 1852, BBFFP.
40. French, diary entry, January 8, 1844, BBFFP.
41. On antebellum Masonry, see Ann Pflugrad-Jackisch, *Brothers of a Vow: Secret Fraternal Orders and the Transformation of White Male Culture in Antebellum Virginia* (Athens: University of Georgia, 2010); Steven C. Bullock, *Revolutionary Brotherhood: Freemasonry and the Transformation of the American Social Order, 1730–1840* (Chapel Hill: UNC, 1998).
42. Francis O. French, diary entry, April 3 and 5, 1850, *Growing Up on Capitol Hill*, 10. French wrote the poem on February 22, 1850; it appeared in Pennsylvania newspapers in March and April. Scrapbook, BBFFP; *Mountain Sentinel* (Ebensburg, Pa.), April 18, 1850.
43. Hamilton, *Prologue to Conflict*, 33; John C. Waugh, *On the Brink of Civil War: The Compromise of 1850 and How It Changed the Course of American History* (Wilmington, Del.: Scholarly Resources, 2003), 8.
44. On Foote generally, see Jon L. Wakelyn, "Disloyalty in the Confederate Congress: The Character of Henry Stuart Foote," in *Confederates Against the Confederacy: Essays on Leadership and Loyalty*, ed. Jon L. Wakelyn (Westport, Conn.: Praeger, 2002), 53–76; John E. Gonzales, "The Public Career of Henry Stuart Foote, 1804–1880" (Ph.D. dissertation, UNC, 1957); George Baber, "Personal Recollections of Senator H. S. Foote," *Overland Monthly* 26 (July–December 1895): 162–71; James P. Coleman, "Two Irascible Antebellum Senators: George Poindexter and Henry S. Foote," *Journal of Mississippi History* 46 (February 1984): 17–27; John E. Gonzales, "Henry Stuart Foote: A Forgotten Unionist of the Fifties," *Southern Quarterly* 1 (January 1963): 129–39; Henry S. Foote, *Casket of Reminiscences* (Washington: Chronicle, 1874); idem, *The Bench and Bar of the South and Southwest* (St. Louis: Thomas Wentworth, 1876). Foote was a "distant cousin" of the historian Shelby Foote. William C. Carter, ed., *Conversations with Shelby Foote* (Jackson: University Press of Mississippi, 1989), 154.
45. Luke Lea of Mississippi was testifying; he said that he had known Foote for about ten years. Benton-Foote Report, 33.
46. Ibid., 7, 10–11, 26, 129. See also J.[ames] S.[hepherd] P.[ike], "Benton, Clay, Foote," April 18, 1850, in *Littell's Living Age* 25 (April 1850): 331.
47. Foote, *Casket of Reminiscences*, 76.
48. See ibid., 187. According to one account, in one of his two duels with S. S. Prentiss, when one of Foote's bullets passed over Prentiss's head, Prentiss called to a small boy watching from a tree: "My son, you had better take care; General Foote is shooting rather wild." *Encyclopedia of Mississippi History: Compromising Sketches of Counties, Towns, Events, Institutions and Persons*, ed. Dunbar Rowland, 2 vols. (Madison, Wis.: Selwyn A. Brant, 1907), 2:469.
49. Oliver Dyer, *Great Senators of the United States Forty Years Ago* (New York: Robert Bonner's Sons, 1889), 140.
50. On the Davis dispute, see James T. McIntosh, ed., *The Papers of Jefferson Davis, 1856–1860* (Baton Rouge: LSU Press, 1974), 2:86, note 38; and Felicity Allen, *Jefferson Davis: Unconquerable Heart* (Columbia: University of Missouri Press, 1999),

163, which quotes a letter from Davis describing how he "knocked him [Foote] down, jumped on him and commenced beating him." On the Cameron dispute, see Dyer, *Great Senators*, 140. On the Fremont dispute, see Foote, *Casket of Reminiscences*, 340–43; Jones, "Personal Recollections," in Parish, *George Wallace Jones*, 273. On the Borland fight, see *Saturday Evening Post*, March 23, 1850; *Daily Evening Transcript* (Boston), March 16, 1850; *Boston Daily Atlas*, March 16, 1850; *Constitution* (Middletown, Conn.), March 20, 1850; *Washington Union*, in *The Independent*, March 28, 1850; *Alexandria Gazette*, March 16, 1850; *Missouri Republican* (St. Louis), March 19, 1850; *New-York Tribune*, March 16, 1850.

51. *Savannah Daily Republican*, April 23, 1850.

52. *Boston Evening Transcript*, April 23, 1850; *Saturday Evening Post* (Philadelphia), March 23, 1850. The verse was modeled on the frequently reprinted Isaac Watts's *Divine and Moral Songs for Children*, a hymnal of sorts first published in 1715. On Borland's fights, see Steven Teske, *Unvarnished Arkansas: The Naked Truth about Nine Famous Arkansans* (Little Rock: Butler Center Books, 2013), 49–57.

53. *Herald* (Port Gibson, Miss.), July 4, 1844, in *The Papers of Jefferson Davis: June 1841–July 1846*, ed. James T. McIntosh, 2:176.

54. David Outlaw to Emily Outlaw, January 9, 1850, DOP.

55. French, diary entry, April 11, 1858, *Witness*, 291. When told that his opponents called him vain, Benton supposedly replied: "G—d—them, I've got something to be vain and egotistical of. I know more than all of them put together." Jones, "Personal Recollections," in Parish, *George Wallace Jones*, 271.

56. Benton to unknown correspondent, 1813, in Robert V. Remini, *Andrew Jackson: The Course of American Empire, 1767–1821* (Baltimore: Johns Hopkins, 1998), 184–86; Dick Steward, *Duels and the Roots of Violence in Missouri* (Columbia: University of Missouri Press, 2000), 62; *Huron Reflector* (Norwalk, Ohio), June 4, 1844.

57. Benton became involved in three disputes with the opposing lawyer Charles Lucas. Lucas called Benton a liar during the case and Benton challenged him to a duel, but Lucas argued that it impinged on his rights at the bar. Nine months later when they clashed again, Benton called Lucas a puppy and Lucas challenged him; Lucas was shot but recovered. Not long after, Lucas's friends began whispering that Benton had been too scared to shorten the distance between the two men on the dueling ground; the two men dueled again, and this time Benton killed Lucas. Smith, *Magnificent Missourian*, 59–65; Steward, *Duels and the Roots of Violence in Missouri*, 58–78.

58. French to Harriette French, April 24, 1834, BBFFP. French assumed that his sister "must have heard of Col. Benton . . . He is the man who had such a fight in Nashville."

59. William Nisbet Chambers, *Old Bullion Benton: Senator from the New West* (Boston: Little, Brown, 1956), 185–86.

60. David Outlaw told his wife that when Benton didn't respond to Butler's challenge, a "peremptory note" was sent via Senator Reverdy Johnson (W-MD) demanding a response by 5:00 p.m., or the matter would be considered closed. Outlaw to Emily Outlaw, August 17, 1848, DOP. For a detailed account of the negotiations, see *New York Herald*, August 15 and 19, 1848; Chambers, *Old Bullion Benton*, 329.

61. David Outlaw to Emily Outlaw, January 17, 1850, DOP; *New Hampshire Sentinel* (Keene), April 25, 1850; Adams, diary entry, April 8, 1840, *Memoirs*, 10:257. Adams, sitting next to Benton at funeral services for a senator, was watching Benton entertain one of his daughters on his knee.

62. George Julian, *Political Recollections*, 92.

63. Adams, *Memoirs*, August 16, 1841, 10:533.

64. On Benton's dictatorial, aggressive personality and Missouri's desire for a "fighting leader," see Perry McCandless, "The Political Philosophy and Political Personality of Thomas H. Benton," *Missouri Historical Review* 2 (January 1956): 145–58. On Benton more generally, see Adam Arenson, *The Great Heart of the Republic: St. Louis and the Cultural Civil War* (Cambridge, Mass.: Harvard University Press, 2011); Elbert B. Smith, *Magnificent Missourian: The Life of Thomas Hart Benton* (New York: J. B. Lippincott, 1958); Chambers, *Old Bullion Benton*; Thomas Hart Benton, *Thirty Years View; or, A History of the Working of the American Government for Thirty Years, from 1820 to 1850*, 2 vols. (New York: D. Appleton, 1856).

65. Henry A. Wise, *Seven Decades of the Union: The Humanities and Materialism* (Philadelphia: J. B. Lippincott, 1872), 137. For references to "bully Benton," see for example *Ohio State Journal* (Columbus), November 16, 1842; *Daily Madisonian* (Washington, D.C.), March 22, 1843; *Baltimore Sun*, March 5, 1847; *Trenton State Gazette*, March 8, 1847.

66. Dyer, *Great Senators of the United States Forty Years Ago*, 203.

67. *Albany Evening Journal*, August 17, 1848; *New York Herald*, August 15, 1848; *Semi-Weekly Eagle* (Brattleboro, Vt.), August 17, 1848. For a good account of the negotiations between—and arrest of—Benton and Butler, see *New York Herald*, August 19, 1848. See also Dyer, *Great Senators*, 203, 200.

68. *Globe*, 30th Cong.,1st Sess., August 12, 1848, 1077.

69. Holt, *The Fate of Their Country*, 71–73; Stegmaier, *Texas, New Mexico, and the Compromise of 1850*, 103, 373, note 13. For some of Foote's proposals, see Stegmaier, *Texas, New Mexico, and the Compromise of 1850*, 93–96; Holt, *Political Crisis*, 86.

70. See esp. Varon, *Disunion!*

71. Ibid., 199–231; and more generally, Mark E. Neely, Jr., "The Kansas-Nebraska Act in American Political Culture: The Road to Bladensburg and the Appeal of the Independent Democrats," in *The Nebraska-Kansas Act of 1854*, ed. John R. Wunder and Joann M. Ross (Lincoln: University of Nebraska Press, 2008), 13–46, esp. 13–23; Amy S. Greenberg, "Manifest Destiny's Hangover: Congress Confronts Territorial Expansion and Martial Masculinity in the 1850s," in *Congress and the Crisis of the 1850s*, ed. Finkelman and Kennon, 97–119; Olsen, *Political Culture and Secession*, 44–54; Kenneth A. Deitreich, "Honor, Patriarchy, and Disunion: Masculinity and the Coming of the American Civil War" (Ph.D. dissertation, Western Virginia University, 2006).

72. On the personal dimensions of sectional rights (and particularly, Southern rights), see Paul D. H. Quigley, "Patchwork Nation: Sources of Confederate Nationalism, 1848–1865" (Ph.D. dissertation, UNC, 2006), 113–37; Wyatt-Brown, *Shaping of Southern Culture*, 177–202; Olsen, *Political Culture and Secession in Mississippi*, 169–95.

73. *Globe*, 31st Cong., 1st Sess., January 22, 1850, 205. New York's *Commercial Advertiser* stated that sometimes the telegraph "works wonderfully well in the transmission of both doings and sayings: and sometimes it works so that we do not know what to make of it." In Clingman's case, "Either the gentleman has talked an inconceivable mass of nonsense, or the telegraph has made him say something very different from his real utterance." *Commercial Advertiser*, January 23, 1850.

74. *Globe*, 31st Cong., 1st Sess., January 22, 1850, 205.

75. Ibid., February 18, 1850, 375–85.

76. Ibid., February 21, 1850, 418.

77. See for example *Daily Union* (Washington), March 1 and 19, 1850; *Trenton State Gazette*, March 1, 1850; *Richmond Whig*, March 1, 1850; *Baltimore Sun*, February 27, 1850; *Philadelphia Inquirer*, March 4, 1850; *Albany Evening Journal*, March 4, 1850.

78. *Philadelphia Inquirer*, March 4, 1850.

79. David Outlaw to Emily Outlaw, March 3, 1850, DOP.

80. David Outlaw to Emily Outlaw, January [?] 1850, DOP.

81. *Philadelphia Inquirer*, March 4, 1850. For a range of opinions, see *Journal of Commerce*, March 4, 1850; *Trenton State Gazette*, March 1, 1850; *Daily Union*, March 1, 1850; *Boston Evening Transcript*, February 28, 1850.

82. Horace Mann to Charles Sumner, March 4, 1849, in Mann, *Life of Horace Mann*, 277. The three fights on the evening of March 4, 1849, pitted Robert Ward Johnson (D-AK) against Orlando Ficklin (D-IL); Richard Kidder Meade (D-VA) against Joshua Giddings (W-OH); and Henry Foote (D-MS) against Simon Cameron (D-PA). Johnson shoved Ficklin over some desks; Meade charged at Giddings; and Foote punched Cameron.

83. David Outlaw to Emily Outlaw, March 4, 1850, DOP. Outlaw described the crowds as "strangers"—suggesting that they weren't local Washingtonians.

84. David Outlaw to Emily Outlaw, March 1, 2, and 3, 1850, ibid; Horace Mann to Samuel Downer, August 17, 1852, in Mann, *Life of Horace Mann*, 380; Mann to E. W. Clap, February 14, 1850, ibid., 289.

85. David Outlaw to Emily Outlaw, December 16, 1849, ibid.

86. John Parker Hale to Lucy Hale, December 22, 1848, John Parker Hale Papers, NHHS.

87. Varon, *Disunion!*, 210. On the parliamentary use of disunion threats to "control government," see ibid., 7–10.

88. French to Henry Flagg French, January 20, 1850, BBFFP. For a similar sentiment from a few years earlier, see William Pitt Fessenden to Ellen Fessenden, February 6, 1842, in *Life and Public Services of William Pitt Fessenden*, 23; Robert J. Cook, *Civil War Senator: William Pitt Fessenden and the Fight to Save the American Republic* (Baton Rouge: LSU Press, 2013), 55.

89. French, diary entry, January 21, 1849, *Witness*, 207–8; French, "To the Hon. J. R. Giddings, upon reading his great speech in the Ho Reps U. S. on Presidential nominations," July 11, 1852, BBFFP.

90. *Liberator*, March 6, 1849; Giddings's diary, March 2–4, 1849, in Stewart, "Joshua Giddings, Antislavery Violence, and Congressional Politics of Honor," 184; *Boston*

Herald, March 6, 1849; *Louisville Daily Journal,* March 10, 1849; Walter Buell, *Joshua R. Giddings: A Sketch* (Cleveland: William W. Williams, 1882), 189–90; *Cabinet* (Schenectady, N.Y.), March 13, 1849.

91. *Globe,* 31st Cong., 1st Sess., February 13, 1850, 343–44. The press noted Hale's unusual flare-up; see for example *Milwaukee Sentinel,* February 16, 1850; *Newark Daily Advertiser,* February 13, 1850.

92. *Globe,* 30th Cong., 1st Sess., May 20, 1848, 511–12.

93. Ibid., 31st Cong., 1st Sess., December 14, 1850, 32.

94. David Outlaw to Emily Outlaw, December 15, 1850, DOP; *Globe,* 31st Cong., 1st Sess., December 15, 1850, 36. Essentially, the House voted for the doorkeeper and sergeant at arms from the Thirtieth Congress to enforce what had been Rule 17 in that Congress. David Outlaw to Emily Outlaw, January 14, 1850, DOP. With a Speaker elected, the House was debating its rules. *Globe,* 31st Cong., 1st Sess., January 14, 1850, 146–48.

95. *Alexandria Gazette,* April 19, 1850.

96. *Commercial Advertiser* (N.Y.), April 19, 1850.

97. *Boston Recorder,* April 25, 1850.

98. *Globe,* 31st Cong, 1st Sess., January 22, 1850, 205. On expansion and sectional rights as personally reconciled realities and not abstractions, see also Morrison, *Slavery and the American West*; Woods, *Emotional and Sectional Conflict.*

99. On the ambiguities of sectionalism and sentiment about national unity and nationalism, see Rogan Kersh, *Dreams of a More Perfect Union* (Ithaca: Cornell University Press, 2001), esp. 141–52; Morrison, *Slavery and the American West.* On the idea of an "affective theory of the Union," see Woods, *Emotional and Sectional Conflict,* 21–31.

100. French to Henry Flagg French, January 20, 1850, BBFFP.

101. David Outlaw to Emily Outlaw, [January 1850,] DOP.

102. Not all confrontations involved two Southerners. William Seward (W-NY) left town when Thomas Jefferson Rusk (D-TX) threatened him over a reneged promise concerning Texas. Walter Stahr, *Seward: Lincoln's Indispensable Man* (New York: Simon and Schuster, 2012), 130–31. Assuring Rusk that Texas could get a better boundary in a bill that was separate from the Omnibus cluster of bills, Seward asked Rusk to draw up a bill, but filed it away and never acted on it. Not long after, Seward voted against a separate bill for Texas. The outraged Rusk threatened to expose Seward as a liar, and may have threatened him with a duel challenge. Seward made vague excuses and left town. My thanks to Walter Stahr for alerting me to this incident.

103. John Raven Mathewes to John C. Calhoun, October 7, 1849, in *The Papers of John C. Calhoun,* ed. Robert L. Meriwether and Clyde N. Wilson (Columbia: University of South Carolina Press, 1959–2003): 27:77. For Foote's confession along these lines, see Foote, *Casket of Reminiscences,* 337. Benton's loyalties were already suspect in Congress; he was one of only two Southern senators not invited to John C. Calhoun's Southern caucus. Sam Houston also wasn't invited, but he went in the hope of tempering extremism. For Benton as traitor, see *Mississippi Free Trader,* June 6 and September 9, 1849; *Richmond Enquirer,* June 8 and 29, November 6, 1849; *Rusk Pioneer* (Rusk, Tex.), July 25, 1849; *Macon Weekly Telegraph,* August 14, 1849.

104. Solon Borland called Benton's attack on Calhoun "an assault upon the South." Borland to Calhoun, August 5, 1849, *Papers of John C. Calhoun* (Columbia: University of South Carolina Press, 2003), 27:13. See also John Raven Mathewes to Calhoun, October 7, 1849; Fitzwilliam Byrdsall to Calhoun, February 11, 1850, ibid., 27:77, 171; and A.Y.P. Garnett to Muscoe Russell Hunter Garnett, June 29, 1849, Papers of the Hunter-Garnett Family, UVA; Garnett vowed "to raise Heaven & earth" to reply to Benton's "attack . . . upon Mr. Calhoun & the South generally."

105. Benton-Foote Report, 4.

106. Henry Stuart Foote, *The Bench and Bar of the South and Southwest* (St. Louis: Soule, Thomas & Wentworth, 1876), 161.

107. *Globe*, 31st Cong., 1st Sess., March 26, 1850, 602–3.

108. David Outlaw to Emily Outlaw, January 17, 1850, DOP.

109. Benton-Foote Report, Senate Representative Com. No. 170, 31st Cong., 1st Sess., July 30, 1850, 45, 50, 56, 57, 80, 87, 88, 121.

110. *Globe*, 26th Cong., 1st Sess., January 18, 1840, 128. Fisher was attacked by Charles Mitchell (W-NY). For other examples, see ibid., June 23, 1840, 481; January 23, 1846, 29th Cong., 1st Sess., 236; 26th Cong., 1st Sess., 128, 269, 313; 26th Cong., 2nd Sess., 328; 27th Cong., 3rd Sess., 277; 29th Cong., 1st Sess., 661. To avoid attacking someone who was absent, some men forewarned their victims of a coming attack. See for example *Globe*, 26th Cong., 2nd Sess., 172; 26th Cong., 1st Sess., 492; 27th Cong., 2nd Sess., 401; 29th Cong., 2nd Sess., 351.

111. On Benton leaving the chamber, see David Outlaw to Emily Outlaw, January 17, 1850, DOP; testimony of Hannibal Hamlin (D-ME), June 20, 1850, Benton-Foote Report, 126.

112. Testimony of Hannibal Hamlin (D-ME), June 20, 1850, Benton-Foote Report, 126.

113. Ibid., 26th Cong., 1st Sess., March 14, 1840, 269. See also ibid., 28th Cong., 1st Sess., January 13, 1844, 139; and ibid., March 18, 1846, 29th Cong., 1st Sess., 521–22. On personal explanations, see also *Hinds*, 5:5064–74, 79; Shelden, *Washington Brotherhood*, 31.

114. As Speaker John W. Davis (D-IN) put it, "Any question which conveyed an imputation on a member, as touching his integrity, was necessarily a question of privilege and must override all others." *Globe*, 29th Cong., 1st Sess., January 10, 1846, 177.

115. *Globe*, 29th Cong., 1st Sess., April 27, 1846, 731.

116. See for example T. P. Chisman to Frederick Lander, April 13, 1860, Frederick W. Lander Papers, LC; *New York Herald*, March 1 and April 14, 1860.

117. Unidentified newspaper article, Scrapbook, ca. 1859–60, Frederick W. Lander Papers, LC.

118. David Outlaw to Emily Outlaw, December 13 and 16, 1849, DOP. On congressional street fights, see the actions of Henry Wilson (R-MA) when William Gwin (D-CA) challenged him to a duel in 1858. Wilson to the editors of the *Saturday Evening Post*, July 7, 1858, reprinted in *NYT*, July 10, 1858. Similarly, William Montgomery (D-PA) offered to fight William English (D-IN) on the street ("but without weapons") after they clashed in 1858; they ended up fighting with a cane (English) and a brick (Montgomery). After one of the 1850 fights—between

William Bissell (D-IL) and Jefferson Davis (D-MS) over whose regiment was more heroic during the war with Mexico—*The New York Herald* predicted a "street collision" because of the District's anti-dueling law. *Herald*, March 1, 1850. Also, during the 1860 dispute between John Potter (R-WI) and Roger Pryor (D-VA), T. P. Chisman thought that as a Northerner, Potter might opt for a street fight. T. P. Chisman to Frederick Lander, April 13, 1860, Frederick W. Lander Papers, LC; *New York Herald*, March 1 and April 14, 1860. After Sumner's caning, Horace Sergent declared a street fight the best alternative for men who wouldn't duel. Sergent to Sumner, May 23, 1856, Charles Sumner Papers, LC. Sumner declared street fights a Southern custom. Sumner, *The Barbarism of Slavery* (N.Y.: Young Men's Republican Union, 1863 reprint with new introduction by Sumner), 43, 55–56. See also Wyatt-Brown, *Southern Honor*, 353.

119. David Outlaw to Emily Outlaw, December 13 and 16, 1849, DOP. With the aid of seconds, Duer and Meade negotiated a mutual apology that was announced on the floor and met with applause. *Globe*, 31st Cong., 1st Sess., December 19, 1850; *Huron Reflector* (Norwalk, Ohio), January 1, 1850.

120. Benton-Foote Report, 22, 28. See also Foote, *Casket of Reminiscences*, 339; Foote says that Senator Thomas Pratt (W-MD) told him that given the public threat, Foote should arm himself.

121. Benton-Foote Report, 30.

122. Ibid., 63. See also *Globe*, 31st Cong., 1st Sess., April 17, 1850, 763. Henry Dodge (D-WI) was speaking.

123. Testimony of General Edny, June 7, 1850, Benton-Foote Report, 118.

124. Ibid.

125. *Liberator* (Boston), May 3, 1850. See also *New-York Tribune*, April 19, 1850.

126. *Globe*, 31st Cong., 1st Sess., April 17, 1850, 762.

127. Ibid.; *Baltimore Sun*, April 18, 1850.

128. Testimony of Albert Gallatin Brown (D-MI), June 24, 1850, ibid., 129.

129. Testimony of Elbridge Gerry, May 3, 1850, ibid., 16. Gerry (D-ME) and James Bradbury (D-ME) examined Benton to see if he was armed.

130. *New York Herald*, April 15, 1858, reprinted from *Washington Union*, April 13, 1858. See also David Brown, *Southern Outcast: Hinton Rowan Helper and the Impending Crisis of the South* (Baton Rouge: LSU Press, 2006), 135–37. Helper was fighting with Francis Burton Craige (D-NC). Brown notes that Wright accused Helper of starting the fight, but that Helper said that Craige was a "bully" who threw the first punch. Helper, author of *The Impending Crisis of the South*, had come to the House to defend his name against a personal attack delivered during debate by Asa Biggs (D-NC); Helper thought that Craige had given damaging personal information to Biggs. For more on this clash, see chapter 7.

131. *Boston Courier*, April 18, 1850, as reprinted in *Littell's Living Age*, April 1850, 331. The piece was signed J.S.P. (James Shepherd Pike).

132. Benton also asked United States District Attorney Philip Fendall to bring the case before the District Criminal Court. *Alexandria Gazette*, April 20, 1850; *Commercial Advertiser* (N.Y.), April 23, 1850.

133. Benton-Foote Report, 16–17, 89.

134. Historians usually cite the Foote-Benton scuffle as a splash of color that brings

the period's political tensions to life, or as political theater aimed at Foote's home audience, arguing that congressmen knew it was just for show. But in fact, the committee report shows that congressmen expected physical violence (people expected Foote to be beaten, and Foote worried about wounding senators if he fired his gun on the floor), and the reputations of Foote and Benton both in Washington and at home were implicated. Some bullying was aimed at both congressional colleagues *and* a home audience; indeed, the two audiences were intertwined, as congressmen themselves well knew.

135. *New York Express*, June 17, 1846, in Menahem Blondheim, *News over the Wires: The Telegraph and the Flow of Public Information, 1844–1897* (Cambridge: Harvard University Press, 1994), 191.

136. On the telegraph, see esp. Blondheim, *News over the Wires*; Richard R. John, *Spreading the News: The American Postal System from Franklin to Morse* (Cambridge, Mass.: Harvard University Press, 1995); Daniel Walker Howe, *What Hath God Wrought*, 1–4, 690–98; Richard B. Kielbowicz, "News Gathering by Mail in the Age of the Telegraph: Adapting to a New Technology," *Technology and Culture* 28 (January 1987): 26–41; David W. Bulla and Gregory A. Borchard, *Journalism in the Civil War Era* (New York: Peter Lang Publishing, 2010), 90–94; Richard R. John, "Recasting the Information Infrastructure for the Industrial Age," in *A Nation Transformed by Information: How Information Has Shaped the United States from Colonial Times to the Present*, ed. Alfred D. Chandler, Jr., and James W. Cortada (New York: Oxford University Press, 2000), 65; idem., *Network Nation: Inventing American Telecommunications* (Cambridge: Harvard University Press, 2010); Baldasty, *Commercialization of News*.

137. *Globe*, 34th Cong., 1st Sess., April 21, 1856, 286 app.

138. Blondheim, *News over the Wires*, 39. Smith's full name was Francis Ormand Jonathan Smith; French named his son Francis Ormand.

139. French, letter to the editor, October 31, 1848, in *Daily Union*, November 1, 1848.

140. French, "To the Editors," *Daily National Intelligencer*, May 31, 1848. He paid a reporter $20.00 to cover the convention, and $10.50 in telegraphic charges.

141. The poem was titled "On the Changes of the World" and included a passage on the telegraph. John Thomas Scharf, *History of Baltimore City and County, from the Earliest Period to the Present Day* (Philadelphia: Louis H. Everts, 1881), 505.

142. French, diary entry, June 18, 1843, *Witness*, 149.

143. Benton-Foote Report, 53–54, 82–83.

144. Ibid., 54–57.

145. Testimony of Jesse Bright, June 8, 1850, ibid., 70. Benton explicitly asked Jesse Bright (D-IN), did Foote "'glide' or 'walk'"? "I should say he walked," Bright replied. Ibid., 119. See also Foote's footnote in the *Globe*, 31st Cong., 1st Sess., April 17, 1850, 762.

146. Benton-Foote Report, 132, 128.

147. See for example *Daily Missouri Republic*, April 29, 1850; *Trenton State Gazette*, April 20, 1850; *National Era* (Washington), April 25, 1850; *Daily Picayune* (New Orleans), April 20, 1850; *Savannah Republican*, April 23, 1850; *Plain Dealer* (Cleveland), May 1, 1850. See also *Daily Ohio State Journal*, April 23, 1850.

148. *Baltimore Sun*, June 24, 1850, in *Daily Missouri Republican*, July 1, 1850.

149. *Richmond Enquirer,* April 26, 1850.
150. *New-York Tribune,* in *Wisconsin Democrat,* May 4, 1850. On Swisshelm's admission to the reporter's gallery, see Donald A. Ritchie, *American Journalists: Getting the Story* (New York: Oxford University Press, 1997); Jane Gray Cannon Swisshelm, *Half a Century: The Memoirs of the First Woman Journalist in the Civil Rights Struggle,* ed. Paul D. Sporer (Chester, N.Y.: Anza Publishing, 2005), 87–88. On Swisshelm's account of the fracas, the *Wisconsin Democrat* wrote: "nobody but a regular woman could make a description of such a scene so interesting. That jerking, nervous, half breathless excitement which would embarrass the narrative of a man only adds piquancy and grace to that of a woman—and they always have words for their ideas and ideas for their words."
151. *Richmond Enquirer,* April 26, 1850.
152. *Washington Reporter* (Pennsylvania), April 24, 1850.
153. *St. Albans (Vermont) Messenger,* April 25, 1850.
154. *Trenton State* Gazette, April 20, 1850; *Evening Transcript* (Boston), April 23, 1850. This article is titled "Yankee Sullivan, New York Hyer, Mississippi Foote, Missouri Benton." Sullivan and Hyer were famous boxers.
155. *Boston Herald,* April 19, 1850.
156. Hamilton, *Prologue to Conflict,* 160.
157. Salma Hale to John Parker Hale, April 12, 1850, John Parker Hale Papers, NHHS.
158. *Articles of Association and Charter from the State of Maryland, of the Magnetic Telegraph Company, Together with the Office Regulations and the Minutes of the Meetings of Stockholders and Board of Directors* (New York: Chatterton & Crist, 1847), 231.
159. French to Henry Flagg French, December 27, 1852, BBFFP.

6. A TALE OF TWO CONSPIRACIES

1. Another passenger later died of injuries. *Boston Herald,* January 7, 1853; *New Hampshire Patriot,* January 12, 1853.
2. French, diary entry, March 27, April 24, 1853, *Witness,* 233, 239.
3. Benjamin Brown French to French, August 9, 1852, BBFFP.
4. *Connecticut Courant* (Hartford), July 10, 1852; *Richmond Whig,* July 9, 1852; *Trenton State Gazette,* June 25 and 26, 1852; *Albany Evening Journal,* June 10, 1852; *Kalamazoo Gazette,* June 11, 1852; *Weekly Journal* (Galveston), June 11, 1852. For a Democratic defense, see *Trenton State Gazette,* June 7, 1852.
5. *National Aegis* (Worcester, Mass.), July 7, 1852. Pierce's original statement was: "No North, no South, no East, no West." *Daily Union,* June 6, 1852.
6. *New-York Tribune,* June 10, 1852; *Litchfield Republican,* June 17, 1852; *Floridian and Journal* (Tallahassee), June 26, 1852; *Daily Alabama Journal,* June 18, 1852; *Daily Atlas* (Boston), July 23, 1852; Wallner, *Franklin Pierce: New Hampshire's Favorite Son,* 147–48; Nichols, *Franklin Pierce,* 161–63. According to Nichols, Pierce's horse reared, banging Pierce's groin against the saddle pommel, inflicting an "excruciating and sense-taking though hardly permanent injury" before falling on Pierce and wrenching his knee; at some point, Pierce passed out. The next

day, though still in pain, he insisted on fighting at the battle of Churubusco; while advancing under fire he twisted his injured knee and fainted again, though when he came to, he allegedly insisted that his men leave him where he was, exposed to enemy fire. The "bottle" accusation originated in the *New-York Tribune* and was so loudly condemned that Greeley retracted it. *Tribune*, June 10 and 11, 1852.

7. Nichols, *Franklin Pierce*, 201–202. A Richmond editor had been asking candidates about their stance on the Fugitive Slave Act. Although not formally a candidate, Pierce knew that his dark-horse candidacy depended on his clarity on this key issue, so he wrote a letter to Major F. T. Lally, an old army friend in the Maine delegation, clearly stating his views.

8. *Connecticut Courant*, July 24, 1852; *Salem Register*, July 15, 1852; *Richmond Whig*, July 16, 1852; *Alexandria Gazette*, July 14, 1852. For defenses of Pierce against such charges, see *Richmond Enquirer*, July 20 and 26, 1852; *Macon Weekly Telegraph*, June 29, 1852. See also Stephen John Hartnett, "Franklin Pierce and the Exuberant Hauteur of an Age of Extremes: A Love Song for America in Six Movements," *Before the Rhetorical Presidency*, ed. Martin J. Medhurst (College Station: Texas A&M University, 2008), 117–20.

9. *New York Evening Post*, June 8, 1852. Countering the Northern Democratic claims, see the Whig *Albany Evening Journal*, June 10 and 14, 1852; *Enquirer* (Richmond), June 15, 1852—for Southern Democrats; *Connecticut Courant*, July 17 and 24, 1852. The alleged speech was in January 1852. For an example of Southern Democrats citing Northern Whigs to prove Pierce's South-friendly sentiments, see *Macon Weekly Telegraph*, June 29, 1852; also ibid., June 15, 1852, on the antislavery petition charge. On Pierce as South-friendly generally, see also *Mississippi Free Trader*, June 23, 1852; *Enquirer* (Richmond), June 25, July 20 and 26, 1852; *Macon Weekly Telegraph*, July 6, 1852; *Enquirer*, July 20, 1852.

10. For example, even as Northern Democratic newspapers praised Pierce for opposing gag rules, the Democratic *Enquirer* praised him for opposing the reception of slavery petitions; *Enquirer*, June 15, 1852.

11. *Daily Union*, June 8, 1852.

12. French, diary entry, January 2, 1853, *Witness*, 227.

13. Wise to Franklin Pierce, June 22, 1852, Franklin Pierce Papers; French to F.O.J. Smith, November 21, 1852, Collection 38, F.O.J. Smith Papers, Collections of the Maine Historical Society.

14. French to F.O.J. Smith, November 21, 1852, Collection 38, F.O.J. Smith Papers, Collection of the Maine Historical Society. French said that he stayed at a hotel where the Indiana, Illinois, New York, and Georgia delegates were staying. On the Convention generally, see Landis, *Northern Men*, 63–71.

15. Wise to Pierce, June 22, 1852, Franklin Pierce Papers. Wise also credited Caleb Cushing with influencing him and the Virginia delegation. Landis details the ardent efforts of the New Hampshire politico Edmund Burke. Landis, *Northern Men*, 61–69. For Wise's account of the fight, see his card for the *Portsmouth Democrat*, reprinted in the *American and Commercial Daily Advertiser* (Baltimore), October 5, 1852; William A. Link, *Roots of Secession: Slavery and Politics in Antebellum Virginia* (Chapel Hill: UNC Press, 2003), 69–70.

16. French to Bess French, July 26, 1852, BBFFP. Emphasis in original.

17. French to F.O.J. Smith, November 21, 1852, Collection 38, F.O.J. Smith Papers, Collections of the Maine Historical Society. Emphasis in original.
18. *Daily Union*, June 19, 1852.
19. French to Henry Flagg French, October 10, 1852, BBFFP. For more of French's electioneering efforts, see French to Pierce, July 15, 23, and August 4, 1852, Franklin Pierce Papers.
20. French to Henry Flagg French, March 13, 1853, BBFFP.
21. *Union* (Washington), June 15, 1852.
22. *Connecticut Courant*, July 10, 1852; *Milwaukee Daily Sentinel*, June 16, 1852; *Alexandria Gazette*, June 17, 1852.
23. Hawthorne to Horatio Bridge, October 13, 1852, in *The Letters, 1843–1853*, ed. Thomas Woodson, L. Neal Smith, and Norman Holmes Pearson (Columbus: Ohio State University Press, 1985), 16:605.
24. Ibid.
25. Pierce received 254 Electoral College votes to Winfield Scott's 42, and 1,601,474 popular votes to Scott's 1,386,580. The Free Soil candidate John Hale received 155,825 votes, and Daniel Webster—though dead—received 7,425—perhaps a desperate vote for compromise. Hartnett, "Franklin Pierce," 121. On Pierce's election and loyalties, see Landis, *Northern Men*, 66–84.
26. Nichols, *Franklin Pierce*, 216.
27. French called the Compromise a compact; July 1, 1855, *Witness*, 262. On the passage of the act as treachery, see Etcheson, *Bleeding Kansas*, chapter 1; Miner, *Seeding Civil War*, chapter 2. On the Kansas-Nebraska Act, generally, see also Malavasic, *The F Street Mess*; Wunder and Ross, *The Nebraska-Kansas Act of 1854*; Roy F. Nichols, "The Kansas-Nebraska Act: A Century of Historiography," *Mississippi Valley Historical Review* 43 (September 1956): 187–212; Varon, *Disunion!*, 251–66; Landis, *Northern Men*, 106–121; and Michael Woods's handy survey, *Bleeding Kansas: Slavery, Sectionalism, and Civil War on the Missouri-Kansas Border* (New York: Routledge, 2016).
28. French, diary entry, July 1, 1855, 260. See also August 3, 1855, 265.
29. Ibid., March 5, 1854, 249.
30. Ibid., January 29, 1854, 244–45.
31. Landis, *Northern Men*, 133.
32. For a doughface-centered look at the Kansas-Nebraska debate, see esp. Landis, *Northern Men*, 106–121.
33. On framing arguments in this debate, see Craig Miner, *Seeding Civil War*; Hartnett, *Democratic Dissent*; Gunja SenGupta, *For God and Mammon: Evangelicals and Entrepreneurs, Masters and Slaves in Territorial Kansas, 1854–1860* (Athens: University of Georgia, 1996).
34. *Macon Weekly Telegraph*, May 30, 1854. On press coverage of Kansas, see esp. Miner, *Seeding Civil War*. As Miner notes, the Kansas debate didn't break neatly along sectional lines; national party loyalties still had some impact. This held true for the press as well as for Congress.
35. See esp. Michael William Pfau, *The Political Style of Conspiracy: Chase, Sumner, and Lincoln* (East Lansing: Michigan State University, 2005); Miner, *Seeding Civil War*.

36. On the press offering the public a "front row seat" to Congress's conflict and machinations, see Miner, *Seeding Civil War*, 239–51.

37. On newspaper growth, see John, *Spreading the News*, 38; Brooke, "'To be 'Read by the Whole People'"; Swift, *The Making of an American Senate*, 167.

38. On national press exposure of sectional furor, see Ratner and Teeter, *Fanatics and Fire-Eaters*; Leonard, *Power of the Press*, 90–96; Miner, *Seeding Civil War*, 37–39; Schudson, *Discovering the News*, chapter 3; Pierce, "Networks of Disunion"; Kielbowicz, *News in the Mail*.

39. See also Miner, *Seeding Civil War*, 240–41, 246–49.

40. French to F.O.J. Smith, November 21, 1852, Collection 38, F.O.J. Smith Papers, Collections of the Maine Historical Society. Emphasis in original.

41. Samuel Kernell and Gray C. Jacobson, "Congress and the Presidency as News in the Nineteenth Century," *Journal of Politics* 49 (November 1987): 1016–35.

42. On Washington reporting, see esp. McPherson, "Reporting the Debates"; Essary, *Covering Washington*; Ritchie, *Press Gallery*; Culver H. Smith, *The Press, Politics, and Patronage*; Marbut, *News from the Capital*; Leonard, *Power of the Press*, chapter 3; Ames, *A History of the National Intelligencer*.

43. The *Congressional Globe* came out weekly, using the type set for the regular *Globe*. The *Register of Debates* came out at the end of every session until 1837, when it ceased publication. In 1848, the Senate hired reporters to cover its proceedings; improvements in stenography enabled them to record virtual verbatim accounts. The House followed suit in 1850. Amer, "The Congressional Record."

44. Baldasty, *Commercialization of News*, 42–43. The *Congressional Record* began publication in 1873. Other Washington newspapers, such as the *Union* and the *Telegraph*, also served as a kind of record, particularly the paper chosen as the president's "organ."

45. French, diary entry, June 19, 1843, *Witness*, 150.

46. *Globe*, 26th Cong., 1st Sess., April 9, 1840, 313. To avoid this problem, some reporters printed insults in the first person, indicating that they themselves weren't responsible for them. For example, the account of an exchange between Eugenius Nisbet (W-GA) and Edward Black (D-GA) shifts into the first person when Black asks if Nesbit is calling him a liar. Ibid., 26th Cong., 2nd Sess., February 18, 1841, 187.

47. For a sense of printing costs, see Smith, *Press, Politics, and Patronage*, 250–55. See also Robert C. Byrd, *The Senate: 1789–1989: Historical Statistics* (Washington, D.C.: GPO, 1993), 675; idem., "Reporters of Debate and the Congressional Record," ibid., 311–26; Hearing Before the Subcommittee on Government Management, Information, and Technology of the Committee on Government Reform, House of Representatives, May 24, 1999, No. 106–91, 4; Jenkins and Stewart, *Fighting for the Speakership*, 48–54. In 1846, Congress began low-bid printing awards. Baldasty, *The Commercialization of News in the Nineteenth Century*, 42.

48. French to unknown correspondent, March 28, 1836, BBFFP. See also French, diary entry, April 10, 1836, *Witness*, 64. Emphasis in original.

49. On the inaccuracy of the *Globe* and *Intelligencer*, see Alexander, *History and Procedure of the House of Representatives*, 101; McPherson, "Reporting the Debates"; *NYT*, April 10, 1860.

50. See for example *Globe*, 31st Cong., 1st Sess., December 13, 1849, 27.
51. Ibid., 33rd Cong., 1st Sess., June 20 and 21, 1854, 1451, 1466.
52. Ibid., 27th Cong., 3rd Sess., February 27, 1843, 353. See also ibid., 27th Cong. 1st Sess., 1, which explains that the appendix "will contain the long speeches, written out by the members themselves."
53. Ibid., 28th Cong., 1st Sess., February 21, 1844, 303–304; ibid., January 1844, 534 app.
54. French, diary entry, May 24, 1838, *Witness*, 86.
55. Ibid., July 17, 1870, 621.
56. Ibid., June 19, 1843, 150. On his reading and writing habits, see for example French to Henry Flagg French, July 3, 1853, BBFFP; French to R. J. Walker, July 31, 1844, BBFFP.
57. *Alexandria Gazette*, June 17, 1854.
58. *Daily National Intelligencer*, July 22, 1854. The *Intelligencer* said the day's average temperature was 94 degrees. French's three (!) thermometers—one at the front door, one in his library, and one in the parlor—read higher.
59. French to Henry Flagg French, December 12, 1847. French was irritated by charges in the Whig press and considered not only "pouncing" but libel suits.
60. Sir John Edwin Mason, "Sir Benjamin Brown French," *Proceedings of the Grand Encampment 18th Triennial Session* (Davenport, Iowa: Griggs, Watson & Day, 1871), 27 app.
61. Adams, diary entry, February 18, 1845, *Diary*, 12:170. Adams was speaking of his speech the day before.
62. Leonard, *Power of the Press*, 78–80; McPherson, "Reporting the Debates," 144; Ritchie, *Press Gallery*, 24.
63. Late in his career, Webster favored the *New York Times* reporter Henry Raymond: "Nobody could ever report my speeches, to make them appear so well as he." Webster to Simeon Draper, undated [post-1851], Henry J. Raymond Papers, NYPL. In 1830, Webster asked the *Intelligencer* editor Joseph Gales to record a speech, then spent a month revising it for print. Benjamin Perley Poore, *Perley's Reminiscences*, 1:116–18; McPherson, "Reporting the Debates," 145. See also Raymond's notes of a conversation with Webster, probably in late 1847 or early 1848, outlining in advance an argument that Webster delivered to the U.S. Supreme Court on January 27, 1848, concerning Rhode Island's Dorr Rebellion. Notes, undated, Henry J. Raymond Papers, NYPL. Thomas Hart Benton did the same with reporters. John Wentworth, *Congressional Reminiscences: Adams, Benton, Calhoun, Clay, and Webster, an Address: Delivered at Central Music Hall, Thursday Eve., March 16, 1882, Before the Chicago Historical Society* (Chicago: Fergus Printing Company, 1882), 47–48.
64. *Globe*, 31st Cong., 1st Sess., March 25, 1850, 592. See also Ritchie, *Press Gallery*, 24; George F. Hoar, *Autobiography of Seventy Years*, 2 vols. (New York: Charles Scribner's Sons, 1903), 144.
65. Adams, diary entry, March 6–17, 1835, *Diary*, 9:216–20; ibid., December 13, 1831, 8:437.
66. Benton-Foote Report, 56. Similarly, Adams referred a reporter for the *Boston Atlas* to the *Intelligencer*; Adams, diary entry, October 16, 1837, *Diary*, 9:414.

67. *Globe*, 26th Cong., 1st Sess., April 2 and 9, 1840, 301, 313–14. The footnote is dated April 10, 1840. See also ibid., May 1, 1840, 372.

68. Ibid., March 31, 1840, 297; McPherson, "Reporting the Debates," 145. Thompson was part of a Whig attack on the *Globe*, along with Edward Stanly (W-NC), William Graves (W-KY), and William Bond (W-OH) in the House, and Henry Clay (W-KY) in the Senate.

69. Gobright, *Recollections of Men and Things*, 402; Gobright became a *Globe* reporter in the winter of 1840. See esp. John Nerone, *Violence Against the Press: Policing the Public Sphere* (New York: Oxford University Press, 1994); Ford Risley, *Abolition and the Press: The Moral Struggle Against Slavery* (Evanston, Ill.: Northwestern University, 2008), esp. chapter 3.

70. Gobright, *Recollection of Men and Things*, 401–402.

71. Thompson is barely reported between March 31 and May 1, 1840; see for example *Globe*, 26th Cong., 1st Sess., 297, 370–71.

72. Ibid., May 1, 1840, 371.

73. *Globe*, 26th Cong., 1st Sess., January 18, 1840, 128; McPherson, "Reporting the Debates," 145.

74. Baldasty, *Commercialization of News*, 48–49.

75. Ibid., 42–43, 49.

76. Ibid., 42–43; Leonard, *Power of the Press*, 92–95; Ratner and Teeter, *Fanatics and Fire-Eaters*, 8–33.

77. *New York Herald*, April 13, 1860.

78. Hazel Dicken-Garcia, *Journalistic Standards in Nineteenth-Century America* (Madison: University of Wisconsin Press, 1989), 98, 175–78; Ratner and Teeter, *Fanatics and Fire-Eaters*, 21.

79. David Outlaw to Emily Outlaw, February 18, 1850, DOP.

80. *New-York Tribune*, May 10, 1854.

81. *Washington Sentinel*, May 12, 1854; *Daily Union* (Washington), May 14, 1854. There was much ranting by Southern congressmen as well. See for example *Globe*, 33rd Cong., 1st Sess., June 8, 1854, 1363.

82. Pike, *First Blows of the Civil War: The Ten Years of Preliminary Conflict in the United States, from 1850 to 1860* (New York: American News, 1879), 230–33. On Pike, see Ritchie, *Press Gallery*, 46–54.

83. *Ohio State Journal*, May 16, 1854.

84. On Campbell, see William E. Gienapp, *The Origins of the Republican Party, 1852–1856* (New York: Oxford University Press, 1987), 242; Robert J. Zalimas, Jr., "'Contest MY Seat Sir!': Lewis D. Campbell, Clement L. Vallandigham, and the Election of 1856," *Ohio History Journal* (Winter–Spring 1997): 5–30.

85. *Globe*, 33rd Cong., 1st Sess., May 11–12, 1854, 1854; *Coldwater (Mich.) Sentinel*, May 19, 1854; *Manufacturers' and Farmers' Journal*, May 15, 1854; Morrison, *Slavery and the American West*, 153–54.

86. Campbell to Pike, May 14, 1854, in Pike, *First Blows of the Civil War*, 230. For an example of such resolves, see "THE VOICE OF NEW YORK!," *Massachusetts Spy*, May 17, 1854.

87. Washburn to Pike, May 13, 1854, in Pike, *First Blows of the Civil War*, 226.

88. Ohioans Campbell, Joshua Giddings, and Salmon Chase also did some stirring

up, launching a statewide campaign for an anti-Nebraska "Convention of the
People" that they hoped "the people" would be willing to call. Chase to William
Schouler, May 25, 1855, in Reinhard H. Luthin, "Salmon P. Chase's Political
Career Before the Civil War," *Mississippi Historical Review* 29 (March 1943):
517–40, quote on 524.

89. Gienapp, *Origins of the Republican Party*, 242.
90. *Ohio State Journal*, November 25, 1854. Campbell won 2,463 votes in Butler
County, 2,414 votes in Preble County, and 4,181 votes in Montgomery County,
giving him a total of 9,058 votes; Democrat Clement Vallandigham won 2,755
votes, 966 votes, and 2,772 votes respectively, giving him a total of 6,493 votes.
See also Morrison, *Slavery and the American West*, 155–56; Potter, *Impending
Crisis*, 175–76.
91. Hudson, *Journalism in the United States*, 522–73.
92. On letter-writers, see Timothy E. Cook, "Senators and Reporters Revisited," in
Loomis, *Esteemed Colleagues*, 169–72; Ritchie, *Press Gallery*, 20–32 and passim;
Wilmer, *Our Press Gang*; Essary, *Covering Washington*, 22–26; Miner, *Seeding
Civil War*, 378–79. On a later period, see Ralph M. McKenzie, *Washington Correspondents Past and Present: Brief Sketches of the Rank and File* (New York: Newspaperdom, 1903). Congressmen were hard put to tell reporters from letter-writers.
Globe, 28th Cong., 1st Sess., January 26, 1844, 194; *Hinds' Precedents*, vol. 5, chapter 148, section 7306–308.
93. "Congressional Manners," *NYT*, April 10, 1860.
94. For a glance at this correlation, see Frank Luther Mott, "Facetious News Writing, 1833–1883," *Mississippi Valley Historical Review* 29 (June 1942): 35–54.
95. "Nominis in Umbra" [French], dateline February 23, 1838, *Chicago Democrat*,
BBFFP.
96. For congressional venting about letter-writers, see for example *Globe*, 28th Cong.,
2nd Sess., March 3, 1845, 388; ibid., 23rd Cong., 1st Sess., March 31, 1834, 280.
97. James Green (D-MO) was speaking. Ibid., 35th Cong., 2nd Sess., January 25,
1859, 574. See also "Black Cats in the Gallery—How Does the Herald Obtain
News," *New York Herald*, January 26, 1859. A year later, members joked about
"black cats" when discussing a leak. *Globe*, 36th Cong., 1st Sess., January 12,
1860, 430; *New York Herald*, January 13, 1860. For a search, see for example
Globe, 36th Cong., 1st Sess., January 12, 1860, 430.
98. Through his close connection with the *Philadelphia Press* editor John W. Forney,
Secretary of State (and future president) James Buchanan (D-PA)—a former
newspaperman himself—wrote occasional letters. Forney, *Public Men*, 195.
When Buchanan was blamed for leaking a copy of the Mexican Treaty to the
press through the *Herald's* letter-writer, President Polk thought that the controversy would teach him "a profitable lesson, and that is that it is dangerous to
have any connection or intercourse with the unprincipled letter writers at Washington." Diary entry, March 27, 1848, *Diary of James K. Polk*, 3:410. Buchanan
also wrote letters attacking Benton during debate over the admission of Oregon.
Meigs, *Life of Benton* (Philadelphia: J. B. Lippincott, 1904), 300–301.
99. *New-York Daily Tribune*, May 15, 1854. See for example *Trenton State Gazette*,
May 15, 1854; *Albany Evening Journal*, May 15, 1854; *Ohio State Journal*, May 23,
1854.

100. *New-York Daily Tribune*, May 15, 1854.
101. See for example *Ohio State Journal*, May 17–18, 1854.
102. *Globe*, 33rd Cong., 1st Sess., May 19, 1854, 1230.
103. *Daily Union* (Washington), May 12, 1854.
104. *Richmond Whig*, May 16, 1854.
105. On the strengthening of popular belief of a Slave Power conspiracy in the 1850s, see esp. Pfau, *Political Style of Conspiracy*, 1–45; Miner, *Seeding Civil War*.
106. The six incidents included a fistfight in a restaurant between Jeremiah Clemens (D-AL) and Willey P. Harris (D-MS); duel negotiations between Francis Cutting (D-NY) and John C. Breckenridge (D-KY); the gun-toting lunge and thrust of Churchwell and Cullom; a scuffle over Indian policy between Mike Walsh (D-NY) and James H. Seward (D-GA); a tussle between James Lane and Ephraim Farley (W-ME) over delaying discussion of far-western territories; and the Campbell-Edmundson confrontation. There were also at least five near misses, including a barely averted duel challenge, two throwings of the lie (producing "great tumult—members running all about the House" and some effective mace wielding), Edmundson's threats against Wentworth, and a face-to-face confrontation between Lewis Campbell and the Speaker over adjourning the House.
107. On the Kansas debate and Southern aggression, see Arnold, "Competition for the Virgin Soil of Kansas"; James L. Huston, *The British Gentry, the Southern Planter, and the Northern Family Farmer: Agriculture and Sectional Antagonism in North America* (Baton Rouge: LSU Press, 2015).
108. On the Slave Power narrative in this period, see esp. Miner, *Seeding Civil War*, 174–75; Fehrenbacher, *Slaveholding Republic*, chapter 6; David Brion Davis, *The Slave Power Conspiracy and the Paranoid Style* (Baton Rouge: LSU Press, 1969); Richards, *The Slave Power*; Foner, *Free Soil*, passim, esp. 90–102; Larry Gara, "Slavery and The Slave Power: A Crucial Distinction," *Civil War History* 15 (March 1969): 5–18; Adam Rothman, "The 'Slave Power' in the United States, 1783–1865," in *Ruling America: A History of Wealth and Power in a Democracy*, ed. Steve Fraser and Gary Gerstle (New York: Cambridge University Press, 2005); Richard H. Sewell, *Ballots for Freedom: Antislavery Politics in the United States, 1837–1860* (New York: Oxford University Press, 1976), 257–65 and passim.
109. *Globe*, 33rd Cong., 1st Sess., March 27 and 31, 1854, 761–64, 825. For the duel correspondence, see *Weekly Herald* (N.Y.), April 8, 1854.
110. *Newark Daily Advertiser*, March 29, 1854.
111. *Connecticut Courant*, April 1, 1854 (printing reports of March 29); *Alexandria Gazette*, March 29, 1854.
112. *St. Albans* (Vt.) *Messenger*, April 6, 1854; *Massachusetts Spy* (Worcester), April 5, 1854; *Salem Register*, April 10, 1854; *Daily Advocate* (Baton Rouge), April 8, 1854.
113. *Philadelphia Inquirer*, March 31, 1854; *Massachusetts Spy*, April 5, 1854; *Albany Evening Journal*, April 3, 1854; *Portland Weekly Advertiser*, April 4, 1854; *Vermont Journal*, April 7, 1854. On the Slave Power plot in the press, see Miner, *Seeding Civil War*, 174–75
114. *Weekly Herald*, April 1 and 8, 1854; *Trenton State Gazette*, April 10, 1854. The Democracy-friendly *Herald* had turned on Pierce for abandoning his promise to stay true to the Compromise of 1850.
115. *Albany Evening Journal*, April 3, 1854; *National Democrat* as quoted in *Portland*

Weekly Advertiser, April 4, 1854; *Vermont Journal,* April 7, 1854. On Cutting as a fighting man, see also *New York Mirror* as quoted in *Alexandria Gazette,* April 1, 1854; *Portland Weekly Advertiser,* April 4, 1854.

116. *Portland Weekly Advertiser,* April 4, 1854.

117. *Alexandria Gazette,* April 1, 1854.

118. *New-York Daily Tribune,* March 7, 1854. Pike had urged Fessenden to hurry down to Washington to give a hell-raising speech that he promised to trumpet. Ritchie, *Press Gallery,* 48.

119. Fessenden to Elizabeth Warriner, March 26, 1854; Fessenden to Ellen Fessenden, March 11, 1854, in Cook, *Civil War Senator,* 88.

120. *National Aegis,* May 17, 1854.

121. Cutting's obituaries in the press almost uniformly mentioned his "difficulty" with Breckenridge, and virtually nothing else about his congressional career. Some noted that he had earned his fame because he'd proven "that Northern men could fight." See for example *San Francisco Bulletin,* June 18, 1870.

122. *Macon Weekly Telegraph,* June 20, 1854; *Richmond Whig,* June 6, July 11, October 10, and December 5, 1854.

123. *Daily Union* (Washington), June 8, 1854.

124. "Obsolete Ideas.—No. 6. By an Old Fogy," *Daily Union,* June 8, 1854; *Boston Courier,* June 12, 1854; *Globe,* 33rd Cong., 1st Sess., June 8, 1854, 1361. See also *Hinds' Precedents,* vol. 3, chapter 81, section 2641.

125. For Northern praise of Cutting's defense of free speech, see for example *Newark Daily Advertiser,* April 12, 1854.

126. Ratner and Teeter, *Fanatics and Fire-Eaters,* 117–18; Harrold, *Border War: Fighting over Slavery Before the Civil War,* 161. See also Pfau, *The Political Style of Conspiracy.* On Everett's resignation, see Ritchie, *Press Gallery,* 48; Matthew Mason, *Apostle of Union: A Political Biography of Edward Everett* (Chapel Hill: UNC Press, 2016). The ill health of Everett and his wife contributed to his resignation.

127. French, diary entry, January 1, 1854, BBFFP. See also Henry Flagg French to French, May 25, 1856, ibid; French, diary entry, February 1, 1857, *Witness,* 276.

128. On their differing opinions, see for example French to Henry Flagg French, June 4, 1854, BBFFP; *New York Evening Post,* March 1, 1854.

129. French, diary entry, July 1, 1855, *Witness,* 260–63.

130. Ibid., March 13, 1855, 255.

131. Ibid., May 7, 1854, March 13, 1855, July 1, 1855, 250, 255, 260.

132. Etcheson, *Bleeding Kansas,* 29.

133. After drafting a series of pro- and antislavery constitutions, Kansas approved a free-state constitution in 1859 and received statehood in 1861. Harrold notes that the outbreak of violence in Kansas in 1855 was an expansion of an ongoing border war instigated by Missourians attempting to prevent slaves from escaping into Kansas. Harrold, *Border War,* 164–65, passim. See also Etcheson, *Bleeding Kansas*; Jeremy Neely, *The Border Between Them: Violence and Reconciliation on the Kansas-Missouri Line* (Columbia: University of Missouri Press, 2007); Michael Fellman, "Rehearsal for the Civil War: Antislavery and Proslavery at the Fighting Point in Kansas," in *Antislavery Reconsidered: New Perspectives on the Abolitionists,* ed. Lewis Perry and Fellman (Baton Rouge: LSU Press, 1979), 287–309.

134. French, diary entry, July 1, 1855, *Witness*, 262.
135. Ibid., January 2, 1855, 253.
136. Ibid., May 25, 1856, 269.
137. Ibid., June 5, 1855, 256.
138. Ronald P. Formisano, *For the People: American Populist Movements from the Revolution to the 1850s* (Chapel Hill: UNC Press, 2008), 198–212; Tyler Anbinder, *Nativism and Slavery: The Northern Know Nothings and the Politics of the 1850s* (New York: Oxford University Press, 1992); Michael Holt, *Political Parties and American Political Development: From the Age of Jackson to the Age of Lincoln* (Baton Rouge: LSU Press, 1992), 112–50; Gienapp, *Origins of the Republican Party*, 69–166; Stephen E. Maizlish, "The Meaning of Nativism and the Crisis of the Union: The Know-Nothing Movement in the Antebellum North," in *Essays on American Antebellum Politics, 1840–1860*, ed. Maizlish and Kushma (College Station: Texas A&M University, 1982).
139. *National Era*, April 19, 1855, taken from a letter to his constituents.
140. French, diary entry, June 10, 1855, *Witness*, 257–58.
141. *Evening Star* (Washington), June 2, 1855.
142. French, diary entry, June 10, 1855, *Witness*, 256–59.
143. *Alexandria Gazette*, June 8, 1855; *Daily Atlas* (Boston), June 8, 1855; *Evening Star*, June 5, 1855; *Ohio State Journal*, May 30, 1855; *The South-western* (Shreveport, La.), May 30, 1855; *NYT*, June 5 and 9, 1855; *Philadelphia Inquirer*, June 9, 1855. For French's insistence that he resigned, see *Intelligencer*, July 16, 1855.
144. *Ohio State Journal*, June 13, 1855; Henry Flagg French to French, June 5, 1855, BBFFP. French must have telegraphed the news to his half brother; in his letter, Henry said he'd telegraph back.
145. French to Pierce, June 30, 1855, BBFFP.
146. French, diary entry, March 13, 1855, *Witness*, 254–55.
147. French to Pierce, June 30, 1855, BBFFP.
148. *Weekly New York Herald*, April 8, 1854.
149. On the wrenching emotions tied to changing parties, see Woods, *Emotional and Sectional Conflict*, 145; Gienapp, *Origins of the Republican Party*, 7–8.
150. French, diary entry, July 1, 1855, *Witness*, 259–61.
151. Ibid., and June 7, 1856, 262, 271.
152. Ibid., July 1, 1855, August 5, 1855, and June 7, 1856, 259–60, 265, 271.
153. Ibid., January 2, 1856, 267. French was referring to Giddings's speech of December 18, 1855, in which he said he was defining party terms. *Globe*, 34th Cong., 1st Sess., 42–45 app.
154. *Boston Traveler*, February 22, 1856; *New York Herald*, May 30, 1856.
155. Bess to French, October 9, 1856, BBFFP.
156. In the midst of French's transition, Cilley's son Jonathan Prince (known as "Prin") visited Pierce and French separately. Prin Cilley to Julia Draper Cilley, [December] 1856, in Anderson, *Breach of Privilege*, 387.
157. Thomas R. Bright, "The Anti-Nebraska Coalition and the Emergence of the Republican Party in New Hampshire: 1853–1857," *Historical New Hampshire* 27 (Summer 1972): 57–88. On the radicalizing impact of Slave Power aggression, see Foner, *Free Soil*, 209–10.
158. See for example the emotional letters of Georgian Hopkins Holsey to the former

congressman Howell Cobb (D-GA) during the 1850 crisis. More than once, Holsey noted that his "heart bleeds at the unavoidable separation." Holsey to Cobb, February 13 and 24, 1849, *Correspondence of Toombs, Stephens, and Cobb*, 151, 153. See also Woods, *Emotional and Sectional Conflict*.

159. James G. Hollandsworth, Jr., *Pretense of Glory: The Life of General Nathaniel P. Banks* (Baton Rouge: LSU Press, 1998), 25. Banks's words as reported in the press were "[L]et me say, although I am not one of that class of men who cry for the perpetuation of the Union, though I am willing in a certain state of circumstances to 'let it slide,' I have no fear for its perpetuation. But let me say, if the chief object of the people of this country be to maintain perpetuate and propagate chattel property in man, in other words, human slavery—this Union cannot stand, and it ought not to stand. (Prolonged applause.)" *Portland Advertiser*, August 21, 1855.

160. [Memorandum on French's poetry,] undated, BBFFP; *Liberator*, November 30, 1860.

7. REPUBLICANS MEET THE SLAVE POWER

1. French, diary entry, November 27, 1860, *Witness*, 336.
2. Ibid., December 4, 1859, 318.
3. Ibid.
4. French to Henry Flagg French, June 4, 1854, BBFFP.
5. French, diary entry, April 25, 1857, *Witness*, 280.
6. See for example ibid., April 25, 1857, 280.
7. On this panoply of Republicans, see Foner, *Free Soil*; Hans L. Trefousse, *The Radical Republicans: Lincoln's Vanguard for Racial Justice* (New York: Alfred A. Knopf, 1969). On racism and Republicans, see Sewell, *Ballots for Freedom*, chapter 13. On the self-interested motives of some abolitionists, see Gara, "Slavery and the Slave Power."
8. Larry Gara, "Antislavery Congressmen, 1848–1856: Their Contribution to the Debate Between the Sections," *Civil War History* (September 1986): 197–207, vote count on 207. On the formation of the Republican Party with a congressional spin, see esp. ibid.; William E. Gienapp, *The Origins of the Republican Party, 1852–1856* (New York: Oxford University Press, 1987); Allan G. Bogue, *The Earnest Men: Republicans of the Civil War Senate* (Ithaca: Cornell University Press, 1981); Trefousse, *Radical Republicans*; Foner, *Free Soil*; Holt, *Political Crisis*; Michael A. Morrison, *Slavery and the American West* (Chapel Hill: UNC Press, 1997); Sewell, *Ballots for Freedom*; Joel Silbey, "The Surge in Republican Power: Partisan Antipathy, American Social Conflict, and the Coming of the Civil War," in *Essays on American Antebellum Politics, 1840–1860*, ed. Stephen E. Maizlish and John J. Kushkia (College Station: Texas A&M University, 1982), 199–229; Heather Cox Richardson, *To Make Men Free: A History of the Republican Party* (New York: Basic Books, 2014).
9. Fehrenbacher, *Slaveholding Republic*, 295–338.
10. Trefousse, *Radical Republicans*; Michael Les Benedict, *A Compromise of Principle: Congressional Republicans and Reconstruction, 1863–1869* (New York: Norton, 1974); Edward Gambill, "Who Were the Senate Radicals?," *Civil War History*

(September 1965): 237–44; David H. Donald, *The Politics of Reconstruction* (Cambridge, Mass.: Harvard University Press, 1984).

11. See esp. Oakes, *The Scorpion's Sting.*

12. Greenberg suggests that aggressive expansionism led to an "unintended victory" for martial manhood that exacerbated sectional conflict in the 1850s. Although she doesn't address this directly, it's noteworthy that the Republican Party and its violent congressional undertow fit this pattern. Greenberg, *Manifest Manhood,* 17.

13. See esp. Kenneth Ira Kersch, *Freedom of Speech: Rights and Liberties Under the Law*; Michael Kent Curtis, *"The People's Darling Privilege": Struggles for Freedom of Expression in American History* (Durham: Duke University Press, 2000).

14. Varon, *Disunion!,* 283; Foner, *Free Soil,* 146.

15. *Globe,* 36th Cong., 1st Sess., December 6, 1859, 24–25; *August Chronicle,* December 10, 1859; *National Intelligencer,* December 7, 1859; *New-York Tribune,* December 9, 1859; *Albany Evening Journal,* December 9, 1859; *Ohio State Journal,* December 13, 1859; *Massachusetts Spy,* December 14, 1859. Only the independent press mentioned weapons, specifically mentioning Laurence Keitt (D-SC) and Edward McPherson (R-PA), Stevens's protégé and friend. See also Hans L. Trefousse, *Thaddeus Stevens: Nineteenth-Century Egalitarian* (Chapel Hill: UNC Press, 1997), 98–99; idem., *Radical Republicans,* 131.

16. The original statement is by Carl Philipp Gottfried von Clausewitz: "War is nothing but a continuation of politics with the admixture of other means." Clausewitz, *On War* (1832–34).

17. French, diary entry, November 27, 1860, *Witness,* 336.

18. Ibid., January 19, 1857, August 25, 1858, March 2, 1861, 275–76, 299–300, 342.

19. Particular friends included Mason Tappan (R-NH), Aaron Cragin (R-NH), John Parker Hale (R-NH), and Daniel Clark (R-NH), among others.

20. For a particularly useful exploration of the difference between being antislavery and anti–Slave Power, see Gara, "Slavery and the Slave Power."

21. French, diary entry, August 5, 1855, *Witness,* 265. French was in Chester talking to Yankee "knowing ones." He was probably referring to the removal of Governor Andrew Reeder and the violence that was likely to result.

22. *Boston Daily Bee,* September 26, 1855.

23. Wilson to Parker, July 23, 1855, in *Life and Correspondence of Theodore Parker,* ed. John Weiss, 2 vols. (New York: D. Appleton, 1864), 2:211; John L. Myers, *Henry Wilson and the Coming of the Civil War* (Lanham, Md.: University Press of America, 2005), 288. For similar forebodings, see Hunt to Samuel B. Ruggles, November 22 and December 23, 1855, in Gienapp, "The Crime Against Sumner: The Caning of Charles Sumner and the Rise of the Republican Party," *Civil War History* 3 (September 1979): 218–45, quote on 218–19; Convers Francis to Sumner, May 29, 1856, Charles Sumner Papers, LC.

24. Keitt to Susanna Sparks, June 6, 1855, in Eric H. Walther, *The Fire-Eaters* (LSU, 1992), 180. On Keitt, see Walther, *The Fire-Eaters*; Stephen W. Berry II, *All That Makes a Man: Love and Ambition in the Civil War South* (New York: Oxford University Press, 2003), 45–80; Holt Merchant, *South Carolina Fire-Eater: The Life of Laurence Massillion Keitt, 1824–1864* (Columbia: University of South Carolina Press, 2014). As defined by Walther, fire-eaters were dedicated to Southern

independence and tended toward violence and showmanship, but not all Southern radicals were fire-eaters. Walther, *Fire-Eaters*, 2. Interestingly, not all declared fire-eaters were violent in Congress.

25. Keitt to Susanna Sparks, July 11, 1855; A. Dudley Mann to Keitt, August 24,
1855, Laurence Massillon Keitt Papers, Perkins Library, Duke University.

26. *Globe*, 34th Cong., 1st Sess., December 24, 1855, 77. On Banks's election as
Speaker, see Fred Harvey Harrington, "The First Northern Victory," *Journal of
Southern History* 5 (1939): 186–205; Joel H. Silbey, "After 'The First Northern
Victory': The Republican Party Comes to Congress, 1855–56," *Journal of Inter-
disciplinary History* 20 (Summer 1989): 1–24.

27. On uproars on the floor during the balloting, see Anson Burlingame to Jennie
Burlingame, January 10, 1856, Anson Burlingame & Family Papers, LC.

28. *Daily Picayune*, January 2, 1856; *Cabinet* (Schenectady), December 25, 1855;
Chicago Daily Tribune, December 27, 1855; *Daily Dispatch*, December 24, 1855;
Poore, *Reminiscences*, 1:466. "Extra Billy" Smith had a mail contract, and made
a tidy sum in extra fees by expanding mail routes.

29. John F. T. Crampton to Lord Clarendon, December 24, 1855, *Private and Confidential: Letters from British Ministers in Washington to the Foreign Secretaries
in London, 1844–67*, ed. James J. Barnes and Patience P. Barnes (Selinsgrove,
Pa.: Susquehanna University Press, 1993), 144.

30. *New-York Daily Tribune*, January 31, 1856. See also *National Era*, February 7,
1856; *New York Daily Times*, January 30, February 13, and June 30, 1856; *Saturday Evening Post*, April 19, 1856; Horace Greeley, *Recollections of a Busy Life*
(New York: J. B. Ford, 1869), 348–50; L. D. Ingersoll, *The Life of Horace Greeley*
(Philadelphia: E. Potter, 1874), 303.

31. Fessenden to unknown, ca. 1856, in *Life and Public Service of William Pitt
Fessenden*, 78–79.

32. Greeley to Charles Dana, January 30, 1856, in *Greeley on Lincoln with Mr. Greeley's Letters to Charles A. Dana and a Lady Friend*, ed. Joel Benton (New York:
Baker & Taylor, 1893), 107; Robert Chadwell Williams, *Horace Greeley: Champion
of American Freedom* (New York: NYU Press, 2006), 183.

33. *Globe*, 34th Cong., 1st Sess., February 2, 1856, 342–43; Giddings to Laura Giddings, February 3, 1856, in Stewart, *Giddings*, 237.

34. *NYT*, February 6, 1856. For similar sentiments about the existence of "a North,"
see Edwin Morgan to his brothers, January 26, 1856, in Hollcroft, "Congressman's Letters," 455.

35. John Swanson to Banks, undated, Nathaniel Banks Papers, LC.

36. Swanson to Brooks, May 30 1856, in Harlan Joel Gradin, "Losing Control: The
Caning of Charles Sumner and the Breakdown of Antebellum Political Cul-
ture" (Ph.D. dissertation, UNC, 1991), 31. Gradin misidentifies the writer as
"Lawson."

37. The best primary accounts of the caning of Sumner are the lengthy accounts of
related debates in the *Globe* and the report of the congressional investigative com-
mittee: House Report No. 182, 34th Cong., 1st Sess., 1856, "Alleged Assault
Upon Charles Sumner." Particularly useful secondary accounts include David
Herbert Donald, *Charles Sumner* (New York: Da Capo Press, 1996), 1:278–311;
Gradin, "Losing Control"; Brooks D. Simpson, "'Hit Him Again': The Caning of

Charles Sumner," in *Compromise of 1850*, ed. Finkelman and Kennon, 202–220; T. Lloyd Benson, *The Caning of Senator Sumner* (Greenville, S.C.: Furman University, 2004); Williamjames Hull Hoffer, *The Caning of Charles Sumner: Honor, Idealism, and the Origins of the Civil War* (Baltimore: Johns Hopkins, 2010). For studies that use the caning as a thematic starting point, see for example Gregg M. McCormick, "Personal Conflict, Sectional Reaction: The Role of Free Speech in the Caning of Charles Sumner," *Texas Law Review* 85 (May 2007): 1519–52; David Tatham, "Winslow Homer's 'Arguments of the Chivalry,'" *American Art Journal* 5 (May 1973): 86–89; James Corbett David, "The Politics of Emasculation: The Caning of Charles Sumner and Elite Ideologies of Manhood in the Mid-Nineteenth Century United States," *Gender and History* 19 (August 2007): 324–45; Manisha Sinha, "The Caning of Sumner: Slavery, Race, and Ideology in the Age of the Civil War," *JER* 23 (Summer 2003): 233–62.

38. Sumner to Henry Raymond, March 2, 1856, Charles Sumner Papers, LC. Interestingly, Sumner didn't care what the topic of his attack would be, noting that "at this moment Kansas is the inevitable point." But he was "smitten" by events in Kansas and eager to "expose this whole crime at great length, and without sparing language." Sumner to William Jay, May 6, 1856; Sumner to Salmon P. Chase, May 15, 1856, ibid.

39. Sumner, "The Crime Against Kansas" (Boston: John P. Jewett, 1856), 5, 17; *Globe*, 34th Cong., 1st Sess., May 20, 1856, 547 app. For Adams: *Globe*, 26th Cong., 2nd Sess., February 4, 1841, 322 app.

40. Le Baron Russell to Sumner, May 11, 1856, in *The Works of Charles Sumner* (Boston: Lee and Shepard, 1873), 4:129.

41. Donald, *Charles Sumner*, 1:289.

42. Preston Brooks to John Hampden Brooks, May 23, 1856, in Robert L. Meriwether, ed., "Preston S. Brooks on the Caning of Charles Sumner," *The South Carolina Historical and Genealogical Magazine* 52 (1951): 2.

43. Donald, *Charles Sumner*, 1:286; James Buffington testimony, Committee Report, 66–67.

44. Donald, *Charles Sumner*, 1:286; *Globe*, 26th Cong., 2nd Sess., February 4, 1841, 322 app. During the investigation of the caning, Representative John Bingham (O-OH) stated that Douglas's comment was taken by many as a request for someone to cane Sumner. Committee Report, 44.

45. *Globe*, July 14, 1856, 34th Cong., 1st Sess., 832 app.

46. On Stanbery, see House Journal, April 21, 1832, 625, as well as ibid., April 16, 17, 19, 23 and May 11, 14.

47. Edmundson testimony, Committee Report, 59–60.

48. Wise to Edward Everett, May 26, 1856, Edward Everett Papers, LC. See also James Mason to George M. Dallas, June 10, 1856, in Gienapp, "The Crime Against Sumner," 221.

49. Committee Report, 60. Edmundson argued that because the Senate had adjourned for the day, the attack wouldn't be as objectionable.

50. Ibid., 3–4, 19. Howell Cobb (D-GA) and Alfred Greenwood (D-AR) signed the minority report; Lewis Campbell (O-OH), Francis E. Spinner (D-NY), and A.C.M. Pennington (O-NJ) signed the majority report.

51. *NYT*, May 23 and 27, 1856; *New York Courier and Inquirer*, reprinted in *NYT*,

May 28, 1856; New York *Commercial Advertiser* reprinted in *Richmond Daily Dispatch*, May 30, 1856. See also Pierce, "Murder and Mayhem: Violence, Press Coverage, and the Mobilization of the Republican Party in 1856."

52. *New Hampshire Statesman*, May 31, 1856. See also *New-York Daily Tribune*, May 24 and 25, 1856. On the linking of Sumner and violence in Kansas, see Gienapp, *Origins of the Republican Party*, 295–303; Miner, *Seeding Civil War*. Years later, Albert Gallatin Riddle (R-OH) made the connection even more blatant: "The senate chamber was a part of Kansas." Riddle, *Life of Wade*, 24. On the idea of a chain of Slave Power assaults, see Pierce, "Murder and Mayhem."

53. *NYT*, May 22, 1856. On national press coverage of the caning, see Lorman A. Ratner and Dwight L. Teeter, Jr., *Fanatics and Fire-Eaters: Newspapers and the Coming of the Civil War* (Chicago: University of Illinois, 2003), chapter 2, 34–48; Donald, *Charles Sumner*, 303–307; Manisha Sinha, "The Caning of Charles Sumner," 233–62; Michael D. Pierson, "'All Southern Society Is Assailed by the Foulest Charges': Charles Sumner's 'The Crime Against Kansas' and the Escalation of Republican Anti-Slavery Rhetoric," *New England Quarterly* 68, no. 4 (December 1995): 531–57; David, "The Politics of Emasculation"; Hoffer, *Caning of Sumner*, 85–95.

54. Reprinted in *The Liberator*, June 13, 1856.

55. From *New York Courier and Enquirer*, quoted in *Daily Atlas* (Boston), May 30, 1856. On the link between "Bloody Kansas," "Bloody Sumner," and the rise of the Republican Party, see Gienapp, "Caning of Sumner," 230–31.

56. *Lowell Daily Citizen and News*, May 29, 1856. On Webb and slavery, see Crouthamel, *James Watson Webb*, 55–56, 99–100.

57. Brooks to Webb, May 26, 1856, James Watson Webb Papers, Sterling Library, Yale University. On Webb's conversion to the Republican Party, see Crouthamel, *James Watson Webb*, 125–35; Gienapp, *Origins of the Republican Party*, 267–68.

58. Frances Seward to her children, May 22, 1856, in Walter Stahr, *Seward: Lincoln's Indispensable Man* (New York: Simon and Schuster, 2012), 161.

59. *NYT*, May 28, 1856. In true Southern style, Andrew Butler (D-SC) worried about the speech's damage to his reputation because he couldn't defend himself if the speech was spread "to the four corners of the globe, where I am not known." *Globe*, 34th Cong., 1st Sess., June 12, 1856, 630 app.

60. Hamlin to Fessenden, May 28, 1856, in *The Life and Times of Hannibal Hamlin*, ed. Charles E. Hamlin (Cambridge: Riverside Press, 1899), 284.

61. Fessenden to Frank, June 15, 1856.

62. Preston Brooks to John Hampden Brooks, June 21 and May 23, 1856, in Meriwether, "Preston S. Brooks on the Caning of Charles Sumner," 4, 3.

63. *Richmond Daily Dispatch*, May 30, 1856.

64. *Globe*, 34th Cong., 1st Sess., May 23, 1856, 1289–90. When Clingman insisted that Campbell's implications were false, Campbell immediately asked, "Does the gentleman mean anything personal by that?" Ibid., 1290.

65. Wise to Edward Everett, May 31, 1856, Edward Everett Papers, LC.

66. Keitt to Sue Sparks, May 29, 1856, Laurence Massillon Keitt Papers, Duke University.

67. "A Well Wisher" to Banks, July 10, 1856, Nathaniel Banks Papers, LC.

68. Shelden's *Washington Brotherhood* skillfully explores bonds between congressmen, depicting Congress as a "bubble" of good feeling (5, 68). Yet, as congressmen themselves attested, they could socialize across sectional lines and still envision a "North" or "South" that was trying to dominate the federal government and degrade their section, and thus had to be stopped at any cost, even to the point of congressional violence. Sociability and hostility weren't mutually exclusive, and a handful of hotheads could push congressmen to extremes in ways that mattered. Along similar lines, Banks didn't appoint a moderate committee to investigate Sumner's caning because the caning meant so *little* to congressmen; quite the opposite, he appointed a moderate committee because the caning meant so much. *Washington Brotherhood*, 142–43.

69. Preston Brooks to John Hampden Brooks, June 21, 1856, in Benson, *The Caning of Senator Sumner*, 133–34. Brooks engaged in formal duel correspondence with Henry Wilson (R-MA), Anson Burlingame (R-MA), and New Yorker James Watson Webb, and he had a friend ask John Woodruff (A-CT) if he was a fighting man. He also insultingly dismissed Calvin Chaffee (A-MA) as not worth fighting, and went looking for Russell Sage (R-NY) and Edwin Morgan (O-NY) at Willard's Hotel, vowing to do them damage, though he never found them. When pressed on his actions the next day, Brooks allegedly claimed to be "excited with wine." *New-York Tribune*, August 22, 1856; *National Aegis*, August 27, 1856; *Liberator*, August 29, 1856; *Chicago Daily Tribune*, August 25, 1856.

70. Keitt and Burlingame exchanged harsh words on June 21, leading to talk of a duel, but no action; Toombs was allegedly planning to attack Benjamin Wade (R-OH) for his harsh words about the caning and about Toombs, who had declared that Sumner got what he deserved. Myers, *Henry Wilson and the Coming of the Civil War*, 326. On Campbell, see ibid., 324.

71. French to Henry Flagg French, June 29, 1856, BBFFP. See also Myers, *Henry Wilson and the Coming of the Civil War*, 324.

72. *Albany Evening Journal*, June 7, 1856. For their correspondence, see *Daily Union*, May 31, 1856.

73. John Bigelow, *Retrospections of an Active Life, 1817–1863*, 5 vols. (New York: Baker & Taylor, 1909), 1:166. Lewis Campbell (R-OH), Burlingame's second, was allegedly told about Cilley's disadvantage by Francis P. Blair (R-MO), who claimed that Cilley's friends wouldn't have shied from him in the North as they had in the South.

74. *New York Herald*, July 23, 1856, quoted in *Boston Traveler*, July 23, 1856. See also Lawrence O'Bryan Branch to Nannie Branch, July 30, 1856, Papers of Lawrence O'Bryan Branch, UVA; "The Carolinian Fire-Eater"—a humorous poem depicting Brooks as a coward—*Liberator*, August 1, 1858; and Brooks's "Canada Song," which first appeared in the *New York Evening Post*, in Benson, *Caning of Senator Sumner*, 200–201. On the Burlingame-Brooks affair, see *National Era*, July 31, 1856; Burlingame, "A Card," *National Intelligencer*, July 21, 1856; Burlingame's account of his dispute in *Daily Union* (Washington), July 23, 1856; James E. Campbell, "Sumner—Brooks—Burlingame, or, The Last Great Challenge," *Ohio Archeological and Historical Quarterly* 34 (October 1925): 435–73.

75. French to Henry Flagg French, July 17, 1857, BBFFP.
76. Jessie Benton Fremont to Elizabeth Blair Lee, July 23, 1856, *The Letters of Jessie Benton Fremont*, ed. Pamela Herr and Mary Lee Spence (Urbana: University of Illinois Press, 1993), 120.
77. Sumner to Joshua Giddings, July 22, 1856, Charles Sumner Papers, LC. For negative coverage, see for example *Boston Herald*, July 21, 1856, and September 13, 1856 and *Lowell Daily Citizen*, July 23, 1856.
78. See for example Rollin H. Neale to Burlingame, July 29, 1856; William Winter to Burlingame, July 28, 1856, Anson Burlingame and Family Papers, LC. See also *New Hampshire Patriot*, October 15, 1856; *Boston Herald*, November 4, 1856, on why Burlingame is the man to elect to Congress because Massachusetts shouldn't send a "milk and water man." Southerners had little respect for Burlingame after the affair. See for example Lawrence O'Bryan Branch to unknown, June 13, 1856, Papers of Lawrence O'Bryan Branch, UVA.
79. Burlingame to Jennie Burlingame, July 13, August 1, 3, 6, and 10, September 1, 1856, Anson Burlingame and Family Papers, LC.
80. *New York Herald*, June 5, 1856. See also Resolutions of citizens of Marshfield, June 2, 1856; Albert Browne to Sumner, June 6, 1856; L. D. Johnson to Sumner, June 7, 1856; Edward Everett to Charles Eames, June 21, 1856, Edward Everett Papers, LC.
81. Irwin Silber, ed., *Songs of the Civil War* (New York: Dover, 1995), 169–70.
82. On the link between the rise of the Republicans and the period's violent events generally, see David Grant, *Political Antislavery Discourse and American Literature of the 1850s* (Newark: University of Delaware, 2012), 102–105; McKivigan and Harrold, eds., *Antislavery Violence*; Pierce, "Murder and Mayhem"; Gienapp, *Origins of the Republican Party*, 348–52; Woods, *Emotional and Sectional Conflict*, chapter 5.
83. Gienapp, *Origins of the Republican Party*, 414. On the election of 1856 as a "victorious defeat" for Republicans, see ibid., chapter 13.
84. See esp. idem., "Crime Against Sumner."
85. For an exploration of the role of emotion in the rise of the Republican Party, see Michael E. Woods, "'The Indignation of Freedom-Loving People': The Caning of Charles Sumner and Emotion in Antebellum Politics," *Journal of Social History* 44 (Spring 2011): 689–705; idem., *Emotional and Sectional Conflict.*
86. "The Sumner Outrage. A Full Report of the Speeches at the Meeting of Citizens in Cambridge, June 2, 1856" (Cambridge: John Ford, Printer, 1856), 6; Seth Webb, Jr., to Charles Sumner, May 23, 1856, Charles Sumner Papers, LC; [Petition and resolutions], Fitchburg, Mass., May 24 and 26, 1856, ibid.
87. "The Sumner Outrage," 6; Students of Union College to Sumner, May 27, 1856, Sumner Papers, LC; *Advertiser* (Portland, Maine), June 3, 1856.
88. Ibid. On the symbolism of Brooks's cane, see Michael E. Woods, "Tracing the 'Sacred Relics': The Strange Career of Preston Brooks's Cane," *Civil War History* (June 2017): 113–32.
89. Preston Brooks to John Hampden Brooks, June 21, 1856, *South Carolina Historical and Genealogical Magazine* 52 (1951): 1–4. See also Henry Ward Beecher's article in the *Washington Star*, June 12, 1856: "With the exception of one or two papers,

the whole South has accepted the act and made it representative! It is no longer Brooks that struck Sumner! He was the arm, but the whole South was the body!"
90. French, diary entry, May 25, 1856, *Witness*, 269.
91. French to Bess French, June 8, 1856, ibid., 327. For Sam's adventure and Fessenden's panicked response, see Fessenden to Sam, June 15, 1856; James Fessenden to Sam, June 16, 1856; idem. to Fessenden, June 25, 1856; Fessenden to Ellen Fessenden, July 6, 1856, all in William Fessenden Papers, Bowdoin College; Cook, *Civil War Senator*, 98. For Sam's narrative of his experience, see Francis Fessenden, *Life and Public Services of William Pitt Fessenden*, 2 vols. (Cambridge: Riverside Press, 1907), 71–78.
92. Foner notes Northern approval of the physical courage of Republicans. *Free Soil*, 146.
93. *New England Farmer* (Boston), July 19, 1856. Some of the resolutions passed by indignation meetings specifically mentioned the long history of Southern "insolence" in Congress. See for example those passed by a meeting in Manchester, N.H., May 28, 1856, Charles Sumner Papers, LC. On support of Northern fighting men, see also Thomas Hicks to Wade, February 2, 1856, and J. H. Baker to Wade, June 2, 1856, Benjamin Franklin Wade Papers, LC. On indignation meetings and the rise of the Republican Party, see Woods, "Indignation of Freedom-Loving People"; idem., *Emotional and Sectional Conflict*, chapters 4 and 5.
94. *Richmond Whig*, February 16, 1858. The *Whig* was commenting on an article in the *Daily Palladium* (Oswego, N.Y.) on February 10, 1858, titled "Don't Kick Him," detailing Wilson's desire to be "Sumnerized"—"kicked or cuffed"—into reelection.
95. *Richmond Whig*, February 16, 1858.
96. Unknown to Lawrence O'Bryan Branch, June 13, 1856, Papers of Lawrence O'Bryan Branch, UVA.
97. *Globe*, 34th Cong., 1st Sess., July 14 and 16, 1856, 831, 838 app.
98. F.O.J. French to Bess French, May 25, 1856, BBFFP.
99. Sargent to Sumner, May 25, 1856, Charles Sumner Papers, LC.
100. Everett to Charles Eames, June 21, 1856, Edward Everett Papers, LC.
101. See for example Lawrence O'Bryan Branch to Nannie Branch, July 30, 1856, Papers of Lawrence O'Bryan Branch, UVA.
102. Winthrop to William Cabell Rives, June 5, 1856, William Cabell Rives Papers, LC.
103. Everett to Charles Eames, June 21, 1856, Edward Everett Papers.
104. French amended the proposal by adding representatives from the territories. *Proceedings of the First Three Republican National Conventions of 1856, 1860, and 1864, Including Proceedings of the Antecedent National Convention Held at Pittsburg, in February, 1856, as Reported by Horace Greeley* (Minneapolis: Charles W. Johnson, 1893), 21–22.
105. French, diary entry, February 1, 1857, *Witness*, 276–77.
106. Article 1, Section 6 of the Constitution provides that "for any speech or debate in either House, [Senators and Representatives] shall not be questioned in any other place."
107. McCormick, "Personal Conflict, Sectional Reaction"; Curtis, *Free Speech, "The People's Darling Privilege."*

108. Unknown to Banks, July 10, 1856, Nathanial Banks Papers, LC.
109. *Globe*, 1856, 1056, in Gradin, "Losing Control," 188. On dangerous words in this period, see also Miner, *Seeding Civil War*, passim.
110. Pierce to Horatio King, November 28, 1860, in Horatio King, "Buchanan's Loyalty," *Century Magazine* 23 (December 1881): 289–97, quote on 292; Pierce to Jacob Thompson, November 26, 1860, *Constitution* (Washington), December 1, 1860.
111. Leonard, *Power of the Press*, 81–82; Chambers, *Old Bullion Benton*, 425, 431, 436, 438.
112. See esp. McCormick, "Personal Conflict, Sectional Reaction," 1519–52.
113. *Lowell Daily Citizen*, June 6, 1856; *Salem Register*, June 9, 1856. Brooks also mentioned Knapp's revolver in his resignation speech, as well as the fact that Linus Comins (R-MA) was armed. *Globe*, 34th Cong., 1st Sess., July 14, 1856, 833 app.
114. Harlow, *Rise and Fall of Kansas Aid*, 16–20.
115. Lewis Clephane, *Birth of the Republican Party, with a Brief History of the Important Part Taken by the Original Republican Association of the National Capital* (Washington: Gibson Bros., 1889), 31. The organization followed in the model of—and possibly grew out of—the Washington Free Soil Association. Both organizations had a reading room on Capitol Hill. Jonathan Earle, "Saturday Nights at the Baileys," *In the Shadow of Freedom*, 94–95.
116. "To Republicans," May 8, 1858, *New-York Tribune*. The announcement—asking Republicans around the country to send cash—was widely reprinted; see for example *Lowell Daily Citizen and News*, May 22, 1858; *National Era*, May 20, 1858.
117. *National Era*, August 5 and September 3, 1858.
118. *Albany Evening Journal*, June 4, 1858.
119. *Globe*, 36th Cong., 1st Sess., March 7, 1860, 161 app. Wade followed his statement by stating that he wouldn't hesitate to fight a duel "in an extreme case."
120. *Globe*, 35th Cong., 1st Sess., March 15, 1858, 101, 105, 109–10 app. Republican protestors that night included William Pitt Fessenden (R-ME), Daniel Clark (R-NH), and William Seward (R-NY), who complained that he had been "crushed continually" for the past eight years.
121. Ibid., 35th Cong., 1st Sess., March 15, 1858, 101, 105, 109–10 app. See also Trefousse, *Wade*, 110–11.
122. [Memorandum], May 26, 1874, Simon Cameron Papers [microfilm]. See also *Zachariah Chandler: An Outline Sketch of His Life and Public Services* (Detroit: Post and Tribune Co., 1880), 145–47.
123. [Speech on the Fourteenth Amendment], May 10, 1866, in *The Selected Papers of Thaddeus Stevens, April 1865–August 1868*, 2 vols. (Pittsburgh: University of Pittsburgh Press, 1997–98) 2:137–42. Quotes are from both the *Globe* version of Stevens's speech and an eight-page draft in his notes; the draft mentions people's names and includes more detail. See also Stevens's speech of January 13, 1865; ibid., 1:522.
124. [Speech on the Fourteenth Amendment], May 10, 1866, in *Selected Papers of Thaddeus Stevens*, 2:137–42.
125. Alexander Stephens to Linton Stephens, February 5, 1858, *Life of Alexander*

Hamilton Stephens, 329–30. See also *Charleston Mercury*, February 11, 1858. Stephens notes, "Nobody was hurt or even scratched, I believe; but bad feeling was produced by it. . . . All things here are tending to bring my mind to the conclusion that the Union cannot or will not last long."

126. *Charleston Mercury*, February 11, 1858. See also *Boston Traveler*, February 11, 1858.

127. Fehrenbacher, *Slaveholding Republic*, passim.

128. Alexander Stephens to Linton Stephens, March 12, 1858, in Richard Malcolm Johnston and William Hand Browne, *Life of Alexander H. Stephens* (Philadelphia: J. B. Lippincott, 1878), 331.

129. On Grow, see James T. Dubois and Gertrude S. Mathews, *Galusha A. Grow: Father of the Homestead Law* (New York: Houghton Mifflin, 1917); Robert D. Ilisevich, *Galusha A. Grow: The People's Candidate* (Pittsburgh: University of Pittsburgh, 1989). On his abrasive manner see ibid., 158. On Keitt, see Stephen W. Berry II, *All That Makes a Man: Love and Ambition in the Civil War South* (Pittsburgh: University of Pittsburgh, 1989); Walther, *Fire-Eaters*, 160–94; Marchant, *Laurence Massillion Keitt*.

130. On the Washburn brothers, see Gaillard Hunt, *Israel, Elihu, and Cadwallader Washburn: A Chapter in American Biography* (New York: Macmillan, 1925).

131. *Globe*, 35th Cong., 1st Sess., February 5, 1858, 603. See also Alexander Hamilton Stephens to Linton Stephens, February 5, 1858, in Richard Malcolm Johnston and William Hand Browne, *Life of Alexander H. Stephens* (Philadelphia: J. B. Lippincott, 1883), 329–30; *NYT*, February 8, 11, and 19, 1858; *New York Herald*, February 13, 1858; *Weekly Champion* (Atchison, Kans.), March 6, 1858. Though later accounts note that Cadwallader Washburn yanked off the wig of William Barksdale (D-MS), Charles Marsh—who seems to have gotten the story from Potter himself—credits Potter. Charles W. Marsh, *Recollections, 1837–1910* (Chicago: Farm Implement News Co., 1910), 119–20.

132. Grow to unnamed relative, February 9, 1858, in Dubois and Matthews, *Galusha A. Grow*, 181–82. See also *NYT*, February 8 and April 15, 1858.

133. *National Era*, March 25, 1858; *Globe*, 35th Cong., 1st Sess., March 15, 1858, 107 app.

134. *Philadelphia Inquirer*, February 8, 1858; *Boston Traveler*, February 11, 1858.

135. *Frederick Douglass' Paper*, February 12, 1858. See also *NYT*, February 8, 1858; *Philadelphia Inquirer*, February 8, 1858; *Boston Evening Transcript*, February 11, 1858; *Milwaukee Sentinel*, February 17, 1858.

136. *Boston Traveler*, February 11, 1858.

137. *NYT*, February 11, 1858.

138. In *Daily Advocate* (Baton Rouge), February 22, 1858.

139. *Charleston Mercury*, February 11, 1858.

140. *Virginia Sentinel*, in *Annapolis Gazette*, June 24, 1858; *Columbus (Georgia) Enquirer*, February 11, 1858; *Charleston Mercury*, February 13, 1858.

141. *Annapolis Gazette*, June 24, 1858.

142. *Virginia Sentinel*, June 24, 1858; *Charleston Mercury*, February 13, 1858; *Columbus* (Georgia) *Enquirer*, February 11, 1858.

143. Laurence Keitt to Ellison Keitt, February 17, 1858, in "Autograph Letters and

Portraits of the Signers of the Constitution of the Confederate States," Charles Colcock Jones, Jr., Papers, Duke University.

144. Thomas Hood, *Quips and Cranks* (London: Routledge, Warne, and Routledge, 1861), 48–54.

145. "The Fight over the Body of Keitt," from *Punch*, in *Tribune*, March 22, 1858. See also *Massachusetts Spy*, March 24, 1858.

146. *Albany Evening Journal*, February 25, 1858.

147. *Lowell Daily Citizen*, February 20, 1858.

148. *Plain Dealer* (Cleveland), February 11, 1858. In John Brougham's play *Pocahontas* there was already a line referring to a fight: "Hold—have done! / Do you think you're in Washington?" (A line that in itself says something.) Brougham added: "These blows must not be applied, / Even from the Administration side."

149. *Lowell Daily Citizen*, March 17, 1858; *Frank Leslie's Illustrated Newspaper*, February 20, 1858. Boxing was America's "preeminent sport" by the 1850s. Elliott J. Gorn, *The Manly Art: Bare-Knuckle Prize Fighting in America* (Ithaca: Cornell University Press, 1986), 129.

150. On *Vanity Fair*, see Frank Luther Mott, *A History of American Magazines, 1850–1865* (Cambridge: Harvard University Press, 1938), 520–29; Edward L. Gambill, "Vanity Fair: 1859–1863," in *The Conservative Press in Eighteenth and Nineteenth Century America*, ed. Ronald Lora and William Henry Longton (Westport, Conn.: Greenwood Press, 1999), 139–45.

151. *Vanity Fair*, January 21 and 28, April 7, February 4, and January 14, 1860.

152. Ibid., December 15, 1860.

153. *New York Herald*, February 14, 1845.

154. Henry Clay Preuss, "Fashions and Follies of Washington Life. A Play. In Five Acts" (Washington, D.C.: Published by the author, 1857). See also Walter J. Meserve, "Social Awareness on Stage: Tensions Mounting, 1850–1859," in *The American Stage*, ed. Ron Engle and Tice L. Miller (New York: Cambridge University Press, 1993), 87–88. Interestingly, in 1862, Preuss was investigated by a House committee for disloyalty to the government. 37th Cong., 2nd Sess., House Report No. 16, "Loyalty of Clerks and Other Persons Employed by Government," January 28, 1862, 5, 8. Preuss worked for the Engineer Bureau.

155. *NYT*, June 26, 1856. See also *The United States Magazine* (July–December 1856): 186; *Wide West* (San Francisco), August 17, 1856; *Brooklyn Daily Eagle*, June 30, 1856; *The Magnet* (London), September 29, 1856.

156. "Life in an American Hotel?," *Punch*, June 28, 1856, 258; *Boston Evening Transcript*, July 12, 1856; *Alexandria Gazette*, July 17, 1856; *Daily Advocate* (Baton Rouge), July 26, 1856; *Washington Reporter* (Pa.), August 27, 1856; *Weekly Wisconsin Patriot* (Madison), August 30, 1856; *Alta California* (San Francisco), September 5, 1856.

157. On humor as a tool of reform, see Barnet Baskerville, "19th Century Burlesque of Oratory," *American Quarterly* 20 (Winter 1968): 726–43. See also Dean L. Yarwood, *When Congress Makes a Joke: Congressional Humor Then and Now* (New York: Rowman & Littlefield, 2004).

158. David Outlaw comments on how congressional violence weakened public confidence in Congress. Outlaw to Emily Outlaw, April 18, 1850, DOP.

159. French to Bess French, June 10, 1860, *Witness*, 327–28.

160. French to Bess French, July 25, 1852, BBFFP.
161. French to Henry Flagg French, May 2, 1852, ibid.
162. See for example the resolutions of Springfield High School, May 30, 1856; George Nourse to Sumner, June 4, 1856; Albert Browne to Sumner, June 6, 1856, all in Charles Sumner Papers, LC.
163. *New York Herald*, January 16, 1860.
164. On the contest generally, see David Brown, *Southern Outcast: Hinton Rowan Helper and the Impending Crisis of the South* (Baton Rouge: LSU Press, 2006), esp. 152–70; Freehling, *Road to Disunion: Secessionists Triumphant*, 250–58, 265–66; Crenshaw, "Speakership Contest"; idem., *The Slave States in the Presidential Election of 1860* (Baltimore: Johns Hopkins, 1945); Manisha Sinha, *The Counterrevolution of Slavery: Politics and Ideology in Antebellum South Carolina* (Chapel Hill: UNC Press, 2000), 208–10; Mary R. Campbell, "Tennessee's Congressional Delegation in the Sectional Crisis of 1859–1860," *Tennessee Historical Quarterly* 19 (December 1960): 348–71.
165. On Helper's book, see esp. David Brown, "Attacking Slavery from Within: The Making of 'The Impending Crisis of the South,'" *Journal of Southern History* 70 (August 2004): 541–76; idem., Brown, *Southern Outcast*.
166. Helper intended to attack Asa Biggs (D-NC), who was absent, so he assaulted Francis Craige (D-NC) instead. Brown, *Southern Outcast*, 134–36.
167. *Globe*, 36th Cong., 1st Sess., December 5, 1859, 3. On the response to Helper in the House, see esp. Brown, *Southern Outcast*, 152–70; Freehling, *Secessionists Triumphant*, 240–45, 250–53. Freehling writes: "It was as if the slaveholders shouted at posterity: Read our speeches on the *Compendium*, instead of using your political science models, to discern our intentions. Then you will understand why we considered Republicans' endorsement of Helper dangerous as well as insulting." Ibid., 251.
168. On the fraught battle to elect a Speaker, see Landis, *Northern Men*, 218–19; Jenkins and Stewart, *Fighting for the Speakership*, 212–24.
169. *Daily Confederation* (Montgomery, Ala.), December 13, 1859.
170. *Globe*, 36th Cong., 1st Sess., January 25, 1860, 572. Wilson was speaking of the Territorial Slave Code. The "tragic strut" was a theatrical term. See Paul Kuritz, *The Making of Theatre History* (Englewood Cliffs, N.J.: Prentice Hall, 1989), 206.
171. *Globe*, 36th Cong., 1st Sess., January 25, 1860, 586. For similar sentiments, see Edwin Morgan to his brothers, December 22, 1855; Schuyler Colfax to Charles Heaton, December 25, 1855, in Hollcroft, "Congressmen's Letters," 451; David M. Potter, *Lincoln and His Party in the Secession Crisis* (New Haven: Yale University Press, 1967).
172. On the importance of a sense of personal insult to the logic of secession, see Wyatt-Brown, *Shaping of Southern Culture*, 177–202; idem., *Yankee Saints and Southern Sinners* (Baton Rouge: LSU Press, 1985), 183–213; Kenneth Greenberg, *Masters and Statesmen: The Political Culture of American Slavery* (Baltimore: Johns Hopkins, 1985), 107–46; Sinha, *Counterrevolution of Slavery*, 207–20.
173. There were fights between John Logan (D-IL) and William Kellogg (R-IL); Robert Toombs (D-GA) and James Doolittle (R-WI); Robert Toombs (D-GA) and Charles Scott (D-CA); Roger Pryor (D-VA) and the *New York Herald* editor James

Gordon Bennett's son James Jr.; Thaddeus Stevens (R-PA) and Martin Crawford (D-GA); John Haskin (ALD-NY) and Horace Clark (ALD-NY); Galusha Grow (R-PA) and Lawrence O'Bryan Branch (D-NC); Roger Pryor (D-VA) and John Sherman (R-OH); and John Hickman (R-PA) and Henry Edmundson (D-VA). On April 12, 1860, the NYT noted that there already had been fifteen "scenes" in Congress. In later years, John Sherman wrote, "It appeared many times that the threatened war would commence on the floor of the House of Representatives." Sherman, *Recollections*, 172.

174. *Richmond Whig*, February 17, 1860. See also Pike, *First Blows of the Civil War*, 486–89; *New-York Tribune*, February 13, 1860.

175. *Manufacturers' and Farmers' Journal* (Providence, R.I.), January 19, 1860.

176. Gist to William Porcher Miles, December 20, 1859, in Crenshaw, "Speakership Contest," 335. Robert Barnwell Rhett, D. H. Hamilton, Keitt, Miles, and possibly others were in contact with Gist concerning the plot. Brown, *Southern Outcast*, 171. Susanna Keitt's March 4, 1861, letter to Mrs. Frederick Brown suggests that Roger Pryor and Thomas Clingman were involved as well. Laurence Massillon Keitt Papers, Duke University. On Gist, see Manisha Sinha, *The Counterrevolution of Slavery*; Steven A. Channing, *Crisis of Fear: Secession in South Carolina* (New York: Norton, 1974).

177. Susanna Keitt to Alexander Sparks, [December 1859], Laurence Massillon Keitt Papers, Duke University. The letter is undated but indicates that Susanna and Keitt are married; they married in May 1859 and returned from a trip to Europe in December. My thanks to Elizabeth Dunn at Duke University for helping me determine the date. On Wise's threat, see also *Lincoln and His Party*, 254–55.

178. See esp. Brown, *Southern Outcast*, 167–68.

179. Ibid., 158–59.

180. On Pennington's election, see Jenkins and Stewart, *Fighting for the Speakership*, 220–23.

181. French, diary entry, February 9, 1860, BBFFP.

182. On the Potter-Pryor clash, see [Rockford, Ill.] *Daily Register*, December 26, 1882; *Chicago Tribune*, December 24, 1882; *Harper's Weekly*, April 21, 1860; *New York Herald*, April 14 and 16, 1860; *Daily Dispatch*, April 16, 1860; *Charleston Mercury*, April 18, 1860; *Chicago Press and Tribune*, April 18, 1860; *NYT*, April 12, 1860; Ben A. Riley, "The Pryor-Potter Affair: Nineteenth Century Civilian Conflict as Precursor to Civil War," *Journal of West Virginia Historical Association* (1984): 30–39; William Hasseltine, "The Pryor-Potter Duel," *Wisconsin Magazine of History* (June 1944): 400–409; Potter to Pryor, April 11, 1860; Gary L. Ecelbarger, *Frederick W. Lander: The Great Natural American Soldier* (Baton Rouge: LSU Press, 2000), 56–61; T. P. Chisman to Frederick Lander, April 12, 1860; Pryor to Potter, April 12, 1860; Potter to Pryor, April 12, 1860; Lander to Chisman, April 12, 1860; Chisman to Lander, April 12, 1860; Pryor to Potter, April 12, 1860; Chisman to Lander, April 13, 1860; in Papers of Frederick W. Lander, LC; W. A. Sugrue[?] to William Porcher Miles, May 22, 1860; contents of Folder 28, William Porcher Miles Papers, UNC.

183. Pryor tangled with the *New York Herald* editor James Gordon Bennett's son

James Jr., John Sherman (R-OH), John Hickman (R-PA), Owen Lovejoy (R-IL), and John Potter (R-WI).

184. Carl Schurz, *The Reminiscences of Carl Schurz*, 3 vols. (New York: McClure, 1907–1908), 2:166.
185. *NYT*, May 16, 1860.
186. Scrapbook, Papers of Frederick Lander, LC; *New York Herald*, April 21, 1860.
187. See for example *Milwaukee Sentinel*, November 6, 1860.
188. Anonymous undated statement, January 1860, Lawrence O'Bryan Branch Papers, UVA; *Boston Evening Transcript*, January 2, 1860; *Constitution* (Washington), January 4, 1860. See also *Boston Traveler*, January 2, 1860; *Commercial Advertiser* (N.Y.), January 3, 1860; *New Albany Daily Ledger*, January 5, 1860; *Frank Leslie's Illustrated Newspaper*, January 14, 1860; *Augusta Chronicle*, January 1, 1860. James Watson Webb's resulting homily on the sins of dueling in the *Courier and Enquirer* irritated the *Herald* enough to detail Webb's dueling history, including an extended discussion of the Graves-Cilley duel. *New York Herald*, January 15, 1860.
189. *Vanity Fair*, "Jonathan's Idees," January 14, 1860, 40.
190. French, diary entry, May 20 and 28, 1860, *Witness*, 322–24; *NYT*, May 21, 1860; *Daily National Intelligencer*, May 22, 1860; *New York Herald*, May 20, 1860.
191. Ibid., May 28, 1860, 324.
192. *Globe*, 36th Cong., 1st Sess., June 4, 1860, 2600; Sumner, *The Barbarism of Slavery. Speech of Hon. Charles Sumner, on the Bill for the Admission of Kansas as a Free State, in the United States Senate, June 4, 1860* (Boston: Thayer and Eldridge, 1860), 117–18.
193. Sumner, "The Barbarism of Slavery" (New York: Young Men's Republican Union, 1863), 79–80.
194. French to Bess French, June 8, 1860, in the July 8, 1860, diary entry, *Witness*, 327. On July 8, French recounted events between June 5 and 27 by incorporating into his diary a series of letters to his wife while she and the children were in New Hampshire.
195. French to Bess French, June 10, 1860, in diary entry, July 8, 1860, *Witness*, 327; Donald, *Charles Sumner*, 357.
196. French to Bess French, June 10, 1860, in diary entry, July 8, 1860, *Witness*, 328.
197. Hammond to Francis Lieber, April 19, 1860, *The Life and Letters of Francis Lieber*, ed. Thomas Sergeant Perry (Boston: James R. Osgood, 1882), 310–11. See also William Porcher Miles to C. G. Memminger, January 23, 1860, in Crenshaw, "Speakership Contest," 332. Miles said he couldn't leave the House at the moment because he wanted to be fighting with the South if there was a "collision."
198. *Globe*, 36th Cong., 1st Sess., January 12, 1860, 434–35. See also *National Era*, January 19, 1860; *Chicago Times and Tribune*, January 13, 1860; *New York Herald*, January 13, 14, and 16, 1860.
199. Schurz, *Reminiscences*, 2:163–4.
200. *Vanity Fair*, January 28, 1860, 76; Schurz, *Reminiscences*, 2:164. See also William Cullen Bryant, "Proof of Our Progress in Civilization," January 19, 1860, in *Power*

for Sanity: Selected Editorials of William Cullen Bryant, 1829–1861, ed. William Cullen Bryant II (New York: Fordham University Press, 1994), 370–73.

201. Crawford to Alexander Stephens, April 8, 1860, in Crenshaw, "Speakership Contest," 335–36.

202. Crenshaw notes that Southern politicians disagreed about where they stood in relation to public opinion; some felt that the people were ready for anything, others felt that they were outstripping their constituents. Ibid.

203. Ibid.

204. Gist to W. P. Miles, December 20, 1859, in ibid., 334–5.

205. E. W. Hazard to Lyman Trumbull, May 23, 1856, Lyman Trumbull Papers, LC.

206. For a similar logic in another era of extreme politics—the 1790s—see Joanne B. Freeman, "The Election of 1800: A Study in the Process of Political Change," *Yale Law Journal* 108 (June 1999): 1959–94.

207. Freehling, *Road to Disunion*, 2:338.

208. Ibid., 337–38, 371; Walther, *Yancey*, 270–71.

209. Susanna Sparks Keitt to Mrs. Frederick Brown, March 4, 1861, Laurence Massillon Keitt Papers, Duke University.

210. *Globe*, 36th Cong., 2nd Sess., December 5, 1860, 10.

211. Ibid., 12.

212. French, diary entry, May 14, 1861, *Witness*, 356.

213. *New-York Tribune*, January 21, 1861.

214. See esp. Potter, *Lincoln and His Party*; Daniel W. Crofts, *Reluctant Confederates: Upper South Unionists in the Secession Crisis* (Chapel Hill: UNC Press, 1989). For a brilliant analysis of the evolving meaning of "disunion" as a prophecy, a threat, an accusation, a process, and then a program, see Varon, *Disunion!*

215. For examples of these speeches, see *Globe*, 36th Cong., 2nd Sess., January 21, 1861, 484–87.

216. *New York Herald*, January 22, 1861. The *Globe* doesn't include those exact words, but Mason's speech makes precisely that point throughout. *Globe*, 36th Cong., 2nd Sess., January 22, 1861, 503.

217. French, diary entries, November 27, 1860, February 3 and April 19, 1861, *Witness*, 336–37, 340–41, 351.

218. Ibid., November 11, 1860, 335.

219. On the credibility of a Baltimore assassination threat, see Harold Holzer, *Lincoln President-Elect: Abraham Lincoln and the Great Secession Winter, 1860–1861* (New York: Simon and Schuster, 2008), 403–405.

220. Ibid., January 1, February 24, and March 1, 1861, 339, 341–43.

221. Ibid., February 26 and March 6, 1861, 343, 348.

222. French's instinct wasn't without merit. On Confederate and Union Masons crossing battle lines to help each other, see Michael A. Halleran, *The Better Angels of Our Nature: Freemasonry in the American Civil War* (Tuscaloosa: University of Alabama, 2010); Allen E. Roberts, *House Undivided: The Story of Freemasonry and the Civil War* (Richmond: Macoy Publishing and Masonic Supply, 1990).

223. Both sides of this correspondence are included in *Proceedings of the Regular Conclave of the Grand Commandery of Knights Templar of the State of Michigan, Held at Detroit Michigan, June 4, A.D. 1861, A. O. 743* (Detroit: H. Barns & Co.,

Printers, 1861), 22–24. See also "The Voice of the Templars of Pennsylvania," *The Masonic Review* 25 (September 1861): 341–46.
224. W. J. Bates to French, May 27, 1861; French to Bates, June 18, 1861, in "The Virginia Templar Secession," *Freemason's Monthly Magazine* 20 (August 1861): 307–309.
225. French, diary entry, March 6, 1861, *Witness*, 348.

EPILOGUE

1. French, diary entry, May 6, 1861, *Witness*, 354–55.
2. Out of a grand total of $454,001.70 sought by Kansas claimants, French awarded $449,498.11. He granted $10,000 or more to five claimants; George Brown, the owner of the *Herald*; Columbus Hornsby, William Hornsby, and Thomas Ferrell, owners of a merchandising warehouse; Shalron W. Eldridge, owner of the Free State Hotel; the estate of the hardware store owner Gaius Jenkins; and Charles Robinson. 36th Cong., 2nd Sess., Rpt. No. 104, Kansas Claims, March 2, 1861, 3 vols., 108–23, 403, 900. See also Dale E. Watts, "How Bloody Was Bleeding Kansas? Political Killings in Kansas Territory, 1854–1861," *Kansas History* 18 (Summer 1995): 116–29.
3. French to Catherine Wells, June 3, 1862, in Michael Spangler, "Benjamin Brown French in the Lincoln Period," *White House History* 8 (Fall 2000): 12. On Lincoln, see also French, diary entry, April 14 and November 24, 1861; January 8, 1862; July 8, 1863, *Witness*, 350, 381, 384, 426.
4. Lincoln first appointed William Wood commissioner, but after accompanying Mary Todd Lincoln on the controversial shopping trip that prompted French's "mission," Wood fell out of grace and French replaced him. *Witness*, 361, note 1.
5. Ibid., December 18, 1861, 383. See also ibid., September 8, 1861, and May 24, 1865, 375, 479; French to Henry Flagg French, October 13, 1861, BBFFP.
6. French, diary entry, December 16, 1861, *Witness*, 382.
7. Ibid. See also French's script of his conversations with the Lincolns in his letter to Pamela French, December 24, 1861, BBFFP; and Jean H. Baker, *Mary Todd Lincoln: A Biography* (New York: Norton, 2008), 187–90. Baker notes that French ultimately buried the expenses in his commissioner budget and a congressional appropriation. Baker, *Lincoln*, 189–90.
8. French, diary entry, December 26, 1869, *Witness*, 608. French seems to have become less admiring of Mary Todd Lincoln over time. Early in their relationship, he noted that she was "imprudent," an "accomplished . . . curiosity," but that much of the gossip about her was untrue. French to Pamela French, December 24, 1861, BBFFP. See also French, diary entry, May 24, 1865, *Witness*, 479.
9. French, diary entry, April 23, 1861, *Witness*, 352.
10. On Washington in wartime, see esp. Winkle, *Lincoln's Citadel*. On Congress, see Bogue, *Congressman's Civil War*; David M. Potter, *Lincoln and His Party*.
11. French, diary entry, June 30, 1861, 361–62.
12. The group included (but wasn't limited to) William Richardson (D-IL), J. R. Morris (D-OH), John A. Gurley (R-OH), Alfred Ely (R-NY), Elihu Washburne (R-IL), Harrison Blake (R-OH), Charles B. Hoard (R-NY), Albert Riddle (R-OH),

William Dunn (R-IN), Benjamin Wade (R-OH), Zachariah Chandler (R-MI), Simon Cameron (R-PA), Henry Wilson (R-MA), Lafayette Foster (OPP-CT), Alexander Rice (R-MA), Charles Delano (R-MA), John Logan (D-IL), and
Sergeant at Arms George T. Brown of the Senate. Albert Riddle claimed to have
promised an Ohio volunteer infantry company that if a battle was fought near
Washington, he would fight alongside them. Riddle, *Recollections of War Times:
Reminiscences of Men and Events in Washington, 1860–1865* (New York: G. P. Putnam's Sons, 1895), 44–45; Samuel Sullivan Cox, *Union-Disunion-Reunion: Three
Decades of Federal Legislation, 1855 to 1885* (Providence: A. & R. A. Reid, 1885),
156–59.

13. Riddle, *Recollections*, 52–53.

14. Charles Lanman, ed., *Journal of Alfred Ely, a Prisoner of War in Richmond*
    (New York: D. Appleton, 1862). See also documents included in William H. Jef-
    frey, *Richmond Prisons, 1861–1862* (St. Johnsbury, Vt.: Republican Press, 1893),
    esp. 75–82.

15. French, diary entry, July 22, 1861, *Witness*, 366.

16. Walther, *Fire-Eaters*, 187–89. On the two fights, see Hans L. Trefousse, *Andrew
    Johnson: A Biography* (New York: Norton, 1989), 404–405 note 18; *Alexandria
    Gazette*, February 12, 1861; *Baltimore Sun*, February 9, 1861; *San Francisco
    Bulletin*, April 1, 1861; *Plain Dealer* (Cleveland), March 13, 1861.

17. Virginia Jeans Laas, ed., *Wartime Washington: The Civil War Letters of Eliza-
    beth Blair Lee* (Urbana: University of Illinois Press, 1999), 23; *Boston Herald*,
    January 12, 1861; *Plain Dealer* (Cleveland), January 12, 1861.

18. *Baltimore Sun*, January 29, 1861; *Plain Dealer* (Cleveland), January 25, 1861;
    Charleston Mercury, January 25 and 28, 1861; William Wesley Woolen, *William
    McKee Dunn: Brigadier-General, U.S.A.: A Memoir* (New York: Knickerbocker
    Press, c. 1887–92), 44–48. Woolen quotes Dunn as saying that if he had killed
    Rust in a duel, "he should have had the same feeling as if he had killed him on
    the field of battle." Woolen, *Dunn*, 47–48.

19. *Chicago Tribune*, February 20, 1861; *NYT*, February 16, 1861.

20. *Globe*, 36th Cong., 1st Sess., March 7, 1860, 1027–34. For talk of a duel, see
    ibid., 1032.

21. *Massachusetts Spy*, February 27, 1861; *New-York Tribune*, February 25, 1861;
    Salem Register, February 25, 1861; *Vermont Journal*, March 2, 1861; *Jamestown
    Journal*, March 1, 1861; *Sandusky Register*, February 25, 1861; *Alexandria Gazette*,
    February 25, 1861. For Van Wyck's second speech, see *Globe*, 36th Cong.,
    2nd Sess., January 29, 1861, 629–32.

22. Proving a negative is inherently difficult if not impossible; in the same way that
    the total number of violent incidents is impossible to ascertain, it's hard to be
    certain regarding their absence. Extensive searching of the same kind that un-
    covered the incidents that shape this volume produced harsh words, a few threat-
    ened duel challenges, and a close call in 1863, when Daniel Voorhees (D-IN)
    followed John Hickman (R-PA) into a hall after being insulted on the House floor,
    but was persuaded by friends to hold back. *New York Herald*, February 20, 1863.

23. *Globe*, 37th Cong., 4th Sess., March 15, 1861, 1464.

24. For example, see the clashes between Martin Conway (R-KS) and Philip Fouke

(D-IL) in December 1861; Henry Burnett (D-KY) and William Richardson (D-IL) in July 1861; Roscoe Conkling (R-NY) and Elihu Washburne (R-IL) in May 1862; Clement Vallandigham (D-OH) and Benjamin Wade (R-OH) in May 1862; and James Moorhead (R-PA) and Albert Gallatin Riddle (R-OH) in February 1863.

25. *NYT*, March 16, 1862. See also *The Round Table*, June 16, 1864.

26. *The Round Table*, June 18, 1864, 2–3. See also *New York Herald*, February 15, 1863.

27. For a sample of such language, see *Globe*, 37th Cong., 2nd Sess., April 26, 1862, 1829. See also "Congressional Trifling and Truculence," *Springfield Republican*, May 3, 1862; "Unparliamentary Conduct in Both Houses of Congress," *New York Herald*, June 16, 1866. Not surprisingly, some Southern newspapers gloried in it: "The Lincoln Senate" and "Rows in the Lincoln House," *Macon Telegraph*, June 17, 1862, and January 17, 1863.

28. *New York Herald*, June 16, 1866.

29. The Confederate Congress met behind closed doors; this sampling of fights may well be just a sampling.

30. Wilfred Buck Yearns, *The Confederate Congress* (Athens: University of Georgia Press, 1960), 15–16. Edmund Dargan of Alabama made the knife attack. Thomas Hanly of Missouri inflicted the committee-room pounding, and William Swan was the umbrella assailant. See also E. Merton Coulter, *The Confederate States of America, 1861–1865*, vol. 7 of *A History of the South* (Baton Rouge: LSU Press, 1950), 143.

31. Wilfred Yearns, *The Confederate Congress*, 15–16; Edward A. Pollard, "The Confederate Congress: A Chapter in the History of the Late War," *The Galaxy* 6 (July 1, 1868, to January 1, 1869): 749–58.

32. *NYT*, October 2, 1864; John E. Gonzales, "Henry Stuart Foote: Confederate Congressman and Exile," *Civil War History* 11 (December 1965): 384–95; idem., "Henry Stuart Foote in Exile," *Journal of Mississippi History* (April 1953): 90–98.

33. Congress had seated two congressmen from Louisiana in 1863 fifteen days before the close of the Thirty-seventh Congress, when their tenure expired. Joseph G. Dawson, *Army Generals and Reconstruction: Louisiana, 1862–1877* (Baton Rouge: LSU Press, 1982), 15.

34. For a detailed account, see 38th Cong., 2nd Sess., House Report No. 10, "Assault upon Hon. William D. Kelley," February 7, 1865; quote on p. 1.

35. 39th Cong., 1st Sess., H. Rpt. 90, July 2, 1866, "Breach of Privilege." On the incident generally, see also Address of Hon. Lovell H. Rousseau to His Constituents (1866); Reply of Gen. Rousseau to Wendell Phillips, *NYT*, May 10, 1867; Josiah B. Grinnell, *Men and Events of Forty Years: Autobiographical Reminiscences of an Active Career from 1850 to 1890* (Boston: D. Lothrop, 1891), 163–70; Marion and Oliver, *Killing Congress*, 208–27; Paul R. Abrams, "The Assault upon Josiah B. Grinnell by Lovell H. Rousseau, *Iowa Journal of History* 3 (July 1912): 383–402; Dan Lee, *Kentuckian in Blue: A Biography of Major General Lovell Harrison Rousseau* (Jefferson, N.C.: McFarland, 2010), 181–89; Charles Payne, *Josiah Bushnell Grinnell*. See *Globe*, 39th Cong., 1st Sess., July 17, 1866, 3882 for James Garfield's (R-OH) summary of the lead-up to the fight.

36. Grinnell, *Men and Events*, 169–70. Fellow Iowans—also at his lodgings that night—gave Grinnell a heavy iron-topped cane. Only three of Rousseau's blows did damage. Rousseau later said, "I did not want to hurt you; I wanted to disgrace you, you damned poltroon." He also noted that he asked for an apology as a warning to Grinnell, "to call his attention to what I was doing." H. Rpt. No. 10, 6, 22, 25.

37. On disgracing the House floor, see H. Rpt. No. 10, 26; on demand for a "fair fight," see ibid., 20–24, 36.

38. *Globe*, 39th Cong., 1st Sess., July 17, 1866, 3882, 3885.

39. Women in Louisville, Kentucky, and St. Louis, Missouri, sent canes. *Alexandria Gazette*, August 4, 1866; *Providence Evening Press*, July 26, 1866; *Commercial Advertiser* (N.Y.), August 3, 1866.

40. *Daily Advocate* (Baton Rouge), July 9, 1866; *Macon Weekly Telegraph*, July 9, 1866.

41. *Lowell Daily Citizen and News*, January 25, 1865; *New Orleans Times*, February 3, 1865; *Chicago Tribune*, January 29, 1865; *Christian Advocate and Journal*, February 2, 1865.

42. Grinnell, *Men and Events*, 163; *Cincinnati Daily Gazette*, April 17, 1872; *Daily Iowa State Register*, September 28, 1867. Grinnell discusses the incident in his memoir to counteract the "hasty public judgment that I should have fought my assailant, and, without his apology, taken the life of a criminal." On the new, more martial ideals of Northern manhood that emerged from the war, see also Arnold, "Virgin Soil of Kansas," 246.

43. See esp. George C. Rable, *But There Was No Peace: The Role of Violence in the Politics of Reconstruction* (Athens: University of Georgia Press, 2007; orig. ed. 1984); Wyatt-Brown, *Shaping of Southern Culture*, 270–95.

44. Simpson, *Good Southerner*, 287–93. Wise's two eldest surviving sons became Republican congressmen; his oldest son died under Wise's command during the war. In 1870, Wise was attacked in the press for his role in the Cilley-Graves duel; he thought it was an attempt to strike at Grant, whom he supported. Wise to unknown correspondent, January 27, 1870, Henry A. Wise Papers, UNC.

45. French, diary entry, March 9, 1862, *Witness*, 390. The song—"The Patriotic Diggers" by Samuel Woodworth—was about digging trenches for protection against the British. Gerry Silverman, *New York Sings: 400 Years of the Empire State in Song* (New York: Excelsior Editions, 2009), 38–39. The reference to the Revolution was "Recollect our dads gave you once a basting."

46. French, diary entry, July 17, 1863, *Witness*, 427; Wallner, *Martyr*, 350–51; Nichols, *Pierce*, 522–23.

47. French, diary entry, March 20, 1864, *Witness*, 447.

48. Ibid, September 25, 1864, and July 10, 1863, 457, 427.

49. Ibid., April 6, 1865, 469.

50. Ibid., April 17, 1865, 474.

51. Cresson, *Journey into Fame*, 108. Cresson, Daniel's daughter, was a noted sculptor like her father.

52. French to George McLaughlin, December 5, 1863, in *History of the Great Western Sanitary Fair* (Cincinnati: C. F. Vent, 1864), 165–66. McLaughlin had asked

French to write a poem for the fair; French declined but sent along the original draft of his Gettysburg hymn and described its composition.

53. French, diary entry, November 22, 1863, BBFFP; French, "Hymn Composed at Gettysburg for the Consecration, Nov. 19, 1863," BBFFP.

54. French to Francis O. French, April 24, 1865, BBFFP; Affidavit of Robert Strong, March 20, 1876, in Ward Hill Lamon, *Recollections of Abraham Lincoln, 1847–1865*, ed. Dorothy Lamon Teillard (Washington: Published by editor, 1911), 272–73.

55. French, diary entry, June 17, 1869, *Witness*, 596.

56. Cresson, *Journey into Fame*, 19.

57. On the details, see Stahr, *Seward*, 435–38.

58. French, diary entries, April 15, 1865, and April 15, 1866, 469–71, *Witness*, 507. Sometime that day, French loaded his revolver; ibid., July 5, 1865, 482. See also his account of that day in "Address Delivered at the Dedication of the Statue of Abraham Lincoln, Erected in Front of the City Hall, Washington, D.C." (Washington: McGill & Witherow, 1868), 12–15. In the speech, he says that he couldn't "leave the inanimate form of him of whom I had seen so much, and whom I loved so well in life." Ibid., 10.

59. French to Francis O. French, April 24, 1865, BBFFP.

60. Ibid.

61. French, diary entry, November 23, 1866, and February 6, 1867, *Witness*, 525, 528.

62. Ibid., February 6, 1867, 528.

63. Ibid., July 17, 1866, and May 26, 1867, 511, 539.

64. Ibid., February 21, 1866, *Witness*, 502–503; French to Andrew Johnson, February 8, 1866, *The Papers of Andrew Johnson: February–July 1866*, ed. Paul H. Bergeron, vol. 10 (Knoxville: University of Tennessee Press, 1992), 57–58.

65. *Globe*, 39th Cong., 2nd Sess., February 23, 1867, 1523–26. French wrote the poem in April 1861. For the poem in broadside form, see repository.library.brown .edu/studio/item/bdr:282409/, accessed June 4, 2015.

66. Act of March 2, 1867, Section 2 (14 Stats., p. 466).

67. French, diary entry, February 24, 1867, 531. See also ibid., February 6, March 3 and 11, 1867, 528, 533.

68. Ibid., May 12, 1867, 539. See also ibid., December 8, 1867, 549. On the elimination of the commissioner, see William C. Allen, *History of the United States Capitol: A Chronicle of Design, Construction, and Politics* (Washington, D.C.: GPO, 2001), 342–43.

69. French, diary entry, March 8, 1868, *Witness*, 560.

70. Emphasis in original; even now, however, French considered having the poem published in future. Ibid., January 31, 1868, 553. He wrote it in August 1867.

71. Ibid., April 2, July 10, and August 2, 1867, 535, 539, 543.

72. French had filled the position from 1847 to 1853. Ibid., November 10, 1867, 548.

73. Ibid., February 10, 1868, 556. See also ibid., June 6, 1869, 594–95.

74. Ibid., November 8, 1868, 584.

75. Ibid., August 15, 1868, 576–77.

76. Ibid., August 26, 1868, and October 10, 1869, 580, 604.

77. Ibid., November 13, 1869, 605–606.
78. Ibid., July 31, 1870, 622.
79. Frank O. French, diary entry, ca. August 14, 1870; F. O. French to Ellen French, August 12, 1870, BBFFP.
80. French, diary entry, August 8, 1870, *Witness*, 622–23. Emphasis in original.
81. Sarita Brady to Anne Ransford French, August 15, 1870, typescript, BBFFP.
82. *Evening Star*, August 12, 1870; *National Intelligencer*, August 15, 1870; *Baltimore Sun*, August 15, 1870; *Daily National Intelligencer*, March 28, 1851.
83. Sarita Brady to Anne Ransford French, August 15, 1870, typescript, BBFFP.
84. *National Republican*, August 24, 1870 (based on typescript in BBFFP). On Lodges of Sorrow, see "Lodges of Sorrow," *Masonic Monthly* 2 (November 1864): 379–80.
85. *NYT*, August 14, 1870.
86. Clipping from *The Home Journal*, November 23, 1861, BBFFP.
87. French, "Reminiscences of Washington: The Old Capitol," *Washington Sunday Herald and Weekly National Intelligencer*, March 13, 1870, in Curtis Carroll Davis, "The 'Old Capitol' and Its Keeper: How William P. Wood Ran a Civil War Prison," *Records of the Columbia Historical Society* 52 (1989): 206–34, quote on 206.
88. *National Freemason* 1 (October 1863): 68–69. French's opening paragraphs describe his intention to describe what he witnessed. He began his memoir of sorts on May 5, 1856; between 1863 and 1865, the *National Freemason* published it serially under the title "Congressional Reminiscences." It doesn't seem to extend past French's first five years in Washington. Ibid., 1 (June 1863); 2 (July 1863); 4 (September 1863); 5 (October 1863); 6 (November 1863); 7 (December 1863); 1 (June 1864); 2 (July 1864); 5 (October 1864); 6 (November 1864); 8 (February 1865); 11 (April 1865).
89. French, "Address Delivered at the Dedication of the Statue of Abraham Lincoln, Erected in Front of the City Hall, Washington, D.C." (Washington: McGill & Witherow, 1868), 14.
90. The recent burst of scholarship on the decline of congressional civility since the 1980s generally argues: Congress is us. Loomis, *Esteemed Colleagues*; Uslaner, *Decline of Comity*; Juliet Eilperin, *Fight Club Politics: How Partisanship Is Poisoning the House of Representatives* (Lanham, Md.: Rowman & Littlefield, 2006); Ahuja, *Congress Behaving Badly*; Mann and Ornstein, *The Broken Branch*.
91. French, "A Vision," June 13, 1869, BBFFP. The poem appeared in the *Civil Service Journal* under the dateline July 31, 1869.

APPENDIX B

1. John Fairfield to Ann Fairfield, January 29, 1836, John Fairfield Papers, LC.
2. Henry A. Wise to Henry A. Wise, December 10, 1856, Wise Family Papers, LC; T. C. Day to John Bigelow, November 25, 1856, John Bigelow Papers, NYPL. See also ibid., December 1, 1856, and a "Quite confidential" memo—allegedly from Jessie B. Fremont—detailing a conversation between F. P. Blair and her father, Thomas Hart Benton. John Bigelow Papers, NYPL.

3. On Potter's attempt to refute newspaper stories about the kicking, see *Globe,* 35th Cong., 1st Sess., February 26, 1858, 889–90; *Chicago Daily Tribune,* March 6 and 8, 1858; *Sandusky Register,* March 12, 1858.

4. For an invaluable discussion of these histories, see Woods, *Emotional and Sectional Conflict,* 4–7; Ayers, *What Caused the Civil War?,* 131–44.

5. See "Note on Method," Freeman, *Affairs of Honor,* 289–93.

6. Particularly helpful in understanding the historical context of emotions is Strange, Cribb, and Forth, *Honour, Violence and Emotions in History,* 1–22. For a fascinating consideration of the role of strong emotions in politics, see Martha C. Nussbaum's *Political Emotions: Why Love Matters for Justice* (Cambridge: Harvard University Press, 2013); and *Anger and Forgiveness: Resentment, Generosity, Justice* (New York: Oxford University Press, 2016). Nussbaum emphasizes the importance of forgiveness and civility over anger; *The Field of Blood* is a story of anger leading to justice.

7. Ayers, *The Thin Light of Freedom,* xxi.

SELECTED BIBLIOGRAPHY

MANUSCRIPT COLLECTIONS

BOWDOIN COLLEGE
Jonathan Cilley Biographical File
William Pitt Fessenden Papers

DUKE UNIVERSITY
Charles Colcock Jones, Jr., Papers
Laurence Massillon Keitt Papers

LIBRARY OF CONGRESS
Nathaniel Banks Papers
John Bell Papers
Blair Family Papers
Breckenridge Family Papers
Anson Burlingame and Family Papers
Simon Cameron Papers
John Jordan Crittenden Papers
Edward Everett Papers
John Fairfield Papers
Benjamin Brown French Family Papers
James Henry Hammond Papers
Frederick W. Lander Papers
Lee-Palfrey Family Papers
Louise McLane Papers
Amasa Junius Parker Papers
Franklin Pierce Papers
Thomas Ritchie Papers

William Cabell Rives Papers
Samuel Lewis Southard Papers
Charles Sumner Collection
Charles Sumner Papers
Robert Augustus Toombs Papers
Nicholas Trist Papers
Lyman Trumbull Papers
Benjamin Franklin Wade Papers
Henry Wilson Papers
Wise Family Papers

MAINE HISTORICAL SOCIETY
F.O.J. Smith Papers

MASSACHUSETTS HISTORICAL SOCIETY
William Schouler Papers

NATIONAL ARCHIVES
24th Cong., 2nd Sess. H. Rpt. No. 24A-D24.1, "R. M. Whitney."

NEW HAMPSHIRE HISTORICAL SOCIETY
Benjamin Brown French to Henry Flagg French Correspondence
John Parker Hale Papers
Isaac Hill Papers
Tristram Shaw Papers

NEW YORK PUBLIC LIBRARY
James Gordon Bennett Papers
Bigelow Family Papers
John Bigelow Papers
James A. Hamilton Papers
George Jones Papers
Henry J. Raymond Papers
F.O.J. Smith Papers

OFFICE OF THE CURATOR OF THE U.S. SENATE
Isaac Bassett Papers

UNIVERSITY OF NORTH CAROLINA
Robert L. Caruthers Papers

Fisher Family Papers
Daniel R. Goodloe Papers
William Porcher Miles Papers
David Outlaw Papers
Robert Barnwell Rhett Papers
Nicholas P. Trist Papers
Henry A. Wise Papers

UNIVERSITY OF VIRGINIA
Lawrence O'Bryan Branch Papers
Hunter-Garnett Family Papers

YALE UNIVERSITY
James Watson Webb Papers

GOVERNMENT DOCUMENTS
Annals of Congress
Biographical Directory of the United States Congress, 1774–Present (Washington,
   D.C.: GPO), bioguide.congress.gov/biosearch/biosearch.asp
Congressional Globe
Hinds' Precedents of the House of Representatives of the United States, 5 vols. (Wash-
   ington, D.C.: GPO, 1907).
House Journal
National Intelligencer
Register of Debates
Roster of Congressional Officeholders and Biographical Characteristics (ICPSR
   7803)
Senate Executive Journal
Senate Journal
22nd Cong. 1st Sess., H. Doc. No. 269, "Abstract of the Returns of the Fifth Census"
   (Washington: Duff Green, 1832).
24th Cong., 2nd Sess., H. Rpt. No. 156, "Memorial of Reuben M. Whitney."
24th Cong., 2nd Sess., H. Rpt. No. 24A-D24.1, "R. M. Whitney."
25th Cong., 2nd Sess., H. Rpt. No. 825, April 21, 1838, "Death of Mr. Cilley—Duel."
28th Cong., 1st Sess., H. Rpt. No. 470, May 6, 1844, "Rencounter Between Messrs.
   White and Rathbun."
31st Cong., 1st Sess., S. Rpt. No. 170, July 30, 1850, "Thomas H. Benton of Missouri
   and Henry S. Foote of Mississippi."
34th Cong., 1st Sess., 1 H. Rpt. No. 182, 1856, "Alleged Assault upon Charles
   Sumner."
34th Cong., 3rd Sess., H. Rpt. No. 29, December 19, 1856, "John L. Wirt."
36th Cong., 2nd Sess., H. Rpt. No. 104, March 2, 1861, "Kansas Claims."
38th Cong., 2nd Sess., H. Rpt. No. 10, February 7, 1865, "Assault upon Hon. William D. Kelley."

39th Cong., 1st Sess., H. Rpt. No. 90, July 2, 1866, "Breach of Privilege."
40th Cong., 2nd Sess., H. Rpt. No. 65, June 20, 1868, "Ventilation of the Hall of the House of Representatives."
108th Cong., 2nd Sess., H. Doc. No. 108-240, January 18, 2008, *Glenn Brown's History of the United States Capitol.*

PUBLISHED PRIMARY SOURCES

"The Campaigns of a 'Conqueror'; or, 'The Man 'Who Bragged High for a Fight.'" [undated broadside].
"Circular from the Executive Committee of the Democratic Association of Washington City," September 1844.
"Death of Cilley," *United States Magazine and Democratic Review* 4 (November–December 1840): 196–200.
The Diaries of John Quincy Adams: A Digital Collection. Massachusetts Historical Society. www.masshist.org/jqadiaries/php/how.
Festival of the Sons of New Hampshire . . . Celebrated in Boston, November 7, 1849. Boston: James French, 1850.
"Manhood Suffrage and the Ballot in America," *Blackwood's Edinburgh Magazine* 101 (April 1867): 461–78.
Memoirs and Services of Three Generations. Rockland, Maine, reprint from *Courier-Gazette*, 1909.
"The National Metropolis," *De Bow's Review* 1 (April 1859).
"A Peep at Washington," *The Knickerbocker; or New York Monthly Magazine*, June 1834.
Permanent Documents of the American Temperance Society, 2 vols. Boston: Seth Bliss, 1835.
"Proceedings of the Annual Town Meeting in Concord, March 12, 13, 14, 15, 1844."
"Proceedings at the Banquet of the Jackson Democratic Association, Washington, Eighth of January, 1852." Washington, D.C., 1852.
"Proceedings of the Congressional Total Abstinence Society." New York: Office of the American Temperance Union, 1842.
Proceedings of the First Three Republican National Conventions of 1856, 1860, and 1864, Including Proceedings of the Antecedent National Convention Held at Pittsburg, in February, 1856, as Reported by Horace Greeley. Minneapolis: Charles W. Johnson, 1893.
Proceedings of the Massachusetts Historical Society, June Meeting, 1898. Boston, 1899.
Proceedings of the Regular Conclave of the Grand Commandery of Knights Templar of the State of Michigan, Held at Detroit Michigan, June 4, A.D. 1861, A. O. 743. Detroit: H. Barns & Co., 1861.
"Scenic and Characteristic Outlines of Congress, I," *National Magazine and Republican Review* 1 (January 1839).
"The Sumner Outrage. A Full Report of the Speeches at the Meeting of Citizens in Cambridge, June 2, 1856." Cambridge: John Ford, Printer, 1856.
"Washington City Forty Years Ago." In *Memoirs of Anne C. L. Botta Written by Her Friends.* New York: J. Selwin Tait & Sons, 1893.
The Works of Charles Sumner, 12 vols. Boston: Lee and Shepard, 1870–83.

Zachariah Chandler: An Outline Sketch of His Life and Public Services. Detroit: Post and Tribune Co., 1880.

Adams, Charles Francis. *Memoirs of John Quincy Adams, Compromising Portions of His Diary from 1795 to 1848,* 12 vols. Philadelphia: J. B. Lippincott & Co., 1874–77.

Adams, John Quincy. "Address of John Quincy Adams to Constituents." Boston: J. H. Eastburn, 1842.

Anderson, Eve, ed. *A Breach of Privilege: Cilley Family Letters, 1820–1867.* Spruce Head, Maine: Seven Coin Press, 2002.

Baber, George. "Personal Recollections of Senator H. S. Foote," *Overland Monthly* 26 (July–December 1895), 162–71.

Barnes, Gilbert H., and Dwight L. Dumond, eds. *Letters of Theodore Dwight Weld, Angelina Grimke Weld and Sarah Grimke, 1822–1844,* 2 vols. New York: D. Appleton-Century Co., 1934.

Barnes, James J., and Patience P. Barnes, eds. *Private and Confidential: Letters from British Ministers in Washington to the Foreign Secretaries in London, 1844–67.* Selinsgrove, Pa.: Susquehanna University Press, 1993.

Bartlett, John Russell. *Dictionary of Americanisms: A Glossary of Words and Phrases Usually Regarded as Peculiar to the United States.* Boston: Little, Brown, 1848.

Benton, Joel, ed. *Greeley on Lincoln with Mr. Greeley's Letters to Charles A. Dana and a Lady Friend.* New York: Baker & Taylor, 1893.

Benton, Thomas Hart. *Thirty Years, View; or, A History of the Working of the American Government for Thirty Years, from 1820 to 1850,* 2 vols. New York: D. Appleton and Co., 1856.

Bigelow, John. *Retrospections of an Active Life, 1817–1863,* 5 vols. New York: Baker & Taylor, 1909.

Boyle, E. M., ed. "Jonathan Cilley of Maine and William J. Graves of Kentucky, Representatives in Congress. An Historical Duel, 1838, as Narrated by Gen. Geo. W. Jones, Cilley's Second." *Maine Historical and Genealogical Recorder* 6 (1889).

Brainerd, Cephas, and Eveline Warner Brainerd, eds. *The New England Society Orations: Addresses, Sermons, and Poems Delivered Before the New England Society in the City of New York, 1820–1885,* 2 vols. New York: The Century Co., 1901.

Brockway, Beman. *Fifty Years in Journalism: Embracing Recollections and Personal Experiences with an Autobiography.* Watertown, N.Y.: Daily Times Printing and Publishing House, 1891.

Brown, George Rothwell, ed. *Reminiscences of Senator William M. Stewart, of Nevada.* New York: Neale Publishing Company, 1908.

Browne, William Hand. *Life of Alexander H. Stephens.* Philadelphia: J. B. Lippincott & Co., 1878.

Bryant, William Cullen II, ed. *Power for Sanity: Selected Editorials of William Cullen Bryant, 1829–1861.* New York: Fordham University Press, 1994.

Buckingham, J. S. *America, Historical, Statistic, and Descriptive,* 3 vols. London: Fisher, Son & Co., 1841.

Chapman, Maria Weston, ed. *Harriet Martineau's Autobiography,* 3 vols. Boston: Houghton, Mifflin and Co., 1877.

Chapple, Joel Mitchell. "Affairs at Washington," *National Magazine,* October 1903.

Clephane, Lewis. *Birth of the Republican Party, with a Brief History of the Important Part Taken by the Original Republican Association of the National Capital.* Washington, D.C.: Gibson Bros., 1889.

Cole, Donald B., and John J. McDonough, eds. *Witness to the Young Republic: A Yankee's Journal, 1828–1870.* Hanover, N.H.: University Press of New England, 1989.

Coleman, Chapman, ed. *The Life of John J. Crittenden, with Selections from His Correspondence and Speeches,* 2 vols. Philadelphia: J. B. Lippincott & Co., 1871.

Cox, Samuel S. *Eight Years in Congress, from 1857–1865: Memoir and Speeches.* New York: D. Appleton and Co., 1865.

———. *Union-Disunion-Reunion: Three Decades of Federal Legislation, 1855 to 1885.* Providence: A. & R. A. Reid, 1885.

Darby, William, and Theodore Dwight, Jr. *A New Gazetteer of the United States of America.* Hartford: Edward Hopkins, 1833.

Deese, Helen R., ed. *Daughter of Boston: The Extraordinary Diary of a Nineteenth-Century Woman: Caroline Healey Dall.* Boston: Beacon Press, 2005.

Dickens, Charles. *American Notes for General Circulation,* 2 vols. London: Chapman and Hall, 1842.

Dickinson, John R., ed. *Speeches, Correspondence, Etc., of the Late Daniel S. Dickinson of New York,* 2 vols. New York: G. P. Putnam & Son, 1867.

Dwight, Timothy. *Travels in New-England and New-York,* 4 vols. New Haven, Conn.: Published by author, S. Converse, Printer.

Dyer, Oliver. *Great Senators of the United States Forty Years Ago.* New York: Robert Bonner's Sons, 1889.

Eckloff, Christian F. *Memoirs of a Senate Page, 1855–1859.* New York: Broadway Publishing Company, 1909.

Feller, Dan, Thomas Coens, and Laura-Eve Moss, eds., *The Papers of Andrew Jackson,* 10 vols. Knoxville: University of Tennessee, 1980–.

Fessenden, Francis. *Life and Public Services of William Pitt Fessenden,* 2 vols. Cambridge, Mass.: Riverside Press, 1907.

Foote, Henry S. *The Bench and Bar of the South and Southwest.* St. Louis: Thomas Wentworth, 1876.

———. *Casket of Reminiscences.* Washington: Chronicle, 1874.

Forney, John Wien. *Anecdotes of Public Men,* 2 vols. New York, 1873–81.

French, Benjamin Brown. "Address Delivered at the Dedication of the Statue of Abraham Lincoln, Erected in Front of the City Hall, Washington, D.C. Washington: McGill & Witherow, 1868.

———. "Application of Parliamentary Law to the Government of Masonic Bodies," *American Quarterly Review of Freemasonry and Its Kindred Sciences* 3 (January 5858 [i.e., 1857]).

———. "Congressional Reminiscences," *National Freemason* (1863–65).

———. [Eulogy for John Quincy Adams]. In "Proceedings in the Board of Aldermen and Board of Common Council, of the City of Washington, on the Occasion of the Death of John Quincy Adams." Washington: John T. Towers, 1848.

———. "Reminiscences of Washington: The Old Capitol," *Washington Sunday Her-*

ald and Weekly National Intelligencer, March 13, 1870, in "The 'Old Capitol' and Its Keeper: How William P. Wood Ran a Civil War Prison," Curtis Carroll Davis, ed. *Records of the Columbia Historical Society* 52 (1989): 206–34.

Friedlaender, Marc, et al., eds., *Diary of Charles Francis Adams*. Cambridge, Mass.: Harvard University Press, 1986.

Furber, George P. *Precedents Relating to the Privileges of the Senate of the United States*. Washington, D.C.: GPO, 1893.

Garfield, James A. [Address at dedication of a monument to Joshua Giddings], July 25, 1870, in *The Works of James Abram Garfield*, ed. Burke A. Hinsdale. Boston: James Osgood and Co, 1882.

Giddings, Joshua. *History of the Rebellion: Its Authors and Causes*. New York: Follet, Foster & Co., 1864.

———. [Speech on Relation of the Federal Government to Slavery]. *Speeches in Congress*. Boston: John P. Jewett and Co., 1853.

Gobright, Lawrence. *Recollection of Men and Things at Washington During the Third of a Century*. Philadelphia: Claxton, Remson & Haffelfinger, 1869.

Gough, John B. *Sunlight and Shadow, or, Gleanings from My Life Work*. London: R. D. Dickinson, 1881.

Graf, Leroy P., Ralph W. Haskins, and Paul H. Bergeron, eds. *The Papers of Andrew Johnson*, 16 vols. Knoxville: University of Tennessee Press, 1992.

Greeley, Horace. *Recollections of a Busy Life*. New York: J. B. Ford & Co., 1869.

Greene, H. W. "Letters Addressed to Francis O. J. Smith, Representative in Congress from Cumberland District, (Me.) Being a Defence of the Writer Against the Attacks Made on Him By That Individual—And A Sketch of Mr. Smith's Political Life." N.p., 1839.

Griffin, G. W., ed. *Prenticeana: or, Wit and Humor in Paragraphs*. Philadelphia: Claxton, Remsen & Haffelfinger, 1871.

Grinnell, Josiah B. *Men and Events of Forty Years: Autobiographical Reminiscences of an Active Career from 1850 to 1890*. Boston: D. Lothrop Co., 1891.

Grund, Francis J. "Society in the American Metropolis." *Sartain's Union Magazine of Literature and Art*, vol. 6 (January–June 1850): 17–18.

Hambleton, James Pinkney. "A Biographical Sketch of Henry A. Wise, with a History of the Political Campaign in Virginia in 1855." Richmond, Va.: J. W. Randolph, 1856.

Hawthorne, Nathaniel. "Biographical Sketch of Jonathan Cilley." *United States Magazine and Democratic Review* 3 (September 1838): 69–77.

———. *Passages from the American Note-Books of Nathaniel Hawthorne*. In *The Works of Nathaniel Hawthorne*, 12 vols. Boston: Houghton, Mifflin, & Co., 1883.

Herr, Pamela, and Mary Lee Spence, eds. *The Letters of Jessie Benton Fremont*. Champaign: University of Illinois, 1993.

History of the New England Society. New England Society of New York. www.nesnyc .org/overview.

Hollcroft, Temple R., ed. "A Congressman's Letters on the Speaker Election in the Thirty-fourth Congress," *Mississippi Valley Historical Review* 43, no. 3 (December 1956): 444–58.

Hood, Thomas. *Quips and Cranks*. London: Routledge, Warne, and Routledge, 1861.

House, Madeline, Graham Storey, Kathleen Tillotson, et al., eds. *The British Academy Pilgrim Edition, The Letters of Charles Dickens*, 12 vols. Oxford: Clarendon Press, 1965–2002.

Howell, Wilber S., ed. *Jefferson's Parliamentary Writings: "Parliamentary Pocket-Book" and a Manual of Parliamentary Practice*. Princeton, N.J.: Princeton University Press, 1988.

Ingersoll, L. D. *The Life of Horace Greeley*. Philadelphia: E. Potter, 1874.

Johnston, Richard Malcolm, and William Hand Browne. *Life of Alexander H. Stephens*. Philadelphia: J. B. Lippincott & Co., 1878.

Jones, George Wallace. "Autobiography." In John Carl Parish, ed. *George Wallace Jones*. Iowa City: State Historical Society, 1912.

———. [Funeral Oration . . . over the Body of Hon. Jonathan Cilley]. *George Wallace Jones*, John C. Parish, ed., Iowa City: State Historical Society, 1912.

Julian, George W. *The Life of Joshua R. Giddings*. Chicago: A. C. McClurg and Co., 1892.

———. *Political Recollections 1840 to 1872*. Chicago: Jansen, McClurg & Co., 1884.

King, Horatio. "History of the Duel Between Jonathan Cilley and William J. Graves." *Collections and Proceedings of the Maine Historical Society* 2 (April 1892): 127–48.

———. *Turning On the Light: A Dispassionate Survey of President Buchanan's Administration, from 1860 to Its Close*. Philadelphia: J. B. Lippincott Co., 1895.

Laas, Virginia Jeans, ed. *Wartime Washington: The Civil War Letters of Elizabeth Blair Lee*. Champaign: University of Illinois, 1999.

Lanman, Charles, ed. *Journal of Alfred Ely, a Prisoner of War in Richmond* (New York: D. Appleton and Co., 1862.

Lieber, Francis. *Letters to a Gentleman in Germany: Written After a Trip from Philadelphia to Niagara*. Philadelphia: Carey, Lea & Blanchard, 1834.

[Lyman, Darius]. "A Former Resident of the South." *Leaven for Doughfaces; or Threescore and Ten Parables Touching Slavery*. Cincinnati: Bangs and Co., 1856.

Mann, Mary T. P., ed. *Life of Horace Mann by His Wife*. Boston: Lee & Shepard, 1904.

Marryat, Frederick. *A Diary in America, with Remarks on Its Institutions*, 3 vols. London: Longman, Orme, Brown, Green & Longman's, 1839.

Marsh, Charles W. *Recollections, 1837–1910*. Chicago: Farm Implement News Co., 1910.

Marshall, Thomas F. "Speeches of Thomas F. Marshall of Kentucky on the Resolutions to Censure John Q. Adams." Washington: Blair & Rives, 1842.

Martineau, Harriet. *Retrospect of Western Travel*. New York: Harper and Brothers, 1838.

———. *Society in America*. Paris: Baudry's European Library, 1837.

McCulloch, Hugh. "Memories of Some Contemporaries." *Scribner's Magazine* 3 (September 1888).

McDonough, John J., ed. *Growing Up on Capitol Hill: A Young Washingtonian's Journal, 1850–1852*. Washington, D.C.: LC, 1997.

McIntosh, James T., Lynda L. Crist, and Haskell M. Monroe, Jr., eds. *The Papers of Jefferson Davis*. Baton Rouge: LSU Press, 1971–2014.

Meriwether, Robert L., ed. "Preston S. Brooks on the Caning of Charles Sumner." *South Carolina Historical and Genealogical Magazine* 52 (1951).

Meriwether, Robert L., and Clyde N. Wilson, eds. *The Papers of John C. Calhoun.* Columbia: University of South Carolina, 1959–2003.

Mills, Robert. *Guide to the Capital of the United States Embracing Every Information Useful to the Visiter, Whether on Business or Pleasure.* Washington, n.p., 1834.

Monroe, Haskell, M. Monroe, Jr., and James T. McIntosh, eds. *The Papers of Jefferson Davis: Volume 1, 1808–1840.* Baton Rouge: LSU Press, 1991 rev. ed.

Moody, Robert E., ed. *The Papers of Leverett Saltonstall, 1816–1845*, 5 vols. Boston: Massachusetts Historical Society, 1984.

Moore, Charles, ed. and comp. *Joint Select Committee to Investigate the Charities and Reformatory Institutions in the District of Columbia.* Washington, D.C.: GPO, 1898.

Palmer, Beverly Wilson, and Holly Byers Ochoa, eds. *The Selected Papers of Thaddeus Stevens, April 1865–August 1868*, 2 vols. Pittsburgh: University of Pittsburgh Press, 1997–98.

Perry, Thomas Sergeant, ed. *The Life and Letters of Francis Lieber.* Boston: James R. Osgood & Co., 1882.

Phillips, Ulrich B., ed. *The Correspondence of Robert Toombs, Alexander H. Stephens, and Howell Cobb*, 2 vols., in *Annual Report of the American Historical Association for 1911.* Washington, D.C.: GPO, 1913.

Pike, James Shepherd. *First Blows of the Civil War: The Ten Years of Preliminary Conflict in the United States, from 1850 to 1860.* New York: American News, 1879.

Plumer, William, Jr. "Reminiscences of Daniel Webster," in *The Writings and Speeches of Daniel Webster*, National Edition, James W. McIntyre, ed., 18 vols. Boston: Little, Brown, 1903.

Poore, Benjamin Perley. *Perley's Reminiscences of Sixty Years in the National Metropolis*, 2 vols. Philadelphia: Hubbard Brothers, 1886.

Preuss, Henry Clay. "Fashions and Follies of Washington Life. A Play. In Five Acts." Washington, D.C.: Published by the author, 1857.

Quaife, Milo Milton, ed. *The Diary of James K. Polk During His Presidency, 1845 to 1849*, 4 vols. Chicago: A. C. McClurg & Co., 1910.

Riddle, Albert Gallatin. *Recollections of War Times: Reminiscences of Men and Events in Washington, 1860–1865.* New York: G. P. Putnam's Sons, 1895.

Sabine, Lorenzo. *Notes on Duels and Duelling.* Boston: Crosby, Nichols, and Co., 1855.

Sala, George A. *My Diary in America in the Midst of War*, 2 vols. London: Tinsley Brothers, 1865.

Sargent, Nathan. *Public Men and Events from the Commencement of Mr. Monroe's Administration, in 1817, to the Close of Mr. Fillmore's Administration, in 1853*, 2 vols. Philadelphia: J. B. Lippincott & Co., 1875.

Schultz, Edward T. *History of Freemasonry in Maryland of All the Rites Introduced into Maryland from the Earliest Time to the Present*, 2 vols. Baltimore: J. H. Medairy & Co., 1885.

Schurz, Carl. *The Reminiscences of Carl Schurz*, 3 vols. New York: McClure, 1907–1908.

Seager, Robert II, James F. Hopkins, and Mary W. M. Hargreaves, et al., eds. *The Papers of Henry Clay*, 11 vols. Lexington: University Press of Kentucky, 1959–92.

Seward, Frederick William. *Autobiography: Seward at Washington, as Senator and Secretary of State*. New York: Derby and Miller, 1891.

———. *Reminiscences of a War-Time Statesman and Diplomat, 1830–1915*. New York: G. P. Putnam's Sons, 1916.

Shanks, Henry Thomas, ed. *The Papers of Willie Person Mangum*. Raleigh: State Department of Archives and History, 1950.

Sherman, John. *John Sherman's Recollections of Forty Years in the House, Senate and Cabinet: An Autobiography*. New York: Werner Co., 1896.

Shulman, Holly C., ed. *The Papers of Dolley Madison Digital Edition*. Charlottesville: UVA Press, 2008.

Simons, John W. *A Familiar Treatise on the Principles and Practice of Masonic Jurisprudence*. New York: Masonic Publishing and Manufacturing Co., 1869.

Sporer, Paul D., ed. *Half a Century: The Memoirs of the First Woman Journalist in the Civil Rights Struggle*. Chester, N.Y.: Anza Publishing, 2005.

Staples, Arthur G., ed. *The Letters of John Fairfield*. Lewiston: Lewiston Journal Co., 1922.

Sumner, Charles. *The Barbarism of Slavery*. New York: Young Men's Republican Union, 1863 reprint with new introduction by Sumner.

———. "The Crime Against Kansas." Boston: John P. Jewett & Co., 1856.

———. *Speech of Hon. Charles Sumner, on the Bill for the Admission of Kansas as a Free State, in the United States Senate, June 4, 1860*. Boston: Thayer and Eldridge, 1860.

Teillard, Dorothy Lamon, ed. *Recollections of Abraham Lincoln, 1847–1865*. Washington: Published by editor, 1911.

Torrence, Clayton, ed. "From the Society's Collections: Letters of Mrs. Ann (Jennings) Wise to Her Husband, Henry A. Wise," *Virginia Magazine of History and Biography* 58, no. 4 (October 1950): 492–515.

Watterston, George. *New Guide to Washington*. Washington: Robert Farnham, 1842.

———. *A Picture of Washington*. Washington: William M. Morrison, 1840.

Weaver, Herbert, and Kermit L. Hall, eds. *Correspondence of James K. Polk*, 10 vols. Nashville: Vanderbilt University, 1969–2004.

Weiss, John, ed. *Life and Correspondence of Theodore Parker*, 2 vols. New York: D. Appleton & Co., 1864.

Wentworth, John. *Congressional Reminiscences: Adams, Benton, Calhoun, Clay, and Webster, an Address: Delivered at Central Music Hall, Thursday Eve., March 16, 1882, Before the Chicago Historical Society*. Chicago: Fergus Printing Company, 1882.

Wheeler, John H. *Reminiscences and Memoirs of North Carolina and Eminent North Carolinians*. Columbus: Columbus Printing Works, 1884.

Whitman, Walt. "Song for Certain Congressmen." In *Whitman: Complete Poetry and Collected Prose*, ed. Justin Kaplan. New York: Library of America, 1982.

Wilkie, F. B. "Geo. W. Jones." *Iowa Historical Record* 2 (April 1887).

Wilmer, Lambert A. *Our Press Gang; or, A Complete Exposition of the Corruptions and Crimes of the American Newspapers*. Philadelphia: J. T. Lloyd, 1860.

Wilson, Clyde N., Shirley Bright Cook, and Alexander Moore, eds. *The Papers of John C. Calhoun*, 28 vols. Columbia: University of South Carolina Press, 2001.

Wilson, Henry. *History of the Rise and Fall of the Slave Power in America*. Boston: Houghton Mifflin, 1874.

Wiltse, Charles M., and Michael J. Birkner, eds. *The Papers of Daniel Webster*. Hanover, N.H.: University Press of New England, 1974–85.

Windle, Mary Jane. *Life in Washington: and Life Here and There*. Philadelphia: J. B. Lippincott & Co., 1859.

Wise, Barton H. *The Life of Henry A. Wise of Virginia, 1806–1876*. New York: Macmillan, 1899.

Wise, Henry A. "Opinions of Hon. Henry A. Wise, Upon the Conduct and Character of James K. Polk, Speaker of the House of Representatives, With Other 'Democratic' Illustrations." Washington, D.C., 1844.

———. *Seven Decades of the Union*. Philadelphia: J. B. Lippincott & Co., 1872.

Wise, John Sergeant. *The End of an Era*. New York: Houghton, Mifflin and Co., 1902.

———. *Recollections of Thirteen Presidents*. New York: Doubleday, Page & Co., 1906.

MAGAZINES

The Century Magazine
DeBow's Review
Freemason's Monthly Magazine
The Galaxy
Harper's New Monthly Magazine
The Knickerbocker; or New York Monthly Magazine
Littell's Living Age
The Masonic Monthly
The Masonic Review
Merchant's Magazine
The National Freemason
The National Magazine and Republican Review
The New-Yorker
Punch
Rural Repository
Scribner's Magazine
United States Magazine and Democratic Review
Vanity Fair

SECONDARY SOURCES

Blocker, Jack S., David M. Fahey, and Ian R. Tyrrell, eds. "Congressional Temperance Society," in *Alcohol and Temperance in Modern History: A Global Encyclopedia*, 1:171–72. Santa Barbara, Calif.: ABC-Clio, 2003.

United States Senate Commission on Art and Antiquities. "Manners in the Senate Chamber: 19th Century Women's Views." Washington, D.C.: GPO, 1980.

Abbott, Carl. *Political Terrain: Washington, D.C. from the Tidewater to Global Metropolis.* Chapel Hill: UNC Press, 1999.

Abrams, Ann Uhry. "National Paintings and American Character: Historical Murals in the Capitol's Rotunda," in *Picturing History: American Painting, 1770–1930,* ed. William Ayres. New York: Rizzoli, 1993.

Abrams, Paul R. "The Assault upon Josiah B. Grinnell by Lovell H. Rousseau." *Iowa Journal of History* 3 (July 1912): 383–402.

Ahuja, Sunil. *Congress Behaving Badly: The Rise of Partisanship and Incivility and the Death of Public Trust.* Westport, Conn.: Praeger, 2008.

Alberta, Tim. "John Boehner Unchained," *Politico,* November/December 2017, www .politico.com/magazine/story/2017/10/29/john-boehner-trump-house-republican -party-retirement-profile-feature-215741.

Aldrich, John H. *Why Parties?: A Second Look.* Chicago: University of Chicago Press, 2011.
———. *Why Parties? The Origin and Transformation of Political Parties in America.* Chicago: University of Chicago Press, 1995.

Alexander, DeAlva Stanwood. *History and Procedure of the House of Representatives.* Boston: Riverside Press, 1916.

Allen, Felicity. *Jefferson Davis: Unconquerable Heart.* University of Missouri, 1999.

Allen, William C. *History of the United States Capitol: A Chronicle of Design, Construction, and Politics.* Washington, D.C.: GPO, 2001.

Allgor, Catherine. *Parlor Politics: In Which the Ladies of Washington Help Build a City and a Government.* Charlottesville: UVA Press, 2000.

Altschuler, Glenn C., and Stuart M. Blumin. *Rude Republic: Americans and Their Politics in the Nineteenth Century.* Princeton, N.J.: Princeton University Press, 2000.

Amer, Mildred L. "The Congressional Record: Content, History and Issues," January 14, 1993, CRS Report for Congress (93-60 GOV).

Ames, William E. *A History of the National Intelligencer.* Chapel Hill: UNC Press, 1972.

Anbinder, Tyler. *Nativism & Slavery: The Northern Know Nothings & the Politics of the 1850s.* New York: Oxford University Press, 1992.

Arenson, Adam. *The Great Heart of the Republic: St. Louis and the Cultural Civil War.* Cambridge, Mass.: Harvard University Press, 2011.

Arnold, Brie Anna Swenson. "'Competition for the Virgin Soil of Kansas': Gendered and Sexualized Discourse about the Kansas Crisis in Northern Popular Print and Political Culture, 1854–1860." Ph.D. dissertation: University of Minnesota, 2008.

Atkins, Jonathan M. *Parties, Politics, and the Sectional Conflict in Tennessee, 1832–1861.* Knoxville: University of Tennessee Press, 1997.

Ayers, Edward L. *The Thin Light of Freedom: The Civil War and Emancipation in the Heart of America.* New York: Norton, 2017.
———. *Vengeance & Justice: Crime and Punishment in the 19th-Century American South.* New York: Oxford University Press, 1984.
———. *What Caused the Civil War? Reflections on the South and Southern History.* New York: Norton, 2005.

Bacon, Donald C. "Violence in Congress," in *The Encyclopedia of the United States Congress,* ed. Donald C. Bacon, Roger H. Davidson, and Morton Keller. New York: Simon and Schuster, 1995, 2062–66.

Baker, Jean H. *Affairs of Party: The Political Culture of Northern Democrats in the Mid-Nineteenth Century.* Ithaca: Cornell University Press, 1983.
————. *Mary Todd Lincoln: A Biography.* New York: Norton, 2008.
Baldasty, Gerald J. *The Commercialization of News in the Nineteenth Century.* Madison: University of Wisconsin Press, 1992.
Balogh, Brian. *A Government Out of Sight: The Mystery of National Authority in Nineteenth-Century America.* New York: Cambridge University Press, 2009.
Barnes, Gilbert Hobbs. *The Antislavery Impulse, 1830–1844.* New York: Harbinger, 1933.
Baskerville, Barnet. "19th Century Burlesque of Oratory," *American Quarterly* 20 (Winter 1968): 726–43.
Bedini, Silvio A. "The Mace and the Gavel: Symbols of Government in America," *Transactions of the American Philosophical Society* 87, no. 4 (1997): 1–84.
Beeman, Richard R. "Unlimited Debate in the Senate: The First Phase," *Political Science Quarterly* 83, no. 3 (September 1968): 419–34.
Belko, W. Stephen. *The Invincible Duff Green: Whig of the West.* Columbia: University of Missouri Press, 2006.
Belohlavek, John M. *Broken Glass: Caleb Cushing and the Shattering of the Union.* Kent, Ohio: Kent State University, 2005.
Bemis, Samuel Flagg. *John Quincy Adams and the Union.* New York: Knopf, 1956.
Benedict, Michael Les. *A Compromise of Principle: Congressional Republicans and Reconstruction, 1863–1869.* New York: Norton, 1974.
Benson, T. Lloyd. *The Caning of Senator Sumner.* Greenville, S.C.: Furman University Press, 2004.
Berry, Stephen W., II. *All That Makes a Man: Love and Ambition in the Civil War South.* New York: Oxford University Press, 2003.
Binder, Sarah A. *Minority Rights, Majority Rule: Partisanship and the Development of Congress.* New York: Cambridge University Press, 1997.
Binder, Sarah A., and Steven S. Smith. "Political Goals and Procedural Choice in the Senate," *Journal of Politics* 60, no. 2 (May 1998): 396–416.
————. *Politics or Principle? Filibustering in the United States Senate.* Washington, D.C.: Brookings Institution Press, 1997.
Blau, Judith R., and Cheryl Elman. "The Institutionalization of U.S. Political Parties: Patronage Newspapers," *Sociological Inquiry* (Fall 2002): 576–99.
Blondheim, Menahem. *News over the Wires: The Telegraph and the Flow of Public Information, 1844–1897.* Cambridge, Mass.: Harvard University Press, 1994.
Bogue, Allan G. *The Congressman's Civil War.* New York: Cambridge University Press, 1989.
————. *The Earnest Men: Republicans of the Civil War Senate.* Ithaca: Cornell University Press, 1981.
Bogue, Allan G., Jerome M. Clubb, Carroll R. McKibbin, and Santa A. Traugott. "Members of the House of Representatives and the Process of Modernization, 1789–1960," *Journal of American History* 63 (September 1976): 275–302.
Bonner, Robert E. *Mastering America: Southern Slaveholders and the Crisis of American Nationhood.* New York: Cambridge University Press, 2009.
Bowman, Shearer Davis. *At the Precipice: Americans North and South During the Secession Crisis.* Chapel Hill: UNC Press, 2010.

Bradley, Cyrus P. *Biography of Isaac Hill.* Concord, N.H.: Published by John Brown, 1835.

Brant, Martha. "The Alaskan Assault," *Newsweek,* October 1, 1995, www.newsweek .com/alaskan-assault-184084.

Brewin, Mark W. *Celebrating Democracy: The Mass-Mediated Ritual of Election Day.* New York: Peter Lang, 2008.

Bright, Thomas R. "The Anti-Nebraska Coalition and the Emergence of the Republican Party in New Hampshire: 1853–1857," *Historical New Hampshire* 27 (Summer 1972): 57–88.

Brooke, John L. "Party, Nation, and Cultural Rupture: The Crisis of the American Civil War," in *Practicing Democracy: Popular Politics in the United States from the Constitution to the Civil War,* ed. Daniel Pearl and Adam I. P. Smith. Charlottesville: UVA Press, 2015.

———. "To Be 'Read by the Whole People': Press, Party, and Public Sphere in the United States, 1789–1840," *Proceedings of the American Antiquarian Society* 110, no. 11 (2002): 41–118.

Brooks, Corey M. *Liberty Power: Antislavery Third Parties and the Transformation of American Politics.* Chicago: University of Chicago Press, 2016.

———. "Stoking the 'Abolition Fire in the Capitol': Liberty Party Lobbying and Antislavery in Congress," *JER* (Fall 2013): 523–47.

Brown, David. "Attacking Slavery from Within: The Making of 'The Impending Crisis of the South,'" *Journal of Southern History* 70 (August 2004): 541–76.

———. *Southern Outcast: Hinton Rowan Helper and the Impending Crisis of the South.* Baton Rouge: LSU Press, 2006.

Brown, Letitia W. *Free Negroes in the District of Columbia, 1790–1846.* New York: Oxford University Press, 1972.

Brown, Norman D. *Edward Stanly: Whiggery's Tarheel "Conquerer."* Tuscaloosa: University of Alabama Press, 1974.

Brown, Thomas. "From Old Hickory to Sly Fox: The Routinization of Charisma in the Early Democratic Party," *JER* 3 (Autumn 1991): 339–69.

Bruce, Dickson. *Violence and Culture in the Antebellum South.* Austin: University of Texas Press, 1979.

Bryan, Wilhelmus B. *A History of the National Capital from Its Foundation Through the Period of the Adoption of the Organic Act,* 2 vols. New York: Macmillan, 1914.

Buell, Walter, ed. *Joshua R. Giddings: A Sketch.* Cleveland: William W. Williams, 1882.

Bulla, David W., and Gregory A. Borchard. *Journalism in the Civil War Era.* New York: Peter Lang Publishing, 2010.

Bullock, Steven C. *Revolutionary Brotherhood: Freemasonry and the Transformation of the American Social Order, 1730–1840.* Chapel Hill: UNC Press, 1996.

Burstein, Andrew. *The Passions of Andrew Jackson.* New York: Random House, 2007.

Byrd, Robert C. *The Senate: 1789–1989: Historical Statistics.* Washington, D.C.: GPO, 1993.

Byron, Matthew A. "Crime and Punishment: The Impotency of Dueling Laws in the United States." Ph.D. dissertation, University of Arkansas, 2008.

Campbell, James E. "Sumner—Brooks—Burlingame, or, The Last Great Challenge," *Ohio Archeological and Historical Quarterly* 34 (October 1925): 435–73.

Campbell, Mary R. "Tennessee's Congressional Delegation in the Sectional Crisis of 1859–1860," *Tennessee Historical Quarterly* 19 (December 1960): 348–71.

Carnes, Mark C. "Middle-Class Men and the Solace of Fraternal Ritual," in *Meanings for Manhood: Constructions of Masculinity in Victorian America*, ed. Marc C. Carnes and Clyde Griffen. Chicago: University of Chicago Press, 1990, 37–52.

———. *Secret Ritual and Manhood in Victorian America*. New Haven: Yale University Press, 1989.

Carson, Barbara G. *Ambitious Appetites: Dining, Behavior, and Patterns of Consumption in Federal Washington*. Washington: American Institute of Architects, 1990.

Chafetz, Josh. *Congress's Constitution: Legislative Authority and the Separation of Powers*. New Haven: Yale University Press, 2017.

Chamberlain, Ryan. *Pistols, Politics and the Press: Dueling in 19th-Century American Journalism*. Jefferson, N.C.: McFarland, 2009.

Chambers, William Nisbet. *Old Bullion Benton: Senator from the New West*. Boston: Little, Brown, 1956.

Channing, Steven A. *Crisis of Fear: Secession in South Carolina*. New York: W. W. Norton, 1974.

Chase, James S. *Emergence of the Presidential Nominating Convention, 1789–1832*. Urbana: University of Illinois Press, 1973.

Clephane, Walter C. "The Local Aspect of Slavery in the District of Columbia," March 6, 1899, in *Records of the Columbia Historical Society* 3 (1900).

Cole, Donald B. *Jacksonian Democracy in New Hampshire*. Cambridge, Mass.: Harvard University Press, 1970.

———. *Martin Van Buren and the American Political System*. Princeton, N.J.: Princeton University Press, 1984.

———. *Vindicating Andrew Jackson: The 1828 Election and the Rise of the Two-Party System*. Lawrence: University Press of Kansas, 2009.

Coleman, James P. "Two Irascible Antebellum Senators: George Poindexter and Henry S. Foote," *Journal of Mississippi History* 46 (February 1984): 17–27.

Cook, Robert J. *Civil War Senator: William Pitt Fessenden and the Fight to Save the American Republic*. Baton Rouge: LSU Press, 2013.

Cook, Timothy E. "Senators and Reporters Revisited," in *Esteemed Colleagues: Civility and Deliberation in the U.S. Senate*, ed. Burdick Loomis. Washington, D.C.: Brookings Institution, 2000, 169–72.

Cooper, Joseph. *Congress and Its Committees: A Historical Approach to the Role of Committees in the Legislative Process*. New York: Garland, 1988.

———. *The Origins of Standing Committees and the Development of the Modern House*. Houston, Tex.: Rice University Press, 1970.

Coulter, E. Merton. *The Confederate States of America, 1861–1865*, vol. 7 of *A History of the South*. Baton Rouge: LSU Press, 1950.

Crenshaw, Ollinger. *The Slave States in the Presidential Election of 1860*. Baltimore: Johns Hopkins, 1945.

———. "The Speakership Contest of 1859–1860: John Sherman's Election as a Cause of Disruption?" *Mississippi Valley Historical Review* 29 (December 1942): 323–38.

Cresson, Margaret French. *Journey into Fame: The Life of Daniel Chester French.* Cambridge, Mass.: Harvard University Press, 1947.

Crofts, Daniel W. *Reluctant Confederates: Upper South Unionists in the Secession Crisis.* Chapel Hill: UNC Press, 1989.

Crouthamel, James L. *James Watson Webb: A Biography.* Middletown, Conn.: Wesleyan, 1969.

Cunliffe, Marcus. *Soldiers and Civilians: The Martial Spirit in America, 1775–1865.* Boston: Little, Brown, 1968.

Curtis, James C. *Andrew Jackson and the Search for Vindication.* Boston: Little, Brown, 1976.

Curtis, Michael Ken. *Free Speech, "The People's Darling Privilege": Struggles for Freedom of Expression in American History.* Durham: Duke University Press, 2000.

David, James Corbett. "The Politics of Emasculation: The Caning of Charles Sumner and Elite Ideologies of Manhood in the Mid-Nineteenth Century United States," *Gender and History* 19 (August 2007): 324–45.

Davis, David Brion. *The Slave Power Conspiracy and the Paranoid Style.* Baton Rouge: LSU Press, 1969.

Deitreich, Kenneth A. "Honor, Patriarchy, and Disunion: Masculinity and the Coming of the American Civil War." Ph.D. dissertation, Western Virginia University, 2006.

Derthick, Martha, ed. *Dilemmas of Scale in America's Federal Democracy.* New York: Cambridge University Press, 1999.

Dicken-Garcia, Hazel. *Journalistic Standards in Nineteenth-Century America.* Madison: University of Wisconsin Press, 1989.

Dion, Douglas. *Turning the Legislative Thumbscrew: Minority Rights and Procedural Change in Legislative Politics.* East Lansing: University of Michigan, 1997.

Donald, David Herbert. *Charles Sumner.* New York: Da Capo Press, 1996.

———. *The Politics of Reconstruction.* Cambridge, Mass.: Harvard University Press, 1984.

Dubois, James T., and Gertrude S. Mathews. *Galusha A. Grow: Father of the Homestead Law.* New York: Houghton Mifflin, 1917.

Durham, Walter T. *Balie Peyton of Tennessee: Nineteenth-Century Politics and Thoroughbreds.* Franklin, Tenn.: Hillsboro Press, 2004.

Dzelzainis, Ella. "Dickins, Democracy, and Spit," in *The American Experiment and the Idea of Democracy in British Culture, 1776–1914,* ed. Ella Dzelzainis and Ruth Livesey. London: Routledge, 2013.

Earle, Jonathan H. *Jacksonian Antislavery and the Politics of Free Soil, 1824–1854.* Chapel Hill: UNC Press, 2004.

———. "Saturday Nights at the Baileys," in *In the Shadow of Freedom: The Politics of Slavery in the National Capital,* ed. Paul Finkelman and Donald Kennon. Athens: Ohio University Press, 2011.

Earman, Cynthia D. "Boardinghouses, Parties, and the Creation of a Political Society, Washington City, 1800–1830." M.A. thesis, LSU, 1992.

———. "A Census of Early Boardinghouses," *Washington History* 12 (2000): 118–12.

Eaton, Clement. "Henry A. Wise, a Liberal of the Old South," *Journal of Southern History* 7, no. 4 (November 1941): 482–94.

———. "Henry A. Wise and the Virginia Fire Eaters of 1856," *Mississippi Valley Historical Review* 21, no. 4 (March 1935): 495–512.

Ecelbarger, Gary L. *Frederick W. Lander: The Great Natural American Soldier.* Baton Rouge: LSU Press, 2000.

Edel, Charles N. *Nation Builder: John Quincy Adams and the Grand Strategy of the Republic.* Cambridge, Mass.: Harvard University Press, 2014.

Erickson, Stephen. "The Entrenching of Incumbency: Reflections in the U.S. House of Representatives, 1790–1994," *Cato Journal* 3 (Winter 1995): 397–420.

Erkkila, Betsy. *Whitman the Political Poet.* New York: Oxford University Press, 1989.

Essary, J. Frederick. *Covering Washington: Government Reflected to the Public in the Press, 1822–1926.* Boston: Houghton Mifflin, 1927.

Etcheson, Nicole. *Bleeding Kansas: Contested Liberty in the Civil War Era.* Lawrence: University Press of Kansas, 2004.

Fehrenbacher, Don E. *The Slaveholding Republic: An Account of the United States Government's Relations to Slavery.* New York: Oxford University Press, 2001.

Fellman, Michael. "Rehearsal for the Civil War: Antislavery and Proslavery at the Fighting Point in Kansas," in *Antislavery Reconsidered: New Perspectives on the Abolitionists*, ed. Lewis Perry and Fellman. Baton Rouge: LSU Press, 1979.

Fenno, Richard F. *Home Style: House Members in Their Districts.* Boston: Little, Brown, 1978.

———. "If, as Ralph Nader Says, Congress Is the 'Broken Branch,' How Come We Love Our Congressmen So Much?" in *Congress in Change: Evolution and Reform*, ed. Norman J. Ornstein. New York: Praeger, 1975.

Finkelman, Paul, and Donald R. Kennon, eds. *Congress and the Crisis of the 1850s.* Athens: Ohio University, 2012.

———. *In the Shadow of Freedom: The Politics of Slavery in the National Capital.* Athens: Ohio University Press, 2011.

Fiorina, Morris P., David W. Rohde, and Peter Wissel. "Historical Change in House Turnover," in *Congress in Change: Evolution and Reform*, ed. Norman J. Ornstein. New York: Praeger, 1975, 24–46.

Foner, Eric. *Free Soil, Free Labor, Free Men: The Ideology of the Republican Party Before the Civil War.* New York: Oxford University Press, 1995.

Foote, Lorien. *The Gentlemen and the Roughs: Manhood, Honor, and Violence in the Union Army.* New York: NYU Press, 2010.

Ford, Lacy K. *Deliver Us from Evil: The Slavery Question in the Old South.* New York: Oxford University Press, 2009.

Formisano, Ronald P. *For the People: American Populist Movements from the Revolution to the 1850s.* Chapel Hill: UNC Press, 2008.

———. "Political Character, Antipartyism and the Second Party System," *American Quarterly* 21 (Winter 1969): 683–709.

———. *The Transformation of Political Culture: Massachusetts Parties, 1790s–1840s.* New York: Oxford University Press, 1983.

Franklin, John Hope. *The Militant South, 1800–1861.* Cambridge, Mass.: Harvard University Press, 1956.

———. *A Southern Odyssey: Travelers in the Antebellum North.* Baton Rouge: LSU Press, 1976; 1991 printing.

Frederick, David C. "John Quincy Adams, Slavery, and the Disappearance of the Right of Petition," *Law and History Review* 9, no. 1 (Spring 1991): 115–55.

Freehling, William W. *The Road to Disunion*, 2 vols. New York: Oxford University Press, 2007.

———. *The South Against the South: How Anti-Confederate Southerners Shaped the Course of the Civil War.* New York: Oxford University Press, 2001.

Freeman, Joanne B. *Affairs of Honor: National Politics in the New Republic.* New Haven: Yale University Press, 2001.

———. "The Election of 1800: A Study in the Process of Political Change," *Yale Law Journal* 108 (June 1999): 1959–94.

Fryd, Vivien Green. *Art and Empire: The Politics of Ethnicity in the United States Capitol, 1815–1860.* Columbus: Ohio University Press, 2001.

———. "Representating the Constitution in the US Capitol Building: Justice, Freedom, and Slavery," in *Constitutional Cultures: On the Concept and Representation of Constitutions in the Atlantic World*, ed. Silke Hensel, Ulrike Bock, Katrin Dircksen, and Hans-Ulrich Thamer. New York: Cambridge University Press, 2012, 227–50.

Gallagher, Gary W. *The Union War.* New York: Cambridge University Press, 2011.

Galloway, George B. *History of the House of Representatives.* New York: Thomas Y. Crowell Company, 1961.

Gambill, Edward. "Vanity Fair: 1859–1863," in *The Conservative Press in Eighteenth and Nineteenth Century America*, ed. Ronald Lora and William Henry Longton. Westport, Conn.: Greenwood Press, 1999, 139–45.

———. "Who Were the Senate Radicals?," *Civil War History* (September 1965): 237–44.

Gamm, Gerald, and Kenneth Shepsle. "Emergence of Legislative Institutions: Standing Committees in the House and Senate, 1810–1825," *Legislative Studies Quarterly* 14, no. 1 (February 1989): 39–66.

Gara, Larry. "Antislavery Congressmen, 1848–1856: Their Contribution to the Debate Between the Sections," *Civil War History* (September 1986): 197–207.

———. *The Presidency of Franklin Pierce.* Lawrence: University Press of Kansas, 1991.

———. "Slavery and the Slave Power: A Crucial Distinction," *Civil War History* 15 (March 1969): 5–18.

Gauker, Ralph H. *History of the Scottish Rite Bodies in the District of Columbia.* Washington, D.C.: Mithras Lodge of Perfection, 1970.

Gienapp, William E. "The Crime Against Sumner: The Caning of Charles Sumner and the Rise of the Republican Party," *Civil War History* 3 (September 1979): 218–45.

———. *The Origins of the Republican Party, 1852–1856.* New York: Oxford University Press, 1987.

———. "'Politics Seem to Enter into Everything': Political Culture in the North, 1840–1860," in *Essays on American Antebellum Politics, 1840–1860*, ed. Stephen E. Maizlish and John J. Kushma. College Station: University of Texas at Arlington, 1982, 15–69.

Gilje, Paul A., *Rioting in America.* Bloomington: Indiana University Press, 1996.

Gillette, Howard, Jr., ed. *Southern City, National Ambition: The Growth of Early Washington, D.C., 1800–1860.* Washington, D.C.: George Washington University Center for Washington Area Studies, 1995.

Gillette, William. *Retreat from Reconstruction, 1869–1879*. Baton Rouge: LSU Press, 1982.

Ginn, Roger. *New England Must Not Be Trampled On: The Tragic Death of Jonathan Cilley*. Camden, Maine: DownEast Books, 2016.

Glassman, Matthew Eric, Erin Hemlin, and Amber Hope Wilhelm. CRS Report R41545, "Congressional Careers: Service Tenure and Patterns of Member Service, 1789–2011," Congressional Research Service, January 7, 2011.

Glover, Lorri. "'Let Us Manufacture Men': Educating Elite Boys in the Early National South," in *Southern Manhood: Perspectives on Masculinity in the Old South*, ed. Lorri Glover and Craig Thompson Friend. Athens: University of Georgia Press, 2004.

Goldfield, David R. "Antebellum Washington in Context: The Pursuit of Prosperity and Identity," in *Southern City, National Ambition: The Growth of Early Washington, D.C., 1800–1860*, ed. Howard Gillette, Jr. Washington, D.C.: George Washington University Center for Washington Area Studies.

Goldman, Ralph M. *The National Party Chairmen and Committees: Factionalism at the Top*. Armonk, N.Y.: M. E. Sharpe, 1990.

Gonzalez, Darryl. *The Children Who Ran for Congress: A History of Congressional Pages*. Santa Barbara, Calif.: Praeger, 2010.

Gonzales, John E. "Henry Stuart Foote: A Forgotten Unionist of the Fifties," *Southern Quarterly* 1 (January 1963): 129–39.

———. "Henry Stuart Foote in Exile—1865," *Journal of Mississippi History* 5 (April 1953): 90–98.

———. "The Public Career of Henry Stuart Foote, 1804–1880." Ph.D. dissertation, UNC, 1957.

Gorn, Elliott J. *The Manly Art: Bare-Knuckle Prize Fighting in America*. Ithaca: Cornell University Press, 1986.

Gradin, Harlan Joel. "Losing Control: The Caning of Charles Sumner and the Breakdown of Antebellum Political Culture." Ph.D. dissertation, UNC, 1991.

Grant, David. *Political Antislavery Discourse and American Literature of the 1850s*. Newark: University of Delaware, 2012.

Grant, Susan-Mary. *North over South: Northern Nationalism and American Identity in the Antebellum Era*. Lawrence: University Press of Kansas, 2000.

Green, Constance McLaughlin. *The Secret City: A History of Race Relations in the Nation's Capital*. Princeton, N.J.: Princeton University Press, 1967.

———. *Washington: Village and Capital, 1800–1878*, 2 vols. Princeton, N.J.: Princeton University Press, 1962.

Greenberg, Amy. "Manifest Destiny's Hangover: Congress Confronts Territorial Expansion and Martial Masculinity in the 1850s," in *Congress and the Crisis of the 1850s*, ed. Paul Finkelman and Donald R. Kennon. Athens: Ohio University, 2012.

———. *Manifest Manhood and the Antebellum American Empire*. New York: Cambridge University Press, 2005.

Greenberg, Kenneth S. *Honor and Slavery: Lies, Duels, Noses, Masks, Dressing as a Woman, Gifts, Strangers, Humanitarianism, Death, Slave Rebellions, the Proslavery Argument, Baseball, Hunting, and Gambling in the Old South*. Princeton, N.J.: Princeton University Press, 1996.

———. *Masters and Statesmen: The Political Culture of American Slavery*. Baltimore: Johns Hopkins, 1985.

Grimsted, David. *American Mobbing, 1828–1861: Toward the Civil War.* New York: Oxford University Press, 1998.

Groosberg, Michael, and Christopher Tomlins, eds. *The Cambridge History of Law in America: The Long Nineteenth Century, 1789–1920.* New York: Cambridge University Press, 2008.

Gugliotta, Guy. *Freedom's Cap: The United States Capitol and the Coming of the Civil War.* New York: Hill and Wang, 2013.

Gustafson, Melanie Susan. *Women and the Republican Party, 1854–1924.* Chicago: University of Illinois Press, 2001.

Hackney, Sheldon. "Southern Violence," *American Historical Review* 74 (1969): 906–25.

Halleran, Michael A. *The Better Angels of Our Nature: Freemasonry in the American Civil War.* Tuscaloosa: University of Alabama Press, 2010.

Hamilton, Holman. *Prologue to Conflict: The Crisis and Compromise of 1850.* Lawrence: University of Kansas Press, 1964.

Hamlin, Charles E., ed. *The Life and Times of Hannibal Hamlin.* Cambridge, Mass.: Riverside Press, 1899.

Harrington, Fred Harvey. "The First Northern Victory," *Journal of Southern History* 5 (1939): 186–205.

Harris, Wilmer C. *The Public Life of Zachariah Chandler, 1851–1875.* Michigan Historical Publications, 1917.

Harrison, Robert. *Washington During the Civil War and Reconstruction: Race and Radicalism.* Cambridge, Mass.: Cambridge University Press, 2011.

Harrold, Stanley. *American Abolitionists.* London and New York: Routledge, 2001.

———. *Border War: Fighting over Slavery Before the Civil War.* Chapel Hill: UNC Press, 2010.

———. *Subversives: Antislavery Community in Washington, D.C., 1828–1865.* Baton Rouge: LSU Press, 2003.

Hartnett, Stephen John. *Democratic Dissent and the Cultural Fictions of Antebellum America.* Chicago: University of Illinois Press, 2002.

———. "Franklin Pierce and the Exuberant Hauteur of an Age of Extremes: A Love Song for America in Six Movements," in *Before the Rhetorical Presidency,* ed. Martin J. Medhurst. Texas A&M University Press, 2008.

Hasseltine, William. "The Pryor-Potter Duel," *Wisconsin Magazine of History* (June 1944): 400–409.

Hay, Melba Porter. "Henry Clay and the Graves-Cilley Duel," in *A Mythic Land Apart: Reassessing Southerners and Their History,* ed. John David Smith, Thomas H. Appleton, and Charles Pierce Roland. Westport, Conn.: Greenwood Press, 1997.

Herman, Bernard L. "Southern City, National Ambition: Washington's Early Town Houses," in *Southern City, National Ambition: The Growth of Early Washington, D.C., 1800–1860,* ed. Howard Gillette, Jr. Washington, D.C.: George Washington University Center for Washington Area Studies, 1995.

Hernon, Joseph M. *Profiles in Character: Hubris and Heroism in the U.S. Senate, 1789–1990.* New York: M. E. Sharpe, 1997.

Hoffer, Williamjames Hull. *The Caning of Charles Sumner: Honor, Idealism, and the Origins of the Civil War.* Baltimore: Johns Hopkins, 2010.

Hollandsworth, James G., Jr. *Pretense of Glory: The Life of General Nathaniel P. Banks.* Baton Rouge: LSU Press, 1998.

Holmes, Stephen. "Gag Rules, or the Politics of Omission," in *Constitutionalism and Democracy*, ed. Jon Elster and Rune Slagstad. New York: Cambridge University Press, 1988.

Holt, Michael F. *The Fate of Their Country: Politicians, Slavery Extension, and the Coming of the Civil War.* New York: Hill and Wang, 2004.

———. *Franklin Pierce.* New York: Henry Holt, 2010.

———. *The Political Crisis of the 1850s.* New York: Norton, 1978.

———. *Political Parties and American Political Development: From the Age of Jackson to the Age of Lincoln.* Baton Rouge: LSU Press, 1992.

———. *The Rise and Fall of the American Whig Party: Jacksonian Politics and the Onset of the Civil War.* New York: Oxford University Press, 1999.

Holzer, Harold. *Lincoln President-Elect: Abraham Lincoln and the Great Secession Winter, 1860–1861.* New York: Simon and Schuster, 2008.

Howe, Daniel Walker. *The Political Culture of the American Whigs.* Chicago: University of Chicago Press, 1979.

———. *What Hath God Wrought: The Transformation of America, 1815–1848.* New York: Oxford University Press, 2007.

Hudson, Frederic. *Journalism in the United States from 1690 to 1872.* New York: Harper & Brothers, 1873.

Hunt, Gaillard. *Israel, Elihu, and Cadwallader Washburn: A Chapter in American Biography.* New York: Macmillan, 1925.

Huston, James L. *The British Gentry, the Southern Planter, and the Northern Family Farmer: Agriculture and Sectional Antagonism in North America.* Baton Rouge: LSU Press, 2015.

———. "The Experiential Basis of the Northern Antislavery Impulse," *Journal of Southern History* 4 (November 1990): 609–40.

Ilisevich, Robert D. *Galusha A. Grow: The People's Candidate.* Pittsburgh: University of Pittsburgh, 1989.

Jackson, George S. *Early Songs of Uncle Sam.* Boston: Bruce Humphries, Publishers, 1962.

Jacob, Kathryn Allamong. *King of the Lobby: The Life and Times of Sam Ward, Man-About-Washington in the Gilded Age.* Baltimore: Johns Hopkins, 2010.

Jenkins, Jeffrey A., and Charles Stewart III. *Fighting for the Speakership: The House and the Rise of Party Government.* Princeton, N.J.: Princeton University Press, 2013.

———. "The Gag Rule, Congressional Politics, and the Growth of Anti-Slavery Popular Politics," paper presented at "Congress and History" conference, MIT, May 30–31, 2003.

Johannsen, Robert W. *To the Halls of the Montezumas: The Mexican War in the American Imagination.* New York: Oxford University Press, 1985.

John, Richard R. *Network Nation: Inventing American Telecommunications.* Cambridge, Mass.: Harvard University Press, 2010.

———. "Recasting the Information Infrastructure for the Industrial Age," in *A Nation Transformed by Information: How Information Has Shaped the United States from Colonial Times to the Present*, ed. Alfred D. Chandler, Jr., and James W. Cortada. New York: Oxford University Press, 2000.

————. *Spreading the News: The American Postal System from Franklin to Morse.* Cambridge, Mass.: Harvard University Press, 1995.

Kaestle, Carl F. *Pillars of the Republic: Common Schools and American Society, 1780–1860.* New York: Hill and Wang, 1983.

Karp, Matthew. *This Vast Southern Empire: Slaveholders at the Helm of American Foreign Policy.* Cambridge, Mass.: Harvard University Press, 2016.

Kennon, Donald R. *American Pantheon: Sculptural and Artistic Decoration of the United States Capitol.* Athens: Ohio University, 2004.

————, ed. *A Republic for the Ages: The United States Capitol and the Political Culture of the Early Republic.* Charlottesville: UVA Press, 1999.

————. *The United States Capitol: Designing and Decorating a National Icon.* Athens: Ohio University, 2000.

Kernell, Samuel. "Toward Understanding 19th-Century Congressional Careers: Ambition, Competition, and Rotation," *American Journal of Political Science* 21 (November 1977): 669–93.

Kernell, Samuel, and Gray C. Jacobson. "Congress and the Presidency as News in the Nineteenth Century," *Journal of Politics* 49 (November 1987): 1016–35.

Kersch, Kenneth Ira. *Freedom of Speech: Rights and Liberties Under the Law.* Santa Barbara, Calif.: ABC-CLIO, 2003.

Kersh, Rogan. *Dreams of a More Perfect Union.* Ithaca: Cornell University Press, 2001.

Kielbowicz, Richard B. "News Gathering by Mail in the Age of the Telegraph: Adapting to a New Technology," *Technology and Culture* 28 (January 1987): 26–41.

————. *News in the Mail: The Press, Post Office, and Public Information, 1700–1860s.* Westport, Conn.: Greenwood Press, 1989.

Kirby, Bruce R. "The Limits of Honor: Party, Section, and Dueling in the Jacksonian Congress." M.A. thesis, George Mason University, 1997.

Kirkpatrick, Jennet. *Uncivil Disobedience: Studies in Violence and Democratic Politics.* Princeton: Princeton University Press, 2008.

Klammer, Martin. *Whitman, Slavery, and the Emergence of Leaves of Grass.* University Park: Pennsylvania State University, 1995.

Klapthor, Margaret B. "Furniture in the Capitol: Desks and Chairs Used in the Chamber of the House of Representatives, 1819–1857," *Records of the Columbia Historical Society, Washington, D.C.,* 69–70 (1969–1970): 192–98.

Klinghard, Daniel. *The Nationalization of American Political Parties, 1880–1896.* New York: Cambridge University Press, 2010.

Koivusalo, Anna. "'He Ordered the First Gun Fired & He Resigned First': James Chesnut, Southern Honor, and Emotion," in *The Field of Honor: Essays on Southern Character and American Identity,* ed. John Mayfield and Todd Hagstette, 196–212. Columbia: University of South Carolina, 2017.

Koschnik, Albrecht. *"Let a Common Interest Bind Us Together": Associations, Partisanship, and Culture in Philadelphia, 1775–1840.* Charlottesville: UVA Press, 2007.

Krotoszynsi, Ronald J. *Reclaiming the Petition Clause: Seditious Libel, "Offensive" Protest, and the Right to Petition the Government for a Redress of Grievances.* New Haven: Yale University Press, 2012.

Landis, Michael T. *Northern Men with Southern Loyalties: The Democratic Party and the Sectional Crisis.* Ithaca: Cornell University Press, 2014.

Lee, Dan. *Kentuckian in Blue: A Biography of Major General Lovell Harrison Rousseau.* McFarland, 2010.

Leonard, Gerald. *The Invention of Party Politics: Federalism, Popular Sovereignty, and Constitutional Development in Jacksonian Illinois.* Chapel Hill: UNC Press, 2002.

Leonard, Thomas C. *The Power of the Press: The Birth of American Political Reporting.* NY: Oxford, 1986.

Levine, Robert S. "'The Honor of New England': Nathaniel Hawthorne and the Cilley-Graves Duel of 1838," in *The Field of Honor: Essays on Southern Character and American Identity,* ed. John Mayfield and Todd Hagstette. Columbia: University of South Carolina Press, 2017.

Link, William A. *Roots of Secession: Slavery and Politics in Antebellum Virginia.* Chapel Hill: UNC Press, 2003.

Litwack, Leon. *North of Slavery: The Negro in the Free States, 1790–1860.* Chicago: University of Chicago Press, 1961.

Loomis, Burdett A., ed. *Esteemed Colleagues: Civility and Deliberation in the U.S. Senate.* Washington, D.C.: Brookings Institution, 2000.

Ludlum, Robert. "The Antislavery 'Gag-rule': History and Argument," *Journal of Negro History* 26 (1941): 203–43.

Lynn, Joshua A. "Half-Baked Men: Doughface Masculinity and the Antebellum Politics of Household." M.A. thesis, UNC, Chapel Hill, 2010.

Maizlish, Stephen E. "The Meaning of Nativism and the Crisis of the Union: The Know-Nothing Movement in the Antebellum North," in *Essays on American Antebellum Politics, 1840–1860,* ed. Stephen E. Maizlish and John J. Kushma. College Station: Texas A&M University Press, 1982.

Malavasic, Alice E. *The F Street Mess: How Southern Senators Rewrote the Kansas-Nebraska Act.* Chapel Hill: UNC Press, 2017.

Malin, James C. *The Nebraska Question, 1852–54.* Michigan: Edwards Brothers, 1953.

Maltzman, Forrest, Lee Sigelman, and Sarah Binder, "Leaving Office Feet First: Death in Congress," *Political Science and Politics* 29 (December 1996): 665–71.

Marbut, F. B. *News from the Capital: The Story of Washington Reporting.* Carbondale: Southern Illinois University, 1971.

Marion, Nancy E., and Willard M. Oliver. *Killing Congress: Assassinations, Attempted Assassinations, and Other Violence Against Members of Congress.* London: Lexington Books, 2014.

Maskell, Jack. "Expulsion, Censure, Reprimand, and Fine: Legislative Discipline in the House of Representatives," CRS Report No. RL31382 (Washington, D.C.: Congressional Research Service, June 27, 2016).

Mason, Sir John Edwin. "Sir Benjamin Brown French," *Proceedings of the Grand Encampment 18th Triennial Session.* Davenport, Iowa: Griggs, Watson & Day, 1871.

Mason, Matthew. *Apostle of Union: A Political Biography of Edward Everett.* Chapel Hill: UNC Press, 2016.

Mayo, Edward L. "Republicanism, Antipartyism, and Jacksonian Party Politics: A View from the Nation's Capital," *American Quarterly* 31 (Spring 1979): 3–20.

McCandless, Perry. "The Political Philosophy and Political Personality of Thomas H. Benton," *Missouri Historical Review* 2 (January 1956): 145–58.

McClure, Clarence. *Opposition in Missouri to Thomas Hart Benton.* Warrensburg: Central Missouri State Teachers College, 1926.

McCormick, Gregg M. "Personal Conflict, Sectional Reaction: The Role of Free Speech in the Caning of Charles Sumner," *Texas Law Review* 85 (May 2007): 1519–52.

McCormick, Richard P. *The Second American Party System: Party Formation in the Jacksonian Era.* New York: Norton, 1966.

McCurry, Stephanie. *Confederate Reckoning: Power and Politics in the Civil War South.* Cambridge, Mass.: Harvard University Press, 2010.

McFaul, John M., and Frank Otto Gatell. "The Outcast Insider: Reuben M. Whitney and the Bank War," *Pennsylvania Magazine of History and Biography* (April 1967): 115–44.

McGerr, Michael E. *The Decline of Popular Politics: The American North, 1865–1928.* New York: Oxford University Press, 1988.

McGiffen, Steven P. "Ideology and the Failure of the Whig Party in New Hampshire, 1834–1841," *New England Quarterly* 59 (September 1986): 387–401.

McKenzie, Ralph M. *Washington Correspondents Past and Present: Brief Sketches of the Rank and File.* New York: Newspaperdom, 1903.

McKivigan, John R., and Stanley Harrold, eds. *Antislavery Violence: Sectional, Racial, and Cultural Conflict in Antebellum America.* Knoxville: University of Tennessee, 1999.

McPherson, Elizabeth G. "Major Publications of Gales and Seaton," *Quarterly Journal of Speech* 31 (December 1945): 430–39.

———. "Reporting the Debates of Congress," *Quarterly Journal of Speech* 28 (April 1942): 141–48.

McPherson, James. "The Fight Against the Gag Rule: Joshua Levitt and Antislavery Insurgency in the Whig Party, 1839–1842," *Journal of Negro History* 48 (1963): 177–95.

Mearns, David C. "A View of Washington in 1863," *Records of the Columbia Historical Society, Washington, D.C.,* 63–65 (1963–1965): 210–20.

Meigs, William Montgomery. *The Life of Thomas Hart Benton.* Philadelphia: J. B. Lippincott Co., 1904.

Meinke, Scott "Slavery, Partisanship, and Procedure: The Gag Rule, 1836–1845," *Legislative Studies Quarterly* 1 (February 2007): 33–58.

Melish, Joanne P. *Disowning Slavery: Gradual Emancipation and Race in New England, 1780–1860.* Ithaca: Cornell University Press, 1998.

Merchant, Holt. *South Carolina Fire-Eater: The Life of Laurence Massillion Keitt, 1824–1864.* Columbia: University of South Carolina Press, 2014.

Mercieca, Jennifer Rose. "The Culture of Honor: How Slaveholders Responded to the Abolitionist Mail Crisis of 1835," *Rhetoric & Public Affairs* 10, no. 1 (2007): 51–76.

Merkel, Benjamin C. "The Slavery Issue and the Political Decline of Thomas Hart Benton, 1846–1856," *Missouri Historical Review* 38 (July 1944): 3–88.

Miller, William Lee. *Arguing About Slavery: The Great Battle in the United States Congress.* New York: Knopf, 1996.

Miner, Craig. *Seeding Civil War: Kansas in the National News, 1854–1858.* Lawrence: University Press of Kansas, 2008.

Monroe, Dan. *The Republican Vision of John Tyler.* College Station: Texas A&M University Press, 2003.

Moore, Powell. "James K. Polk: Tennessee Politician," *Journal of Southern History* 17 (November 1951): 493–516.

Morrison, Michael A. *Slavery and the American West: The Eclipse of Manifest Destiny and the Coming of the Civil War.* Chapel Hill: UNC Press, 1997.

Morton, John D. "'A High Wall and a Deep Ditch': Thomas Hart Benton and the Compromise of 1850," *Missouri Historical Review* 94 (October 1999): 1–24.

Mott, Frank Luther. "Facetious News Writing, 1833–1883," *Mississippi Valley Historical Review* 29 (June 1942): 35–54.

———. *A History of American Magazines, 1850–1865.* Cambridge, Mass.: Harvard University Press, 1938.

Muelder, Owen W. *Theodore Dwight Weld and the American Anti-Slavery Society.* Jefferson, N.C.: McFarland & Co., 2011.

Myers, John L. *Henry Wilson and the Coming of the Civil War.* Lanham, Md.: University Press of America, 2005.

Nash, Gary B. "The Philadelphia Bench and Bar, 1800–1861," *Comparative Studies in Society and History* 7, no. 2 (January 1965): 203–20.

Neely, Jeremy. *The Border Between Them: Violence and Reconciliation on the Kansas-Missouri Line.* Columbia: University of Missouri Press, 2007.

Neely, Mark E., Jr. "The Kansas-Nebraska Act in American Political Culture: The Road to Bladensburg and the *Appeal of the Independent Democrats,*" in *The Nebraska-Kansas Act of 1854,* ed. John R. Wunder and Joann M. Ross. Lincoln: University of Nebraska Press, 2008.

———. *The Boundaries of Political Culture in the Civil War Era.* Chapel Hill: UNC Press, 2005.

Nerone, John. *Violence Against the Press: Policing the Public Sphere.* New York: Oxford University Press, 1994.

Nichols, Roy Franklin. *Franklin Pierce: Young Hickory of the Granite Hills.* Philadelphia: University of Pennsylvania Press, 1931.

———. *The Disruption of American Democracy.* New York: Collier Books Edition, 1962; orig. pub. 1948.

———. "The Kansas-Nebraska Act: A Century of Historiography," *Mississippi Valley Historical Review* 43 (September 1956): 187–212.

Nisbett, Richard E., and Dov Cohen. *Culture of Honor: The Psychology of Violence in the South.* Boulder, Colo.: Westview Press, 1996.

Nussbaum, Martha C. *Anger and Forgiveness: Resentment, Generosity, Justice.* New York: Oxford University Press, 2016.

———. *Political Emotions: Why Love Matters for Justice.* Cambridge, Mass.: Harvard University Press, 2013.

Nye, Russell B. *Fettered Freedom: Civil Liberties and the Slavery Controversy, 1830–1860.* East Lansing: Michigan State University Press, 1963.

Oakes, James. *Freedom National: The Destruction of Slavery in the United States, 1861–1865.* New York: Norton, 2014.

———. *The Scorpion's Sting: Antislavery and the Coming of the Civil War.* New York: Norton, 2015.

Oertel, Kristen T. *Bleeding Borders: Race, Gender, and Violence in Pre–Civil War Kansas.* Baton Rouge: LSU Press, 2009.

Olsen, Christopher J. *Political Culture and Secession in Mississippi: Masculinity, Honor, and the Antiparty Tradition, 1830–1860*. New York: Oxford University Press, 2000.

Ornstein, Norman, and Thomas E. Mann. *The Broken Branch: How Congress Is Failing America and How to Get It Back on Track*. New York: Oxford University Press, 2008.

Parkerson, Donald H., and Jo Ann Parkerson. *The Emergence of the Common School in the U.S. Countryside*. Lewiston, N.Y.: Edwin Mellen Press, 1998.

Parsons, Lynn Hudson. *The Birth of Modern Politics: Andrew Jackson, John Quincy Adams, and the Election of 1828*. New York: Oxford University Press, 2009.

Pasley, Jeffrey. "Minnows, Spies, and Aristocrats: The Social Crisis in Congress in the Age of Martin Van Buren," *JER* 27 (Winter 2007): 599–653.

———. "Printers, Editors, and Publishers of Political Journals Elected to the U.S. Congress, 1789–1861," pasleybrothers.com/newspols/congress.htm.

Payne, Charles E. *Josiah Bushnell Grinnell*. Iowa City: State Historical Society of Iowa, 1938.

Peterson, R. Eric, Jennifer E. Manning, and Erin Hemlin, "Violence Against Members of Congress and Their Staff: Selected Examples and Congressional Responses," CRS Report, 7-5700, R41609 (Washington, D.C.: Congressional Research Service, January 25, 2011).

Pfau, Michael William. *The Political Style of Conspiracy: Chase, Sumner, and Lincoln*. East Lansing: Michigan State University Press, 2005.

Pflugrad-Jackisch, Ann. *Brothers of a Vow: Secret Fraternal Orders and the Transformation of White Male Culture in Antebellum Virginia*. Athens: University of Georgia, 2010.

Pierce, Katherine A. "Murder and Mayhem: Violence, Press Coverage, and the Mobilization of the Republican Party in 1856," in *Words at War: The Civil War and American Journalism*, ed. David B. Sachsman, S. Kittrell Rushing, and Roy Morris, Jr. West Lafayette, Ind.: Purdue University Press, 2008, 85–100.

———. "Networks of Disunion: Politics, Print Culture, and the Coming of the Civil War." Ph.D. dissertation, University of Virginia, 2006.

Pierson, Arthur Tappan. *Zachariah Chandler: An Outline Sketch of His Life and Public Services*. Detroit: Post and Tribune, 1880.

Pierson, Michael D. "'All Southern Society Is Assailed by the Foulest Charges'": Charles Sumner's 'The Crime Against Kansas' and the Escalation of Republican Anti-Slavery Rhetoric," *New England Quarterly* 68, no. 4 (December 1995): 531–57.

Pitkin, Hanna F. *The Concept of Representation*. Berkeley, University of California Press, 1972.

Polsby, Nelson W. "The Institutionalization of the U.S. House of Representatives," *American Political Science Review* 62 (March 1968): 144–68.

Potter, David M. *The Impending Crisis: 1848–1861*. New York: Harper, 1976.

———. *Lincoln and His Party in the Secession Crisis*. New Haven: Yale University Press, 1967.

Price, H. Douglas. "Careers and Committees in the American Congress: The Problem of Structural Change," in *The History of Parliamentary Behavior*, ed.

William O. Ayedelotte Princeton, N.J.: Princeton Legacy Library, 2015; orig. pub. 1977, 3–27.

———. "Congress and the Evolution of Legislative 'Professionalism,'" in *Congress in Change* New York: Praeger, 1975, 14–27.

Proctor, John C. *Washington Past and Present: A History*, 5 vols. New York: Lewis Historical Publishing Co., 1930.

Quigley, Paul D. H. "Patchwork Nation: Sources of Confederate Nationalism, 1848–1865." Ph.D. dissertation, UNC, 2006.

Rable, George C. *But There Was No Peace: The Role of Violence in the Politics of Reconstruction.* Athens: University of Georgia Press, 2007; orig. ed. 1984.

———. *Damn Yankees!: Demonization and Defiance in the Confederate South.* Baton Rouge: LSU Press, 2015.

———. "Slavery, Politics, and the South: The Gag Rule as a Case Study," *Capitol Studies* 3 (1975): 69–87.

Radomsky, Susan. "The Social Life of Politics: Washington's Official Society and the Emergence of a National Political Elite, 1800–1876," 2 vols. Ph.D. dissertation, University of Chicago, 2005.

Ratner, Lorman A., and Dwight L. Teeter, Jr. *Fanatics and Fire-Eaters: Newspapers and the Coming of the Civil War.* Urbana: University of Illinois Press, 2003.

Reddy, William M. *The Navigation of Feeling: A Framework for the History of Emotions.* New York: Cambridge University Press, 2001.

Reed, Henry Hope. *The United States Capitol: Its Architecture and Decoration.* New York: Norton, 2005.

Reed, John S. "Below the Smith and Wesson Line: Southern Violence," in *One South: An Ethnic Approach to Regional Culture.* Baton Rouge: LSU Press, 1982, 139–53.

Remini, Robert V. *Andrew Jackson: The Course of American Empire, 1767–1821.* Baltimore: Johns Hopkins, 1998.

———. *The Election of Andrew Jackson.* New York: J. B. Lippincott, 1963.

———. *Martin Van Buren and the Making of the Democratic Party.* New York: Columbia University Press, 1959.

———. *Henry Clay: Statesman for the Union.* New York: Norton, 1991.

Richards, Leonard L. *"Gentlemen of Property and Standing": Anti-Abolition Mobs in Jacksonian America.* New York: Oxford University Press, 1970.

———. *The Life and Times of Congressman John Quincy Adams.* New York: Oxford University Press, 1986.

———. *The Slave Power: The Free North and Southern Domination, 1780–1860.* Baton Rouge: LSU Press, 2000.

Richardson, Heather Cox. *To Make Men Free: A History of the Republican Party.* New York: Basic Books, 2014.

Riddle, Albert Gallatin. *Life of Benjamin Franklin Wade.* Cleveland: Williams Publishing Co., 1888.

Riley, Ben A. "The Pryor-Potter Affair: Nineteenth Century Civilian Conflict as Precursor to Civil War," *Journal of West Virginia Historical Association* (1984): 30–39.

Risley, Ford. *Abolition and the Press: The Moral Struggle Against Slavery.* Evanston, Ill.: Northwestern University Press, 2008.

Ritchie, Donald. *American Journalists: Getting the Story.* New York: Oxford University Press, 1997.

———. *Press Gallery: Congress and the Washington Correspondents.* Cambridge, Mass.: Harvard University Press, 1991.

Roberts, Allen E. *House Undivided: The Story of Freemasonry and the Civil War.* Richmond: Macoy Publishing and Masonic Supply, 1990.

Roberts-Miller, Patricia. "Agonism, Wrangling, and John Quincy Adams," *Rhetoric Review* 25, no. 2 (2006): 141–61.

———. *Fanatical Schemes: Proslavery Rhetoric and the Tragedy of Consensus.* Tuscaloosa: University of Alabama Press, 2009.

Robinson, Elwyn Burns. "The 'Pennsylvanian': Organ of the Democracy," *Pennsylvania Magazine of History and Biography* 3 (1938): 350–60.

Rorabaugh, W. J. *The Alcoholic Republic: An American Tradition.* New York: Oxford University Press, 1979.

Rothman, Adam. "The 'Slave Power' in the United States, 1783–1865," in *Ruling America: A History of Wealth and Power in a Democracy,* ed. Steve Fraser and Gary Gerstle. New York: Cambridge University Press, 2005.

Rugemer, Edward B. "Caribbean Slave Revolt and the Origins of the Gag Rule: A Contest between Abolitionism and Democracy, 1797–1835," in *Contesting Slavery: The Politics of Slavery in the New American Nation,* ed. John Craig Hammond and Matthew Mason. Charlottesville: UVA Press, 2011.

Ryan, Mary. *Civic Wars: Democracy and Public Life in the American City During the Nineteenth Century.* Berkeley: University of California Press, 1997.

Sachsman, David B., S. Kittrell Rushing, and Roy Morris Jr., eds. *Words at War: The Civil War and American Journalism.* West Lafayette, Ind.: Purdue University Press, 2008.

Sampson, Robert. *John L. O'Sullivan and His Times.* Kent, Ohio: Kent State University Press, 2003.

Schudson, Michael. *Discovering the News: A Social History of American Newspapers.* New York: Basic Books, 1981.

Scott, Pamela. *Temple of Liberty: Building the Capitol for a New Nation.* New York: Oxford University Press, 1995.

Seitz, Don C. *Famous American Duels.* New York: Thomas Y. Crowell Co., 1929.

SenGupta, Gunja. *For God and Mammon: Evangelicals and Entrepreneurs, Masters and Slaves in Territorial Kansas, 1854–1860.* Athens: University of Georgia Press, 1996.

Sewell, Richard H. *Ballots for Freedom: Antislavery Politics in the United States, 1837–1860.* New York: Oxford University Press, 1976.

———. *John P. Hale and the Politics of Abolition.* Cambridge, Mass.: Harvard University Press, 1965.

Shade, William. "Political Pluralism and Party Development: The Creation of a Modern Party System, 1815–1852," in *The Evolution of American Electoral Systems,* ed. Paul Kleppner, Walter Dean Burnham, Ronald P. Formisano, Samuel P. Hays, Richard Jensen, and William G. Shade. Westport, Conn.: Greenwood Press, 1981, 77–111.

Shalhope, Robert E. "Thomas Hart Benton and Missouri State Politics: A Re-Examination," *Bulletin of the Missouri Historical Society* 25 (April 1969): 171–91.

Shelden, Rachel A. *Washington Brotherhood: Politics, Social Life, and the Coming of the Civil War.* Chapel Hill: UNC Press, 2013.

Sheppard, Steve, ed. *The History of Legal Education in the United States: Commentaries and Primary Sources,* 2 vols. Pasadena, Calif.: Salem Press, 1999.

Shields, Johanna Nicol. *The Line of Duty: Maverick Congressmen and the Development of American Political Culture, 1836–1860.* Westport, Conn.: Greenwood Press, 1985.

Silbey, Joel H. "After 'The First Northern Victory': The Republican Party Comes to Congress, 1855–56, *Journal of Interdisciplinary History* 20 (Summer 1989): 1–24.

———. *The American Political Nation, 1838–1893.* Stanford, Calif.: Stanford University Press, 1991.

———. *Martin Van Buren and the Emergence of American Popular Politics.* Lanham, Md.: Rowman & Littlefield, 2002.

———. *Storm over Texas: The Annexation Controversy and the Road to Civil War.* New York: Oxford University Press, 2005.

———. "The Surge in Republican Power: Partisan Antipathy, American Social Conflict, and the Coming of the Civil War," in *Essays on American Antebellum Politics, 1840–1860,* ed. Stephen E. Maizlish and John J. Kushkia. College Station: Texas A&M University Press, 1982.

Simpson, Brooks D. "'Hit Him Again': The Caning of Charles Sumner," in *Congress and the Compromise of the 1850s,* ed. Paul Finkelman and Donald R. Kennon. Athens: Ohio University Press, 2012.

Simpson, Craig M. *A Good Southerner: The Life of Henry A. Wise of Virginia.* Chapel Hill: UNC Press, 1985.

Sinha, Manisha. "The Caning of Sumner: Slavery, Race, and Ideology in the Age of the Civil War," *JER* 23 (Summer 2003): 233–62.

———. *The Counterrevolution of Slavery: Politics and Ideology in Antebellum South Carolina.* Chapel Hill: UNC Press, 2000.

———. *The Slave's Cause: A History of Abolition.* New Haven: Yale University Press, 2016.

Smith, Culver H. *The Press, Politics, and Patronage: The American Government's Use of Newspapers, 1789–1875.* Athens: University of Georgia Press, 1977.

Smith, Elbert B. *Magnificent Missourian: The Life of Thomas Hart Benton.* New York: J. B. Lippincott, 1958.

Snay, Mitchell. *Gospel of Disunion: Religion and Separatism in the Antebellum South.* Chapel Hill: UNC Press, 1997.

Spangler, Michael. "Benjamin Brown French in the Lincoln Period," *White House History* 8 (Fall 2000), 4–17.

Spofford, Harriet Prescott. "The Messenger Boys at the Capitol," *Harper's Young People* 63 (January 11, 1881).

Springer, Keith L. "Cold Water Congressmen: The Congressional Temperance Society Before the Civil War," *Historian* 27, no. 4 (1965): 498–515.

Stahr, Walter. *Seward: Lincoln's Indispensable Man.* New York: Simon and Schuster, 2012.

Stegmaier, Mark J. *Texas, New Mexico, and the Compromise of 1850: Boundary Dispute and Sectional Crisis*. Kent, Ohio: Kent State University Press, 1996.

Steward, Dick. *Duels and the Roots of Violence in Missouri*. Columbia: University of Missouri Press, 2000.

Stewart, James Brewer. "Christian Statesmanship, Codes of Honor, and Congressional Violence: The Antislavery Travails and Triumphs of Joshua Giddings," in Paul Finkelman and Donald R. Kennon, eds., *In the Shadow of Freedom: The Politics of Slavery in the National Capital*. Athens: Ohio University Press, 2011.

———. *Joshua R. Giddings and the Tactics of Radical Politics*. Cleveland: Press of Case Western Reserve University, 1970.

Stott, Richard. *Jolly Fellows: Male Milieus in Nineteenth-Century America*. Baltimore: Johns Hopkins, 2009.

Strange, Carolyn, Robert Cribb, and Christopher E. Forth, eds. *Honour, Violence and Emotions in History*. London: Bloomsbury, 2014.

Struble, Robert Struble, Jr. "House Turnover and the Principle of Rotation," *Political Science Quarterly* 4 (Winter 1979–80): 649–67.

Summers, Mark W. *The Press Gang: Newspapers and Politics, 1865–1878*. Chapel Hill: UNC Press, 1994.

Sundquist, James L. *Dynamics of the Party System: Alignment and Realignment of Political Parties in the United States*. Washington, D.C.: Brookings Institute, 1983.

Swift, Elaine K. *The Making of an American Senate: Reconstitutive Change in Congress, 1787–1841*. East Lansing: University of Michigan Press, 2002.

Tatham, David. "Winslow Homer's 'Arguments of the Chivalry,'" *American Art Journal* 5 (May 1973): 86–89.

Thayer, Shelly A. "The Delegate and the Duel: The Early Political Career of George Wallace Jones," *Palimpsest* 5 (September–October 1984): 178–88.

Theriault, Sean M., and Barry R. Weingast. "Agenda Manipulation, Strategic Voting, and Legislative Details in the Compromise of 1850," in *Party, Process, and Political Change in Congress*, ed. David Brady and Matthew McCubbins, 2 vols. Stanford, Calif.: Stanford University Press, 2002.

Thompson, Margaret Susan. *The "Spider Web": Congress and Lobbying in the Age of Grant*. Ithaca: Cornell University Press, 1985.

Thomsen, Jacqueline. "GOP Lawmaker Once Held a Knife to Boehner's Throat," *The Hill*, October 29, 2017, thehill.com/blogs/in-the-know/in-the-know/357743 -gop-lawmaker-once-held-a-knife-to-boehners-throat.

Tilly, Charles. *The Politics of Collective Violence*. New York: Cambridge University Press, 2003.

Tomich, Dale W., ed. *The Politics of the Second Slavery*. Albany: State University of New York Press, 2016.

———. *Through the Prism of Slavery: Labor, Capital, and World Economy*. Lanham, Md.: Rowman & Littlefield, 2004.

Trachtenberg, Alan. *Lincoln's Smile and Other Enigmas*. New York: Hill and Wang, 2007.

Trefousse, Hans L. *Andrew Johnson: A Biography*. New York: Norton, 1989.

———. *The Radical Republicans: Lincoln's Vanguard for Racial Justice*. New York: Knopf, 1969.

———. *Thaddeus Stevens: Nineteenth-Century Egalitarian*. Chapel Hill: UNC Press, 1997.

SELECTED BIBLIOGRAPHY   425

Tyrell, Ian R. *Sobering Up: From Temperance to Prohibition in Antebellum America, 1800–1860.* Westport, Conn.: Greenwood Press, 1979.

Uslaner, Eric M. "Comity in Context: Confrontation in Historical Perspective," *British Journal of Political Science* 21 (1991): 45–77.

———. *The Decline of Comity in Congress.* Ann Arbor: University of Michigan Press, 1993.

———. "Is the Senate More Civil Than the House?" in *Esteemed Colleagues: Civility and Deliberation in the U.S. Senate,* ed. Burdett A. Loomis. Washington, D.C.: Brookings Institution, 2000, 32–55.

Van Cleve, George William. *A Slaveholders' Union: Slavery, Politics, and the Constitution in the Early Republic.* Chicago: University of Chicago Press, 2010.

Varon, Elizabeth R. *We Mean to Be Counted: White Women and Politics in Antebellum Virginia.* Chapel Hill: UNC Press, 1998.

Vollweiler, Albert T. "The Nature of Life in Congress (1850–1861)," *Quarterly Journal of the University of North Dakota* 6, no. 1 (October 1915): 145–58.

Wakelyn, Jon L. "Disloyalty in the Confederate Congress: The Character of Henry Stuart Foote," in *Confederates Against the Confederacy: Essays on Leadership and Loyalty,* ed. Jon L. Wakelyn. Westport, Conn.: Praeger, 2002.

Wallner, Peter A. *Franklin Pierce: Martyr for the Union.* Concord, N.H.: Plaidswede, 2007.

———. *Franklin Pierce: New Hampshire's Favorite Son.* Concord, N.H.: Plaidswede, 2004.

Walther, Eric H. *The Fire-Eaters.* Baton Rouge: LSU Press, 1992.

———. *The Shattering of the Union: America in the 1850s.* Lanham, Md.: Rowman & Littlefield, 2004.

Ward, John William. *Andrew Jackson: Symbol for an Age.* New York: Oxford University Press, 1955.

Wawro, Gregory J., and Eric Schickler. *Filibuster: Obstruction and Lawmaking in the U.S. Senate.* Princeton, N.J.: Princeton University Press, 2006.

Weinbaum, Paul O. "Mobs and Demagogues: The New York Response to Collective Violence in the Early Nineteenth Century." Ph.D. dissertation, University of Rochester, 1974.

Wells, Harwell. "The End of the Affair? Anti-Dueling Laws and Social Norms in Antebellum America," *Vanderbilt Law Review* 54: 1805–47.

Widmer, Edward L. *Young America: The Flowering of Democracy in New York City.* New York: Oxford University Press, 1999.

Wilentz, Sean. *The Rise of American Democracy: Jefferson to Lincoln.* New York: Norton, 2005.

Williams, Robert Chadwell. *Horace Greeley: Champion of American Freedom.* New York: NYU Press, 2006.

Winkle, Kenneth J. *Lincoln's Citadel: The Civil War in Washington, D.C.* New York: Norton, 2013.

Wirls, Daniel. "The 'Golden Age' Senate and Floor Debate in the Antebellum Congress," *Legislative Studies Quarterly* 2 (May 2007): 193–222.

———. "'The Only Mode of Avoiding Everlasting Debate': The Overlooked Senate Gag Rule for Antislavery Petitions," *JER* (Spring 2007): 115–38.

Wongsrichanalai, Kanisorn. *Northern Character: College-Educated New Englanders,*

Honor, Nationalism, and Leadership in the Civil War. New York: Fordham University Press, 2016.

Wood, Nicholas. "John Randolph of Roanoke and the Politics of Slavery in the Early Republic," *Virginia Magazine of History and Biography* 2 (Summer 2012): 106–43.

Woods, Michael E. *Emotional and Sectional Conflict in the Antebellum United States.* New York: Cambridge University Press, 2014.

———. "'The Indignation of Freedom-Loving People': The Caning of Charles Sumner and Emotion in Antebellum Politics," *Journal of Social History* 44 (Spring 2011): 689–705.

———. "Tracing the 'Sacred Relics': The Strange Career of Preston Brooks's Cane," *Civil War History* (June 2017): 113–32.

———. "What Twenty-First-Century Historians Have Said About the Causes of Disunion: A Civil War Sesquicentennial Review of the Recent Literature," *JAH* (September 2012): 415–39.

Wunder, John R., and Joann M. Ross., eds. *The Nebraska-Kansas Act of 1854.* Lincoln: University of Nebraska Press, 2008.

Wyatt-Brown, Bertram. "The Abolitionists' Postal Campaign of 1835," *Journal of Negro History* 50 (October 1965): 227–38.

———. "Andrew Jackson's Honor." *Journal of the Early Republic* 17 (Spring 1997): 1–35.

———. "Honor, Humiliation, and the American Civil War," in *A Warring Nation: Honor, Race, and Humiliation in America and Abroad,* ed. Bertram Wyatt-Brown. Charlottesville: UVA Press, 2014.

———. *The Shaping of Southern Culture: Honor, Grace, and War, 1760s–1880s.* Chapel Hill: UNC Press, 2001.

———. *Southern Honor: Ethics and Behavior in the Old South.* New York: Oxford University Press, 1982.

———. *Yankee Saints and Southern Sinners.* Baton Rouge: LSU Press, 1985.

Wyly-Jones, Susan. "The 1835 Anti-Abolition Meetings in the South: A New Look at the Controversy over the Abolition Postal Campaign," *Civil War History* 47 (2001): 289–309.

Yacovone, Donald. "Abolitionists and the 'Language of Fraternal Love,'" in *Meanings for Manhood,* ed. Mark C. Carnes and Clyde Griffen. Chicago: University of Chicago Press, 1990, 85–95.

Yarwood, Dean L. *When Congress Makes a Joke: Congressional Humor Then and Now.* New York: Rowman & Littlefield, 2004.

Yearns, Wilfred. *The Confederate Congress.* Athens: University of Georgia Press, 1960.

Young, James Sterling. *The Washington Community, 1800–1828.* New York: Harcourt, 1966.

Zaeske, Susan. *Signatures of Citizenship: Petitioning, Antislavery, and Women's Political Identity.* Chapel Hill: UNC Press, 2003.

———. "'The South Arose as One Man': Gender and Sectionalism in Antislavery Petition Debates, 1835–1845," *Rhetoric & Public Affairs* 12 (2009).

Zagarri, Rosemarie. "The Family Factor: Congressmen, Turnover, and the Burden of Public Service in the Early American Republic," *JER* 2 (Summer 2013): 283–316.

Zalimas, Robert J., Jr. "'Contest MY Seat Sir!': Lewis D. Campbell, Clement L. Vallandigham, and the Election of 1856," *Ohio History Journal* (Winter–Spring 1997): 5–30.

Zelizer, Julian, ed. *The American Congress: The Building of Democracy.* New York: Houghton Mifflin, 2004.

ACKNOWLEDGMENTS

The biggest disjuncture in writing this book was the network of support and friendship that bolstered my study of violence and nastiness. From start to finish, friends, family, and colleagues unselfishly gave their support, counsel, and wisdom. The thanks offered here can't begin to do them justice.

When I was first seeking (and finding) my topic, the J. Franklin Jameson fellowship from the American Historical Association and the Library of Congress was essential; the ability to spend several months at the Library rummaging through the papers of congressmen revealed and fleshed out the trail of violence at the heart of this book. For that early support, I am eternally grateful. The Dirksen Congressional Center also provided funding at an early crucial point. And the American Council of Learned Societies and the Dorothy and Lewis B. Cullman Center for Scholars and Writers at the New York Public Library offered support that was transformative, not only funding and guiding a year of research and writing, but also introducing me to a cohort of warm and wonderful writers and scholars, some of them now dear friends. Adrien LeBlanc and Joel Kaye offered sage advice and cheered from the sidelines for years; Mark Stevens was a wonderful partner in intellectual crime at the center, as were Jennifer Vanderbes and Han Ong, and I had several idea-shaping lunches with Jim Oakes. Our fearless leader Jean Strouse was wise, encouraging, nurturing, and writing-savvy all in one. My thanks to all for their generous intellectual and emotional support (and the scotch-filled end-of-writing-day confabs as well).

Many librarians and curators were exceedingly generous with their time and wisdom, particularly in Washington, this book's ground zero. In the Manuscript Division at the Library of Congress, the Civil War and Reconstruction specialist Michelle Krowl helped me access and use French's writings (and seemed to enjoy getting to know French almost as much as I did). The reference librarian Bruce Kirby not only helped me with my research, but also gave me a copy of his fine master's thesis on the Cilley-Graves duel and accompanied me to the "mountaintop" (the Smithsonian gun storage room) to see the Cilley-Graves rifles. The man who showed us those rifles—David

Miller, Curator of Armed Forces History at the National Museum of American History—went out of his way to display and decode an array of weapons that were popular with congressmen; many years later, he stepped forward again to provide photographs of a few of those weapons for use as illustrations. Senate Historian Emeritus Don Ritchie toured me around the Capitol's open and closed spaces as I chatted about who hit whom in what corner for what reason. From the U.S. Senate Commission on Art, Curator Diane Skvarla offered visual fodder, and Scott Strong generously sent me an ongoing stream of materials on congressional set-tos. From the Office of the House Historian, Associate Historian Kenneth Kato, Historian Matthew Wasniewski, and Historian Emeritus Ray Smock were wonderfully hospitable as I rummaged through their files. Without these wonderful Washington folk, I couldn't have found the ground-level reality of the antebellum Congress.

The Library of Congress's invaluable abridged edition of French's diary—*Witness to the Young Republic: A Yankee's Journal, 1828–1870*, edited by Donald B. Cole and John J. McDonough—led me to another person who helped me envision French's world. Peter S. French, the great-great-grandson of the man at the heart of this book, not only answered my questions, but welcomed me into his home, showed me some of French's belongings, and provided me with a family tree. Great thanks are also due to Peter for giving French's writings to the Library of Congress many years ago. When we first met, he couldn't believe that anyone would read them. Hopefully, this book will show him the benefits when someone does. Thanks also to Roger Ginn, who sent me a copy of his study of Jonathan Cilley.

Many others stepped forward at key moments to solve mysteries and answer questions. Dayle Dooley at the Congressional Cemetery was kind enough to photograph French's grave so I could see its wording. Long after I had left the New Hampshire Historical Society, the librarian William Copeley helped me decode a letter from afar. The librarian Elizabeth Dunn at the David M. Rubenstein Rare Book and Manuscript Library at Duke University helped me track down some details in Lawrence Keitt's life. Heartfelt thanks are also due to the folks at the Massachusetts Historical Society, the Rauner Special Collections Library at Dartmouth College, the National Archives, the Southern Historical Collection at UNC Chapel Hill, the British Library, the Special Collections and Archives at Bowdoin College Library, and the Huntington Library. In this digitized age, these archives and libraries are irreplaceable centers of study staffed by expert librarians and archivists and containing invaluable holdings that often can't be found in any database. For those reasons and more, they deserve applause. Former Clerk of the House of Commons Sir Malcolm Jack discussed clerkiness with me over a wonderfully informative lunch. Kathy White was host extraordinaire during my extended research trip to North Carolina, showing me the sights and pointing me to much good food. Michael Donaldson, the general manager of the Franklin Hotel in Chapel Hill, did me a great kindness in facilitating my stay. To all of these people, I offer my heartfelt thanks.

I'm also in the debt of the many historians and scholars who provided insights over the years. Michael Les Benedict, Dan Feller, Michael Grow, Pauline Maier, Joseph Meisel, Randy Roth, Tony Rotundo, Walter Stahr, and Julian Zelizer were exceedingly generous with their time and knowledge. (Dan generously advanced me information about Henry Wise, and was my partner in crime in poking fun at him.) I'm particularly indebted to Peter Onuf, Edward Ayers, John Demos, James Brewer

Stewart, Frank Cogliano, and R. B. Bernstein for reading the manuscript and providing essential and deeply appreciated feedback. Peter read it more than once, offering his crystallizing-as-always feedback as well as ongoing encouragement. He has shaped my work and thinking in more ways than he can ever know. Ed kept me on an even keel between North and South while being wonderfully supportive. John—enthusiastic from the start—supported this project in countless ways and coached me on the fine art of storytelling. Jim couldn't have been more supportive not only of the project, but of what he called my "anthropological" approach to political history; his enthusiasm was—and is—gratefully appreciated. Frank offered to read the book years ago, and generously did so at the last minute, when I was almost done. And Richard listened to me talk (and occasionally panic) about this book for many years, an eternally calm and soothing voice as well as a source of sage advice and counsel. I'm more grateful than I can say for the support of these friends and colleagues. They represent the best of what the profession of history has to offer, as well as the best of friends.

My colleagues at Yale have been unfailingly interested and encouraging. In the History Department, Dan Kevles, David Blight, Ed Rugemer, and Naomi Lamoreaux cheered me on; Alejandra Dubcovsky and Joanne Meyerowitz provided vital moral support (plus, as a fellow early Americanist, Alejandra offered great feedback, as did Ed). David Mayhew and I had some informative Congress lunches. Akhil Amar asked some key questions. The Legal Theory Colloquium, the Yale Early American Historians Colloquium (YEAH), the Race and Slavery Working Group, and the Gilder Lehrman Center workshopped parts of this book (YEAH more than once), and the book is much the better for it. In addition, three American history librarians lent a helping hand: Greg Eow and David Gary were invaluable in tracking down obscure materials, and James Kessenides, along with Research Data Support Specialist Joshua Dull, took the time to show me how to use the ICPSR database.

This brings me to the remarkable students at Yale. How can I thank them? They were more important to this project than they know. Undergraduates and graduate students have heard material from this book for many years, and have offered wonderful insights along the way. When my momentum slowed or my energy flagged, their interest urged me on. Graduate students Michael Blaakman, Zach Conn, and James Shinn deserve special notice. Skilled historians of early and antebellum America who have a way with a pen, they read an early version of this book and offered extensive feedback (over New Haven pizza, of course). James went the extra mile, doing a second reading toward the end of the project. I can't thank them enough for their input as well as their support. Working with people like Ml, Zach, and James makes teaching at Yale the joy that it is.

Outside of Yale, a host of other groups workshopped parts of this book. The American Political History Seminar at Princeton, the Columbia Seminar on Early American History, the Congress and History conference at the Massachusetts Institute of Technology, the National Council for History Education, and the Charles Warren Center at Harvard helped me hash things out. Pauline Maier, who attended my session at the Warren Center, was particularly encouraging. Over the course of many years, she was a much-loved mentor and friend. I wish that I could show her the end product. Also, great thanks to my fellow members of the Little Summit: Amy Chazkel, Seth Fein, Chris Hill, and Pablo Piccato. Their keen insight and advice made an enormous difference in the early phases of this project; their friendship and encouragement made those phases fun. The wonderful people at the OpEd Project—which is working to boost the presence of women in the arena of public commentary—were invaluable at a key point in this project; Katie Orenstein, Chloe Angyl, and Mary Curtis helped me find the best ways to use my work about the past to comment on the present, and I thank them.

I wasn't always a barrel of laughs in the many years that it took me to write this book, so I want to offer my heartfelt thanks and apologies to any and all friends and colleagues I've inconvenienced as I've hidden myself away to write. Thanks to everyone at BackStory for their encouragement and patience in putting up with my ongoing need to "finish the book." Thanks, too, to the friends who listened to me talk for years on end about congressmen behaving badly. Janice Norian, Kristen Walters, Anne Marie Alino, Lisa Bloom, Donna Saleh, and Alan Mowatt never failed to cheer me on. Honor Sachs supported me through some trying times and sent kick-ass encouragements to write. Beth Wrightson and Kelly Allgaier were the truest of friends through times high and low. Ted Weinstein offered sage publishing advice. I couldn't have written this book without their friendship and support. My fellow "gym rats" at In-Shape in North Haven— and particularly Bob Strathdee—were equally enthusiastic, even in the midst of lifting weights. Rudy Williams, Tony Delfi, Emir Graciano, Adam Ufret, and Efrain Burgos were friends through it all, listening to a good many fight stories and urging me forward. Muffie Meyer and Ron Blumer urged me forward as well, even when I vanished into my writing hole, as did Gloria Sesso. Mel McCombie, Harris Friedman, and their feathered little Dickens were dedicated supporters and friends. Helen Lankenau had many words of wisdom. In many ways, Doris Silverman's advice and support were the backbone of my writing process. And finally, the folks at Meredith's Bread in Kingston, New York, deserve a shout-out; their "magical biscotti" (as I call them) were my ritualistic prewriting breakfast, and though I've thanked them on many a Saturday morning at the local farmer's market, now it's official because I've put it in writing.

In the final phases of writing this book, two people deserve special mention and special thanks. When my project became a book that needed a home, my agent, Wendy Strothman, was a tireless advocate and advisor, and she generously gave the book a final read in my last week of writing. My editor, Alex Star, was deeply engaged with my book from the outset, offering crucial editorial advice and encouragement; it has been a joy to work with him. Indeed, my heartfelt thanks to all of the wonderful people at Farrar, Straus and Giroux, including the wonderful Dominique Lear, Stephen Weil, and Jonathan Lippincott, who designed this book.

Thanks to my family as well, who never failed in their faith in me. My brothers, Richard and Marc, and my sister-in-law Joanne Keegan were ace advisors; Marc went out of his way to encourage me to tell a good story. My mother enthusiastically and appreciatively listened to me read bits of the book aloud, which meant a lot. My father, market researcher that he is, couldn't wait to advertise the end result. My niece, Olivia, didn't really help me with this book, but I love her—so here she is.

And finally, much love to my cockatiel Boo, my constant writing companion. He came into my life when I started this book and died when I ended it. Throughout it all, he sat by my side, giving my manuscript a dubious side-eye and laughing along with me when I found a particularly egregious bit of mayhem. As goofy as it is to credit a pet in one's acknowledgments, Boo merits it. He witnessed it all.

INDEX

Page numbers in *italics* refer to illustrations.